MODERN TELEMETRY

Edited by **Ondrej Krejcar**

INTECHOPEN.COM

Modern Telemetry
Edited by Ondrej Krejcar

CBS, Edition **2017**

Published by InTech
Janeza Trdine 9, 51000 Rijeka, Croatia

Publishing Process Manager Iva Lipovic

Technical Editor InTech DTP team

Cover Designer InTech Design Team

Image Copyright Pongphan.R, 2011. Used under license from Shutterstock.com

Additional hard copies can be obtained from orders@intechopen.com

Modern Telemetry, Edited by Ondrej Krejcar
p. cm.
ISBN 978-953-307-415-3

INTECH

open science | open minds

Contents

Contents

Contents

Preface

Telemetry problematic is based on knowledge of various disciplines like Electronics, Measurement, Control and Communication along with their combination as Computer Networks etc. This fact leads to a need of studying and understanding of these principles before the usage of Telemetry on selected problem solving. Spending time is however many times returned in form of obtained data or knowledge which telemetry system can provide.

Usage of telemetry can be found in many areas from military through biomedical to real medical applications. Modern way to create a wireless sensors remotely connected to central system with artificial intelligence provide many new, sometimes unusual ways to get a knowledge about remote objects behaviour.

This book is intended to present some new up to date accesses to telemetry problems solving by use of new sensors conceptions, new wireless transfer or communication techniques, data collection or processing techniques as well as several real use case scenarios describing model examples.

The book is split to several sections containing one or more chapters. The text starts with a first section "Sensors" (contain 4 chapters) describing new sensor architectures, communication strategies between them as well as description of same modern ways to develop sensors.

Second section "Telemetry Data Mining" introduces problems related to telemetry, satellite, autonomy, etc. This section contains one very well structured chapter.

Telemetry Use Cases focused on the theme of biomedical, medical, animal as well as military, are considered in following four sections containing the rest 16 chapters. These chapters deals with many real cases of telemetry issues which can be used as a cookbooks for Your own telemetry related problems.

Ondrej Krejcar, Ph.D.
VSB - Technical University of Ostrava,
Faculty of Electrical Engineering and Computer Science,
Department of Measurement and Control,
Centre for Applied Cybernetics,
Poruba, Czech Republic

Part 1

Sensors

1

Optical Fiber Sensors

Marcelo M. Werneck[1] and Regina Célia S. B. Allil[1,2]
[1]Federal University of Rio de Janeiro-Instrumentation and Photonic Laboratory-Electrical Engineering Program-COPPE
[2]Brazilian Army Technology Center-Biological Defense Laboratory-Chemical, Biological and Nuclear Defence Division
Brasil

1. Introduction

Telemetry is a technology that allows remote measurement and monitoring of data. It normally refers to one-way direction of information, that is, from the sensor to the interrogation system or data logger system. Telemetry could be defined as a sub-class of telecom, a more complex way of exchanging information such as Internet, telephone calls or video transmission.

Telecommand, the counterpart of telemetry, occurs when the remote systems require remote instructions and data to operate, which means that the information goes on the other direction.

Telemetry finds applications in aerospace, automotive, consumer, engineering, industrial manufacturing, medical, military, electric power industry etc.

Although the term telemetry commonly refers to wireless data transfer mechanisms (e.g. using radio or infrared systems), it also encompasses data transferred over other media, such as a telephone or computer network, optical link or other wired communications.

In the applications mentioned above and particularly in the electric power industry, we find normally protocols that can be either bidirectional or mono directional, such as Fieldbus, RS-485, Ethernet, 4-20 mA, 0-10 V, all working in a twisted-pair basis. These protocols, although being among us for many decades, have disadvantages, particularly when applied to the electric power industry. One of these disadvantages is that data transmitted through electric wires normally need electric energy at the sensor end, or in other words, the transducer needs to be powered in order to measure and transmit data. However, it occurs that sometimes providing electric energy at the sensor location is difficult for it could be far away from any appropriated power supply. This happens in long high voltage transmission lines or along pipe-lines or in deep ocean, for instance. The other problem with these protocols is that they electrically connect the sensor location with the interrogation location. The main consequence of this is that short circuits due to malfunctioning or atmospheric discharges can easily be transferred to the operation room and furthermore putting the substation personnel and equipment at risk.

With the invention of the practical optical fiber in the 70´s the world watched a boom in the telecommunication technology. In the 80´s, with the popularity of optical fiber technology, scientists started to develop a new class of sensors and transducers: the optical fiber sensors. They came offering many advantages over the other technologies and soon started to be applied in telemetry with very good return in costs, maintenance and efficiency.

In conclusion, when it comes to telemetry, optical fibers perform telemetric measurements at distances much longer than conventional telemetry protocols and media. Additionally, due to its virtually infinite capacity to multiplex, one can mix different kinds of signals in one single fiber therefore saving many kilometers of copper wires, which is also welcome by the maintenance personnel.
In this article we will concentrate on applications of telemetry over optical fiber and on optical fiber sensors which encompass telemetry and sensor in one single media.

2. Optical fiber sensors

Optical fiber sensors (OFS) came just after the invention of the optical fiber in the 70's. At the beginning of this era, optical devices such as laser, photodetectors and the optical fibers were very expensive, adequate only to the already saturated telephone network in which companies would pay any price to transmit more information and more telephone calls. With the great diffusion of the optical fiber technology in the 80´and on, optoelectronic devices became less expensive, what favored their use in OFS.
OFS can be applied in many branches of the industry but we will concentrate here their applications through our experience in the electric power industry.
In this area, the operators need to measure and monitor some important physical parameters that include:

- Strain (με)
- Vibration of structures and machines
- Electric current (from A to kA)
- Voltage (from mV to MV)
- Impedancy (μΩ)
- Leakage current of insulators (μA to mA)
- Temperature
- Pressure
- Gas concentration
- Distance between stationary and rotating or moving parts

Some of these parameters, depending on where they are located, are very difficult or even impossible to be conventionally monitored because of a well-known paradigm of the electrical power industry: An electric sensor cannot be close enough to a high potential in order to break the electric rigidity of the air, which is about 1 kV/cm. This would cause a short circuit when the current would flow from high voltage to ground potential by the sensor's connecting wires. The best option to avoid this catastrophic effect is the OFS, because the fiber is made of dielectric materials and therefore it is possible to be placed very close or even touch a high potential conductor and they do not necessary need electrical power at the sensor location.
OFS can be built using several physical principles and materials. They have specific characteristics that are well exploited when applied to the electric power industry and in this case OFS offer a large number of advantages over conventional sensors. The most important are:

- High immunity to EMI
- Electrical insulation
- Absence of metallic parts
- Local electrical power not required
- Lightweight and compactness

- Easy maintenance
- Chemically inert even against corrosion
- Work over long distances
- Several sensors can be multiplexed on the same fiber

The high immunity to electromagnetic interference (EMI) is a strong requirement for sensing in electromagnetic contaminated environments, e.g. RF-field and high electric and magnetic fields present in power lines.

The insulation is another special requirement, because as these sensors are inherently electrically insulated (dielectric) and do not require external power, this means that there is no electric path from the power line to ground, which means high personnel security. Therefore the optical fiber sensors can work at high electrical potentials and in potentially explosive environments.

Optical fibers can be used as sensors by modifying a fiber so that the measurand interferes on the guided light and modulate light parameters such as intensity, phase, polarization, wavelength, or transit time of light over the fiber. Sensors that vary the intensity of light are the simplest, since only a simple source and detector are required.

We can divide OFS in three basic categories: intrinsic, extrinsic and evanescent field based.

Extrinsic fiber optic sensors use an optical fiber, normally multi-mode, to transmit modulated light from either a non-fiber optical sensor or an electronic sensor connected to an optical transmitter. In this case the optical fiber is used only to transmit light to and from the sensor. This kind of sensor sometimes is called hybrid sensor for it enclosures different technologies such as optics and electronics.

In intrinsic sensors the light does not leave the fiber and the light modulation takes place inside the fiber. This kind of sensor presents the major benefit to have the ability to reach otherwise inaccessible places and without the need of electrical energy at the sensing location.

The third category is the evanescent field based sensor. Due to the total internal reflection phenomenon that occurs in the core-cladding interface of the fiber, the light propagating in the fiber has two components - an oscillatory field in the core and an exponentially decaying field in the cladding. The latter field, referred to as the evanescent field, is the key to sensing and is based on the modulation of the light amplitude in the core of the fiber by the optical properties of the surrounding medium.

When developing an OFS we can use the fiber for: a) conducting light; b) to be the sensor itself; and c) for both applications, that is, sensing and conducting light to and from the sensing area.

An optical fiber is a thin, flexible, transparent glassy filament that acts as a waveguide, or "light pipe", to transmit light from the light source to the photodetector located at the two ends of the fiber. They are mainly used for telecom and sensing but find many uses in the industry, research sciences, medicine, entertainment etc.

By the 70's all telephone cables and microwave links in the planet were already saturated. The solution came when Charles Kao and George Hockham of the British company Standard Telephones and Cables (STC) promoted the idea that the attenuation in the existing optical fibers could be reduced below 20 decibels per kilometer (dB/km), making fibers a practical communication medium. They proposed that the attenuation in fibers available at the time was caused by impurities that could be removed by chemical processes. They correctly and systematically theorized the light-loss properties for optical fiber, and pointed out the right material to use for such fibers — silica glass with high purity. This discovery earned Kao the Nobel Prize in Physics in 2009.

The crucial attenuation limit of 20 dB/km was first achieved in 1970 by researchers at the American glass maker Corning Glass Works, now Corning Incorporated. They demonstrated a fiber with 17 dB/km attenuation by doping silica glass with titanium. A few years later they produced a fiber with only 4 dB/km attenuation using germanium dioxide as the core dopant. Such low attenuation allowed optical fiber to be used in telecom from the 80's until today when the telecom fiber presents an attenuation of only0.25 dB/km.
Although polymeric optical fibers (POF) are around us much longer than silica fibers, only in the last decade they start to attract attention for LANs and small industrial networks and their use for sensors has just emerged few years ago. Figure 2.1 shows the different diameters as comparing POFs with silica fibers.

Fig. 2.1. Relative comparison of diameters in different kinds of fibers. SI-POF=step-index polymeric optical fiber; PCS=plastic cladding silica fiber; MM Silica=multimode silica fiber; SM silica=single mode silica fiber; PF-GI-POF=perflorinated graded-index POF. The light color represents the cladding and dark color the core.

The first report of poly-metil-meta-acrylate (PMMA) POF dates from 1968 when Du Pont presented a POF with an attenuation of 500 dB/km. From then on several laboratories are keeping trying to decrease the attenuation in order to apply POF in telecom. Figure 2.2 shows the results of those efforts.

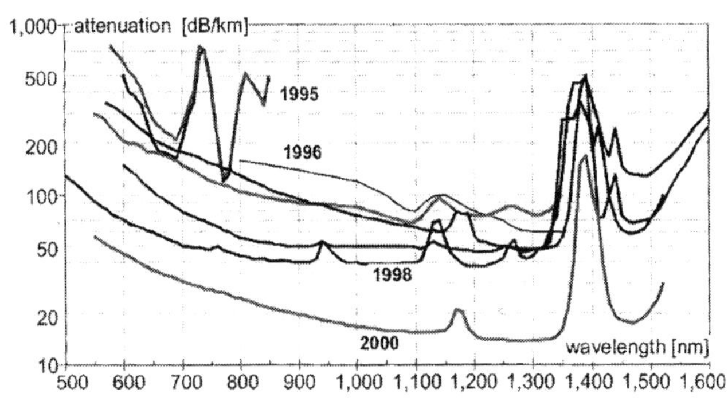

Fig. 2.2. History of the attenuation improvement of PF-GI-POF.

Comparing POF and silica fibers by the attenuation, silica fibers are much better. However, when constructing a fiber sensor using POF instead of silica, we have some additional advantages:

- Maintenance costs
- More resistance to strain
- Cheaper peripherical components
- Easy handling
- No need of special skill for splicing and connectorization

Due to their larger diameter, it is simpler to work with open optics and easy handling. POFs are cheaper than their counterpart as well as the peripheral components and devices, such as connectors, LEDs and photodetectors. They also present more resistance to strain (larger modulus of elasticity) which means more reliable networks. Finally, many interfaces can be built in laboratory what makes the maintenance cost much lower than when dealing with silica fibers.

Of course POFs have disadvantages too. POF only transmits visible and near infrared light, so we cannot use the available technology of telecommunications such as 1300 nm and 1500 nm telecom windows. Additionally, POF has a very high attenuation in the visible spectrum (see Fig. 2.3).

The other issue is the temperature because plastic materials cannot withstand high temperatures as much as glasses. POFs can operate only up to 70 to 85°C. However, some specials POFs have been developed mainly for harsh environment such as in car networks. In these applications POFs have to withstand temperatures as much as 150°C. Table 1 shows some examples.

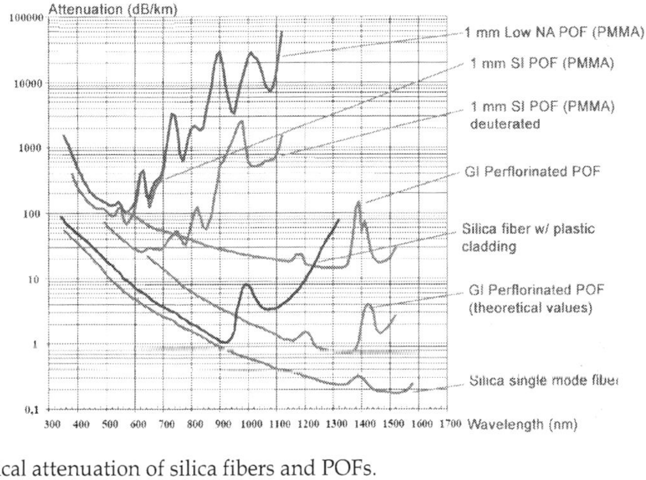

Fig. 2.3. Optical attenuation of silica fibers and POFs.

The attenuation of silica fibers is negligible for sensing distances (around 1 km), but when using a POF for transmitting light, the first thing to have in mind is the high attenuation the POF impinges to the light.

3. Case studies

This section will present real applications of OFS and telemetry in the electrical power industry. The techniques presented here have been tested in the field mainly in high voltage transmission lines, in substation equipments and in hydroelectric generators, all in a connected-to-the-grid basis.

3.1 Application of POF and ruby for temperature measurement in an electric power substation

3.1.1 Introduction

Temperature is a very important parameter for the electric power industry because insulators, copper conductors, iron core of transformers, insulating oil and every equipment are very sensitive to the temperature which has to be kept under strict control during all times. Nevertheless, when dealing with high voltage, sometimes one cannot use conventional electric sensors particularly when working near high voltage areas. This case reports the development of a temperature sensor system using the fluorescence technique.

The fluorescence effect can be used as an indicator and generate a signal proportional to a specific parameter need to be monitored. In the same way, fluorescent materials can be used as sensors. It is well known that the fluorescence decay time of some crystals is proportional to the temperature. Therefore, one way to build a temperature sensor is by the measurement of the time constant of the exponential decay that produces a linear relationship with the temperature.

Optical fibre sensors offer a large number of advantages over conventional sensors such as high immunity to electromagnetic interference, electrical isolation and the absence of metallic parts, a strong requirement for sensing in electromagnetic contaminated environments, e.g. RF/microwave. The sensor probes are inherently electrically insulated system and external power is not required for their operation, they can work at high electrical potentials and in potentially explosive environments. It can be made as lightweight, compact, disposable of low cost and is highly chemically inert even against corrosion.

The fluorescence based sensors offer the advantage of a near-zero background, because the wavelength of the emitted light is always larger than that of the excitation light, which makes then in principle much more sensitive and error immune than those that change only the absorption when the temperature varies [Asada and Yuki, 1994, Grattan and Zhang, 1995]. Previously, experiments with commercial polystyrene fluorescent fibres as temperature sensor were done [Ribeiro et al., 2003]. Although it features some advantages as compatibility with standards POFs, a weak fluorescence signal with time-decay < 100 ns was measured, thus requiring a much complex electronics. Furthermore, the polystyrene can withstand only up to ~70°C thus limiting its usefulness for the electrical energy industry. Ruby has been used for fluorescence thermometry because it is of low cost, easily available, POF compatible, requires low cost source (blue or green ultra-bright LEDs), Si-based photodetection and simple electronics. Additionally it presents strong intensity and long lifetime of fluorescence signal. The fluorescence peaking at 694 nm wavelength features a long-decay time of 2-4 ms. Persegol and co-workers [Persegol et al., 1999] described a POF-based temperature sensor in the range -20°C to +120°C with an accuracy of ± 2°C for early detection of faults in medium-voltage (36 kV) substations. They used heavily-doped ruby powder packaged at the POF end as fluorescent material pumped with a green LED. Two POF-probe were used, one for pumping the ruby and the other for bringing the fluorescence back to the photodetector.

In this case study we describe the temperature sensor prototype development based on the ruby crystal and a one-probe-POF for "low" and "high" temperatures. Low cost passive and active components as couplers, connectors, adapters, LEDs etc were used. Ruby crystals are geometrically compatible with standard POFs and even after cutting and polishing it remains at low cost.

3.1.2 The prototype

Fig. 3.1.1 shows a top view picture of the temperature sensor prototype (conditioning equipment) where the key components are assigned. The LED package was polished almost reaching the semiconductor chip thus maximizing the light caption. Light launching was made through butt-coupling the polished LED and a carefully terminated POF. Optical pulses of 32 ms time-width from the LED were generated to pump the ruby crystal at 15.6 Hz. A miniature 1x2 POF-coupler is used to send pump pulses toward the ruby crystal glued at the end of the POF-probe and to collect the fluorescence toward the Si-photodetector.

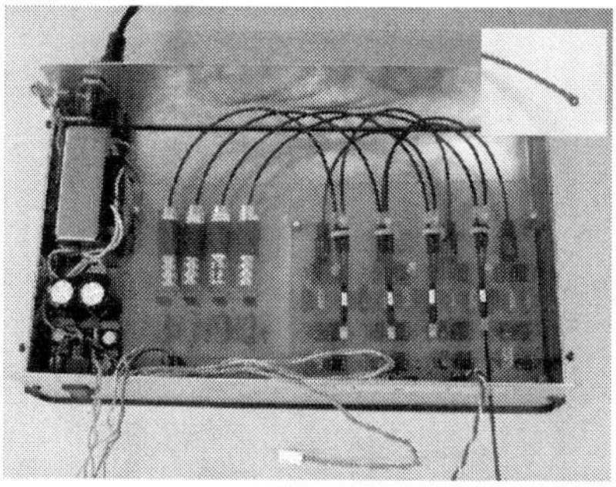

Fig. 3.1.1. Top view picture of the temperature sensor prototype (conditioning equipment).

Fig. 3.1.2 shows the picture of the one-POF-probe with 4 mm in diameter. The POF was terminated at the other end with a standard HP plastic connector. With this configuration, it can be detached from the conditioning equipment box. The fluorescence response from the crystal, passing through the same POF, was conveyed into the other port of the coupler. Due to the back reflections at the many optical interfaces, the fluorescent signal could have been buried under the intense excitation signal. Thus, in order to avoid a saturation of the detection stage and to enable the fluorescence response to be detected exclusively, a red long-pass filter was placed before the Si photodiode. The electrical signal generated from the photodiode is amplified and processed.

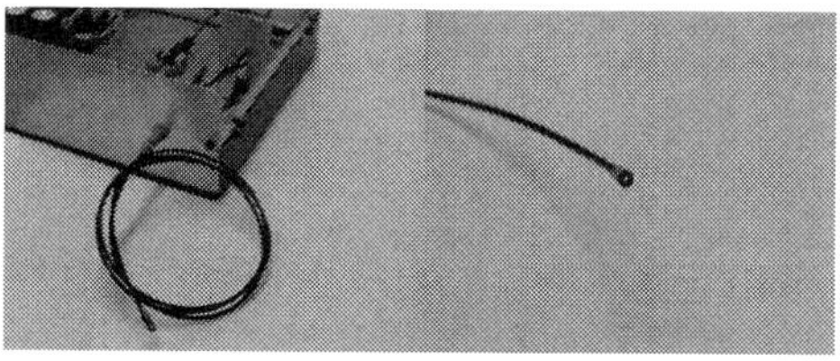

Fig. 3.1.2. Picture of the miniaturised POF-probe with hemispherical ruby crystal.

The field prototype probe (Fig. 3.1.3) was designed to work in the field under 25 kV. The POF with the ruby crystal is inserted inside the probe up to its tip where it touches the copper conductor of the coil.

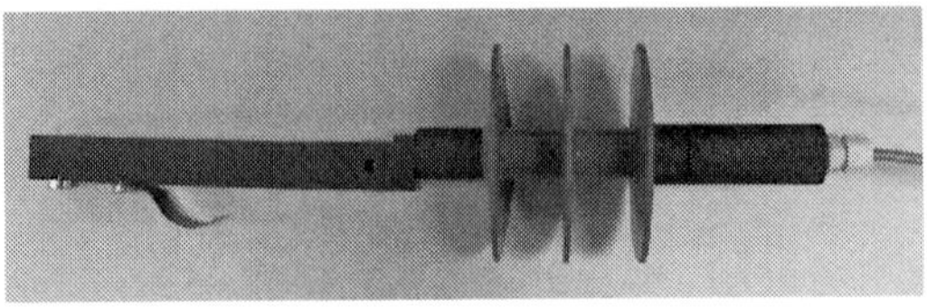

Fig. 3.1.3. High voltage probe.

3.1.3 Prototype tests

Fig. 3.1.4 shows in the top the oscilloscope trace of the square shape pump pulses. Bottom trace shows the fluorescence signal at room temperature exhibiting a clear exponential time-decay.

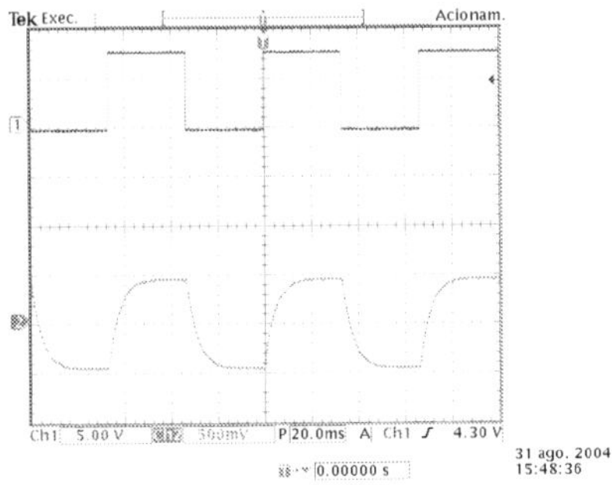

Fig. 3.1.4. Oscilloscope traces of pump (top) and fluorescent (bottom) light signals at room temperature (23°C).

The exponential decay shown in Fig. 3.1.4 can be expressed as:

$$P(t) = P_0 \exp[-t/\tau(T)]$$

where $P(t)$ is the output light power at a time t, P_0 is the light power at t=0 and $\tau(T)$ it the time-decay constant at temperature T. Fig 3.1.5 shows the measurements of fluorescence time-decay τ against the temperature T with a typical relaxation time of about 5.0 ms.

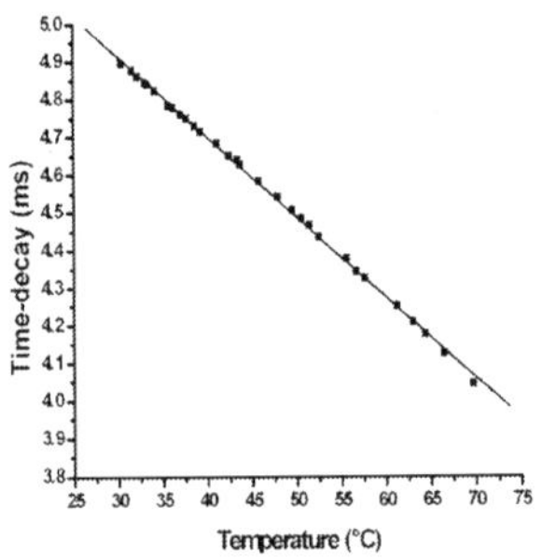

Fig. 3.1.5. Fluorescence time-decay against the temperature.

From the straight line slope shown in Figure 3.1.5 the sensitivity is calculated to be 22.5 μs/°C corresponding to an estimated temperature resolution of ~1°C. A sensitivity of 9 μs/°C has been reported in the literature. However, our sample presented a larger sensitivity probably due to the re-absorption phenomena [Persegol et al., 1999].
Plastic materials cannot withstand high temperatures as much as glasses. Standard POFs usually can operate up to 70 to 85°C. However, some special POFs have been developed mainly for harsh environment as in car networks applications. Some of those "high-temperature" POFs had been disclosed in the literature but still impose severe limitations for temperature sensing [Ribeiro et al., 2003].
Table 1 shows the attenuation given by the manufacturer for three POFs (Mitsubishi Rayon Company) corresponding to centre wavelengths of blue/green LEDs and ruby R-line (694 nm).

Fiber Type	470 nm	525 nm	694 nm
EH4001 (datacom-grade)	~ 0.10 dB/m	~ 0.10 dB/m	> 0.40 dB/m
DH4001 (heat-resistant, 115°C)	0.95 dB/m	0.48 dB/m	0.40 dB/m
FH4001 (heat-resistant, PC core, 125°C)	4.00 dB/m	2.70 dB/m	1.30 dB/m

Table 1. Attenuation of three POFs at some key wavelengths. PC = polycarbonate.

From Table 1 one can see that the EH4001 POF-probe attenuation is the same despite the use of blue or green LED regarding a maximum temperature of 85°C for which this POF can withstand.
Table 2 shows comparatively the attenuations for 10m of POF-probe length when a maximum temperature of 110°C is allowed to be reached.

	470 nm (pump) + 694nm (fluorescence)	525 nm (pump) + 694nm (fluorescence)
EH 4001	1.0 + 4.0 = 5.0 dB	1.0 + 4.0 = 5.0 dB
DH4001	9.5 + 4.0 = 13.5 dB	4.8 + 4.0 = 8.8 dB
FH4001	40.0 + 13.0 = 53.0 dB	27.0 + 13.0 = 40.0 dB

Table 2. Attenuation for 10 m of POF-probe for different pump wavelengths.

Fibers type DH4001 and FH4001 can withstand up to 115°C and 125°C, respectively. However, our choice as "high temperature" POF-probe was the heat resistant-grade DH4001 (1 mm core with black XPE jacket) because it features total attenuation of 8.8 dB that is much smaller than 40.0 dB presented by FH4001 regarding the green LED as the excitation light source.

3.1.4 Field installation

The system has been installed at the harmonic filter of Furnas Substation in the city of Ibiúna, State of São Paulo, Brasil to allow the technicians to monitor the temperature in four points of the coil of this reactor in real time. If the temperature reaches 80°C an alarm is issued in order to shut down the transmission line. Fig 3.1.6 shows one of the four installed sensors, Fig. 3.1.7 shows the coil with two of the sensors and Fig. 3.1.8 shows the control software which screen shows the graph of the four temperatures as well as the ambient temperature.

Fig. 3.1.6. One of the four sensors installed on the top of the coil.

Fig. 3.1.7. The reactor coil and the sensors installed.

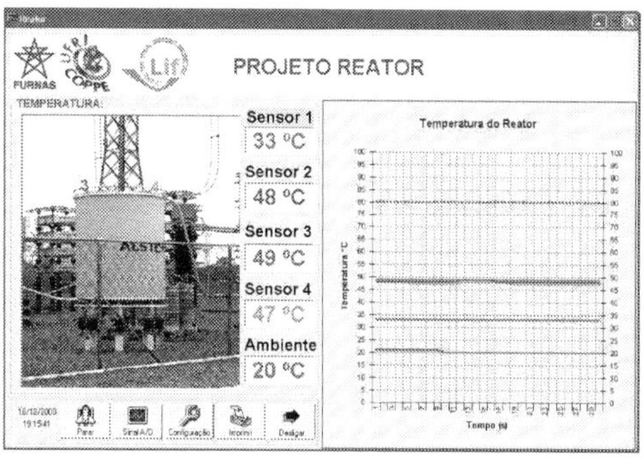

Fig. 3.1.8. Control software screen showing the graph of the four temperatures as well as the ambient temperature.

3.1.5 Results

Figures 3.1.9 and 3.1.10 show the graphs of the measurements taken at two different dates.

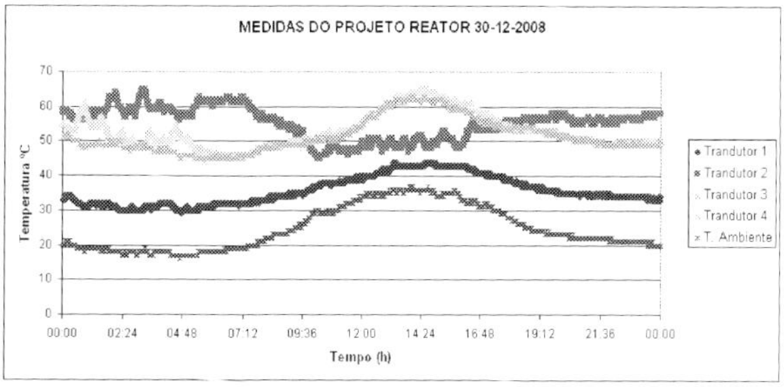

Fig. 3.1.9. Temperature monitored by the four transducers.

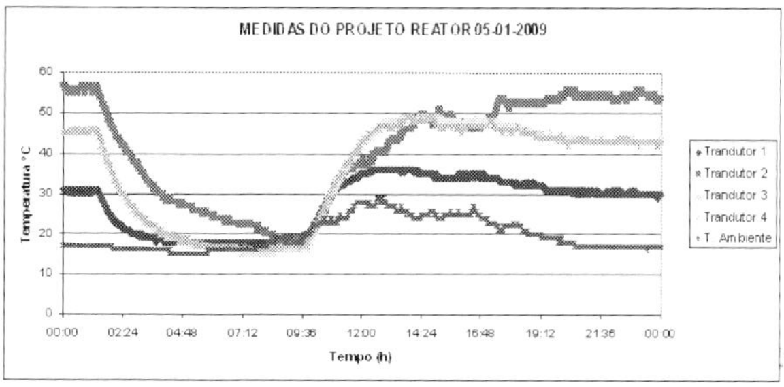

Fig. 3.1.10. Temperature monitored during an electric power shortage.

3.1.6 Concluding remarks

Experimental results of a simple and low cost four-point temperature POF sensor prototype based on time-decay of the ruby fluorescence pumped with blue (or green) ultra-bright LED are presented. The major drawbacks of polymer optical fibres are their restricted temperature range and relatively high losses. However many applications do not exceed a temperature of more than 100ºC and requires a sensing distance smaller than 10 m. The best choice for temperatures up to 115ºC was the DH4001 as the POF-probe pumped with green LED. The developed prototype is quite compatible with a 1-mm-core silica fibre or a hybrid POF + silica fibre-probe where the later may be put in contact with the hot surface to be sensed.

3.2 Application of a POF-based current sensor for measuring leakage current in 500 kV transmission line

3.2.1 Introduction

The leakage current of insulators in a high voltage transmission line is due to the increasing conductive deposited yielded by environment pollution. The more common pollution is the salt-spray produced by winds in areas close to sea shore. The salt deposit on the insulator surface offers to the electrical current alternative paths to the ground, thus connecting the high voltage to ground potential. Although this current is only a few tens of milliamperes, when multiplied by the total number of insulators located in that particular transmission line, the total leakage current can reach so high values that can trigger over current protection devices leading to electrical power line interruption. When an electric arc occurs,

it is called "flashover", leading occasionally to the destruction of the whole insulator [Kanashiro and Burani, 1996].
An optoelectronic sensor for real time leakage current monitoring of high-voltage (500kV) power lines insulators was developed as a continuation of a study presented on the 2003 POF Conference (Werneck et al, 2003). The leakage current drives an ultra-bright green LED. The optically intensity-encoded data measurement is coupled to a POF and transmitted from the high potential to ground potential. After demodulation, the RMS value of the leakage current and waveforms are sent to a remote station using a GPRS code in a cell-phone platform. This case study shows the sensing system, the telemetry technology and the results obtained.
The continuous monitoring of leakage current levels yields parameters to establish an operational preventive strategy of cleaning or substitution of insulators placed inside the area with favorable conditions to flashover occurrence.
Usually, in order to monitor leakage current, it is applied a resistor (Briggs, 1976; Amarh, 2001) or an induction coil (Maraio, 1992). However, these methods need the connection to potential, allowing electromagnetic interference and risks to personnel. In order to circumvent this problem it has been proposed the development of an optoelectronic system using plastic optical fiber (POF) technology. This method has some advantages, such as it does not suffer electromagnetic interference effect; it is of low cost, light weight and does not need power supply to work.
With this system in operational status it will bring benefits such as energy losses monitoring and increasing the grid reliability. It also promotes optimization of insulators washing causing therefore a reduction of maintenance cost.

3.2.2 System description and methods

The sensor previously developed and presented in the 2003 POF Conference was used for 13.8 kV whereas this same technology is now used for a 500 kV transmission line in the city of São Luis, State of Maranhão, Brazil. Fig. 3.2.1 shows the schematic diagram of the system.

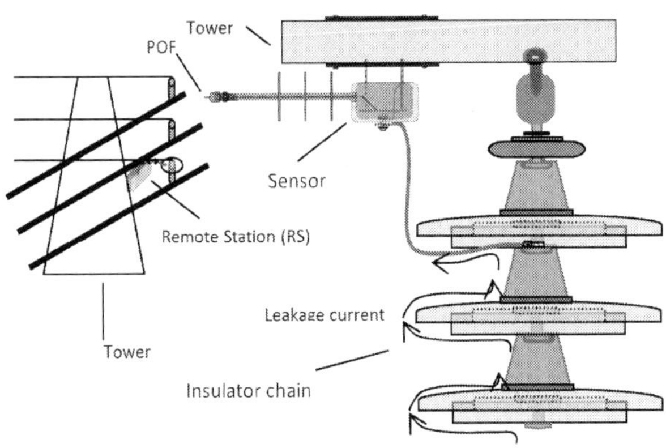

Fig. 3.2.1. Schematic diagram of the system

The main problem is the insulation of the whole system, since at this so high voltage, nearly everything conducts, including POFs. Therefore, we should place the sensor at or near ground potential.

The method proposed to monitor the leakage current of high-voltage circuits is based on the fact that all leakage current flows through all insulator sectors (see Fig. 3.2.1). Therefore if we measure the current from the last section of the insulator to ground, we are actually measuring the leakage current and with the sensor connected at a low voltage level. Fig. 3.2.2 shows the location where the control and transmission box is installed and the location where the sensor is installed at the insulator chain of a 500 kV transmission line tower.

(a) (b)

Fig. 3.2.2. The arrows show the location where the control and transmission box is installed and the location where the sensor is installed.

3.2.3 The transducer

The leakage current supplies energy enough to optically power a high efficient blue-green-LED (Marcou, 1997). The leakage current modulates the LED output power that is transmitted to the receptor by means of a specially protected POF. The emitted light from the LED is amplitude and wavelength modulated. In this work it was applied only amplitude modulation/demodulation technique.

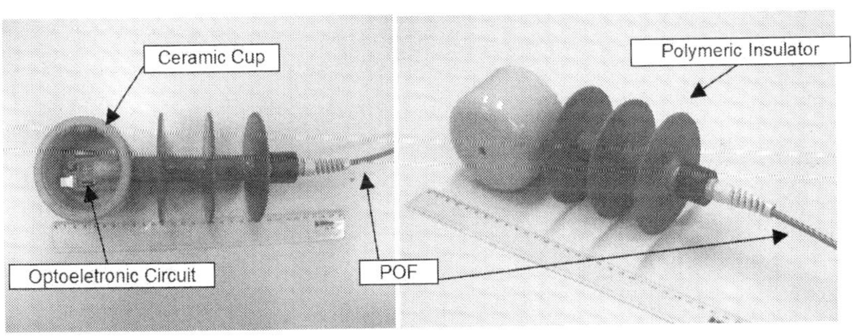

Fig. 3.2.3. Picture of the POF-based leakage current sensor

The optical signal is detected by the receptor circuit, inside the Remote Station that performs the half cycle demodulation. Fig. 3.2.3 shows pictures of the transducer which was designed to be connect to the test-insulator. Calibration and measurement procedures of leakage waveforms were made under controlled laboratory conditions by a salt-spray chamber aiming to simulate the real conditions of the field.

3.2.4 Remote station

The Remote Station contains the sensor interrogation system the CPU and the cell-phone transmitter. The electronic hardware is composed by the followings modules: CPU board associated to the datalogger system; power supply; battery and cell phone (see Fig. 3.2.4). The RS, designed to work under field conditions, is attached at the metallic structure located at medium height of the tower (see Fig. 3.2.2a).

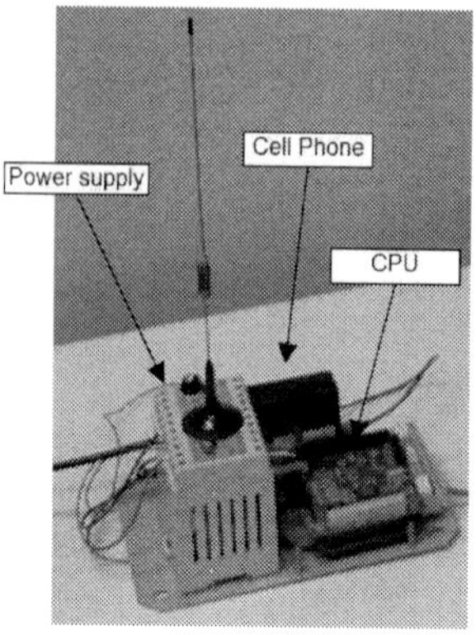

Fig. 3.2.4. Electronic hardware inside of Remote Station: power supply, battery, datalogger, CPU and cell phone.

3.2.5 The software

The software is responsible for establishing the communication between RS (installed in field) and any authenticated computer connected to the Internet. The signals are acquired, processed and stored in memory. In another cycle, the data is sent to the remote computer via modem. Another program is responsible for remote updates of the local software. This feature is particularly important because the monitoring place is about 2000 km away from the Laboratory and very often a new update of the local program has to be installed in the system and this is done remotely. Fig. 3.2.5 shows the remote screen as seen in our laboratory.

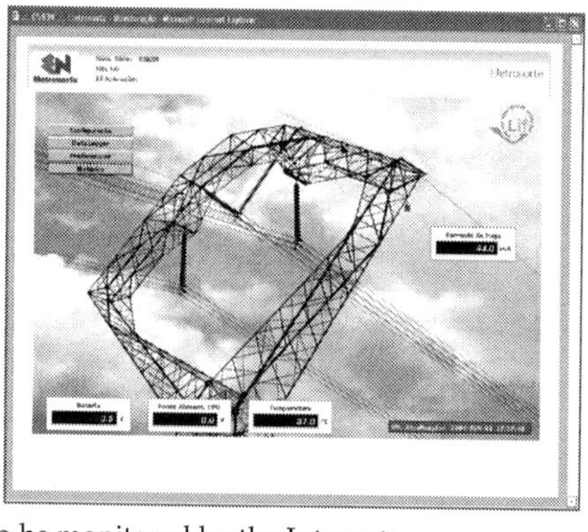

Fig. 3.2.5. Main screen to be monitored by the Internet.

3.2.6 Results

The monitoring process is based on block dataset transference, which is related with values sampled from specific time interval. Figure 3.2.6 shows a set of data downloaded from the system's website.

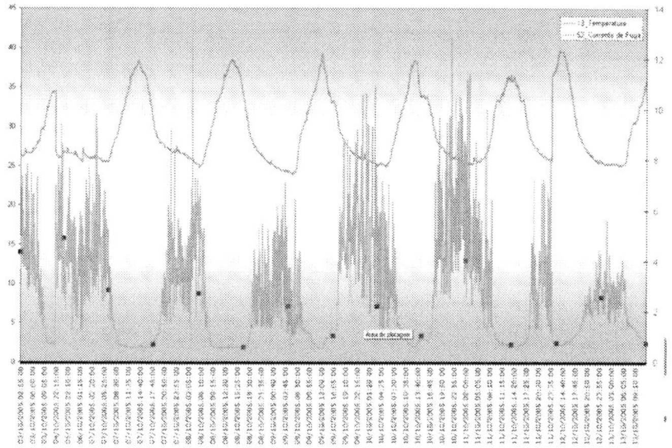

Fig. 3.2.6. Results downloaded from the system's website. The upper trace is the ambient temperature and the lower trace is the leakage current.

3.2.7 Discussion and conclusions

The LED/POF technology applied in thr leakage current sensor presents some advantages over other techniques adopted in last years, i.e.: efficient, easy to handle, robust and reliable. Despite problems described on the literature, optical amplitude modulation technique applied to fiber optic sensing proved to be efficient enough to obtain the leakage current so that the use of frequency modulation technique proposed as alternative technique was not necessary (Culshaw& Dakin, 1989 and 1997).

The objectives of this project were reached, however, in order to this technique be of any usefulness to the company, it necessary to transform the data into information. This means to establish parameters which can determinate the real status of the insulator regarding the leakage current allowed to flow to the ground. After such parameter has been established, it will be possible to issue the "washing procedures" alarm, meaning that if the set of insulators were not washed immediately, a flashover may occur. The establishment of these parameters would produce the logistic insertion of this activity in company, reducing the risk probability of an insulator failing. To create these parameters it would be necessary to analyze a great diversified amount of data from different critical points of maritime pollution inside the company operation area. Thus, it would be possible to determinate the optimum point to intervention (washing of insulators). On the other hand, it could be possible to establish an analytical relationship between different kinds of insulators under same pollution conditions, aiming at the creation of a "performance indicator" to each insulator under the same conditions. This analytic methodology could supply most adequate insulator to specific geo-meteorological region.

3.3 Hybrid optoelectronic sensor for current and temperature monitoring in overhead transmission lines

3.3.1 Introduction

Transmission line (TL) capacity is determined by the maximum power transmitted from the source to the load. Since the line voltage is always fixed, this capacity is in fact the maximum current capable to flow in the TL. Normally, during the project, this maximum power is established and the whole project is built around this parameter. When the energy demands grow, technicians are worried to infringe standards of security and performance, such as wire temperature and sag (conductor-to-ground distance).

The sag is a very important parameter since it is directly related to the current: the higher the current, the higher the conductor temperature, and so thermal expansion, consequently decreasing the conductor-to-ground distance. Nevertheless, the conductor temperature does not depend only on the electrical current. It is strongly dependent on environmental features such as wind velocity and direction, ambient air temperature, pollution, cable construction, rain and snow conditions [Douglas and Thrash, 2007]. So, TL maximum sag characteristic is determined always considering the worst case aiming the best safety conditions.

With the increasing demand for electrical energy, especially in developing countries, the idea to utilize the full transmission capacity of already existing TL, instead of built new ones, is quite attractive. The idea behind this project, which will be confirmed by data collected from the system in the field, is that the temperature of the conductor depends on current and weather conditions, but the sag only depends on the conductor temperature, regardless the weather conditions.

The system operates in two stages. The first stage will provide the measurement of three parameters: line current, conductor temperature and sag. This system will be installed in one or two TL towers for sufficient period of time to acquire data at all possible situations. This information will make it feasible to establish a set of calibration curves which will relate sag distance with conductor temperature, and sag distance with line current. The sag will be measured by taken photographs of a target hung on the middle of the catenary. A neural network recognizes the target on the picture and calculates its distance from a background reference.

Since the sag is dependent on line current and conductor temperature, on the second stage of the project only current and temperature sensors will remain installed on the TL tower. Thus, technicians will be able to infer the sag value exclusively from the latter parameters. The conductor-sag distance, acquired using the digital processing of digital camera images, plus the data regarding conductor current and temperature, will enable the development of a catenary behavior estimation algorithm, for each monitored and calibrated TL conductor cable, hence eliminating the necessity of constant monitoring.

3.3.2 System description

The system is comprised of three monitoring sub-systems: a temperature sensor, a current sensor and a conductor-sag monitoring sub-system. These three sub-systems will be installed on a 138 kV transmission line tower, in order to monitor the sag between this tower and the next one, being this conductor sag a strategic and representative one. Once the effectiveness of this method is confirmed, the system will be reproduced and taken to monitor problematic sags in the company's transmission lines.

The current transformer and the temperature system are composed by two subsystems: the one in ground potential and the one in high voltage (138 kV); the latter is optically powered by the former in the following manner: in ground potential a laser injects 830 nm light in a multimode ordinary telecommunications optical fiber. This fiber is directed to the high potential subsystem through a specially designed 138 kV polymeric insulator. At the high potential level, the laser light is converted into electric energy through a conventional silicon photodetector. This energy powers all electronic circuits embarked on the high voltage level: current and temperature sensors, microcontroller and fiber optic serial transmitter. The transmitter relays the data collected to the ground potential through another multi-mode optical fiber that is also insulated by the previously mentioned 138 kV insulator.

A Rogowski coil, a helical coil sensor uniformly wound on a relatively long non-magnetic strip [Tumanski, 2007], is used as a current sensor, which offers advantages compared to conventional current transformers, such as linearity and easy handling [Ward and Exon, 1993]. The cable temperature measurement is implemented through a conventional LM35 integrated circuit, which is very simple and inexpensive. The sensors' electrical output signals are digitalized and processed by means of a low-power microcontroller and sent to a receiving system located at the low-voltage region using a LED operating at 850 nm wavelength, connected to a multimode 62.5/125-μm optical fiber.

3.3.3 Power over fiber link

All the circuits located in the high voltage area are optically powered; a laser module at the low-voltage area launches up to 1W optical power at 830 nm in another multimode 62.5/125-μm fiber, conducting the energy to the photovoltaic power converter remotely situated. Power and data channels can be combined into a single optical fiber linking both high and low voltage areas [Böttger et al, 2008]; however, in this monitoring system for TL an option for dedicated fiber cables was made [Tardy et al, 1995 and Pember et al, 1995]. A general view of the system is presented in Fig. 3.3.1.

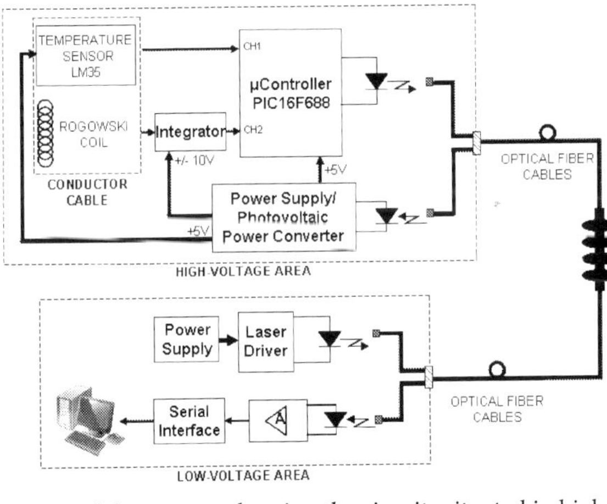

Fig. 3.3.1. General view of the system, showing the circuits situated in high and low voltage regions.

The system is comprised of the following sub-modulus: the laser module located at the low voltage region, 830 nm operating wavelength, and controlled by a driver which can manage the launch of up to 1 W optical power; a 40m-long-62.5-μm multimode optical fiber to guide the optical power; and a photovoltaic power converter (PPC), which is an array of semiconducting diodes.

Optical attenuation is a key issue when photonic power is used. Fiber splices and connectors were implemented to incorporate the 40 m optical waveguide into the power-over-fiber link, including the isolator showed in Figure 3.3.1, between the laser and the PPC on the other end. The estimated losses for the fiber splices and the connector are 0.01dB and 0.30dB, respectively; the optical fiber attenuation for the first transmission window should also be considered, accounting approximately 0.12dB (forty meters long). Consequently, the total estimated attenuation in the power-over-fiber link is 0.43dB, which does not affect the system operation. Since the system is installed outdoors, according to the international standard IEC 60529, the circuits and optical connectors are allocated inside an IP66 rated enclosure, providing increased long-term functionality and greater protection against dust and humidity. The electronic system placed close to the conductor cable was designed to perform two main functions: provide electrical power to the sensors and data processing elements, carry out the digital-to-analog conversion and the communication between high and low voltage regions. The PPC provides 3.5 V that is raised to 5 V using a DC-DC converter. Another DC-DC converter provides the symmetric ±10 V to the Rogowski coil integrator circuit. A low-consumption microcontroller executes data acquisition, treatment and communication between low and high voltage areas. A RMS-to-DC operation is effectuated on the Rogowski coil integrator signal, which produces a sinusoidal function proportional to the current, prior to the microcontroller 10 bit analog-to-digital conversion. The data are serially transmitted at 9600 bps via a 850 nm LED (see Figure 3.3.2). The light signal is coupled to a 40-m-62.5-μm optical fiber, dedicated for data transmission.

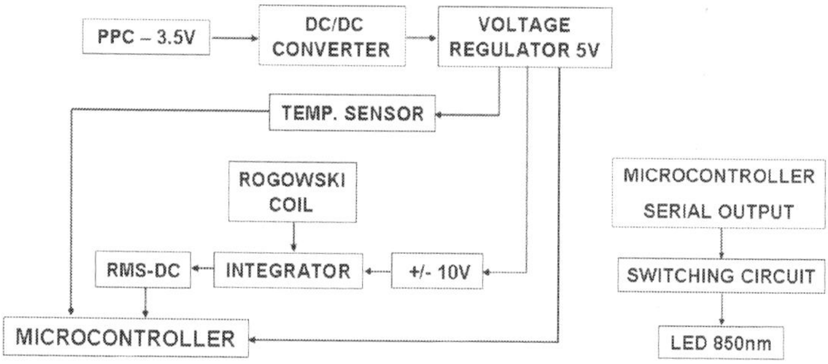

Fig. 3.3.2. High voltage area circuit general view: (Left) microcontroller inputs and voltage levels, Right) communications schematic.

The low voltage area circuit, located at a base station, performs the optical-to-electrical conversion by a high speed PIN photodiode, operating in photovoltaic mode, using the technique suggested by Werneck and Abrantes [2004]. Before the serial transmission to the instrumentation computer, the signal is converted to EIA-232 levels. Fig. 3.4.1 shows the low voltage area schematic for the monitoring system communications section. Energy to drive the laser for photonic power, which is also situated at the low voltage area, and for the data treatment circuits, after the optical-to-electrical conversion, will be provided by solar energy. Batteries, charged by a solar panel, supply electrical power to the circuits.

3.3.4 Conclusions

It has been shown that the proposed monitoring system for transmission line cables measurement of temperature and current provides reliable data. Since silica optical fiber cables are utilized in communications and power supply links, insulation between the sensor head and the user operation site is guaranteed, eliminating the use conventional copper cabling.

The measured values were compared with reference values, the latter being outfitted by commercial measurement laboratory instruments; and small errors were observed, for both current and temperature data. For an even more reliable study of the system accuracy, a calibration using tracked instruments must be carried out.

Future works include the system field installation, in Piracicaba TL, which requires the improvement of system mechanical robustness, and the addition of the sag monitoring subsystem. It is expected that the data collected, together with the sag information, will provide support for the development of an algorithm for the estimation of conductor-sag values.

3.4 Optical high voltage sensor based in fiber Bragg grating and PZT piezoelectric ceramics

3.4.1 Introduction

Electric power facilities, such as substations, rely on instrument transformers for their functionality and protection. They are divided into voltage transformers (VT) and current transformers (CT) for measuring and controlling voltage and current, respectively. The role of the instrument transformer is to provide accurate signals for protection, control and metering systems, including revenue metering. These requirements place stringent demands on the accuracy and reliability of the instrument transformer to guarantee the correct functionality for protection systems and precise measurement for metering purposes.

Created over a century ago, they are reliable for over-voltage and over-current protection; allow 0.2% revenue metering accuracy and their behavior is well known under both normal and abnormal conditions. Nevertheless, these pieces of equipment are made entirely of copper, ceramic and iron with all empty spaces filled with oil, which are weighty materials, producing bulky, heavy and clumsy equipment. On top of that, they tend to explode without prior warning, resulting in the potential destruction of nearby equipment by pieces of sharp ceramics and furthermore putting the substation personnel at risk.

Optical voltage transducers offer many improvements on traditional inductive and capacitive voltage transformers such as linear performance and wider dynamic range, lighter weight, smaller size and improved safety.

The optical-fiber sensors industry has grown in recent years, and most of the efforts involving the sensors industry focused the use of Fiber Bragg Grating (FBG) as a sensor element. Among the parameters of interest most of the works found in the literature focus on temperature, strain, pressure, displacement, acceleration, vibration, voltage and current.

The behavior of optical current transformer (OCT) and optical voltage transformer (OVT) applied on electric power transmission system has been widely discussed in the literature because they present advantages when compared with conventional transformers. The innovations coming from the optical transformers circumvent problems such as the risk of explosion, high weight, electric safety, insulation oil, difficulty of installation, etc [Sawa et al, 1990, Cease et al, 1991, Werneck and Abrantes, 2004, and De Nazaré and Werneck, 2010].

However, the main drawback is still the high cost of this new technology, not only for acquisition but also maintenance, demanding specialty skills uncommonly available among company personnel. With this motivation, this case relates the development of a high voltage measuring system to be used as the core of a 13.8-kV-class OVT for the electric power industry application using a PZT(Lead Titanate Zirconate) crystal as voltage transducer and FBG as strain measuring sensor. This new technology can be developed at a cost fully compatible with conventional CTs and VTs.

FBG technology is one of the most popular choices for optical-fiber sensor for strain or temperature measurements due to their simple manufacturing, besides it is relatively easy to deal with and reliable. The use of piezoelectric ceramics in the last decade due to piezoelectric characteristics and transducer properties has attracted interest to electric power systems measurements because of their properties to convert electrical energy to mechanical energy [Niewczas et al, 2005, Yao and Yi, 2006 and Allil and Werneck, 2011].

This study relates to the development of a high voltage sensor system using a PZT piezoelectric crystal as transducer and an FBG as a sensor for an optical voltage transformer for 13.8-kV-class. In the present contribution, a voltage was applied in a combined PZT and FBG sensor by using a high voltage source. This voltage acts on the PZT ceramic causing a mechanical deformation and by using a FBG as interrogation system, the spectrum of the reflected light from the FBG is captured and demodulated to obtain a sinusoidal signal proportional to the applied voltage.

The results showed a linear relationship between the applied voltages to the PZT-FBG sensor with the reflected Bragg wavelength shift. The easy implementation and the low cost of the equipment used prove the viability of this project for applications in the electric power industries.

From previous experimental studies it has been proven that the exposure to ultraviolet radiation during the FBG inscription process decreases the silica yield strength, furthermore, when stretching the FBG to bond it to the stress element, it is necessary to remove the optical fiber coating, and this process can degrade the fiber strength [Miyajima, 1982, Olshansky, Maurer, 1976 and Kurkjian et al, 1989].

To study the mechanical strength and the fiber resistance to strain, in a previous paper [Ribeiro and Werneck, 2010] we measured the tensile strength of silica optical fiber. By providing information about mechanical strength it is possible to obtain a maximum life span for these devices.

3.4.2 Experimental setup

As mentioned above, we used a PZT crystal as voltage transducer and a FBG as strain measuring sensor. The experimental setup of the FBG-PZT sensor system is shown in Fig. 3.4.1. The ceramic stack was built using ten 4-mm-thick PZT rings, with d_{33} = 300 pm/V separated by 0.2-mm thick copper electrodes where the contacts were fixed. The electrodes were arranged on both sides of the ceramic discs and were connected in a parallel line. The ceramic disks were glued together separated by the cooper plates using EPO-TEK 302-3M resin and kept in the oven for 3 hours at a temperature of 65°C for the cure. A double aluminum structure was used to accommodate the ceramic stack and the 82-mm-length sensor was glued on the top of it.

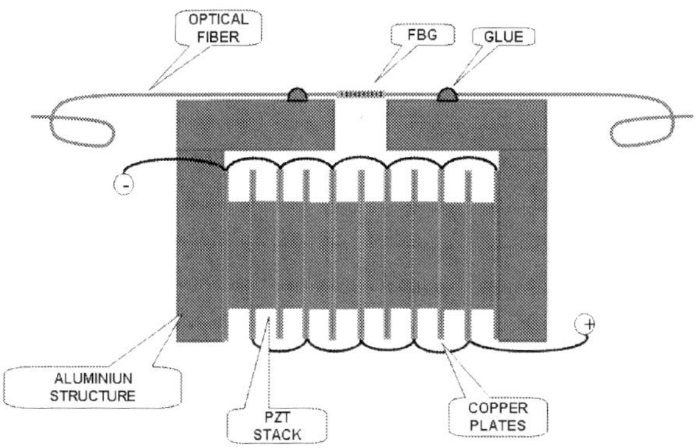

Fig. 3.4.1. Schematic diagram of the FBG-Piezostack.

For improving isolation for high voltage the entire assembly was immersed in a bath of insulating oil. The FBG with central wavelength of 1532.9 nm was stretched to 1535.18 nm as shown in Fig. 3.4.2, before bonded to the aluminum structure to allow measurements in both directions, that is augmenting and retreating PZT thickness.

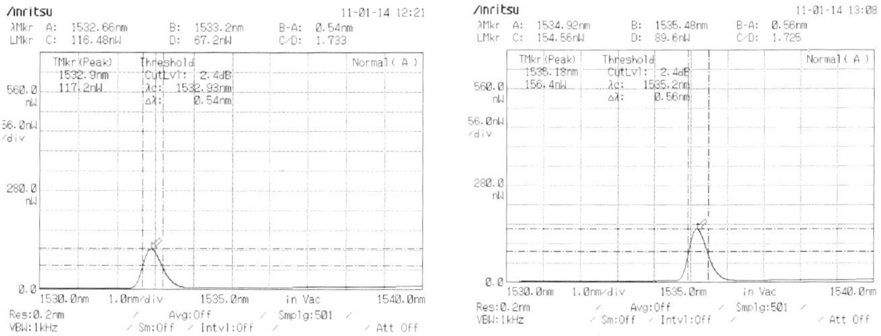

Fig. 3.4.2. (a) The FBG reflection spectrum before bonded to the aluminum base and (b) after bonded.

Notice that by bonding the FBG on the PZT stack as we described, we would have the strain on the FBG equals to the strain on the PZT. This is because, although the total displacement is bigger, so is the length of the fiber, yielding therefore the same strain.
Since the fiber is bonded to the ends of the stack, the displacement previewed by (8) will be transmitted to the fiber, so that

$$\Delta L_{PZT} = \Delta L_{FBG} \quad (1)$$

Now combining (5), (8) e (9) and considering $\Delta T=0$ (constant temperature environment), we achieve:

$$\Delta\lambda_B=\lambda_B(1-\rho_e)\ nd_{33}V/L \tag{2}$$

Substituting the PZT constants of Table 3 in (10) we have the following sensitivity for the applied DC voltage:

$$\Delta\lambda_B/\Delta V=128.3\ pm/kV \tag{3}$$

Notice that the larger the L_{FBG}, the greater the strain experienced by the FBG and consequently, the greater the sensitivity.

Physical and dielectric properties	Value
PZT	
PZT type	PZT4
Ceramic Shape	Ring
Piezoeletric strain constant	d_{33}=300 pm/V
Thickness of ceramic	w =4 mm
Maximum allowed direct field strength	1-2 kV/mm
Maximum allowed reverse field strength	350-500 V/mm
Curie Temperature (T_c)	325°C
Number of elements in stack	n=10
FBG	
Bragg wavelength	λ_B = 1535.18 nm
Photo-elastic coefficient	ρ_e =0.22
Coefficient of thermal expansion	α=0.55 x 10^{-6}/°C
Thermo-optic coefficient (dn/dT)	η=8.6 x 10^{-6}/°C
Length of FBG	L=28 mm

Table 3. FBG and PZT Parameters

3.4.3 Optical setup for DC high voltage input

A DC voltage was applied on the PZT crystal terminals by using a high voltage supply and the displacement of the PZT was converted into variations of the Bragg central wavelength. The interrogation system for DC voltage measurements is schematically illustrated in Fig. 3.4.3. The light from an amplified spontaneous emission (ASE) ranging from 1520 nm to 1610 nm was used to illuminate the sensor and a commercial interrogation system from FOS&S model Spectral Eye 400, with accuracy of 2.0 pm was used to measure the reflected FBG spectrum accordingly to the sensor displacement.

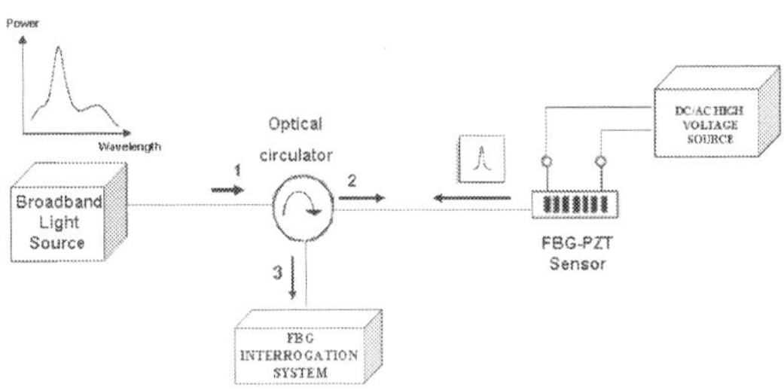

Fig. 3.4.3. Schematic diagram of experiment setup for DC voltage.

For the first experiment, only DC voltages were applied to the PZT in order to measure the Bragg displacement accurately by the interrogation system. Eq. 9 was used to calculate the maximum voltage to be applied to the PZT ceramic and do not exceed the allowed value, accordingly with the Table 3.

$$V = E.d_{ij} \tag{4}$$

By applying a DC voltage to the PZT and recording the respective Bragg shift we can see the linear relationship between the applied voltage and the central Bragg wavelength (Fig. 3.4.4). The results show that the measured sensitivity was of 91.5 pm/kV and the correlation coefficient (R2) were 0.999.

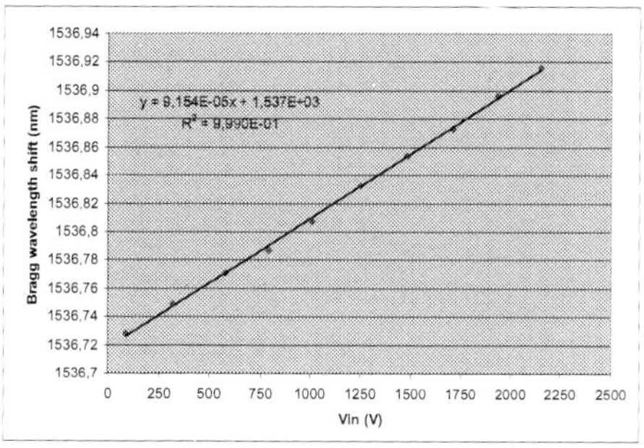

Fig. 3.4.4. FBG-PZT sensor curve when a DC voltage is applied

3.4.4 The optical setup with a AC voltage power supply

Fig. 3.4.5 represents the interrogation system for AC voltage measurements. Since the optical spectrum analyzer is too slow to respond to the 60-Hz line frequency, the central wavelength variation can be obtained by using a photo-detector. The light from the ASE illuminates the FBG-PZT sensor via an optical circulator. The reflected spectrum of the sensor pass through the Fabry-Perot tunable filter (FFP-TF) with 0.89 nm bandwidth, nominal finesse of 130 and 116 nm of free spectral range (FSR). The light signal enters an amplified photo-detector with designed for detection of light signal over 700 nm - 1800 nm. The AC output signal is monitored by an oscilloscope. The FFP filter was tuned in 1540.04 nm by applying a voltage of the 7.2 volts. This point indicates that the FFP filter is matched with the FBG sensor on the stack and the intensity of light at the photo-detector is at maximum.

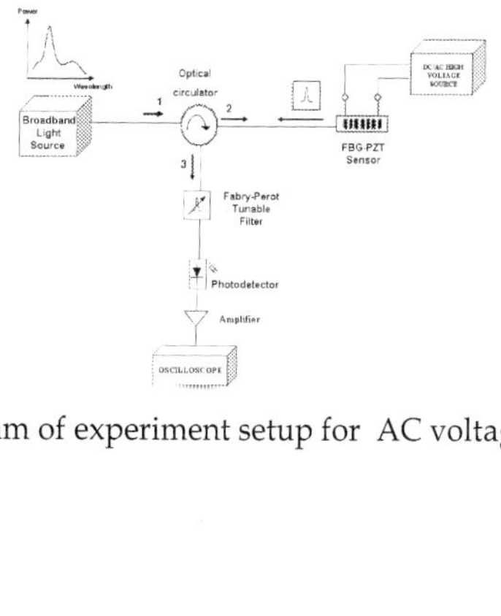

Fig 3.4.5. Schematic diagram of experiment setup for AC voltage.

From Fig. 3.4.6 we can see a linear relationship between the AC voltage applied to the FBG-PZT sensor and the output signal. A high voltage source was used to supply the input signal ranging from 0 kV to 2 kV at the terminals of the PZT electrodes, and on Figure 3.4.7 we can see the sequence of screens of the oscilloscope when an increment of AC voltage is applied to the PZT terminals.

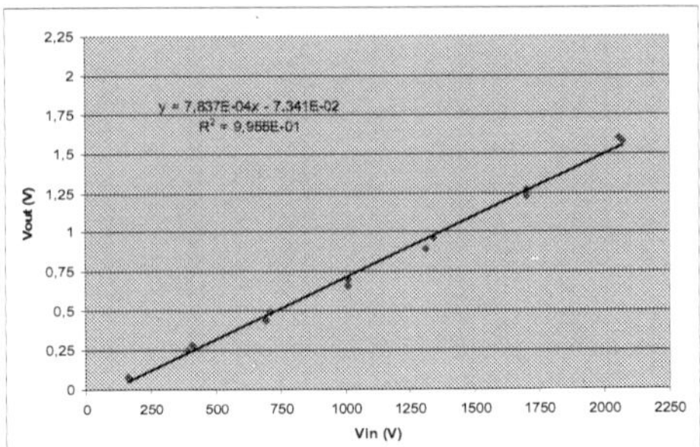

Fig. 3.4.6. Relationship between the input AC voltage versus output signal

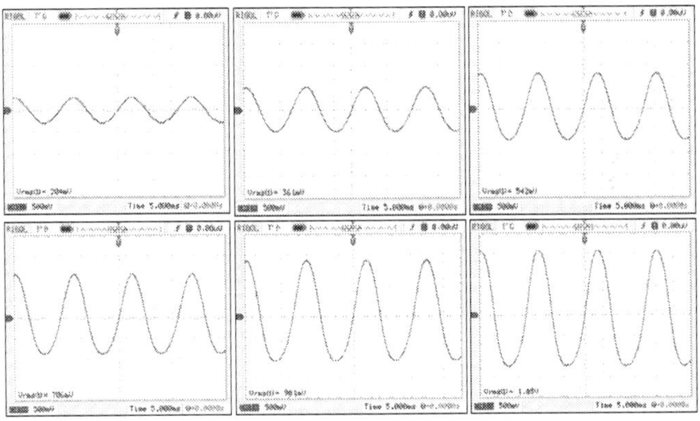

Fig. 3.4.7. Photodetector output signal for each increment of the AC voltage applied (Vrms)

3.4.5 Mechanical and temperature stability

All mechanicals parts are very rigid, including the PZT ceramics and the FBG itself which presents a Young modulus of 70 GPa, close to that of steel as measured in section II. In an OVT the vibrations are mainly of 60 Hz, due to magnetic movement of the transformer core. However, in the case of an optical CT, there is no iron core to vibrate and then this equipment is noiseless and does not present this kind the vibrations.

Figure 3.4.8 shows the results for several acquisitions employing the sensor, where a low dispersion of results when a DC voltage is applied on the terminals of the sensor can be observed. However, it is important to notice that one degree Celsius in temperature change will cause an approximately 14 pm Bragg wavelength displacement. Therefore, temperature compensation is important in DC/AC applications because the drift caused by temperature variation will affect not only the sensor response, but also all parts of the transducer, producing unwanted drifts. However for DC only, a simple high-pass filter easily filters out temperature drifts from the output signal. A picture of the sensor on the high voltage rig is shown in Fig. 3.4.9.

This experiment provided information for the mathematical model developed in section IV and showed a good repeatability in sets of measurements and a correlation coefficient R^2=0,997.

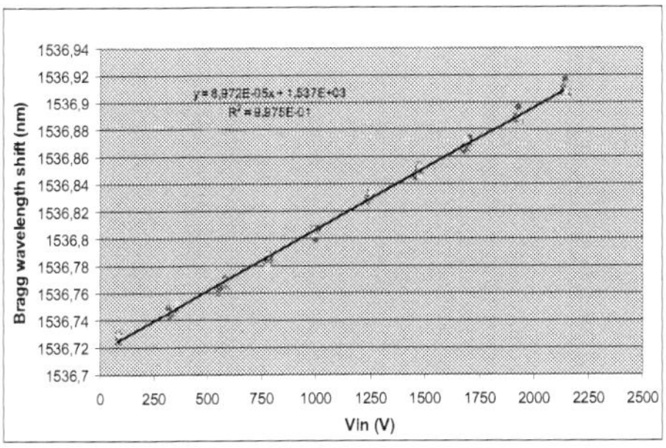

Fig. 3.4.8. FBG-PZT sensor curve when a DC voltage is applied

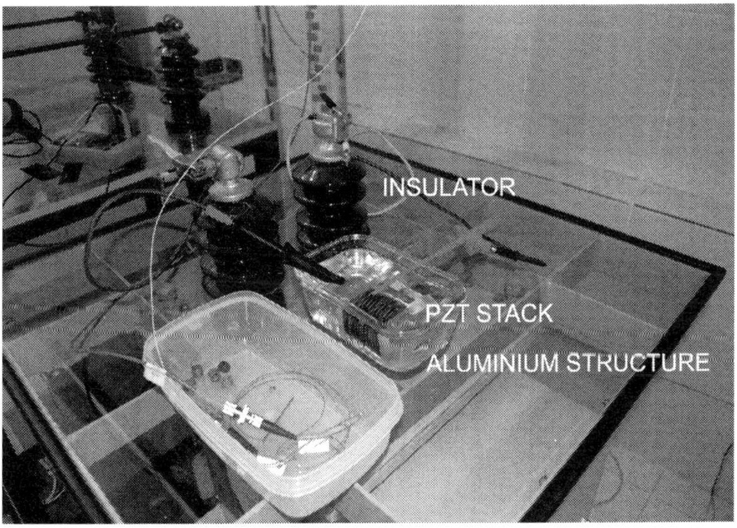

Fig. 3.4.9. Photograph of the FBG-PZT sensor.

3.4.6 Conclusions

In this work, it was presented the development of an optical high voltage transformer based in FBG and PZT piezoelectric ceramics for use on a 13.8 kV-Class electric power transmission system The advantages of piezoelectric material with the characteristics of a sensor fiber Bragg grating is employed. For the assembly of the prototype used, the aluminum structure was designed in order to support a larger number of ceramic rings and thus increase the longitudinal displacement of the material by improving the resolution of the demodulation system. An aspect to be considered is related to the maximum field strength allowed according to the manufacturer's specifications restricting the voltage applied to the sensor, an aspect that can be solved with a capacitive divider. Despite this limitation, the results make it viable the use of this technology for monitoring power substations. In order to improve the system and increase accuracy, a more appropriate setup is under development. An increased longitudinal displacement can be obtained with a new prototype sensor based on ceramics with a higher piezoelectric charge constant and by encapsulation of the sensor by increasing the sensitivity.

3.5 Fiber Bragg grating temperature sensor system applied to large air cooled hydrogenerators

3.5.1 Introduction

This project describes the research, project, construction, calibration, installation and operation of a fiber Bragg grating based fiber-optic system applied to a hydro-electric generator to perform a continuous monitoring of temperature. After being deployed for two and a half years, the system has proved itself to be capable of reliably and accurately measuring and monitoring temperatures inside the generator, even taking into consideration the harsh environment of the stator. The results were considered satisfactory, demonstrating the usefulness of the fiber-optic system in power generation equipment.

The technology of power generation by hydro-electric plants (HEP) in Brazil has reached a high level of sophistication and investment. Nowadays about 73% of all electric energy produced in the country is from HEPs, including very large ones such as Itaipu and Tucuruí with 14 and 8.3 GW respectively. This figure will increase further with the already in construction Rio Madeira Complex whose 88 turbines will produce over 6.8 GW and Belo Monte (11.3 GW) in licensing processes.

This electric grid represents a very high capital invested which is also of very expensive maintenance. Each minute down time of any piece of equipment could cost the energy providers thousands of dollars from profit losses of undelivered energy and also from several types of fines applied by the National Electric Power Agency which they are subjected to.

For this reason the reliability of equipment has become a highest priority and many control systems have been designed to protect and perform real time diagnosing for prompt shutdown or warnings in case of faults.

The main control parameter in any HEP or substation is, of course, the electric current that can rise without limits in case a short-circuit or excess load occurs. The second parameter in importance is the voltage that may present surges or transients due to switching or atmospheric discharges. The third parameter, normally a consequence of the current, is the temperature that must be under severe observation since rises above 100°C can accelerate aging of the insulating material and conductors or even destroy them, causing a general failure of the generators or transformers. Paradoxally, since current and voltage maintain their values approximately the same all over the HEP, there are much more temperature control points in a HEP than there are for current or voltage.

With the idea of decreasing the amount of copper wires, facilitating the maintenance, possibility of remote sensing and consequently decreasing costs, we designed a fiber-optic multiplexed temperature sensor for application in large air cooled HEP. The system has the objective to cover all temperature monitoring needs of a HEP that would also overcome some the disadvantages presented by the conventional RTD (resistive temperature detector) network.

The Eletronorte, the largest electric energy producer in Brazil, contracted the Instrumentation and Photonics Laboratory, at the Federal University of Rio de Janeiro to project, test and install a complete FBG system to monitor the temperatures inside hydro-generator.

This paper relates the world's first real application, test and operation of a FBG temperature sensor array inside a fully operational and connected-to-the-grid hydro-electric power generator.

3.5.2 Hydrogenerator temperature monitoring

Although hydro-generators are very reliable, the temperature monitoring of these machines is a well-established procedure. The reason for this is that the stator windings, cooper and insulation, age over time and tend to degrade when the machine operates at relatively high temperatures such as the in the range 100-120°C [Stone, G. C., 1999]. Keeping the temperature below these limits is not easy because large hydrogenerators stators and rotor can weigh as much as 1,000 tons and 1,700 tons, respectively, and as a consequence, these machines have a big thermal time constant.

For keeping the temperature below these limits, large hydro-electric machines of 40 MW or more are normally air cooled. These generators are supplied with a closed air-cooling circuit where the air is cooled by a water refrigerated radiator. In this type of generator the air temperature is monitored before and after it passes through the radiators.

The temperature monitoring of the cooling air or directly inside the stator winding conductors are the most reliable methods of assuring the proper operation of power generator [Stone, G. C., 1999] and for these measurements, the most popular sensor is the Pt-100, meaning 100 Ω platinum resistance sensor, also known as RTD. These sensors are placed at various locations within the generator, for instance, in the cooling air passages, inside the lubricant and hydraulic oil pipes, in the bearings and also inserted into the slots of the stator core, summing up to about fifteen or more sensors for each machine.

These reliable, accurate and relatively inexpensive sensors are in use by the industry for almost a century and perfectly fulfill all temperature monitoring needs of a HEP. They have disadvantages, though, that can be mentioned: a) sensitivity to electromagnetic interference (EMI), demanding low pass filters; b) tendency to carry the high voltage of the generator to the control room if short circuits occur; c) tendency to burn inside the slots of the stator winding where they cannot be replaced. Additionally, each sensor is driven by a three wire harness that needs to go all the way from the machine to the control room where a large rack with many modules receives each sensor harness. For larger distances it is necessary to use a current loop to carry the information signals, therefore a terminal box must be installed close to the sensor location with amplifiers, filters and converters to 4-to-20 mA, for example. In a relatively large HEP with ten generators, there are many terminal boxes, harnesses, plug-in modules and racks all over the plant with hundreds of kilometers of electric wires. This is the principal aspect where a multiplexed sensor array can help, as with only a few fiber-optic cables the system can manage all temperature check points of the whole plant.

The feasibility of application FBG sensors in electric machines for temperature monitoring has been the theme of many recent works. One of them is the paper from a Siemens AG engineer team [Theune, et al., 2002] in which the authors investigate the application of FBG sensors embedded into the stator core of a generator on a test bench. This test demonstrated the viability of the FBG technique applied to generators. More recently, the internal temperatures of oil-immersed power transformers were measured by FBG arrays extending the application of this kind of fiber-optic sensor in electric machines [Kim et al., 2008, Wei-gen et al, 2008 and Ribeiro et al, 2008]

3.5.3 FBG theory

Fiber Bragg Grating (FBG) technology is one of the most popular choices for optical fiber sensors for strain or temperature measurements due to their simple manufacture (UV photo-inscribed) and relatively strong reflected signal strength. They are formed by a periodic modulation of the index of refraction of the fiber core along the longitudinal direction and can be produced by various techniques [Othonos and Kalli, 1999 and Meltz et al., 1989].

Since the strain or temperature measurands are encoded into wavelength shifts, these sensors are also self-calibrated because wavelength is an absolute parameter. Thus these sensors do not drift on the total light levels, losses in the connecting fibers and couplers or light source power. Additionally, the wavelength encoded nature of the output also allows the use of wavelength division multiplexing technique (WDM) by assigning each sensor to a different wavelength range of the available light source spectrum.

In the FBG, due to the periodic modulation of the index of refraction, light guided along the core of the fiber will be weakly backwards reflected by each grating plane. The contribution of the reflected light from each grating plane will add up with each other in the backward direction. This addition can be constructive or destructive, depending on whether the wavelength of the incoming light satisfies or not the Bragg condition, given by:

$$\lambda_B = 2n_{eff} \cdot \Lambda \qquad (1)$$

Where, n_{eff} is the effective index of refraction of the fiber core and Λ is the modulation period of the index of refraction.

Equation (1), also known as the Bragg reflection wavelength, is the peak wavelength of the narrowband spectral component reflected by each FBG of the array. The FWHM (full-width-half-maximum) or bandwidth of this reflection depends on several parameters, particularly the grating length. Typically, the FWHM is 0.05 to 0.3 nm in most sensor applications. Equation 30 also shows that the Bragg wavelength is a function of Λ and n_{eff}. Thus we conclude that a longitudinal deformation due to an external force can change both Λ and n_{eff}, the later by the photo-elastic effect and the former by increasing the pitch of the grating.

Equivalently, a variation of temperature can also change both parameters, by thermal dilation and by the thermo-optic effect respectively.
With such a device, by injecting a spectrally broadband source of light into the fiber, a narrowband spectral component at the Bragg wavelength will be reflected by the grating. In the transmitted light, this spectral component will be missed but the remaining of this light can be used to illuminate other FBGs in the same fiber, each one tuned in a different wavelength. The final result of such arrangement is that we will have at the beginning of the fiber all Bragg peak reflections of each FBG, each one in its specific wavelength range.
Now, by designing the proper interface, measurands can be made to impinge perturbation on the grating resulting in a shift in the Bragg wavelength which can then be used as a parameter transducer.
Starting from the theorem of the conservation of energy and momentum, after a series of algebraic manipulations, very well detailed in [Othonos and Kalli, 1999], one arrives to the following equation, which establishes the relationship between the Bragg wavelength, strain and temperature applied to the FBG:

$$\frac{\Delta\lambda_B}{\lambda_B} = (1-\rho_e)\varepsilon_z + (\alpha+\eta)\Delta T \qquad (2)$$

Where, ε_z is the longitudinal strain; ΔT is the temperature variation; ρ_e is the photo-elastic coefficient; α is the thermal expansion coefficient and η is the thermo-optic coefficient, representing the temperature dependence of the refractive index (dn/dT). For materials with positive thermal expansion coefficient, the index of refraction normally decreases with temperature. These parameters have the following values for a silica fiber with a germanium doped core:

$\rho_e=0.22$;
$\alpha=0.55 \times 10^{-6}/°C$;
and $\eta=8.6 \times 10^{-6}/°C$.

Since we want to measure only the temperature, we must protect the fiber against strain by placing the grating portion of the fiber inside a protective tubing, for instance. Thus the sensitivity of the grating for temperature at the wavelength range of 1550 nm is, after substituting the constants in (2):

$$\frac{\Delta\lambda_B}{\Delta T} = 14.18\frac{pm}{{}^0C} \qquad (3)$$

This theoretical value, though, is not absolute as each FBG of the same fabrication batch will present slightly different sensitivities, as we will see later in the following sections.

3.5.4 Calibration of sensors

Before installing the sensors into the generator they had to be calibrated because, as already mentioned, (3) is not valid for all FBGs as they may have different thermo-optic coefficients and they are tuned into different wavelengths.

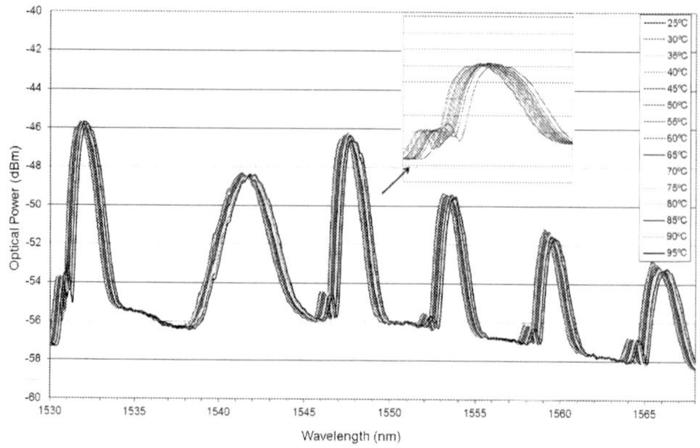

Fig. 3.5.1. Superimposed wavelength shift of each FBG as temperature varies from 25°C to 95°C.

The calibration procedure of the sensors followed two steps. In the first set of measurements, the six sensors were calibrated simultaneously by immersion into a temperature controlled bath and the Bragg wavelengths were monitored along with the temperature in order to calculate the sensitivity of each sensor, as predicted by (3).

This first set of measurements allowed us to observe and measure the Bragg shift of each FBG as a function of temperature in the range of 25°C to 95°C. Fig. 3.5.1 shows all Bragg reflection of each temperature superimposed. In this experiment it is important to make sure that each pulse does not enter the neighbor's range during its displacement.

From this data the software calculates the center wavelength of each Bragg reflection and plots the Bragg shift versus temperature for each FBG, producing the graph shown in Fig. 3.5.2.

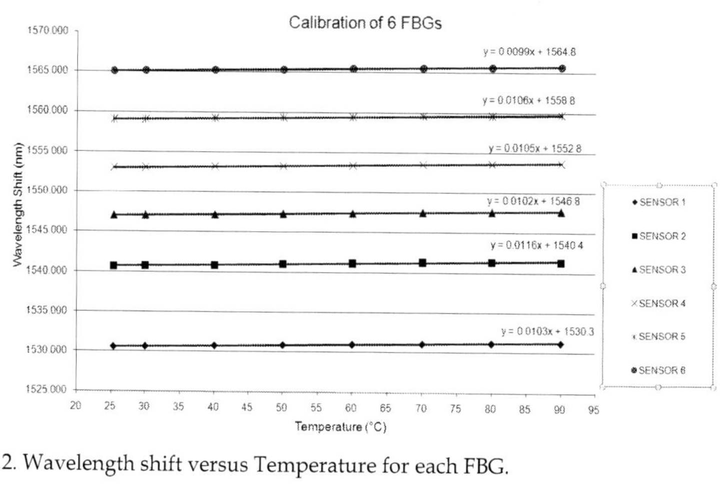

Fig. 3.5.2. Wavelength shift versus Temperature for each FBG.

Table 4 summarizes the information acquired from the last experiment.

Sensor #	Theoretical Sensitivity (pm/°C)	Measured Sensitivity (pm/°C)	Wavelength @ 25°C (nm)
1	14.00	10.3	1530,534
2	14.10	11.6	1540,667
3	14.16	10.2	1547,027
4	14.21	10.5	1553,035
5	14.27	10.6	1559,063
6	14.32	9.9	1565,090

Table 4. Theoretical and measured sensitivities of each FBG.

Notice in Table 4 that, as predicted by (3), the theoretical sensitivities are different from those obtained in the calibration experiment. But, since all FBGs were made out of the same optical-fiber reel, α, the silica coefficient of temperature should be the same for all FBGs produced from that fiber. The other parameter in (3) is η, the thermo-optic coefficient, representing the temperature dependence of the refractive index (dn/dT). Equation (1) teaches us that λ_B is a function of n_{eff}, the average index of refraction between the pristine fiber core and that of the ultra-violet-irradiated core. Recall that during the FBG fabrication, the radiation time for each FBG inscription is not the same as the operator turns off the laser only when she observes the Bragg reflection above a certain level. Since the UV irradiation modifies the index of refraction of the fiber core, it is possible that it could also modify differently the values of η in each FBG, ending up to the slightly dispersed sensitivities found above. However, to the best of our knowledge, there is no mention of this effect whatsoever in the literature.

The data obtained from Fig. 3.29 also allow us to calculate the linear relationship between wavelength and temperature for each FBG. These equations were fed into the software in order to calculate the temperature of each sensor.

The second step of the calibration procedure was the comparison between the calculated temperatures by the optical interrogator software with the calibrated temperatures of each FBG, as given by a precision thermometer. From this experiment it was possible to calculate the inaccuracy of the measurement which was less than 0.5°C, quite sufficient for this application. The correlation coefficient of the linear curve fitting was 0.9994 as shown in Fig. 3.5.3.

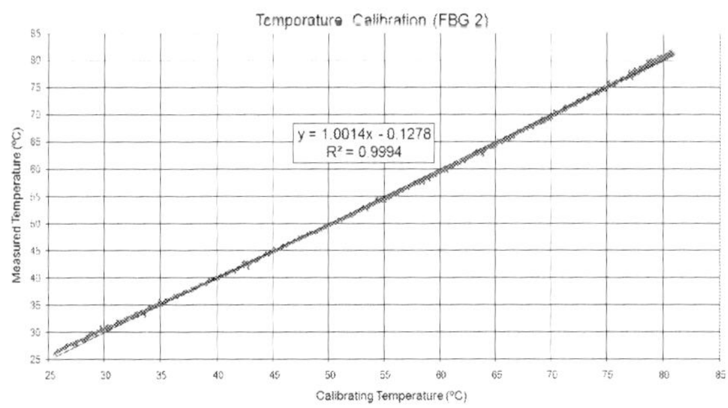

Fig. 3.5.3. Calibration of FBG 2.

3.5.5 Installation of sensors and results

The HEP chosen for this experiment was the UHE-Samuel, at Brazil`s far west city of Porto Velho, close to the border with Bolivia. UHE-Samuel is located at the Jamari River, a tributary of the Madeira River, which in turn, is one of the major tributaries of the Amazon River. The UHE-Samuel generates 216 MW and counts with five Kaplan-type turbines generating each one about 42 MW.

The system began to be installed in the generator number five in November 2007. This process was performed in two opportunities: during a five-day shutdown of the machine for maintenance and in another five-day window for retrofit (exchange of rectifiers).

For the installation of the sensors inside the stator it is obviously necessary to turn off the machine, which is not an easy task. This is because, as the majority of HEPs in Brazil, UHE-Samuel is a national-grid-connected HEP therefore to be turned off, one needs a special authorization issued by the National System Operator. The request is normally dispatched six months in advance, and if granted, the machine is allowed to be turned off during a five-day window.

The machine, which operates at a normal temperature around 95ºC, needs 24 hours to drop its temperature to about 45ºC in order to be possible to enter inside the stator hall to install the sensors. The stator environment can be considered to be one of the worst places a sensor can be installed in. Its average temperature is about 95ºC peaking up to 110ºC with an air humidity close to 100%; it presents a dense oily atmosphere; a very high electro-magnetic interference at a few millimeters from 15 kV conductors carrying a current of 2 kA; vibrations of every kind up to 0.3 G and among heavy parts that are frequently assembled and disassembled using heavy tools with huge force. How can so a fragile sensor, such as a 125-μm-diameter-glass-optical-fiber-sensor, be installed in such harsh environment and even though keep its reliability during the expected 40-years life span?

A FBG used as a temperature sensor presents a very small time constant because it has a small mass. In order to protect this sensor and do not deteriorate such a valuable parameter the sensor was installed loosely inside a thin U-form copper tubing in order to allow a good heat transfer between the cooling air and the optical fiber, as shown in Fig. 3.5.4. The tubing, which also protects the fiber against strain, goes out and back again from an IP65 polymeric enclosure.

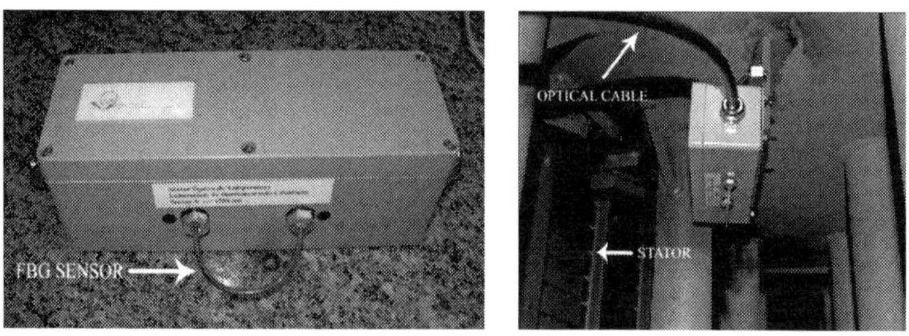

Fig. 3.5.4. Box containing the fiber-optic splices with the FBG inside the U-shape copper tubing (left) and installed inside the generator (right).

An adequate fiber-optic cable connected all six boxes as they were installed around the stator winding behind of each radiator of the generator. The optical cable was then placed within the existing cable trays along with other electric cables following all the way up, from the generator to the HEP control room where the optical interrogator and an industrial PC were installed.

The optical interrogation setup consists of a broad band optical source that illuminates all FBGs in the array. The return signal of each FBG is detected by an optical spectrum analyzer (OSA) that identifies the center wavelength of each FBG reflection pulse. The OSA communicates with an industrial PC via RS-232 interface, running a LabView software for calculation and storage of the temperatures. The PC publishes all data into the company's Intranet that automatically and instantaneously become available to the HEP central software control. Fig. 3.5.5 shows the block diagram of the system.

However, the proposed system goes much further in ambition. After the approval of the current system, the proposed project planes to use this technology to fulfill all temperature needs of the HEP, including turbines, air, oil and water ducts and other electrical equipment as well at the substation (see Fig. 3.5.6). Since a single optical fiber cable can monitor about 16 or more sensors, it is just necessary one cable per equipment for all temperature measurements. The system is also intended to access the Internet so as to be able to be accessed remotely, even from another location. This is especially advantageous for automatic unmanned substations.

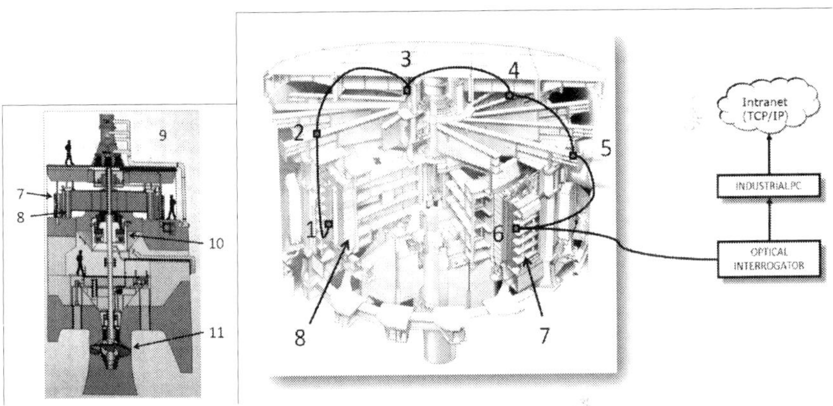

Fig. 3.5.5. Depiction of a cross-section of the hydro-generator (left). Generator in detail with sensors connected to the interrogation system (right). 1 to 6) FBG sensors; 7) Radiator; 8) Stator; 9) Machine room; 10) Bearing; 11) Kaplan turbine.

Shortly after the installation we noticed that the last two FBGs in the fiber-optic cable were not identified by the optical interrogator, probably due a malfunction of the optical connectors. But there was no time to open up again the inspection windows of the stator as the machine was programmed to start up immediately. Since then, the machine did not stop again as our requests for shutting down were not granted so far. Currently, at the time of writing this article, the machine is in operation for two and a half years and the fiber-optic system is monitoring normally four radiators. The results of the measurements are sent periodically to the company's head-quarters in Belém, some 1,800 km north and from there to our laboratory located in Rio de Janeiro, 2,400 km south.

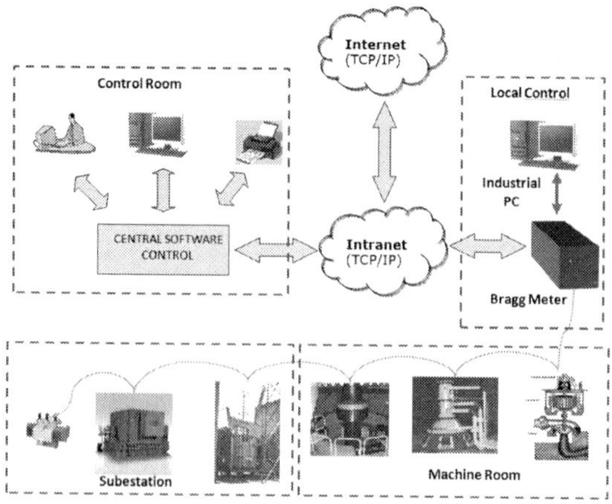

Fig. 3.5.6. Proposed extension of the system including all monitoring needs of the hydro-electric plant.

Just after the installation the system started the monitoring the temperatures, producing the graph shown in Fig. 3.5.7. We can observe all signals superimposed at about 33ºC.

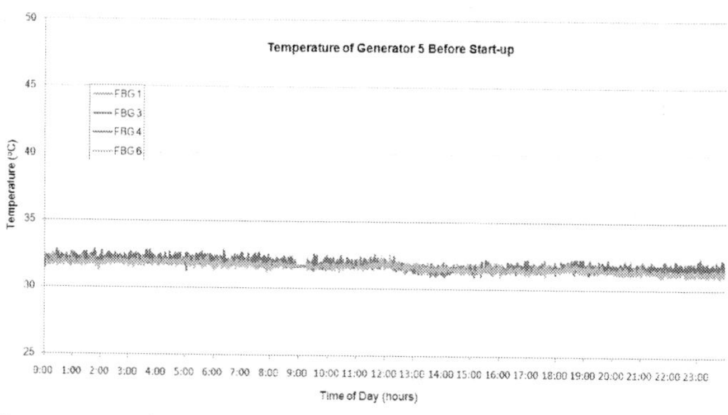

Fig. 3.5.7. Temperature of generator 5 before start up.

After the installation the machine was several times started up and down in test procedures. The graph in Fig. .45 shows the evolution of the temperature during the last start up test of the generator. Notice that, differently than in Figure 3.5.8, the temperatures of the radiators were not the same before start up. This is because the machine was working before with differenttemperatures around the stator, which is normal as it will be seen later. At 9 AM the turbine was opened to the dam and the machine started-up. The temperature at FBG 3 rose from around 35ºC to 85ºC while the turbine accelerated up to 90 rpm until in phase with the 60 Hz grid frequency. Then, at 6 PM the generator was switched to the national grid and the temperature rose again up to 95ºC, stabilizing thereafter.

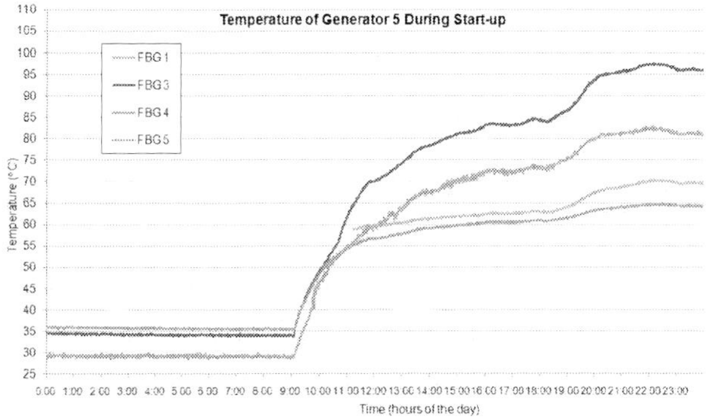

Fig. 3.5.8. Temperature evolution of generator 5 during start up.

Fig. 3.5.9 shows the temperature of the generator in normal operation. At this time the generator was producing 22 MW with an average water flow of 82 m^3/s.

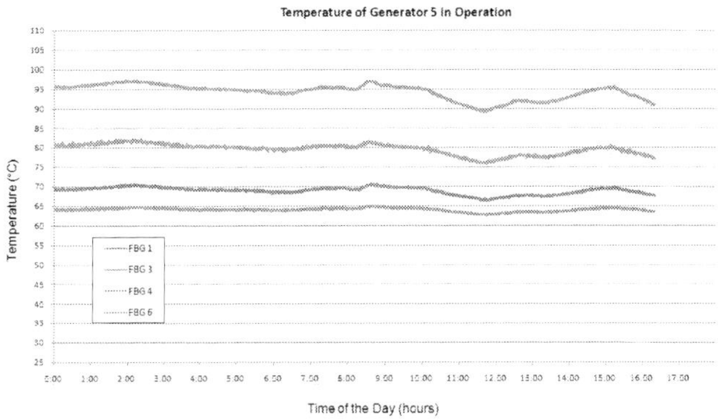

Fig. 3.5.9. Temperature of generator 5 in operation.

As in Fig. 3.5.8, we can still observe in Fig. 3.5.9 a difference in temperature between different sections of the generator. For explaining this behavior it is necessary first to understand how the cooling system works. The cold water from the bottom of the dam is taken by a pipe and, after a chlorine treatment, it feeds the radiators, one after the other, in a row. But as the water pipe goes around the stator feeding each radiator, the water loses pressure so that the first radiator has a higher water flow than the second, and so on until the water reaches the last radiator which receives much less water. Therefore, each section of the stator is cooled down to different temperatures leading to the behavior observed in Fig. 3.5.8 and Fig. 3.5.9. Of course a load unbalance between the phases would also lead to different temperatures but in a 5-machine plant with all generators interconnected this would be very difficult to happen.

Observing Fig. 3.5.9 it is possible to notice that, even in steady state the generator temperatures vary along the time, with all temperatures following the same pattern. This is how the generator responds to the energy demands by the load.

3.5.6 Conclusions

This case described the world's first real application, test and operation of a FBG temperature sensor array inside a fully operational and connected-to-the-grid hydro-electric power generator. The FBGs sensors were installed inside the generator in November 2007 and are in continuous operation since then. The system was capable to measure and monitor reliably and accurately temperatures inside the generator even considering the harsh environment of the stator generator.

With this system in operation a large reduction of installation and maintenance costs could be avoided since many kilometers of electric wire would be saved.

Another conclusion of such experiment is that it is very difficult to conciliate research and commercial interests. Scientists working with power generation find enormous difficulties in having machines turned off, particularly those connected to the national grid. Power operation authorities are so much concerned about system reliability and energy production without discontinuities that often refuse any kind of research proposals that could, in any way, put in jeopardy machines integrity or interrupt energy production.

4. References

R. C. S. B. Allil and M. M. Werneck, "Optical High Voltage Sensor based in Fiber Bragg Grating and PZT Piezoeletric Ceramics", *IEEE Transactions on Instrumentaion and Measurement"*, Vol. 60 , Issue 7, 2011

K. Asada and H. Yuki, "Fiber optic temperature sensor", 3rd POF'94, p. 49-51, Yokohama, Japan (1994).

J. B. Briggs, "Leakage current monitoring system and method", U.S. Patent 3,947,759 (1976).

G. Böttger, M. Dreschmann, C. Klamouris, M. Hübner, M. Röger, A. W. Bett, T. Kueng, J. Becker, W. Freude and J. Leuthold, "An optically powered video camera link", *IEEE Photonic Tech. Letters*, vol. 20, no.1, pp. 39-41, Jan. 2008.

T. W. Cease, J. G. Driggans, and S. J. Weikel, "Optical voltage and current sensors used in a revenue metering system", *IEEE Transactions on Power Delivery* Vol. 6, Issue 4, pp. 1374-1379, October 1991.

D. A. Douglas and R. Thrash, "Sag and tension of Conductor - The Electric Power Engineering Handbook", CRC Press/IEEE Press. 2007.

S. Tumanski, "Induction coil sensors-a review", *Measurement Science and Technology*, vol. 18, no. 3, R31-R46, March 2007.

F. Amarh, "Electric transmission line flashover prediction system", PhD Thesis, Arizona State University, May (2001).

K. T. V. Grattan and Z. Y. Zhang, "Fiber Optic Fluorescence Thermometry", Chapman &Hall, London (1995).

R. W. Hertzberg, *Deformation and Fracture Mechanics of Engineering Materials*, Wiley; 4rd edition, Chapter 4, December 1995.

IEC 60793-1-1 "*Opticals fibres - Part 1-1: Measurement methods and test procedures - General and guidance*", International Electrotechinical Commission, 2008.

A. D. Kersey, M. A. Davis, et al. "Fiber grating sensors. Journal of Ligthwave Technology," N°.8, 1997, pp. 1442-1463.

B. Jaffe, R. S. Roth, and S. Marzullo, "Piezoeletric porperties of lead zirconate-lead titanate solid-solution ceramics",J.Appl.Phys., vol.25, pp. 809-810; June, 1954.

A. G. Kanashiro e G. F. Burani, "Leakage Current Monitoring of Insulators Exposed to Marine and Industrial Pollution", IEEE International Symposium on Electrical Insulation, 271-274, Quebec, Canada, (1996).

C. R. Kurkjian, J. T. Krause, M. J. Matthewson, "Strength and Fatigue of Silica Optical Fibers", *Journal of Light Techonology*, pp: 1360-1370, Vol.7, N° 9, September 1989.

R. A. Maraio, A. T. McMahon and H. B. Hart Jr., "Method and detector for identifying insulator flashover", U. S. Patent 5,136,248 (1992).

D. A. Ward and J. L. T. Exon, "Using Rogowski coils for transient current measurements", *Eng. Sci. Education J.*, vol. 2, pp. 105-113, 1993.

J. Marcou (editor), "Plastic Optical Fibers: Practical Applications", Club des FibresOptiquesPlastiques, Wiley & Sons, France (1997).

B. Culshaw& J. Dakin (editors), Optical Fiber Sensor, Artech House, London, 1989 and 1997.

J. N. Mitchell, "Limits of electrical power generation by transmission of light through optical fibers", Applied Physics Division - Southwest Research Institute, 2004, San Antonio, USA.

M. R. Speigel, "Statistics", McGraw-Hill of Brazil, Rio de Janeiro, 1971.

Y. Miyajima, "Studies on High-Tensile Proof Tests of Optical Fibers", *Journal of Lightwave Techonology*, pp. 340-346, Vol. LT-1, N° 2, June 1983

De Nazaré, F. V. B., Weneck, M.M., "Development of a monitoring system to improve ampacity in 138kV transmission lines using photonic technology", *IEEE Transmission and Distribution Conference and Exposition*, 2010, pp.1-6.

P. Niewczas, L. Dziuda, G. Fusiek, and J. R. Mc Donald, "Design and Evaluation of a Preprototype Hybrid Fiber-Optic Voltage Sensor for Remotely Interrogated Condition Monitoring System", *IEEE Transactions on Instrumentaion and Measurement*, vol.54, no.4, augsut 2005.

R. Olshansky, R. D. Maurer, "Tensile strength and fatigue of optical fibers", *Journal of Applied Physics*, pp. 4497-4499, Vol. 47, N° 10, October 1976.

A. Othonos, "Fiber Bragg gratings," Rev. Sci. Instrum, N°.68, 1997, pp. 43094341, 1997.

J. A. Gallego-Juarez, "Piezoelectric ceramics and ultrasonic transducers" J. Phys. E: Sci. Instrum. 22, pp. 804-816, (1989).

S. J. Pember, C. M. France, B. E, Jones, "A multiplexed network of optically powered, addressed and interrogated hybrid resonant sensors", Sensors and Actuators A, 46 47, pp. 474-477, 1995.

D. Persegol, J.L. Lovato and V. Minier, "Thermal diagnosis of medium voltage switchboards: a cost-effective multi-pointPOF sensor", 8th POF'99, p. 256-259, Chiba, Japan (1999).

R. M. Ribeiro, L.A. Marques-Filho and M.M. Werneck, "Fluorescent plastic optical fibers for temperature monitoring", 12th POF'03, p. 282-285, Seattle, USA (2003).

B. Ribeiro and M. M. Werneck, "Tensile Response of re-coated Optical Fibers using a recoating machine" *XXXIII Brazilian Meeting on Condensed Matter Physics*, May 2010.

T. Sawa, K. Kurosawa, T. Kaminishi and T. Yokota, "Development of optical instrument transformers", *IEEE Transactions on Power Delivery* Vol. 5, No. 2, pp. 884-891, April 1990.

A. Tardy, A. Derossis and J. P. Dupraz, "A current sensor remotely powered and monitored through an optical fiber link", *Optical Fiber Technology*, vol. 1, pp. 181-185, 1995.

M. M. Werneck, C. C. Carvalho, Ricardo M. Ribeiro and Fernando L. Maciel, "High-voltage current sensing based hybrid technology". Proceedings of the 12th International POF Conference 2003, pp 50-53, University of Washington, Seattle, EUA, September 14-17, 2003.

M. M. Werneck, A. C. S. Abrantes, "Fiber-optic-based current and voltage measuring system for high-volatge distribution lines", *IEEE Transactions on Power Delivery* 19 (3): 947-951 Jul 2004.

J. G. Werthen, A. G. Andersson, S. T. Weiss and H. O. Björklund, "Current measurements using optical power", IEEE Transmission and Distribution Conference, 1996, pp. 213-218.

J. G. Werthen, M. Cohen, "Photonic power: delivering power over fiber for optical networks", International Conference on Photonics in Switching, Oct. 2006.

Y. Yao and B. Yi, "FBG Based Voltage Measurement using PZT Modulation,"International Conference Wireless Communications, Networking and Mobile Computing, pp. 1-4, September 2006.

2

Communication Strategies for Various Types of Swallowable Telemetry Capsules

Jin-Ho Cho and Sang Hyo Woo
School of Electrical Engineering and Computer Science, Kyungbook National University, South Korea

1. Introduction

In this chapter, introducing some of the ideas, potentialities, and limitations of swalowable telemetry capsule systems. The telemetry systems were widely used for animal research while the subject can do its regular activities [1-9]. Therefore, it is an ideal method to collect the data of migration path and environmental data. In order to collect the data, the telemetry system has to be attached or implanted to the subjects and transmits the signal throughout the antenna. For the human patients, most of physiological signal from outside of the body did not need telemetry systems, because the signal was easily distorted when the patients were moving. Therefore, the telemetry systems are used when the device is implant into the patients and then collect the data. Since the implantation of the device is extremely difficult work, using the telemetry system is limited for scientific researches and a commercial medical telemetry device was not advent.

Since the implantable telemetry systems is limited by the regulations and safety issue, the scientists look forward to develop a disposable capsule that resemble a medical pill and automatically measure the various philological data after swallow it. There are many frontier researches about the telemetry capsules. Some of the capsule measured the intraluminal pressure from inside of the gastro intestine while the capsule goes naturally flow toward to aboral direction [10-14]. Since the physician gets the intraluminal data, it was hard to assume a location of the capsule such as the capsule is in the middle of a duodenum or jejunum?

Another capsule can measure pH signals from the gastro intestine. This capsule provides the meaningful data to diagnosis many diseases such as the gastroesophageal reflux. These capsules also measure the pH signal while it is naturally flow and does not provide location information. While most of the capsules was measuring the signal when the capsule was naturally flow toward to aboral direction, a bravo capsule can stop at the esophagus and measuring the pH difference [15-19]. Other capsules measures the core temperature [20, 21], which is a bit higher than skin temperature.

Unlike above applications, a capsule endoscopy is a revolutionary product that captures inside of the gastro images and transmits it throughout the RF transmitter [22-26]. In order to get clear images, the data rate of the RF transmitter has to be sufficiently high while the power consumption is still low that could be active by small coin batteries. The frontier of this field is Given Image company products and it could monitor not only the small intestine but also the esophagus and colon.

Due to success of the capsule endoscopy, there are many trails to develop the capsule that has surgical operation, medical treatment, and locomotion abilities [27-33]. Most of researches are focused to give locomotion ability by using a magnet, actuator, and electrical stimuli. The aim of locomotion research is to observe a suspicious area because the capsule is naturally goes down to the aboral direction. Other researches do increasing friction to stop the capsule at the suspicious area [34, 35]. Also, there are many interesting capsules are developing such as a bleeding detection [36], assembling capsule[37], and biopsy [37].
From above description, application of the swallowable telemetry capsule is abundant and it is rapidly cutting its edges. In order to transmit the physiological data or control the capsule, a telemetry system is essential part for stable module. In this chapter, a basic telemetry methods are describe in 2.1 to 2.2 and describe important points for swallowable capsule in the 2.6. Therefore, the reader who is familiar of a communication technique should skip the 2.1~2.5 and read the 2.6 directly.

2. Telemetry system

Telemetry is a technology that allows remote measurement, control, and reporting of information. In order to transmit the data throughout radiation, concept of the modulation have to be known.

2.1 Modulation methods

Modulation is the process of varying one or more properties of a high-frequency periodic waveform, called the carrier signal, with respect to a modulating signal. Fig. 1 shows block diagram of the modulation where the signal is modulated by the carrier signal. There are the three key parameters of the modulation, which is amplitude, phase, and frequency. Typically a high-frequency sinusoid waveform is used as carrier signal, but a square wave pulse train may also occur. Fig. 2 (a) depicts the modulation result that the baseband signal ($m(t)$) is up converted by carrier frequency ($\cos(w_c t)$). The negative frequency is generated and bandwidth of the signal is remained.

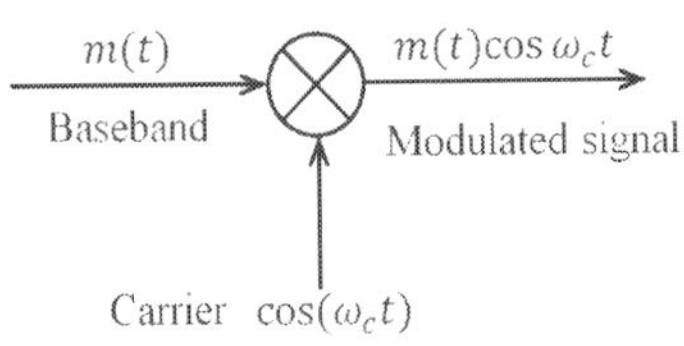

Fig. 1. Block diagram of the modulation.

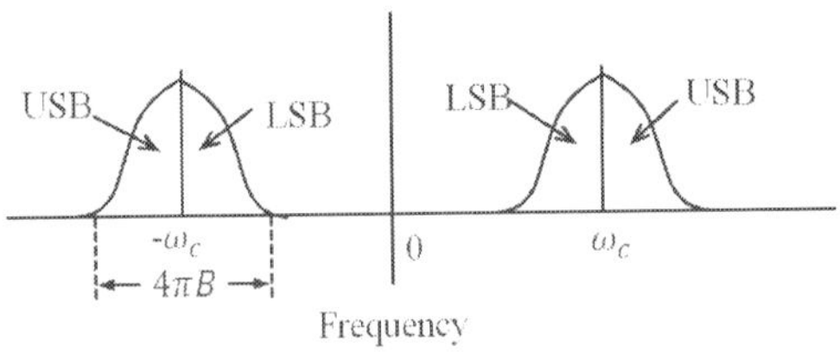

Fig. 2. Spectrum of frequency up converting.

Fig. 3 depicts common analog modulation methods that is known as amplitude modulation (AM), frequency modulation (FM), and phase modulation (PM). The latter two types of modulation are similar, and belong to the class of modulation known as the angle modulation.

The AM is characterized by the fact that amplitude of carrier signal is varied in proportion to the baseband signal. In the fig. 3 (c) depicts modulated AM signal and it could be easily see the amplitude of the signal is varying with the baseband signal. The FM conveys information over a carrier wave by varying its instantaneous frequency. In the fig. 3 (d) depicts the frequency of the carrier signal is changed from the baseband signal. The PM is a form of modulation that represents information as variations in the instantaneous phase of a carrier wave. In the fig. 3 (e) depicts that the phase of the signal is varying with the baseband signal.

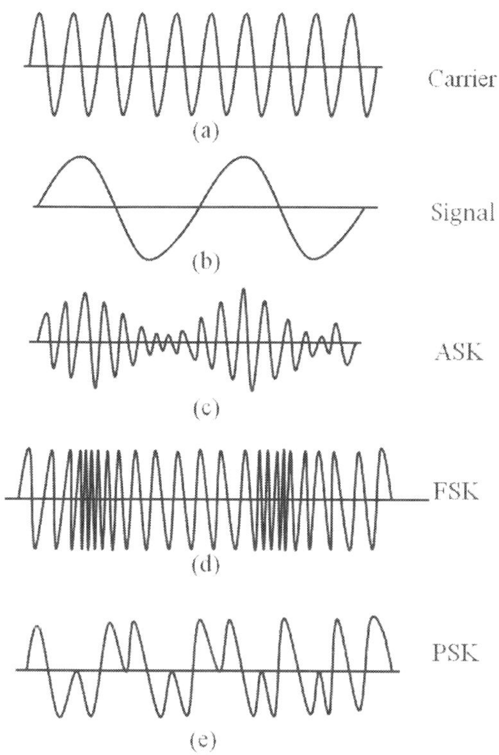

Fig. 3. Simple example of the modulated signal.

With using analog modulation system, the super heterodyne system is widely used due to its simplicity, cheap, and high performance. Fig. 4 depicts the super heterodyne system that uses frequency mixing or heterodyning to convert a received signal to a fixed intermediate frequency (IF). With using the IF, it is easily tuning the channel and can reduce performance of the band filters.

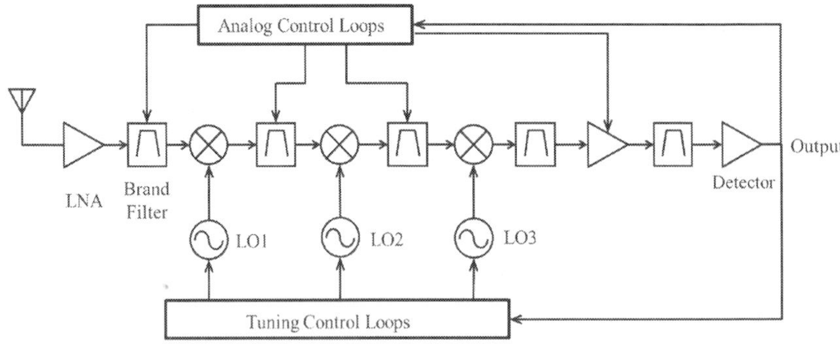

Fig. 4. Block diagram of traditional super heterodyne detection system.

Unlike analogy modulation, the digital modulation uses digitalized baseband signal and in-phase/quadrature (I/Q) modulator, which can actually create the AM, FM, and PM modulation with in one hardware. The fig. 5 depicts the I/Q modulator and demodulator system that has two mixer with same carrier signal with -pi/2 lag. The I/Q modulator can modulate a carrier with a waveform that changes the carrier's frequency slightly; you can treat the modulating signal as the phasor. It has both a real and an imaginary parts, or an in-phase (I) and a quadrature (Q) part. Now construct a receiver that locks to the carrier, and you can decipher information by reading the I and Q parts of the modulating signal.

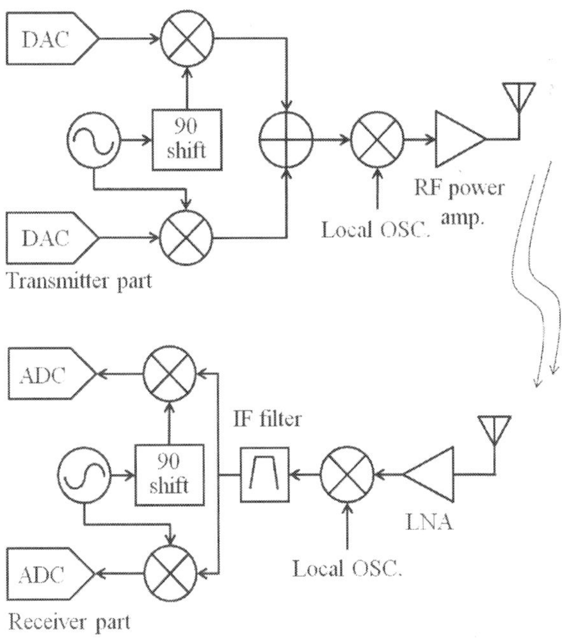

Fig. 5. I/Q modulator and demodulator.

With help the I/Q modulator, various digital modulation is generated such as BPSK, O-PSK, GMSK, and QAM. The Fig. 6 depicts that the BPSK signal that vary with input baseband signal. Unlike analogy modulation, the digital modulation uses digitalized baseband signal and the modulated signal is discontinued.

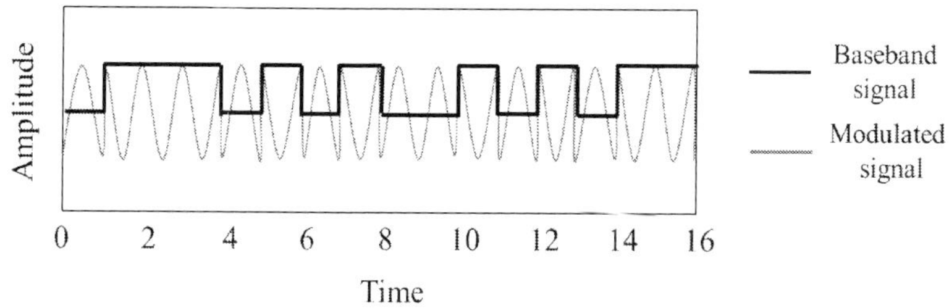

Fig. 6. I/Q modulator and demodulator.

2.2 Spread spectrum

A spread-spectrum system is a process other than the information signal to expand, or spread, the bandwidth of the signal. The spread-spectrum method is that breaks the data signal into little pieces using some kind of code, and the transmitted signal with wide bandwidth. Therefore, it is hard to tap and find the signal. There are four types are used for spectrum spreading such as direct sequence, frequency hopping, time hopping, and frequency chirp.

Fig. 7 depicts a direct sequence spread spectrum (DSSS) technique is that multiply the data by the pseudonoise (PN) code, and spreading the energy of the original signal into a much wider band. The spread signal resemble the white noise, which looks like wide band noise, and it could be dispreading when PN code is known.

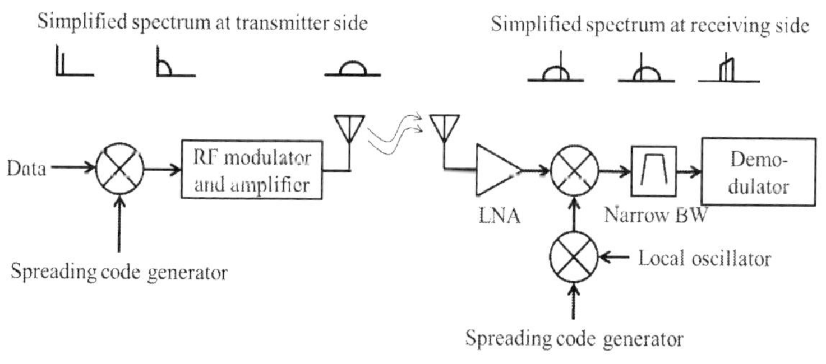

Fig. 7. Diagram of direct-sequence spread spectrum.

Another method to spread spectrum is using frequency-hopping spread spectrum (FHSS). The FHSS is a method of transmitting radio signals by rapidly switching a carrier among many frequency channels, using a pseudorandom sequence. Fig. 8 depicts the block diagram of the FHSS. Unlike the DSSS, the spectrum the FHSS shows vary shape impulses and disappear immediately.

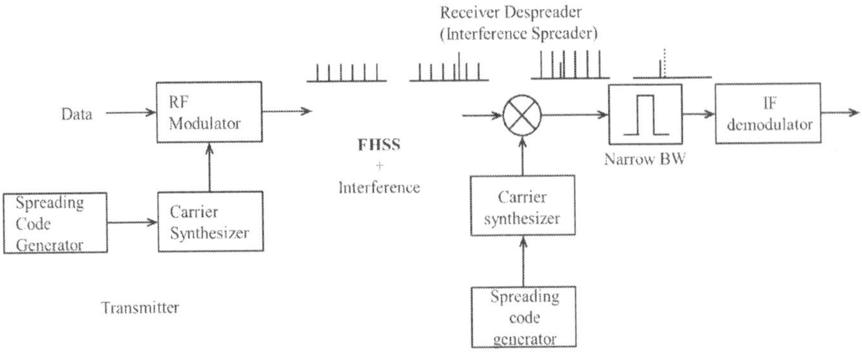

Fig. 8. Block diagram of frequency-hopping spread spectrum.

Orthogonal frequency-division multiplexing (OFDM) is a frequency-division multiplexing (FDM) scheme used as a digital multi-carrier modulation method. A large number of closely-spaced orthogonal sub-carriers are used to carry data. The fig. 9 depicts the difference between the spectrum of FDM and OFDM. Since the FDM have to avoid the superposition its frequency band to other, the OFDM use the sub-carrier are orthogonal to each other.

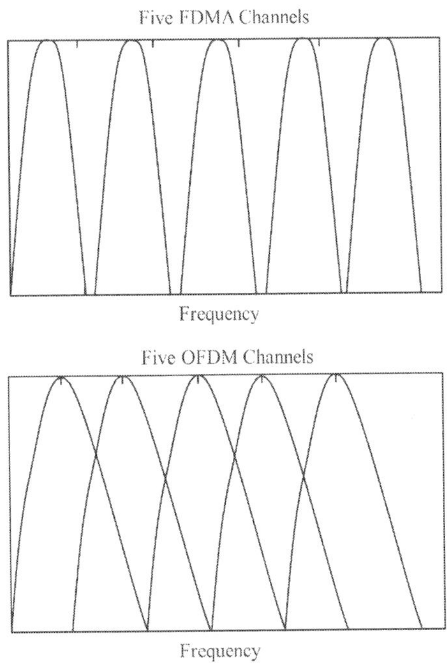

Fig. 9. Spectrum difference of the FDM and OFDM.

The OFDM use an inverse FFT to compute parallel data for giving a set of complex time-domain samples. These samples are then quadrature-mixed to passband in the standard way. The real and imaginary components are first converted to the analogue domain using digital-to-analogue converters (DACs); the analogue signals are then used to modulate cosine and sine waves at the carrier frequency, respectively. These signals are then summed to give the transmission signal. Above descriptions are depicted in the fig. 10.

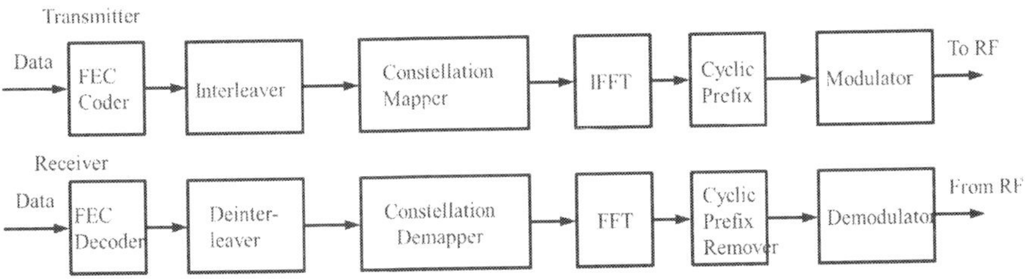

Fig. 10. Block diagram of the OFDM.

2.3 Software-Defined Radio spread spectrum

A software-defined radio system (SDR) is a radio communication system where components that have been typically implemented in hardware such as mixer and detectors. The strong advantage of the SDR is that it can modulate/demodulate various type of communication without additional hardware. The fig. 11 depicts the concept of the SDR that it could receive various modulated signal by one hardware.

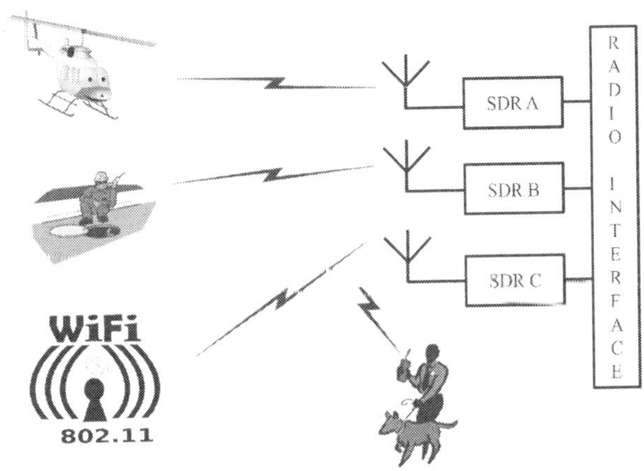

Fig. 11. Concepts of the SDR.

Since the concept of the SDR can directly receive the analog signal from the antenna, the ideal scheme is not completely realized because of limits of the analog to digital conversion (ADC). The ADC speed and resolution is not high enough to receiver RF or IF stage signal. Therefore, most of low end SDR use super-heteroine structure and it is depicts in the Fig. 12.

Recently, many high speed and accuracy ADC is developed and eliminate IF stage and directly receive the signal from IF signal.

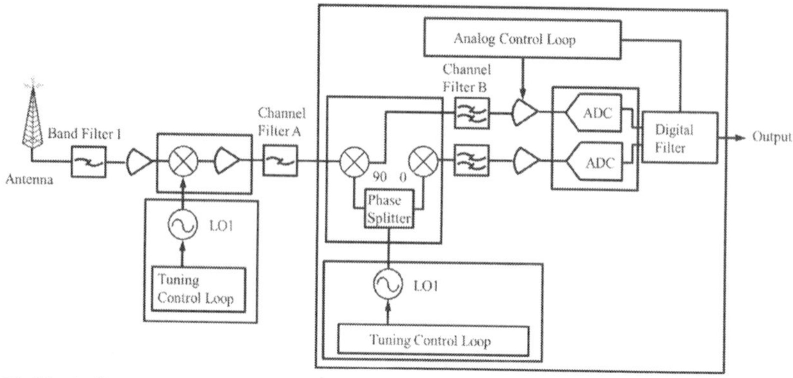

Fig. 12. Block diagram of the SDR.

2.4 Ultra-wideband communication

Ultra-wideband is a radio technology that can be used at very low energy levels for short-range high-bandwidth communications by using a large portion of the radio spectrum. The UWB uses high frequency with low power density which is typically -41 dBm/MHz and does not arrowed to use frequency below 2.6 GHz to reduce possibility of collision. The fig. 13 depicts the FCC indoor mask which is limitation of RF power for the UWB.

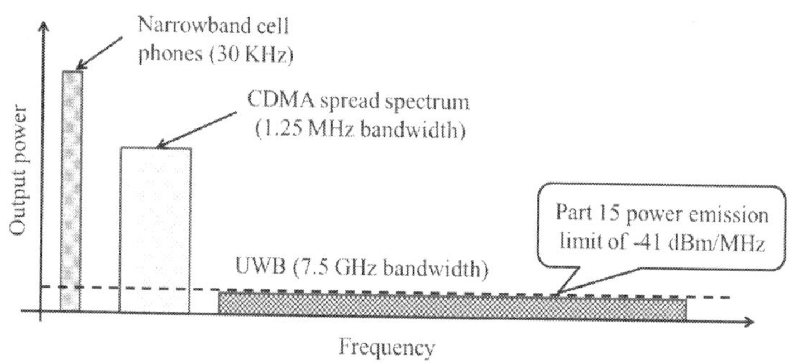

Fig. 13. Band width comparison between commercialized communication and UWB.

In order to follow the regulation, most of the UWB signal is generated by nth derivative of the Gaussian pulse shape. The fig. 14 depicts multiple pulse shapes of the UWB and its equation is shown as

$$p(t) = \frac{A}{\sqrt{2\pi\sigma^2}} e^{(-t^2/2\sigma^2)} \tag{1}$$

Where A,t, and σ are amplitude, time and spread of the Gaussian pulse.

Hence the time which the signal is actually transmitting is very short, the power consumption of the UWB is very low and it is easy to achieve the time division multiplex (TDM).

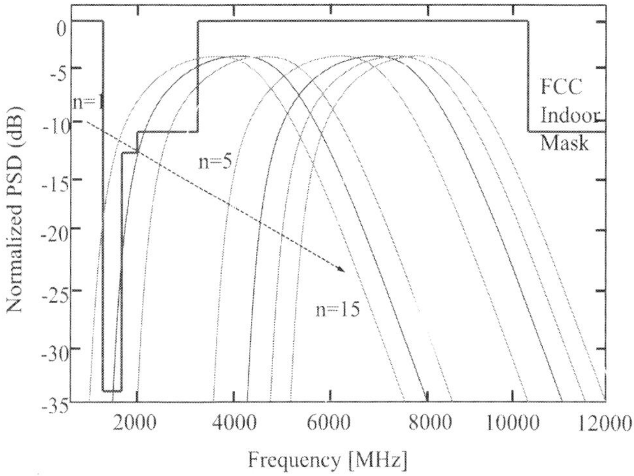

Fig. 14. PSD of higher order derivatives of the Gaussian pulse for UWB indoor systems.

Fig. 15 (a) depicts a conventional RF communication and Fig. 15 (b) depicts a UWB communication system. Unlike the conventional RF transceiver, the UWB requires less hardware and can easily convert the analog signal to digital.

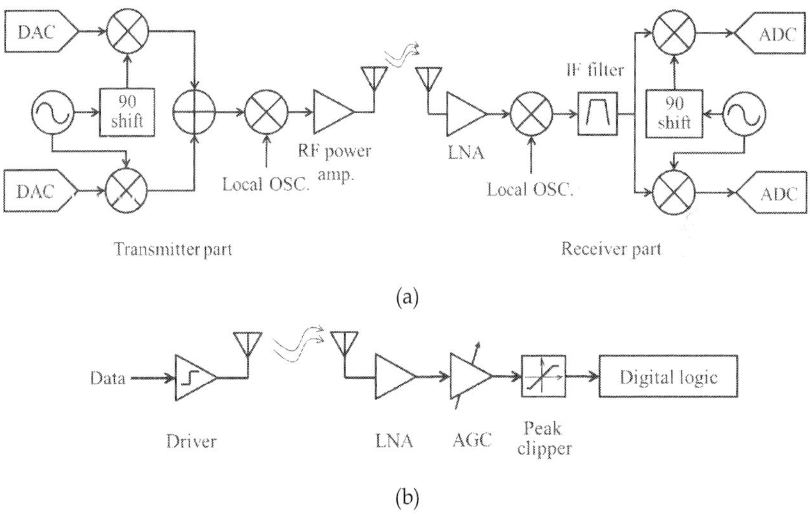

Fig. 15. UWB communication. (a) Conventional communication. (b) UWB communication.

2.5 Body Area Network

A Body Area Network (BAN) is a term used to describe the application of wearable computing devices that transmit data throughout the human body. Since the human body is a much better transmission medium comparing than air, the transceiver can be activated by using low power. Therefore, the information can be transmitted to another person when two people are shaking hands. Since the concept of the BAN is for communication throughout the surface of the skin, there is a trail for using this technology for the capsule endoscopy.
The company Intromedic reported on a capsule that transmits data by using a BAN. The capsule has two electrodes that can touch the inside of the gastrointestinal tract and transmit the data throughout the human body. A receiver was attached at the surface of the human body using the ECG electrodes.

2.6 Application of a swallowable capsule

In order to design a telemetry system, the RF frequencies have to be chosen based on the attenuation, data rate, maximum permissible exposure (MPE), and antenna efficiency. Since the human body mostly consists of saline, the RF power is attenuated in various parts of the human body. Fig. 16 depicts the attenuation constants for various parts of the human body. The attenuation is proportionally increased with frequency. Among the various parts of the human body, the small intestine shows the highest attenuation and the fat shows the lowest attenuation factor.
An application such as capsule endoscopy, which captures the image from the inside of the gastrointestinal tract and wirelessly transmits it to the outside, focuses on penetrating the RF power from the small intestine. Unfortunately, the small intestine attenuates a great deal of RF power and it is thus necessary to transmit a high RF power from the small capsule. High RF power will reduce the working time of the capsule endoscopy, and the MPE should be taken into consideration.

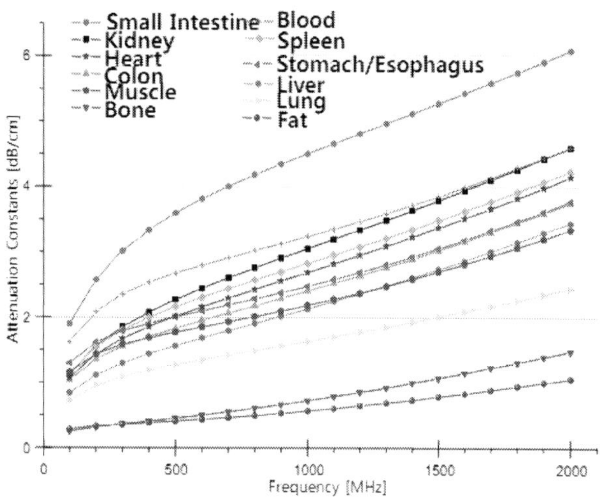

Fig. 16. The attenuation constants for various parts of the human body.

The MPE is the highest power or energy density of an RF source that is considered safe, i.e. that has a negligible probability for creating damage. Since the MPE is regulated from the outside of the body, it could be used as a guideline for the amount of RF radiation inside the body.

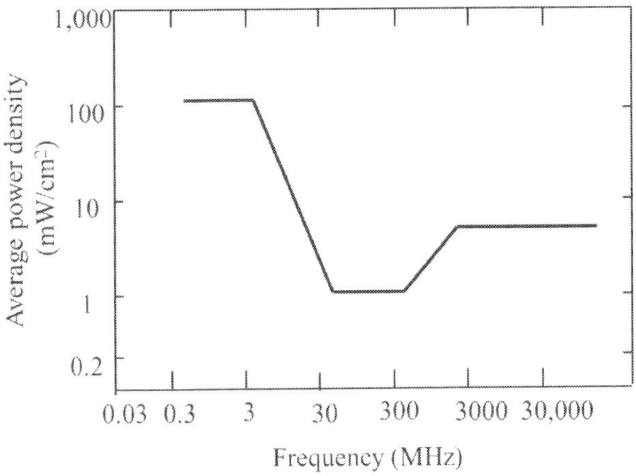

Fig. 17. The maximum permissible exposure regulation.

In order to determine the RF band, the body attenuation, MPE, and data rate have to be considered. Since the antenna efficiency is extremely low at low frequencies (<100 MHz), the length of the antenna has to be longer than the size of the small pill. However, the low frequency modulation requires less power consumption and radiation power because the human body does not attenuate the low frequency. Therefore, early capsule type telemetry systems were designed to use the FM method and used a long and flexible antenna. Since early telemetry systems did not require a high data rate, this was sufficient except for the repulsion of its shape.

With the advent of capsule endoscopy, the data rate has to be increased so as to be sufficient enough for transmission of gastrointestinal images. Fig. 18 shows an example of capsule endoscopes. The analog type can transmit the National Television Standards Committee (NTSC) format, which is widely used for analog TV transmission, and the physician can monitor the inside of the gastrointestinal tract as if watching an analog television. Since the NTSC uses the analog transmission technology, it could provide a high fame rate (30 frame/s) but it is weak to channel noise; further, restoration of the data is impossible. Fig 18 (b) shows digital type capsule endoscope that could transmit 640×480×8 resolution images by using a digital transmitter. Since a digital receiver can restore the data from environmental noises, the frame rate of the capsule is reduced to 1 frame/s. Fig. 18 (c) shows images taken from the ileum and esophagus by using a digital type transmitter capsule.

In order to transmit at a high data rate, the RF frequency has to be increased so as the make the antenna effective. For capsule endoscopy, the 430 and 1200 MHz the industrial, scientific and medical (ISM) bands are widely used to transmit the signal. These bands can transmit higher data rate than the FM band and the human body attenuation is moderate enough to allow the signal to penetrate the body. Also, the size of the antenna should be small enough that it can be inserted into the capsule. For these reasons, the Federal Communications Commission (FCC) decided to create the Medical Implant Communication Service (MICS) for the use of the frequency band between 402 and 405 MHz for communication with medical implants. It allows bidirectional radio communication with pacemakers or other electronic implant devices.

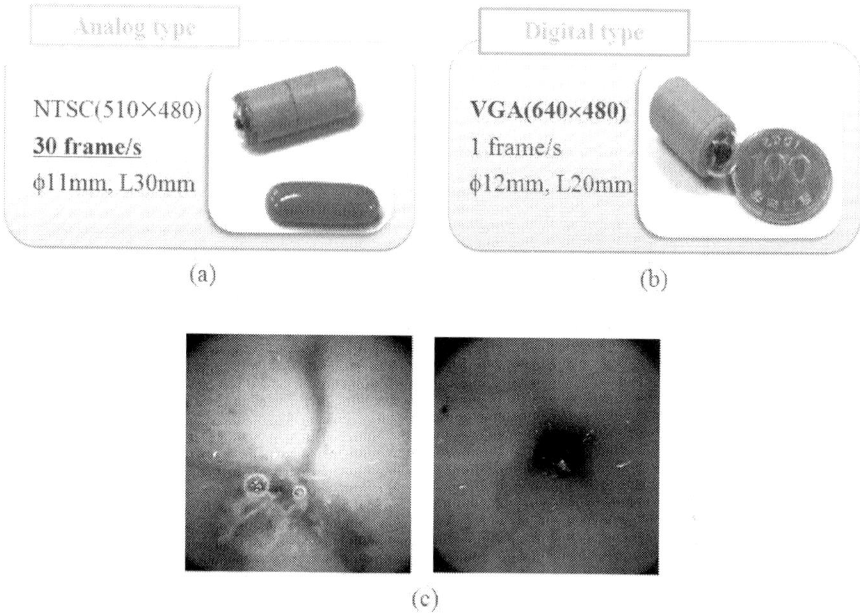

Fig. 18. Example of capsule endoscopy. (a) NTSC format transmitter. (b) VGA resolution transmitter. (c) Image taken from the VGA resolution transmitter capsule.

2.4 GHz is widely used for commercial WLAN, and there are many commercial antennas and transceivers for it. Unfortunately, the body attenuation at the 2.4 GHz is too high that it could attenuate up to -50 dBm at a 15 cm body thickness. Therefore, the 2.4 GHz band is not suitable for uses with implants or swallowable telemetry systems. Table 1 summaries the RF frequency efficiency of the various RF bands.

Most swallowed capsule designs have used conventional modulation such as FM or AM because of their simplicity. Since capsule telemetry is not widely used, encrypt and spread spectrums were not taken into account. Also, the concept of the UWB fits well with capsule endoscopy because the transmitter does not require a large space and power consumption is lower than that of the conventional transmitters. However, the human body attenuates high frequency signals, and this cannot be overcome by using equalization. There is one trial using UWB for capsule endoscopy, and the frequency was reduced to 800 MHz and a transceiver was implemented. Even though this proposed system violates the regulation of the UWB, it could be useable if the upper frequency were limited.

Comparatives	300 MHz Range	400 MHz Range	900 MHz Range	1200 MHz Range	2400 MHz Range
Safety level	Best		Best		Moderate
MPE [dBm/cm²]	0	1.25	4.78	6.02	6.99
Attenuation	Best		Good		Worst
15 cm Body attenuation [dB/cm²]	14	15	20	24	41
Power transmission	Best		Good		Worst
Availability		ISM Band	ISM Band		ISM Band
Antenna Size efficacy	Worst		Good		Best

Table 1. RF frequency efficiency of the various the RF bands

Another method is using an OFDM that can transmit a large bandwidth within a limited frequency band, but it requires FFT/IFFT modules that consume too much power. Since the capsule uses small batteries that typically have a capacity of less than 100 mAh, it is not easy to implement a low power FFT/IFFT block.

The SDR method is good for the swallowable capsule because it can support the various types of transmission signals. When the SDR is developed, patients will only need to receive signals in one receiver from many transition sources. When the protocols of swallowable capsule are open, this could become possible.

Table 2 summarizes various types of telemetry systems for capsules. Various modulation methods, frequencies, and RF power levels were used for various applications. Usually, FM modulation is used for moderate data rates and AM is used for simple and low power purposes. In additionally, SDR and UWB appear feasible but their details have not been fully described.

Reference	Frequency (MHz)	Data rate (kbps)	Modulation	Power consumption (mW)	RF power (dBm)
Thone et al.	144	2000	FSK	-	- 18
Chen et al.	433	267	FSK	24	-
Wang et al.	-	-	AM	125	Variable
Kfouri et al.	UHF	250	-	-	-
Park et al.	315	-	AM	-	-
Mackay et al.	433	-	FM	15.5	-
Woo et al.	1200	2000	SDR	-	-
Lee et al.	1200	2000	FSK	29.7	-
Intromedic	-	-	Manchester code	-	-

Table 2. Various types of applications of swallowable telemetry capsule

3. Conclusion

In this chapter, brief explanations of modern communication strategies are explained and the limitations of their use in swallowable telemetry systems are described. Selections of the RF band and modulation methods are described and compared with each other. Since the human body attenuates high frequency RF power, their use in sophisticated communication is limited.

4. Acknowledgment

I'd like to thank Qun Wei and Zia Moth-Un-Din for their support of drawing the pictures. This book was supported by a grant of the Institute of Biomedical Engineering Research, Kyungpook National University, Republic of Korea.

5. References

[1] Dinslage, S., J. McLaren, and R. Brubaker, *Intraocular pressure in rabbits by telemetry II: Effects of animal handling and drugs.* Investigative Ophthalmology & Visual Science, 1998. 39(12): p. 2485-2489.

[2] Hawkins, P., *Telemetry in the field: Practical refinements to improve animal welfare.* Comparative Biochemistry and Physiology a-Molecular & Integrative Physiology, 2007. 146(4): p. S84-S84.

[3] Johnson, D.S., et al., *Continuous-time correlated random walk model for animal telemetry data.* Ecology, 2008. 89(5): p. 1208-1215.

[4] Johnson, D.S., et al., *A general framework for the analysis of animal resource selection from telemetry data.* Biometrics, 2008. 64(3): p. 968-976.

[5] Kong, W., et al., *A semi-implantable multichannel telemetry system for continuous electrical, mechanical and hemodynamical recordings in animal cardiac research.* Physiological Measurement, 2007. 28(3): p. 249-257.

[6] Kutsch, W., *Telemetry in insects: the "intact animal approach".* Theory in Biosciences, 1999. 118(1): p. 29-53.

[7] Nations, C.S. and R.C. Anderson-Sprecher, *Estimation of animal location from radio telemetry data with temporal dependencies.* Journal of Agricultural Biological and Environmental Statistics, 2006. 11(1): p. 87-105.

[8] Salvatori, V., et al., *Estimating temporal independence of radio-telemetry data on animal activity.* Journal of Theoretical Biology, 1999. 198(4): p. 567-574.

[9] Walisser, J., et al., *Optimizing Telemetry Stock Animal Quality: Implementation of Monthly Signal Checks and Assessment of Transmitter Battery Life.* Journal of the American Association for Laboratory Animal Science, 2010. 49(5): p. 721-721.

[10] Ko, W.H., et al., *Studies of MEMS Acoustic Sensors as Implantable Microphones for Totally Implantable Hearing-Aid Systems.* IEEE Transactions on Biomedical Circuits and Systems, 2009. 3(5): p. 277-285.

[11] Yoon, K.W., et al., *Telemetry capsule for pressure monitoring in the gastrointestinal tract.* Ieice Transactions on Fundamentals of Electronics Communications and Computer Sciences, 2006. E89a(6): p. 1699-1700.

[12] Browning, C., et al., *A New Pressure Sensitive Ingestible Radio Telemetric Capsule.* The Lancet, 1981. 318(8245): p. 504-505.

[13] Mackay, R.S. and B. Jacobson, *Endoradiosonde.* Nature, 1957. 179(4572): p. 1239-1240.
[14] Connell, A.M. and E.N. Rowlands, *Wireless Telemetering from the Digestive Tract.* Gut., 1960. 1(3): p. 266-272.
[15] Banerjee, R. and D.N. Reddy, *Bravo capsule pH monitoring.* American Journal of Gastroenterology, 2006. 101(4): p. 906-906.
[16] Belafsky, P.C., et al., *Wireless pH testing as an adjunct to unsedated transnasal esophagoscopy: The safety and efficacy of transnasal telemetry capsule placement.* Otolaryngology-Head and Neck Surgery, 2004. 131(1): p. 26-28.
[17] Chaw, C.S., E. Yazaki, and D.F. Evans, *The effect of pH change on the gastric emptying of liquids measured by electrical impedance tomography and pH-sensitive radiotelemetry capsule.* International Journal of Pharmaceutics, 2001. 227(1-2): p. 167-175.
[18] Pandolfino, J.E., *Bravo capsule pH monitoring.* American Journal of Gastroenterology, 2005. 100(1): p. 8-10.
[19] Holloway, R.H., *Capsule pH monitoring: is wireless more?* Gut, 2005. 54(12): p. 1672-1673.
[20] Thorne, P.S., C.P. Yeske, and M.H. Karol, *Monitoring Guinea Pig Core Temperature by Telemetry during Inhalation Exposures.* Toxicological Sciences, 1987. 9(3): p. 398-408.
[21] O'Brien, C., et al., *Telemetry pill measurement of core temperature in humans during active heating and cooling.* Medicine and Science in Sports and Exercise, 1998. 30(3): p. 468-472.
[22] Iddan, G., et al., *Wireless capsule endoscopy.* Nature, 2000. 405(6785): p. 417-417.
[23] Svarta, S., et al., *Diagnostic yield of repeat capsule endoscopy and the effect on subsequent patient management.* Canadian Journal of Gastroenterology, 2010. 24(7): p. 441-444.
[24] Spada, C., et al., *Capsule endoscopy in Italy: An unbalanced review of the literature.* International Journal of Technology Assessment in Health Care, 2010. 26(3): p. 354-356.
[25] Spada, C., et al., *PillCam Colon Capsule Endoscopy (PCCE) for Colon Exploration: A Single Centre Italian Experience.* Gastrointestinal Endoscopy, 2010. 71(5): p. Ab203-Ab203.
[26] Woo, S.H., et al., *High Speed Receiver for Capsule Endoscope.* Journal of Medical Systems, 2010. 34(5): p. 843-847.
[27] Menciassi, A., et al. *Single and multiple robotic capsules for endoluminal diagnosis and surgery.* in *Biomedical Robotics and Biomechatronics, 2008. BioRob 2008. 2nd IEEE RAS & EMBS International Conference on.* 2008.
[28] Quirini, M., et al., *Design and Fabrication of a Motor Legged Capsule for the Active Exploration of the Gastrointestinal Tract.* Mechatronics, IEEE/ASME Transactions on, 2008. 13(2): p. 169-179.
[29] Byungkyu, K., et al. *Inchworm-Like Microrobot for Capsule Endoscope.* in *Robotics and Biomimetics, 2004. ROBIO 2004. IEEE International Conference on.* 2004.
[30] Elisa, B. and et al., *Evaluation of friction enhancement through soft polymer micro-patterns in active capsule endoscopy.* Measurement Science and Technology, 2010. 21(10): p. 105802.
[31] Quirini, M., et al., *Feasibility proof of a legged locomotion capsule for the GI tract.* Gastrointestinal Endoscopy, 2008. 67(7): p. 1153-1158.
[32] Woo, S.H., et al., *Implemented edge shape of an electrical stimulus capsule.* International Journal of Medical Robotics and Computer Assisted Surgery, 2009. 5(1): p. 59-65.

[33] Park, H.J., et al., *New method of moving control for wireless endoscopic capsule using electrical stimuli.* Ieice Transactions on Fundamentals of Electronics Communications and Computer Sciences, 2005. E88a(6): p. 1476-1480.

[34] Glass, P., E. Cheung, and M. Sitti, *A Legged Anchoring Mechanism for Capsule Endoscopes Using Micropatterned Adhesives.* Biomedical Engineering, IEEE Transactions on, 2008. 55(12): p. 2759-2767.

[35] Woo, S.H., T.W. Kim, and J.H. Cho, *Stopping mechanism for capsule endoscope using electrical stimulus.* Medical & Biological Engineering & Computing, 2010. 48(1): p. 97-102.

[36] Nagaoka, T. and A. Uchiyama. *Development of a small wireless position and bleeding detection sensor.* in *Microtechnology in Medicine and Biology, 2005. 3rd IEEE/EMBS Special Topic Conference on.* 2005.

[37] Menciassi, A. and P. Dario. *Miniaturized robotic devices for endoluminal diagnosis and surgery: A single-module and a multiple-module approach.* in *Engineering in Medicine and Biology Society, 2009. EMBC 2009. Annual International Conference of the IEEE.* 2009.

[38] http://www.intromedic.com/.

[39] Gao, Y.J., et al., *Endoscopic capsule placement improves the completion rate of small-bowel capsule endoscopy and increases diagnostic yield.* Gastrointestinal Endoscopy, 2010. 72(1): p. 103-108.

[40] Kim, H.M., et al., *A Pilot Study of Sequential Capsule Endoscopy Using MiroCam and PillCam SB Devices with Different Transmission Technologies.* Gut and Liver, 2010. 4(2): p. 192-200.

[41] Lee, J., et al., *CPLD based bi-directional wireless capsule endoscopes.* Ieice Transactions on Information and Systems, 2007. E90d(3): p. 694-697.

[42] Yuan, G., et al. *Low power ultra-wideband wireless telemetry system for capsule endoscopy application.* in *Robotics Automation and Mechatronics (RAM), 2010 IEEE Conference on.* 2010.

[43] Thone, J., et al., *Design of a 2 Mbps FSK near-field transmitter for wireless capsule endoscopy.* Sensors and Actuators a-Physical, 2009. 156(1): p. 43-48.

[44] Xinkai, C., et al., *A Wireless Capsule Endoscope System With Low-Power Controlling and Processing ASIC.* Biomedical Circuits and Systems, IEEE Transactions on, 2009. 3(1): p. 11-22.

[45] Kfouri, M., M. Kfouri, and M. Kfouri, *Toward a miniaturised wireless fluorescence-based diagnostic imaging system.* IEEE J. Selected Topics in Quantum Electronics, 2008. 14.

[46] MacKay, R.S., *Bio-Medical Telemetry: Sensing and Transmitting Biological Information from Animals and Man.* 1998: John Wiley & Sons.

3

Inductively Coupled Telemetry in Spinal Fusion Application Using Capacitive Strain Sensors

Ji-Tzuoh Lin, Douglas Jackson, Julia Aebersold, Kevin Walsh, John Naber and William Hnat
University of Louisville
USA

1. Introduction

Titanium or stainless steel rods are implanted to stabilize vertebrae movement during spinal fusion surgery, which allows bone grafts to fuse two or more vertebrae. Radiograph images (x-rays), computed tomography scans (CT) and magnetic resonance imaging (MRI) procedures are used to assess fusion progress and diagnose problems during patient recovery. However, the imaging techniques yield subjective results (Vamvanij et al.,1998) and as a consequence, result in unnecessary exploratory surgeries to ascertain the efficacy of the spinal fusion surgery. As the grafted bone fuses, the bending strain of the implanted rods decreases as the load is transferred to the fused vertebrae (Kanayama et al., 1997). Strain is measurable on the spinal fusion fixture, normally a stainless or titanium rod. In other words, the amount of strain is an indicator of the load applied to the rod. Therefore, it is proposed that the strain on the implant rods can be used as an alternative and non-invasive method to monitor the progress of spinal fusion (Hnat et al., 2008).

This chapter will demonstrate the realization of a telemetric strain measurement system for the spinal fusion detection as illustrated in Fig. 1. The system is composed of three major components: a sensitive strain sensor, a battery free transducer circuit that wirelessly interfaces the strain sensor, and an external interrogating reader that provides power to the implant as well as collects strain information from the transducer circuit. Research has shown that less power is consumed by a capacitive sensor than the resistive counterpart (Puers, 1993). In addition, the sensors require high sensitivity to eliminate the need for amplification that would require additional power. Therefore, the novel capacitive strain sensors are developed to meet both the power and sensitivity demand. Additional, in making the measurements a bodily-like situation, the sensor system, including the transducer circuit, is assembled on a housing (Aebersold et al., 2007) that is capable of transferring the strain from the rod to the sensor and accommodating for the size constrain. The testing loads on the rods will be provided by a material test system (MTS) with a corpectomy model fixture.

Although most strain sensors are capable of measuring axial strain due to tension and compression or their equivalents derived from bending, a sensitive bending strain sensor that only responds to bending strain is also desirable for spinal fusion purpose. The strain sensor is expected to measure 1000 με based on an adult of 200 pounds in a corpectomy model under bending with 2 stainless spinal fusion rods (6.4 mm in diameter and 50.8 mm long) implanted (Gibson, 2002).

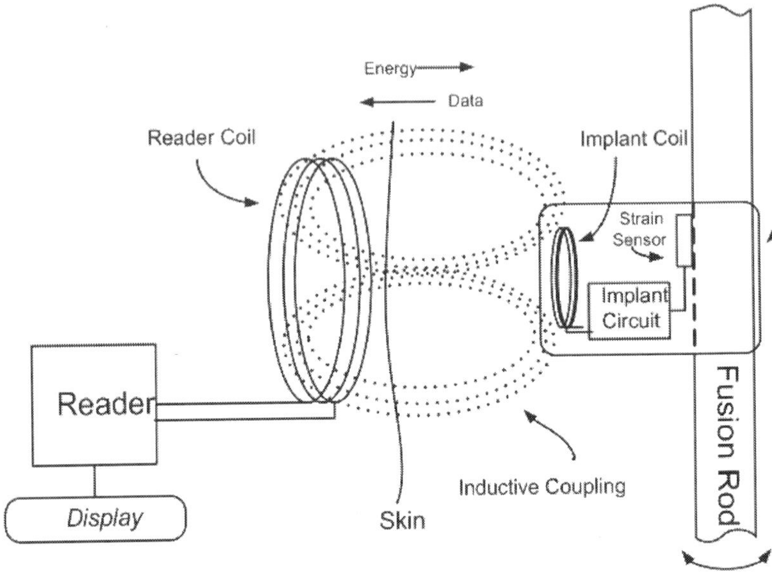

Fig. 1. A strain gauge telemetry application in spinal fusion.

MEMS capacitive sensors using wireless data transmission have been evaluated in many applications such as humidity (DeHennis & Wise, 2005; Harpster et al., 2002;), temperature (DeHennis & Wise, 2005) and pressure sensing devices (Akar et al., 2001; Chatzandroulis et al., 2000; DeHennis & Wise, 2002, 2005; Strong et al., 2002). The telemetry approach to monitor strain uses inductively coupled battery-less technology similar to the technology used in Radio Frequency IDentification (RFID) devices (Finkenzeller, 1999). Some examples of the early applications are shown in Table 1. The inductively coupled wireless system with sensing capability needs not only the working passive telemetry circuitry, but also both the sensor interface circuitry and the sensor themselves. A fully integrated implanted sensor system was realized (Chatzandroulis et al., 2000) with a capacitive pressure sensor and an application-specific integrated circuit (ASIC) chip that controls RF modulation and converts capacitance variations into frequency variations. Suster et al. developed a wireless strain detection with the transducer coil size of 3-inch coaxial to the interrogating reader (Suster et al., 2005). However, this transducer coil size is not desirable for spinal fusion implant. Research using this technique coupled with MEMS sensors has become widespread in biomedical applications. It is a promising approach for orthopedic implant sensors and the key is a highly sensitive capacitive sensor (Benzel et al., 2002).

Author, year	Chatzandroulis et al. 2000	DeHennis et al. 2002	DeHennis et al. 2005	Suster et al. 2005
Method	Backscattering	Backscatterin, C-F converter	Backscattering, C-F converter	Backsctteringt, C-F, F-V converter
Sensor	Capacitive pressure	Capacitive sensor	Capacitive sensor	Capacitive strain sensor
Range			4cm	1 inch
Frequency	40.68MHz	800KHz	3.18MHz	50MHz
Secondary coil			4.5mmx7.5mm	Co-axial 3 inches coils
Applications	Pressure sensor	Pressure	Pressure, humidity and temperature	Strain
Overall sensor and circuit size	450μm in diameter 2mm x 2mm	2mmx2mm sensor on chip with circuit	4.5mmx7.5mmx1mm	1000μm
Mounting	ASIC chip		On silicon	On silicon
Testing method				3-point bending
Circuit type	C/F converter	CMOS ring oscillator	Current source and relaxation oscillator	Voltage output
Number of channels	1	3 channels	3 channels	1 channel
Reader type	MC68HC705 micro-controller	Class E amplifier	Class E amplifier	
Strain/pressure range				1000 μs
Dynamic/static		Dynamic/static	Dynamic/static	Dynamic/static
Capacitance range		5pF - 33pF	0.5pF-6pF	440fF

Table 1. Some details of the inductively coupled detection systems

In the next sections, the highly sensitive MEMS bending strain sensor will be described in great detail followed by the system circuitry and the testing methods.

2. The MEMS strain sensors

This section focuses on the development and fabrication of the custom bending strain capacitive sensing element needed for the spinal fusion measurement implant (SFMI) applications. This application requires a high bending strain sensitivity with enough nominal capacitance to avoid loss due to parasitic capacitance, compatibility with an inductively powered circuit, and suitable dimensions for system packaging. The sensitive bending strain sensor is expected to be packaged in a housing container that attaches to the diameter spinal fusion rod. The distance between two vertebrae is about 25.4 mm in the lumber region, making the maximum length of the housing limited to approximately 12 mm long. Therefore, it is desirable that the sensor length be less than 10 mm. The housing is installed between two pedicle screws and needs to transfer the bending strain from the rod to the sensor as described in (Aebersold et al. 2007). The curved surface of the rod is compensated with the 2 mm thick plastic housing which conforms to the rod and is trimmed 1 mm down to provide a flat area of 2 mm x 10 mm for the sensor to mount.

Certain characteristics were primarily considered when reviewing limited examples of previous parallel plate capacitive strain sensors in the literature. The basic concept of the capacitive strain sensor features a pair of metalized parallel plates with a dielectric gap. The sensing mechanism manifests itself in varying either the area of the plate, the gap between the plates, or the dielectric medium between the plates. A number of parallel plate sensor designs with a variable air gap were analyzed in the early 90's (Procter & Strong 1992). These sensors generally exhibited low nominal capacitance and sensitivity due to the large gap. In an attempt to increase the nominal capacitance in a non-air gap design, it was demonstrated by a sensor with a parallel plate structure and a thick-film dielectric material (Arshak et al., 1994). The dielectric film between the two plates was compressed during bending, thus expanding the film in area and decreasing the thickness from the perspective of the electrodes. These changes in the film geometry lead to a high gauge factor of 75-80 with a 15-25 μm gap based on a uniform model. The capacitive gauge factor is defined by the fractional change in capacitance with respect to strain. This thick-film dielectric produced both capacitive and resistive responses to strain making this approach electrically unique, but undesirable for the SFMI application due to power consumption. In another design, more effort was involved to invoke the change in permittivity of a dielectric material resulting in a gauge factor of 3.5 to 6, with a 150 μm gap (Arshak et al., 2000). This variable permittivity approach exhibits limited sensitivity that showed no dependency on its dimension (the gauge factor is constant and only depends on the "piezocapacitive" effect). This low gauge factor approach would require additional circuitry that is not desired for this implant design.

2.1 The bending sensor theory

The mechanism of sensing pure bending on a test substrate is described in two folds: the capacitance and the strain condition imposed on the sensor, as illustrated in Fig. 2. Assuming the bending sensor is attached to a steal cantilever with length L and thickness R in an elastic bending.

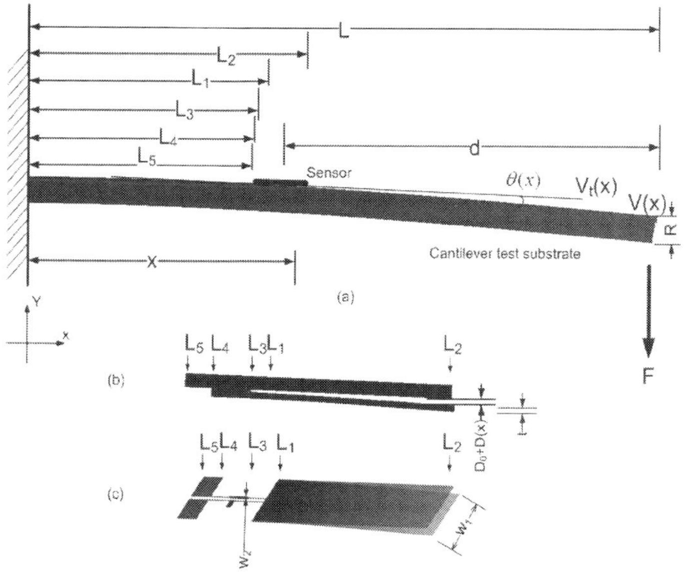

Fig. 2. The sensor on a substrate bar under bending. (b) The sensor's gap D_0+D(x), zoomed in from above, varies as a function of position x. (c) shows the respect metal coordinates on the cantilever substrate.

The capacitance from two parallel electrode plates is given by

$$C = \varepsilon_0 \varepsilon_r \frac{A}{D} \tag{1}$$

where A is the area, D is the distance between two parallel plates, ε_0 is the permittivity and ε_r is the dielectric constant of the material between the plates. In order to measure the strain magnitude, a cantilever test substrate is utilized. For strain and capacitance calculations, it is assumed that the dimensions of the cantilever test substrate very large compared to the sensor and that the sensor is firmly affixed to the substrate. For a cantilever beam, the moment of inertia, I, is given by

$$I = \frac{WT^3}{12} \tag{2}$$

where, W is the beam width and T (or R as shown in Fig. 1) is the beam thickness. For a beam in uniaxial state of stress, the strain at any point on any surface under bending is given by a textbook (Hibbleer, 1997),

$$\varepsilon = \frac{\sigma}{E} = \frac{Mc}{EI} = \frac{6Fd}{EWT^2} \tag{3}$$

where σ is the stress on the surface, E is the Young's modulus of the steel bar substrate, M is the bending moment, c is the distance from the neutral axis to the surface, F is the force applied at the free end of the beam and d is the sensor location from the free end of the beam. The sensor location on the beam is given by

$$d = L \quad \frac{L_4 + L_2}{2} \tag{4}$$

where L is the length of the cantilever substrate, L_4 and L_2 are the longitudinal boundaries that define the bottom beam of the sensor. Fig. 2a shows the sensor location on the bent cantilever test substrate. Fig. 2b is the side view of a bending condition of the sensor design depicted in Fig. 2c, showing the sensor's metal layer coordinates and the widened gap, D_0+D(x). Figs. 2c also shows the details of the top and bottom electrode while under bending for the designs of interest. The initial sensor capacitance is given by

$$C_0 = \varepsilon_0 \varepsilon_r \frac{w_1(L_2 - M_1)}{D_0} + \varepsilon_0 \varepsilon_r \frac{w_2(M_1 - L_1)}{D_0} + C_p \tag{5}$$

where L_1 marks the beginning of the metal layer on the bottom electrode, L_2 not only represents the boundary of the sensor but also the end of the metal layers on both the bottom and top electrode beams and therefore, L_2-L_1=L_0 is the effective electrode length. With various designs, M_1 is a variable that represents the start of the metal layer on the top electrode beam and also ends the trace that connects the electrode to the pad on the bottom beam. Therefore, $w_1(L_2\text{-}M_1)$ represents the area of the overlapping metal plates, $w_2(M_1\text{-}L_1)$ the area of the metal trace, and D_0 the initial spacing between the plates (see Figs. 2b-2c). The first term represents the capacitance of the overlapping metal plates. The second term is the capacitance of the trace between the electrode and the pad. The third term, C_p, is the parasitic capacitance of the metal traces between L_1 and L_3 combined with the planar pads between L_4 and L_5. L_3 is also the pivot point where the gap starts and L_5 is the physical boundary of the top electrode beam. Capacitance calculations for planar pads indicate that the third term is 0.035 pF (Baxter, 1997). In order to estimate sensor sensitivity to strain, the capacitance change caused by an applied strain is calculated using standard beam equations. The sensor metal plate attached to the beam will follow the beam deflection while the initially parallel plate will remain straight under deformation. The deflection of a cantilever beam and the attached sensor metal plate is given by (Hibbleer, 1997),

$$v(x) = \frac{-F}{6EI}(3Lx^2 - x^3) \tag{6}$$

where the $v(x)$, as seen in Fig. 2a, is the vertical displacement at position x on the beam. The initially parallel plate remains straight and its position is represented by a line tangent to the deformed beam at the pivot point of the sensor. The tangent line (see Fig. 2a) is given by

$$v_t(x) = \theta(x)x + b \tag{7}$$

where $\theta(x)$ is the slope at x and b is a constant determined by a boundary condition. The slope is determined from the first derivative of the deflection and given by

$$\theta(x) = \frac{-F}{2EI}(2Lx - x^2) \tag{8}$$

At the sensor pivot point, L_3, from Fig. 4b, the deflection of the two metal plates is equal, providing the boundary condition

$$v_t(L_3) = v(L_3) \tag{9}$$

The constant b from (7) is solved by combining (6), (8) and (9) at point L_3 and becomes

$$b = \frac{F}{6EI}\left(3LL_3^2 - 2L_3^3\right) \tag{10}$$

Therefore, the tangent line is expressed as

$$v_t(x) = \frac{-F}{2EI}\left(2LL_3 - L_3^2\right)x + \frac{F}{6EI}\left(3LL_3^2 - 2L_3^3\right) \tag{11}$$

The increased gap (see Fig. 2b) between the two electrode plates is a function in the x-direction and expressed as

$$D(x) = v_t(x) - v(x) \tag{12}$$

The capacitance change is determined by calculating the average distance between the two metal plates of the strain sensor. The average displacement, in addition to the initial gap, between main metal layers is expressed as

$$D_1 = D_0 + \frac{1}{(L_2 - M_1)}\int_{M_1}^{L_2} (v_t(x) - v(x))dx \tag{13}$$

where M_1 is where the sensing portion of metal starts and L_2 where it ends. The capacitance due to the trace has an average displacement of D_2, which is expressed as

$$D_2 = D_0 + \frac{1}{(M_1 - L_1)}\int_{L_1}^{M_2} (v_t(x) - v(x))dx \tag{14}$$

where the metal stops at L_1. Capacitance, due to beam deformation, C_f, is given by

$$C_f = \varepsilon_0\varepsilon_r \frac{w_1(L_2 - M_1)}{D_0 + D_1} + \varepsilon_0\varepsilon_r \frac{w_2(M_1 - L_1)}{D_0 + D_2} + C_p \tag{15}$$

Combining (3), (13), (14) and (15), yields

$$C_f = \varepsilon_0\varepsilon_r \frac{w_1(L_2 - M_1)}{D_0 + \dfrac{\varepsilon(L(L_2^3 - M_1^3) - \frac{1}{4}(L_2^4 - M_1^4) + (3L_3^2L - 2L_3^3)(L_2 - M_1) + (\frac{3}{2}L_3^2 - 3L_3L)(L_2^2 - M_1^2))}{3dT(L_2 - M_1)}}$$

$$+ \varepsilon_0\varepsilon_r \frac{w_2(M_1 - L_1)}{D_0 + \dfrac{\varepsilon(L(M_1^3 - L_1^3) - \frac{1}{4}(M_1^4 - L_1^4) + (3L_3^2L - 2L_3^3)(M_1 - L_1) + (\frac{3}{2}L_3^2 - 3L_3L)(M1^2 - L_1^2))}{3dT(M_1 - L_1)}} + C_p \tag{16}$$

Based on the equation above, the bending strain sensor is analytically formulated and to be compared with the fabricated MEMS sensor in the following section.

2.2 Strain sensor fabrication

The sensor fabrication process is illustrated in Fig. 3. The materials include borosilicate glass (Pyrex Corning 7740, 500 μm thick) and silicon wafers (p-type, (100), 1-10 ohm-cm, double side polished, 310 μm thick). Fabrication began with clean glass and silicon substrates as shown in Figs. 3a and 3c. An electrode, traces, and a pair of contact pads were patterned onto the glass substrate by sputtering 0.02 μm chromium for adhesion layer followed by 0.2 μm of gold. The metal trace leading to the bonding area makes electrical contact with the silicon side electrode after anodic bonding. Wet etching was used to pattern the metal (Fig. 3b).The silicon wafer was wet oxidized (Fig. 3d), patterned using photolithography and etched with buffered oxide etch (BOE) solution to form an oxide mask for silicon surface machining. The wafer was etched using potassium hydroxide (KOH) at 85°C (approximately 0.7 μm / minute) to form recessed features and created the initial gap spacing. The etching mask was removed using BOE leaving two

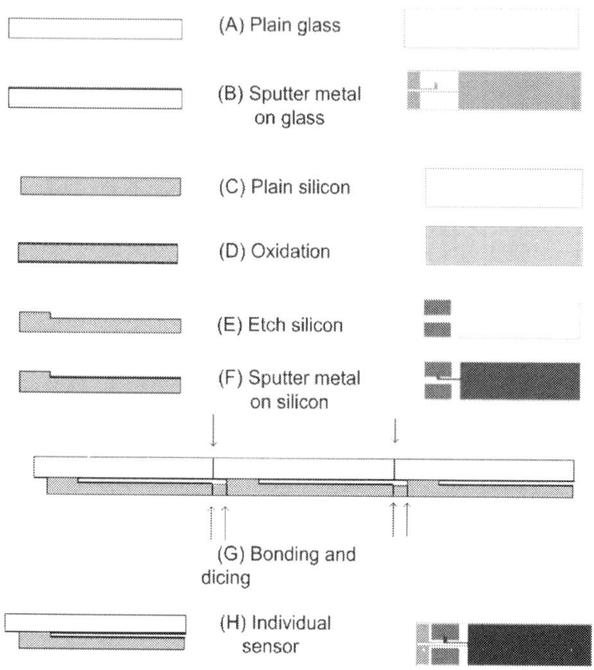

Fig. 3. Cantilever bending strain sensor fabrication process. Illustrations on the left are the side views and on the right are the top views. (a) Pyrex (Coring 7400) glass, (b)sputter of Au/Cr on glass as one electrode, (c) silicon substrate, (d) oxidation of the silicon as the etching mask, (e) etching silicon with KOH to create platforms for anodic bonding with glass, (f) sputter Au/Cr on silicon as the other electrode, (g) side view of partial dicing (arrows marks) after glass and silicon are anodically bonded, (h) the individual sensor after final separation, noting the gap between the two electrodes.

silicon islands, which function as anchor platforms for the anodic bonding interface, as seen in Fig. 3e. An electrode and trace were then sputtered and patterned onto the silicon using the previously described metallization process. The small contact area on the raised anchor connected the pad on the glass plate with the electrode on the silicon plate via the traces, as seen in Fig. 3f.

The glass and silicon wafers were stacked with the metal surfaces facing each other and visually aligned using a mask aligner. Methanol was used to temporarily maintain alignment. The substrates were anodically bonded at 450 °C on a grounded hotplate using a pointed probe to selectively place a -1000 V source on the glass, as shown in Fig. 3g. A gap is created between the electrodes on glass and silicon. This technique of selectively applying the electric field and bonding pressure prevented the recessed spaces from bonding to each other due to thermally induced warpage and electrostatic attraction. An automated dicing saw equipped with a 250 μm thick diamond blade was used to separate the individual sensor die from the bonded wafers. The silicon substrate was diced nearly through at the area above the contact pads. This was accomplished by limiting the depth of the cut and using the dicing alignment marks previously patterned on the silicon. Cuts to individually remove the sensors were similarly made from the silicon and glass substrate leaving approximately 30 μm of each substrate's depth (Fig. 3g). Care was taken to avoid chipping and prevent debris from filling the sensor gap. The sensors were separated from the wafer manually by flexing them to break the remaining thin substrate (Fig. 3h).

Sensors with less than 3 μm gap have been fabricated, but with unreliable capacitance values and low yield. It is because of the collapsing of the two electrodes during the anodic bonding process. In an effort to maintain high nominal capacitance, preserve sensitivity and promote linearity, a sensor with an electrode area of 2 mm x 4 mm, and a gap of 3 μm was fabricated for final SFMI prototyping. This sensor was tested on a spinal fusion rod with a near-linear response, as shown in Fig. 4.

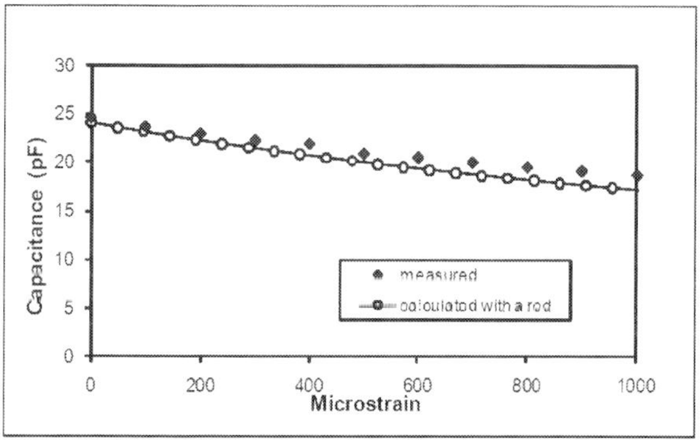

Fig. 4. Comparison of the calculation and experimental results of a strain sensor glued to a spinal fusion rod.

Gauge factor is defined as

$$GF = \frac{\frac{dC}{C}}{\varepsilon} \quad (2)$$

where dC/C is the fractional change of capacitance and ε is the strain. Using a linear fit of the differential capacitance data graphed in Fig 5, the gauge factor was ploted and calculated to be 252 for 0 to 1000 με. This value is extremly high in comparison to the current literature (Arshak 1994, 2000; Proctor & Strong 1992). By comparison, piezoresistive gauges typically provide a gauge factor less than 200 (Fraden, 1995) even at the cost of high temperature sensitivity.

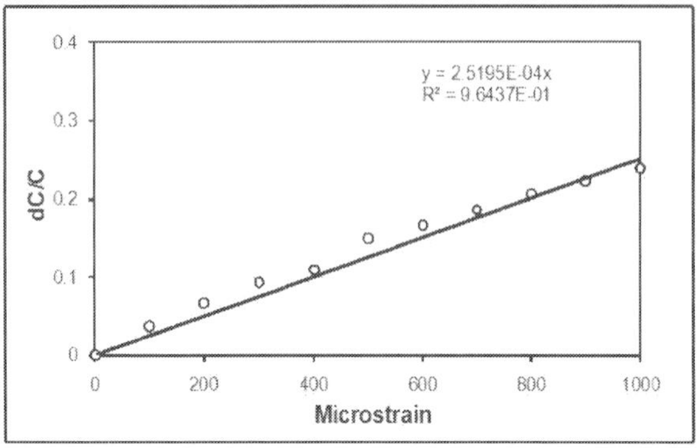

Fig. 5. Comparison of the calculation and experimental results of a strain sensor glued to a spinal fusion rod.

3. The transducer circuit

The transducer circuit is an inductively coupled, load modulated design similar in concept to Radio Frequency IDentification tags used for inventory and security. The 125 kHz magnetic field sourced by the interrogating reader induces a voltage in the LC tank of the implant. The LC tank (1 cm diameter, 600 turns) is resonant at 125 kHz. The AC voltage is then rectified, filtered, and regulated using a low quiescent power regulator. A supply of 3VDC, 28 μA is required to power the oscillator circuit described above and a frequency divider circuit composed of flip-flops. The oscillator frequency is divided to less than 1/20 the carrier frequency so that detection is simplified. The frequency divider also buffers the oscillator signal so that it can drive the gate of a MOSFET placed across the LC tank. The MOSFET acts a load that modulates the 125 kHz tank output at the divider output frequency. A diagram that shows the functionality can be seen in Fig. 6(a).

As it is functioned as an oscillator in Fig. 6(a), a capacitance to frequency (c-f) converter is used to convert the strain signal to a signal that can be transfered wirelessly. The c-f circuit is comprised of a pair of CMOS inverters (Lancaster, 1997) and can be seen in detail in Fig. 6(b). The oscillator produces a periodical voltage due to the charging and discharging of the RC across a threshold of an inverter input. The frequency of the RC oscillator is expressed as $F=2.3R_tC$, where C is the variable capacitor, or a capacitive strain sensor, and R_t is the matched resistance of the oscillator. The resistor R_I is to unload the RC network from clamping effect of protection diodes in the inverter. It will also result in a nearly square duty cycle and make the frequency less dependent of power supply variations. R_I is normally set about 10 times as higher as R_t to minimize the effect of the protection diodes. The oscillator oscillates empirically at 20 kHz with 20 pF capacitor and 100 kOhm resistor.

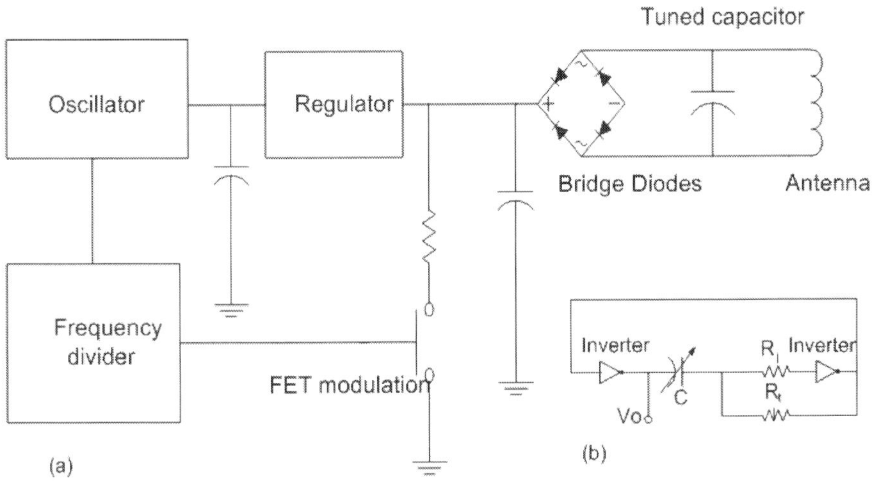

Fig. 6. The block diagram of the (a) transducer circuit and (b) oscillator circuit.

4. The interrogating reader

The interogating reader operating on 12 VDC, 175 mA provides the 125 kHz magnetic field for the implant, as illustrate in Fig. 7. The reader antenna is 24 cm in diameter and is tuned to 125 kHz. An EM Microelectronic (Marin, Switzerland), EM4095 IC contains an on-chip oscillator, antenna driver, and a demodulation circuit. The output of the demodulator is measured using an Agilent 53131A counter and logged with a computer based data acquisition system.

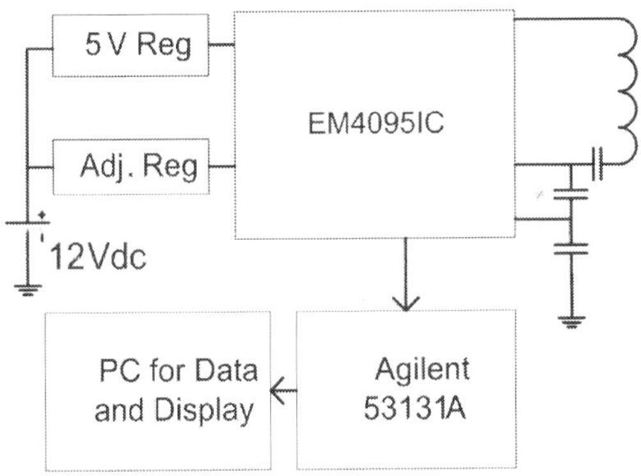

Fig. 7. The block diagram of the power reader.

4.1 Detection region

In the region of detection, see Fig. 8, the implant receives enough power to operate from the magnetic field sourced by the reader. There is no degradation of strain sensing performance if sufficient DC power is available from the regulator. However at the far end of the region, planar and axial alignment becomes very important. With distance from the reader, inductive coupling is reduced thereby reducing the AC voltage across the LC tank and thus the modulated signal amplitude. The data signal also relies on the same low coupling between the implant and the reader. It is necessary to have a sensitive reader to detect the implant at the far end of the region.

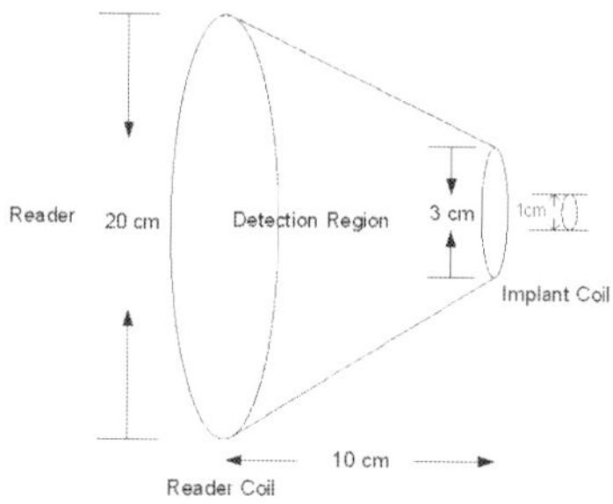

Fig. 8. The detection region is within the cone shape.

5. The testing methods

The corpectomy model was used to evaluate the strain measurement system prior to spine testing. This model has similar bending to a four-point bending model therefore the rod strain does not change significantly along the length of the rod. A single metal foil strain gauge reference was attached to the rod adjacent to the housing for comparison to the transducer system. Comparing the metal foil reference gauge to the spinal fusion sensor placed in close proximity is justified. Figure 9 shows the sensor assembly on a housing without a container cover.

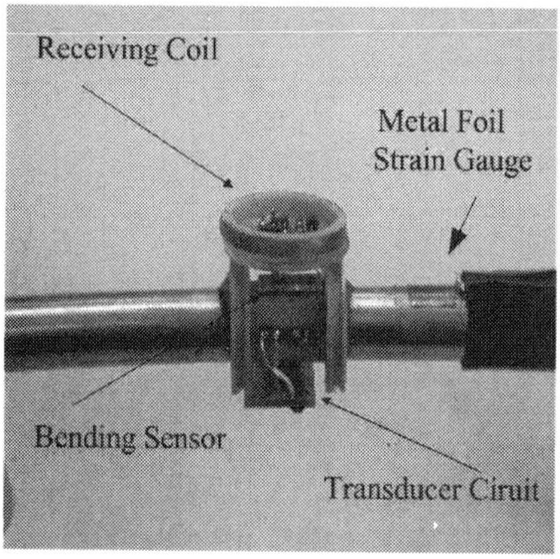

Fig. 9. The transducer sensor system on a housing that attaches to a stainless rod before a hermetically sealed container is assembled.

The strain measurement system was tested using a corpectomy model designed as a simplified mechanical analog of a spine section and then will be tested using a human spine. Figure 10 shows a free body diagram of the forces and bending moments applied to the spinal rods through the pedicle screws due to loading of the hard plastic blocks. Note that when the spinal fusion rods are fastened to the fixtures, often the initial strain is introduced and recalibrated. On the first test, the corpectomy apparatus was assembled inside a clear acrylic water tank without water on the MTS machine for application of the load; the sensor system was oriented facing out to be detected. The MTS machine's dynamic motion only changes 3 mm in the detection distance between the interrogating reader and the strain sensor. The read range was limited to 10 cm due to the reader design used and the sensor coil design constraints. A more optimal reader would increase the range. For other applications where a larger coil diameter is acceptable the range would be increased as well.

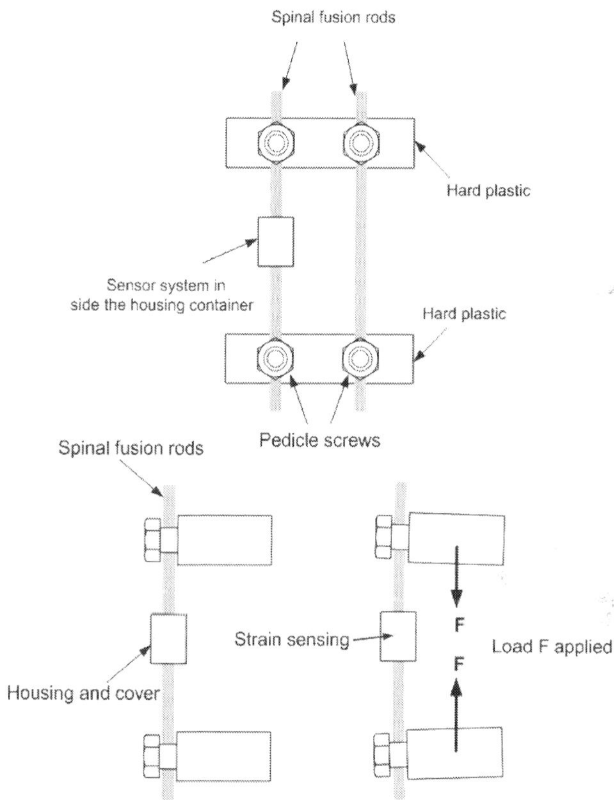

Fig. 10. The corpectomy model: front view, top and side view, bottom.

The data acquisition is obtained with LabView software, an interfacing program designed to transfer and record live data between instruments and computer by National Instrument. The strain information is recorded by the commecial metal foil strain gauge through a strain

indicator (Measurement group model P-3500). The frequency output from the wireless strain sensor system measurement is obtained through the digital universal counter (Agilent 53131A). In normal use, the response time for the strain indicator is 0.5 second, and the universal counter about 0.2 second. However, with the Labview interface the response time for the universal counter changes to 2.3 seconds but does not change for the strain indicator. The lag in time in the acquisition of the frequency data from the sensor system will cause false information when recording a drastic dynamic motion. In order to have a consistent and corresponding readings for the referred strain and the frequency output, a delay or pause in the live measurement is needed. Therefore, the MTS machine is programmed to pause 5 seconds at every increment of load for the frequency output to stabilize. Both the strain and the frequency data then are taken at the same time frame as the Material Test Machine.
The result of the telemetry strain sensor detection in Fig. 11 shows good linearity with R^2= 0.99. The gauge factor is calculated to be 249 up to 1000 micro-strain, with R^2=0.96 as see in Fig. 12. Similar gauge factor of 252 in the capacitance mode was measured in section 2. The frequency mode also exhibits high gauge factor without any amplification.

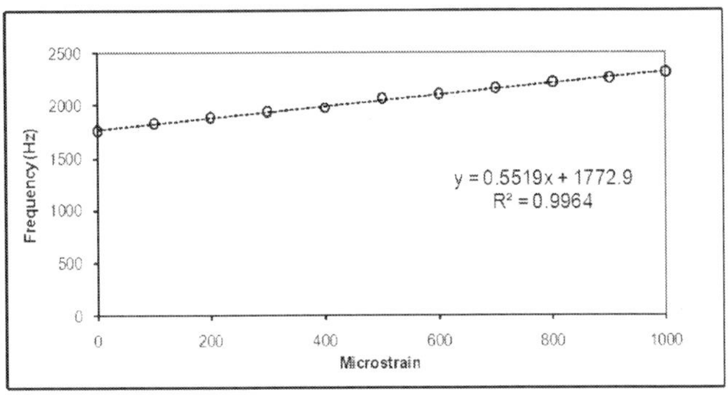

Fig. 11. The demodulate frequency responses from the sensor transducer shows a linear response due to bending test of the corpectomy model.

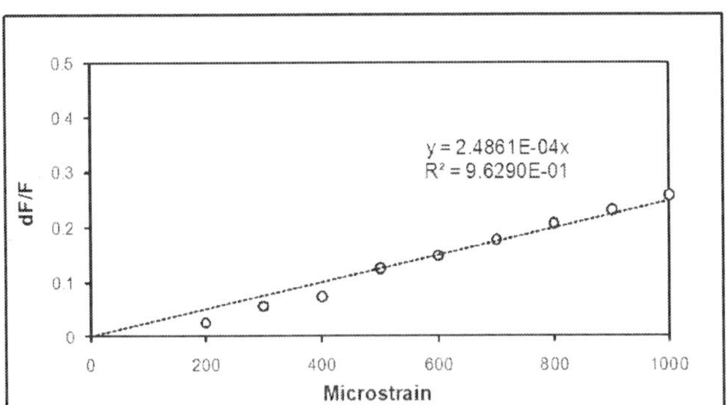

Fig. 12. The plot shows a linear gauge factor 249 in the frequency domain.

5.1 Water tank test

For the next application in water tank test, the sensor is expected to be in a fluidic environment. To protect from the influence of water or water vapor, the system was hermetically sealed in a container made of nylon and painted heavily with silicone and polyethylene. The container protected the device during corpectomy testing where it is submerged in a water tank used to simulate the body and during spine testing where it is in contact with tissue.

Caution has been taken for the temperature difference between water and ambient. A temperature dependent test on the sensor shows that the frequency drift from 1752 to 1778 Hz from 0 °C to 22.2 °C and vice versa with no strain at the rate of about 1.8 Hz/ °C. The interrgating reader was not moved at about 10 cm from the sensor system, through water, glass and air. The difference of the readings before the introduction of water and after was unnoticeable. The corpectomy model in water test was successful in showing the repeatability for the cyclic loads. It aslo suggestes that measurements were possible in conditions present in-vivo. The tests of the corpectomy model in water tank were successful in showing that measurements were possible in conditions present in-vivo.

5.2 Excise spine test

A discectomy was performed on an excised spine from a cadaver and was constrained and loaded in a MTS system to simulate a 113.4 kg (250 lb) patient. The excised spine was potted using a liquid lead/bismuth alloy (Cerro Products, Bellefont, PA) and attached to a MTS Bionix mechanical testing system. A custom-built test apparatus was used to apply anatomic loads to the spine. The intact spine was tested by applying loads ranging from 100 to 200 N in an increasing and decrease manner with a 5-second period of pause at every increment to accommodate the detection speed of the system. The disc between L3 and L4 was surgically removed to simulate an unstable spine prior to fusion surgery, and the test sequence repeated. The comparison of results before and after the disk is removed are shown in Fig. 13.

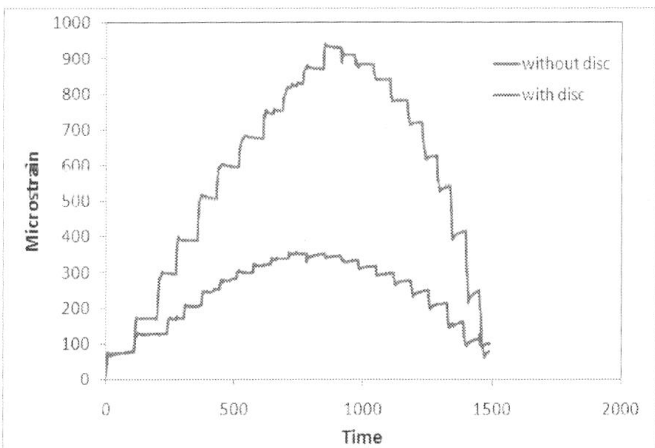

Fig. 13. Measured strains during excised spine testing.

With the same loading steps on the spine from MTS, the spinal fusion rods experienced less strain increment in the spine with the disk than that in the spine with the disk removed.

From the wireless transmision data along with the referred metal foil strain gauge, it is suggested that the spinal fusion rods showed that roughly one third of the load were shared by the intact spine after the spine is fused. The telemetry system clearly shows the rigidity of the intact spine.

6. Conclusion

A telemetry system using a capacitive strain sensor has been developed for the detection of spinal fusion monitoring. The strain sensor was made using MEMS process with high sensitivity and reduced size that serves the purpose for strain detection on the spinal fusion rod. The cantilever structure of the sensor is composed of two parallel plates, galss and silicon, respectively, with a narrow gap D_0 (3 μm) and a conjoint end. The bending strain sensor has the characteristics of high nominal capacitance (20 pF), high sensitivity, and compact dimensions (2 mm x 7 mm x 0.8 mm). It utilizes a variable gap configuration comprised of silicon and glass beams that are bonded at one end and open at the opposing end. This type of structure has been tested to withstand a strain range of 0 to 1000 με. The inductive link between the implant circuit and the reader was sufficient for supplying power to the implant circuit and extracting data at 10 cm distance. A specific sensor has a linear gauge factor of 252 in the capacitive domain and 249 in the frequency domain. Measurements made through air and water with a corpectomy model produced a linear response consistent with a metal foil reference gauge. The strain measurement system was also tested with the corpectomy model designed as a simplified mechanical analog of a spine section and was then tested using a human spine. For the biomechanics application, the sensor is expected to be in a fluidic environment. The tests of the corpectomy model placed in water tank were successful in showing that measurements were possible in conditions present in-vivo. The read range was limited to 10 cm due to the reader design used and the sensor coil design constraints. Finally, a test performed using a human spine showed the wireless implant detected strain roughly one third of the load were shared by the intact spine after the spine is fused.

7. Acknowledgment

The authors would like to express the appreciation to Tommy Roussel, Tom Carroll, Don Yeager, John C. Jones, Dr. Michael Voor, Dr. Rolando Puno and Robert L Burden for their assistance with the modeling, test setups and surgery performance.

8. References

Aebersold, J.W.; Hnat, W.P.; Voor, M.J.; Puno, R.M.; Jackson, D.J.; Lin, J.T.; Walsh, K.M.& J.F. Naber (2007). Development of a strain transferring sensor housing for a lumber spinal fusion detection system, J. Med. Devices 1 (June 2007) 159-164.

Akar, O. ; Akin, T.& Najafi, K. (2001) A wire less batch sealed absolute capacitive pressure sensor, Sensor and Actuator A 95 (2001) 29-38.

Arshak, K.I.; Collins, D. & Ansari, F. (1994). New high gauge-factor thick-film transducer based on a capacitor configuration, Int. J. Electronics, 1994 vol. 77 No. 3, 387-399.

Arshak, K.I.; McDonagh, D. & Durcan, M.A. (2000). Development of new capacitive strain sensors based on thick film polymer and cement technologies, Sensors and Actuators A 79 (2000) 102-114.

Baxter, L. K. (1997). Capacitive Sensors: Design and applications, IEEE press, New York, 1997 pp 17-73

Benzel, E. & Ferrara, L. ; Roy, S. & Fleischman, A. (2002) Clinical Neurosurgery, 49, 209-225 (2002).

Chatzandroulis, S.; Tsoukalas, D., & NeuKomm P. A. (2000) A miniature pressure system with a capacitive sensor and a passive telemetry link for use in implantable applications, Journal of Microelectromechanicalsystems Vol.9 No.1 March 2000.

DeHennis, A.& Wise, K.D. (2002), A double-sided single-chip wireless pressure sensor, Digest IEEE conference on MEMS, (January 2002) Las Vegas. Pp 252-255. (2002) A Passive-Telemetry-Based pressure sensing system, Digest of the Solid-state Sensor and Actuator Workshop, (June 2002) Hilton Head,

DeHennis, A.& Wise, K.D. (2005). A wireless microsystem for the remote sensing of pressure, temperature, and relative humidity, J. of MEMS Vol. 14, NO. 1 February 2005 12-22.

Vamvanij, V.; Fredrickson, B.E.; Thorpe, J.M.; Stadnick, M.E.& Yuan, H.A. (1998). Surgical treatment of internal disc disruption: an outcome study of four fusion techniques, Journal of Spinal Disorders, Oct.11 (5) (1998) 375-382.

Finkenzeller, K. (1999). RFID Handbook: Radio-frequency identification fundamentals and applications, John Wiley & Sons, 1999 p 38.

Fraden, J. (1996) Hanbook of Modern Sensors (Springer-Verlag, New York, 1996)

Gibson, H. (2002). Measurement and finite element modeling of spinal rod strain, Master thesis, Dept of Mechanical Engineering University of Louisville, May 2002.

Harpster, T.J.; Hauvespre, S.; Dokmeci, M. R. & Najafi, K. (2002). A passive humidity monitoring system for in situ remote wireless testing of micropackages, J. of MEMS. Vol.11 No.1 February (2002) 61-67.

Hibbeler, R.C. (1997). Mechanics of Materials, Prentice Hall, New Jersey, 3rd ed., 1997 pp 584

Hnat, W.; Walsh, K. & Naber J. (2008). US Patent No 7357037.

Kanayama, M.; Cunningham, B.W.; Weis, J.C.; Parker, L.M.; Kanoda, K. & McAfee, P.C. (1997). Maturation of the posterolateral fusion and its effect on load-sharing of spinal instrumentation, Journal Bone and Joint Surgery Am. Vol. 79 (11) (1997) 1710-1720.

Lancaster, D. (1997). CMOS cookbook, Howard W. Sams & Co. Inc. pp 226.

Lin, J.-T.; (2006). Development of a telemetry spinal fusion sensor system, Ph.D. Dissertation, Electrical Engineering, University of Louisville, Louisville, KY.

Lin, J.-T.; Walsh, K. ; Jackson, D.; Aebersold, J.; Crain, M.; Naber, J. F. & Hnat, W. P. (2007). Development of capacitive pure bending strain sensor for wireless spinal fusion monitoring, Sens. Actuators,A,138 (2007) 276-28

Procter, E.& Strong, E. (1992) Capacitance strain gauges: strain gauge technology, Elsevier, 1992, PP 301-323.

Puers, R. (1993) Capacitive Sensor: When and how to use them, Sensors and Actuators A 37-38 (1993) 93-105.

Strong, Z.A.; Wang, A.W. & C.F. Mcconagh (2002). Hydrogel-actuated capacitive transducer for wireless biosensors, Biomed. Microdev. 4:2, (2002) 97-103.

Suster, M.; Chaimanonart,; N.; Guo,J.; Ko, W. H. & Young, D. J. (January 2005). Remote-Powered high-performance strain sensing microsystem, Technical Digest, the 18th IEEE International Conference on Micro Electro Mechanical Systems, Miami, Florida, January 2005, pp.255-258.

4

Ubiquitous Piezoelectric Sensor Network (UPSN)-Based Concrete Curing Monitoring for u-Construction

Seunghee Park and Dong-Jin Kim
Department of Civil and Environmental Engineering/u-City Design and EngineeringSungkyunkwan University
Cheoncheon-dong Jangan-gu Suwon
Republic of Korea

1. Introduction

Recently, there has been increasing demand for high-rise buildings or wide-span bridges. These structures are constructed with a mount of mass concrete. However, the concrete might be susceptible to brittle fracture if the curing process is inadequate. Therefore, to prevent this drawback, it is essential to predict the strength development of concrete during the curing process. In addition, real-time monitoring of the curing strength is important for reducing the construction time and cost because it can determine the appropriate curing time to achieve sufficient strength to progress to the next phase safely. The in-situ strength of concrete structures can be determined with a high precision by performing the strength testing and/or material analysis on core samples removed from the structure (Irie et al., 2008). However, this method might destroy the concrete structure. Therefore, a range of methods based on the thermal, acoustical, electrical, magnetic, optical, radiographic, and mechanical properties of the test materials have been developed to monitor the strength development without damaging the host structures (ACI Committee 228, 2003; Lamind and Pielert, 2006; Metha and Monterio, 2005). These methods typically measure certain properties of concrete from which the strength and/or elastic constants can be estimated. Among these techniques, several methods using a Schmidt hammer or an integrated temperature have been normally used. However, these are unsuitable for use at construction sites because they do not allow real-time monitoring of the curing process of concrete structures at inaccessible places.

The recent advent of smart materials, particularly piezoelectric materials, can provide a solution for the real-time monitoring for strength development. Electromechanical impedance techniques that employ piezoelectric materials have emerged as a potential tool for the implementation of a built-in monitoring system for civil infrastructures (Park G. et al., 2000, 2003; Park S. et al. 2005, 2006, 2011). This technique utilizes high-frequency structural excitation, which is typically > 20 kHz from surface-bonded PZT (Lead-Zirconate-Titanate) patches, to sensitively monitor the changes in the mechanical impedance of the test structures. Furthermore, the recent advances in online monitoring, including actuation and sensing, on-board computing, and radio-frequency (RF) telemetry, have improved the accessibility of the impedance method for in-field measurements. Lynch et al. (2004) designed a wireless active sensing unit to monitor civil structures, which was constructed of off-the-shelf components and had the ability to command active sensors and actuators from a computational core combined with wireless transmission and sensing circuits, embedded algorithm to process the acquired data, and structural status broadcasting. Grisso and Inman (2005) designed a DSP (Digital Signal Processor) based prototype to provide wireless assessment of thermal protection systems. It was able to directly detect damages by analyzing variations of the electrical impedance of PZT sensors bonded to the structure. The obtained impedance signals were compared with the pre-stored baseline and a statistical damage index was calculated. Mascarenas et al. (2007) proposed a wireless sensor node which consists of a miniaturized impedance measuring chip, a microprocessor, and a radio-frequency identification (RFID) module. Low cost impedance measuring chip actuated the structure through a PZT and measured the structural impedance response, and RFID module delivered the diagnostic result to a base station. Park S. et al. (2009) improved the wireless sensor node of Mascarenas et al. (2007) by adding two multiplexer IC chips for 16 channels for the cases of multiple sensors in a small region and by embedding signal processing algorithms in the microcontroller unit (MCU) for both structural damage identification and sensor self-diagnosis. Research groups at Los Alamos National Lab recently developed a compact impedance-based wireless sensing device (WID3) for low power operation (Overly et al. 2007, 2008), which requires around 60 mW of power to operate. Here, a wake-up capability was combined for low power operation. Taylor et al. (2009a, b) extended the capability of the WID3 by implementing a module with low-frequency A/D and D/A converters to measure low-frequency vibration data for multiple SHM techniques. It is wirelessly triggered by a mobile agent for use in the mobile-host-based wireless sensing network. Min et al. (2010) developed a multi-functional wireless sensor node integrating piezoelectric actuating, sensing, signal processing, temperature compensating, and energy harvesting modules.

In this context, this study presents a series of efforts to confirm the applicability of the electromechanical impedance technique using both wired and wireless systems for online monitoring on the strength-development during the curing process of concrete.

2. Electromechanical impedance based concrete strength estimation

As already described, in order to manage effectively the construction process of the concrete structures, online monitoring of the concrete strength-development is strongly required. To end this, this study employs the electromechanical impedance-based structural health monitoring (SHM) methodology because the electromechanical impedance can represent the mechanical properties of a host structure. The strength variation developed during the curing process can be observed throughout the electromechanical impedance measurements.

2.1 Strength development due to concrete curing process

Concrete achieves its strength through a hydraulic process known as hydration. With the addition of the correct amount of water, the cement gels into a paste that glues sand and aggregates together to form hardened concrete. The curing of concrete involves maintaining a proper moisture vapor transmission rate (2% mvtr) immediately after concrete placement as well as throughout the ensuing period of approximately 28 days. Fig. 1 shows a typical strength development curve (Shariq et al., 2010).

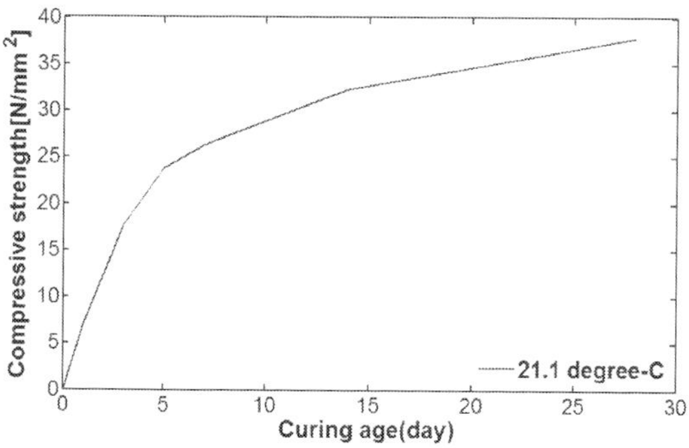

Fig. 1. Typical Strength Development Curve

2.2 Electromechanical impedance modeling

The electromechanical impedance-based SHM techniques have been developed as a promising tool for real-time structural damage assessment on critical members of large structural systems (Park G. et al., 2003, Koo et al., 2009, Taylor et al., 2009a, 2009b, Mascarenas et al., 2009). They make use of piezoelectric sensors such as piezoceramic (PZT) and macro-fiber composite (MFC) patches, which form a collocated sensor and actuator, often referred to as a self-sensing actuator (Giurgiutiu, 2007). The basis of this active sensing technology is the energy transfer between the actuator and the host mechanical system. If a PZT attached on a structure is driven with a sinusoidal voltage, it causes the local area of the structure to vibrate (the converse piezoelectric effect). And the structural response causes an electrical response in the PZT (the direct piezoelectric effect). Liang et al. (1996) first proposed a one-dimensional analytical model of this setup as in Fig. 2, and showed that the electrical admittance (inverse of the electrical impedance), Y(ω), of a PZT is directly correlated to the local mechanical impedance of the host structure, Zs(ω), and that of a PZT patch, Za(ω), in most applications as

$$Y(\omega) = G(\omega) + jB(\omega) - j\omega C\left(1 - \kappa_{31}^2 \frac{Z_s(\omega)}{Z_s(\omega) + Z_a(\omega)}\right) \qquad (1)$$

where G is the conductance (real part); B is the susceptance (imaginary part); C is the zero-load capacitance of a PZT; and κ31 is the electromechanical coupling coefficient of a PZT. Given that the mechanical impedance and the material properties of the PZT stay constant, the equation shows that a change in the structure's mechanical impedance directly results in a change in the electrical impedance measured by the PZT. Since damages cause a change in the structure's local mass, stiffness, or damping properties and consequently its mechanical impedance, the structure's mechanical integrity can be assessed by monitoring the PZT's electrical impedance. It should be noted that the admittance function, Y(ω), is a complex number. Bhalla et al. (2002) demonstrated that the real part of the measured admittance is more sensitively changed due to the structural damage condition as compared to the imaginary part. On the other hand, Park G. et al. (2006) found out that the imaginary part can be more effectively used for piezoelectric sensor self-diagnosis.

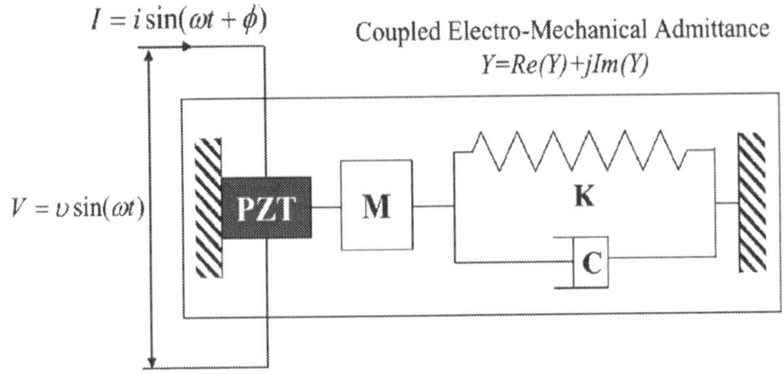

Fig. 2. 1-D Model used to derive electromechanical admittance of a PZT bonded to a structure (Liang et al. 1996)

2.3 Self-sensing based wired impedance measurement method

In this study, impedance measurement systems are based on a self-sensing technique, as shown in Fig. 3. A self-sensing circuit as described in Fig. 3 is suitable for use in cast-in-site concrete because it is inexpensive and has sufficient accuracy to measure the development of strength, even though the impedance signal is less accurate than other impedance measurement methods. The self-sensing circuit board consists of a single PZT patch, and a voltage divider, such as a resister or capacitor to acquire the output voltage.

The impedance is measured in three steps based on the self-sensing circuit as follows: (1) the input voltage (V_i) generated from an arbitrary waveform generator (AWG) is applied to the free surface of the PZT sensor; (2) the output voltage from the self-sensing circuit (V_o) is measured using a digitizer (DIG); and (3) the admittance, which is the inverse of impedance, is derived from the input voltage, output voltage, and reference capacitance (C_r). The output voltage from the self-sensing circuit consists of the input voltage and mechanical response of the structure (V_r). Although the amplitude of the mechanical responses of the structure is small enough to ignore, the output voltage is dominated by the input voltage and can be approximated as follows (Lee and Sohn, 2006)

$$V_o(t) = \frac{C_p}{C_p + C_r}\left[V_i(t) + V_p(t)\right] \simeq \frac{C_p}{C_p + C_r} V_i(t) \tag{2}$$

where C_p is the PZT capacitance and C_r is the reference capacitance of the self-sensing circuit. From Eq. (2), the impedance of structure (Z) is derived as follows:

$$Z(\omega) = \frac{V_p(\omega)}{I(\omega)} = [iwC_p]^{-1} \simeq \left[i\omega C_r\left(\frac{V_o(\omega)}{V_i(\omega) - V_o(\omega)}\right)\right]^{-1} \tag{3}$$

Thus, the impedance explained at Eq. (1) could be measured by Eq. (3) using the self-sensing circuit displayed in Fig. 3.

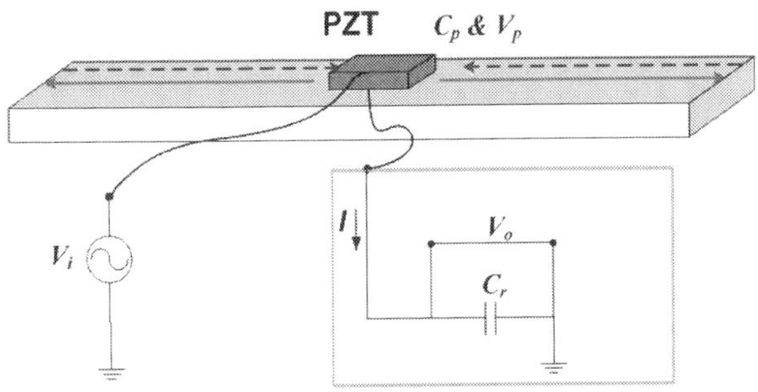

Fig. 3. Schematic diagram of a self-sensing circuit

3. Development of wireless impedance sensor nodes

The recent advances in wireless online monitoring integrating actuation and sensing, on-board computing, and radio-frequency (RF) telemetry improved the accessibility of the electromechanical impedance method for in-field measurements. In this study, the multi-functional wireless sensor node developed by Min et al. (2010) was utilized.

3.1 Subsystems of wireless impedance sensor nodes

To measure the electromechanical impedances, impedance analyzers such as HP4294A are conventionally used. However, they are not quite suitable for field applications to online SHM because they are bulky (approximately 25 kg) and expensive (approximately 40,000 USD). Thus, research on the impedance based SHM technique trends toward development of self-contained sensors and wireless active sensor nodes with all required functions including actuating/sensing, data processing, damage assessments and sensor self-diagnostics on the sensor board as well as power management with energy harvesters. Recently, Analog Devices© developed an integrated impedance converters, AD5933 (www.analog.com). It is equipped with a 12-bit analog-to-digital converter (ADC), a digital-to-analog converter (DAC) and a discrete Fourier transform (DFT) functionality. The frequency generator allows an external complex impedance with range of 100 Ω to 10MΩ to be excited with a known frequency of up to 100 kHz. AD5933 is just of a penny size, thus it provides a solution for self-contained miniaturized impedance measuring. Therefore, AD5933 has been used as a core component in developing a wireless impedance sensor node for SHM applications (Mascarenas et al. 2007, 2009, Overly et al. 2007, 2008, Taylor et al. 2009a, b, Park S. et al. 2009, Min et al. 2010). The wireless sensor node, proposed in this study, has extended the previous researches for multifunctional and environment-friendly uses in the impedance-based SHM (Mascarenas et al. 2007, Park S. et al. 2009). It was designed by adding: (1) optimal arrangement of each chip for low power consumption, (2) energy harvester equipped with solar panels, (3) peer-to-peer communication by using a RF transceiver of CC2420, which enables to construct the ubiquitous sensor network, (4) internal algorithms for operations, which are optimized by using microcontroller-dependent instruction codes to boost the sensor node's capability and (5) miniaturized hardware system fabricated as a printed circuit board (PCB) for a high quality prototype and enclosed by waterproof plastic box for applications to real structures. The proposed wireless sensor node is composed of four functional subsystems: (1) sensing interface, (2) computational core, (3) wireless transceiver and (4) power supply. The "sensing interface" includes an interface to which a piezoelectric sensor and a temperature sensor can be connected, and an impedance chip (AD5933) for exciting a piezoelectric sensor and measuring the impedance signals. Here, NTC (Negative Temperature Coefficient) disc thermistor is equipped for temperature sensing on the structure near a piezoelectric sensor. It is a low-cost and small-size resistance type device, and is suitable for temperature ranges from -20 °C to +120 °C with reference resistance of 10 kΩ at 25 °C. The "computational core" consists of a microcontroller and a serial flash memory for computational tasks and system operations with various embedded algorithms. Through embedding technologies in microcontroller, the wireless traffic can be reduced and the survival rate of transmitted data can be increased. In this sensor node, ATmega128L is adopted because it is one of high performance and low power 8-bit microcontrollers, and has 128 kilobytes of in-system self-programmable flash program memory (www.atmel.com). The "wireless transceiver" is an integral component of the wireless system, which is composed of a RF transceiver (CC2420), a balun transformer, and an antenna to communicate with a base station (Kmote-B radio module) and/or other wireless sensor nodes and to broadcast the structural condition. CC2420 is a single chip 2.4 GHz IEEE 802.15.4 compliant RF transceiver designed for low-power and low-voltage wireless applications (www.ti.com). It provides a low-cost and highly integrated solution for robust wireless communication and extensive hardware support for packet handling, data buffering and burst transmission. These features reduce the load on the host controller and allow CC2420 to interface low-cost microcontrollers. The sensor node can be operated by one of three type "power supply" systems: 5 V AC-plug DC adapter, 3.6-7.2 V battery, or 5 V solar power system. The power can be monitored on the microcontroller using a general ADC, which transforms the analog signals acquired from batteries to the digital signals. For stable power supply to the sensor node during operations, LDO (Low-dropout regulator) is mounted for providing a fixed 3.3 V reference output to the sensor node. Solar power system for energy harvesting consists of single crystalline silicon solar cells (120 × 60 mm2) to generate the maximum power for its size, two AA Ni- MH rechargeable batteries to stand high temperature and overcharging under sunlight and to last up to 1000 charge/discharge cycles, and a step-up DC/DC solar controller to protect the appliances and the batteries with over discharge prevention circuit. Fig. 4 shows the impedance sensor node developed in this study and its block diagram, and the features are described in Table 1. The developed impedance sensor node was tested on the several operational conditions to determine the actual in-service power consumption. A multimeter was placed in line on the node's positive voltage terminal. The current draw during each condition was recorded as: 1.3 mA in idle state, 25.8 mA during measurement, 15.2 mA during calculation, and 27.3 mA during transmission, which indicates that the maximum required power is approximately 90 mW with 3.3 V.

It is slightly larger than the required power of 60 mW by Overly et al. (2008), which may be caused by additionally equipped NTC thermistor for temperature sensing, three LEDs for informing the node status by twinkling with different colors, and other operation subsystems. The required power may be reduced further with proper use of sleep modes in Overly et al. (2008).

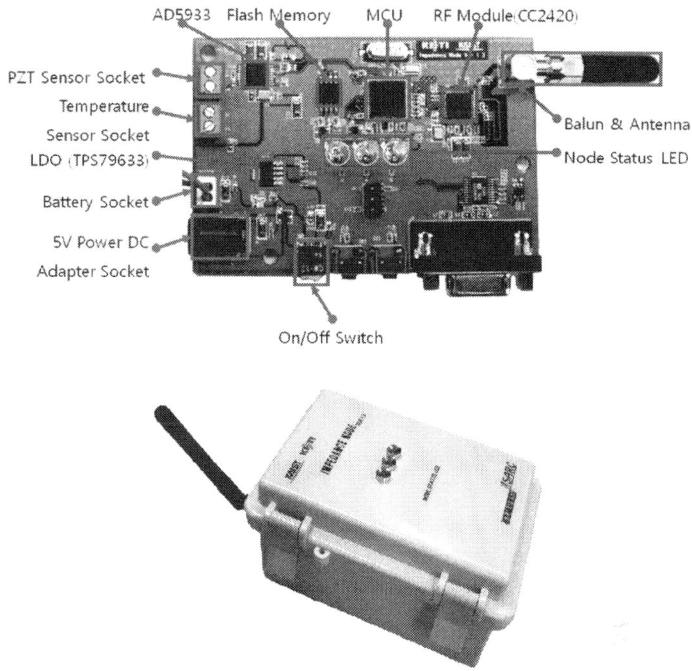

(a) Subsystem and enclosure

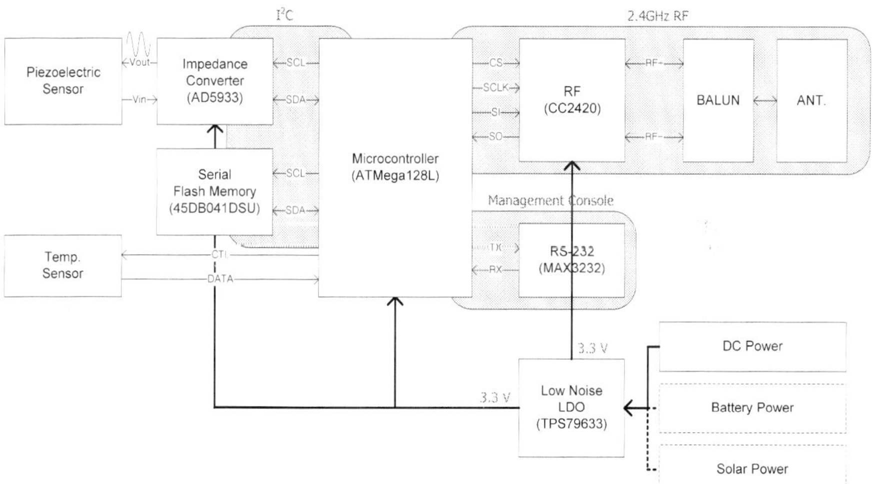

(b) Block diagram

Fig. 4. Proposed wireless impedance sensor node

Output Frequency Range	1 ~ 100 kHz
Output Frequency Resolution	> 1 Hz
Impedance Range	1 kΩ ~ 1 MΩ
Temperature Range	-40 ~ 125 °C
Temperature Resolution	> 0.03 °C
On-Board Processing	Yes (MCU : ATMega128L)
Operating Frequency	2.4 GHz IEEE 802.15.4 / Zigbee RF Transceiver
Outdoor Transmission Range	150 m
Power Supply Options	• 5V AC-plug DC Adapter • Commercial batteries (3.6-7.2V) • 2AA Ni-MH rechargeable battery with Solar Panels (3V)
Feature	150 x 100 x 70 (mm) ; 310 (g)

Table 1. Features of the proposed wireless impedance sensor node

3.2 Data control and on-board data analysis

TinyOS is the most typical open-source operating system designed for wireless embedded sensor networks. It features a component-based architecture which enables rapid innovation and implementation while minimizing code size as required by the severe memory constraints inherent in sensor networks.

The proposed sensor node is based on TinyOS for system operation. On the other hand, the server is controlled by users through MATLAB® software, which is a high-level language and interactive environment to perform computationally intensive tasks faster than traditional programming languages such as C, C++, or FORTRAN, and includes a number of mathematical functions including Fourier analysis, filtering, signal processing and serial communications. Moreover, it provides GUI (graphical user interface) development environment, from which the user can easily change the control variables and monitor the wirelessly transmitted raw and/or processed data, temperature and node status such as battery condition. The serial communication is established between a server and a base station using two service daemons, which are cross-complied using Cygwin. These daemons provide a Linux-like environment for Windows, and enable to communicate between MATLAB® (Windows) and base station/sensor node (TinyOS).

For continuous and autonomous SHM using wireless sensor nodes, it is strongly required to construct the embedded data analysis system. More power-efficient wireless SHMs could be achieved, if the measured impedance is analyzed on microcontroller of the sensor node and only the analyzed results Table 1 Features of the proposed wireless impedance sensor node could be wirelessly sent to a base station. Especially, this fact is crucial for self-powered wireless sensor nodes incorporating several kinds of energy harvesters. In the proposed sensor node, multifunctional algorithms are implemented for temperature/power measurement, impedance measurement and analysis engine for both structural damage detection and sensor self-diagnosis, as shown in Fig. 5.

The impedance measurement block consists of the TWI library, AD5933 control library and the default sweep function (512 points) library. Using raw data from the impedance measurement block, the embedded analysis engine optionally performs the analysis for structural damage detection and sensor self-diagnosis. Two algorithms are embedded on the microcontroller for the structural status monitoring: the RMSD metric and the temperature compensated CC metric calculated by EFS method. Sensor self-diagnosis is simply carried out calculating the slope of the imaginary part of admittance. Here, the baseline impedance is stored at the serial flash memory. Depending on input arguments, the users can get raw or processed data from the designated sensors.

3.3 Self-powered wireless system incorporated with solar cells

Power scavenging enables "place-and-forget" wireless sensor node. Considering that the necessary cost and efforts for battery maintenance and replacement may over-shadow the merits of the wireless SHM system, the ability to scavenge energy from the environment is a quite important and it permits deploying self-powered sensor nodes onto inaccessible locations. Thus, many researchers have shown interest in power scavenging and the related technologies have steeply grown. Especially, the solar power is most often used, which is produced by collecting sunlight and converting it into electricity.

This is done by using solar panels, which are large flat panels made up of many individual solar cells. In this study, a solar power system for operating a wireless sensor node is designed with single crystalline silicon solar cells (120 × 60 mm2), two AA Ni-MH rechargeable batteries (1.2 V × 2ea), and a step-up DC/DC solar controller, considering one-time measurement per day. A step-up DC/DC solar controller offers 4.8 V reference output from a lowered battery voltage of more than 2 V.

This solar power system provides maximum 750 mW, which may be enough to operate the developed sensor node of 90 mW. If the larger power is needed for more frequent measurements per day, the recharging capacity of the solar power system may be increased by using higher-efficient and bigger size solar panels and higher-voltage batteries. To validate the ability of the solar power system, a simple experiment has been carried out on an aluminum plate as shown in Fig. 6. A macro-fiber composite (MFC) patch of 47 × 25 × 0.267 mm3 (2814P1 Type; Smart Material©) was surface-bonded to the aluminum specimen of 50 × 1,000 × 4 mm3. The MFC is a relatively new type of PZT transducer that exhibit superior ruggedness and conformability compared to traditional piezoceramic wafers. At the beginning, the batteries were fully recharged by an electric battery charger. Then, the experiment started at 00:00 am on 6 September, 2009. Raw impedance signals and the processed structural damage detection results were wirelessly transmitted to a base station at every 10:00 am for five days. The weather condition was changed in five days as follows: sunny (19.6-31.1 °C; cloud 0.8), mostly cloudy (20.9-27.9 °C; cloud 7.6), partly cloudy (21.0-29.8 °C; cloud 5.3), partly cloudy (17.9- 28.6 °C; cloud 4.3), and partly cloudy (14.5-28.5 °C; cloud 6.8). Fig. 7 shows the voltage level in two AA rechargeable batteries during five days, which was measured every one hour.

Although the voltage steeply declined during the measurement of impedances and on-board calculation of damage index, it was almost fully recovered in one hour under sun light.

It may indicate that it is able to operate the sensor node several times per day. The recharged voltage remained on stable condition under sun light, but it decreased at 0.005 V/hour at night. When cloudy, the solar cells could not be recharged due to the lack of sun light, but it shortly returned to stable condition as the sun rose. From the above results, it may be concluded that the solar power system is able to provide a solution for maintenance-free wireless sensor nodes in spite of sensitive reaction to the environment, which would be complemented by development of the more efficient energy scavenging technologies.

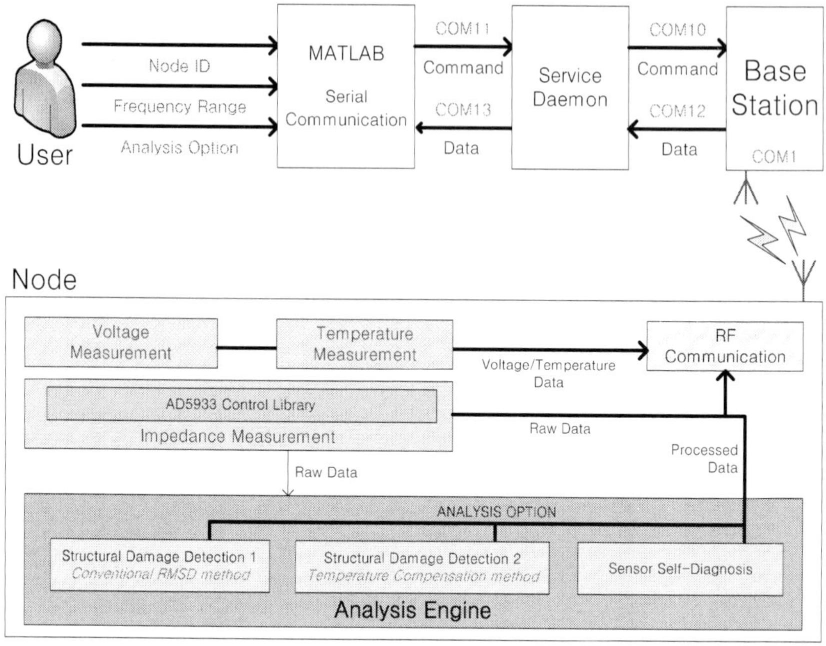

Fig. 5. Overall command/data flow of embedded software

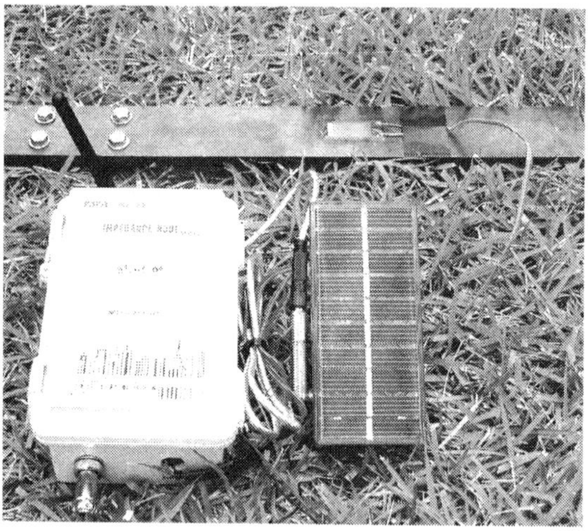

Fig. 6. Sensor node with a solar panel

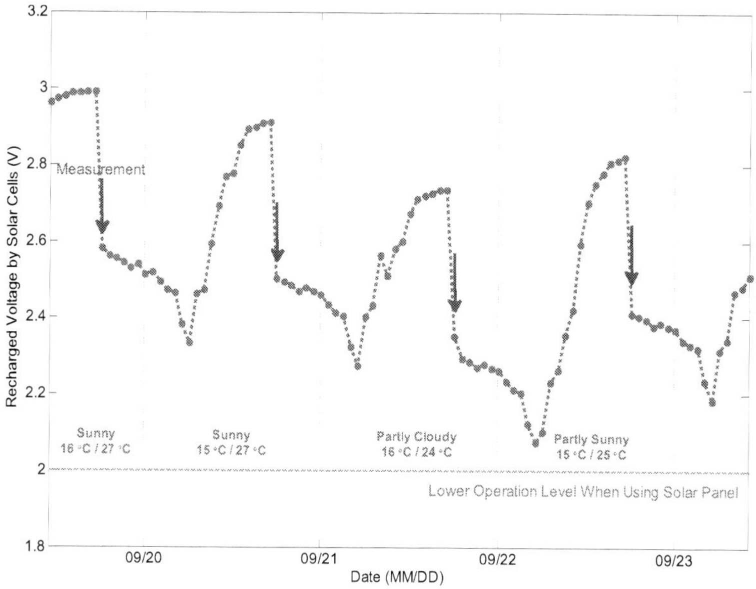

Fig. 7. Voltage monitoring of a wireless SHM system with solar cells

4. Experimental verification

In order to verify the feasibility of the proposed electromechanical impedance technique for online monitoring of the strength developed during the curing process of the concrete structures, a series of experimental studies have been carried out using both wired and wireless systems.

4.1 Experimental setup and test procedure

Two types of concrete cylinders with design strength of 60MPa and 100MPa were prepared to measure the impedance signals during the curing process of concrete, as shown in Fig. 8. The cylinders were developed by isothermal air curing. PZT sensors, 20 mm × 20 mm × 0.508 mm in size, were attached to the concrete cylinders. The PZT sensors were installed on the cylinders in the first 24 hours after casting. Since concrete is a non-conducting material, a conducting copper paste was applied to the specimen before bonding the PZT sensor to the host structure. The PZT patches were bonded to the top center of the cylinder surface, as shown in Fig. 8. The experimental setup for the wired impedance measurement system consisted of cylinders with the PZT sensors, a self-sensing circuit board and a DAQ system (PXI 1042Q, National Instruments Inc.). The DAQ system consisted of an Arbitrary Waveform Generator (AWG), a Digitizer (DIG), embedded controller and data acquisition software (LabVIEW). The wireless system was comprised of the cylinders with the PZT sensors, a wireless sensor node, a RF receiver (KETI), and a laptop computer equipped with data acquisition software (MATLAP), as shown in Fig. 9, 10.

(a) 60MPa Concrete specimen

(b) 100MPa Concrete specimen

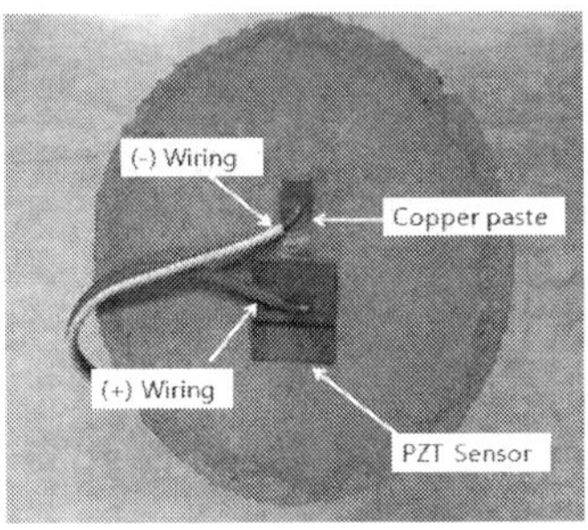

(c) PZT attached concrete specimen

Fig. 8. Test specimen: High Strength Concrete Cylinders

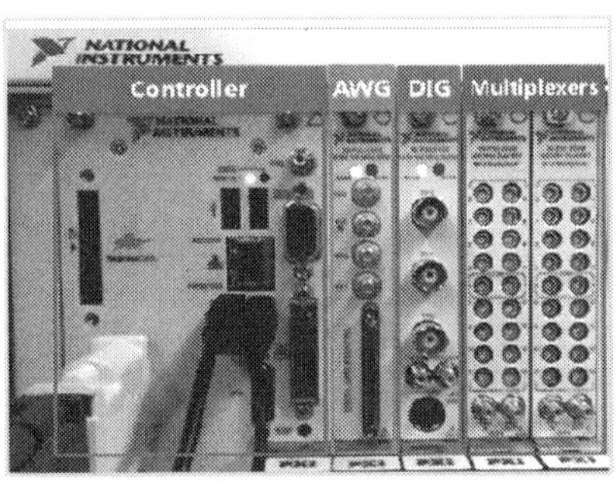

(a) NI-PXI DAQ system

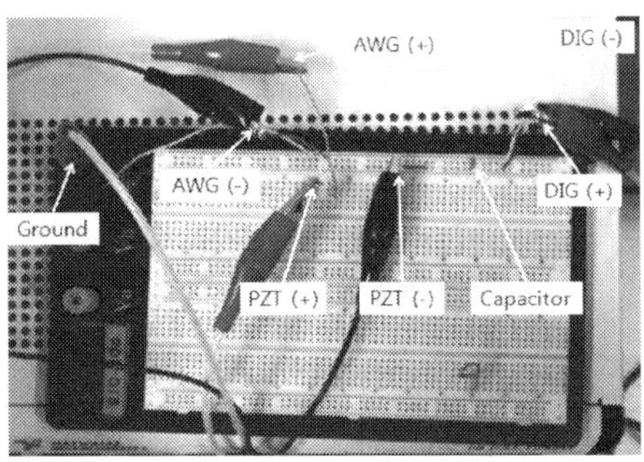

(b) Self-sensing circuit

Fig. 9. Wired impedance measuring system

(a) Wireless impednace sensor node (b) RF reciever

Fig. 10. Wireless impedance measuring system

The frequency ranges so the shift in the resonant frequencies could be observed clearly in the measured impedance signals were determined to be 45 kHz ~ 50 kHz for the 60MPa cylinder and 35 kHz ~ 40 kHz for the 100MPa cylinder. The first test was carried out 3 days after mixing because before 3 days, the piezoelectric sensors could not be attached completely. Subsequent tests were performed at 5, 7, 14, 21 and 28 days. In particular, days 3, 7, 14, and 28 are important days in evaluating the in-place compressive strength in the construction codes of many countries. Three cylinders for each group were tested using the wired and wireless systems simultaneously to compare their performance. To improve the signal to noise ratio, the signals were acquired 3 times and averaged.

4.2 Impedance variations due to curing process

The strength of the concrete results from the hydration process of the concrete. During hydration, the mechanical properties of the concrete, such as strength, impedance etc., changed. The impedance technique for monitoring the strength development of concrete employs the change in the mechanical impedance during the hydration process. Figs. 11 and 12 show the measured impedance signals from the wired and wireless systems at six different curing ages. In addition, each dataset was normalized to the maximum value. First, the results from the 60MPa are reported. The resonant frequencies in the impedance signals shifted gradually to the right side with increasing curing age (Fig. 11) due to strength development of the concrete. This confirmed that the impedance technique can be used to monitor the strength development of concrete. In Fig. 12, the impedance data from the 100MPa specimens showed a similar pattern to that obtained from the 60MPa specimens. Although wireless data has some noises, the quantity of the shift in the resonant frequency measured using the wired and wireless system was similar. The noises of wireless data are caused by the resolution problem of wireless sensor node. The frequency resolution can be fixed at a certain level (in this study, that is 1Hz) when NI PXI equipment is used. However, the wireless sensor node can sample with maximum 512 points. In this study, the frequency band of the measured signal is 5kHz with 500 sampling points. Hence, the frequency resolution is 10Hz when the wireless sensor node is used. However, these bumps can be negligible because these cannot affect to the patterns from the curing process. Therefore, the applicability of a wireless impedance measuring system to monitor the curing process of concrete was established.

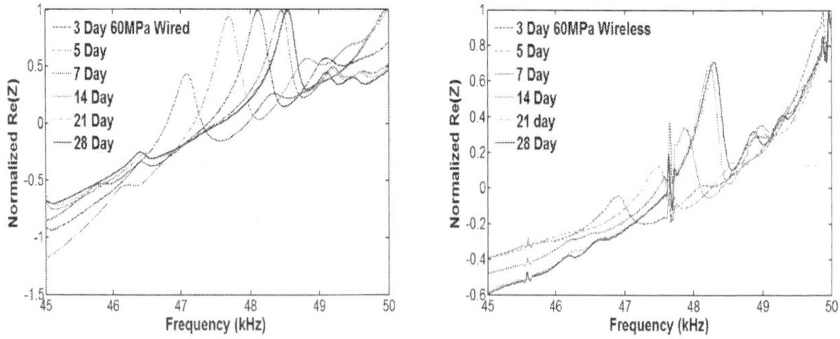

(a) Wired data (b) Wireless data

Fig. 11. Impedance variation measured at 60MPa concrete cylinder

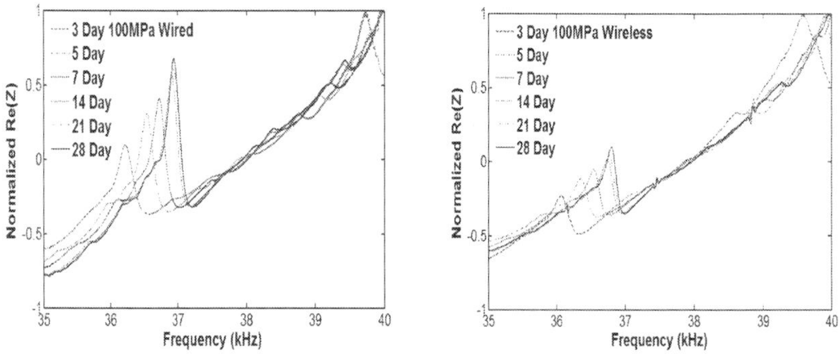

(a) Wired data (b) Wireless data

Fig. 12. Impedance variation measured at 100MPa concrete cylinder

4.3 Signal processing for the impedance variation

Two methods, resonant frequency and cross-correlation coefficient, were applied to examine the trend of the impedance variations more precisely:

4.3.1 Resonant frequency shift

To visualize the curing process of the concrete, the resonant frequency shift (RFS), derived as Eq. (4), at each curing age was plotted, as shown in Fig. 13.

$$RFS = \frac{f_i - f_o}{f_o} \tag{4}$$

where f_i is the current resonant frequency of the impedance data at each measurement day, and f_o is the resonant frequency of the 3rd day measured impedance data as a baseline.

The resonant frequency increased in both cases 60MPa and 100MPa. All the resonant frequency shift data was normalized to the maximum value. As the curing process progressed, the strength of the cylinder increased during the hydration process. Since the resonant frequency is associated with the strength of a concrete cylinder, the resonant frequency in the impedance signals of the cylinder increased with increasing cylinder strength. In addition, the change in resonant frequency measured using the wired system and wireless system were similar in 60MPa and 100MPa. Fig. 1 shows a typical strength development curve of 30MPa at a curing temperature of 21.1 °C to compare these results with the typical strength development of curing concrete. The changing patterns between the increasing resonant frequency and the development of the compressive strength were similar. Also the RFS of wired and wireless represent similar pattern. Therefore, the RFS of the impedance can be used to monitor the strength development of the concrete.

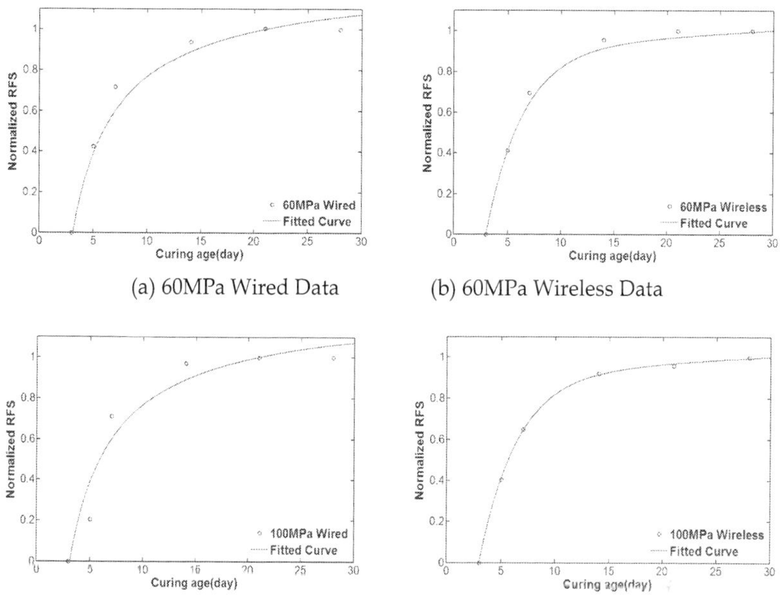

(a) 60MPa Wired Data (b) 60MPa Wireless Data

(c) 100MPa Wired Data (d) 100MPa Wireless Data

Fig. 13. Resonant frequency shift-based estimate of strength development

4.3.2 Cross-correlation coefficient

In addition to the RFS, the cross-correlation coefficient index (1-CC) was calculated to provide quantitative information. The 1-CC values were derived using the following equation:

$$1-CC=1-\frac{1}{N\ 1}\frac{\sum_{i=1}^{N}(\mathrm{Re}(Z_{i,0})-\mathrm{Re}(\overline{Z_0}))(\mathrm{Re}(Z_{i,1})-\mathrm{Re}(\overline{Z_1}))}{\sigma_{Z_0}\sigma_{Z_1}} \quad (5)$$

where $Z_{i,0}$ is the impedance function at the baseline (the impedance data of 3rd day), $Z_{i,1}$ is the current impedance at each measured day, and $\sigma_{Z_0}, \sigma_{Z_1}$ are the standard deviations of each dataset, respectively. The data was normalized to the maximum value. Fig. 14 shows the 1-CC data of 60MPa and 100MPa respectively. The 1-CC data shows the same pattern with a commercial strength development curve (Fig. 1). Also, the wired data and wireless data has similar pattern. Therefore, the 1-CC value can provide more reliable quantitative information on strength development.

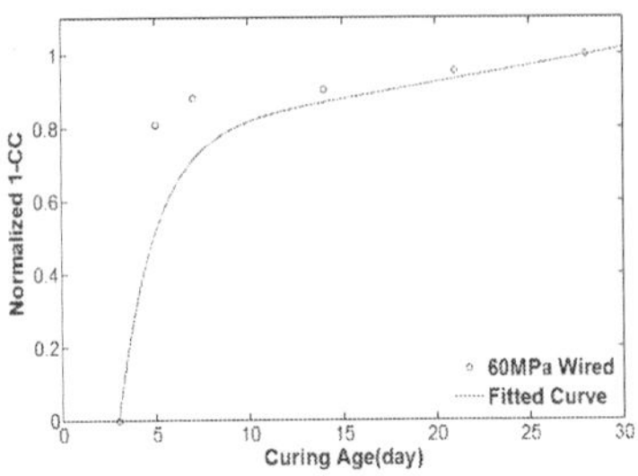

(a) 60MPa Wired Data

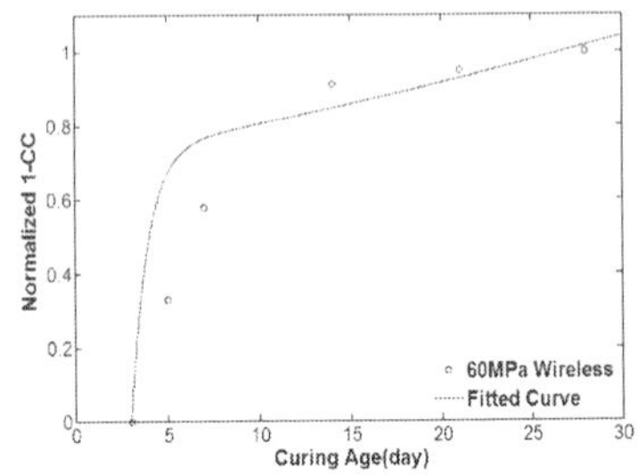

(b) 60MPa Wireless Data

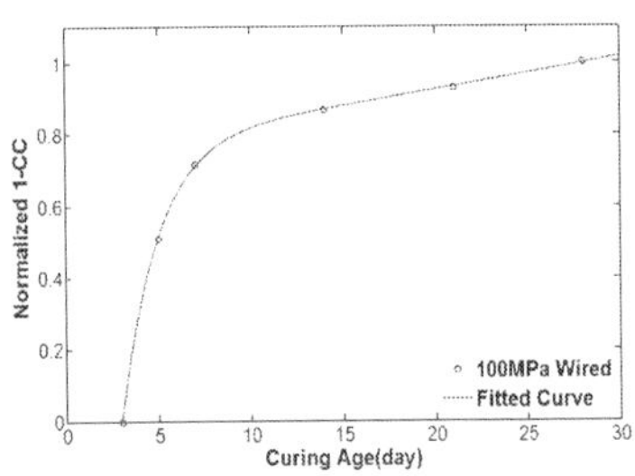

(c) 100MPa Wired Data

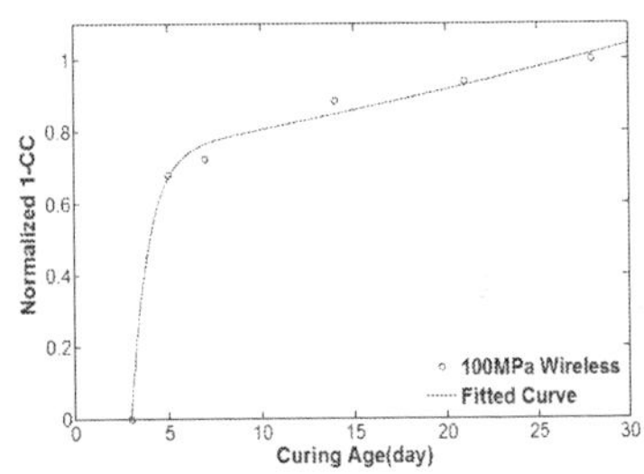

(d) 100MPa Wireless Data

Fig. 14. 1-CC-based estimate of strength development

5. Conclusion

This study evaluated the application of PZT sensors for monitoring the strength development of high strength concrete. The applicability of the conventional impedance measuring technique, which is normally used to detect damage, was extended to monitor the curing process of concrete. The impedance signals were obtained at six different curing ages. The compressive strengths of the test concrete cylinders were also evaluated by considering the resonant frequency variations and cross-correlation coefficient. Based on the experimental results, the resonant frequencies in the impedance signals shifted gradually to the right side with increasing curing time, which confirms the applicability of impedance measurements to monitor the strength development of concrete. The largest deviation of the resonant frequency shift was observed between days 3 and 5, and the change decreased with time. In addition, the 1-CC values increased due to strength development during the curing process. A wireless impedance system showed similar results to that of the wired impedance system. Therefore, a wireless system that can improve the applicability to a construction site can be used to monitor the strength development of concrete. Consequently, the wireless strength development monitoring system for concrete can be employed comfortably in construction sites. Furthermore, piezoelectric sensors that monitor the strength development can be used for structural health monitoring (SHM) after construction. In addition, embedded curing monitoring and a SHM system for high strength concrete can be developed to improve the applicability and efficiency of this system.

6. Acknowledgment

This study was supported by National Nuclear R&D Program through the National Research Foundation of Korea (NRF) funded by the Ministry of Education, Science and Technology (2010-0025889) and u-City Master and Doctor Support Project funded by Ministry of Land, Transport and Maritime Affairs (MLTMA). This all-out support is greatly appreciated.

7. References

ACI Committee 228. (Nov 1, 2003)). *In-place methods to estimate concrete strength report,* American Concrete Institute, MI, USA

Bhalla, S., Naidu, A.S.K. and Soh, C.K. (2002). Influence of structure-actuator interactions and temperature on piezoelectric mechatronic signatures for NDE, *Proceedings of the ISSS-SPIE International Conferences on Smart Materials Structures and Systems,* ISSN 0277786X, Bangalore, December 2002.

Giurgiutiu, V. (July 1, 2007*). Structural health monitoring: with piezoelectric wafer active sensors,* Elsevier/Academic Press, ISBN 9780120887606, Amsterdam

Grisso, B.L. and Inman, D.J. (2005). Developing an autonomous on-orbit impedance-based SHM system for thermal protection systems, *Proceedings of the 5th Int'l Workshop on Structural Health Monitoring,* Stanford, CA, September.

Irie, H., Yoshida, Y., Sakurada, Y., and Ito, T. (2008). Non-destructive-testing Methods for Concrete Structures, *NTT Technical Review.* Vol. 6, No. 8, (May 2008), pp. 1-8

Koo, K.Y., Park, S., Lee, J.J. and Yun, C.B. (2009). Automated impedance-based structural health monitoring incorporating effective frequency shift for compensating temperature effects, *Journal of Intelligent Material Systems and Structures,* Vol. 20, No. 4, pp.367- 377, ISSN 1045389X

Lamond, J. F. and Pielert, J. H. (2006). Significance of tests and properties of concrete and concrete-making materials, *ASTM International,* Vol. 169, pp. 667, ISSN 00660558

Lee, S.J., and Sohn, H. (2006). Active self-sensing scheme development for structural health monitoring, *Smart Materials and Structures,* Vol. 15, No. 6, pp. 1734-1746, ISSN 09641726

Liang, C., Sun, F.P. and Rogers, C.A. (1996). Electro-mechanical impedance modeling of active material systems, *Smart Materials and Structures,* Vol. 5, No. 2, pp. 171-186, ISSN 09641726

Lynch, J.P., Sundararajan, A., Law, K.H., Sohn, H. and Farrar, C.R. (2004). Design of a wireless active sensing unit for structural health monitoring, *Proceedings of the SPIE Annual Int'l Symposium on Smart Structures and Materials,* ISSN 0277786X, San Diego, CA, March.

Mascarenas, D.L., Todd, M.D., Park, G. and Farrar, C.R. (2007). Development of an impedance-based wireless sensor node for structural health monitoring, *Smart Materials and Structures,* Vol. 16, No. 6, pp. 2137-2145, ISSN 09641726

Mascarenas, D.L., Park, G., Farinholt, K., Todd, M.D. and Farrar, C.R. (2009). A low-power wireless sensing device for remote inspection of bolted joints, *Proceedings of the Institution of Mechanical Engineers, Part G: Journal of Aerospace Engineering*, Vol. 223, No. 5, pp. 565-575, ISSN 09544100

Mehta, P. K. and Monterio, P. J. M. (Sep 30, 2005). *Concrete: microstructure, properties, and materials. 3rd ed.*, McGraw-Hill, ISBN 0071462899, New York,

Min, J., Park, S., Yun, C.-B., and Song, B. (2010). Development of Low-cost Multi-functional Wireless Impedance Sensor Nodes, *Smart Structures and Systems*, Vol. 6, No. 5-6 pp. 689-709

Overly, T.G., Park, G., Farrar, C.R. and Allemang, R.J. (2007). Compact hardware development for structural health monitoring and sensor diagnostics using admittance measurements, *Proceedings of the IMAC-XXV: A Conference & Exposition on Structural Dynamics*, Orlando, FL, February 2007.

Overly, T.G., Park, G., Farinholt, K.M. and Farrar, C.R. (2008). Development of an extremely compact impedance-based wireless sensing device, *Smart Materials and Structures*, Vol. 17, No. 6., 065011, ISSN 09641726

Park, G., Cudney, H. H. and Inman, D. J. (2000), Impedance-based health monitoring of civil structural components, *Journal of Infrastructure and Systems,* Vol. 6, No. 4, pp.153-160, ISSN 10760342

Park, G., Sohn, H., Farrar, C.R. and Inman, D.J. (2003). Overview of piezoelectric impedance-based health monitoring and path forward, *Shock and Vibration Digest*, Vol. 35, No. 6, pp. 451-463, ISSN 05831024

Park, G., Farrar, C.R., Rutherford, A.C. and Robertson, A.N. (2006). Piezoelectric active sensor self-diagnostics using electrical admittance measurements, *Journal of Vibration and Acoustics*, Vol. 128, No. 4, pp. 469-476, ISSN 10489002

Park, S., Ahmad, S., Yun, C.-B., and Roh, Y. (2006). Multiple Crack Detection of Concrete Structures Using Impedance-based Structural Health Monitoring Techniques, *Journal of Experimental Mechanics*, Vol. 46, pp.609-618.

Park, S.,, Kim, J.-W., Lee, C.-G., and Park, S.-K. (2011). Impedance-based Wireless Debonding Condition Monitoring of CFRP Laminated Concrete Structures, *NDT&E International*, Vol. 44, pp. 232-238

Park, S., Shin, H.H. and Yun, C.B. (2009), Wireless impedance sensor nodes for functions of structural damage identification and sensor self-diagnosis, *Smart Materials and Structures*, Vol. 18, No. 5, 055001, ISSN 09641726

Park, S., Yun, C.-B., and Roh, Y. , and Lee, J.-J. (2005). Health monitoring of steel structures using impedance of thickness modes at PZT patches, *Journal of Smart Structures and Systems*, Vol. 1, No. 4, pp.339-353.

Shariq, M., Parasad, J. and Masood, A. (2010). Effect of GGBFS on time dependent compressive strength of concrete, *Construction and Building Materials,* Vol. 24, No. 8 pp. 1469-1478, ISSN 09500618

Taylor, S.G., Farinholt, K.M., Park, G. and Farrar, C.R. (2009a). Wireless impedance device for electromechanical impedance sensing and low-frequency vibration data acquisition, *Proceedings of the SPIE Annual International Symposium on Sensors and Smart Structures Technologies for Civil, Mechanical, and Aerospace Systems*, ISBN 978-081947552-7, San Diego, CA, March 2009

Talyor, S.G., Farinholt, K.M., Flynn, E.B., Figueiredo, E., Mascarenas, D.L., Moro, E.A., Park, G., Todd, M.D. and Farrar, C.R. (2009b). A mobile-agent-based wireless sensing network for structural monitoring applications, *Measurement Science and Technology*, Vol. 20, No. 4, 045201, ISSN 09570233

Part 2

Telemetry Data Mining

5

Telemetry Data Mining with SVM for Satellite Monitoring

Yosuke Fukushima
Institute of Space and Astronautical Science, Japan Aerospace Exploration Agency, Japan

1. Introduction

The aim of this chapter is to provide readers with a basic knowledge of satellite monitoring and data mining for anomaly detection using a support vector machine (SVM) technique. The author describes the design and implementation of an SVM and an example of the use of the satellite hardware anomaly detection to discover instability in the attitude rate bias of a gyro sensor. This anomaly is caused by a change in the characteristic parameter of the gyro hardware: a statistical parameter related to noise specifications. The detection is demonstrated using telemetry data that have been sent by an actual science satellite.

This chapter is divided into three sections: first, the author describes the target satellite and the basic mathematical modelling and formulation of attitude dynamics of the satellite. In the formulation, kinematics and model parameter estimation technique using Kalman filter method is described to provide readers the key parameter; the drift parameters of attitude rate gyro, which are to be dealt with in the following sections in detail. Estimation of unknown parameter of the formulation is also shown using actual telemetry data. This scheme called observers is most popular method for almost every satellite. Second, a brief introduction of the SVM technique is given and followed by a design and implementation of the SVM technique to the gyro bias instability detection. This analysis and calculation are performed using a set of real telemetry data are given. Finally, a software architecture is proposed that will make it easier to migrate SVM software into an onboard computer as a step toward realizing onboard autonomy.

Although the formulation developed in this chapter is concerned with attitude rate sensors of a particular satellite, this approach can be applied to other types of remote systems; a remote system that is designed to be operated by human operators in a distant site by communicating using telemetry systems. This type of onboard autonomous system monitoring seems to be promising not only in all remote systems that are working at server circumstances such as space or deep underwater but also in some consumer products such as cars and trains.

2. Onboard satellite health monitoring

In this section, knowledge of attitude determination of a satellite is given by modelling and analysis of an actual satellite attitude motion in detail. It is necessary to understand meaning and mechanism of estimation of characteristic parameters of hardware as health indicators of satellite systems throughout operations. To dealing with change in value of such parameters, a complete set of analytical process of attitude determination is shown. The telemetry data used in this chapter was obtained in an actual satellite operation.

2.1 Aurora science small satellite REIMEI

The Institute of Space and Astronautical Science, Japan Exploration Agency (ISAS/JAXA) has launched a series of scientific satellites including planetary spacecraft as well as astronomical observation satellites. Although the missions have achieved fruitful scientific results, these satellites, including our own M-V launch vehicle, have cost nearly 160 million dollars and taken over eight years to develop. As a result, the launch frequency of scientific satellites has decreased significantly in the last decade. In addition to these large and expensive missions with a long development time, an inexpensive mission with a short development time involving a small piggyback satellite has been planned. This satellite should be an effective tool for demonstrating new technology and performing scientific observations.

A small satellite named "REIMEI" was developed from 2000 and was launched to a height of 610 Km by the Dnepr Launching Vehicle from Baikonur Cosmodrome launch site in Kazakhstan on August 24, 2005 (Saito et al., 2005). Since then it has followed a near Sun synchronous orbit. The Japanese word "REIMEI" means dawn, and the satellite name was chosen to celebrate the new era of high-performance small satellites developed in Japan. REIMEI's mission objective is to observe dynamic aurora phenomena using the three spectrum imagers (MAC) and two particle analysers (E/ISA) installed onboard. Observations are carried out with the aim of studying the small-scale dynamics of terrestrial aurora, namely, their spatial distributions and time variations, and their correspondence to the spectral properties and spatial distributions of charged particles. Figure 1 shows the flight configuration of REIMEI. There are two solar-concentrated deployable paddles on the top surface that can generate a power of 150 W, three camera lens holes for MAC in the black-kapton-covered front surface, and E/ISA are installed covered by the silver-Teflon-lined right surface.

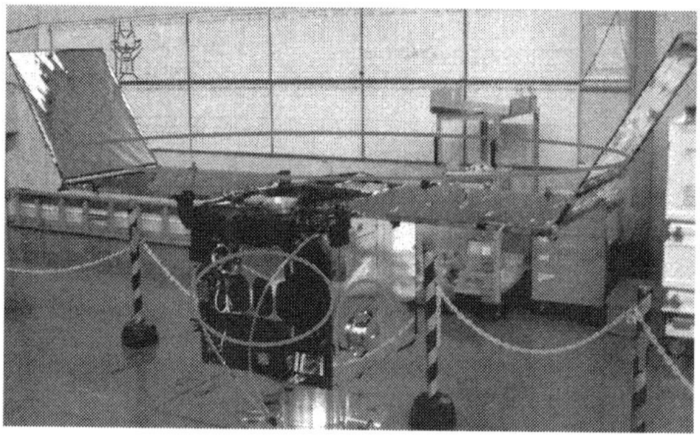

Fig. 1. Flight configuration of REIMEI

2.2 Attitude control requirements

REIMEI has a bias-momentum three-axis attitude control subsystem (ACS) to meet the requirements: the attitude control accuracy should be less than 0.5 degree, and the attitude determination accuracy should be less than 0.05 degree. These requirements are specified for one of the most important observation modes, the image/particle simultaneous observation mode, in which E/ISA detect particles to count their number as well as to measure their energy, while MAC captures aurora phenomena emerging at a magnetic line foot-point, where the aurora is energized by the particles observed.

ACS inputs data from sensors such as the spin type sun sensor (SSAS), the two-dimensional sun sensor (NSAS), the star tracker (STT), the three-axis geomagnetic field aspect sensor (GAS), and three-axis fibre-optic gyroscopes (FOGs). On the other hand, ACS outputs data to actuators such as the small momentum wheel (WHL), which provides the satellite with bias momentum (0.5 Nms), and the three-axis magnetic torquers (MTQ). Figure 2 shows the flight models of FOG of REIMEI.

ACS can be divided into two function blocks: the attitude control and the attitude determination blocks. Since several papers have been published (Sakai et al., 2006a; Fukushima et al., 2006) dealing with the REIMEI attitude control block that refer to its algorithm, formulation, and flight results, here we will focus on the attitude determination block illustrated in Fig.3. The inputs for the attitude determination block are the angular increment angle data measured by FOG and the five star vectors measured by STT. The outputs are the attitude and the attitude rate of REIMEI, which are expressed in an inertial coordinate system. Attitude is expressed using quaternions in this paper and is propagated by the integration of an initial or current attitude quaternion using the attitude rate with respect to time. The attitude rate is also called the angular velocity. Note that the attitude rate is calculated from both FOG outputs and the FOG bias. The FOG bias is residual output when FOG is motionless in the inertial coordinate system.

Fig. 2. Flight models of three FOGs assembled on one aluminium plate.

An error correction procedure must be installed into the attitude determination block since there will be a modeling error or observation error in the a priori initial attitude, the attitude rate observed by FOG, and the star vectors obtained by STT. For example, if the FOG bias is not suitably taken into account in the attitude propagation, the attitude rate error will accumulate to a value that will corrupt the attitude propagation. In addition, the FOG bias fluctuates with respect to time and temperature of FOG. Thus, REIMEI has a Kalman filter programmed in the attitude determination block to simultaneously estimate the attitude estimation error and the FOG bias estimation error.

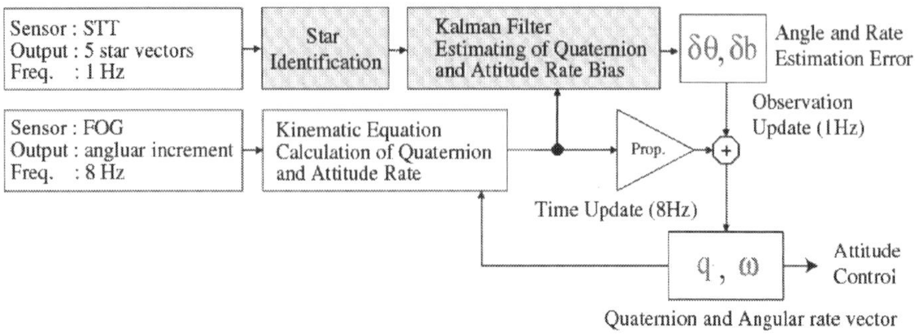

Fig. 3. Diagram of attitude control of REIMEI

2.3 Attitude kinematics and attitude determination

An extended Kalman filter (EKF) theory was employed to determine the attitude and attitude rate simultaneously. This filter algorithm is based on an attitude uncertainty model in rotating body coordinates that is discretized with intervals equal to the attitude update time interval. The algorithm estimates both the attitude estimation error angle theta and the attitude rate bias b. Bias b is also called FOG bias.

The satellite rotation equation and the relation between the attitude rate and the FOG bias are given by

$$\dot{q} = \frac{1}{2}\Omega(\omega)q \tag{1}$$

$$\omega = \omega_{FOG} - b \tag{2}$$

$$\dot{b} = 0, \tag{3}$$

where q is a quaternion vector, ω is an attitude rate vector, b is an rate bias vector, and ω_{FOG} is an attitude rate vector measured by FOG. $\Omega(\omega)$ is the following well-known 4x4 skew matrix

$$\Omega(\omega) = \begin{pmatrix} 0 & \omega_3 & -\omega_2 & \omega_1 \\ -\omega_3 & 0 & \omega_1 & \omega_2 \\ \omega_2 & -\omega_1 & 0 & \omega_3 \\ -\omega_1 & -\omega_2 & -\omega_3 & 0 \end{pmatrix} \tag{4}$$

If q is considered as reference, the state equations can be linearized around q. In other words, q can be regarded as an ideal determined attitude under the condition that there is no noise or uncertainties when Eqn. 1 is integrated with respect to time.

2.4 Estimation variables

First, it is necessary to define estimation variables and formulate state equations expressed in terms of these variables. In this paper, the attitude estimation error vector and FOG bias estimation error vector are used for this purpose. The attitude estimation error vector $\delta\theta = [\delta\theta_1 \quad \delta\theta_2 \quad \delta\theta_3]$ represents the difference between the estimated attitude and the actual attitude, while θ represents small rotation angles with respect to the X, Y, and Z axes. The FOG bias estimation error vector $\delta b = [\delta b_1 \quad \delta b_2 \quad \delta b_3]^T$ represents the difference between the estimated bias and the actual bias with respect to the X, Y, and Z axes.
According to Farrenkopf's paper (Farrenkopf, 1978), the following equations hold.

$$\delta\dot{\theta} = \omega - \dot{\theta} - (b + n_v) \tag{5}$$

$$\delta\dot{b} = n_u \tag{6}$$

where n_v and n_u have the following statistics characteristics.

$$E[n_v(t)n_v(\tau)] = \sigma_v^{\,2}\delta(t-\tau) \tag{7}$$

$$E[n_u(t)n_u(\tau)] = \sigma_u^{\,2}\delta(t-\tau) \tag{8}$$

The constants σ_v and σ_u indicate the level of FOG bias drift and the random walk characteristics, respectively. They are usually estimated through experiments or given by the manufacturers.
Since we did not measure the precise alignment between FOG and STT, there is probably some misalignment that may cause the attitude rate of one axis to have a non zero projection onto the other axes. In addition, there are unobservable parameters of FOG in principle; thus, b should be regarded as the net equivalent bias vector.

2.5 Formulation of attitude determination

Figure 4 shows the update sequence in EKF. There are two types of update: the time update with an 8 Hz cycle and the observation update with a 1 Hz cycle. Since the state variables are updated in these cycles, their accuracy will vary during estimation. In the time update steps, the attitude is propagated by the integration of q using the small Euler angle approximation for the three axes $\Delta\phi = [\Delta\phi_1 \quad \Delta\phi_2 \quad \Delta\phi_3]$. $\Delta\phi$ is the incremental angle data including both the bias and the misalignment uncertainty. ω_{FOG} is obtained by dividing $\Delta\phi$ by the propagation time interval. In the observation update steps, the estimation is performed by subtracting $\delta\theta$ and δb from the calculated θ and b is obtained from the latest observation update using Eqns. 2 and 3. After that, θ is recalculated by integrating the sum of the $\Delta\phi$ sampled during the STT update time interval.

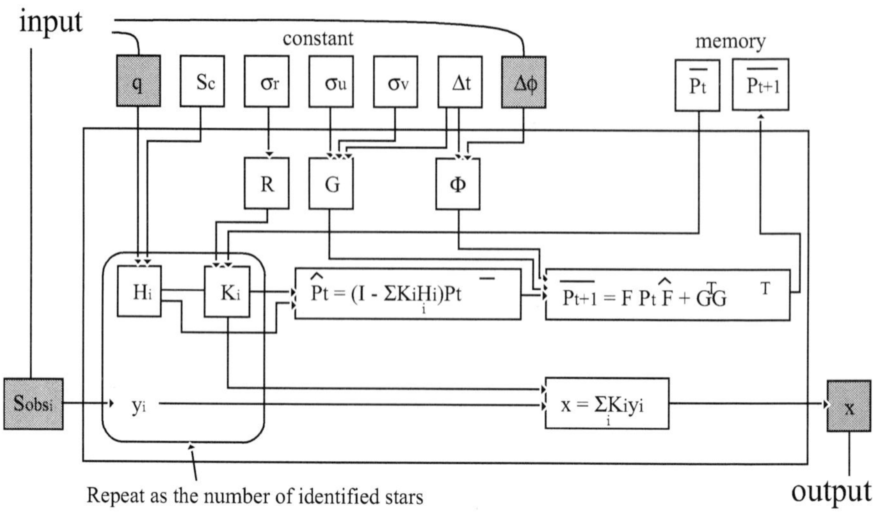

Fig. 4. EKF block diagram showing data-flow

Observations are made by obtaining a residual vector y expressed as

$$y = S_{obs} - \left(\delta\theta C S_c + n_r\right) \tag{9}$$

$$= S_{obs} + \left(C S_C\right)\delta\theta - n_r \tag{10}$$

$$\delta\theta = \begin{bmatrix} 0 & \delta\theta_3 & -\delta\theta_2 \\ -\delta\theta_3 & 0 & \delta\theta_1 \\ \delta\theta_2 & -\delta\theta_1 & 0 \end{bmatrix} \tag{11}$$

where "~" indicates the tilde operator used to form a 3x3 skew matrix from a 3x1 vector, S_{obs} is the observed star vector, S_c is the corresponding catalog star vector, and C is the direction cosine matrix of the satellite composed using q. The observation noise vector n_r can be expressed as follows using the delta function:

$$E\left[n_r(t)n_r(\tau)\right] = \sigma_r^{\,2}\delta(t-\tau) \tag{12}$$

Figure 11 shows a block diagram of EKF (Farrenkopf, 1978). The symbols G, R, and K are described as follows. x is a state vector composed from $\delta\theta$ and δb. The state transition matrix of x can be written as

$$x(t+\Delta t) = \Phi x(t) = \begin{bmatrix} \Delta\phi & -\Delta t I \\ 0 & I \end{bmatrix} \begin{bmatrix} \delta\theta(t) \\ \delta b(t) \end{bmatrix} \tag{13}$$

Since we apply the reset-type Kalman filter (Ninomiya et al, 1994), x is the zero vector; in other words, x will be reset to zero after every observation update.
G is the process error matrix written as follows:

$$G = \begin{bmatrix} \left(\sigma_v^2 + \frac{\sigma_u^2 \Delta t^2}{3} \right) \Delta t I & -\frac{\sigma_u^2 \Delta t^2}{2} I \\ -\frac{\sigma_u^2 \Delta t^2}{2} I & \sigma_u^2 \Delta t I \end{bmatrix} \tag{14}$$

H is the observation matrix written as follows:

$$H = \left[(CS_c) \quad 0_{2\times 2} \right] \tag{15}$$

R is the following observation noise matrix:

$$R = \begin{bmatrix} \sigma_r & 0 \\ 0 & \sigma_r \end{bmatrix} \tag{16}$$

K is the following Kalman gain matrix:

$$K_i = \overline{P}(t) H_i^T \left(H_i \overline{P}(t) H_i^T + R \right)^{-1} \tag{17}$$

where suffix i is the sequence number of the identified stars.
The observation update shown in Fig.4 is performed up to i so that the inverse of a matrix larger than 3x3 does not appear in Eqn.17.
We have now defined all the matrices required for EKF. Even if the EKF process must be turned off for some reason, the time update process should be continued using Eqns.2 and 3 every 125 ms.

2.6 Flight results of attitude determination

The attitude determination system of REIMEI mainly depends on the STT, which has 3 arcmin accuracy. If the STT is not available, the FOGs take the role of the principal sensor to acquire the current satellite attitude by propagation. Two periods in which the STT is available and not available follow each other cyclically as illustrated in Fig. 5. In science operations, the earth enters the field of view (FOV) of the STT when the satellite attitude is controlled at a fixed value and pointing in a particular direction with respect to an inertial coordinate system. The durations of the periods when the STT is unavailable (STT-OFF period) and available (STT-ON period) are 67 min and 30 min, respectively.
This EKF has been operating as expected for more than five years (from Sep. 2005 to Mar. 2011) and no serious failures have occurred. The observed stars were scattered inside STT-FOV, in other words, they were not gathered within a small area of STT-FOV, resulting in attitude error correction being performed efficiently. Figure 6 shows a sample of EKF telemetry data including the determined quaternion vector q, the observed error angle vector $\delta\theta$, and the attitude rate bias vector b. REIMEI performed Z-axis maneuvers at 1:30 and 2:40 on Aug 5, 2006. There are four $\delta\theta$ data for the identified stars viewed by STT. Note

that the $\delta\theta$ in Fig. 6 were calculated from y shown in Fig. 4. The observed error angle includes the effects of n_r.

The resultant accuracy drived from obtained telemetry are attitude determination is 0.04 deg $\pm 0.003(\sigma)$ and accuracy of rate bias is 0.1 deg/h $\pm 0.08(\sigma)$, respectively. The accuracy of b can be evaluated using the first several $\delta\theta$ data obtained shortly after beginning the STT-ON period. $\delta\theta$ for the first several data are equivalent to the angle given by the sum of the STT output errors, which can be modelled by a Gaussian, and the cumulative error angle of $\delta b \Delta t$. In other words, if δb is sufficiently larger than the STT noise, then we can regard the first $\delta\theta$ as $\delta b \Delta t$. Note that the accuracy may vary depending on the operation maneuverer plan, for example, how long STT has been turned off due to observation attitude requirements, or how rapidly the attitude is changing. However, the accuracy of estimation is typical for the most frequent observation operations using the telemetry data.

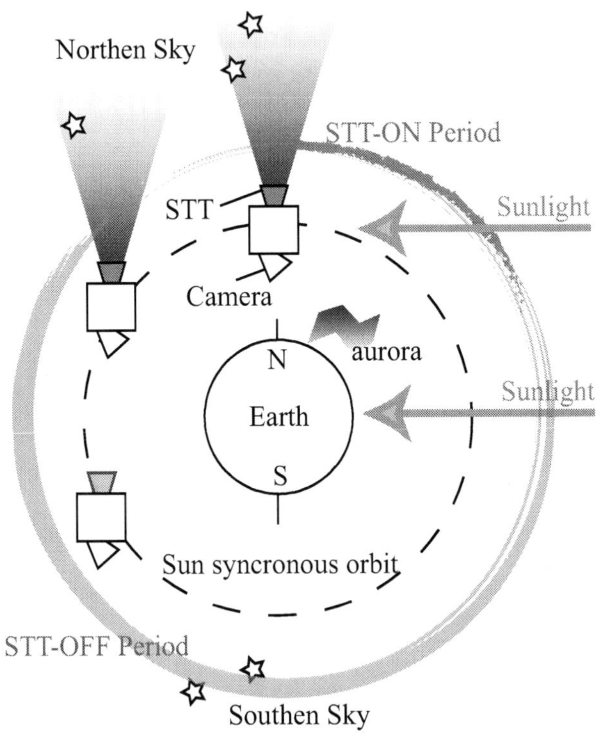

Fig. 5. STT-ON and STT-OFF operation: since the attitude of the satellite is fixed in an inertial coordinate system during the observation periods, STT must be turn on and off cyclically to prevent the Earth's albedo (reflection of the sunlight) from coming inside STT-FOV. This is one of a specific limitation of the use of STT in REIMEI system.

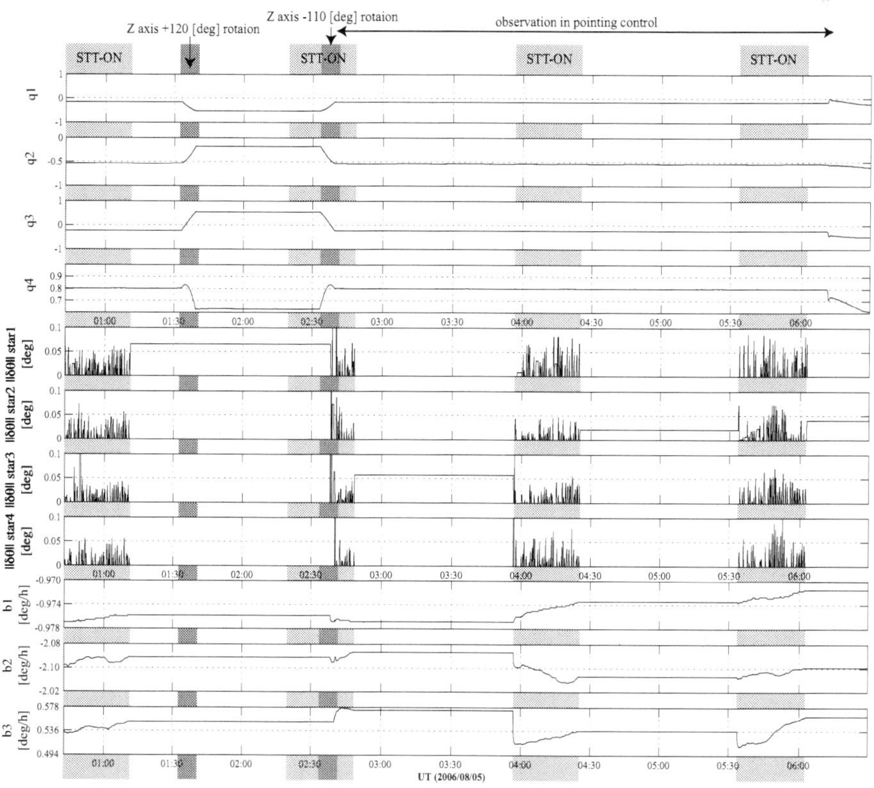

Fig. 6. Attitude and bias estimation results from actual telemetry data

3. FOG Bias instability problem

The accuracy of satellite attitude estimation depends only on the FOG data during the 30 min of STT-OFF periods; thus, the bias stability of the FOGs is a crucial factor in maintaining the accuracy. With several STTs onboard, such limitation to the accuracy of attitude would not exist. Owing to their small weight and volume, small satellites have little capacity for onboard components, and it is not unusual for a small satellite to have only one sensor or one actuator onboard, whereas most satellites have several sets onboard.

Although the attitude is estimated sufficiently accurately to meet the requirements of the mission during the STT-ON periods, this is not the case during the STT-OFF periods. The cumulative attitude error caused by the bias estimation error increases to a value exceeding the requirements.

There are two sources of bias estimation error: the Kalman filter tuning performance and the bias instability. In REIMEI system, the bias is modelled using Farrenkopf's gyro dynamic model shown in the section 2.4.

3.1 Accuracy of bias drift estimation

Since the parameters σ_v and σ_u were previously carefully tuned using a flight software simulator and actual flight telemetry data, the results of attitude estimation and FOG bias estimation for the REIMEI satellite were sufficiently good to ensure operation without any problems until about 18 months after the launch.

To maintain the estimation performance, it is necessary to continually monitor the temperature of the FOGs (Sakai et al., 2006b). Changes in temperature have a strong effect on the stability of the FOGs. Figure 7 shows an example of changes in bias observed in the telemetry data (Fukushima et al., 2006). Although these FOGs were well calibrated and their thermal environment has been controlled by heaters, some minor problems have arisen in bias estimation since Nov. 2007.

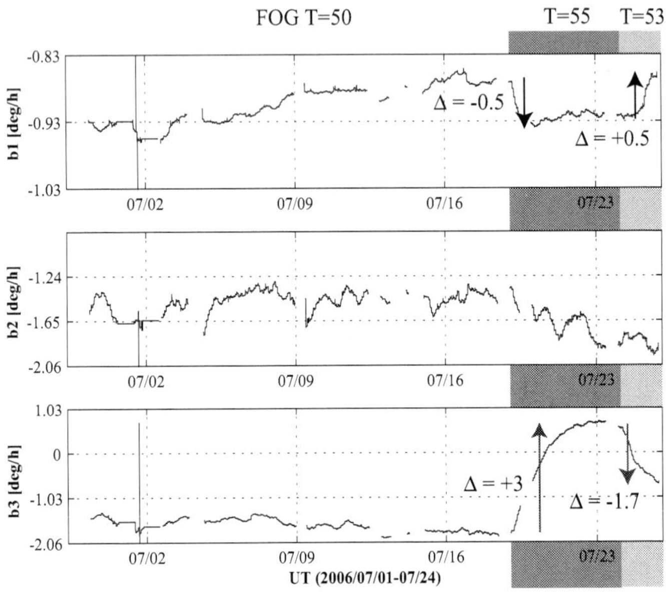

Fig. 7. FOG bias drift caused by change in FOG temperature

The accuracy of the estimated bias can be evaluated using the attitude error. This error can be observed at the moment when the STT is switched on. The attitude error is defined as the angular difference between the observed star vectors and the corresponding theoretical star vectors calculated using the onboard star catalog and the satellite attitude. This angular difference of propagation can be regarded as being equal to the cumulative error caused by the bias estimation error during the STT-OFF periods. Figure 8 is a schematic drawing of the cumulative propagation error, with its standard deviation σ_θ formulated using σ_v, σ_u, and the deviation of the STT observation data σ_n.

$$\sigma_\theta^2 = \sigma_n^2 + \sigma_v^2 T + \frac{1}{3}\sigma_u^2 T^2 \tag{18}$$

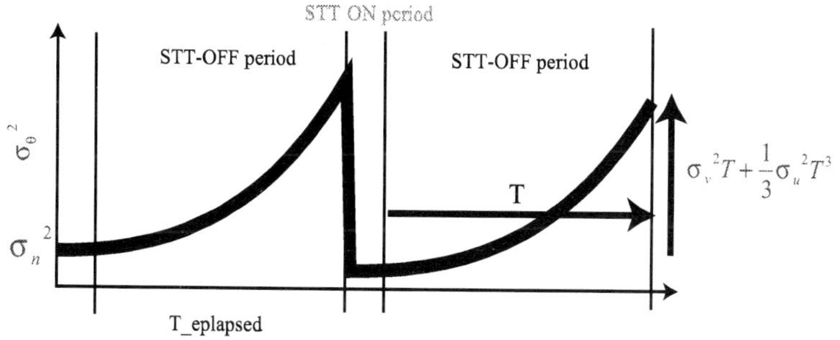

Fig. 8. Cumulative propagation error caused by bias drift of FOGs

3.2 Bias instability observed in telemetry data

The angular difference between the star vectors observed using the STT and the corresponding theoretical star vectors should be monitored during STT-ON periods to verify the accuracy of the STT data. If there is a problem with the STT, this angular difference will increase.

Figure 9 shows several examples of time history plots of the angular difference on the same axes. The horizontal axis is the time elapsed from the moment when the STT is switched on, while the vertical axis is the angular difference. We can observe two types of angular difference data on this plot. The data points plotted on or near the vertical axis (t=0) are the angular difference of propagation, and the data points near the center of this plot, with times of about 480 s to 1200 s, show the angular difference of the STT.

Figures 10 and 11 show time history plots of these two types of angular difference obtained over the last two years (2007 and 2008). From these plots, we can conclude that (1) the STT does not appear to be developing any signs of problems and (2) the bias estimation error has increased discontinuously several times, i.e., some unknown factors have affected the stability of the characteristic parameters, σ_v and σ_u , of the FOGs.

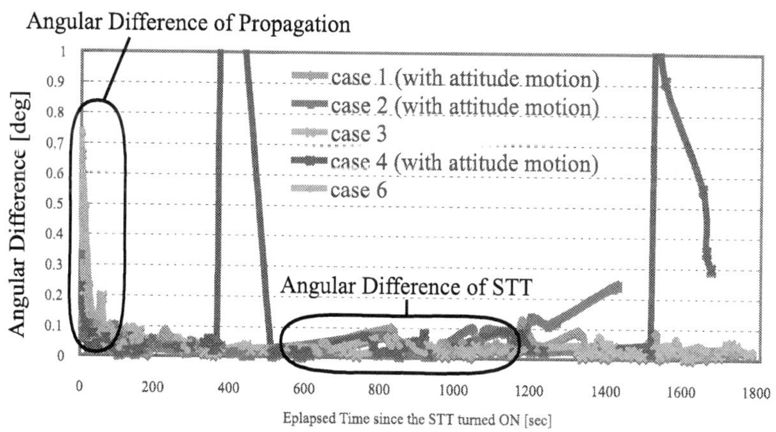

Fig. 9. Angular difference plots overlaid aligned for each start from STT-On event to the left

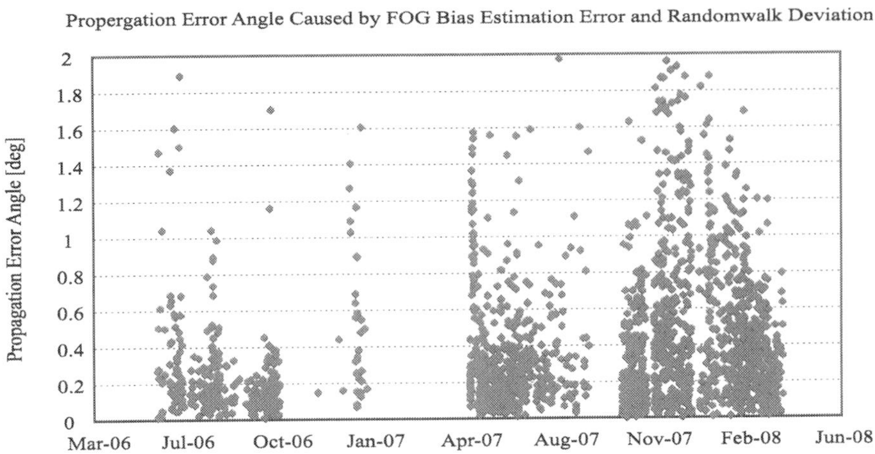

Fig. 10. Trend of angular difference of propagation

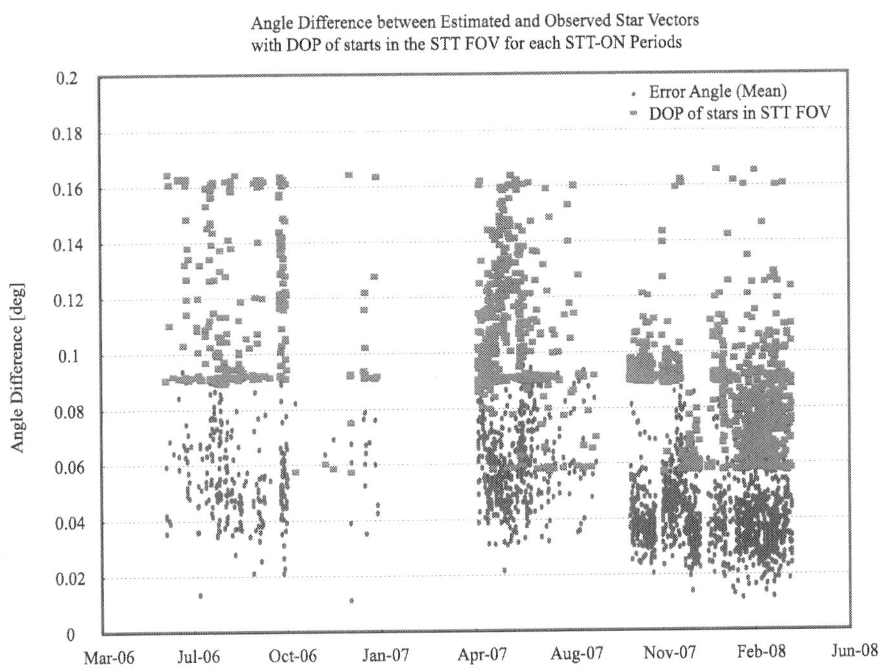

Fig. 11. Trend of angular difference of STT

We can see that the angular difference of the STT appeared to be larger during some periods in Fig. 11. This difference can be explained using the dilution of precision (DOP) of stars. The DOP of stars is defined in this paper as an index of how stars are aligned in the FOV of the STT; its formula is given as follows:

$$DOP_{stars} = \sqrt{trace\left(H^T H\right)^{-1}} \tag{19}$$

where H is the observation matrix used in the Kalman filter of this system. The larger, the value of DOP, the less accurate the attitude estimation, similarly to the DOP used in the accuracy analysis of the Global Positioning System. The DOP indicates how stars are seen in the FOV of the STT, which affects the accuracy of attitude determination. The degradation of accuracy of attitude estimation over time is inevitable for such a system with only one STT.

4. Detection of changes in FOG bias using SVM

It has been needed to find any weak sign of event that would link to some system troubles. Such demand called failure detection, a sub category of system monitoring, has been researched for ground systems as well as onboard systems in many fields. Having experience of working for years as an operator of REIMEI, the author also has felt such for failure detection only for system failure but also for detection of degrade of performance: signs of changes in specification that there is no error but something seems to be wrong. In this section, an example of such failure detection is shown using a problem of degrade of FOG bias drifting in REMEI.

4.1 Signs of changes in bias

Figure 12 shows time history plots of the angular difference of propagation and the angular difference of the STT over 2 years, which are plotted over different time spans such as one month, ten days, and one day.

From the statistics for these time spans, it is easy to observe the level of fitness of the EKF parameters. By taking statistics over a longer time span, randomness can be reduced. For example, there is no sign of parameter mismatch before Oct. 2006, but an event occurred in Oct. 2006; the difference between the median and mode of the distribution of the angular difference of propagation has been increasing since Nov. 2006. The median indicates the accuracy of bias estimation, while the mode indicates the random-walk error of bias drift.

According to these time history plots over 2 years, it can be concluded that the EKF parameters have been mismatched with the actual state of the FOGs since Oct. 2006. This means that the characteristics of the FOG bias changed at that time. The most probable reason for the bias error is that the degradation of fibre transparency due to radiation became sufficiently large to cause bias instability. However, this degradation is still considered to have a limited effect according to the results of radiation tests performed before the launch; there must be another factor causing this degradation.

From the operator's viewpoint, one month is a too long period to take any measures to prevent the degradation of accuracy of attitude determination. Any parameter mismatch must be noticed as soon as possible rather from the analysis of monthly statistics.

4.2 Support vector machine

The easiest way to rapidly detect signs of bias change is to shorten the time span of statistics to ten days or one day. However, the shorter the time span, the less accurate the statistical results. Thus, it is necessary to define a threshold for determining whether or not the level of fitness of parameters is acceptable before calculating short-time-span statistics using the telemetry data.

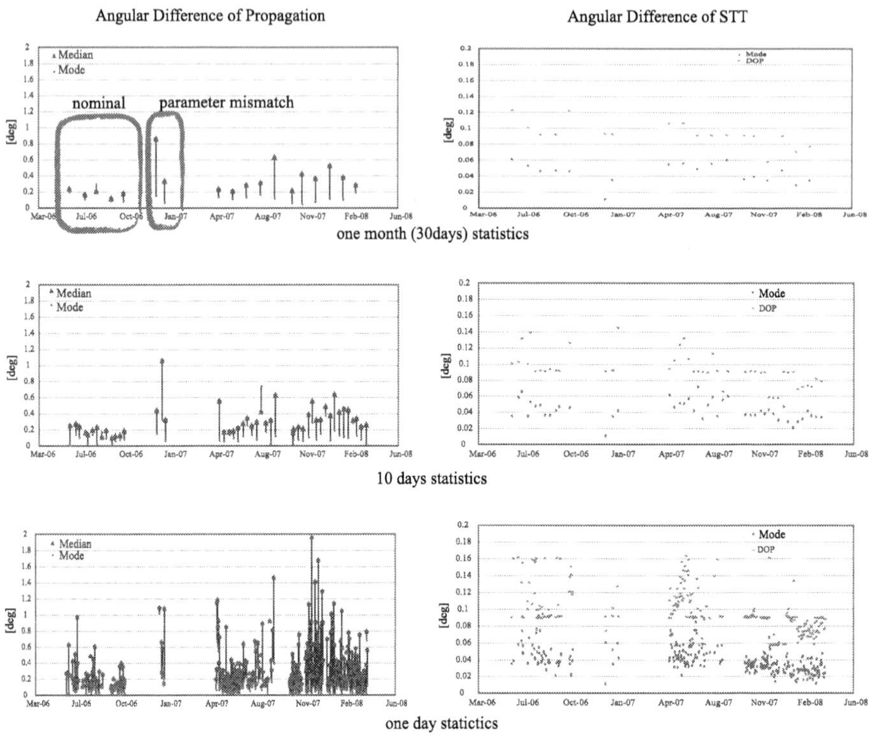

Fig. 12. Trend plots of the angular difference for two years time span

The support vector machine (SVM) technique is one of the most practical methods of detecting such signs from telemetry data. It is a popular discrimination scheme used in many fields. The SVM technique is a type of supervisory learning method (Cristianini & Shawer-Tylor, 2000). It is thus necessary to carry out a training process before using it for discrimination, which is shown in Fig. 13. The SVM technique is as follows: in Step 1, a telemetry data set that was obtained before the change in bias is prepared. This data set is treated as a no-error (OK) data set. In Step 2, a telemetry data set is prepared that contains some signs indicating that the parameters are unsuitable. This data set is treated as an erroneous (NG) data set. In Step 3, using these data sets as training data sets, support vectors are calculated. The kernel function is a simple linear function for this case. Using the support vectors, the entire telemetry data set (test data set) can be classified as an OK data set or an NG data set, i.e., it can be established whether or not the current parameters are tuned appropriately.

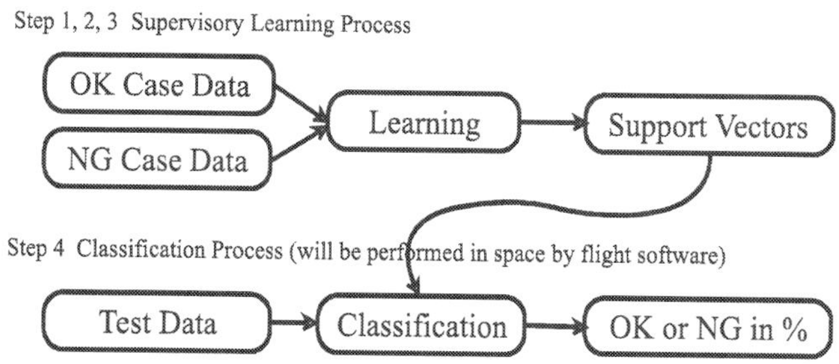

Fig. 13. The 4 steps to make up a SVM

The angular difference of propagation and the DOP of stars shown in Fig. 14 were selected as the training data set to test the performance of the SVM technique. Even though the SVM was generated using one month of statistical data, it detected a change in bias for ten days of statistical data as well as one month of statistical data. A summary of this detection is shown in Fig. 15. Since Mar. 2007, the parameters have been changed several times to reduce the angular difference of propagation to a sufficiently small value to meet the mission requirements. All these changes were detected in the results.

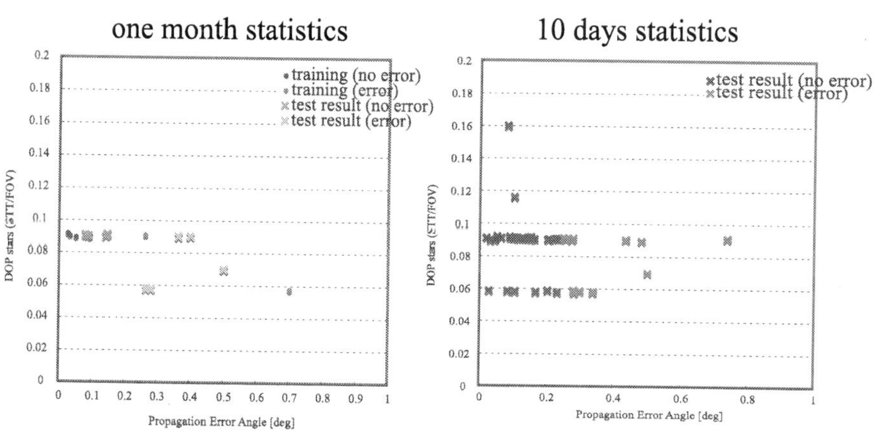

Fig. 14. Two plots of propagation error angle vs DOP starts calculated using deferent statistics. These plots show the discrimination performance how the SVM generated using training data can judge the state of FOG bias using test data.

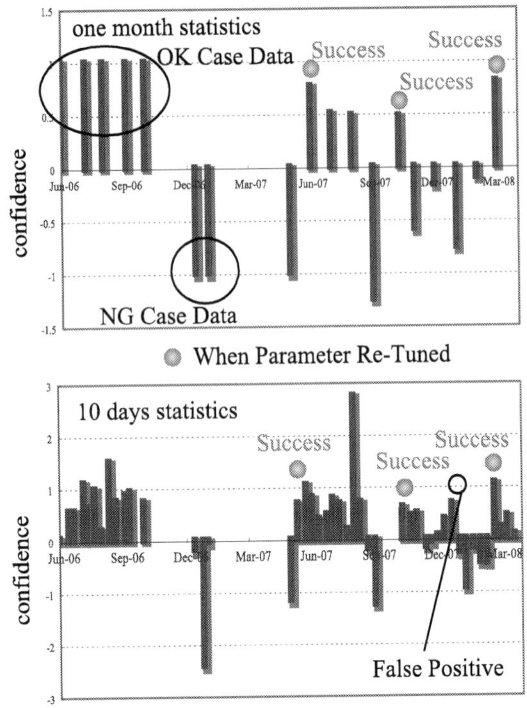

Fig. 15. Classification results by the SVM generated using OK and NG data sets. The result using one month statistics case successfully detects all the changes in FOG bias drifts, while the 10 days statistics case have one false positive detection (miss detection of change in FOG bias).

5. Onboard software architecture

If onboard system monitor is implemented on flight software, it is necessary to consider what software architecture should be employed. Most hardware control tasks must run in a fixed time interval or by triggered as a response to an event while satisfying strict timing requirements. In other words, such a control task must run as a real-time task. On the other hand, system monitoring shown in previous sections does not have such limitations. Since timing requirements for hardware control and system monitoring are different, corresponding software should be implemented in different level of tasks.

To implement flight software clearly structured as multiple tasks running in parallel without unexpected mutual interventions, layered programming approach is suitable. Although there are many researches on this topic, the three-layer structure programming is considered in this chapter as basic software architecture (Rabideau et al., 1999). because such structure is simple, popular, and has a variety of applications even in space systems (Balzano & Isaacs, 2006). The architecture consists of a deliberator layer, an executor layer, and a driver layer as shown in Fig. 16. The driver layer manages data interfaces with hardware in a real-time manner by performing tasks, such as serial data port handling and interruption signal handling. This layer should be implemented to perform real-time tasks on a real-time OS. The deliberator layer processes all the input data such as environment measurement data, hardware status data, and operation commands and determines the next action to be taken. The executor layer connects input and output data between the executor and driver layers by interpreting the stream of abstract data such as operator commands (for examples GO or STOP) into the hardware data stream (ON or OFF) and vice versa. It also manages the issue of commands, i.e., when and where to send the data.

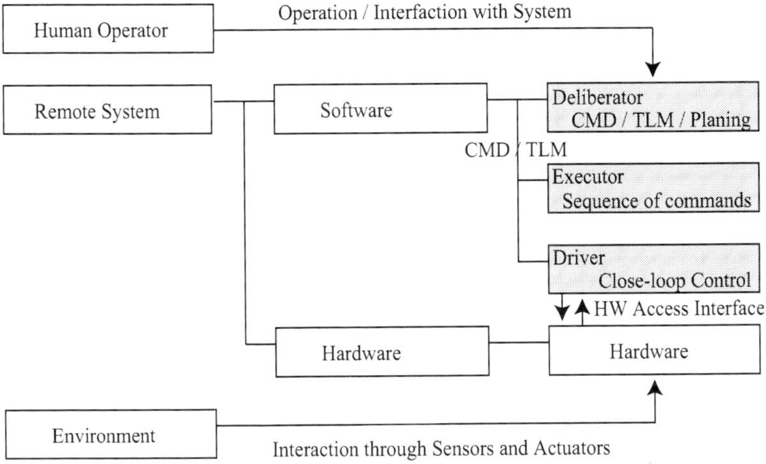

Fig. 16. The three-layer architecture for remote system software consisting of Deliberator, Executor, and Driver functions.

A human operator at a remote station communicates with a remote system by telecomands (CMD) and telemetry (TLM). The operator reads TLM data to determine the event that has occurred at the remote system and then sends CMDs so that the system can operate as planned to achieve its mission goals, resulting in a human-in-the-loop control system. To make the remote system autonomous, the deliberator layer should behave in the same way as the human operator. If this can be achieved, the lower layers will act in the same way under both a human operator and autonomous control. If this situation can be realized, the system can be considered to have the ability to make its own decisions.

Here is an example to show how to implement such architecture in Fig. 17. The driver and executor layers is implemented as real-time tasks running on a real-time OS and the deliberator is implemented as a script engine running on the same OS so that it is easy to communicate between the three layers by an intertask communication mechanism provided by the OS kernel. The reason why a script engine is used on the deliberator layer is that it is expected that algorithms for system monitoring such as SVM should change its target according to operation purposes and circumstances of the system: many algorithms should be loaded to detect many potential failures throughout its mission. FOG bias drift detection was explained in this chapter, but it is not only possible trouble on onboard hardware. Using usual tasks programmed in C/C++, it is hard to change onboard algorithm for system monitoring after starting up the system. However, script engines seem to be an only option to change algorithm frequently. By changing the script, the algorithms can be changed without affecting other running tasks such as hardware controls.

The requirements of time and memory for a script engine to run with multiple real-time tasks have been too great for its realization on an actual onboard computer so far. However, owing to recent technical advances, such a script engine can be installed in a spacecraft project. The author recommends T-Kernel as the OS kernel, which is expected to become a standard real-time OS, and JavaScript as the script engine to run on T-Kernel (Fukushima & Mita, 2011). Figure 16 depicts the proposed software architecture.

Most space systems can accept such commands that a software internal variable should be substituted by some value like "a_hardware_switch = 1". With the proposed script engine, it is possible to send commands by another form: an expression of a logic such as "IF a variable = value THEN do something", i.e., a program fragment. If space systems can accept a logic-type command, the system will have the capability to self-update dynamically; a script code sent by a logic-type command can modify the prescribed behaviours of the system. So far, software updates have only been achieved by stopping and reloading the entire software or by applying memory data patches on the running software code, despite the concern that these methods of updating have some risk of corrupting the system. Thus, such logic-type commands are clearly advantageous for our proposed software architecture.

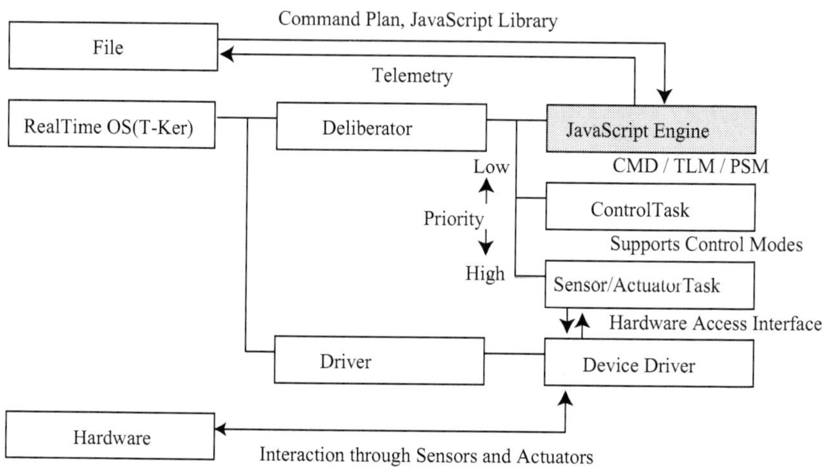

Fig. 17. A sample recommended implementation of the three-layer architecture for a remote system using a real-time OS with the deliberator that is realized by the help of a text-script engine, such as JavaScript, to provide onboard dynamic and self-update mechanism for users.

6. Conclusion

This chapter shows an experimental implementation of telemetry data processing to obtain a hidden event using a data mining technique. As a concrete example, detection of signs of actual satellite attitude sensor hardware failure was considered.

As preparation of treatment of practical data analysis commonly performed in satellite operations, a basic concept and practice of quantitative telemetry data analysis was demonstrated using REIMEI satellite data. By this preparation, the reader understood what the

FOG bias drift means and how it can be estimated from telemetry data of attitude motion. Then, an SVM was designed and tested to monitor the instability of the FOGs in the REIMEI satellite using 2 years of telemetry data. The result shows that the SVM can detect changes in bias with a simple linear kernel. Thus, the classification part of the SVM logic can be implemented on the flight software without difficulty. As a hint for actual implementation onboard software, the three-layer architecture for onboard software was explained.
The flight software version of the SVM using a script engine has not yet been tested in the REIMEI satellite, and the author is waiting for an opportunity to carry out an in-flight experiment. It appears that SVMs can be used as a standard autonomous software component not only for onboard software even in small satellite systems but also for monitoring telemetry data. Thus, the author conducted an experiment to export this concept of system monitoring onto an autonomous underwater vehicle as concept verification activities and obtain sound results as it was expected. However, the most fruitful result expected area seems to space systems and it is the final destination of this research.

7. References

Balzano, V. & Zak, D. (2006). Event-drvien Jamses Space Webb Space Telescobe operations using on-board JavaScripts, *Proceedings of SPIE,* 6274, 62740A, Orlando, FL, USA, May 24, 2006

Cristianini, R. & Shawe-Tylor, J. (2000). *An Introduction to Support Vector Machines,* Cambridge University Press, ISBN 978-052-870-19-3, Cambridge, UK

Farrenkopf, R. L. (1978). Analytic steady-state accuracy solutions for two common spacecraft attitude estimators, *Journal of Guidance, Control, and Dynamics,* Vol.1, No.4, pp. 282-284, ISSN 0731-5090

Fukushima, Y. & Mita, M. (2011). A New Approach to Onboard Mission Replanning Using Orthogonal Arrays, Proceedings of *2011 IEEE/ASME International Conference on Advanced Intelligent Mechatronics,* Budapest, Hungary, July, 2011

Fukushima, Y. (2008). Onboard Sensor and Actuator Failure Detection using SVM for Autonomy of Small Satellite Systems. *Proceedings of the 9th International Symposium on Artificial Intelligence and Robotic Automation in Space,* Los Angels, CA, USA, January, 2008

Fukushima, Y.; Sakai, S. & Saito, K. (2006). Flight Performance of the REIMEI Microsatellite Attitude Determination System, *Proceedings of the Small Satellite Systems and Services,* ESA-SP-625, Sardignia, Italy, September, 2006

Ninomiya, K.; Hasimoto, T.; Kii, T.; Muranaka, N.; Uo, M.; Maeda, K. & Saitoh, T. (1994). In-Orbit Performance of ASCA Satellite Attitude Control System, *Proceedings of 17th Annual AAS Rocky Mountain,* Keystone, CO, USA, February 2 - 6, 1994

Rabideau, G. ; Knight, R. ; Chien, S. ; Fukunaga, A. & Govindjee, A. (1999). Iterative Repair Planning for Spacecraft Operations in the ASPEN System, *Proceedings of 5th International Symposium on Artificial Intelligence, Robotics, and Automation in Space,* Noordwijk, The Netherlands, June, 1999

Saito, H.; Mizuno, T.; Tanaka, K.; Sone, Y.; Fukuda, S.; Sakai, S.; Okuizumi, N.; Mita, M.; Fukushima, Y.; Hirahara, M.; Asamura, K.; Sakanoi, T.; Miura, A.; Ikenaga, T. & Masumoto, Y. (2005). AN-OVERVIEW AND INITIAL IN-ORBIT STATUS OF "INDEX" SATELLITE, *56th International Astronautical Confernce,* IAC-05-B5.6.B.05, Fukuoka, Japan, 2005

Sakai, S.; Fukushima, Y. & Saito, K. (2006). In-orbit Performance Evaluation of Temparature Controlled Small Fiber Optical Gyro on Microsatellite REIMEI, *18th International Conference on Optical Fiber Sensors Topical Meeting*, TuE3, Cancun, Mexico, October 23, 2006

Sakai, S.; Fukushima, Y.; Saito, H. & Kaneda, R. (2006). Studies on Magnetic Attitude Control System for the REIMEI Microsatellite, AIAA Guidance, Navigation, and Control Conference and Exhibit, AIAA-2006-6450, Keystone, CO, August 21 - 24, 2006

Part 3

Biomedical Telemetry

6

Radio-Telemetry in Biomedical Research - Radio-Telemetry Blood Pressure Measurements in Animal Models of Hypertension, How It Revolutionized Hypertension Research

Pierre Dumas, Dan Chiche, Johanne Tremblay, Ondřej Šeda, Junzheng Peng and Pavel Hamet
Centre for Ecogenomic Models of Human Diseases/CRCHUM, Technopôle Angus
Canada

1. Introduction

Radiotelemetry is employed in several fields to circumvent several issues: areas difficult or dangerous to access, monitoring of dangerous processes, need for secret monitoring. In biological sciences, telemetry is mainly useful because it decreases the observer bias and interference. In the field of medicine, the current research is mostly aimed at findings the cause and appropriate cures to common diseases. Common diseases are widely prevalent diseases for which we know only partially the causes and for which, as a consequence, we only propose treatments to alleviate the symptoms or their impacts on target organs. The common examples of such diseases to name a few are: diabetes, cancer(s), obesity, multiple sclerosis and hypertension, not to mention most of the psychiatric illnesses. They are characterized by a strong genetic component and a strong environmental influence since their prevalence is markedly influenced by age, diet, exercise or other environmental stressors. This important environmental modulation makes them more difficult to study. Therefore, our goal here will be to illustrate the challenge of studying environment-modulated traits. With hypertension as an example, we will describe the use and benefits of employing radiotelemetry in hypertension research in order to be able to subtract the role of the environment or, conversely to quantify its impact on blood pressure. In the current post-genome era, with enough financial support and colleagues from around the world, it has never been easier to design and perform huge genome-wide association studies to try to unveil the genetic determinants of common diseases. Each month, hundreds of loci are reported that are associated with a higher prevalence of diseases and single nucleotide polymorphisms covering the entire genome are proposed to be in linkage with disease genes. We also know that very few of these proposed loci end up being truly associated with diseases in replication studies and we will present the current arguments pro and against this approach in the field of hypertension. This, we hope, will illustrate the point that we want to make in this chapter: in order to perform valid genome-wide association studies in human or genetic studies in animal models to uncover the genetic determinants of common diseases, it is essential to clearly define the studied phenotype(s) and to ensure that their measurements are performed accurately with the least amount of confounders or artefacts.

Our contribution to this book entitled "Telemetry" will not be of a technical nature nor will it systematically review in all details the merit of telemetry in our field of research because it would go beyond the scope of this book and would not be suited for a broad audience. We direct the interested readers to the review of Kurtz and colleagues (2005) for that purpose. We are presenting here an aspect of what we think is the most important contribution of telemetry in our field, its use to monitor blood pressure free of stress artefacts or on the contrary, its use to evaluate the contribution of this environmental "stress".

2. Blood pressure and hypertension

High blood pressure is a major risk factor for cardiovascular diseases. Because of its impact on cardiovascular diseases, their complications and the cost associated, it is important to evaluate its prevalence accurately. This essential data can then help design public health policies aimed at controlling high blood pressure in the population. With the example of recent Canadian epidemiological studies, we will try to demonstrate how the methods used to record blood pressure can affect the relative prevalence in the study population with direct consequences on public health policies. Our aim is to illustrate the importance of good phenotyping, a major challenge in hypertension research.

2.1 Definition and prevalence of hypertension

Blood pressure is a continuous quantitative trait genetically determined but under the strong influence of the environment. It is a consistent and independent risk factor for cardiovascular and renal diseases. At least one third of adult United States population have hypertension defined as systolic blood pressure ≥ 140 mm Hg, diastolic blood pressure ≥ 90 mm Hg and/or current use of antihypertensive medication (Brown et al., 2001). It is a major risk factor for premature cardiovascular morbidity and mortality (Lawes et al., 2008). Epidemiologic studies have indicated that, for people 40–69 years of age, each increase of 20 mm Hg in usual systolic blood pressure is associated with a doubling of mortality rates for stroke and ischemic heart disease (Lewington et al., 2002). Hypertension is considered by the World Health Organization to be the number one risk factor for death in the world in both developed and developing countries, responsible for an estimated 7.5 million deaths per year (12.8% of all deaths).

2.2 Situation in Canada

The prevalence of hypertension in Canada was recently assessed in four population-based studies between 1986 and 2009 (Table 1). Blood pressure measurement was performed in all but one study (Canadian Community Health Survey). An automated device, BpTRU was used for the two most recent studies (Leenen et al., 2008; Wilkins et al., 2010), whereas blood pressure was measured by a trained nurse in the other one (Joffres et al., 2001). The Canada Heart Health Study (Joffres et al., 2001) has been conducted from 1986 to 1992 as a population-based cross-sectional study to estimate the prevalence and distribution of elevated blood pressure among Canadian adults. A probability sample of 23,111 men and women aged 18 to 74 years were selected from the health insurance registers in each province. Mean of all available blood pressure measurements from four measurements was used. The rate of subjects with hypertension, defined by systolic BP at or above 140 mmHg or diastolic BP at or above 90 mmHg or treatment for hypertension was 21.1%. The proportion of hypertensive subjects unaware of their hypertension was 43%. The level of hypertensive subjects aware but not treated and not controlled was 22% while 21% percent were treated and not controlled, and only 13% were treated and controlled. At that time, although the prevalence of hypertension was similar in Canada and the United States, levels of awareness, treatment and control were higher in the United States. Leenen et al. (2008) have conducted a survey to evaluate the current prevalence and management of hypertension among adults in the province of Ontario. Blood pressures, measured with an automated device, were obtained for 2,551 of the respondents (age 20–79 years). Hypertension, defined as systolic blood pressure of 140 mm Hg or more, diastolic blood pressure of 90 mm Hg or more, or treatment with an antihypertensive medication, was identified in 21.3% of the population overall (23.8% of men and 19.0% of women). Prevalence increased with age, from 3.4% among participants 20–39 years of age to 51.6% among those 60–79 years of age. Hypertension was more prevalent in black people and people originating from South Asia than among white people; hypertension was also associated with higher body mass index. Among hypertensive participants, 65.7% were undergoing treatment with control of hypertension, 14.7% were undergoing treatment but the hypertension was not controlled, and 19.5% were not receiving any treatment (including 13.7% who were unaware of their hypertension).

The latest Canadian report was published in 2010 by Wilkins et al (2010) with cycle 1 of the Canadian Health Measures Survey, conducted from March 2007 through February 2009 in 15 sites across Canada. This survey comprised a population-based sample and included direct BP measures using an automated device. During an interview, 3,514 subjects were asked two questions about BP: whether they had high BP diagnosed by a health professional and whether they had taken "medicine for high blood pressure" in the past month. BP measures were obtained at a mobile examination centre a few days after the initial interview. BP values were calculated by taking the average of the last five of six measures (taken one minute apart) of valid BP measurements. Results among adults aged 20 to 79 years showed that hypertension (systolic BP higher than or equal to 140 or diastolic BP higher than or equal to 90 mmHg, or self-reported recent medication use for high BP) was present in 19%. Of those with hypertension, 83% were aware, 80% were taking antihypertensive drugs, and 66% were controlled. With regards to the significant progress observed compared to Joffres et al report (1992), the authors conclude that their results are consistent with the large improvements in diagnosis, treatment and drug prescriptions for hypertension that have recently occurred in Canada (Campbell et al., 2009; Hemmelgarn et al., 2008). In the late 1990s, extensive efforts have been underway in Canada to improve physician and public awareness of the importance of diagnosis, treatment and control of hypertension, including the Canadian Hypertension Education Program (http://www.hypertension.ca/chep), yet the author cautioned against a potential overestimation of this change, particularity as it makes Canada being out of the range of other countries.

Table 1 reports the main results from these 4 studies. When measured, the prevalence of hypertension is quite stable between 19 and 21.3%. The rate of hypertensive patients unaware of their condition has dramatically decreased from 43% to 16.6%. In addition, the rate of treated and controlled hypertensive patients among hypertensive population seems to have dramatically increased as well from 13% to 65.9%. This trend was still observed in treated hypertensive population taking into consideration the differences in the number of hypertensive patients aware of their condition and treated. Nevertheless, this comparison must be interpreted with caution since there are many differences in methodological approaches, mainly the use of an automated device known to report lower BP values.

Name, author	Data collection and sample representation	Blood pressure measurement	Definition of hypertension	Study Period	Preva-lence	Hypertensive unaware [1]	Treated and controlled [1]	Treated and controlled [2]
Canadian Heart Health Surveys, Joffres et al., 1992	Population based, 18-74 year, Interview and clinic visit	Two BP measurements: one at the beginning of the interview and one at the end, twice, 2 weeks apart. The BP was measured by a trained nurse. Standardization for identification of the Korotkoff sounds. Correctly sized cuffs were used. Quiet for 5 min, sitting position, Right arm (if possible) The mean BP (four measurements for most participants) was used.	Mean SBP/DBP of 140/90 mm Hg or medication	1986-1992	21.1%	43%	13%	38%
Canadian Community Health Survey Campbell et al., 2008	Canadians aged 12 and over. 65,000 representative of 121 Health Regions Computer-Assisted Personal Interview or Telephone Interview	None	Population aged 12 and over who report that they have been diagnosed by a health professional	2001, 2003, 2005, 2007, (yearly)	16.4% (2008)	NA	NA	NA
Ontario Survey on the Prevention and Control of Hypertension 2006, Leenen et al., 2008	Random dwellings, 2551 participants, 20-79 years, Ontario	Arm circumference measured for selection of cuff. Cuff placed on left arm. Seated and quiet for 5 minutes. 6 measures and 5 records using BpTRU	Mean SBP/DBP of 140/90 mm Hg or treatment with antihyperten sive drugs	Published in 2008	21.3%	13.7%	65.7%	77%
Canadian Health Measures Survey, Wilkins et al., 2010	Population based, Interview, home and mobile center visits, 20-79 years	BpTRU - Average of the last five measures of a set of six taken one minute apart.	Mean SBP/DBP of 140/90 mm Hg or self-reported recent medication use for high BP.	2007-2009	19%	16.6%	65.9%	82%

[1]Among hypertensive population; [2]Among treated for hypertension population.

Table 1. Recent Canadian population-based studies estimating the prevalence of hypertension.

2.3 Measurement bias

It is well recognized that the method used for BP measurement has a very significant impact on the results. As an example, we compared Joffre et al. (2001) results to that of Wilkins et al. (2010) in the younger group age (respectively 18 to 34, and 20 to 39) where the prevalence of hypertension is very rare (below 5%) with limited impact on mean systolic and diastolic BP. Mean SBP are significantly higher in male and female in Joffres et al. publication when compared to Wilkins et al.: in the range of 120/110 (male/female) as compared to 110/101, respectively. Similarly, DBP are 75/70 versus 72/67, respectively. Therefore, the remarkable improvement in the proportion of hypertensive subjects that are treated and controlled should be considered with caution, given the facts that the BP measurement protocols were different, with the most recent publications reporting lower BP values. An important advantage of an automated device is that it enables BP to be measured in the absence of another person. Its use, therefore, eliminates observer errors such as digit bias, zero preference and incorrect deflation rates, and also reduces "white coat hypertension". However, this specific device discard the first two readings, leading to elimination of highest pressures and these numbers were never validated for outcomes. According to the 2010 CHEP Recommendations for the Management of Hypertension (Hackam et al., 2010), home SBP values >135 mmHg or DBP values >85 mmHg using an automated device should be considered elevated and associated with an increased overall mortality risk analogous to office SBP readings of >140 mmHg or DBP >90 mmHg. Hence, maybe less emphasis should be put on the 140/90 mm Hg threshold with the more and more systematic use of automated devices for BP measurements in a controlled environment.

Thus, one should asks if these measurements are really reflecting the 'usual' blood pressure of an individual, knowing that the protocol demands that the first two values (always higher) be discarded and that the measurement be performed in a silent closed room without an observer. Does it really reflect the 'true' blood pressure and its minute-to-minute variability? Therefore, there is clearly a need to assess precisely blood pressure in humans since its 'usual value' as so much to do with the risk of cardiovascular events. Telemetric determination of blood pressure in human to assess its 'true values', its variations over time and the effect of antihypertensive medications would indeed be welcomed.

2.4 Portapres, the only system that comes close to telemetry for blood pressure determination in humans

Protocols and recommendations for blood pressure measurement in humans are available and they provide information for procedures in the clinical settings or at home and insist on the training of the observer (Pickering et al., 2005). Among the methods described, they cite the 100-year old auscultatory method employed with a stethoscope and a sphygmomanometer. It is based on the Korotkoff technique and uses a cuff placed around the upper arm and inflated above systolic pressure to occlude the brachial artery. The stethoscope is used to listen to the sounds of the pulsatile blood flow while the cuff is slowly deflated. Despite its accuracy, the classic mercury sphygmomanometer tends to disappear because of the hazard from mercury and is replaced by aneroid or hybrid sphygmomanometer. Other technologies and automated devices are also available, and the interested reader is directed to the review by Pickering et al. (2005) for details. Of note, the Korotkoff technique tends to underestimate the systolic blood pressure and overestimate the diastolic blood pressure when compared to intra-arterial pressure (Holland & Humerfelt, 1964). With technology advances, battery-powered automated devices are now available to measure and record ambulatory blood pressure. They employ the same upper arm cuff and, because of the time required for one measurement they cannot record rapid changes in blood pressure. Furthermore, a maximum of four measurements per hour for 24 hours are usually obtained because of the annoyance of having the device squeeze the arm at regular interval. Nevertheless, ambulatory blood pressure monitoring can be very useful for diagnostic to ascertain blood pressure level outside the clinic. It also provides good information about blood pressure pattern during sleep.

There is, however, a method for blood pressure determination in humans that comes close to a telemetric method: the finger cuff method of Peñaz (1973). It is available commercially under the name Finapres or Portapres (Wesseling et al., 1995; Finapres Medical Systems BV, Amsterdam, The Netherlands). Despite being cumbersome, the Portapres enables reading to be recorded over 24 hours while the subject is ambulatory (Omboni et al., 1995; Parati et al., 1996). A photoplethysmograph under a finger cuff detects the pulsation of the blood flow. The inflation is continuously adjusted by a servo-loop according to the output of the plethysmograh to keep the output constant. As a result, the artery is kept in a partially open state. The pressure oscillations of the cuff were found to resemble to the intra-arterial pressure curve. Hence, this method gives an accurate estimate of the rapid changes in blood pressure although it usually underestimates 'true' systolic and diastolic pressures. Monitoring of blood pressure variations may prove to be of high clinical significance as several reports indicate a striking relationship between blood pressure variability and stroke (Rothwell, 2010; Rothwell et al., 2010).

In conclusion, the techniques for blood pressure determination in humans provide relatively accurate values of systolic and diastolic blood pressure. But, for most of them, quality measurements and reproducibility are greatly dependent on good calibration of the equipment, the environment where the measurements are taking place and training of the personnel performing them. Finally, only the finger-cuff method provides high accuracy of blood pressure changes with a high, beat-to-beat, measurement frequency. Since it is not invasive and enables recording in ambulatory subjects in their real life activities, this is the closest to a telemetric method when it comes to blood pressure determination in humans. In addition we should not hide that its cost and the technical expertise it requires are also something it shares with telemetry…

2.5 Methods to unveil the genetic basis of hypertension - Need to define high blood pressure

With what we have presented in mind, we will now conclude this section by presenting the challenges that our field of research is facing. Hypertension stems from a combination of genetic and environmental factors. The blood pressure variance commonly attributed to the genetic component is estimated between 30% and 50% (Havlik et al., 1979). Moreover, from twin or family aggregation studies, the sibling recurrence risk of hypertension is estimated at 2,5 to 3,5 (relative risk of developing hypertension if a sibling is affected) (Tobin et al., 2007). This clearly demonstrates the important genetic basis of the disease. With the sequencing of the human genome in 2000 and the progress of the HapMap project, we entered the «genomic era». Nowadays, there are about one million single nucleotide polymorphisms available without counting other genetic polymorphisms like copy number variants. These can be used for genome-wide association studies (GWAS) to characterize thousands of individuals from cases and control population in order to localize the genetic differences associated with the disease or related quantitative traits. In the field of hypertension, several large GWAS and many meta-analyses of GWAS were performed. Many loci on several chromosomes associated with hypertension were unveiled (for review, see Dominiczak & Munroe, 2010). Despite these successes, critics from the community state that only a very small amount of the blood pressure variance is explained by each of these variants (about 1 mm Hg of systolic and 0,5 mm Hg of diastolic pressure). They rightfully ask: can such small-effect alleles have such an important population-wide role to play in the aetiology of the disease? And, with regard to the very high cost of these GWAS, is it worth continuing in the same direction with bigger and bigger study populations (Kurtz, 2010)? The proponents of the GWAS insist that the progress made in understanding the pathophysiology of the disease are important whereas the opponents argue that none of the current high-blood pressure drug-target were unveiled with GWAS and that finding thousands of common genetic variants with minute effects on blood pressure is of no use for the development of new drugs or the understanding of the disease.

While recognizing the power of GWAS and the fine-mapping capabilities of the current genomic technologies, we think that the accumulation of data from large studies is of no use if this data is not accurate and reliable. Currently, significant efforts are spent to standardize large population studies (Knoppers et al., 2008). On the long term, this would permit the merging of several studies with similar design in order to pool the data and increase the statistical power. In addition to standardization, we think also that the definition of the traits to be phenotyped is cardinal to any study. Only when that is done precisely and agreed on can the methods for measuring them be standardized. As we have seen from the Canadian experience, in an effort to standardize blood pressure measurements in the clinic as well as for the multicentre GWAS, more and more automated devices were employed in rigorous conditions with rejections of the first, higher, blood pressure values. As a result, the prevalence of hypertension has dramatically decreased in the last ten years. On the optimistic side, it may indicate an impact of the public health campaign and compliance to drug regimen by the patients. On the other hand, it may just reflect 'wrong' phenotyping. As we will demonstrate in the remaining of this chapter, because up to 70% of the blood pressure variance can be of environmental origin, it is essential to take the impact of the environment into account. If it is somewhat subtracted by 'overstandardization', blood pressure values may underestimate the 'true' blood pressure, and we may end up never finding high blood pressure genes because very few people will ever display high blood pressure in those settings. We should also mention the fact that studies rarely try to discriminate between supine, standing or seated blood pressure and that the blood pressure medication is usually not withdrawn prior to measurements because of the risks (ethical concerns) or the cost of monitoring the patients during that time. For instance, we have shown that the impact of the *fto* gene on blood pressure is dependent on the body position (sympathetic modulation) and responsive to stress (Pausova et al., 2009). As we will try to demonstrate in animal models of hypertension, we think that it is important to understand what we are measuring. We will now present a section explaining how to study genes that are sensitive to the environment and how to measure the traits that are modulated by the environment. We will then show how telemetry is suitable to achieve this very specific endeavour in research with animal models with some examples from our group.

3. Genes X environment interactions, impact on blood pressure and development of hypertension

Up to 70% of blood pressure variance is attributed to the environment. The impact of the environment can be seen as additive or in interaction with genes. Figure 1 summarizes the possible contributions of genes and environment to hypertension.

In the first case (a), the genes and the environment exert their influence on blood pressure independently. Thus, a disease gene (Gd) and a deleterious environment (Ed) would act separately to cause hypertension in an additive manner. In the second case (b), the environment is not "deleterious" *per se*. Its influence will depend on environment-sensitive genes (Gs). These are called susceptibility genes. They are not disease genes by themselves, they only permit the environment to reveal or amplify its impact. This is the G × E interaction. The best example in the field of hypertension is salt-sensitivity where only salt-sensitive individuals are displaying hypertension consecutive to a higher intake of salt in the diet (Weinberger, 1990).

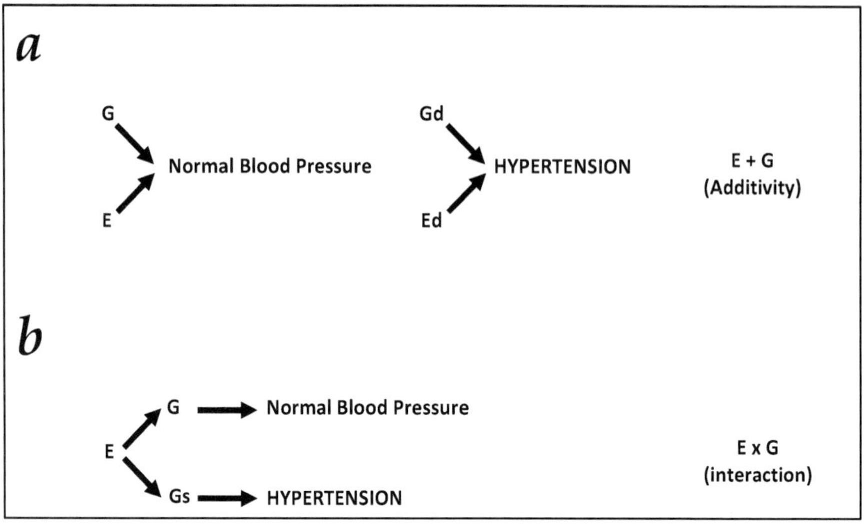

Fig. 1. Gene and environment in hypertension.

3.1 How to approach the genes X environment interactions – Concept of genetic susceptibility to the environment

Thus, while a genetic polymorphism could be associated with an increased risk of developing a disease, a differential response to the environment could define a susceptibility to this environment. This environmental susceptibility being modulated by environment-sensitive genes, we proposed the concept of *genetic susceptibility to the environment* (Hamet, 1996; Hamet et al., 1998; Pausova et al., 1999). The hallmark of a susceptibility gene is that it cannot be coined normal or abnormal since its expression *per se* will not cause the disease. Environment-sensitive variants of these genes will reveal their impact only when the organism is subjected to the specific triggering environment. We will now present the basis of the genes × environment interactions (adapted from Lynch & Walsh, 1997). Figure 2 shows the phenotypic response of 3 different variants of an environment-sensitive gene (called genotypes or alleles) in the presence of 2 different environments.

In Figure 2.a, the phenotypic response is enhanced in the presence of the 2nd environment. This response, however, is identical for the 3 genotypes (the curves are parallel). In contrast, in figures 2.b, c and d, the genetic variance is modified by environment '2', which is translated by an increase (Figure 2.b and c) or a decrease (Figure 2.d) in genetic variance between the 3 genotypes. In addition, the rank can be modified with the most sensitive genotype in one environment becoming the least sensitive in another environment (Figure 2.c and d). In all these 3 cases, the differential impact of the environment is allele-dependent. The increase in genetic variance observed with the environment '2' for figures 2.b and c is essential if one wants to unveil genetic susceptibilities.

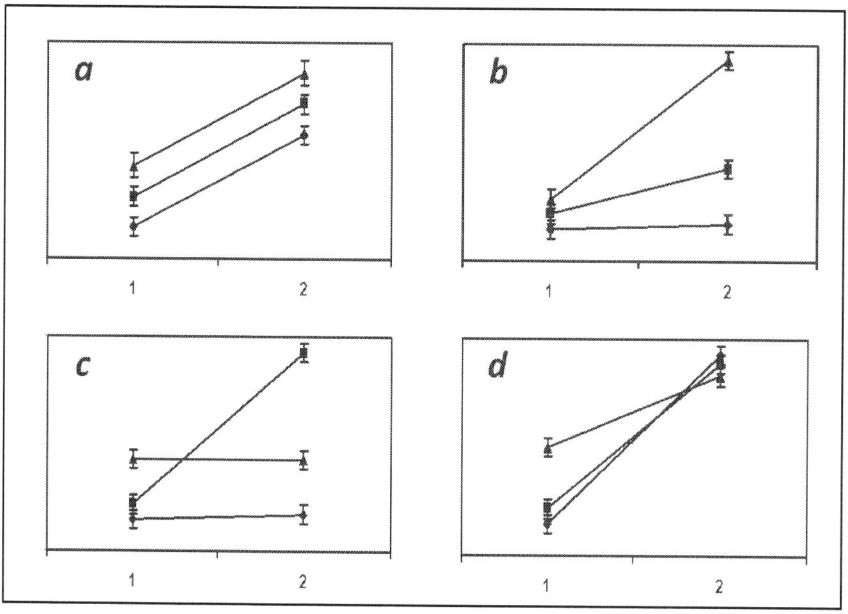

Fig. 2. Gene × environment interactions. Phenotypic expression of 3 different genotypes (alleles) when measured in 2 different environments (1, 2); adapted from Lynch & Walsh, 1997.

It is important at this point to distinguish the impact of the environment that needs to be assessed for its contribution to the disease from the environmental variance that is the variance due to the measurements and is represented by the error bars on the graphs. For instance, in Figure 2, the genetic variance varies depending on the environment whereas the environmental variance does not change. The ratio of the genetic variance over the total variance (genetic + environmental variance) is called 'heritability' and the higher the heritability, the higher the contribution of genes to the studied trait. Technically, this means that when searching for genetic determinants of a disease, one should work with traits displaying a high heritability. However, heritability is not static, especially when considering susceptibility genes. As can be seen from Figure 2, while the environmental variability does not change (error bars), the genetic variance can be modified depending on the environment. Therefore, the key to study the contribution of susceptibility genes is to find the conditions where the genetic variance is at its maximum (for instance, Figure 2.b, environment 2). Because such conditions are not necessarily seen *a priori* in an experimental set-up, it is essential to challenge the model by changing the environment in which the trait of interest is measured. In hypertension research, that can be translated by the use of different diets or drugs in order to blow-up the differences in blood pressure and find the genes responsible for the differential effect.

This understanding is fundamental for selecting the parameters that will allow appreciating the influence of the environment in an experimental setting. This is the area where, we think, radiotelemetry can be the most useful in hypertension research. We will demonstrate later how the currently accepted methods for measuring blood pressure in animal models are not only adding artefacts and biases to the measurements, but how they are creating them because of their nature and the standard protocols employed.

3.2 Stress as an important environmental modulator of hypertension

We will now describe the genetic susceptibility to stress and its effects on blood pressure and hypertension development since it is among the most important environmental factor impacting hypertension (Hamet & Tremblay, 2002). The concept of stress was first defined and described by Hans Selye (1956). He called it "the general adaptation syndrome" or G.A.S. It is defined by 3 phases: the alarm reaction, the resistance period and the exhaustion stage. He demonstrated the role of the sympathetic nervous system with the stimulation of the hypothalamic-pituitary-adrenal axis and the surge of the stress hormones cortisol and cathecholamines. While he was proposing that different stressors would always induce the same response, Henry (1992) showed that the neuroendocrine response is dependent on the perceived stress. For instance, when the stress is bearable, the response will be characterized by a secretion of noradrenalin. In contrast, when the stress persists and is overwhelming, a depressive state will appear. It is characterized by the strong stimulation of the pituitary-adrenal axis with intense secretion of cortisol and high levels of ACTH while the cathecholamines are unchanged. This, in turn, induces a sustained renin secretion, promoting a gradual and steady increase in blood pressure. When this increase is chronic, it leads to hypertension.

3.3 Psychosocial stress and cardiovascular diseases

Alexander (1939) suggested a link between emotional stress and the development of hypertension. For instance, people exposed to an ever changing environment see their blood pressure rise gradually (Gutmann & Benson, 1971). The relationship between the stress of modern life and common diseases started to be more systematically assessed (Cobb & Rose, 1973) and the Health Examination Survey (HES) and Health Examination and Nutrition Survey (HANES) allowed evaluating the link between the perceived stress at work with infarct prevalence. In 4,833 men enrolled in these studies, the results showed that job strain and absence of latitude and decisional power was perceived as a psychological stress that was significantly associated with an increased prevalence of infarct in this cohort (Karasek et al., 1988). A similar study on 2,556 men showed that the job strain was associated with increased prevalence of hypertension and left ventricular hypertrophy, a risk factor for infarct and cardiovascular diseases (Schnall et al., 1990). Data from the Framingham cohort showed that anxiety was predictive of a future hypertensive state in middle aged men followed for 20 years. This relationship was not verified in women however (Markovitz et al., 1993). There was therefore a need to better define psychosocial stress and standardize research protocols to draw reliable and reproducible results. More recent studies reported similar findings related to job stress with interactions with blood pressure-modulating genes (Ohlin B et al, 2008; Yu et al., 2008).

3.4 Psychogenic stress

It is well-recognized that stressful events such as wartime, natural disasters or more commonly hard living conditions are associated to a rise in arterial pressure in sufferers. A need for a test mimicking this perceived stress was necessary to characterize and understand the possible causal relationship between psychogenic stressors (i.e. from psychological origin) and the development of hypertension. The blood pressure response of two standardized tests correlated highly (0,8) with the blood pressure at work (Morales-Ballejo et al., 1988). These standardized tests were a math test and a timed competitive video game test where subjects had to increase their score after each successfully reached levels. The strong correlation with "real-life" blood pressure made these tests good surrogates for everyday life stressors.

In addition to changes in blood pressure and heart rate, Anderson and colleagues (1987) showed a significant increase in blood flow in the arm of children from hypertensive parents during a math test, suggestive of changes in vascular resistance. Interestingly, physical exercise (isometric hand contractions) and math test in hypertensive were both able to increase circulating catecholamines and vasopressin but only the math test induced a rise in plasma renin and aldosterone levels (Sakamoto at al., 1992). For the authors, the activation of the renin-angiotensin-aldosterone system by this psychogenic test made the kidney a stress-sensitive target organ in susceptible hypertensive subjects.

3.5 Enhanced stress response is predictive of hypertension – Concept of genetic susceptibility to stress

The hemodynamic response to stressors is highly heritable (Hassan et al., 2009) and may help distinguish susceptible individuals. Falkner et al. (1979) observed an enhanced response of hemodynamic parameters in normotensive teens from hypertensive parents following a mental stress test. This enhanced response could predict who would become hypertensive later in life (Falkner et al., 1981). Normotensive men with a positive family history of hypertension showed an increased diastolic blood pressure after isometric handgrip testing when compared to controls without a family history of hypertension (Widgren et al., 1992). Similarly, the microcirculation response to local heat stress and skin blood flow is altered in normotensive with family history of hypertension (Gryglewska et al., 2010). In a cohort of adults and their children followed for six years, this increased response to stress was the strongest in the subjects found to display the highest diastolic and systolic blood pressure six years later. This was true in the adult and the boys, but not the girls of the cohort (Matthews et al., 1993). Maybe this sexual dimorphism reflected the young age of the children (20 years) at the end of the study. Presumably, the girls would be protected whereas their mothers (mean age, 48) would not be anymore because of menopause. Thus, the response to a psychogenic stress could be used as a tool to predict a future hypertension status in normotensive children with a positive family history of hypertension. In this case, blood pressure *per se* is not important; it is blood pressure in response to a specific change of environment (stress test) that proved to be the strongest marker. It comes back to what we tried to demonstrate earlier: the right question must be asked and the right measurements performed. Here, the change in environment (stress test) allowed revealing the genetic susceptibility (increase of genetic variance). If the enhanced response to stress can produce a transient or sustained increase in blood pressure as we have seen, it can also impact on the development of other cardiovascular pathologies. For instance, the hypersensitivity of the sympathetic nervous system has been proposed as a 'switch' responsible for the future decrease of cardiac function (Middlekauff et al., 1997), with endogenous catecholamines stimulating left ventricular hypertrophy. This has been shown in normotensive children of hypertensive parents (Trimarco et al., 1985). Thus, the continuous stimulation of the sympathetic nervous system by various stressors over a certain threshold could induce a rise in blood pressure and permanent changes in the cardiovascular system resulting in an irreversible hypertensive state (Capone et al., 2011;

Thayer et al., 2010; Kuneš et al., 1990; Markel, 1985). Furthermore, genetic polymorphisms of tyrosine hydroxylase, the rate-limiting enzyme in catecholamines synthesis, are directly linked to the levels of the stress response (Rao et al., 2008). Thus, this neurogenic hypertension would result from the various environmental and genetic influences on the cardiovascular system. Therefore, the differential response to stress would define sensitive or resistant individuals. **Because it is based on sensitivity genes, we call it the genetic susceptibility to stress**.

In the previous paragraphs, we wanted to introduce this concept of *genetic susceptibility to stress* and insist on the fact that it is an essential component of hypertension development. Therefore, we think that it is not possible to study hypertension and the genetic basis of hypertension and ignore the impact of this environmental component. The rest of our review will demonstrate the essential role of telemetry in hypertension research in monitoring and dissecting this component, a goal that was impossible to achieve before the advent of telemetric measurement of blood pressure.

4. Animal models in hypertension research

Animals were first studied to understand normal physiology, especially when necropsy on human beings was forbidden by the Church. Soon, it became evident that animals could suffer from most of the same ailments as humans. It then became natural to study diseases in animals in order to draw parallels with the human disease counterpart and test treatments. With the discovery of the laws of genetics by Mendel and their re-discovery at the beginning of the 20th century, the breeding of animals for selection of desired traits had now a scientific basis. At that time, mice were very popular as pets and breeders rivalled to produce strains with unique and "desirable" aesthetic characteristics. In order to perpetuate these characteristics in the next generations, brother-sister mating was performed over several generations. This gave rise to the first inbred lines, many of them still available today. The reader can refer to Beck et al. (2000) for a complete review. This massive breeding of mice by amateur breeders and scientists gave also rise to surprising discoveries: animals that were plagued with genetic ailments. Because the strains were inbred, the study of the disease was then possible on multiple animals displaying the same phenotype and over time. It was the beginning of modern biological science. Mice are very good genetic models of diseases, but rats were always the preferred model for physiology because of their "practical size". For organ size, blood drawing and any kind of measurements, rats provide more "research material", are bigger, sturdier, and, not the least, less aggressive than mice. This explains why the rat and mostly the Spontaneously Hypertensive Rat (SHR) is *the* animal model for hypertension research. The SHR was developed by Okamoto and Aoki (1963) by selective breeding of hypertensive males and females from their Wistar colony. The original inbred strain was then distributed to the NIH and institutes around the world. Because of this world-wide distribution, the SHR became the most popular animal model for the study of hypertension. The drawback of this popularity and wide distribution is that several substrains were generated since 1962, either by breeding errors or simply due to genetic drift. For instance, a vendor, Taconic Farms, has a salt-sensitive substrain of SHR (SHR-S) available from its IBU-3 colony (Mozaffari et al., 1991). This sole example simply to illustrate that, even within the same strain, there can be significant genetic differences impacting the studied phenotype. Furthermore, this example of salt-sensitivity illustrates an environmental susceptibility not usually present in SHR. As a result, researchers should be aware of the heterozygosity of the strain and be able to monitor the differential impact of salt or it may go unnoticed and create bias in analysis and results inconsistencies. Other rat inbred strains were developed for the study of hypertension. We will not go into details as it is not the goal of this chapter, but we should not forget to mention the Dahl salt-sensitive and salt-resistant rat and the Milan hypertensive rat among the most popular models. For review, please see Bader (2010). With the advent of these models and the sequencing of the rat genome, discoveries in the rat can be directly verified in humans, and several quantitative trait loci mapped on the rat genome were also described in humans. The review of Stoll and Jacob (2001) about rat models of hypertension and their relationship to human hypertension is suggested as well as the review of Kwitek et al. (2001) for a description and usage of the synteny between rat, human and mouse genomes.

4.1 Animal models to study the stress response

Several animal models can be used to study the stress response and the choice is dependent on the stressor to be employed and the expected outcomes. For instance, chronic immobilisation of the arm for a period of 15 months induced a gradual rise in blood pressure in monkeys (Kuneš et al., 1990). This hypertensive state persisted even when the animals were freed from that restraint and was observed in conscious or anaesthetized monkeys. For short-term and more ethically-acceptable studies, rats are the model of choice. Several stressors can induce hypertension: introduction of an intruder into the cage (Mitra et al., 2011), conflictual situation like food consumption followed by an electric shock (Friedman & Dahl, 1977), cold stress applied to the floor of the cage (Kanayama et al., 1979) and a psychogenic stress, immobilisation (Kvetnansky et al., 1970). Interestingly, in the SHR, immobilisation will induce a rise in blood pressure to levels higher than what is observed in normotensive WKY rats (Grundt et al., 2009; Yamori et al., 1969). McMurtry and Wexler (1981) have shown that ether, heat and immobilisation induce an increase of several biochemical markers of the stress response, with the SHR being more sensitive than the Sprague-Dawley control. SHR was then considered a model of 'neurogenic' hypertension similar to what is seen in humans (Folkow, 1982). Therefore, this hypersensitivity to stress found in SHR and also in hypertensive mice (Davern et al., 2010) may be involved in the development of hypertension by lowering the threshold at which a stimulus is perceived as a real stress. The higher stress response resulting can affect several pathways and organs and will contribute to the development of hypertension. Of note, the stress gene expression is enhanced in SHR as compared to WKY and Brown-Norway rats after a 1-hour immobilisation stress, and the genetic difference points to the heat-shock transcription factor *hstf* (Dumas et al., 2000a & 2000b). Others have reported differences in blood flow or increase in sympathetic nerve activity associated with sodium retention in SHR following stress (Yamamoto et al., 1987; Koepke & DiBona, 1985). All these genes and mechanisms can be involved in the development of hypertension.

In conclusion, hypertension research is performed mostly on the SHR rat, an animal that was bred for its spontaneous hypertension. We now know that the various colonies kept by vendors or institutions around the world do present some important genetic differences, several of them impacting blood pressure and hypertension development. Furthermore, SHR is a stress-sensitive model that mimics neurogenic hypertension. Therefore, because this hypersensitivity to stress and genetic differences pertaining to salt-sensitivity may impact the development of hypertension in SHR, it seems essential to study these environmental susceptibilities when studying hypertension in SHR or, to the least, be aware of these confounders in blood pressure measurements and data analysis. This is where telemetric measurement of blood pressure could be a very useful tool.

5. Blood pressure measurement in mouse and rat

An essential requirement for hypertension research in animal models is the ability to reliably and accurately monitor blood pressure and its slight variations in unanaesthetized conscious animals. The choice of a research methodology and the techniques to be used will be dependent on the specific research goals. Thus, a given method for measuring blood pressure may be well suited for one type of study and not recommended or useful for another. Furthermore, the more expensive and technologically-advanced technique is not necessary the best to employ. For instance, if there is a need to monitor rapid changes in blood pressure consecutive to the intravenous injection of a test compound, telemetry is most suitable because it can record almost instantly the changes in blood pressure. This is particularly true for fast and short-acting substances. Inversely, if one wants to study the changes in target organs consecutive to a long-term treatment with a new vasoactive drug, a sole determination close to the end of the treatment with a non-invasive and 'coarse' method such as tail-cuff should be enough to assess if the test article behaved as expected in the treated animals. We will now review the methods for blood pressure measurement in rodents with an emphasis on the most commonly used technique, the indirect tail-cuff method, and the state-of the art non-invasive telemetric method. Again, the interested readers will be directed to the review by Kurtz et al. (2005), Zhao et al. (2011) or Feng & DiPetrillo (2009) for details and information on other methods.

Ruban D. Buñag started his 1983 review of blood pressure measurement techniques in rats by «A rat's tail is a slender appendage on which the weight of so much research in hypertension hangs, yet blood pressure measurements recorded from it are usually taken for granted, often abused, but seldom discussed» (Buñag RD, 1983). This is the commentary of someone who had first-hand experience of the available techniques for blood pressure determination in animal models of hypertension. At that time, the only available techniques were direct puncture of an artery under light anaesthesia (usually the carotid artery) or the indirect tail-cuff method.

5.1 Indirect method in conscious rodents: The tail-cuff method (Williams et al., 1939)

Often cited as «the tail-cuff method» without further details, this method is an adaptation of the indirect method used in humans. In humans, physicians wrap a cuff around the arm of the patient. With the stethoscope, they can hear the heartbeats while deflating the cuff (Korotkoff sounds). When done correctly, the beats are audible only when the cuff pressure is smaller than the systolic pressure or higher than the diastolic pressure. Thus, these limits represent respectively the systolic and diastolic values of blood pressure of the individual. In order to achieve the measurement, one needs an artery (here, the brachial artery), a cuff to squeeze the artery and interrupt the blood flow and a device to perceive and monitor the blood flow during inflation and deflation (the stethoscope). This key technique to many diagnostic procedures is performed everyday by physicians in their offices and in the hospitals around the world. Its ease of use and the knowledge it brings to assess the condition of the patients makes it probably one of the most important techniques available to physician, even in the era of computers and scanners. The ease of use of the indirect blood pressure determination in humans comes mostly from the fact that the blood pressure determination is performed in conscious subjects and uses a non-invasive procedure on the arm.

How can it be adapted to rodent models of hypertension? In a straightforward adaptation in the animals, researchers considered using the tail in rats and mice as the «organ» around which a cuff could be wrapped (limbs can be employed for bigger animals such as dogs), hence the name «tail-cuff method». In a mouse, the tail is irrigated by one ventral artery and 2 lateral caudal veins. The rats possess the same vascular architecture with the addition of a dorsal vein. Therefore, the cuff squeezes the tail to a pressure greater than systolic pressure, and a sensor distal to the cuff is placed to detect the return of the blood flow as the cuff is deflated. Several sensors are available on the market, with some more sensitive than others. In all cases however, only the systolic blood pressure can be perceived with this method. Furthermore, because the only tail artery is on the ventral side, positioning of the sensor is critical to get a good signal. The strength of the signal is also dependent on the position of the cuff and sensor on the tail: the closest to the animal (proximal), the better the signal. Therefore, one can imagine that the size of the cuff must be adapted to the size of the tail, and the position of the cuff must be standardized, at least within the same experiment. To our knowledge, these precautions are rarely mentioned as most authors will only say "*blood pressure was performed as previously mentioned*" without further details. But these are the least of the culprits that are impacting the measurement with the tail-cuff method. In the light of what we have presented, we will put the emphasis on a major issue responsible for most problems and artefacts: the mandatory use of restraint cages in order to be able to perform this fine tuning on conscious animals. For a detailed depiction of all the other pitfalls of the tail-cuff method, please refer to Buñag (1983).

Recommended for non-invasive detection or screening of:
Frank systolic hypertension
Substantial group differences in systolic blood pressure
Substantial changes in systolic blood pressure over time
High-throughput screening of large numbers of animals when large differences in blood pressure are expected
Not recommended for:
Assessing small differences in blood pressure
Quantifying relationships between blood pressure and other variables
Studying blood pressure-independent effects of any intervention
Measuring blood pressure variability
Measuring diastolic or pulse pressure
Measuring blood pressure in conscious rodents
Measuring blood pressure in stress-sensitive animals
Monitoring possible hemodynamic effects from rapid and short-acting substances

Table 2. Recommendations for the use of indirect methods for measuring blood pressure in animals (adapted from Kurtz et al., 2005)

5.1.1 Effect of restraint on blood pressure determination: Increase in cardiovascular response and in body temperature

In order to be able to install the cuff and record blood pressure, mice and rats are put in restrainers with the tail hanging out. As we have shown at paragraph 4.2, immobilisation stress is considered a psychogenic stress. In the rat, it induces a rapid increase in heart rate and blood pressure, and it has been shown that this increase is higher in SHR when compared to normotensive controls (Yamori et al., 1969; Irvine et al., 1997). Immobilisation also induces an increase in body temperature in the rat (Gollnick & Iannuzzo, 1968; Briese & De Quijada, 1970; Stewart & Eikelboom, 1979; Singer et al., 1986), in the mouse and in the rabbit (Snow & Horita, 1982). In humans, psychogenic stressors also induce a rise in body temperature in addition to the rise of blood pressure and heart rate (Marazziti et al., 1992). The rise in body temperature induced by immobilisation is also stronger in SHR than in normotensive WKY (Berkey et al., 1990, Morley et al., 1990). At room temperature, non-stressed body temperature has been shown to be identical (Berkey et al., 1990) or higher in SHR as compared to WKY (Price & Wilmoth 1990). Wilson at al. (1977) indeed suggested that the basal temperature threshold of SHR is modified, thus explaining its abnormal temperature response to stress. Price and Wilmoth (1990) reported a higher vascular sensitivity to norepinephrine in SHR and O'Leary and Wang (1994) showed a decreased vasodilation in the tail vessels in SHR. Together, these 2 mechanisms could explain the higher temperature reached during immobilisation stress and the inability to go back to baseline rapidly after the stress. Therefore, the stronger temperature response to immobilization in SHR could serve as a marker of stress susceptibility. Indeed, we have found the genetic determinants of this enhanced stress response in hypertensive rats and observed a strong sexual dimorphism in the SHR, the Y chromosome from hypertensive origin contributing significantly to this enhanced response (Dumas et al., 2000a). Because a similar abnormal response has also been reported in humans subjected to psychogenic stress, and because this abnormal response correlates with the future hypertensive status of these individuals, it is important 1) to characterize and to be able to recognize this stress response and 2) to employ methods of blood pressure determination devoid of this important confounder.

5.1.2 Effect of heating on blood pressure determination

In rodents, there are 3 veins and one artery in the tail. However, because its length usually equals that of the body in mouse and rats, most of the time, no blood is flowing through these vessels because of the heat-loss that would result. Hence, the tail serves mainly for thermoregulation. Therefore, when attempting to determine blood pressure with the tail-cuff method, in addition to the restrainer, heating of the animal to temperatures between 30 and 37°C is mandatory in order to get a significant blood flow into the tail. This heat stress thus adds to the body temperature increase due to stress and some animals may die even with prior training to the experimental conditions (Gross & Luft, 2003).

5.1.3 Thermosensitivity and hypertension

Schlager (1974) have reported a higher heat sensitivity in the spontaneously hypertensive mouse (SHM) mice as compared to controls. SHR also presents an increased thermosensitivity (Wilson et al., 1977; Wright et al., 1978; McMurtry & Wexler, 1983). This thermosensitivity persists in culture and is already present in neonatal cardiomyocytes, indicatives of a primary genetic defect not consecutive to high blood pressure (Hamet et al., 1985). Malo from our group (1989) has unveiled the existence of the thermosensitivity locus *tms* associated with hypertension in SHM. When anaesthetized SHM mice were immersed in a 44°C water bath, their body temperature increase was faster (1,74 +/- 0,04°C versus 1,13 +/- 0,03°C degree per minute, p<0,001) and their survival decreased when compared to control mice. This was indicative of a defect in temperature regulation in this strain. When subjected to a 5-min conditioning at a non-lethal 40°C temperature for 20 consecutive days, SHM mice exhibited a 20 mm Hg lower blood pressure as compared to non-treated SHM, and this effect was reversed upon the interruption of this pre-conditioning (Malo et al., 1990).

5.1.4 Seasonal temperature and the development of cardiovascular diseases

It is interesting to note that seasonal temperature itself has an impact on mortality and incidence of cardiovascular diseases. For instance, it is known for a long time that there is an inverse relationship between outside average temperature and blood pressure levels (Rose, 1961; Hata et al., 1982). In Montreal (Canada), where outside temperature varies from -24°C to 27 °C on a yearly average, a study on 2,000 patients with a total of 42,813 blood pressure readings showed a significant inverse relationship between blood pressure and average outside temperature (Kuneš et al., 1991). More recently, a 1°C reduction in daily mean temperature was associated with a 2% cumulative increase in risk of myocardial infarction over the current and following month, with the strongest effects observed after lags of 1 and 2 weeks (Bhaskaran et al., 2010). In many countries, death rates in winter are 10-25% higher as compared to the rest of the year (Curwen, 1991). When corrected for confounders, only temperature showed a constant correlation strongly suggestive of causality. Therefore, stressors that are impacting body temperature should not be seen merely as a side effect of immobilisation. We do think that these must be taken into account when measuring blood pressure and techniques for blood pressure determination that are minimizing stress and its manifestation must be favoured.

5.1.5 Conditioning to restraint stress

It was recognized that restraining is stressful and it has been proposed that seven days of training to the procedure would alleviate the effect of stress and enable the measurements of 'usual' blood pressure in the animals. The idea is the animals would get used to the restrainer and to the manipulation of their tails and display less stress-induced changes in their cardiovascular parameters following conditioning. Gross and Luft (2003) have shown that this conditioning period had no effect in mice. With mice implanted with telemetry transmitters, they have shown that heart rate, systolic and diastolic blood pressure at day 1 was not different than after 10 days of 30-minutes conditioning in the restrainers. A similar absence of conditioning was previously reported for rats (Bazil et al., 1993; Irvine et al., 1997).
This clearly demonstrates that immobilization of rodents in order to measure blood pressure will induce significant artefacts, that training does not prevent these bias and can further modulate the blood pressure in ways not consistent with what is sought. Furthermore, because the stress sensitivity may differ between strains, subtle differences in blood pressure may be missed. Finally, as we have seen, the different thermosensitivity of various strains of rodents in addition to the blood pressure-modulating effect of heat are two significant confounders that could ruin an experimental protocol. Hence, we think that the 'tail-cuff blood pressure method' can only be used when large blood-pressure differences (>= 15-20 mm Hg) are expected in the experimental setting when the restrainer effects become minor as compared to the effects of the tested hypothesis.

5.2 Direct non-invasive method: Radiotelemetry

Radiotelemetry for blood pressure monitoring in animals requires the surgical implantation of a catheter in a suitable artery, usually the carotid or femoral artery. The transmitter itself is inserted in the abdominal cavity (for rats) or under the skin (for mice). Interestingly, with the miniaturization of electronic components and probably because of the pressure of animal rights activists, there has been an impressive decrease in the number of publications using telemetry in large animals (cats, dogs, swine, monkeys) and a significant increase in those employing rodents (Kramer et al., 2001). Our own experience is with the transmitters from Data Sciences International (DSI, St-Paul, MN, USA), but other manufacturers are present on the market. For a review of the progress in radiotelemetry in small animals, please refer to Kramer et al. (2001). Similarly, the interested reader can consult the original publication by Mills et al. (2000) describing the characteristics of the mouse transmitters from DSI as well as the review article by Huetteman & Bogie (2009) that describes in details the surgical procedures to implant DSI transmitters in rats and mice.

Because of the surgery needed for the installation of the transmitters, radiotelemetry can be considered an invasive technique. But, at the same time, when recovery from surgery is optimal, it is the least invasive method since the measurements are achieved in the usual environment without external stressors such as the direct intervention of the technician. Furthermore, measurements are performed not only on undisturbed animals, but also in freely moving animals, which contrasts with all the other measurement techniques. Indwelling catheters attached to tethering devices is the only method allowing some movement of the conscious animals but generates noise and stress and does not come close to what can be achieved by telemetry. Blood pressure can be performed continuously on a beat-to-beat basis and during the night, a period not always practical for the experimenter. It allows the monitoring of the circadian rhythm impact and greatly reduces the variation in the mean blood pressure when data are averaged over several hours. For instance, Van Vliet (2003) has shown that the 95% confidence interval of the mean of 24 hours of blood pressure measurements in a group of 9 mice was 8 mm Hg as compared to 14 mm Hg for 30-minutes average and 22 mm Hg for a single time point. In SHR, systolic blood pressure is 20-40 mm Hg higher and heart rate 100 bpm faster when assessed by tail-cuff or directly by indwelling catheters (Bazil et al., 1993). In mice, while the tail cuff results are highly correlated with direct arterial pressure ($r=0,86$, $p<0,01$), the tail-cuff values are 20 mm Hg higher on average (Krege et al., 1995). For both species, the lowest blood pressure values are obtained with implantable radiotelemetry because the method is devoid of stress and performed in freely moving animals without anaesthesia (Irvine et al., 1997; Mills et al., 2000; Kuneš et al., 2008).

Recommended for:	
	Measuring blood pressure in conscious unrestrained animals
	Measuring blood pressure continuously over time
	Measuring blood pressure variability
	Quantifying hypertension or changes in blood pressure
	Quantifying relationship between blood pressure and other variables
	Studying blood pressure-dependent and independent effects following interventions

Table 3. Recommendations for the use of telemetry for measuring blood pressure in animals (adapted from Kurtz et al., 2005).

Table 3 summarizes the recommended use and advantages that apply to direct blood pressure measurements methods and especially to telemetry. The only application for which the AHA indicates that direct methods are not recommended is for screening of large number of animals and/or when large blood pressure effects are expected. The reasons why these methods are not recommended are their cost and the technical skills that are required to perform them successfully and reproducibly. They are, however far superior scientifically.

6. Radiotelemetry to study gene × environment in hypertension – Experience from our laboratory

Hypertension is an important contributor of mortality and morbidity in humans. Our understanding of the aetiology of the disease is incomplete and the search for the genetic determinants is complicated by the fact that blood pressure is very labile, with important changes occurring within seconds and minutes. As we have shown, blood pressure is hard to assess reproducibly without bias when performing epidemiological studies or GWAS. These problems are in part due to the important environmental component modulating blood pressure. Among these environmental modulators, psychogenic stress exerts a major influence. In experimental research using rodents, we have shown that the usual tail-cuff method for blood pressure determination induces stress and increases body temperature, two major modulators of blood pressure and hypertension. Therefore, we think that telemetry is the only technique to ascertain blood pressure with the least amount of bias. It is also the only technique allowing the measurement of the stress component modulating blood pressure. The few examples below will try to illustrate the level of refinement and robustness that can be achieved in hypertension research when the environmental influences are understood and telemetry the method employed for assessing blood pressure.

6.1 Diet and stress modulation of hypertension

The work by Šedová et al. (2004) from our group illustrates the various concepts that we have presented here and take advantage of telemetric measurement of blood pressure to draw conclusions that would have been impossible to obtain otherwise. The manuscript describes the effects of diet-induced obesity in the SHR. Because the cardiovascular response to stress is a significant predictor of hypertension, it looked more specifically at the effects of the diet on the stress response and the global impact on cardiovascular morbidity. In order to do so, adult male SHR were fed a high fat diet for 12 weeks. Blood pressure and heart rate were measured by telemetry at week 0 and week 12. In addition to basal blood pressure recorded for 3 consecutive days each time, blood pressure determination in response to a 30-minutes immobilisation stress was also performed at weeks 0 and 12.

As expected, immobilisation stress in restrainers for 30 minutes was able to increase blood pressure and heart rate in both groups. While there was no difference in the blood pressure response to stress in both groups between week 0 and 12, there was a significant lag in the return to the baseline after stress in the high-fat diet group at week 12 as compared to week 0. This was significant for systolic and diastolic blood pressure as well as for heart rate. No difference was observed in the response to stress in the control animals in the stress or post-stress periods. Furthermore, because it allowed the measurement of the circadian pattern of blood pressure, telemetry could reveal a blood pressure increase during the night in the animals receiving the high-fat diet as compared to the normal-chow fed controls. As we have seen from the immobilisation stress data, this would have been impossible to detect with a one-time recording in stressful conditions by the tail-cuff method. Needless to say, measuring blood pressure during stress and after stress with any other techniques could not have yielded such results. We think that telemetry is the most appropriate mean for measuring blood pressure in this kind of work involving the modulation of blood pressure by environmental stressors. We also want to underline the fact that stress is always present when dealing with blood pressure measurements in rodents. Given its impact on blood pressure, it has to be taken into consideration even when it is not specifically under study.

This example is a good illustration of the study of the gene × environment interactions: We had to increase the genetic variance in order to be able to monitor changes that would not be visible otherwise. The first challenge was the use of an obesity-inducing diet that revealed differences in blood pressure response to stress and in the night period of the circadian pattern. The second challenge was the stress test where we could observe a delay in the return to the baseline in the high-fat diet treated rats. This is very interesting in the light of another finding: an augmentation of the cardiac mass in the rats fed a high fat diet. With the telemetric data, we can hypothesize that the increase in cardiovascular reactivity observed in the night (active period of the rats) and following a stress could explain an increased workload for the heart and the hypertrophy after only 12 weeks of high-fat diet. The effect of the diet would thus be more important when the animals are awake, active and experiencing daily stressors. This interpretation would be impossible without the telemetric data.

6.2 Genetic determinants of emotionality and stress response in mice

Some strains of mice such as the A/J strain display high anxiety levels. The A/J and C57Bl6 strains are the progenitors of the recombinant congenic strains AcB/BcA. With the help of this recombinant congenic strains panel, Thifault et al. (2008) unveiled quantitative trait loci of the stress response and of emotionality in mice. For the stress response, a 30-minute immobilisation stress was carried out. In these mice, it is characterized by two phases: initial hypothermia followed by thermogenesis. For emotionality, open-field test (number of fecal boli) and elevated plus maze (enclosed arm duration and emergence latencies) were employed. The results unveiled several genomic loci associated with the differential response in the recombinant congenic strains panel. Of major interest, stress loci overlapped with candidate loci for cardiovascular diseases. For instance, the BcA70 strain showed a down regulation of the *Atp1a2* gene in the heart and brain as compared with the parental C57Bl6 strain ($p<0,001$ and $p<0,05$, respectively), and this is in accordance with the high emotionality of the knock-outs for that gene and its involvement in salt-sensitive hypertension.

These remarkable data, resulting from complex analysis of genomic and phenotypic results would not have been possible without telemetry. The body temperature recordings from the stress test were performed with the telemetry implants and a strain distribution pattern over 2,5°C was obtained and could be used to unveil significant loci associated. This temperature difference could not have been monitored with precision with any other means. As for blood pressure, telemetry allowed the monitoring of body temperature continuously and the circadian pattern was obtained. It showed a significant strain x diet effect with the AcB strains (mostly A/J background) displaying a lower body temperature under high-salt diet, and the strain differences were steeper during the dark phase of the circadian cycle. Again, these subtle observations would not have been possible without continuous monitoring by telemetry.

This study unveiled genetic loci responsible for the differential responses to many of the stressors and tests performed. Since it is easy to get spurious association with genetic markers, good phenotyping is essential if one wants to rely on the results. Given the important consequences if one wants to pursue the study of a candidate locus, we think that telemetry is essential for quality phenotyping in genetic research.

6.3 Dissection of hypertension: Positional cloning of quantitative trait loci for blood pressure

Finally, we should not forget to mention the work from Alan Deng who dissects hypertension in the rat and was able to find several significant blood pressure quantitative trait loci (Deng, 2007). His systematic approach uses telemetry as the sole method for blood pressure determination. The blood pressure values are obtained from adult rats from inbred strains. He does, however, perform several genetic manipulations in order to be able to reveal the loci. This approach allowed him to report several loci, the chromosomal position of which are later refined by producing sub-congenics animals (Chauvet et al., 2008). He was also able to reveal some gene-diet interactions and gene-gene interactions. For instance, he was able to demonstrate that a minor effect locus (named C18QTL1) could exert a major effect when it was transferred onto another genetic background. The normotensive Lewis rat genetic background was preventing this locus from exerting its full effect (Charron et al., 2005). This indicates that the normotensives also possess high blood pressure genes, but their effects are counterbalanced by 'normotensive' genes. This demonstrates the genetic buffering capacity of the genome and probably explains why the GWAS performed in humans do not yield the desired major high blood pressure loci: the population are displaying genetic heterogeneities that dilute the loci effects.

7. General conclusion

In this review, we have tried to demonstrate the importance of the environmental component of hypertension. When recognizing this importance, we think that it becomes easier to select the right tools to measure blood pressure in animal models as well as in humans. Human studies tend to indicate a decrease of the prevalence of hypertension whereas it may only be the reflection of the new standardized methods for the measurement of blood pressure devoid of stress. We have shown that rodents used for hypertension research are also stress sensitive and that the most commonly used method for blood pressure determination exacerbates the stress perceived by the animals: it increases blood pressure and body temperature. Since we have presented evidences indicating that stress and temperature can in turn be involved in the development of hypertension, it seems essential to subtract their influence when studying hypertension. Therefore, we think that telemetry is the sole method to perform blood pressure measurement in animal models of hypertension because it enables to subtract the stress artefacts or, conversely, to study them. Furthermore, no genetic studies should be performed in animals if telemetry is not used to characterize the blood pressure levels. Some differences are small and inadequate phenotyping could ruin a GWAS by revealing spurious statistical associations and diverting researchers to wrong candidate genes. On the other side, in an effort to standardize the techniques and eliminating human interference and bias, human epidemiological and genetic studies tend to eliminate the stress component from the measurement of blood pressure. As we have shown, this approach is desired in animal studies especially because we are dealing with inbred strains and can test our hypothesis is several backgrounds. Small effect blood pressure loci have more chance of being 'true' and can be verified in congenics in several backgrounds. Paradoxically, in human research, we think that reducing stress results in narrowing the range of available blood pressure (decrease of genetic variance). It may thus explain why no major blood pressure loci were found despite the increased size of the study populations in recent studies. Maybe this is a mistake and, because of the genome buffering, none of the hypertensive genes would ever manifest themselves in such conditions. Therefore, we do think that telemetry is the State-of-the-Art method for blood pressure determination. But, first, we think that the right question must be asked before any blood pressure determination attempt. Only with well-defined goals and phenotype will a blood pressure method easy to select and the results obtained valid and reproducible. It is especially true if one wants to find "high blood pressure" genes (Korner, 2010).

8. References

Alexander F 1939. Emotional factors in essential hypertension. Presentation of a tentative hypothesis. *Psychosom Med*;1:173-179.

Anderson EA, Mahoney LT, Lauer RM & Clarke WR. Enhanced forearm blood flow during mental stress in children of hypertensive parents. *Hypertension*;10:544-549.

Bader M 2010. Rat models of cardiovascular diseases. *Methods Mol Biol*;597:403-414.

Baskaran K, Hajat S, Haines A, Herrett E, Wilkinson P & Smeeth L 2010. Short term effects of temperature on risk of myocardial infarction in England and Wales: time series regression analysis of the Myocardial Ischaemia Natonal Audit Project (MINAP) registry. *BMJ*;341:c3823.

Bazil MK, Krulan C & Webb RL 1993. Telemetric monitoring of cardiovascular parameters in conscious spontaneously hypertensive rats. *J Cardiovasc Pharmacol*;22:897-905.

Beck JA, Lloyd S, Hafezparast M, Lennon-Pierce M, Eppig JT, Festing MF & Fisher EM 2000. Genealogies of mouse inbred strains. *Nat Genet*;24(1):23-25.

Berkey DL, Meeuwsen KW & Barney CC 1990. Measurement of core temperature in spontaneously hypertensive rats by radiotelemetry. *Am J Physiol*;258:R743-R749.

Briese E & De Quijada MG 1970. Colonic temperature of rats during handling. *Acta Physiol Latinoam*;20:97-102.

Brown MA, Davis GK & McHugh L 2001. The prevalence and clinical significance of nocturnal hypertension in pregnancy. *J Hypertens*;19:1437-1444.

Buñag RD 1983. Facts and fallacies about measuring blood pressure in rats. *Clin Exp Hypertens*;A5(10):1659-1681.

Campbell NR, So L, Amankwah E, Quan H, Maxwell C & Canadian Hypertension Education Program Outcomes Research Task Force 2008. Characteristics of hypertensive Canadians not receiving drug therapy. *Can J Cardiol*;24(6):485-490.

Campbell NR, Brant R, Johansen H, Walker RL, Wielgosz A, Onysko J, Gao RN, Sambell C, Phillips S, McAlister FA & Canadian Hypertension Education Program Outcomes Research Task Force 2009. Increases in antihypertensive prescriptions and reductions in cardiovascular events in Canada. *Hypertension*;53:128-134.

Capone C, Faraco G, Park L, Cao X, Davisson RL & Iadecola C 2011. The cerebrovascular dysfunction induced by slow pressor doses of angiotensin II precedes the development of hypertension. *Am J Physiol Heart Circ Physiol*;300(1):H397-H407.

Charron S, Lambert R, Eliopoulos V, Duong C, Ménard A, Roy J & Deng AY 2005. A loss of genome buffering capacity of Dahl salt-sensitive model modulate blood pressure as a cause of hypertension. *Hum Mol Genet*;14(24)3877-3884.

Chauvet C, Charron S, Ménard A, Xiao C, Roy J & Deng AY 2008. Submegabase resolution of epistatically quantitative trait loci for blood pressure applicable for essential hypertension. *J Hypertens*;26(5):893-901.

Cobb M & Rose RM 1973. Hypertension, peptic ulcer, and diabetes in air traffic controllers. *JAMA*;224:489-492.

Curwen M 1991. Winter mortality: a British phenomenon? *Health Trends*;22:169-175.

Davern PJ, Jackson KL, Nguyen-Huu TP, La Greca L & Head GA 2010. Cardiovascular responses to aversive and nonaversive stressors in Schlager genetically hypertensive mice. *Am J Hypertens*;23(8):838-844.

Deng AY 2007. Positional cloning of quantitative trait loci for blood pressure: How close are we? A critical perspective. *Hypertension*;49:740-747.

Dominiczak AF & Munroe PB 2010. Genome-wide association studies will unlock the genetic basis of hypertension. Pro side of the argument. *Hypertension*;56:1017-1020.

Dumas P, Pausova Z, Kren V, Krenova D, Pravenec M, Dumont M, Ely D, Turner M, Sun Y, Tremblay J & Hamet P 2000a. Contribution of autosomal loci and the Y chromosome to the stress response in rats. *Hypertension*;35:568-573.

Dumas P, Sun Y, Corbeil G, Tremblay S, Pausova Z, Kren V, Krenova D, Pravenec M, Hamet P & Tremblay J 2000b. Mapping of the quantitative trait loci (QTL) of differential stress gene expression in rat recombinant inbred strains. *J Hypertens*;18:545-551.

Falkner B, Onesti G, Angelakos ET, Fernandes M & Langman C 1979. Cardiovascular response to mental stress in normal adolescents with hypertensive parents: Hemodynamics and mental stress in adolescents. *Hypertension*;1:23-30.

Falkner B, Kushner H, Onesti G & Angelakos ET 1981. Cardiovascular characteristics in adolescents who develop essential hypertension. *Hypertension*;3:521-527.

Feng M & DiPetrillo K 2009. Non-invasive blood pressure measurement in mice. *Methods Mol Biol*;573:45-55.

Folkow B 1982. Physiological aspects of primary hypertension. *Physiol Rev*;62:347-504.

Friedman R & Dahl LK 1977. Psychic and genetic factors in the etiology of hypertension. In *Stress and the heart*. D Wheatley Ed, pp. 137-156. Raven Press, ISBN- 0890041512, New York.

Gollnick PD & Iannuzzo CD 1968. Colonic temperature response of rats during exercise. *J Appl Physiol*;24:747-750.

Gross V & Luft FC 2003. Exercising restraint in measuring blood pressure in conscious mice. *Hypertension*;41:879-881.

Grundt A, Grundt C, Gorbey S, Thomas MA & Lemmer B 2009. Strain-dependent differences of restraint stress-induced hypertension in WKY and SHR. *Physiol Behav*;97:341-346.

Gryglewska B, Necki M, Cwynar M, Baron T & Grodzicki T 2010. Local heat stress and skin blood flowmotion in subjects with familial predisposition or newly diagnosed hypertension. *Blood Press*;19(6):366-372.

Gutmann MC & Benson A 1971. Interaction of environmental factors and systemic blood pressure. A review. *Medicine*;50:543-550.

Hackam DG, Khan NA, Hemmelgarn BR, Rabkin SW, Touyz RM, Campbell NR, Padwal R, Campbell TS, Lindsay MP, Hill MD, Quinn RR, Mahon JL, Herman RJ, Schiffrin EL, Ruzicka M, Larochelle P, Feldman RD, Lebel M, Poirier L, Arnold JM, Moe GW, Howlett JG, Trudeau L, Bacon SL, Petrella RJ, Milot A, Stone JA, Drouin D,

Boulanger JM, Sharma M, Hamet P, Fodor G, Dresser GK, Carruthers SG, Pylypchuk G, Burgess ED, Burns KD, Vallée M, Prasad GV, Gilbert RE, Leiter LA, Jones C, Ogilvie RI, Woo V, McFarlane PA, Hegele RA, Tobe SW & Canadian Hypertension Education Program 2010. The 2010 Canadian Hypertension Education Program recommendations for the management of hypertension: part 2 - therapy. *Can J Cardiol*;26(5) :249-258.

Hamet P, Tremblay J, Pang SC, Walter SV & Wen YI 1985. Primary vs secondary events in hypertension. *Can J Physiol Pharmacol*;63:380-386.

Hamet P 1996. Environmentally-regulated genes of hypertension. *Clin Exp Hypertens*;18:267-278.

Hamet P, Pausova Z, Adarichev V, Adaricheva K & Tremblay J 1998. Hypertension : genes and environment. *J Hypertens*;16 :397-418.

Hamet P & Tremblay J 2002. Genetic determinants of the stress response in cardiovascular disease. *Metabolism*;51(6 suppl 1):15-24.

Hassan MO, Bayoumi RA, Lopez-Alvarenga JC, Snieder H, Jaju D, Al-Yahyaee S, Al-Hadabi S, Comuzzie AG & Albarwani S 2009. Heritability of hemodynamic reactivity to laboratory stressors in a homogenous Arab population: 'Oman Family Study'. *Twin Res Hum Genet*;12(6):541-548.

Havlik RJ, Garrison RJ, Feinleib M, Kannel WB, Castelli WP & McNamara PM 1979. Blood pressure aggregation in families. *Am J epidemiol*;110 :304-312.

Hata T, Ogihara T, Maruyama A, Mikami H, Nakamaru M, Naka T, Kumahara Y & Nugent CA 1982. The seasonal variation of blood pressure in patients with essential hypertension. *Clin Exp Hypertens*;A4:341-354.

Hemmelgarn BR, Cehn G Walker R McAlister FA, Quan H, Tu K, Khan N & Campbell N 2008. Trends in anthypertensive drug prescriptions and physician visits in Canada between 1996 and 2006. *Can J Cardiol*;24:507-512.

Henry JP 1992. Biological basis of the stress response. *Int Physiol Behav Sci*;27:66-83.

Holland WW & Humerfelt S 1964. Measurement of blood pressure: comparison of intra-arterial and cuff values. *Br Med J*;2(5419):1241-1243.

Huetteman DA & Bogie H 2009. Direct blood pressure monitoring in laboratory rodents via implantable radio telemetry. *Methods Mol Biol*;573:57-73.

Irvine RJ, White J & Chan R 1997. The influence of restraint on blood pressure in the rat. *J Pharmacol Toxicol Methods*;38:157-162.

Joffres MR, Hamet P, Rabkin SW, Gelskey D, Hogan K & Fodor G 1992. Prevalence, control and awareness of high blood pressure among Canadian adults. Canadian Heart Health Surveys Research Group. *Can Med Assoc J*;146(11) :1997-2005.

Kanayama N, Khatun S, Belayet H, She L & Terao T 1999. Chronic local cold stress to the soles induces hypertension in rats. *Am. J Hypertens*;12:1124-1129.

Karasek RA, Theorell T, Schwartz JE, Schnall PL, Pieper CF & Michela JL 1988. Job characteristics in relation to the prevalence of myocardial infarction in the US Health Examination Survey (HES) and the Health and Nutrition Examination Survey (HANES). *Am J Public Health*;78:910-918.

Koepke JP & DiBona GF 1985. Central beta-adrenergic receptors mediate renal nerve activity during stress in conscious spontaneously hypertensive rats. *Hypertension*;7:350-356.

Korner PI 2010. The phenotypic patterns of essential hypertension are the key to identifying "high blood pressure" genes. *Physiol Res*;59(6):841-857.

Kramer K, Kinter L, Brockway BP, Voss H-P, Remie R & Van Zutphen BLM 2001. The use of radiotelemetry in small laboratory animals: Recent advances. *Contemporary topics*;40(1):8-16.

Krege JH, Hodgin JB, Hagaman JR & Smithies O 1995. A noninvasive computerized tail-cuff system for measuring blood pressure in mice. *Hypertension*;25:1111-1115.

Kuneš J, Demin AN, Jelinek J, Capek K & Belkaniya GS 1990. Stress hypertension in monkeys. *Physiol Bohemoslov*;30:417-423.

Kuneš J, Tremblay J, Bellavance F & Hamet P 1991. Influence of environmental temperature on the blood pressure of hypertensive patients in Montreal. *Am J Hypertens*;4:422-426.

Kuneš J, Dobešová Z, Musilová A, Zídek V, Vorlíček J, Pravenec M, Křen V & Zicha J 2008. Hemodynamic characterization of recombinant inbred strains: twenty years later. *Hypertens Res*;31:1659-1668.

Kurtz TW, Griffin KA, Bidani AK, Davisson RL & Hall JE 2005. Recommendations for blood pressure measurement in humans and experimental animals. Part 2: Blood pressure measurement in experimental animals. A statement for professionals from the subcommittee of professional and public education of the American heart association council on high blood pressure research. *Hypertension*;45:299-310.

Kurtz TW 2010. Genome-wide association studies will unlock the genetic basis of hypertension. Con side of the argument. *Hypertension*;56:1021-1025.

Kvetnansky R, Weise VK & kopin IJ 1970. Elevation of adrenal tyrosine hydroxylase and phenylethanolamine-N-methyl transferase by repeated immobilization in rats. *Endocrinology*;87:744-749.

Kwitek AE, Tonellato PJ, Chen D, Gullings-Handley J, Cheng YS, Twigger S, Scheetz TE, Casavant TL, Stoll M, Nobrega MA, Shiozawa M, Bento Soares M, Sheffield VC & Jacob HJ 2001. Automated construction of high-density comparative maps between rat, human, and mouse. *Genome Res*;11:1935-1943.

Lawes CM, Vander HS & Rodgers A 2008. Global burden of blood-pressure-related disease, 2001. *Lancet*;371(9623):1513-1518.

Leenen FH, Dumais J, McInnis NH, Turton P, Stratychuk L, Nemeth K, Lum-Kwong MM & Fodor G 2008. Results of the Ontario survey on the prevalence and control of hypertension. *Can Med Assoc J*; 178(11):1441-1449.

Lewington S, Clark R, Qizilbash N, Peto R & Collins R 2002. Age-specific relevance of usual blood pressure to vascular mortality: a meta-analysis of individual data for one million adults in 61 prospective studies. *Lancet*;360:1903-1913.

Lynch M & Walsh B 1997. Genotype X environment interaction. In *Genetics and analysis of quantitative traits*. pp. 657-685. Sinauer and Associates Publisher, ISBN-0-87893-481-2, Sunderland (MA).

Malo D, Schlager G, Tremblay J & Hamet P 1989. Thermosensitivity, a possible new locus involved in genetic hypertension. *Hypertension*;14:121-128.

Malo D, Pang SC, Schlager G, Tremblay J & Hamet P 1990. Decrease of blood pressure in spontaneously hypertensive mice by heat treatment. *Am J Hypertens*;3:400-404.

Marazziti D, Di Muro A & Castrogiovanni P 1992. Psychological stress and body temperature changes in humans *Physiol Behav*;52:393-395.

Markovitz JH, Matthews KA, Kannel WB, Cobb JL & D'Agostino RB 1993. Psychological predictors of hypertension in the Framingham study. Is there a tension in hypertension? *JAMA*;270:2439-2443.

Markel' AL 1985. Genetic model of stress-induced arterial hypertension. *Izv Akad Nauk SSSR Biol*;3:466-469.

Matthews KA, Woodall KL & Allen MT 1993. Cardiovascular reactivity to stress predicts future blood pressure status. *Hypertension*;22:479-485.

McMurtry JP & Wexler BC 1981. Hypersensitivity of spontaneously hypertensive rats (SHR) to heat, ether and immobilization. *Endocrinology*;108:1730-1735.

McMurtry JP & Wexler BC 1983. Hypersensitivity of spontaneously hypertensive rats to heat and ether before the onset of high blood pressure. *Endocrinology*;112:166-171.

Middlekauff HR, Nguyen AH, Negrao CE, Nitasche EU, Hoh CK, Natterson BA, Hamilton MA, FOnarow GC, Hage A & Moriguchi JD 1997. Impact of acute mental stress on sympathetic nerve activity and regional blood flow in advance heart failure. Implications for 'triggering' adverse cardiac events. *Circulation*;96:1835-1842.

Mills PA, Huetteman DA, Brockway BP, Zwiers LM, Gelsema AJM, Schwartz RS & Kramer K 2000. A new method for measurement of blood pressure, heart rate, and activity in the mouse by radiotelemetry. *J Appl Physiol*;88:1537-1544.

Mitra A, Crump EM, Alvers KM, Robertson KL & Rowland NE 2011. Effect of high-fat diet on stress responsiveness in borderline hypertensive rats. *Stress*;14(1):42-52.

Morales-Ballejo HM, Eliot RS, Boone JL & Hughes JS 1988. Psychophysiologic stress testing as a predictor of mean daily blood pressure. *Am Heart J*;116 (2 pt 2):673-681.

Morley RM, Conn CA Kluger MJ & Vander AJ 1990. Temperature regulation in biotelemetered spontaneously hypertensive rats. *Am J Physiol*;258:R1064-1069.

Mozaffari MS, Jirakulsomchok S, Shao ZH & Wyss JM 1991. High-NaCl diets increase natriuretic and diuretic responses in salt-resistant but not salt-sensitive SHR. *Am J Physiol*;260:F890-F897.

Ohlin B, Berglund G, Nilsson PM & Melander O 2008. Job strain, job demands and adrenergic beta1-receptor-polymorphism : a possible interaction affecting blood pressure in men. *J Hypertens*;26(8):1583-1589.

Okamoto K & Aoki K 1963. Development of a strain of spontaneously hypertensive rats. *Jpn Circ J*;27:282-293.

O'Leary DS & Wang G 1994. Impaired thermoregulatory cutaneous vasodilation in spontaneously hypertensive rats. *J Appl Physiol*;77 :692-696.

Omboni S, Smit AAJ & Wieling W 1995. Twenty four hour continuous non-invasive finger blood pressure monitoring: a novel approach to the evaluation of treatment in patients with autonomic failure. *Br Heart J*;73:290-292.

Parati G, Frattola A, Di Rienzo M & Mancia G 1996. Blood pressure variability. Importance in research and in clinical hypertension. *Arq Bras Cardiol*;67:131-133.

Pausova Z, Tremblay J & Hamet P 1999. Gene-environment interactions in hypertension. *Curr Hypertens Rep*;1 :42-50.

Pausova Z, Syme C, Abrahamowicz M, Xiao Y, Leonard GT, Perron M, Richer L, Veillette S, Smith GD, Seda O, Tremblay J, Hamet P, Gaudet D & Paus T 2009. A common variant of the FTO gene is associated with not only increased adiposity but also elevated blood pressure in French Canadians. *Circ Cardiovasc Genet*;2(3):260-269.

Peñaz J 1973. Photoelectric measurement of blood pressure, volume and flow in the finger. *Digest of the International Conference on Medicine and Biological Engineering*:104.

Pickering TG, Hall JE, Appel LJ, Falkner BE, Graves J, Hill MN, Jones DW, Kurtz T, Sheps SG & Roccella EJ 2005. Recommendations for blood pressure measurement in humans and experimental animals. Part 1: Blood pressure in humans. A statement for professionals from the subcommittee of professional and public education of the American Heart Council on High Blood Pressure Research. *Hypertension*;45:142-161.

Price JM & Wilmoth FR 1990. Elevated body temperature and increased blood vessel sensitivity in spontaneously hypertensive rats. *Am J Physiol*;258:H946-H953.

Rao F, Zhang L, Wessel J, Zhang K, Wen G, Kennedy BP, Rana BK, Das M, Rodriguez-Flores JL, Smith DW, Cadman PE, Salem RM, Mahata SK, Schork NJ, Taupenot L, Ziegler MG & O'Connor DT 2008. Adrenergic polymorphism and the human stress response. *Ann N Y Acad Sci*;1148:282-296.

Rose G 1961. Seasonal variation in blood pressure in man. *Nature*;189:235.

Rothwell PM 2010. Limitations of the usual blood pressure hypothesis and importance of variability, instability, and episodic hypertension. *Lancet*;375:938-948.

Rothwell PM, Howard SC, Dolan E, O'Brien E, Dobson JE, Dahlöf B, Sever PS & Poulter NR 2010. Prognostic significance of visit-to-visit variability, maximum systolic blood pressure, and episodic hypertension. *Lancet*;375:895-905.

Sakamoto H, Imataka K, Nishimura H & Fujii J 1992. Hematological and pressor hormone responses to mental stress in essential hypertensive patients: a comparison with isometric handgrip exercise. *Hypertens Res*;15:33-39.

Schlager G 1974. Selection of blood pressure levels in mice. *Genetics*;76:537-549.

Schnall PL, Pieper C, Schwartz JE, Karasek RA, Schlussel Y, Devereux RB, Ganau A, Alderman M, Warren K & Pickering TG 1990. The relationship between 'job strain', workplace diastolic blood pressure, and left ventricular mass index. Results of a case-control study. *JAMA*;263:1929-1935.

Šedová L, Bérubé J, Gaudet D, Dumont M, Tremblay J, Hamet P & Pausová Z 2004. Diet-induced obesity delays cardiovascular recovery from stress in spontaneously hypertensive rats. *Obes Res*;12:1951-1958.

Selye H 1956. The stress of life. Pp. 25-43. McGraw Hill, New-York.

Singer RC, Harker CT, Vander AJ & Kluger MJ 1986. Hyperthermia induced by open-field stress is blocked by salicylate. *Physiol Behav*;36:1179-1182.

Snow AE & Horita A 1982. Interaction of apomorphine and stressors in the production of hyperthermia in the rabbit. *J Pharmacol Exp Therap*;220:335-339.

Stoll M & Jacob HJ 2001. Genetic rat models of hypertension: Relationship to human hypertension. *Curr Hypertens Rep*;3:157-164.

Stuart J & Eilkelboom R 1979. Stress masls the hypothermic effect of naloxone in rats. *Life Sci*;25:1165-1172.

Thayer JF, Yamamoto SS & Brosschot JF 2010. The relationship of autonomic imbalance, heart rate variability and cardiovascular disease risk factors. *Int J Cardiol*;141(2):122-131.

Thifault S, Šeda O, Sun Y, Fortin A, Skamene E, Lalonde R, Tremblay J & Hamet P 2008. Genetic determinants of emotionality and stress response in AcB/BcA recombinant congenic mice and *in silico* evidence of convergence with cardiovascular candidate genes. *Hum Mol Genet*;17:331-344.

Tobin M, Sheehan N, Samani N & Burton PP 2007. The genetic epidemiology of hypertension. In *Genetics of Hypertension*. Birkenhager WH & Reid J Eds, pp. 5-28. Elsevier, ISBN-9780444514561, Amsterdam, The Netherlands.

Trimarco B, Ricciardelli B, De Luca N, De Simone A, Cuocolo A, Galva MD, Picotti GB & Condorelli M 1985. Participation of endogenous catecholamines in the regulation of left ventricular mass in progeny of hypertensive parents. *Circulation*;1:38-46.

Van Vliet BN, Chafe LL & Montani JP 2003. Characteristics of 24 h telemetered blood pressure in eNOS-knockout and C57Bl/6J control mice. *J Physiol*;549(pt1):313-325.

Ward R 1990. Familial aggregation and genetic epidemiology of blood pressure. In *Hypertension: Pathophysiology, Diagnosis and Management*. Laragh JH & Brenner BM, pp. 81-100. Raven Press, ISBN-10 0781701570, New York.

Weinberger MH 1990. Clinical studies of the role of dietary sodium in blood pressure. In *Hypertension: Pathophysiology, Diagnosis and Management*. Laragh JH & Brenner BM, pp. 1999-2010. Raven Press, ISBN-10 0781701570, New York.

Wesseling KH, De Wit B, Van der Hoeven GMA, Van Goudoever J & Settels JJ 1995. Physiocal, calibrating finger vascular physiology for Finapres. *Homeostasis*;36 :67-82.

Widgren BR, Wikstrand J, Berglund G & Andersson OK 1992. Increased response to physical and mental stress in men with hypertensive parents. *Hypertension*;20:606-611.

Wilkins K, Campbell NR, Joffres MR, McAlister FA, Nichol M, Quach S, Johansen HL & Tremblay MS 2010. Blood pressure in Canadian adults. *Health Rep*;21(1) :37-46.

Williams JR, Harrison TR & Grollman A 1939. A simple method for determining the systolic blood pressure of the unanesthetized rat. *J CLin Invest*;18:373-376.

Wilson JR, Wilson LM & Dicara LV 1977. Evidence for an elevation in thermoregulatory set-point in the SHR. *Proc 2nd Int Symposium on SHR*;6:376-384.

Wright G, Knecht E & Toraason M 1978. Cardiovascular effects of whole-body heating on spontaneously hypertensive rats. *J Appl Physiol*;45:521-527.

Yamamoto J, Nakai M & Natsume T 1987. Cardiovascular responses to an acute stress in young-to-old spontaneously hypertensive rats. *Hypertension*;4:362-370.

Yamori Y, Matsumoto M, Yamabe H & Okamoto K 1969. Augmentation of spontaneous hypertension by chronic stress in rats. *Jpn Circ J*;33:399-409.

Yu SF, Zhou WH, Jiang KY, Gu GZ & Wang S 2008. Job stress, gene polymorphism of beta2-AR, and prevalence of hypertension. *Biomed Environ Sci*;21(3):239-246.

Zhao X, Ho D, Gao S, Hong C, Vatner DE & Vatner SF 2011. Arterial pressure monitoring in mice. *Curr Protoc Mouse Biol*;1:105-122.

Recent Advances in Telemetry Monitoring and Analysis for Laboratory Animals

Masayoshi Kuwahara
The University of Tokyo, Japan

1. Introduction

Measurement of physiological parameters in laboratory animals plays an important role in evaluating the biomedical applications. It has been widely known that a telemetry system is useful for these studies, because the telemetry system can obtain physiological measurements from conscious and unrestrained laboratory animals. Maurey was the first to report on a telemetry experiment in the scientific literature (see Mackay, 1970). Mackay wrote the experiment as follows: *"A rubber bulb detects the shortening of the pectoral muscle of a pigeon by its thickening the pneumatic signal traveling a rubber tube to a bulb pushing a stylus on a smoked arum. A flapping vane at the wingtip opens and closes an electric contact to indicate the relative duration of the period of elevation and depression of the wing."* One of the first telemetry experiments with the use of a radio signal is reported by Barr (1954). From the late 1950's, several research groups have developed radio-telemetry devices for laboratory animals (Gold & Malcolm, 1957; Essler & Folk, 1961; Franklin, et al., 1964). Although telemetry technology for monitoring laboratory animals have already existed since the early 1950's as described above, fully implantable and reliable telemetry devices for monitoring physiological functions in laboratory animals have been made commercially available since the late 1980's. Advances and further miniaturization of the implantable devices in the beginning of 1990's have provided to measure electrocardiogram (ECG), electromyogram (EMG), electroencephalogram (EEG), blood pressure (BP), body temperature (BT), and locomotor activity (LA). Therefore, the number of publications in which radio-telemetric results in laboratory animals has been tremendously increased for 2 decade. In these days, many companies commercially supply the radio-telemetry implants for monitoring physiological parameters.

In this report, I would like to introduce a newly developed telemetry system in Japanese company and some useful software to analyze ECG data in the fields of cardiology and pathophysiology as well as pharmacology and toxicology. Further, I describe some experimental studies using a telemetry system and applications.

2. Newly developed telemetry system

The telemetry system for rat and mouse consists of an implantable transmitter (ATE-01S) with a pair of flexible leads, a telemetry receiver (ATR-1001) and connected acquisition system (Softron ECG Processor; EP95) to personal computer (Fig. 1).

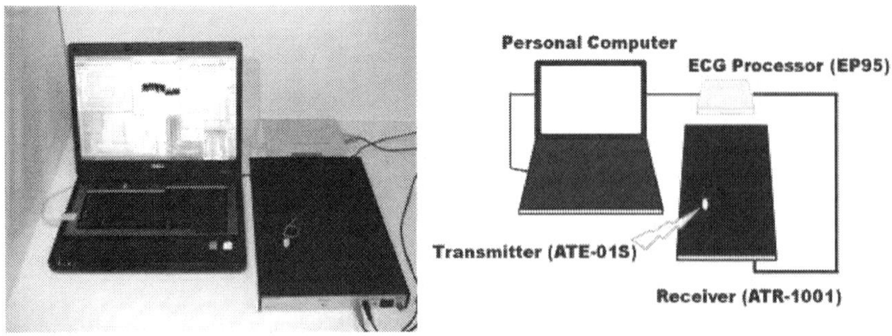

Fig. 1. Picture and schematic drawing of a newly developed telemetry system for recording ECGs. A telemetry transmitter is on a telemetry receiver.

The implantable transmitter consists of a hermetically sealed plastic housing with a biocompatible silastic coating, occupying a volume of less than 1.9 ml and weighing approximately 3.8 g. Each transmitter contains an amplifier, a battery, radio-frequency electronics, a pair of flexible leads with 20 cm and a magnetically activated switch which allows the device to be turned on and off either *in vivo* or *ex vivo*. The transmitter passes the ECG signal to a receiver located beneath the animal cage via radio signal. The data acquisition system records and stores the raw telemetered data into the hard disk for subsequent analysis as described below (Section 4).

3. Transmitter implantation

In many studies, the typical implantation procedure for monitoring ECG is positioning the body of the transmitter in the peritoneal cavity of the laboratory animals. However, we usually implant a telemetry transmitter for ECG chronically into the notal subcutanea under pentobarbital sodium anesthesia (40 mg/kg, intraperitoneally), because this procedure can easily perform and much less invasive and/or damaged for laboratory animals than in the peritoneal cavity procedure. Before making the incision in the skin of the animal, we use a clipper to remove the hair from the operation area of the anesthetized animal. The animal is placed on a hot plate to avoid hypothermia during procedure, and the operation area is sterilized with iodine. A 1.0-1.5 cm long incision in the skin is made, and transmitter is implanted into the subcutaneous area as shown in Fig. 2. Both electrodes are situated in the direction of the head of the animal. Paired electrodes of the transmitter are placed under the skin of the dorsal and ventral thorax to record the apex-base (A-B) lead ECG. When both electrodes are fixed on their places, the transmitter is activated by a magnet close to the transmitter body. When the battery of the transmitter is switched on, the heart beats are clearly audible within a few seconds. To complete the operation, the incision of skin is closed with absorbable suture or Michel clips.

4. Software for recording and analyzing of ECG from many points of view

Softron ECG processor can connect to a telemetry receiver as well as a bioelectrical amplifier, a data recorder and a Holter ECG recorder for recording and analysis of ECGs. Many useful softwares are provided to record and analyze ECGs. In this section, I introduce these softwares.

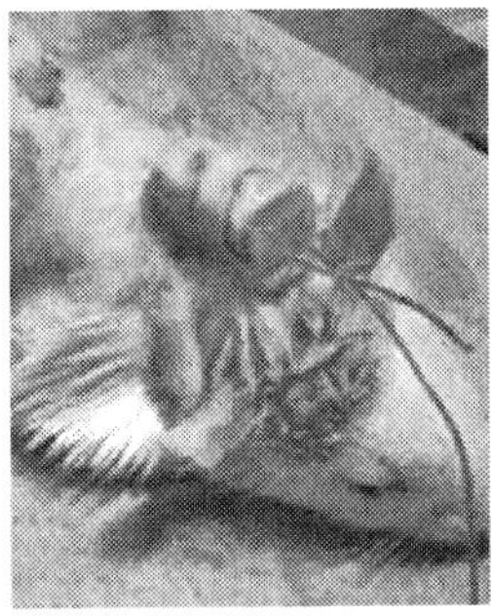

Fig. 2. Picture of a transmitter implantation in rat.

4.1 SP2000

SP2000 consists of the acquisition program and basic analyzing program for ECGs. The acquisition program can collect the data for a specific length of time or continuously and save it on the computer's hard drive. The acquisition program consists of a Config, Waveln, Replay, Edit, Print etc as shown in Fig. 3.

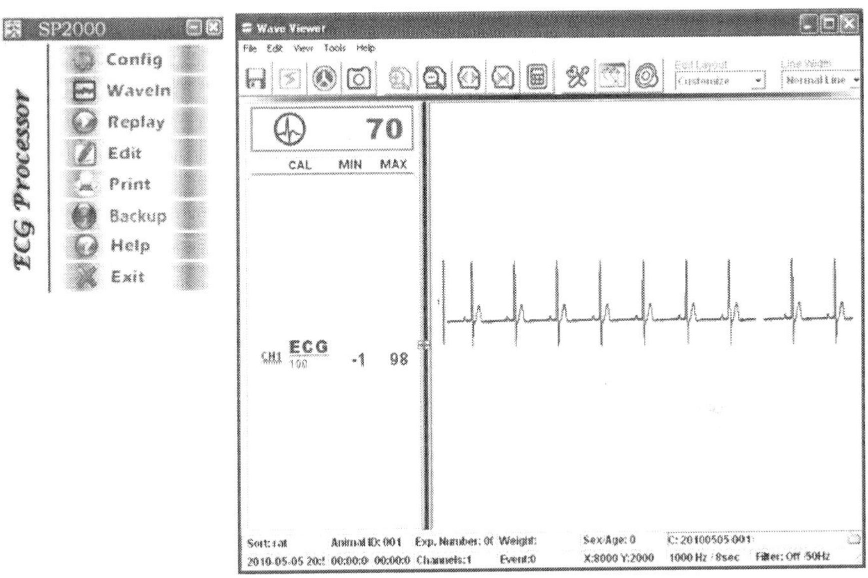

Fig. 3. Main menu (left) and Waveln screen (right) of SP2000.

The Config (Configulation module) allows users to create a file that contains settings for detecting and collecting data signals during a study and to modify an existing configuration file for use in a different study. To record ECG waves, Waveln is opened after setting of configulaton. The analyzing program calculates the points and characteristic values of an

ECG: characteristic points of the P, Q, R, S, T waves as well as the time intervals between these different points by Edit screen as shown in Fig. 4. The program can operate in automatic detection of complexes directly from the ECG signal. This detection is based on the presence of a R wave peak.

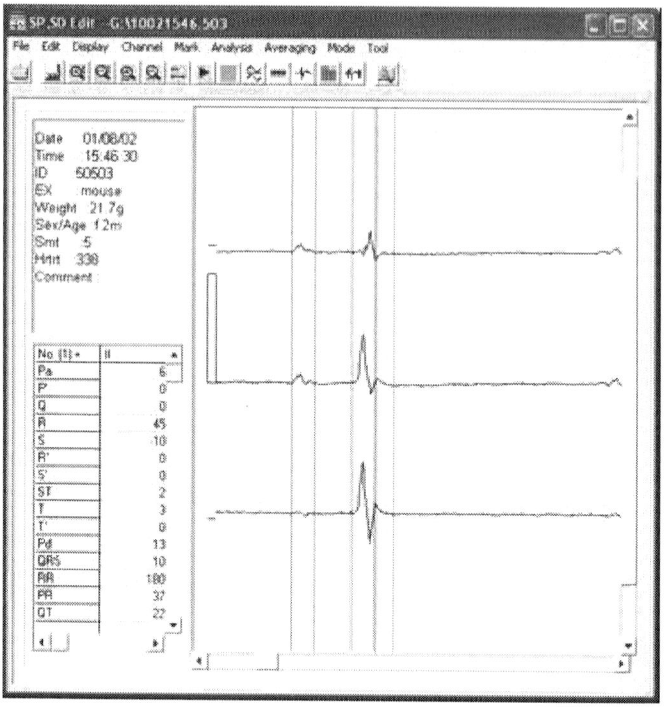

Fig. 4. Edit screen of a mouse ECGs.

4.2 SBP2000

Although SP2000 is specific software for ECG, SBP2000 can record and analyze not only ECG but also intra ventricular pressure, blood pressure, blood flow and respiration. Operation is almost the same as SP2000.

4.3 SHL-2W

SHL-2W is prepared for advanced analysis of arrhythmias for ECG. This software analyzes arrhythmias such as premature ventricular contraction (PVC), premature atrial contraction (PAC), ventricular tachycardia (VT), ventricular fibrillation (VF), Pause, etc based on patterns of QRS complex from long term recording ECGs obtained by the telemetry and Holter ECG recorder. Fig. 5 shows an example of mouse ECG recorded using the telemetry system. Some arrhythmias such as PVC are observed in this ECG. High lightened part is also shown below as an expanded window.

Fig. 6 is Print Preview window. ECGs are able to print out as compress waves.

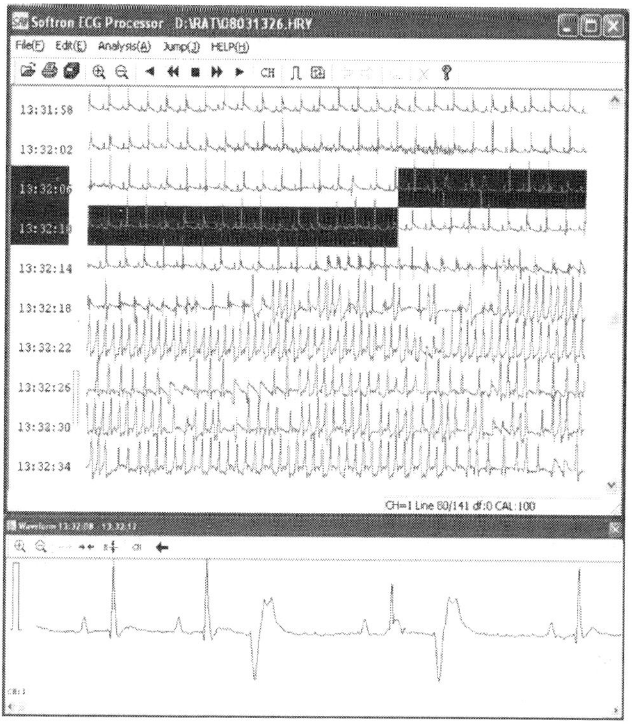

Fig. 5. Long term ECGs of mouse represent with SHL-2W window.

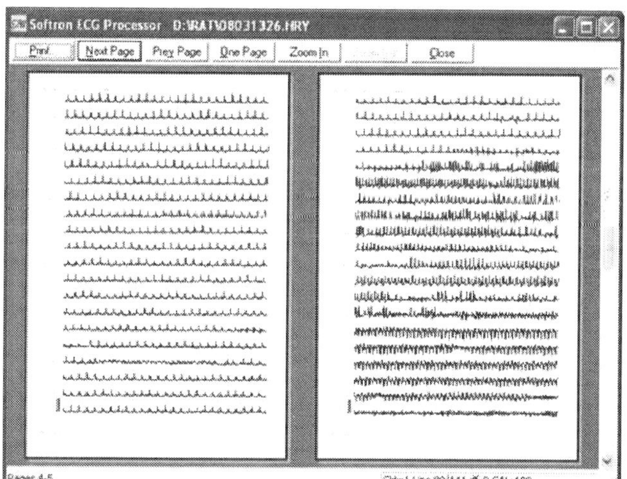

Fig. 6. Print preview window of compress ECGs.

4.4 SRV-2W

SRV-2W is prepared for analysis of heart rate variability (HRV). I describe detail of the HRV in the next session. Breafly, this software detects R waves and calculated the R-R interval tachogram as the raw HRV in sequence order as shown in Fig. 7. Lorentz plots are also able to display.

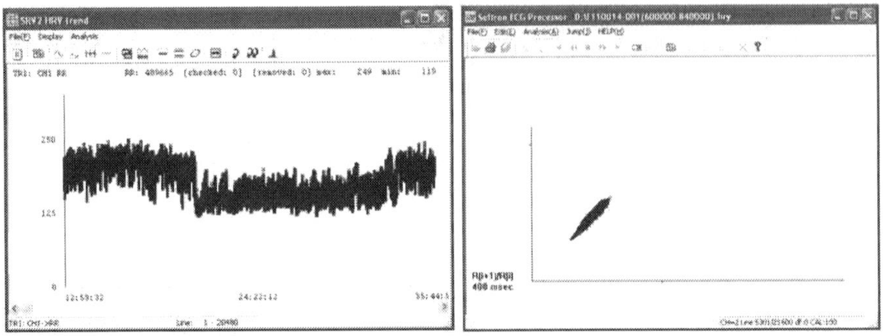

Fig. 7. Tachogram of the R-R interval (left) and example of Lorentz plots.

From this tachogram, the average and instantaneous power spectra are obtained by the fast Fourier transform as shown in raight and left of Fig. 8, respectively. The software calculates many index of values of HRV as shown in Fig. 8.

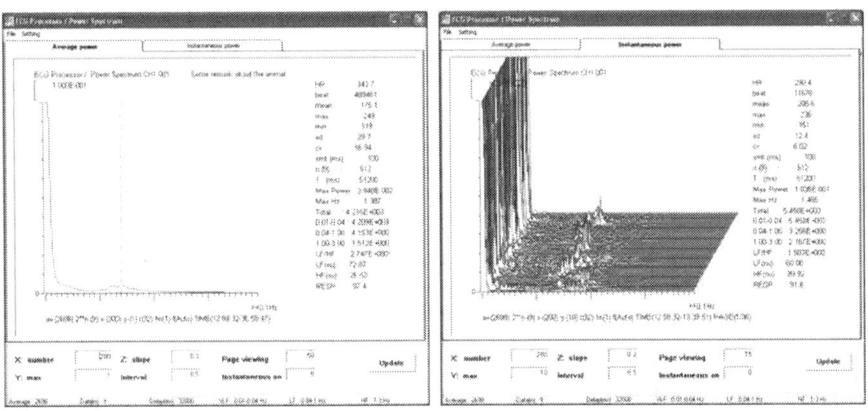

Fig. 8. Examples of average power spectrum (left) and 75 instantaneous power spectra (right) in mouse.

4.5 Other applications

For further analysis of ECGs such as RR-QT relationship, software for Bootstrap method can apply after analyzing all of the waves. This software is useful to detect QT prolongation induced by drugs. Moreover, software for signal average electrocardiogram is developed to detect ventricular late potential.

5. Heart Rate Variability (HRV)

Power spectral analysis of HRV has been studied and applied in not only human beings but also many animal species. In this section, I describe HRV in itself and methods for analysis of HRV.

5.1 What HRV is

Heart rate being regulated by autonomic nervous system and endocrine system, is known to be affected with changes in postures, with exercise, with changes in psychological states. But heart rate is also known to fluctuate around the mean heart rate even in a stable condition. For example, when we inhale heart rate rises and when we exhale heart rate drops. This fluctuation of heart rate is known as respiratory sinus arrhythmia, and it occurs because burst rate at the sino atrial node changes according to respiration cycle. This kind of rhythmic fluctuation of the heart rate under stable condition, brought about by naturally occurring physiological perturbations such as respiration, blood pressure, and thermo-regulation, is recognized as HRV. Considering that the principle systems involved in regulating the heart rate are mainly the sympathetic and parasympathetic nervous system, it has been suggested that the analysis of HRV could lead to noninvasive assessment of the tonic autonomic regulation of the heart rate.

5.2 Analysis of HRV

Since HRV reflects cardiac autonomic outflow, attempts have been made to assess this outflow by analyzing HRV. Time domain analysis with the use of standard deviation of R-R interval has been proposed as measures of parasympathetic activity. But this is a nonspecific quantifier of HRV and we cannot analyze the factors which produce this variability. To solve this problem, frequency domain analysis with the use of power spectrum has proven useful to sort out the variability into components which the whole variability is consisted of. In this method, the variability is mathematically transformed into frequency components, and the power of each frequency is calculated. In this way, we can understand which frequency components make up the variability and how much influence they have on the whole.

Example of a power spectrum of HRV in human is shown in Fig. 9. In human beings, three major components can be observed. One in the low frequency (LF) area of 0.04-0.15 Hz, one in the high frequency (HF) area of around 0.20 Hz and one below the LF. The LF power which is the components between 0.04-0.15 Hz in human, reflect the heart rate fluctuating at a cycle of about 10 seconds. This component is said to be the result of the Mayer wave of arterial pressure reflecting on the burst rate of the sino atrial node through baroreflex (Scher, 1977). Both the sympathetic and parasympathetic outflow are considered to regulate the LF components (Akselrod, et al., 1981; Task Force of the European Society of Cardiology and the North American Society of Pacing and Electrophysiology, 1996). The HF power which is the components between 0.15-0.40 Hz in human, derives from respiratory sinus arrhythmia (Hirsch & Bishop, 1981). The frequency of the component is this area coincides with the frequency of respiration. This component is said to be the respiratory system ad afferent signals from receptors in the lung influencing the cardiovascular system. Only the parasympathetic outflow is considered to regulate the HF components (Akselrod, et al., 1981; Task Force of the European Society of Cardiology and the North American Society of Pacing and Electrophysiology, 1996).

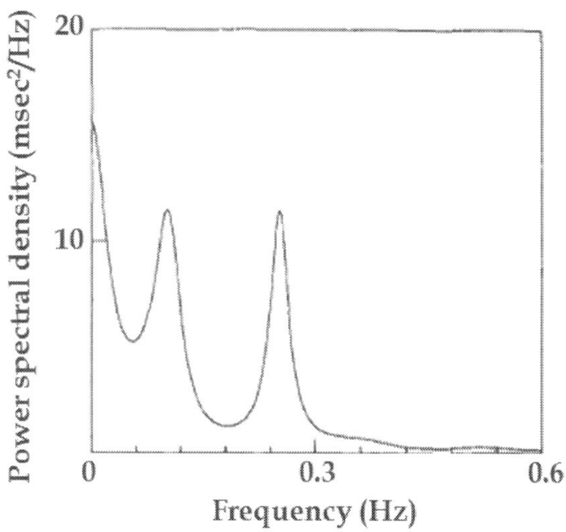

Fig. 9. Power spectrum obtained from human

6. Applications of power spectral analysis of HRV in laboratory animals

HRV has provided increasing interest as a noninvasive index of autonomic nervous activity (Task Force of the European Society of Cardiology and the North American Society of Pacing and Electrophysiology, 1996). Because we thought that the power spectral analysis of HRV from the ECG recorded by a telemetry system may be more reliable for assessing autonomic nervous activity than that recorded by a tethering system. Therefore, we have recorded ECGs for this analysis by the telemetry system from many laboratory animals including mouse, rats, guinea pigs, rabbits, and miniature pigs to investigate autonomic nervous function in these animals. First, we have established the characteristics of HRV in the normal animals. Second, we applied to some pathophysiological studies. In this section, I would like to show the results of these studies.

6.1 Characteristics of HRV in the normal animals

An off-line analysis was performed on an ECG processor analyzing system (SRV-2W, Softron) and a microcomputer using ECG data stored on a hard disk recorded by a telemetry system from many laboratory animals. The computer program first detected R waves and calculated the R-R interval tachogram as the raw HRV in sequence order. From this tachogram, data sets of 512 points were resampled at defined time as each animal species. Time of resampling differed according to their heart rate. The length of this tachogram has been selected as the best compromise between the need for a large time series, in order to achieve greater accuracy during computation, and the desire for short time periods. We then applied each set of data to the Hamming window and the fast Fourier transform to obtain the power spectrum of the fluctuation. The power spectrum has unit of msec^2/Hz. The integral over LF areas was calculated as the LF power and HF areas as the

HF power. These powers have units of msec^2. The ratio of LF power and HF power (LF/HF) was also calculated and this is unitless.

All animals shared a characteristic pattern in their power spectrum analysis. Representative power spectra of HRV in each animal species are shown in Fig. 10.

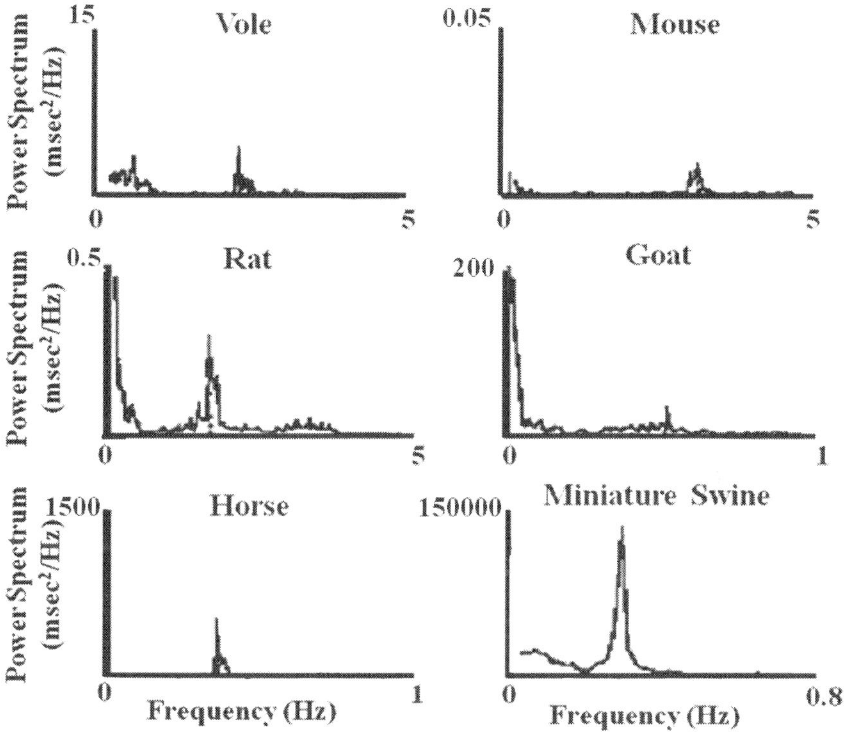

Fig. 10. Representative power spectra obtained from many animal species

There were two major spectral components of LF and HF spectra for HRV. Since the HF power is represented by the component corresponding to respiration, the range of HF was set so that the respiration rate would be included in it. As for the LF, the upper limit was set at the same frequency as the lower limit of HF. The lower limit of LF was set according to the resampling time of the R-R interval time series. In the method of fast Fourier transform, the components at very low frequencies include noise from the data analyzed and makes that part unreliable. The frequency range which includes this noise is in relation to the resampling time. With this in mind, we have set the lower limit of LF according to the limit we observed to be a reliable one. On the basis of these data, two frequency bands of interest were decided in each animal species as shown in Table 1.

The values of HRV in each animal species obtained from our experiments are also summarized in Table 2.

Species	LF (Hz)	HF (Hz)
Mouse	0.1-1.0	1.0-5.0
Vole	0.1-1.0	1.0-5.0
Rat	0.04-1.0	1.0-3.0
Guinea pig	0.07-0.7	0.7-3.0
Rabbit	0.01-0.4	0.4-1.0
Dog	0.04-0.15	0.15-1.0
Goat	0.04-0.2	0.2-1.0
Miniature pig	0.01-0.07	0.07-1.0
Thoroughbred horse	0.01-0.07	0.07-0.6

Table 1. Frequency band determined to each animal species.

Species	HR (bpm)	LF ($msec^2$)	HF ($msec^2$)	LF/HF	References
Mouse	576	1.9	0.5	4.9	Ishii et al. (1996)
Vole	458	32	45	0.8	Ishii et al. (1996)
Rat	337	14.1	2.1	6.5	Kuwahara et al. (1994)
Guinea pig	244	6.0	1.7	4.0	Akita et al. (2002)
Miniature pig	92	1987	2924	1.0	Kuwahara et al. (1999)
Thoroughbred horse	33	1536	173	6.8	Kuwahara et al. (1996)

Table 2. The values of HRV obtained from each animal species.

6.2 Pathophysiological studies

In the previous section, I have shown the characteristics of power spectrum of HRV in various animal species. The HF component corresponding to the frequency of respiration and the LF component which seemed reflect the arterial blood pressure oscillations were observed in each animal species. From these results, we have suggested that these components could be used for assessment of cardiac autonomic outflow as utilized in human beings. Then, we have applied this method to pathophysiological studies in animals.

6.2.1 Animal models for diseases

Spontaneously hypertensive rats (SHR) have been extensively studied as a model of essential hypertension. Young SHR show an arterial blood pressure not different from that of their normotensive progenitors, the Wistar-Kyoto rats (WKY). The irreversible hypertension in the SHR occurs only at the more advanced age of 3 months. Therefore, we studied power spectral analysis of HRV throughout the developmental stages in the SHR and WKY, hypothesizing that an altered neural outflow may trigger hypertension in the SHR. As shown the results in Fig. 11, the HF power increased with age without significant difference between the two strains. Although the LF power tended to increase with age in both strains, the LF power in the SHR was significantly larger than that in the WKY after 6 weeks of age. The level of the LF/HF ratio in the SHR was almost twice that in the WKY after 3 weeks of age. Furthermore, at 6 weeks of age, systolic blood pressure became significantly higher in the SHR than in the age-matched WKY, and this significant difference between them persisted throughout the experimental period. These results suggest that the predominant sympathetic activity from prehypertensive stages may play an important role in the development of irreversible hypertension in the SHR (Kuwahara, et al., 1996).

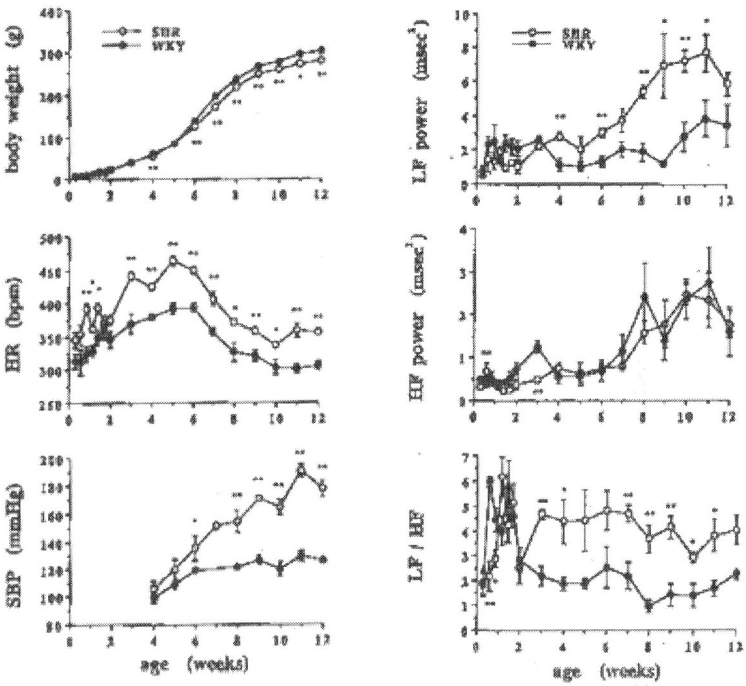

Fig. 11. Changes in body weight, heart rate (HR), systolic blood pressure (SBP), LF power, HF power, and LF/HF ratio in SHR and WKY during the developmental stages.

Asthma has been characterized by intermittent reversible airway obstruction, airway inflammation, and airway hyperresponsiveness. Asthma is also thought to be associated with abnormal autonomic nervous function, because there is markedly increased bronchial sensitivity to cholinergic and non-adrenergic non-cholinergic constrictors, and decreased sensitivity to β_2-adrenergic and non-adrenergic non-cholinergic dilators (Barnes, 1992). Bronchial-hypersensitive (BHS) and bronchial-hyposensitive (BHR) strain guinea pigs are spontaneous model animals of airway hyper- and hyposensitivity (Mikami, et al., 1991). We considered that these animal models might provide new insight into the regulatory roles of autonomic nervous function in asthma. As shown the results in Fig. 12, the autonomic nervous activity in BHS showed a daily pattern, although BHR did not show such rhythmicity. The HF power in BHS was higher than that in BHR throughout the day. The LF/HF ratio in BHS was lower than that in BHR throughout the day. These results suggest that parasympathetic nervous activity may be predominant in BHS (Akita, et al., 2004).

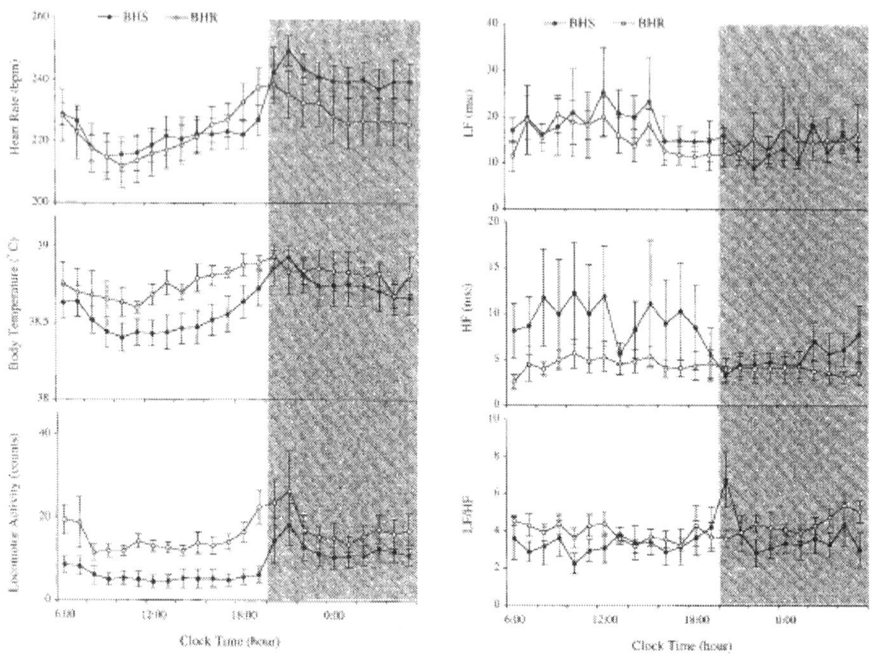

Fig. 12. Changes in hourly averaged values of heart rate, body temperature, locomotor activity, LF power, HF power, and LF/HF ratio in BHS and BHR.

The Zucker-fatty rat showing hyperphagia due to mutation of the leptin receptor gene is a well-established model of insulin resistance (Chau, et al., 1996; Phillips, et al., 1996). Plasma glucose and blood pressure in Zucker-fatty rats are relatively similar to those in Zucker-lean rats (Jermendy, et al., 1996; Pamidimukkala & Jandhyal, 1996). These characteristics show that the Zucker-fatty rat may be suitable for research on effects of insulin resistance on autonomic nervous function. Therefore, we conducted to clarify autonomic nervous function in these animal models. As shown the results in Fig. 13, heart rate in Zucker-fatty rats was lower than that in Zucker-lean rats, but there were no significant differences in the HF and LF power, and LF/HF ratio between Zucker-fatty and Zucker-lean rats. These results suggest that the autonomic nervous function of insulin-resistant Zucker-fatty rats remain normal from the aspect of power spectral analysis of HRV (Towa, et al., 2004).

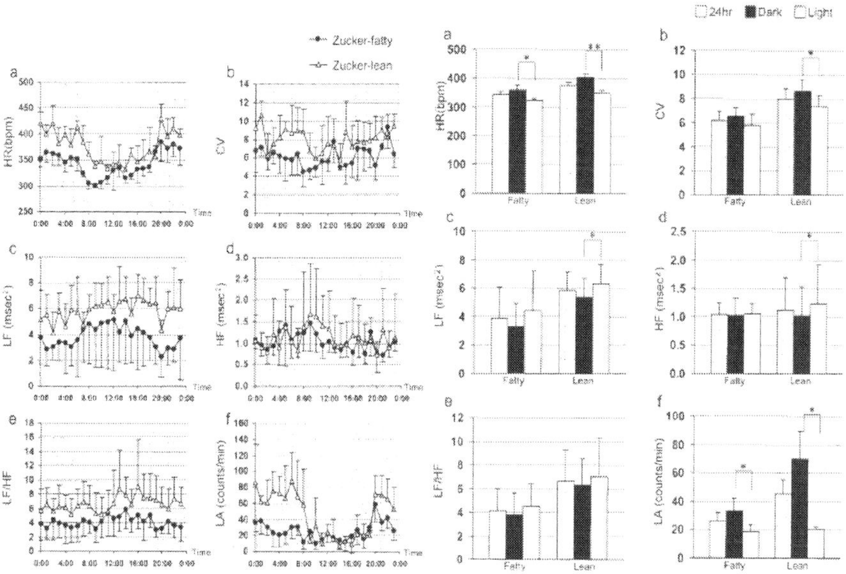

Fig. 13. Heart rate, coefficient variance (CO), LF power, HF power, LF/HF ratio, and locomotor activity (LA) of hourly averaged values (left) and averaged 24 hour, dark and light period (right) in Zucker-fatty and Zucker-lean rats.

6.2.2 Effects of drug and food

Various epidemiological reports indicate that consumption of foods rich in polyphenols is associated with lower incidence of cardiovascular diseases (Hertog, et al., 1993; Manach, et al., 2005). Cacao beans are consumed widely as cocoa or chocolate and are known to be rich in polyphenolic substances containing primarily procyanidins that are the oligomers of flavonoids (Porter, et al., 1991). Because the autonomic nervous system is an important regulatory mechanism for the cardiovascular function, we sought to determine the effect of cacao liquor polyphenol on the cardiovascular and autonomic nervous functions in an animal model of familial hypercholesterolaemia. Kurosawa and Kusanagi-hypercholesterolaemic rabbits exhibit hypercholesterolaemia from birth due to lack of low-density lipoprotein (LDL) receptors and spontaneously develop atherosclerosis (Kurosawa, et al., 1995). We hypothesize that cacao liquor polyphenols increase the depressed HRV and restore the cardiovascular function in the process of development of atherosclerosis in this animal model. After 6 months of dietary administration of cacao liquor polyphenols, heart rate (HR) and systolic blood pressure (SBP) were lowered (Table 3). The HF power in the control group was significantly decreased with aging, but that in the cacao liquor polyphenol group was not significantly different with aging. These results suggest that cacao liquor polyphenols may play an important role to protect cardiovascular and autonomic nervous functions (Akita, et al., 2008).

Group	HR (bpm)	SBP (mmHg)	LF(msec2)	HF(msec2)	LF/HF
5 months control	196.9	93.9	80.6	12.0	7.6
5 months cacao	197.7	85.7	88.2	9.8	14.0
10 months control	226.4	96.1	41.5	4.0	10.9
10 months cacao	185.2	75.9	51.0	5.0	9.9

Table 3. Effects of cacao liquor on cardiovascular and autonomic nervous functions.

Taurine is one of the most abundant free amino acids in animal tissues (Jacobsen, & Smith, 1968) and possesses many important physiological roles. Because antihypertensive action of taurine by suppression of sympathetic overactivity was reported (Sato, et al., 1987), we evaluated effects of taurine on cold-induced hypertension which is a prototypical model of environmentally induced hypertension. After the 7 days control period, both taurine (1%) administrated and control groups of rats were exposed a cold temperature. There were no differences in heart rate, blood pressure, but parasympathetic nervous function was somewhat predominant in taurine group before cold exposure. Heart rate and blood pressure in both groups increased greatly by cold exposure. Heart rate in taurine group was much higher than that in control group (Fig. 14). The LF and HF powers were decreased by cold exposure in both groups. Although no differences were observed in the LF power, decrease of the HF power in taurine group was greater than that in control group. The HF power was reduced, but the LF power of blood pressure variability (BP-LF; index of sympathetic nervous activity) was increased by onset of cold exposure. BP-LF and HF power were gradually increased in chronic stage of cold exposure. Almost the same responses in these parameters were observed between control and taurine groups except time course changes in onset or offset to cold exposure. These results suggest that taurine may provide some reservoir for cardiovascular and autonomic nervous functions to cold stress in rats (Kuwahara, et al., 2009).

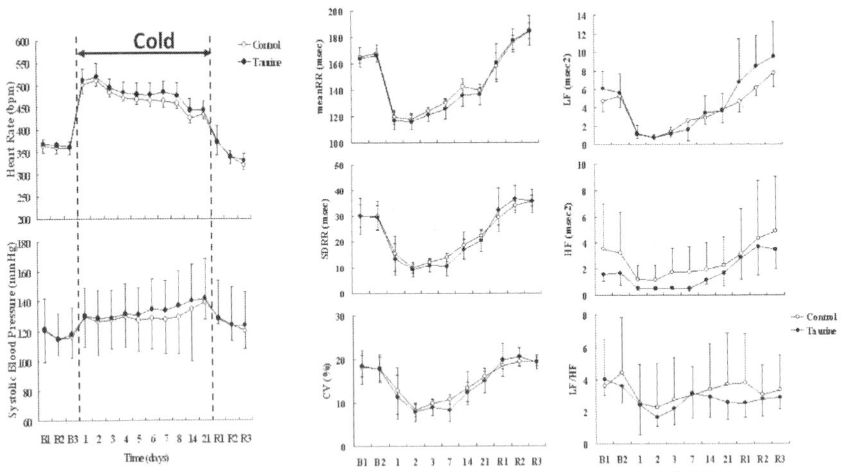

Fig. 14. Effects of taurine on heart rate, systolic blood pressure (left) and autonomic nervous function (middle and right) to cold exposure in rats.

6.2.3 Stress and psychological effects

Individual animal responses to acute and chronic stress are interesting in both experimental and industrial animals from the point of view of animal well-being. Breeding circumstances such as mixing are known to be accompanied by increased agonistic behaviour and may result in social stress (Muller, & Ladewig, 1989). Therefore, we investigated heart rate and autonomic nervous function in miniature swine to clarify the effects of pair housing of animals. As shown the results in Fig. 15, when two miniature swine were housed together, heart rate and the LF/HF were significantly increased throughout the day. Although these changed gradually recovered to basal levels, these parameters had not completely returned to basal levels even after 2 weeks. Heart rate and autonomic nervous activity returned to basal levels about 2 weeks after re-housing. These results suggest that it takes miniature swine at least 2 weeks to adapt to different circumstances. Furthermore, the power spectral analysis of HRV can be used as a useful method in a study for answering controversial issues related to stress response (Kuwahara, et al., 2004).

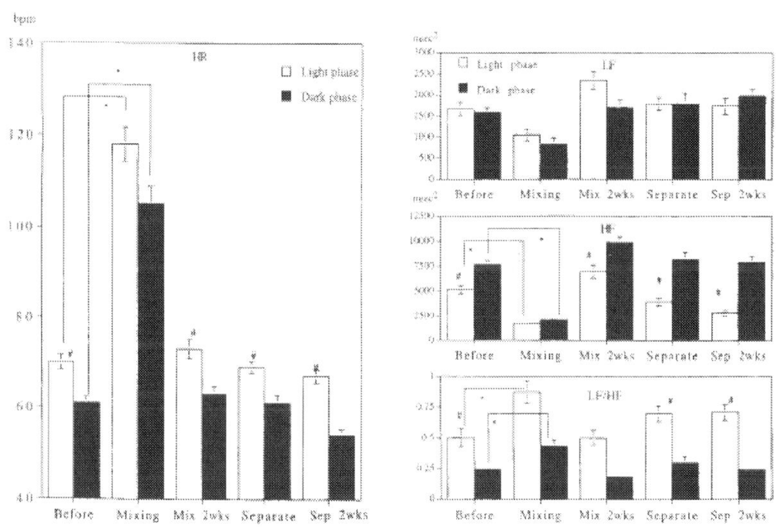

Fig. 15. Light and dark phase values of heart rate(left), LF power, HF power, and LF/HF ratio (right). Before mixing (Before), ont eh day of mixing (Mixing), 2 weeks after mixing (Mix 2wks), on the day of separation (Separate), 2 weeks after separation (Sep 2 wks).

Psychological stress is a risk factor increasing cardiovascular morbidity and mortality (Rosengren, et al., 1991; Ruberman, et al., 1984). The effects of psychological stress on electrical activity of the heart are largely mediated by the autonomic nervous system (Sgoifo, et al., 1997). We evoked anxiety-like or fear-like states in rats by means of classical conditioning and examined changes in autonomic nervous activity using a power spectral analysis of HRV. Anxiety-like states resulted in a significant increase in heart rate, LF power, and LF/HF ratio. Fear-like states resulted in a significant increase in heart rate and a significant decrease in HF power with no significant change in both LF power and LF/HF ratio. These results suggest that autonomic balance becomes predominant in sympathetic nervous activity in both anxiety-like and fear-like states. These changes in rats correspond to changes which are relevant to cardiovascular diseases under many kinds of psychological stress (Inagaki, et al., 2004).

6.2.4 Hypoxia and inflammation

Hypoxia induces a range of behavioural, cardiopulmonary, hormonal and neural responses. Although a small number of studies have investigated to hypoxia exposure in conscious rats, most have used anesthetized animals for short term hypoxia. Therefore, the time courses of changes in cardiovascular and autonomic nervous functions during acclimatization to hypoxia were studied in conscious rats. As shown the results in Fig. 16, the heart rate, HF power of HRV (HR-HF) and LF power of blood pressure variability (BP-LF) were significantly increased after 1 h of hypoxia. Both heart rate and the BP-LF decreased after this initial increase. On the first day of hypoxia, heart rate and BP-LF were significantly lower than those of the control rats. Subsequently, these values altered so that they were similar to the control after 14 days of hypoxia. These results suggest that a sequence of dynamic interactions between sympathetic and parasympathetic nervous activities might have important roles in the regulation cardiovascular function during acclimatization to hypoxia (Kawaguchi, et al., 2005).

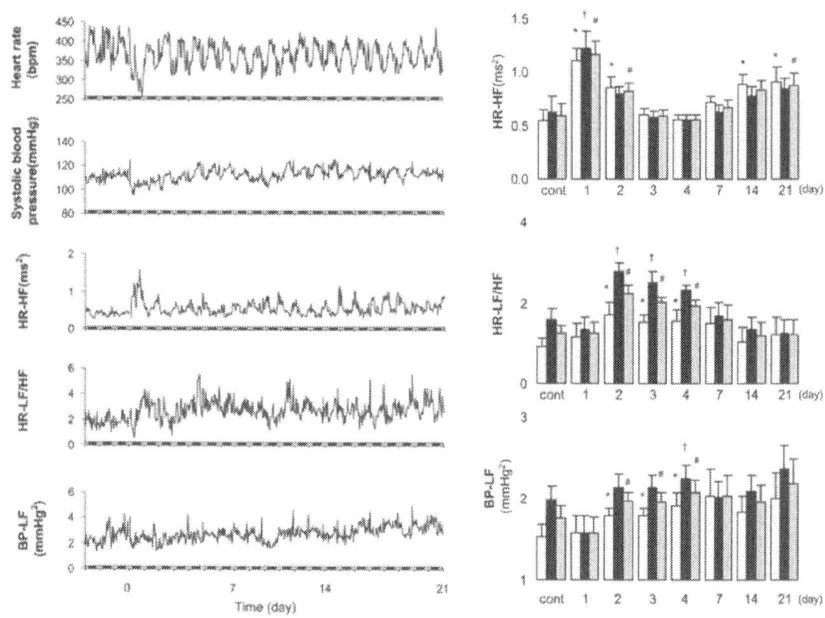

Fig. 16. Representative traces of cardiovascular and autonomic nervous function s during a 21-day period of hypoxia (left) and autonomic nervous function during acclimatization to hypoxia (right). Control data (Cont) were obtained in normoxic conditions from 2 days before hypoxic exposure. Open, solid and gray columns indicate the light, dark and overall periods, respectively.

A neural efferent vagus nerve-mediated mechanism, termed 'cholinergic anti-inflammatory pathway' (CAP), that can suppress the overproduction of pro-inflammatory cytokines such as TNF-α and IL-1β has been described (Borovikova, et al., 2000; Rosas-Ballina, & Tracey, 2009). CAP inhibits unrestrained inflammatory response and improves survival in variety of experimental lethal models. However, limited research has been done yet to examine the mechanisms of activating CAP on bio-behavioral changes. We hypothesize that stimulation of CAP may attenuate the endotoxin-induced septic changes in bio-behavioral function by not only reducing the production of the early proinflammatory cytokines but also maintaining autonomic nervous function as a neuroimmune interaction. Therefore, we evaluated bio-behavioral activity changes in biotelemetry rats to clarify pathophysiological mechanisms of CAP. Autonomic nervous activity was also analyzed by power spectral analysis of HRV. There were no remarkable changes on nicotine treatment in heart rate and autonocimc nervous activity before LPS administration (Fig. 17). Nicotine significantly

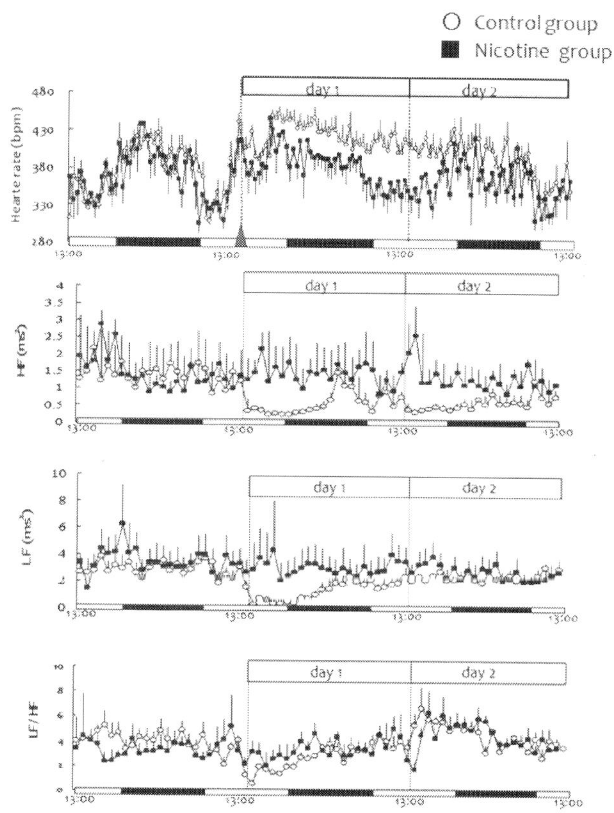

Fig. 17. Effect of nicotine (0.4 mg/kg, i.p.) on LPS (1.0mg/kg, i.p) -induced changes in heart rate, HF and LF power and LF/HF ratio. Arrow indicates LPS injiction point. Control group (open symbols) and nicotine-treated group (filled symbols).

improved survival in LPS-induced endotoxemia. Survival rates of the control and nicotine groups were 67% and 100%, respectively. Heart rate showed increases a few hours after LPS administration in the both control and nicotine groups. Although the elevated heart rate persisted for almost 2 days after LPS injection in the control group, heart rate returned to the baseline value and the diurnal variation was not affected in the nicotine group. The control group showed significant decrease in the HF and LF powers after LPS administration. Lower values of the HF power were continued more than one day. But in the nicotine group, autonomic nervous activity was not affected by LPS injection and index of these values were kept at the base line. Nicotine significantly attenuated LPS-induced changes in heart rate and autonomic nervous activity. These changes were accompanied by significant inhibition of TNF-α and IL-1β gene expression and protein synthesis. However the LPS-induced physiological responses persisted much longer than cytokine production. The plausible explanation is that autonomic nervous activity was lowered by LPS injection for a longer time. These results suggest that the efficacy of nicotine treatment in protecting autonomic nervous system seems likely to have a very important role especially after the acute phase of systemic inflammatory responses (Kojima, et al., 2011).

7. Conclusion

This chapter presents a newly developed telemetry system, analyzing software, and studies using these applications. The telemetry system has become commonly used tool to monitor many kinds of functions in the fields of physiology and pathophysiology as well as pharmacology and toxicology. Moreover, the power stectral analysis of HRV is useful to evaluate autonomic nervous functoin in nromal and disesed laboratory animals. Although further studies will be necesarry to clarify the mechanisms of pathgenesis of many diseases and the effects of many factors on bio-physiological functions of laboratry animals, these methods may become powerful tools to solve these problrems.

8. Acknowledgment

The author is grateful to Softron and Primetech corporation the dedicated supports and assistance for our studies.

9. References

Akita, M., Ishii, K., Kuwahara, M., & Tsubone, H. (2002). Power Spectral Analysis of Heart Rate Variability for Assessments of Diurnal Variation of Autonomic Nervous Activity in Guinea Pigs. Exp. Anim. 51(1): 1-7, 2002.

Akita, M., Kuwahara, M., Itoh, F., Nakano, Y., Osakabe, N., Kurosawa, T., & Tsubone, H. (2008). Effects of Cacao Liquor Polyphenols on Cardiovascular and Autonomic Nervous Functions in Hypercholesterolaemic Rabbits. Basic Clin. Pharmacol. Toxicol. 103(6): 581-587.

Akita, M., Kuwahara, M., Nishibata, R., Mikami, H., & Tsubone, H. (2004). The Daily Pattern of Heart Rate, Body Temperature, Locomotor Activity, and Autonomic Nervous Activity in Congenitally Bronchial-hypersensitive (BHS) and Bronchial-hyposensitive (BHR) Guinea Pigs. Exp. Anim. 53(2): 121-127.

Akselrod, S., Gordon, D., Ubel, F.A., Shannon, D.C., Berger, A.C., & Cohen, R.J. (1981) Power Spectrum Analysis of Heart Rate Fluctuation: a Quantitative Probe of Beat-to beat Cardiovascular Control. Science 213: 220-222.

Barnes, P.J. (1992). Neural Mechanisms in Asthma. Br. Med. Bull. 48: 149-168.

Barr, N.L. (1954). The Radio Transmision of Physiological Information. Milit. Surg. 114(2); 79-83.

Borovikova, L.V., Ivanova, S., Zhang, M., Yang, H., Botchkina, G.I., Watkins, L.R., Wang, H., Abumrad, N., Eaton, J.W., & Tracey, K.J. (2000). Vagus Nerve Stimulation Attenuates the Systemic Inflammatory Response to Endotoxin. Nature. 405:458-462.

Chau, N.P., Bauduceau, B., Chanudet, X., Larroque, P., & Gautier, D. (1994). Ambulatory Blood Pressure in Diabetic Subjects. Am. J. Hypertens. 7: 487-491.

Essler, W.O., & Folk, G.E., Jr. (1961). Determination of Physiological Rhythms of Unrestrained Animls by radio Telemetry. Nature 190: 90-91.

Franklin, D.L., Watson, N.W., & Van Citters, R.L. (1964). Blood Velocity Telemertered from Unththered Animals. Nature 203: 528-530.

Gold, D.C., & Malcolm, J.L. (1957). Action Potentials Recorded by Radio Transmission from the Cortex of Non-anaesthetized, Unrestrained, Cat. J. Physiol. 135: 5P.

Hertog, M.G., Feskens, E.J., Hollman, P.C., Katan, M.B., & Kromhout, D. (1993). Dietary Antioxidant Flavonoids and Risk of Coronary Heart Disease: the Zutphen Elderly Study. Lancet 342: 1007-1011.

Hirsch, & Bishop, (1981). Respiratory Sinus Arrythmia in Humans: How Breathing Patterns Modulate Heart Rate. Am. J. Physiol. 241: H620-H629.

Inagaki, H., Kuwahara, M., & Tsubone, H. (2004). Effects of Psychological Stress on Autonomic Control of Heart in Rats. Exp. Anim. 53(4): 373-378.

Ishii, K., Kuwahara, M., Tsubone, H., & Sugano, S. (1996). Autonomic Nervous Function in Mice and Voles (Microtus arvalis): Investigation by Power Spectral Analysis of Heart Rate Variability. Lab. Anim. 30(4): 359-364.

Jacobsen, J.G., & Smith, L.H. (1968). Biochemistry and Physiology of Taurine and Taurine Derivatives. Physiol Rev 48: 424-511.

Jermendy, G., Ferenczi, J., Hernandez, E., Farkas, K., & Nadas, J. (1996). Day-night Blood Pressure Variation in Normotensive and Hypertensive NIDDM Patients with Asymptomatic Autonomic Neuropathy. Diabetes Res. Clin. Pract. 34: 107-114.

Kawaguchi, T., Tsubone, H., Hori, M., Ozaki, H., & Kuwahara, M. (2005). Cardiovascular and Autonomic Nervous Functions during Acclimatization to Hypoxia in Conscious Rats. Auton. Neurosci.117(2): 97-104.

Kojima, H., Ito, K., Tsubone, H., & Kuwahara, M. (2011). Nicotine Treatment Reduces LPS-Induced Sickness Responses in Telemetry Monitoring Rats. J. Neuroimmunol. 234: 55-62.

Kurosawa, T., Kusanagi, M., Yamasaki, Y., Senga, Y., & Yamamoto, T. (1995). New Mutant Rabbit Strain with Hypercholesterolemia and Atherosclerotic Lesions produced by Serial Inbreeding. Lab. Anim. Sci. 45: 385-392.

Kuwahara, M., Hashimoto, S., Ishii, K., Yagi, Y., Hada, T., Hiraga, A., Kai, M., Kubo, K., Oki, H., Tsubone, H., & Sugano, S. (1996). Assessment of Autonomic Nervous Function by Power Spectral Analysis of Heart Rate Variability in the Horse. J. Auton. Nerv. Syst. 60: 43-48.

Kuwahara, M., Hashimoto, S., Tsubone, H., & Sugano, S. (1996). Developmental Changes of Autonomic Nervous Activity in Spontaneously Hypertensive Rats: Investigation by Power Spectral Analysis of Heart Rate Variability. J. Ambulatory Monitoring 9(1): 51-58.

Kuwahara, M., Kawaguchi, T., Ito, K., & Tsubone, H. (2009). Effects of Taurine on Cardiovascular and Autonomic Nervous Functions in Cold Exposed rats. Advances in Experimental Medicine and Biology 643: 533-540.

Kuwahara, M., Suzuki, A., Tsutsumi, H., Tanigawa, M., Tsubone, H., & Sugano, S. (1999). Power Spectral Analysis of Heart Rate Variability for Assessment of Diurnal Variation of Autonomic Nervous Activity in Miniature Swine. Lab. Anim. Sci.. 49(2): 202-208.

Kuwahara, M., Tsujino, Y., Tsubone, H., Kumagai, E., Tsutsumi, H., & Tanigawa, M. (2004). Effects of Pair Housing on Diurnal Rhythms of Heart Rate and Heart Rate Variability in Miniature Swine. Exp. Anim. 53(3): 303-309.

Kuwahara, M., Yayou, K., Ishii, K., Hashimoto, S., Tsubone, H., & Sugano, S. (1994). Power Spectral Analysis of Heart Rate Variability as a New Method for Assessing Autonomic Activity in the Rat. J. Electrocardiol. 27(4): 333-337.

Mackay, R.S. (1970). In: Biomedical Telemetry: Sensing and Transmitting Biological Information from Animals and Man. John Wiley and Sons, Inc., New York, USA.

Manach, C., Mazur, A., & Scalbert, A. (2005). Polyphenols and Prevention of Cardiovascular Diseases. Curr. Opin. Lipidol. 16: 77-84.

Mikami, H., Nishibata, R., Kawamoto, Y., & Ino, T. (1991). Selective Breeding of Two Lines of Guinea Pigs Differing in Bronchial Sensitivity to Acetylcholine and Histamine Exposure. Exp. Anim. 45: 195-202.

Muller, C., & Ladewig, J. (1989). Behavior and Heart Rate of Heifers Housed in Tether Stanchions without Straw. Phisiol Behav 46: 751-754.

Pamidimukala, J., & Jandhyala, B.S. (1996), Evaluation of Hemodynamics, Vascular Reactivity and Baroreceptor Compensation in the Insulin Resitant Zucker Obese Rats. Clin. Exp. Hypertens. 18: 1089-1104.

Phillips, M.S., Liu, Q., Hammond, H.A., Dugan, V., Hey, P.J, Caskey, C.J., & Hess, J.F. (1996). Leptin Receptor Missense Mutation in the Fatty Zucker rat. Nat. Genet. 13: 18-19.

Porter, L.J., Ma, Z., & Cgan, B.G. (1991). Cacao Procyanidins: Major Flavonoids and Identification of Some Minor Metabolites. Phytochamistry 30: 1657-1663.

Rosas-Ballina, M., & Tracey, K.J. (2009). Cholinergic Control of Inflammation. *J. Internal Med.* 265:663-679.

Rosengren, A., Tibblin, G., & Wilhelmsen, L. (1991). Self-perceived Psychological Stress and Incidence of Coronary Artery Disease in Middle-aged Men. Am. J. Cardiol. 68; 1171-1175.

Ruberman, W., Weinblatt, E., & Goldberg, J.D. (1984). Psychosocial Influences on Mortality After Myocardial Infarction. N. Eng. J. Med. 311; 552-559.

Sato, Y., Ando, K., & Fujita, T. (1987). Role of Sympathetic Nervous System in Hypotensive Action of Taurine in DOCA-salt Rats. Hypertension 9: 81-87.

Scher, A.M. (1977). Carotid and Aortic Regulation of Arterial Blood Pressure. Circulation 56: 521-528.

Sgoifo, A., de Boer, S.F., Westenbroek, C., Maes, F.W., Beldhuis, H., Suzuki, T., & Koolhaas, J.M. (1997). Incidence of Arrhythmias and Heart Rate Variability in Wild-type Rats Exposed to Social Stress. Am. J. Physiol. 273; H1754-H1760.

Task Rorce of the Euroopean Society of Cardiology and the North Amirican Society of Pacing and Electrophysiology. (1996). Heart Rate Variability: Standards of Measurement, Physiological Interpretation, and Clinical Use. Circulation 93: 1043-1065.

Towa, S., Kuwahara, M., & Tsubone, H. (2004). Characteristics of Autonomic Nervous Function in Zucker-fatty Rats: Investigation by Power Spectral Analysis of Heart Rate Variability. Exp. Anim. 53(2): 137-144, 2004.

8

Advances in Management of Poultry Production Using Biotelemetry

Takoi K. Hamrita and Matthew Paulishen
University of Georgia
USA

1. Introduction

In this chapter, the authors review recent developments in the use of biotelemetry in poultry production. The chapter begins with an overview of advancements in biotelemetry and outlines the types of equipment that are commercially available as well as those adapted and developed by researchers primarily for use in farm animals. The authors then highlight the significant milestones achieved by the scientific community in using biotelemetry towards a more holistic poultry production guided by birds' physiological responses to environmental stressors. In particular, the authors discuss efforts at the University of Georgia towards building the next generation closed-loop poultry environmental controller which responds directly and in real-time to physiological needs of the birds.

Biotelemetry is defined as the remote detection and measurement of physiological, bioelectrical, and behavioral variables to monitor function, activity, or condition of conscious unrestrained humans or animals. This encompasses a broad range of techniques of varying invasiveness including video monitoring, non-contact thermometry, radio tracking and the use of internally or externally mounted remote sampling systems (Morton et al., 2003). Biotelemetry is not a new concept and it was first introduced by Einthoven in 1903 when he measured the electrocardiogram using immersion electrodes remotely connected to a galvanometer via telephone lines (Cromwell et al., 1973, as cited in Hamrita et al., 1998). In later years, NASA played a big role in the advancement of biotelemetry by using it to transmit astronaut biomedical data such as heart rate and body temperature to earth. In (N. F. Güler & Übeyli, 2002), the authors provide a detailed history of early uses and developments of biotelemetry.

Biotelemetry consists of sensing the variable of interest from the animal using miniature sensors or transducers. These can be placed on the animal, ingested by the animal, or implanted inside the animal by means of injection or surgery. The output of the sensor or transducer is modulated to a form which can be transmitted wirelessly over a distance from the animal to a receiver using an embedded transmitter. The received signal is demodulated and the measured variable extracted through proper signal conditioning and calibration by the data acquisition system. Biotelemetry data has been transmitted through every medium including air, vacuum, water, and biologic tissue using a variety of modulating carriers such as electromagnetic waves (especially at radiofrequency- hence the name radiotelemetry), light, and ultrasound (N. F. Güler & Übeyli, 2002). By far the most common carriers of biotelemetry data are radio waves. Due to the proliferation of biotelemetry in recent years, the Federal

Communications Commission (FCC) has allocated dedicated frequency bands for biotelemetry use in the VHF range, generally over 100 MHz. Typically variables that have been monitored through biotelemetry fall in four categories: (1) Bioelectrical such as ECG, EMG, and EEG; (2) physiological such as blood pressure, blood flow, and temperature; (3) behavioral such as activity levels; and (4) chemical such as pH.

Through biotelemetry, it is possible to continuously monitor multiple physiological variables without handling or restraining the animal and attaching it to wires and probes. This reduces stress and physiological disturbance of animals by removing the influence of the measurement procedure and thereby improving the quality of data. This also allows for unattended operation reducing labor. Also, animals instrumented with implanted telemetry are free of infections that result from exteriorized catheters and lead wires (N. F. Güler & Übeyli, 2002). Biotelemetry provides the opportunity to increase the frequency of observation or continuously monitor multiple variables over extended periods of time therefore significantly increasing access to larger amounts of physiological data. Additionally, biotelemetry makes possible real-time processing of collected data and the ability to act on it. Knowing how key parameters are changing in real-time in animals allows, for instance, faster adjustment of feeding times to activity rhythms, more objective identification of the preference/tolerance margins towards environmental variables and precise assessment of the impact of environmental or operational changes (Baras & Lagardère, 1995). Lastly, biotelemetry reduces bias and observation influence, therefore contributing to more accurate measurements (Eigenberg et al., 2008). These characteristics of biotelemetry have improved a wide range of applications and enabled new possibilities that were previously unimaginable.

It is however worth mentioning that telemetry can cause suffering to animals in the short and long term if appropriate procedures and refinements are not implemented. In (Morton et al., 2003), the authors state that telemetry is often presented as a refinement, in that it can reduce or eliminate stress caused to animals but like all other procedures on animals, it also needs to be refined. They indicate that the impact of telemetry on animals in practice depends on whether or not surgery is used; the devices used; whether the technique restricts the subjects' abilities to express a range of desirable behaviors; and whether ways of refining both procedures and husbandry were fully researched. The authors provide a 40-page report detailing ways to refine both husbandry and procedures in telemetry applications to minimize suffering and improve welfare of animals. Similarly in (Hawkins et al., 2004), the authors detail husbandry refinements for telemetry procedures.

2. Biotelemetry systems

In this section, we describe the basic principles of biotelemetry systems and survey existing systems which are available for physiological monitoring. The discussion will include both commercially available systems as well as those developed by researchers. The review of commercially available systems is restricted to those used for livestock animals.

A typical biotelemetry system consists of the following components: (1) transmitter, (2) receiver/decoder, and (3) data acquisition unit. The sensor and the transmitter are usually combined into one unit which is implanted in or ingested by the animal. The transducer detects the physiological variable and converts it into a form which can modulate the signal from the transmitter. An antenna at the receiving end is necessary for proper recovery of the transmitted signal. The main role of the receiver is to decode or demodulate the signal, i.e.

convert it to the original signal being measured. Dedicated multichannel programmable receivers with computer interfacing capabilities are now commercially available. Some of these receivers could accommodate as many as 100 transmitters at different carrier frequencies. The data acquisition system turns the received signal into measurements of the variable being monitored based on the calibration information provided by the user. The data acquisition system is usually interfaced with a computer to provide a user-friendly interface which facilitates control of the measurements as well as storage of the collected data (Hamrita et al., 1997). In earlier stages of biotelemetry, researchers used data loggers mounted on animals (Hahn et al., 1990, Feddes & Deshazer, 1993, Harris et al., 2001, and Eigenberg et al., 2002, all as cited in Lowe et al., 2007) to record and store the collected data (Lowe et al., 2007). More recently, most systems use remote data transmission (Gedir, 2001, as cited in Lowe et al., 2007; Lacey et al., 2000a; Brown-Brandl et al., 2003; Silva et al., 2005). In some applications, researchers have mixed data logging in the implant as well as transmission to a data acquisition system (Lowe et al., 2007).

Modulation methods used most in biotelemetry systems include frequency modulation (FM) where frequency of the carrier varies proportionally to the signal being transmitted; amplitude modulation (AM) where amplitude of the carrier varies proportionally to the signal; and pulse modulation where the carrier is a series of pulses. There are several types of pulse modulation techniques including pulse amplitude modulation (PAM) where the amplitude of the pulse varies proportionally, pulse width modulation (PWM) where the pulse width varies proportionally to the signal, and pulse-interval modulation (PIM) where the carrier signal is turned on and off at a rate that is proportional to the variable being transmitted.

Proper signal amplification within the transmitter unit is performed and, depending on the transmission media, may include a miniature "coil" or "whip" antenna for radio communications, an LED for infrared or visible light communications, or an ultrasonic transducer for acoustic communications. When multiple transmitters are used, each transmitter sends its output signal at a different carrier frequency so that outputs of different transmitters are not mixed. However, it is common to measure multiple variables within the same transmitter and have each variable modulate the carrier frequency differently. In the case of AM and FM modulation, this is called frequency multiplexing. In the case of pulse modulation, this is called time multiplexing (N. F. Güler & Übeyli, 2002). Using a light carrier has been shown to provide high bandwidth communication, and is relatively more immunity from interference (Ackermann et al., 2006).

In biotelemetry systems, long operational life of the wireless sensor unit is an essential requirement. These systems have typically been powered using either batteries embedded inside the transmitter units or through external power sources. External powering of biotelemetry sensors includes RF power from a base unit and inductive powering based on magnetic coupling (Ko et al., 1977, de N. Donaldson & Perkins, 1983, Vanschuylenbergh & Puers, 1996, and Jeutter, 1983, all as cited in N. F. Güler & Übeyli, 2002). For sensor units powered using internal batteries, the size of the device often constrains both the operational life and the transmission range. For a given chemistry, there is a generally proportional relationship between battery size and energy storage capacity, so that smaller sized batteries have shorter useful lives in a given device. Concerning RF transmitters, the useable range often shrinks with the size of the transmitter due to decreased space for signal amplification circuitry and efficient antennae. In addition, the power consumption of the device tends to increase proportionally with the intended transmission range, the sensor sampling frequency, and the data transmission rate. To prolong the life of the battery in an implanted biotelemetry system, some researchers have experimented with remote power switching (Varosi et al., 1989, as cited in Hamrita et al., 1998; Leung et al, 1986, as cited in N. F. Güler & Übeyli, 2002).

In order to select the best transmitter for a given application, all the factors discussed above have to be taken into consideration and sometimes compromises must be made. For more in-depth reviews and overviews of biotelemetry systems, the reader is referred to the following sources (Hamrita et al., 1997; Akyildiz et al., 2002; Budinger, 2003; Güler, N. F. & Übeyli, 2002; Hawkins et al., 2004; Luong et al., 2008; Morton et al., 2003; Ruiz-Garcia et al., 2009; Strydis, 2005; Wang et al., 2006; Wathes et al., 2008).

A variety of biotelemetry equipment is available for detecting, monitoring, and storing various variables. Some of these systems are designed to be implanted inside the animal, others are to be ingested by the animal, and others are to be attached to the animal. Some are widely used in human medicine, while others are currently intended solely for animals. The transmitters in these biotelemetry systems vary in size, resolution, range, communication links, sampling rate, number of channels, number of sensors per transmitter, and power consumption. They may consist of many different types of sensors such as temperature, biopotential, and acoustic monitoring, and visible and infrared imaging, which are able to monitor a wide variety of electrical, physiological, chemical, and behavioral conditions. The table below provides a survey of commercially available systems. Note that the communication link used in all these systems is based on radio frequency.

2.1 Commercial biotelemetry systems

Manufacturer	Implantable/ Ingestible/ Attachable	Intended subject	Sensor types	Number of sensors per transmitter	Power requirements/ battery life	Data transmission range
HQ Inc. formerly HTI Technologies	Ingestible	Capsule for human ingestion	Temperature	1	Integrated battery with unknown life	Short range
Remo Technologies Limited	Implantable (some attachable)	Small modules (can be less than 10 grams or even sub-gram)	EEG, ECG, EMG, skin temperature, limb angle, acceleration	Up to 3 biopotential channels plus temperature with some models supporting additional channels	Integrated battery with multiple month life	300 mm
DSI (Data Sciences International)	Implantable	Mouse to large animal	EEG, ECG, EMG, temperature, pressure, activity	Up to 4 biopotential channels plus integrated temperature, pressure, and activity sensors	Integrated batteries with lives from 1.5 to 12 months (some models with replaceable batteries)	-
Telonics	Attachable collars	Birds to elephants	Location with some models offering GPS, ambient temperature, and mortality sensing	Varies with models	Integrated batteries with up to multi-year lives depending on transmission schedule	Long range (many miles)

Table 1a. Commercial Biotelemetry Equipment Providers

Manufacturer	Implantable/ Ingestible/ Attachable	Intended subject	Sensor types	Number of sensors per transmitter	Power requirements/ battery life	Data transmission range
AVM Instrument Company	Implantable and Attachable (collars, ear tags, and glue-on modules)	Hissing cockroaches to tortoises and elk	Location with some models offering temperature, activity, mortality sensing, and sleep/end of hibernation sensing	Varies with model	Integrated batteries with lives from 2 days to 7 years	Long range (many miles)
Mini Mitter	Implantable transponder	Mice to humans	Heart rate, temperature, and gross motor activity depending on model	Up to 3	Passive transponder powered by receiver and only active when in proximity to receiver/ logger	Very short range (12 cm)
Telemetry Research	Implantable	Animals 200 grams and over	Pressure and/or biopotential channels	Up to 3	Integrated batteries - rechargeable in-situ by inductive charger	Up to 5 meters
emka Technologies	Implantable devices and Attachable collars	Animals 200 grams and over	EEG, ECG, EMG, temperature, activity, respiration, sympathetic nerve activity, pressure (implanted and non-invasive versions)	Up to 8 for emkaPack and up to 2 for implantable devices	emkaPack uses two replaceable AA/R6 alkaline batteries for up to 80 hours of use	Up to 5 meters
BlueBox Sensors	Implantable sensors	-	Oxygen, Nitric Oxide, and glucose	-	-	-
Advanced Telemetry Systems	Implantable and Attachable (collars, ear tags, and glue-on modules)	Many sizes and species	Location with some models offering GPS, temperature, activity, and mortality sensing	Varies with model	Integrated battery (months to years depending on pulse rate of transmitter)	Long range (many miles)
TSE Systems	Implantable and Attachable	All sizes of lab animals up to human	ECG, EEG, EMG, EOG, temperature, activity, etc.	Up to 4	-	-

Table 1b. Commercial Biotelemetry Equipment Providers

2.2 Biotelemetry systems developed by researchers

Although there is a wide variety of commercially available biotelemetry equipment, many researchers from various fields have had to design and develop their own biotelemetry systems in an attempt to improve on existing commercially developed ones (I. Güler & Kara, 1996; Wouters et al, 1994, and Kettlewell et al, 1997, as cited in Strydis, 2005; Ackermann et al., 2006; Silva et al., 2005) or to meet specific monitoring needs (Lowe et al., 2007; Quwaider et al, 2010; Cross et al., 2004). In some cases, circuitry is added to give more intelligence to the sensor itself (Puers, 1999; Wouters et al, 1994, as cited in Strydis, 2005). It is also common for researchers to adapt commercially available systems for their applications. For instance in (Eigenberg et al., 2008), the authors adapted a biomedical temperature measurement system for animal use.

In (I. Güler & Kara, 1996), the authors designed and implemented a novel biotelemetry system for biomedical applications which is based on digital data processing and transmission as opposed to existing systems which rely on analog data transmission. The motivation behind this design was to provide high noise immunity and better synchronization between the transmitters and the receiver. The transmitter digitizes analog physiological signals, converts them into serial form and transmits them via an FM transmitter. The receiver amplifies and pulse-shapes the received data, converts it into 8-bit parallel form and then into analog signal. The system showed a stable and high performance within a distance of 100 m.

In (Lowe et al., 2007), the authors designed, built and tested a dual mode telemetric logging system to monitor, transmit and record physiological waveforms (electrocardiogram (ECG), electroencephalogram (EEG) and respiration) from farm animals during commercial transport and slaughter. The system combined telemetry with a logging device, small enough to be mounted on a variety of species including poultry. The motivation behind this design is that in some situations where no reliable radio link could be established, the telemetry system is capable of logging several minutes of data. The developed system had a radio communication range of several meters.

In (Quwaider et al., 2010), the authors designed and developed a novel wireless body-mounted sensor to remotely monitor the location and activity of unrestrained laying hens. In the study, laying hens were fitted with a lightweight (10 g) wireless body-mounted sensor to monitor their location in space relative to key resources and general level of physical activity. Sensor data were validated by correlating them to video-based observations of the sensor-wearing hen.

In (Cross et al., 2004), the authors presented the design of an automated biotelemetry based vaginal controlled release drug delivery system for cows. The intravaginally located device is a low-invasive platform that detects estrus while providing external control of variable drug delivery. The device consists of off the shelf components and allows for monitoring of temperature, pressure, activity, and light intensity. A two-way radio link allows communication with a base station.

In (Wouters et al, 1994, as cited in Strydis, 2005), the authors implemented a complex design to address the need for reliable injectable telemetry sensor systems for large-scale animal husbandry applications featuring extreme miniaturization and ultra-low power consumption as well as increased flexibility, versatility and intelligence. The authors achieved increased intelligence and multi-purpose use of implantable transponders by using a combination of software (through a miniature off-the-shelf microprocessor (MP)) and hardware through a customized generic Sensor Interface Chip (SIC). To conserve power, the authors have the microprocessor operate in a sleep mode most of the time except when data is being collected. The SIC includes a battery check circuit which monitors the voltage-level of the battery and creates an alert if this level is lower than a specific user defined level. The system has the capability of storing data on the on-chip memory or sending it remotely to the receiver. Additionally, through several commands the user can fine-tune sensor and battery operation. The authors in (Puers, 1999) conducted a study dealing with the merits of such an approach. The author in (Strydis, 2005) conducted a more in depth review of this study which was used as a basis for our brief review.

In (Ackermann et al., 2006), the authors addressed the need in some biotelemetry applications for high bandwidth communication. For example, transmitting 100 channels of neural waveform data for a cortical prosthetic control system may require up to 40 Mbps for a 100-channel array. Other applications may also require high rate transcutaneous data transfer, including cochlear implants, visual prosthetics and cortical stimulation sensory prosthetics. The authors considered various high rate transcutaneous data transmission methods such as the use of percutaneous wires, acoustic energy, and RF, but they opted for the use of optical telemetry for three reasons. According to them: (1) Optical telemetry is a mature, well-established technology: fiber-optic and free-air optical communication systems are common in consumer goods and are quite well understood. (2) The optical portion of the EM spectrum is unregulated worldwide for communications purposes, and interference from other sources can be made insignificant. (3) Feasibility of high rate optical transcutaneous data transfer has been established and used for several biomedical applications such as in neuromuscular stimulators (Taylor et al., 2002 [5], as cited in Ackermann et al., 2006), artificial hearts or implanted cardiac assist devices (Mitamura et al., 1990 [6], Miller et al., 1992[7], and Inoue et al., 1998 [8], all as cited in Ackermann et al., 2006), bladder stimulators (Sawan et al., 1997 [9], as cited in Ackermann et al., 2006), laboratory animal monitoring systems (Kudo et al., 1988 [10], as cited in Ackermann et al., 2006), and neural recording systems (Goto & Nakagawa, 2002 [11]; and Larson, 1999 [12], as cited in Ackermann et al., 2006).

In (Kettlewell et al., 1997, as cited in Strydis, 2005), the authors devised a multichannel, radiotelemetry system for continuous monitoring of ECG, deep-body temperature and respiratory movements. Preliminary tests of a prototype device have been performed in poultry. In designing this system, the authors gave active consideration to package size and weight, robust construction, large transmission range and low power consumption. Also, the authors actively sought to deliver a device compliant with regulations and specifications defined by the Department of Trade and Industry (DTI, UK). The implantable transmitter is not an integrated chip and/or micro-machined device, but rather a package of individual components. The signal from the respiratory sensor is superimposed upon the temperature signal by amplitude modulation and, then, mixed with the ECG signal. Superimposed, analog data from three channels are FM modulated and transmitted from the telemetry implant to an external system for further handling. The author in (Strydis, 2005) conducted a more in depth review of this study which was used as a basis for our brief review.

In (Bae et al., 2008), the authors designed and built a radio receiver to monitor pulse signals from multiple temperature transmitters. The receiver provides serial communication and analog voltage output and is optimized for real-time monitoring and control based on temperature telemetry sensors. Calibration of the radio receiver with commercial temperature transmitters provided an accuracy within ±0.1°C.

In recent years, some researchers in the biotelemetry field have experimented with wireless sensor networks. Sensor networks offer various advantages over using individual sensors (Silva et al., 2005): (1) Sensor networks greatly improve the accuracy of information obtained from collaboration among sensor nodes and real-time information processing at those nodes (Min, R. et al., 2002, as cited in Silva et al., 2005); (2) distributed data processing in these networks has the potential of improving the accuracy of vast quantities of sensing information (Asada et al., 2000, as cited in Silva et al., 2005); (3) through sensor networks, data can be integrated to provide a rich, multi-dimensional view of the system monitored; (4) sensor networks function accurately when an individual sensor fails making them more robust and reliable. In (Silva et al., 2005), the authors developed a wireless sensor network prototype to monitor physiological responses of livestock. The system uses a novel low-cost wireless communication protocol named Wireless Floating Base Sensor Network (FBSN) protocol. The sensor implant measures physiological responses from digital sensors, digitalizes data, and transmits it to the base module. The base module in turn, using an FBSN protocol, controls data collection from different animal modules and stores the data. The equipment was validated through an experiment to monitor bovine brain electrical activity in six free moving animals although the system was designed with the ability to monitor other physiological responses in any number of animals.

3. Use of biotelemetry in poultry production research

Poultry production has changed radically from the traditional flock running loose in the farmyard to a system where the majority of production is carried out in large confined facilities. Animals that are grown indoors are more susceptible to stress and diseases. Environmental stresses cause substantial economic losses due to increased mortality, downgrading and condemnations of carcasses and associated problems of environmental pollution, reduced production, reduced feed intake and body weight gain, and impaired immune function (Payne, 1966, as cited in Green & Xin, 2009; Mader et al., 2002, Brown-Brandl et al., 2003, and Hahn, 1999a, 1999b, all as cited in Silva et al., 2005). Poultry researchers and ultimately poultry growers need to understand how the birds respond to environmental stressors to make improved management decisions. Externally noticeable responses to environmental stressors are usually preceded by internal physiological responses, such as a change in body core temperature and/or heart rate, which often provide the first stress indicators. These physiological responses, if measured properly, are the ultimate indicators of stress and they allow us to detect stress at much earlier stages. Technological advances in biotelemetry have fueled the notion among researchers that management of poultry production could be significantly improved through real-time physiological monitoring of the birds. Hence, during the last ten years or so, biotelemetry has been successfully used in a wide range of research pertaining to poultry production. This section highlights some of this research through various examples. In particular, we highlight efforts at the University of Georgia towards building the next generation closed-loop poultry environmental controller which responds directly and in real-time to physiological responses of the birds.

3.1 Biotelemetry validation studies in poultry

Many poultry biotelemetry studies were aimed at validating new commercially available telemetry systems and measurement techniques, and have clearly demonstrated their effectiveness for accurate continuous monitoring of poultry physiology. The majority of these studies were concerned with monitoring of temperature.

In (Brown-Brandl et al., 2003), the authors conducted a comparative evaluation of a telemetry-based deep body temperature measurement system (HQ, Inc., West Palmetto, Fla.) for use in poultry research as well as research involving livestock. Three independent laboratories conducted the evaluation. For poultry, the deep body temperature measurements sensors were of the ingestible type allowing for short-term monitoring. The authors developed and used computational algorithms to filter out spurious data. After careful consideration, the authors concluded that due to the cost of the system, the surgeries involved (in some applications), and the need for data filtering, careful consideration has to be given to ensure that telemetry is the proper method for the experiment.

In (Hamrita et al., 1997), the authors evaluated the use of a biotelemetry system (Mini Mitter, Bend, Oregon; Telonics, Inc, Mesa, Arizona) with implanted transmitters in measuring deep body temperature of poultry under various ambient temperature conditions. The sensors successfully detected body temperature variations due to diurnal rhythm, as well as noticeable responses in deep body temperature to step changes in ambient temperature.

In (van den Brand & van de Belt, 2006), the authors validated the use of a biotelemetry temperature monitoring system in a chicken embryo. In this preliminary study, the authors determined the impact of the implanted temperature transponder on embryo mortality as well as the optimal location (air cell, albumen, or yolk) and day of implantation in the egg. The authors determined that implantation of telemetric temperature transponders in eggs is possible, but not at all sites and all days of incubation.

In (Lacey et al., 2000a), the authors used a telemetric deep body temperature measurement system to measure deep body temperature of poultry under various ambient temperature and relative humidity conditions. Results showed that the measured responses were consistent among all birds, significantly different for the different environmental conditions, and a change in response from one set of conditions to the other was clearly attributed to the change in ambient conditions and not to fluctuations in the measurement system or in between bird variation.

3.2 Poultry stress studies using biotelemetry

Many studies were concerned with monitoring and evaluating physiological and behavioral responses of poultry under various stressful environmental stimuli and management conditions to (1) gain a better understanding of poultry thermoregulatory responses; (2) improve management practices; and (3) evaluate the effectiveness of various environmental conditions. The most studied environmental variable is temperature with a few studies focusing on humidity and air velocity. Poultry response variables that have been examined include deep body temperature (Kettlewell et al., 1997; Hamrita et al., 1998; Lacey et al., 2000a, 2000b; Mitchell et al., 2001, as cited in Silva et al., 2005; Brown-Brandl et al., 2001, as cited in Wang et al., 2006; Blanchard et al., 2002; Yanagi et al., 2002a, 2002b; Brown-Brandl et al., 2003, Tao & Xin, 2003a, 2003b; Crowther et al., 2003; Khalil et al., 2004; van den Brand & van de Belt, 2006; Hamrita & Hoffacker, 2008; Leterrier et al., 2009); brain and heart activity (Blanchard et al., 2002; Crowther et al., 2003; Aubert et al., 2004; Khalil et al., 2004; Lowe et al., 2007; von Borell et al., 2007; Coenen et al., 2009); and physical activity (Khalil et al., 2004; Quwaider et al., 2010). The majority of studies were concerned with deep body temperature responses to heat stress. Heat stress results from the inability of birds to thermoregulate and maintain homeostasis under elevated ambient temperatures and humidity (Green & Xin, 2009).

In (Leterrier et al., 2009), the authors used biotelemetry to monitor and evaluate poultry deep body temperature responses to various treatments of stressful room temperature conditions. The purpose of the study was to investigate the effects of prior exposure to high temperatures on the birds' acclamation to heat stress. The authors experimented with exposing birds to heat stress at various stages in their lives and used both deep body temperature and observations of panting behavior to assess their state. Telemetry sensors were implanted in the body cavity.

In (Hamrita et al., 1997), the authors investigated poultry deep body temperature responses to stressful changes in ambient temperature. The experiment proved that noticeable changes in deep body temperature occurred under heat stress conditions. In (van den Brand & van de Belt, 2006), the authors were concerned with monitoring temperature of chicken embryo under natural brooding conditions in an effort to determine artificial incubation conditions.

In recent years, heart rate and heart rate variability have been increasingly used in animal research to study disease, stress, characteristics, and welfare of animals. In (von Borell et al., 2007), the authors provide an excellent comprehensive review of the use of heart rate monitoring in farm animal studies. This study was commissioned by the "measuring welfare" working group of the EU whose concerted action on 'Measuring and Monitoring Welfare' (COST Action 846) has identified heart rate as a key research area with the potential to "contribute to our understanding and interpretation of stress and welfare status in farm animals". Their "Heart Rate and Heart Rate Variability Task Force" conducted the study in which they outlined the appropriate methodologies for heart rate monitoring and analysis in different species, and identified areas of future research. They determined that for poultry (and avian in general), monitoring and analysis of heart rate has been used in very few studies. This scarcity is attributed to the difficulty of obtaining high quality data and the lack of fundamental research to evaluate the physiological meaning of heart rate variability indices. They cite a few heart rate studies focused on the development of cardiac rhythms (Pearson et al., 1998 [210], Moriya et al., 1999 [211], 2000 [212], 2002 [213], and Tazawa et al., 2002 [214, 215], all as cited in von Borrell et al., 2007); a study used to better understand the relationship between coping style and feather pecking (Korte et al., 1999 [29], as cited in von Borell et al., 2007); an other study to show that exposure to high levels of carbon dioxide in 2-week old broilers increases the incidence of cardiac arrhythmias (Korte et al., 1999 [218], as cited in von Borell et al., 2007); and a study in quail to understand how they respond to emotional stress (Gaudinière et al., 2005 [220], as cited in von Borell et al., 2007).

In (Crowther et al., 2003), the authors evaluated the use of heart rate and skin temperature as indicators of stress in ostriches during night transportation. Literature has identified a number of stressors that have negative impacts on the welfare of ostriches during transportation such as vibration and movement, heat stress, and dehydration and suggested that ostrich welfare during transit might be improved by using darkened vehicles. Comparisons were made between transportation during the day and at night. Statistical tests suggested that heart rate and skin temperature measurements recorded during the night were lower than those recorded during the day. The conclusion was drawn that transporting ostriches at night is potentially beneficial for the reduction of stress and maintenance of welfare.

In (Aubert et al., 2004), the authors monitored heart rate and heart rate variability of poultry embryos at the end of incubation to test the hypothesis that autonomic nervous cardiac modulation is present at the end of development.

In (Quwaider et al., 2010), the authors used a wireless accelerometer-based body-mounted sensor to remotely monitor the location and activity of unrestrained laying hens to enable care givers to visually assess the health, welfare, or movement of hens or to follow a particular hen over time. Sensor data concerning hen's proximity to specific resources such as nest boxes, perches, water, and feeders were validated by correlating them to video-based observations of the sensor-wearing hen. An 84% overall agreement between sensor data and video data was consistently obtained.

In (Coenen et al., 2009), evaluated the welfare implications of euthanizing broilers with three gas mixtures in commercial application of controlled atmosphere stunning. Free moving birds were instrumented with electrodes to measure brain activity (electroencephalogram, EEG) and heart rate. These signals were recorded using a custom-built telemetry-logging system worn by each bird in a spandex backpack.

In (Blanchard et al., 2002), the authors used biotelemetry for intermittent physiological monitoring of poultry on different diets and under changing lighting conditions. The purpose was to determine whether measurements of poultry electrocardiograms (ECG) and temperature over extended periods of time could provide useful physiological information about broilers at risk for sudden death syndrome, and therefore give some insight into the underlying mechanisms of the syndrome. Transmitters were implanted subcutaneously at the base of the right side of the neck with ECG leads placed over the right shoulder and left groin areas.

In (Khalil et al., 2004), the authors used biotelemetry to monitor heart rate, body temperature, and locomotor activity of hens as stress indicators to evaluate the effects of sudden changes to different management factors, such as food withdrawal and reduction to lighting hours. The authors determined that sudden changes in a management program have significant measurable impact on the birds.

In (Yanagi et al., 2002a), the authors used biotelemetry to evaluate poultry deep body temperature responses to heat stress and the use of surface wetting for its relief. An environmental control and measurement system was developed for this study consisting of automatic control of air temperature and relative humidity, manual setting of air velocity, and continuous monitoring of surface and core body temperatures of the animal. Animal surface temperatures were monitored with an infrared thermal imager, deep body temperatures were monitored with a surgery-free telemetric sensing unit, and animal behavior was recorded using surveillance video. The authors advocated for a variable application rate of water depending on the environment's thermal conditions. They used the system to determine water evaporation rate of the hens cooled by intermittent partial surface wetting at various temperature, relative humidity, and air velocity combinations and quantified the animals' physiological responses to the cooling scheme. In a similar study (Tao & Xin, 2003b), the authors measured the effects of surface wetting on broilers with an ingestible wireless telemetry device, and digital imaging.

A high level of relative humidity is commonly known as an exacerbating factor in poultry heat stress problems (Brown et al., 1997, as cited in Hamrita, 2000a). However, as stated in (Shlomo et al, 1995, as cited in Lacey, 2000a), its exact effects have not been "clearly elucidated." Hence, more research efforts are required to better understand the combined effects of ambient temperature and relative humidity on poultry and to incorporate this knowledge in optimizing poultry housing management and control. Information on the interactive effects of ambient temperature, relative humidity, and ventilation rates on poultry subjected to heat stress is meager (Yanagi et al., 2002a). Humidity can aggravate the adverse effect of high temperature (Steinbach, 1971, as cited in Tao & Xin, 2003a) because animals increasingly rely on latent heat loss with rising temperature (Tao & Xin, 2003a).

In (Lacey et al., 2002a), the authors used a telemetric deep body temperature measurement system to determine the effects of stressful ambient temperature and relative humidity conditions on poultry. Three levels of ambient temperature (31, 34, and 37 °C) and two

levels of relative humidity (50 and 80%) were considered. Results showed that the effects of ambient temperature and relative humidity on mean deep body temperature of broilers are cumulative. Higher relative humidity increases the effective ambient temperature experienced by the bird and results in raised deep body temperature.
In (Tao & Xin, 2003a), the authors monitored continuously using biotelemetry core body temperature responses of poultry to acute exposure to multiple thermally challenging environmental conditions. The conditions consisted of 18 factorial combinations of three dry-bulb air temperatures, two dew point temperatures, and three air velocities. Based on the measurements, the authors developed a temperature-humidity-velocity index (THVI) to describe the synergistic effects of the environmental variables on the birds. The authors classified the states of the birds into normal, alert, danger, or emergency and expressed them in terms of the THVI.

3.3 Modeling poultry physiological responses

Continuous biotelemetry monitoring of poultry provides dynamic responses that define relationships with environmental variables. Combining continuous environmental records and response measures allows models to be constructed to predict future outcomes for a range of inputs (Eigenberg et al., 2008). Some researchers have studied predictability of physiological responses of poultry to various environmental variables. (Aerts et al., 1998) used a recursive regression model to predict 15 min ahead heart rate responses to changes in AT and light-dark alternations. In (Lacey et al., 2000c), the authors used artificial neural network models to predict deep body temperature (DBT) responses of broilers to stressful step changes in ambient temperature. Experiments were conducted using a telemetry system to measure DBT responses of birds under various stress conditions. The collected data was used to train and test various neural network architectures, and the Elman-Jordan was determined to be most suitable. The ability of the developed models to predict DBT responses to AT schedules not used in training and/or responses from a bird not used in training was examined. The models performed reasonably well when predicting responses of a different bird to AT schedules used in training. The models performed well when predicting responses of a bird used in training to new AT schedules. However, predictions of the models were less accurate when dealing with a different AT schedule on a different bird. The authors concluded that using a larger data set with more birds and more AT schedules would likely lead to improved DBT predictions. Results of this study indicate that neural networks could potentially be used for predicting the impact of heat stress conditions on bird physiology.

3.4 Environmental control of poultry housing using telemetric real-time physiological feedback

Environmental control is an important factor in the alleviation of heat stress in poultry environments. Several studies have been reported in the literature for computer-based environmental control of the poultry housing environment. In most of these studies, the environmental variables of interest are temperature, humidity, static pressure, and ventilation rates (Timmons et al., 1995, Mitchell, 1986, 1993, Allison et al., 1991, Timmons, 1987, Flood, 1991, Zhang, 1993, Geers et al., 1984, and Berckmans et al., 1986, all as cited in Hamrita & Mitchell, 1999) with temperature being the most widely studied variable. The most basic and common form of control in these reported studies aims at maintaining temperature in the environment within a desired range by controlling ventilation and heating rates (Hamrita & Mitchell, 1999). In most cases, the control actions are based on feedback measurements of ambient temperature collected from a single location in the building using a thermistor or a thermocouple (Aerts et al., 1996, as cited in Hamrita & Mitchell, 1999). Other more advanced studies have emerged which were concerned with developing control strategies that would increase economic efficiency of the poultry house through optimization (Timmons et al., 1986, as cited in Hamrita & Mitchell, 1999), incorporation of natural wind speed (Simmons and Lott, 1993 as cited in Hamrita & Mitchell, 1999), reducing energy costs by controlling temperature with a 24 hour integration period (Timmons et al., 1995, as cited in Hamrita & Mitchell, 1999), and acclamation (Davis et al., 1991, as cited in Hamrita & Mitchell, 1999).

Perhaps the most important factor that has been neglected in the above control strategies is the animal itself. A number of researchers have pointed out the potential for improvement by gaining insight into the physiological responses of the animals to environmental stressors (Aerts et al., 1996, as cited in Hamrita et al., 2008; Hamrita et al., 1997; Goedseels et al., 1992, and Barnett & Hemsworth, 1990, as cited in Lacey et al., 2000c). The authors in (Hamrita & Mitchell, 1999) called for the use of new dynamic control strategies which rely on real-time physiological feedback from the birds.

To our knowledge, the only research effort so far which has explored poultry environmental control using real-time physiological feedback from the birds is at the University of Georgia. In this program, several studies were conducted to establish a link between deep body temperature (DBT) and environmental variables (Hamrita et al., 1997, Hamrita et al., 1998, Lacey et al., 2000a, 2000b, 2000c, and Hamrita & Hoffacker, 2008). Through these studies, it was determined that DBT is a significant, measurable, effective, and predictable indicator of heat stress in poultry. These studies culminated in the design of a poultry housing environmental controller using DBT as a real-time feedback variable. The study described in (Hamrita & Hoffacker, 2008) established precedence for an environmental controller which responds directly and in real-time to birds physiological responses. Using an experimental tunnel ventilation enclosure placed inside an environmentally controlled chamber, implanted radio telemetry sensors, and a programmable logic controller, a proportional-integral type feedback controller was designed to maintain poultry DBT, under stressful ambient temperature conditions, below a given threshold by controlling air velocity rates. The results indicated that (1) air velocity has a measurable, dynamic, and almost immediate impact on DBT of birds under heat stress; and (2) DBT of heat-stressed broilers can be maintained below a set point by varying air velocity using feedback control. These preliminary results suggest that using DBT as a feedback variable to manipulate air velocity within poultry housing is a promising approach.

4. Use of biotelemetry in other fields

Other fields have preceded poultry in the use of biotelemetry and studies of the use of biotelemetry in other species are available for wildlife, livestock, fish, laboratory animals and humans. A quick survey of some of these studies may be a useful source of information for poultry research as they contain interesting equipment and methodologies.

A broad survey of the literature seems to indicate that the most advanced use of biotelemetry is in human medicine. There has been increased interest in the medical field in remote patient monitoring driven by the need for real-time patient data and the ability to monitor multiple patients simultaneously (Tan et al., 2009). Several studies in the literature have surveyed advances in biotelemetry in the medical field and they give insight into the advanced state of medical biotelemetry equipment and its applications (Akyildiz et al., 2002; N. F. Güler & Übeyli, 2002; Budinger, 2003; Lewis & Goldfarb, 2003; Strydis, 2005; Byrne & Lim, 2007; Luong et al., 2008; Ruiz-Garcia et al., 2009; Lin et al., 2010; Yilmaz et al., 2010).

5. Conclusion

This chapter provided, through a large number of examples, a comprehensive overview of the use of biotelemetry in poultry production. The chapter outlined the types of equipment that are commercially available as well as those adapted and developed by researchers for use in poultry production research. Many poultry biotelemetry studies were aimed at validating new commercially available telemetry systems and measurement techniques and have clearly demonstrated their effectiveness for accurate continuous monitoring of poultry physiology. The majority of these studies were concerned with the monitoring of deep body temperature. Biotelemetry has been successfully used in a wide range of research pertaining to poultry production. Many studies were concerned with monitoring and evaluating physiological and behavioral responses of poultry under various stressful environmental stimuli and management conditions to (1) gain a better understanding of poultry thermoregulatory responses; (2) improve management practices; and (3) evaluate the effectiveness of various environmental conditions. Continuous biotelemetry monitoring of poultry provides dynamic responses that define relationships with environmental variables. These relationships have been described using mathematical models constructed to predict future outcomes for a range of inputs. A pioneer study used biotelemetry to design an environmental controller which maintains poultry deep body temperature, under stressful ambient temperature conditions, below a given threshold by controlling air velocity rates. This study is the first step in designing the future poultry environmental controller which responds directly and in real time to the birds' physiological responses.

6. References

Ackermann, D. M., Smith, B., Kilgore, K. L., & Peckham, P. H. (2006). Design of a high speed transcutaneous optical telemetry link. *Proceedings of the 28th IEEE EMBS Annual International Conference*, ISBN 1-4244-0033-3, New York City, USA, Aug 30-Sept 3, 2006

Aerts, J. M., Berkmans, D., & Schurmans, B. (1998). Predicting the heart rate of broiler chickens based on a combination of a telemetry sensor and mathematical identification techniques. *Proceedings of the 1998 Annual Meeting of the Institute of Biological Engineering*, USA, July 10-12, 1998

Akyildiz, I. F., Su, W., Sankarasubramaniam, Y., & Cayirci, E. (2002). Wireless sensor networks: a survey. *Computer Networks*, Vol. 38, No. 4, (March 2002), pp. 393-422, ISSN 1389-1286

Aubert, A., Beckers, F., Ramaekers, D., Verheyden, B., Leribaux, C., Aerts, J.-M., & Berckmans, D. (2004). Heart rate and heart rate variability in chicken embryos at the end of incubation. *Experimental Physiology*, Vol. 89, No. 2, (February 2004), pp. 199-208, ISSN 0958-0670

Bae, Y., Yang, H., & Min, W. (2008). Real-time monitoring of poultry deep body temperature using a custom-built RF receiver. *Proceedings of the 4th International Symposium on*

Machinery and Mechatronics for Agriculture and Biosystems Engineering, Taichung, Taiwan, May 27-29, 2008

Baras, E. & Lagardère, J.-P. (1995). Fish telemetry in aquaculture: review and perspectives. *Aquaculture International*, Vol. 3, No. 2, (June 1995), pp. 77-102, ISSN 0967-6120

Blanchard, S. M., Degernes, L. A., DeWolf, Jr., D. K., & Garlich, J. D. (2002). Intermittent bioelectric monitoring of electrocardiograms and temperature in male broilers at risk for sudden death syndrome. *Poultry Science*, Vol. 81, No. 1, (June 2002) pp. 887-891, ISSN 0032-5791

Brown–Brandl, T. M., Yanagi, Jr., T., Xin, H., Gates, R. S., Bucklin, R. A., & Ross, G. S. (2003). A new telemetry system for measuring core body temperature in livestock and poultry. *Applied Engineering in Agriculture*, Vol. 19, No. 5, (September 2003), pp. 583-589, ISSN 0883-8542

Budinger, T. F. (2003). Biomonitoring with wireless communications. *Annual Review of Biomedical Engineering*, Vol. 5, No. 1, (August 2003), pp. 383-412, ISSN 1523-9829

Byrne, C., & Lim, C. L. (2007). The ingestible telemetric body core temperature sensor: a review of validity and exercise applications. *British Journal of Sports Medicine*, Vol. 41, No. 3, (March 2007), pp. 126-133, ISSN 0306-3674

Coenen, A. M. L., Lankhaar, J., Lowe, J. C., & McKeegan, D. E. F. (2009). Remote monitoring of electroencephalogram, electrocardiogram, and behavior during controlled atmosphere stunning in broilers: Implications for welfare. *Poultry Science*, Vol. 88, No. 1, (January 2009), pp. 10-19, ISSN 0032-5791

Cross, P. S., Künnemeyer, R., Bunt, C. R., Carnegie, D. A., & Rathbone, M. J. (2004). Control, communication and monitoring of intravaginal drug delivery in dairy cows. *International Journal of Pharmaceutics*, Vol. 282, No. 1-2, (September 2004), pp. 35-44, ISSN 0378-5173

Crowther, C., Davies, R., & Glass, W. (2003). The effect of night transportation on the heart rate and skin temperature of ostriches during real transportation. *Meat Science*, Vol. 64, No. 4, (August 2003), pp. 365-370, ISSN 0309-1740

Eigenberg, R. A., Brown-Brandl, T. M., & Nienaber, J. A. (2008). Sensors for dynamic physiological measurements. *Computers and Electronics in Agriculture*, Vol. 62, No. 1, (June 2008), pp. 41-47, ISSN 0168-1699

Green, A. R. & Xin, H. (2009). Effects of stocking density and group size on thermoregulatory responses of laying hens under heat-challenging conditions. *Transactions of the ASABE*, Vol. 52, No. 6, (December 2009), pp. 2033-2038, ISSN 0001-2351

Güler, I. & Kara, S. (1996). A low-cost biotelemetry system for long time monitoring of physiological data. *Journal of Medical Systems*, Vol. 20, No. 3, (June 1996), pp. 151-156, ISSN 0148-5598

Güler, N. F., & Übeyli, E. D. (2002). Theory and applications of biotelemetry. *Journal Of Medical Systems*, Vol. 26, No. 2, (April 2002), pp. 159-178, ISSN 0148-5598

Hamrita, T. K., Hamrita, S. K., Van Wicklen, G., Czarick, M., and Lacy, M. (1997). Use of biotelemetry in measurement of animal responses to environmental stressors. ASAE Paper No. 974008, St. Joseph, Michigan

Hamrita, T. K., Van Wicklen, G., Czarick, M., & Lacy, M. (1998). Monitoring poultry deep body temperature using biotelemetry. *Applied Engineering in Agriculture*, Vol. 14, No. 3, (May 1998), pp. 327-331, ISSN 0883-8542

Hamrita, T. K. & Mitchell, B. (1999). Poultry Environment and Production Control and Optimization: A Summary of Where We Are and Where We Want to Go. *Transactions of the ASAE*, Vol. 42, No. 2, (Month 1999), pp. 479-483, ISSN 0001-2351

Hamrita, T. K. & Hoffacker, E. C. (2008). Closed-loop control of poultry deep body temperature using variably air velocity: a feasibility study. *Transactions of the ASABE*, Vol. 51, No. 2, (April 2008), pp. 663-674, ISSN 0001-2351

Hawkins, P., Morton, D. B., Bevan, R., Heath, K., Kirkwood, J., Pearce, P., Scott, L., Whelan, G., & Webb, A. (2004). Husbandry refinements for rats, mice, dogs and non-human primates used in telemetry procedures. *Laboratory Animals*, Vol. 38, No. 1, (January 2004), pp. 1-10, ISSN 0023-6772

Kettlewell, P. J., Mitchell, M. A., & Meeks, I. R. (1997). An implantable radio-telemetry system for remote monitoring of heart rate and deep body temperature in poultry. *Computers and Electronics in Agriculture*, Vol. 17, No. 2, (May 1997), pp. 161-175, ISSN 0168-1699

Khalil, A. M., Matsui, K., & Takeda, K. (2004). Influence of sudden changes in management program on physiological and behavioral parameters in hens. *Animal Science Journal*, Vol. 75, No. 3, (May 2004), pp. 253-259, ISSN 1740-0929

Lacey, B., Hamrita, T. K., Lacy, M. P., & Van Wicklen, G. L. (2000a). Assessment of poultry deep body temperature responses to ambient temperature and relative humidity using an on-line telemetry system. *Transactions of the ASAE*, Vol. 43, No. 3, (June 2000), pp. 717-721, ISSN 0001-2351

Lacey, B., Hamrita, T. K., Lacy, M. P., Van Wicklen, G. L., & Czarick, M. (2000b). Monitoring deep body temperature responses of broilers using biotelemetry. *Journal of Applied Poultry Research*, Vol. 9, No. 1, (Spring 2000), pp. 6-12, ISSN 1056-6171

Lacey, B., Hamrita, T. K., & McClendon, R. W. (2000c). Feasibility of using neural networks for real-time prediction of poultry deep body temperature responses to stressful changes in ambient temperature. *Applied Engineering in Agriculture*, Vol. 16, No. 3, (May 2000), pp. 303-308, ISSN 0883-8542

Leterrier, C., Colina, Y., Collin, A., Bastianelli, D., Constantin, P., & de Basilio, V. (2009). Effects of late room temperature increases on body temperature and panting behaviour in chicken. / Effets d'elevations tardives de la temperature ambiante sur la temperature corporelle et l'hyperventilation chez le poulet. *World Poultry Science Association (WPSA), Proceedings of the 8th Avian French Research Days*, St Malo, France, March 25-26, 2009

Lewis, B., & Goldfarb, N. (2003). The advent of capsule endoscopy -- a not-so-futuristic approach to obscure gastrointestinal bleeding. *Alimentary Pharmacology & Therapeutics*, Vol. 17, No. 9, (May 2003), pp. 1085-1096, ISSN 0269-2813

Lin, C. T., Ko, L. W., Chang, M. H., Duann, J. R., Chen, J. Y., Su, T. P., & Jung, T. P. (2010). Review of Wireless and Wearable Electroencephalogram Systems and Brain-Computer Interfaces -- A Mini-Review. *Gerontology*, Vol. 56, No. 1, (January 2010), pp. 112-119, ISSN 0304-324X

Lowe. J. C., Abeyesinghe, S. M., Demmers, T. G. M., Wathes, C. M., & McKeegan, D. E. F. (2007). A novel telemetric logging system for recording physiological signals in unrestrained animals. *Computers and Electronics in Agriculture*, Vol. 57, No. 1, (May 2007), pp. 74-79, ISSN 0168-1699

Luong, J. H. T., Male, K. B., & Glennon, J. D. (2008). Biosensor technology: Technology push versus market pull. *Biotechnology Advances*, Vol. 26, No. 5, (September 2008), pp. 492-500, ISSN 0734-9750

Morton, D. B., Hawkins, P., Bevan, R., Heath, K., Kirkwood, J., Pearce, P., Scott, L., Whelan, G., & Webb, A. (2003). Refinements in telemetry procedures. *Laboratory Animals*, Vol. 37, No. 4, (October 2003), pp. 261-300, ISSN 0023-6772

Puers, R. (1999). Sensor, sensor interfacing and front-end data management for stand-alone microsystems. *Journal of Micromechanics and Microengineering*, Vol. 9, No. 2, (June 1999), ISSN 0960-1317

Quwaider, M. Q., Daigle, C. L., Biswas, S. K., Siegford, J. M., & Swanson, J. C. (2010). Development of a wireless body-mounted sensor to monitor location and activity of laying hens in a non-cage housing system. *Transactions of the ASABE*, Vol. 53, No. 5, (October 2010), pp. 1705-1713, ISSN 0001-2351

Ruiz-Garcia, L., Lunadei, L., Barreiro, P., & Robla, J. I. (2009). A Review of Wireless Sensor Technologies and Applications in Agriculture and Food Industry: State of the Art and Current Trends. *Sensors*, Vol. 9, No. 6, (June 2009), pp. 4728-4750, ISSN 1424-8220

Silva, A. C. de S., Arce, A. I. C., Souto, S., & Costa, E. J. X. (2005). A wireless floating base sensor network for physiological responses of livestock. *Computers and Electronics in Agriculture*, Vol. 49, No. 2, (November 2005), pp. 246-254, ISSN 0168-1699

Strydis, C. (2005). Implantable microelectronic devices: A comprehensive study. *MSc Thesis in Computer Engineering*, Delft University of Technology, The Netherlands, June, 2005

Tan, R., McClure, T., Schulam, P., & Schmidt, J. (2009). Development of a minimally invasive implantable wireless vital signs sensor platform. *Studies In Health Technology And Informatics*, Vol. 142, No.1, (January 2009) pp. 380-385, ISSN 0926-9630

Tao, X., & Xin, H. (2003a). Acute synergistic effects of air temperature, humidity, and velocity on homeostasis of market-size broilers. *Transactions of the ASAE*, Vol. 46, No. 2, (April 2003), pp. 491-497, ISSN 0001-2351

Tao, X., & Xin, H. (2003b). Surface wetting and its optimization to cool broiler chickens. *Transactions of the ASAE*, Vol. 46, No. 2, (April 2003), pp. 483-490, ISSN 0001-2351

van den Brand, H., & van de Belt, K. (2006). Using telemetry to measure chicken embryo temperature: developing the technique. *Proceedings of the 12th European Poultry Conference*, Verona, Italy, September 10-14, 2006

von Borell, E., Langbein, J., Despres, G., Hansen, S., Leterrier, C., Marchant-Forde, J., Marchant-Forde, R., Minero, M., Mohr, E., Prunier, A., Valance, D., & Veissier, I. (2007). Heart rate variability as a measure of autonomic regulation of cardiac activity for assessing stress and welfare in farm animals -- A review. *Physiology & Behavior*, Vol. 92, No. 3, (October 2007), pp. 293-316, ISSN 0031-9384

Wang, N., Zhang, N., & Wang, M. (2006). Wireless sensors in agriculture and food industry--Recent development and future perspective. *Computers and Electronics in Agriculture*, Vol. 50, No. 1, (January 2006), pp. 1-14, ISSN 0168-1699

Wathes, C. M., Kristensen, H. H., Aerts, J.-M., & Berckmans, D. (2008). Is precision livestock farming an engineer's daydream or nightmare, an animal's friend or foe, and a farmer's panacea or pitfall? *Computers and Electronics in Agriculture*, Vol. 64, No. 1, (November 2008), pp. 2-10, ISSN 0168-1699

Yanagi, Jr., T., Xin, H., & Gates, R. S. (2002a). A research facility for studying poultry responses to heat stress and its relief. *Applied Engineering in Agriculture*, Vol. 18, No. 2, (March 2002), pp. 255-260, ISSN 0883-8542

Yanagi, Jr., T., Xin, H., & Gates, R. S. (2002b). Measurement and control system for studying animal-environment interactions. *Proceedings of the World Congress of Computers in Agriculture and Natural Resources*, Iguacu Falls, Brazil, March 13-15, 2002, pp. 374-380

Yilmaz, T., Foster, R., & Hao, Y. (2010). Detecting Vital Signs with Wearable Wireless Sensors. *Sensors*, Vol. 10, No. 12, (December 2010), pp. 10837-10862, ISSN 1424-8220

9

Applications of Telemetry in Small Laboratory Animals for Studying Cardiovascular Diseases

Valdir A. Braga[1] and Melissa A. Burmeister[2]
[1]*Federal University of Paraíba*
[2]*Sanford-Burnham Medical Research Institute*
[1]*Brazil*
[2]*United States*

1. Introduction

Telemetry is a state-of-the-art method of monitoring physiological functions in awake and freely moving laboratory animals, while minimizing stress artefacts. Currently, telemetry systems are employed for measurements of blood pressure, heart rate, blood flow, electrocardiogram, respiratory rate, sympathetic nerve activity, body temperature and many other biological signals in a wide range of animal species including rats, mice, dogs, rabbits, gerbils, hamsters, monkeys, guinea pigs and pigs (Kramer et al., 2001; Butz & Davisson, 2001; Galvin et al., 2006; Moons et al., 2007; Hess et al., 2007; Shaw et al., 2007; Greene et al., 2008). Although telemetry technology has existed for at least 50 years, it has only been in the last decade or so that affordable, reliable, and user friendly commercial products have been available for monitoring physiological signals in the laboratory setting. In particular, the use of telemetry for measuring blood pressure in mice and rats has aided researchers in discovering fundamental mechanisms involved in the physiology and pathophysiology of cardiovascular diseases such as hypertension, heart failure and pre-eclampsia (Kramer & Kinter, 2003; Zimmerman et al., 2004; Hoffman et al., 2008, Burmeister et al., 2011). Moreover, drug discovery for treating hypertension has significantly benefited from telemetry since it allows for drug effects to be investigated chronically and longitudinally. In the first part of this chapter, we will discuss the significant contributions of telemetry towards advancing the field of cardiovascular physiology/pathophysiology, emphasizing chronic studies using several experimental models of hypertension. In the second part, we will discuss the benefits of using telemetry in regards to animal welfare and some strategies to refine the telemetry technique in order to reduce the cost and the number of animals used in experiments while improving animal welfare.

2. Use of telemetry in rodents for cardiovascular research

The techniques for measuring arterial blood pressure in experimental animals have improved considerably over the past decades, and several methods are now available. Arterial blood pressure is often measured to assess the reactivity of the cardiovascular system to a treatment (e.g., to a drug or stress) or as an endpoint in itself (e.g., studies of hypertension). The manner in which blood pressure is measured varies from laboratory to laboratory, and the specific values obtained, their reliability and appropriate interpretation, are strongly influenced by the approach selected. These approaches can be divided into indirect and direct methods.

Indirect methods refer to non-invasive methods of blood pressure measurement. Until recently, the most common indirect method for measuring arterial blood pressure in rodents has been the tail-cuff plethysmography, which consists of a tail-cuff device in combination with blood flow sensor (Kim et al., 1995). The major drawbacks of the tail-cuff method are that it measures only systolic pressure and requires training and physical restraint of the animal. In addition, some degree of warming of the animal is usually used to ensure that the tail blood flow is sufficient for a measurement to be made. Even when minimal external warming is used, the combination of restraint and warming may lead to significant increases in core body temperature (Buñag, 1984). Since both restraint and warming constitute stresses that may affect blood pressure, the values of blood pressure obtained with the tail-cuff technique may reflect not only the animals' general blood pressure level, but also the reactivity of blood pressure to the stress of the procedure.

Direct methods refer to techniques by which arterial blood pressure is measured directly with the aid of a sensor device implanted invasively within the arterial system. The most widely used sensor device in animal studies has been the saline-filled catheter, whose distal end is connected to a calibrated pressure transducer (Van Vliet et al., 2000; Braga et al., 2007). The disadvantages to the fluid-filled catheter method requires rodents to be tethered and handled, catheter patency limitations prevent long-term measurements (i.e., for no longer than one week) and the mobility of the animal is considerably restricted. In addition, there is a potential for infection, potential for loss of catheter patency (e.g., clotting), leading to a degradation or loss of the blood pressure signal, and a limited dynamic response, which makes detection of the true systolic and diastolic pressures challenging in small animals with high heart rates.

The recent development of miniature, implantable radiotelemetric devices offers the possibility of long-term, hands-off blood pressure measurement in untethered rodents living in their home cages (Mills et al., 2000). Implantable telemetry devices suitable for use in small laboratory animals provide several advantages over other methods of blood pressure measurement. These advantages include the ability to obtain blood pressure recordings in conscious, unstressed, freely moving animals, the ability to obtain continuous recordings (24 h/day), the ability to obtain high-fidelity recordings, due to a frequency response that exceeds that of traditional saline-filled catheter systems, and the long-term patency of the catheter, which may be used for many weeks or months without loss of the signal or fidelity of the recordings. Therefore, telemetry has become the "gold standard" for measuring blood pressure in laboratory animals (Kurtz et al., 2005). Figure 1 illustrates a blood pressure tracing acquired using telemetry in a rat.

Original blood pressure tracings from a rat 21 days following implantation of a telemetric device showed in different time scales (0.5, 2 and 30 s).

One important aspect that may limit the use of telemetry is cost. For many investigators with limited funding, the cost of purchasing telemetry equipment and that of the necessary periodic factory refurbishment of telemeters may be prohibitive. Companies are working on developing more cost-effect devices, but they still have a long way to go. However, for chronic experiments, telemetry may be cost-effective when compared to other methods.

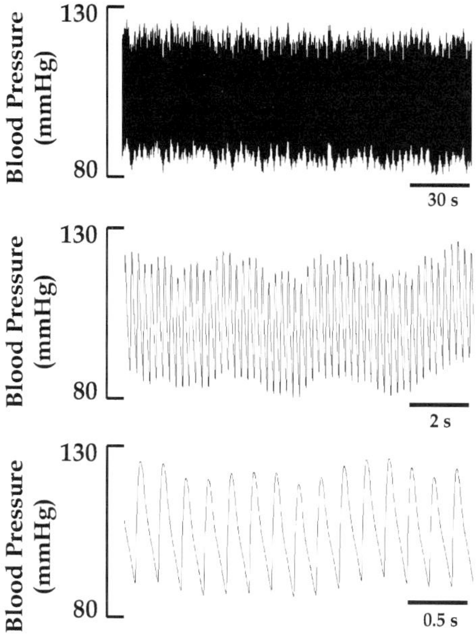

Fig. 1. The feasibility of telemetry for accurate blood pressure measurement.

Relative to a chronic catheter, tether, and swivel system in laboratory animals, the telemetry system requires little day-to-day maintenance, however, and may, therefore, be less labor-intensive and lead to savings in this regard. On the other hand, the cost of factory refurbishment of telemeters depends very much on the pattern of use of the telemetry devices and may represent high costs to researchers. The average nominal battery life of telemeters is 6-8 months depending on the model. However, battery life can be extended by turning off the telemeter when not in use by the use of a magnetic switch, allowing the battery life to be distributed over a longer period of time. More importantly, with care, the telemeter can be explanted, cleaned, recalibrated, resterilized, and reimplanted a number of times without factory refurbishment, thereby maximizing the use of the device and minimizing the cost incurred per animal. The extent to which the telemeters can be reused before refurbishment will depend on the nature and length of the experimental protocol, as well as the care used in implanting and explanting the device. Thus, telemeters can be particularly cost effective when used for multiple short-term implants in rats, with refurbishment costs dropping below US$20 per implantation (Van Vliet et al., 2000).

2.1 Application of telemetry for studying hypertension

The advent of commercially available wireless telemetric technology for blood pressure measurements in laboratory animals has been a significant advancement in hypertension research. The technique has been widely validated and is now available for use in virtually all laboratory animals from mice to monkeys. Of note, its greatest use thus far has been in the rat, the species that has most frequently been used in cardiovascular research.

Telemetric devices have the advantage of allowing for chronic, direct and accurate measurements of blood pressure without the need for restraint. Because of their unlimited capacity for continuous data acquisition over months, telemetry systems also provide the ability to measure blood pressure 24 hours per day, 7 days per week. As a result, continuous direct measurements of blood pressure using telemetry permit diurnal variations in blood pressure to be quantified.

In mammals, the circadian rhythms of behaviour, physiology and metabolism are generated by an internal biological clock mainly located in the suprachiasmatic nucleus of the anterior hypothalamus (Meijer & Rietveld, 1989). The endogenous timekeeping function of the suprachiasmatic nucleus is complemented by its role in the entrainment of circadian rhythms to environmental stimuli. Among the numerous environmental factors acting as synchronizers for the entrainment of endogenous circadian rhythms, the daily light/dark cycle appears to be the most potent factor (Morin, 1994). The information about light/dark cycle is transmitted from the retina to the suprachiasmatic nucleus, which drives the daily rhythm in secretion of the pineal hormone, melatonin (Rusak & Bina, 1990; Morin, 1994), and allows organisms to synchronize the circadian rhythms of behaviour and physiology.

Arterial blood pressure and heart rate exhibit circadian rhythms in both animals (Van Den Buuse, 1994) and humans (Mancia et al., 1983). Specifically, blood pressure and heart rate are lower during periods of rest compared to those of activity, which is related to the day/night rhythm (Conway et al., 1984). In addition, it is well known that life-threatening cardiovascular events such as sudden cardiac death, stroke and myocardial infarction most frequently occur in the early morning hours and are related to the seasonal changes (Marler et al., 1989; Chasen & Muller, 1998). Although various mechanisms may be responsible for these disturbances, they all appear to coincide with the period of increase in the 24-h blood pressure rhythm (Muller et al., 1989).

The advent of telemetry has helped to elucidate how the circadian rhythm influences blood pressure and heart rate in laboratory animals. For example, studies by Zang et al. (2000) demonstrated that rats exposed to a reduction in the photoperiod by changing the light/dark ratio from 12/12h to 8/16h presented altered blood pressure and heart rate variations in a 24h-cycle and that the magnitude of the changes depended on the direction of the extension of the dark period. In addition, transgenic rats with a deficit in brain angiotensin presented a poor adaptation to changes in light/dark cycles when compared to rats with an intact brain renin-angiotensin system (Campos et al., 2006). Furthermore, spontaneously hypertensive rats instrumented with telemeters and treated with various beta blockers displayed gender differences in regards to the drugs' effects on daily variations in blood pressure and heart rate (Grundt et al., 2006). Along these lines, studies employing telemetry demonstrated that treatment with angiotensin-(1-7) agonist alters the circadian rhythm and baroreflex control in spontaneously hypertensive rats (Wessel et al., 2007). In addition to the studies performed in rats, telemetry studies have demonstrated that type 2 diabetic mice exhibit hypertension and disrupted blood pressure and heart rate oscillations during the normal circadian rhythm (Su et al., 2008). Figure 2 shows data generated from recording blood pressure using telemetry for one hour during the day and one hour during the night in a group of rats, illustrating the ability to evaluate diurnal and nocturnal variations in blood pressure.

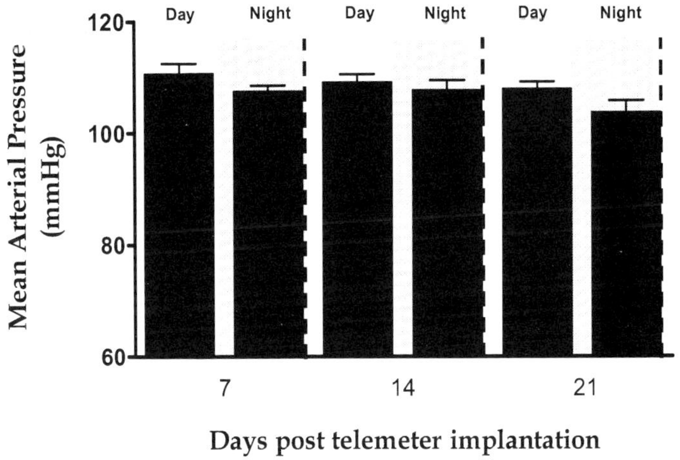

Fig. 2. Effect of the circadian rhythm on blood pressure variations.

Blood pressure values from a group of rats acquired during the day and during the night over 21 days illustrating the application of telemetry for studying diurnal and nocturnal blood pressure variations.

The convenience and reliability of telemetry methodology in cardiovascular research are reflected in the increasing frequency of its utilization by laboratories worldwide. In addition to its application for establishing the extent and duration of the cardiovascular effects of pharmaceutical agents, it has been applied to address unanswered questions in which conventional indirect measurements had yielded inconsistent and often conflicting data. More importantly, it has opened new areas of investigation such as long-term neuro-humoral and cardiovascular regulation of blood pressure and its variability, which were previously beyond the limitations of indirect measurement techniques in rats and mice.

One important application of telemetry is in understanding the pathogenesis of hypertension-associated target organ damage. Although it is generally believed that hypertension contributes to target organ damage, the quantitative relationships have remained controversial since target organ damage is a complex phenomenon thought to be influenced by both blood pressure-dependent and -independent mechanisms. For example, studies performed by Supowit et al. (2005) employing telemetry for studying hypertension-induced end organ damage in hypertensive alpha-calcitonin gene-related peptide knockout mice demonstrated that these transgenic mice presented marked vasculitis in the heart with thickening and inflammation of the vessel walls when compared to hypertensive wild type controls. In addition, transgenic mice presented myocarditis and focal epicarditis with areas of myocardial necrosis. Moreover, the kidneys of these transgenic mice exhibited prominent glomerular changes including congestion of the capillary loops, focal mesangial and crescent proliferation, and focal histocytic infiltration. Finally, urinary microalbumin was significantly higher in the hypertensive alpha-calcitonin gene-related peptide knockout compared to hypertensive wild-types. These findings suggest that deletion of the alpha-calcitonin gene-related peptide gene renders the heart and kidneys more vulnerable to hypertension-induced end organ damage.

Recently, telemetry has been employed for chronic blood pressure measurements up to several months in transgenic, knockout and inbred mouse strains in order to identify the mechanisms underlying different forms of hypertension. Figure 3 shows the development of hypertension in a mouse model of essential hypertension achieved by chronic infusion of angiotensin-II, where blood pressure has been measured daily for 21 days.

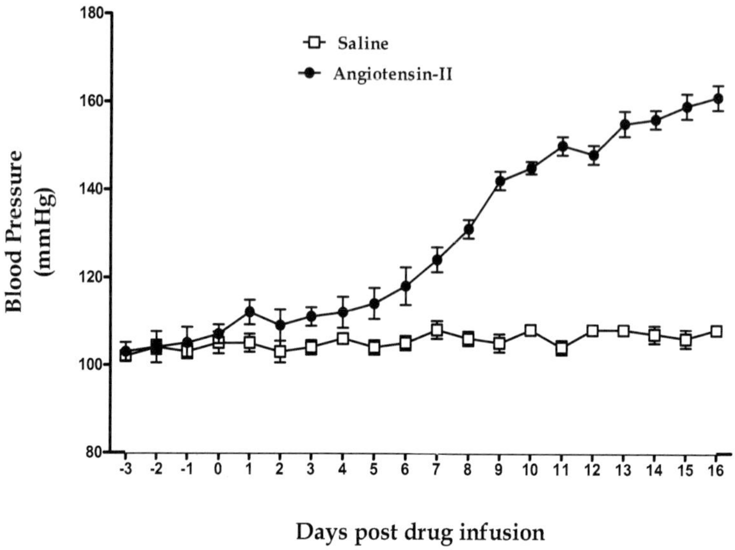

Fig. 3. Use of telemetry in experimental models of hypertension.

Daily blood pressure showing the gradual development of angiotensin-II-dependent hypertension in mice instrumented with telemetric devices and subcutaneously infused with saline or angiotensin-II.

One of the first studies reporting the application of telemetry for studying hypertension in mice was performed by Carlson & Wyss (2000). While developing the technique, the authors demonstrated that although carotid and aortic placements of the telemetry probe provided equally accurate monitoring of arterial pressure and heart rate, the carotid placement yielded a much greater success rate. They also demonstrated that exposure to a high salt diet increased both the amplitude of the arterial pressure rhythm and the average mean arterial pressure, as would be predicted from previous studies in salt-resistant rats. These findings indicated that telemetric recording of long-term arterial pressure and heart rate could be a powerful tool with which to define the mechanisms underlying hypertension in mice. Subsequent studies by Butz & Davisson (2001) further extended the use of telemetry for dissecting the mechanisms underpinning hypertension to pregnant and non-pregnant transgenic and wild type mice. Specifically, they demonstrated the feasibility of continuously monitoring blood pressure before, during and after pregnancy in mice via left carotid artery implantation, which did not interfere with conception, gestation, delivery or postnatal care of pups.

Following these pioneering studies, which set the ground for using telemetry in mice to understand mechanisms underlying hypertension, many other studies combined the advantages of telemetry with the increasing ability to easily and rapidly develop transgenic mouse strains. For example, telemetry has been used to examine hypertension, heart rate variability and baroreflex sensitivity in angiotensin-2-dirupted mice (Gross et al., 2000), hypertension in beta-adducin-deficient mice (Marro et al., 2000),]circadian rhythm effects on blood pressure in eNOS-knockout mice (Van Vliet et al., 2003), menopause-associated hypertension in follitropin receptor knockout mice (Javeshghani et al., 2003), hypertensive response to acute stress in interleukin-6 knockout mice (Lee et al., 2004), hypertension in D4 dopamine receptor-deficient mice (Bek et al., 2006), endothelial dysfunction and elevated blood pressure in MAS gene-deleted mice (Xu et al., 2008), and so on. We recently published an article where we associated virus-mediated gene transfer to the central nervous system, blood pressure recordings using telemetry, and in vivo bioluminescence technology for longitudinal tracking the expression of the redox-regulated activation of activator protein-1 (AP-1), a nuclear transcriptional factor, during the development of renovascular hypertension in mice (Burmeister et al., 2011). Therefore, there are unlimited possibilities for employing different technique combinations associated to telemetry to unravel the mechanisms underlying hypertension.

2.2 Scientific articles Involving telemetry for studying hypertension

The number of articles published using telemetry to study hypertension in mice has steadily increased in the last decade. Figure 4A shows the evolution of the number of articles published in Pubmed (www.pubmed.com) from 2000 to 2010 using the key words "telemetry", "hypertension" and "mice". This number is even greater if the key word "hypertension" is changed to "blood pressure" (Figure 4B), and other combinations yield different numbers. Interestingly, this positive trend seems to be reversing with regard to studies using rats, as illustrated in Figures 5A and 5B.

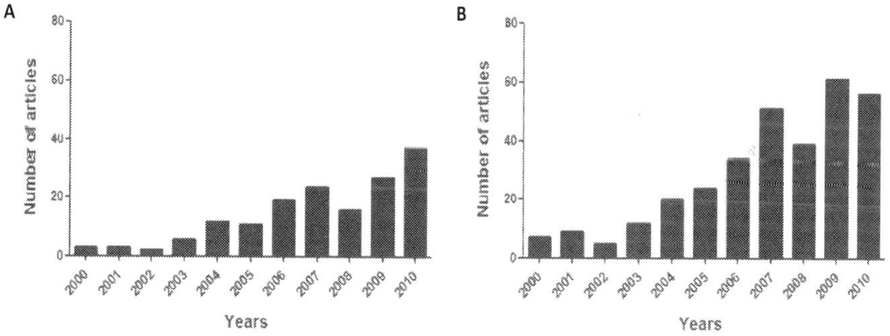

Fig. 4. Publications involving telemetry and mice.
A. Number of articles published in Pubmed from 2000 to 2010 found using the key words "telemetry, hypertension and mice." B. Number of articles published in Pubmed from 2000 to 2010 searched using the key words "telemetry, blood pressure and mice".

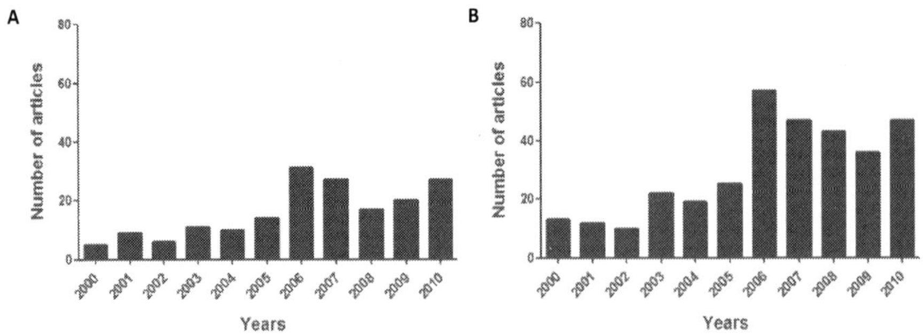

Fig. 5. Publications involving telemetry and rats.
A. Number of articles published in Pubmed from 2000 to 2010 found using the key words "telemetry, hypertension and rat." B. Number of articles published in Pubmed from 2000 to 2010 found using the key words "telemetry, blood pressure and rat."

3. Contribution of telemetry for the animal welfare and refinement

Promoting animal welfare by minimizing pain and distress are important factors to consider in order to acquiring reliable and physiologically accurate results from experimental rodent models of hypertension, as for any other disease models. It is widely recognized that telemetry can reduce stress to animals since it reduces or eliminates the requirement for external instrumentation, restraint or tethering. Telemetry also provides objective biological evidence of animal well-being such as variations in heart rate, blood pressure and body temperature, variations in which may reflect acute or chronic discomfort, stress, distress, pain and fear. In addition, the return of variables such as heart rate to normal circadian rhythms can be used as indicators of physiological recovery and readiness for experimental procedures. When compared to other conventional cardiovascular measurement methods, telemetry offers several advantages including, but not limited to, the 1) elimination of the confounding effects of stress introduced by handling, restraint and anaesthesia; 2) reduction in the number of animals used by 60% to 70%; and (c) unrestricted collection of continuous data for months without the need for any additional manipulation.

The effect of telemetry on an animal's welfare depends on the nature of the technique chosen for implantation and the mass and volume of the device. One of the classic methods described for telemetric device implantation is the abdominal aorta approach, where the blood pressure catheter is inserted into the abdominal aorta, while the body of the transmitter is positioned in the peritoneal cavity (Mills et al., 2000). This method has been refined since it was first proposed. For example, studies performed by Johnston et al. (2007) have assessed the effect of several interventions on postsurgical recovery of food and water intake, core body temperature and locomotor activity. Whereas some of the interventions were associated with increased mortality (such as administration of the postoperative xylazine reversal agent atipamezole), others were either detrimental (such as use of the abdominal lubricant carboxymethylcellulose) or had little or no effect on recovery (such as thermal support).

An alternative approach to the abdominal aorta method places the pressure sensing catheter in the aorta, via the left carotid artery, and the transmitter body subcutaneously on the back at the midscapular region (Carlson & Wyss, 2000) or along the right flank (Butz & Davisson, 2001). Studies from Kaidi et al. (2007) compared the two different techniques in mice. The authors demonstrated that, in left carotid-implanted mice, 80% survived surgery and recovered well. In contrast, only 57% of mice implanted with the abdominal aortic technique survived surgery, and some presented lethal complications. Both techniques had similar recovery times for body weight and food consumption, with a comparable return of normal circadian rhythm by day 6 post-surgery and similar cardiovascular baseline values. Six out of the eight left carotid-implanted mice remained in good health and had good pressure signal for at least 100 days post-surgery, while most of the abdominal aortic-implanted mice had lost the pressure signal within 14–49 days post-surgery. The authors concluded that left carotid artery implantation in mice is superior to the abdominal aorta technique and is more appropriate for long-term telemetry studies, especially in smaller animals. In agreement with this, Butz & Davisson (2001) suggested the use of the left carotid artery implantation approach for studies involving pregnant mice.

In addition to the surgical technique employed for implanting the device, the mass of the implanted device is equally important. Adding additional mass to an animal's body can have significant physiologic effects and can cause distress and discomfort, particularly in small species such as rodents. For instance, increasing the mass in abdominal viscera can compromise diaphragmatic movement and alter breathing pattern. In the short term, changes in body mass and behavior after implantation surgery in mice indicate that their well-being is impaired during the first days after surgery. An animal may require 5 to 7 days to regain its normal circadian rhythm (Butz & Davisson, 2001). Restoration of well-being follows the same time course in rats implanted with transmitters. Therefore, telemetric devices should be as lightweight as possible, although it may be difficult to establish general principles on the appropriate device size and mass.

Considering that the size and shape of the device must avoid or minimize any compromise of normal physiologic function or welfare of the animal, the use of telemetric devices designed for mice in rats affords some remarkable advantages as described by Braga & Prabhakar (2009). For example, implantation of the smaller telemeter is easier because the diameter of the catheter tip is smaller than that for the device designed for rats, thus, facilitating insertion into the abdominal aorta. Another important advantage is the size of the animal that can be implanted: the mouse telemeter can be implanted in animals as small as 17 g, whereas the rat telemeter is only appropriate for animals weighing at least 175 g. Therefore, the approach proposed by Braga & Prabhakar (2009) would be useful for blood pressure studies in neonates and young rats. In addition, the mouse device occupies much less space in the abdominal cavity, as shown in Figure 6, allowing for better accommodation of the internal organs around the transmitter. This feature would be particularly relevant for researchers investigating cardiovascular physiology and physiopathology during pregnancy (such as pre-eclampsia). As important disadvantages to consider, the transmitters designed for mice are more expensive and have a considerably shorter battery life than do the rat transmitters. The costs for a long-term experiment might be increased by 70% to 100% when using the mice transmitter. The main points that must be taken into account for designing such studies are the battery life of the mice transmitter, which is about 6 wk of continuous recording (compared to 17 wk for the rat transmitter), and the costs for refurbishing the transmitter (that is, replacing catheters and recharging batteries) are considerably higher.

These advantages and disadvantages should be taken into consideration when designing chronic experiments using different transmitter types.
It is important to highlight that telemetry improves data quality and quantity, which can lead to a reduction in the number of animals required for each study. In toxicology and pharmacology, telemetry may also be able to identify dose-limiting effects of a compound evidenced by subtle changes in blood pressure or heart rate so that higher dosing studies are not required. However, reducing animal numbers can also increase animal suffering, and it is important to be aware of this and make sure that it does not happen. For example, as implant miniaturization has progressed, sensor functionality has increased such that individual devices may increase in size because more parameters are being measured. Larger batteries may be required, which also makes devices more bulky. These devices will be heavier and require more invasive surgery to implant them. Therefore, it is imperative to ensure that animal numbers have been reduced as far as possible by taking the better quality and quantity of data obtained using telemetry into account when designing experiments. It also important to recognize that there can be a 'trade off' between reduction and refinement, e.g. where fewer animals are used but devices are more bulky or complex. Finally, the impact on each animal should be considered, and reducing numbers at the expense of individual suffering avoided.

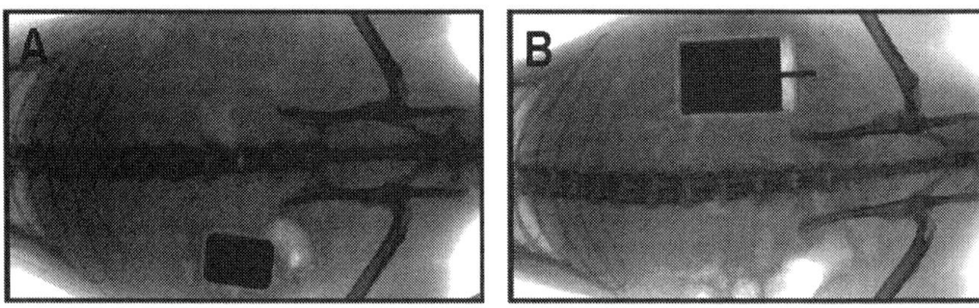

Fig. 6. Refinement of the surgical approach and size of the implanted device.

Radiographic pictures acquired from two different rats implanted with either the mouse (A) or the rat telemetric device (B). Pictures are from first author's personal collection.
New developments in telemetry research can lead to refinements in procedures and/or reductions in animal numbers so it is essential to ensure that progress is monitored and techniques and equipment are updated whenever possible. Some ways to keep updated are using the World Wide Web and attending telemetry user group meetings. It is, however, important to use information from the web or user groups very critically, as it may not be properly refereed or refereed at all. Uncritical use could lead to welfare problems or undermine scientific validity. Further information on refinement husbandry and telemetry procedures for measuring blood pressure in laboratory animals have been described in details by Morton et al. (2003) and Hawkins et al. (2004).

4. Conclusion

Here we have reviewed how advancements in telemetric monitoring of blood pressure and heart rate have led to several major discoveries in the field of cardiovascular research, primarily hypertension and associated pathologies. The benefits of telemetry as a reliable method for measuring in vivo blood pressure in small laboratory animals are further heightened by the advantages that the technique provides regarding cost effectiveness and animal welfare. Until recently, the most commonly used techniques for monitoring blood pressure in conscious rats and mice were a tail cuff device or an exteriorized catheter connected to a pressure transducer. There are, however, considerable drawbacks associated with each of these methods that make them undesirable as accurate means of obtaining blood pressure measurements. Namely, the accuracy of blood pressure measurements using tail cuff are significantly affected by environmental factors as well as by any physiological or pharmacological factor that influences blood flow in the tail, nor does the method allow for continuous blood pressure recordings. Although exteriorized catheters do allow for blood pressure to be measured continuously, decreasing catheter patency is a problem that usually limits the duration of reliable recordings.

Physiologic data collection using telemetry has many advantages over older methods such as restraints, cuffs, tethers, etc. Data are free from physiological and psychological stress- and anaesthesia-induced artefact. Furthermore, telemetry is more cost-effective and less labor-intensive when compared to tail cuff and exteriorized catheters, and there is an increased chance of capturing occasional and transient events over a long period. There is also a reduction in the number of animals required due to more and better quality data. As a result, the technique has proven to be an extremely valuable tool for researchers, especially those in the fields of cardiovascular physiology and pharmacology, where the use of telemetry for measuring blood pressure, cardiac activity, heart rate, body temperature and locomotor activity in rodents has been sufficiently validated.

Continually evolving refinements in telemetry methodology will undoubtedly aid researchers in acquiring high quality, physiologically relevant data and contribute to groundbreaking discoveries that may, ultimately, lead to therapeutics.

5. Acknowledgment

We would like to thank Mr. Antonio Silva Santos for his technical assistance and the Conselho Nacional de Desenvolvimento Científico e Tecnológico (CNPq/Brazil) for funding support.

6. References

Bek, M.J., Wang, X., Asico, L.D., Jones, J.E., Zheng, S., Li, X., Eisner, G.M., Grandy, D.K., Carey, R.M., Soares-da-Silva, P. & Jose, P.A. (2006). Angiotensin-II type 1 receptor-mediated hypertension in D4 dopamine receptor-deficient mice. *Hypertension*, Vol. 47, No. 2, pp. 288-95, ISSN 0194-911X.

Braga, V.A., Soriano, R.N., Braccialli, A.L., de Paula, P.M., Bonagamba, L.G., Paton, J.F. & Machado, B.H. (2007). Involvement of L-glutamate and ATP in the neurotransmission of the sympathoexcitatory component of the chemoreflex in the commissural nucleus tractus solitarii of awake rats and in the working heart-brainstem preparation. *The Journal of Physiology*, Vol. 581, No. 3, pp. 1129-45, ISSN 0022-3751.

Braga, V.A. & Prabhakar, N.R. (2009). Refinement of telemetry for measuring blood pressure in conscious rats. *Journal of the American Association for Laboratory Animal Science*, Vol. 48, No. 3, pp. 268-71, ISSN 1060-0558.

Burmeister, M.A., Young, C.N., Braga, V.A., Butler, S.D., Sharma, R.V. & Davisson, R.L. (2011). In vivo bioluminescence imaging reveals redox-regulated activator protein-1 activation in paraventricular nucleus of mice with renovascular hypertension. *Hypertension*, Vol. 57, No. 2, pp. 289-97, ISSN 0194-911X.

Buñag, R.D. (1984). Measurement of blood pressure in rats. In: W. de Jong (Ed.), Handbook of Hypertension, Volume 4: Experimental and genetic models of hypertension (pp. 1–12). Elsevier, New York, ISBN 0444897151.

Butz, G.M. & Davisson, R.L. (2001). Long-term telemetric measurement of cardiovascular parameters in awake mice: a physiological genomics tool. *Physiological Genomics*, Vol. 5, No. 2, pp. 89-97, ISSN 1094-8341.

Campos, L.A., Plehm, R., Cipolla-Neto, J., Bader, M. & Baltatu, O.C. (2006). Altered circadian rhythm reentrainment to light phase shifts in rats with low levels of brain angiotensinogen. *American Journal of Physiology - Regulatory, Integrative and Comparative Physiology*, Vol. 290, No. 4, pp. R1122-7, ISSN 0363-6119.

Carlson, S.H. & Wyss, J.M. (2000). Long-term telemetric recording of arterial pressure and heart rate in mice fed basal and high NaCl diets. *Hypertension*, Vol. 35, No. 2, pp. E1-5, ISSN 0194-911X.

Chasen, C. & Muller, J.E. (1998). Cardiovascular triggers and morning events. *Blood Pressure Monitoring*, Vol. 3, No. 1, pp 35–42, ISSN 1359-5237.

Conway, J., Boon, N., Davies, C., Jones, J.V. & Sleight, P. (1984). Neural and humoral mechanisms involved in blood pressure variability. *Journal of Hypertension*, Vol. 2, No. 1, pp. 203–208, ISSN 0263-6352.

Gauvin, D.V., Tilley, L.P., Smith, F.W. Jr. & Baird, T.J. (2006). Electrocardiogram, hemodynamics, and core body temperatures of the normal freely moving laboratory beagle dog by remote radiotelemetry. *Journal of Pharmacological and Toxicological Methods*, Vol. 53, No. 2, pp. 128-39, ISSN 1056-8719.

Greene, A.N., Clapp, S.L. & Alper, R.H. (2008). Timecourse of recovery after surgical intraperitoneal implantation of radiotelemetry transmitters in rats. *Journal of Pharmacological and Toxicological Methods*, Vol. 56, No. 2, pp. 218-22, ISSN 1056-8719.

Gross, V., Milia, A.F., Plehm, R., Inagami, T. & Luft, F.C. (2000). Long-term blood pressure telemetry in AT2 receptor-disrupted mice. *Journal of Hypertension*, Vol. 18, No. 7, pp. 955-61, ISSN 0263-6352.

Grundt, C., Meier, K. & Lemmer, B. (2006). Gender dependency of circadian blood pressure and heart rate profiles in spontaneously hypertensive rats: effects of beta-blockers. *Chronobiology International*, Vol. 23, No. 4, pp. 813-29, ISSN 0742-0528.

Hawkins, P., Morton, D.B., Bevan, R., Heath, K., Kirkwood, J., Pearce, P., Scott, L., Whelan, G., Webb, A. & Joint Working Group on Refinement. (2004). Husbandry refinements for rats, mice, dogs and non-human primates used in telemetry procedures. Seventh report of the BVAAWF/FRAME/RSPCA/UFAW Joint Working Group on Refinement, Part B. *Laboratory Animals*, Vol. 38, No. 1, pp. 1-10, ISSN 0023-6772.

Hess, P., Rey, M., Wanner, D., Steiner, B. & Clozel, M. (2007) Measurements of blood pressure and electrocardiogram in conscious freely moving guineapigs: a model for screening QT interval prolongation effects. *Laboratory Animals*, Vol. 41, No. 4, pp. 470-80, ISSN 0023-6772.

Hoffmann, D.S., Weydert, C.J., Lazartigues, E., Kutschke, W.J., Kienzle, M.F., Leach, J.E., Sharma, J.A., Sharma, R.V. & Davisson, R.L. (2008). Chronic tempol prevents hypertension, proteinuria, and poor feto-placental outcomes in BPH/5 mouse model of preeclampsia. *Hypertension*, Vol. 51, No. 4, pp. 1058-65, ISSN 0194-911X.

Javeshghani, D., Touyz, R.M., Sairam, M.R., Virdis, A., Neves, M.F. & Schiffrin, E.L. (2003). Attenuated responses to angiotensin II in follitropin receptor knockout mice, a model of menopause-associated hypertension. *Hypertension*, Vol. 42, No 4, pp. 761-7, ISSN 0194-911X.

Johnston, N.A., Bosgraaf, C., Cox, L., Reichensperger, J., Verhulst, S., Patten, C. Jr & Toth, L.A. (2007). Strategies for refinement of abdominal device implantation in mice: strain, carboxymethylcellulose, thermal support, and atipamezole. *Journal of the American Association for Laboratory Animal Science*, Vol. 46, No. 2, pp. 46-53, ISSN 1060-0558.

Kaïdi, S., Brutel, F., Van Deun, F., Kramer, K., Remie, R., Dewé, W., Remusat, P., Delaunoism A. & Depelchin, O. (2007). Comparison of two methods (left carotid artery and abdominal aorta) for surgical implantation of radiotelemetry devices in CD-1 mice. *Laboratory Animals*, Vol. 41, No. 3, pp. 388-402, ISSN 0023-6772.

Kim, H.S., Krege, J.H., Kluckman, K.D., Hagaman, J.R., Hodgin, J.B., Best, C.F., Jennette, J.C., Coffman, T.M., Maeda, N. & Smithies, O. (1995). Genetic control of blood pressure and the angiotensinogen locus. *Proceedings of the National Academy of Sciences of the United States of America*, Vol. 92, No. 1, pp. 2735–2739, ISSN 0027-8424.

Kramer, K., Kinter, L., Brockway, B.P., Voss, H.P., Remie, R. & Van Zutphen, B.L. (2001). The use of radiotelemetry in small laboratory animals: recent advances. *Contemporary Topics in Laboratory Animal Science*, Vol. 40, No. 1, pp. 8-16, ISSN 1060-0558.

Kramer, K. & Kinter, L.B. (2003). Evaluation and applications of radiotelemetry in small laboratory animals. *Physiological Genomics*, Vol. 13, No. 3, pp. 197-205, ISSN 1094-8341.

Kurtz, T.W., Griffin, K.A., Bidani, A.K., Davisson, R.L., Hall, J.E. AHA Council on High Blood Pressure Research, Professional, & Public Education Subcommittee. (2005). Recommendations for blood pressure measurement in animals: summary of an AHA scientific statement from the Council on High Blood Pressure Research, Professional, and Public Education Subcommittee. *Arteriosclerosis, Thrombosis, and Vascular Biology*, Vol. 25, No. 1, pp. 478–479, ISSN 1079-5642.

Lee, D.L., Leite, R., Fleming, C., Pollock, J.S., Webb, R.C. & Brands, M.W. (2004). Hypertensive response to acute stress is attenuated in interleukin-6 knockout mice. *Hypertension*, Vol. 44, No. 3, pp. 259-63, ISSN 0194-911X.

Mancia, G., Ferrari, A., Gregorini, L., Parati, G., Pomidossi, G., Bertinieri, G., Grassi, G., Di Rienzo, M., Pedotti, A. & Zanchetti, A. (1983). Blood pressure and heart rate variabilities in normotensive and hypertensive human beings. *Circulation Research*, Vol 53, No. 1, pp 96–104, ISSN 0009-7330.

Marler, J.R., Price, T.R. & Clark, G.L. (1989). Morning increases in onset of ischemic stroke. *Stroke*, Vol. 20, No. 1, pp. 473–476Meijer, J.H. & Rietveld, W.J. (1989). Neurophysiology of the suprachiasmatic circadian pacemaker in rodents. *Physiological Reviews*, Vol. 69, No. 1, pp. 671–707, ISSN 0031-9333.

Marro, M.L., Scremin, O.U., Jordan, M.C., Huynh, L., Porro, F., Roos, K.P., Gajovic, S., Baralle, F.E. & Muro, A.F. (2000). Hypertension in beta-adducin-deficient mice. *Hypertension*, Vol. 36, No. 3, pp. 449-53, ISSN 0194-911X.

Meijer, J.H. & Rietveld, W.J. (1989). Neurophysiology of the suprachiasmatic circadian pacemaker in rodents. *Physiologival Reviews*, Vol. 69, No. 3, pp. 671-707, ISSN 0031-9333.

Mills, P.A., Huetteman, D.A., Brockway, B.P., Zwiers, L.M., Gelsema, A.J.M., Schwartz, R.S. & Kramer, K. (2000). A new method for measurement of blood pressure, heart rate, and activity in the mouse by radiotelemetry. *Journal of Applied Physiology*, Vol. 88, No. 1, pp. 1537–1544, ISSN 8750-7587.

Moons, C.P., Hermans, K., Remie, R., Duchateau, L. & Odberg, F.O. (2007). Intraperitoneal versus subcutaneous telemetry devices in young Mongolian gerbils (Meriones unguiculatus). *Laboratory Animals*, Vol. 41, No. 2, pp. 262-9, ISSN 0023-6772.

Morin, L.P. (1994). The circadian visual system. *Brain Research*, Vol. 67, No. 1, pp. 102–127, ISSN 0006-8993.

Morton, D.B., Hawkins, P., Bevan, R., Heath, K., Kirkwood, J., Pearce, P., Scott, L., Whelan, G., Webb, A., British Veterinary Association Animal Welfare Foundation, Fund for Replacement of Animals in Medical Experiments, Royal Society for the Prevention of Cruelty to Animals & Universities Federation for Animal Welfare. (2003). Refinements in telemetry procedures. Seventh report of the BVAAWF/FRAME/RSPCA/UFAW Joint Working Group on Refinement, Part A. *Laboratory Animals*, Vol. 37, No. 4, pp. 261-99, ISSN 0023-6772.

Muller, J.E., Tofler, G.H. & Stone, P.H. (1989). Circadian variation and triggers of onset of acute cardiovascular disease. *Circulation*, Vol. 79, No. 1, pp. 733–743, ISSN 0009-7322.

Rusak, B. & Bina, K.G. (1990). Neurotransmitters in the mammalian circadian system. *Annual Review of Neuroscience*, Vol. 13, No. 1, pp. 387–401, ISSN 0147-006X.

Shaw, M.B., Herndon, C.D., Cain, M.P., Rink, R.C. & Kaefer, M. (2007). A porcine model of bladder outlet obstruction incorporating radio-telemetered cystometry. *British Journal of Urology International*, Vol. 100, No. 1, pp. 170-4, ISSN 2042-2997.

Su, W., Guo, Z., Randall, D.C., Cassis, L., Brown, D.R., Gong, M.C. (2008). Hypertension and disrupted blood pressure circadian rhythm in type 2 diabetic db/db mice. *American Journal of Physiology - Heart and Circulatory Physiology*, Vol. 295, No.4, pp. H1634-41, ISSN 0363-6135.

Supowit, S.C., Rao, A., Bowers, M.C., Zhao, H., Fink, G., Steficek, B., Patel, P., Katki, K.A. & Dipette, D.J. (2005). Calcitonin gene-related peptide protects against hypertension-induced heart and kidney damage. *Hypertension*, Vol. 45, No. 1, pp. 109-1, ISSN 0194-911X.

Van den Buuse, M. (1994). Circadian rhythms of blood pressure, heart rate, and locomotor activity in spontaneously hypertensive rats as measured with radio-telemetry. *Physiology & Behavior*, Vol. 55, No. 1, pp. 783–787, ISSN 0031-9384.

Van Vliet, B.N., Chafe, L.L., Antic, V., Schnyder-Candrian, S. & Montani, J.P. (2000). Direct and indirect methods used to study arterial blood pressure. *Journal of Pharmacological and Toxicological Methods*, Vol. 44, No. 2, pp. 361-73, ISSN 1056-8719.

Van Vliet, B.N., Chafe, L.L. & Montani, J.P. (2003). Characteristics of 24 h telemetered blood pressure in eNOS-knockout and C57Bl/6J control mice. *The Journal of Physiology*, Vol. 549, No. 1, pp 313-25, ISSN 0022-3751.

Wessel, N., Malberg, H., Heringer-Walther, S., Schultheiss, H.P. & Walther, T.J. (2007). The angiotensin-(1-7) receptor agonist AVE0991 dominates the circadian rhythm and baroreflex in spontaneously hypertensive rats. *Journal of Cardiovascular Pharmacology*, Vol. 49, No. 2, pp 67-73, ISSN 0160-2446.

Xu, P., Costa-Goncalves, A.C., Todiras, M., Rabelo, L.A., Sampaio, W.O., Moura, M.M., Santos, S.S., Luft, F.C., Bader, M., Gross, V., Alenina, N. & Santos, R.A. (2008). Endothelial dysfunction and elevated blood pressure in MAS gene-deleted mice. *Hypertension*, Vol. 51, No. 2, pp. 574-80, ISSN 0194-911X.

Zhang, B.L., Zannou, E. & Sannajust, F. (2000). Effects of photoperiod reduction on rat circadian rhythms of BP, heart rate, and locomotor activity. *American Journal of Physiology - Regulatory, Integrative and Comparative Physiology*, Vol. 279, No. 1, pp. R169-78, ISSN 0363-6119.

Zimmerman, M.C., Lazartigues, E., Sharma, R.V. & Davisson, R.L. (2004). Hypertension caused by angiotensin II infusion involves increased superoxide production in the central nervous system. *Circulation Research*, Vol. 95, No. 2, pp. 210-6, ISSN 0009-7330.

Part 4

Medical Telemetry

10

Use of Telemetric EEG in Brain Injury

Marcio Furtado[1], Franco Rossetti[2] and Debra Yourick[3]
[1]Clinical Research Management Inc.,
[2]National Research Council,
[3]Science Education and Strategic Communications,
Walter Reed Army Institute of Research
United States of America

1. Introduction

Telemetry technology allows remote measurement and recording of signals such as biopotentials. This technology offers the advantage of long-term EEG recordings without causing unnecessary distress, as happens in EEG systems where implanted leads connect to the recording device through a cable. The EEG recordings can be used to detect changes in the brain activity after a traumatic event. The use of telemetry for EEG acquisition is the most reliable option in experimental studies due to the reduction of animal stress. Besides its current disadvantages, such as a reduced number of channels when compared to tethered EEG, telemetry can allow us to distinguish oscillatory brain patterns that become pathological after a neurological injury. Normal brain oscillatory synchronization can be correlated with cognitive function and behavioral state. However, abnormal brain oscillations can be caused by pathologies characterized by dysfunction of the cholinergic system and trauma, leading to epilepsy. This phenomenon is the result of abnormal hypersynchronous firing in certain neuronal populations in the brain. Although not all kinds of brain injury can induce epilepsy, the spike/wave activity present during epileptic seizures is of special relevance, because severe brain injury can, in most cases, induce epilepsy.

The combination of EEG acquired through telemetry and video is widely used for assessment of epileptic focus, to distinguish epileptic seizures from psychogenic non-epileptic seizures, re-assessment for potential surgery to treat epilepsy and to study animal models. Nevertheless, the assessment of the long-term EEG changes that occur after brain injury is a challenge, because a large amount of data is accumulated. Reducing the sampling rate and/or the recording schedule is not an option since each subject may respond differently to the injury and treatment. Furthermore, seizure-like events do not occur in pre-determined periods, therefore arbitrary sampling would compromise acquisition and analysis. In order to acquire reliable results, one requires a good estimation of duration and frequency of seizures and/or the duration of sleep stages. Several studies have addressed the need for analytical tools capable of optimally performing spectral analyses and, in this chapter, we evaluate the advantages and disadvantages of some available tools. The reduction and removal of artifacts in the acquired data, spectral decomposition of the signal using fast Fourier and wavelet transforms, and batch-processing will also be discussed. We will provide a view of the role of telemetric EEG technology in neuroscience, focusing on the study of brain injury induced by chemical means. Approaches to assess long-term EEG changes, choices of acquisition parameters, and tools to analyze the EEG data will be introduced.

2. Uses of telemetry technology

The advance of remote recording of physiological data, such as biopotentials, by radio (Holter and Generelli, 1949) was a great advancement in the field of physiology. Telemetry has been used to assess physiological measures through the recording of biopotentials of subjects in remote locations for decades (Fischler & Frei, 1963; Hambrecht *et al*, 1963; Lee *et al*, 1964; Vreeland *et al.*, 1963). The aerospace industry, NASA and the former USSR used telemetry to record electrocardiogram (ECG), electroencephalogram (EEG) and electromyogram (EMG) during different missions (Akulinichev & Baevskii, 1964; Blanc, Gravier, & Geier, 1967; Caldwell & Lewis, 1995; Frostjr *et al*, 1975; Helvey *et al*, 1964) with the objective to monitor pilots/astronauts, collecting information regarding changes in physiological parameters.

The technologies for recording of biopotentials remotely have been improving in parallel with different technologies. For example, the development of the transistor made possible the design of small and relatively power-efficient circuits, allowing small devices to be implanted (Jacobson and Mackay, 1957). Kamp (1984) described the use of a miniaturized 8-channel EEG amplifier combined with a standard radio transmitter/receiver system to record long-term EEG at the patient's residence. Van der Weide and Kamp (1984) created a system to record long-term home EEG in epileptic patients using radio telemetry transmitted over a regular telephone line. Wroe and co-workers (1987) combined telemetry and recording using a standard cassette system, allowing monitoring of epileptic patients in the clinic. Peng and colleagues (2001) used a regular telephone network to send data from a 20-channel EEG system to a monitoring center where the data could be stored and analyzed. Frequency resolution is very important when acquiring EEG signals and the use of frequency modulation (FM) technology allowed a higher sampling rate. Neihart & Harrison (2004) created an FM transmitter (433 MHz) powered by an inductive link (transcutaneous) to send biopotential data to a monopole antenna. A wireless multichannel recording system was designed by Mohseni and colleagues (2005) and featured integrated circuit AC amplification, DC input stabilization, time-division-multiplexing (each signal has a "timeslot") and wireless FM transmission (0.05-6 kHz). Rizk and co-workers (2007) designed and implemented a single-chip to function as a 96-channel, brain-machine interface. The interface uses bidirectional communication, sampling the signals at 31.25 kHz and digitally suiting it for transmission, fulfilling the requirements for an implantable system. However, the newest existing techniques to implement brain-computer interfaces still face problems such as gliosis surrounding the implant and biocompatibility. Visual and auditory replacements and hand and limb prosthetics could revolutionize medicine, but there is still a long way to go (Rothschild, 2010). Finally, optical technology can potentially be used to transmit local field potential data (LFP) more accurately. Wei & Ziaie (2009) accomplished it designing a system composed of a printed circuit board (2.2 x 2.2 cm) to accommodate 4 amplifiers, 16 light-emitting diodes (LED) and a CCD camera to record the signal coming from the LED at 30 frames per second allowing reconstruction of a simulated LFP.

2.1 The use of EEG telemetry to detect clinical seizures in patients

The choice of what telemetry system to use in the clinic must be made according to the physician's expectations and requirements for an EEG system. The physician will determine the level of sophistication required for their EEG system (Schomer, 2006). In any case, although controversial, the EEG can be a potential marker to help in the diagnosis and classification of seizures if monitored continuously. Meierkord (1992) used video-EEG telemetry to identify frontal lobe epilepsy and differentiate it from pseudo-seizures in patients. Overall, the seizure duration was short (up to 60 sec) and inter-ictal epileptiform EEG activity was identified as well as ictal abnormalities. In a similar effort, Raymond and colleagues (1999) were able to distinguish epileptic seizures from "non-epileptic" seizures. They described that even though it is unusual, some patients may display both epileptic seizures and "non-epileptic" seizures. They combined video-EEG telemetry and MRI (not simultaneous) to help in diagnosis and, interestingly, in 12 of 14 patients, the first seizure was "non-epileptic", suggesting that long-term monitoring is necessary to avoid pitfalls in the diagnosis. Moreover, there are situations when patients do not show structural anomalies in the MRI (Scott *et al.*, 1999) but the EEG reveals epileptiform patterns. In these specific cases, although the telemetric EEG does not show a clear cut identification of the epileptogenic site (due to the spatial resolution limitation), it is still a valuable tool. In an attempt to increase the spatial resolution of the EEG, Gross and co-workers (2000) used closely spaced electrodes to study frontal lobe epilepsy (32-64 channels) and found abnormalities that were apparent with 10-20 electrodes. Nevertheless, independent of the number of channels, it is very important to precisely evaluate the video-EEG recordings and, if necessary, review it. In a re-assessment of data collected during 17 months from 121 patients (video-EEG telemetry), Alsaadi and colleagues (2004) changed the diagnosis of 24% of the patients after re-analyzing the data.

2.2 The use of EEG telemetry to study behavior and detect seizures in animal models

Telemetry has been shown to be extremely useful in animal models, allowing approaches that could be considered non-ethical in humans. Several studies were conducted specifically to verify the efficacy of new technologies that allow miniaturization of the telemetry system. Both the study of normal physiological events such as thermoregulation, sleep and circadian cycle (Herold *et al.*, 1998) and the mechanisms of different neuropathologies can be explored through the use of telemetric EEG in animal models. Dimpfel and colleagues (1988) performed the implantation of bipolar electrodes in cortical and sub-cortical structures of rats to allow long-term recording of EEG after different drug treatments, such as amitriptyline, imipramine, amitriptylinoxide, amphetamine, diazepam, haloperidol and LSD. Cotugno and co-workers (1996) described a method to surgically implant telemetry transmitters in rats and record the EEG. The transmitter is implanted in a dorsal subcutaneous pocket and two stainless steel electrodes placed in the skull are connected to the transmitter through a subcutaneous tunnel. The EEG is then collected by an antenna located in a receiver positioned under the animal.

Fitzgerald and colleagues (2003) adapted a method to record EEG in rats through telemetry and perform real-time fast Fourier transform. They used a Data Sciences International system (DSI; St. Paul, Minn.) to send raw EEG of rats injected with atropine, caffeine, ketamine or pentobarbarbital to an oscilloscope (DataSys 7200, Gould Instrument Systems, Valley View, Ohio) with storage, fast Fourier transform (FFT) and averaging features. Then, they calculated the relative power peaks for atropine (< or =5 Hz), caffeine (7.5 Hz) and ketamine (induced a shift from 5 to 10 Hz to < 5 Hz). Bastlund and co-workers (2004) used telemetry to record cortical EEG, EMG, and temperature for long-term monitoring (5-8 weeks) of epileptiform activity in rats injected with either pentylenetetrazole or kainic acid. Weiergräber and colleagues (2005) while studying transgenic mouse models of epilepsy and sleep disorders, used EEG recorded through telemetry playing a crucial role in the neurological characterization of various transgenic mouse models and giving valuable information about epilepsies and sleep disorders in humans. They emphasized that without restraint from tethered EEG systems, the subjects can be observed without interference in their physiology.

Williams and co-workers (2006) used a three EEG channel system (DSI; St. Paul, Minn.) to record interictal spikes and epileptiform activity in the cortex and hippocampus of rats. They studied the model of kainic acid-induced seizures and long-term telemetric EEG recording to investigate epileptogenesis. According to them, although the chance to perform prolonged recordings is a great advantage, the cost, surgical complexity and frequency resolution of the system are listed as disadvantages. Obviously, collecting the data is just the first step, and throughout the use of the same system, White and colleagues (2006) tested different algorithms to process very large EEG data files acquired over 13 days. They concluded that the quality of the EEG and the type of analysis method employed can affect the positive predictive value (PPV, or true positives divided by the sum of true positives and false positives) and sensitivity (true positives divided by the sum of true positives and false negatives). In that sense, both implantation surgery accuracy and telemetry device integrity may be very important factors.

Lapray and colleagues (2008) presented a cost-effective and reusable telemetry system to record EEG in rats. The system allows a sampling rate of 500 Hz (bi-directional) and a range of up to 3 meters. The data transmission rate is roughly 115 kbps and the receiver connected to a computer through the USB port. The software developed by the group allows the recording of simultaneous video, opening the possibility to efficiently correlate behavior and EEG patterns. Finally, the study not only of EEG, but also action potentials during normal behavior, can be benefited by telemetry. It is known that the activity of place cells is highly correlated with the animal's spatial position (O'Keefe and Speakman, 1987; O'Keefe *et al.*, 1998). A very innovative system was created by Chen and co-workers (2008) that used telemetry to record brain potentials in 3D mazes to investigate the role of hippocampal place cells in rats. The wireless technology used was Bluetooth which allowed a range of 5 meters and sampling at up to 10 kHZ, drastically increasing the frequency resolution and satisfying the conditions to have single unit recordings.

3. Distinguishing pathological from normal oscillatory brain patterns

The identification of physiologically relevant brain wave patterns is indispensable when doing EEG studies. In essence, oscillatory brain patterns can be classified as normal (non-pathological) or abnormal (pathological) brain oscillations. For example, normal brain oscillatory synchronization is highly correlated with mental process, perception, memory and behavioral states, such as sleep (Singer, 1999; Engel *et al.*, 2001; Pareti and De Palma, 2004; Gross *et al.*, 2004; Cantero and Atienza, 2005; Schnitzler and Gross, 2005). By comparison, abnormal brain oscillations are usually associated with dysfunctions, such as, cholinergic system imbalances and epilepsy (Traub, 2003; Timofeev and Steriade, 2004; Schnitzler and Gross, 2005). When spike/wave activity is present in the EEG, it is defined as an epileptiform pattern. It might not necessarily mean that the subject developed epilepsy, since this pathology is characterized by spontaneous recurrent seizures (SRS). The spike/wave activity occurs due to hypersynchronous firing in certain regions of the brain that are then called an "epileptic focus" (Engel, 1993). Depending on the affected area, the manifestations can be sensory, motor, or cognitive. The limbic regions are the most frequently affected areas, including the hippocampus, amygdala, pyriform cortex, and cortex (Turski *et al.*, 1983b; Carpentier *et al.*, 1990; Petras, 1994; Scremin *et al.*, 1998; Shih *et al.*, 2003). The situation becomes critical if the seizure is sustained for a prolonged period without significant interruption or recovery. When such an event takes place, the subject is experiencing *status epilepticus* (SE) and can years later display SRS. Under these circumstances, appropriate treatment is anticonvulsant therapy and monitoring (*i.e.* continuous video-EEG) in order to try to interrupt the process of epileptogenesis.

3.1 Normal brain oscillatory synchronization

Various types of brain oscillations can be identified during the circadian cycle. A simplification of these types is exemplified in Fig. 1. Among normal function during the circadian cycle, sleep is of great importance and, obviously, sleep scoring or staging is fundamental as a tool in understanding normal and pathological situations. Gottesmann, (1992) described seven sleep-waking stages in the rat: 1 - attentive walking with dorsal hippocampus theta; 2 - quiet waking without theta pattern; 3 - sleep with cortical slow waves of increasing amplitude; 4 - deeper sleep with cortical spindles that progressively increase in number and amplitude; 5 - pre-paradoxal sleep events with high amplitude spindles that occur in parallel with thalamic sensory transmission to cortex; 6 - paradoxical sleep (eye movements are absent); 7 - paradoxical sleep with the characteristic rapid eye movements (REM). Since manual sleep scoring is laborious and time-consuming, several attempts have been made to automate this process. Gross and co-workers (2009) designed a MATLAB toolbox to perform semi-automated sleep scoring. The system is able to distinguish the states of waking, non-REM (NREM), transition-to-REM, and REM sleep if EEG and EMG are recorded simultaneously. Methods describing details for optimal EEG acquisition calibration, electrode application, signal filtering and power spectral analysis for sleep research were described by Campbell (2009).
The search for the substrates of normal brain oscillations and its correlation with cognitive function, neurochemistry and behavioral states has been studied for several decades. Graf & Kastin, (1984) pointed that peptides can play a role, for example, in sleep, EEG and circadian patterns. Neurons that secrete orexins (excitatory neuropeptide hormones) are likely to be very important in promoting wakefulness during the circadian cycle and in controlling the transition to REM sleep. Also, hormones, like estradiol, can decrease sleep and increase locomotion (Mong *et al.*, 2003). Among the neuroanatomical areas that play a role on sleep, the locus coeruleus is very important, generating brain states such as alertness. Its activation changes the EEG activity from typical non-alert patterns to alert patterns. The locus coeruleus also has a role in attention processes by changing the sensory responses of neocortical neurons and participating in orienting responses occurring in the forebrain that are closely linked to event-related potentials (Foote *et al.*, 1991). EEG studies indicated that the noradrenergic connections from the locus coeruleus excite the upper brain areas, while activation of serotonergic pathways inhibits the same areas. A population of cholinergic neurons can induce and maintain paradoxical sleep and also induce a rapid and transient elevation of alertness (Kayama and Koyama, 1998). In other words projections from the locus coeruleus work as the arousal system. The suprachiasmatic nucleus located in the hypothalamus can also modulate sleep (Dijk and Duffy, 1999). The hypothalamic ventrolateral preoptic area and pons/basal forebrain can play a role on both arousing and sleep-inducing neuronal networks. The mentioned structures could play a role as an ON/OFF switch or transition from sleep to awake state and vice-versa. During sleep, one

subpopulation of pontine neurons discharges during REM stage exclusively and another subpopulation stops its firing activity during REM (Sinton and McCarley, 2004). Finally, the so-called sleep spindles occur due to cyclical interactions between thalamo-cortical and thalamo-reticular neurons (McCormick and Bal, 1997).

Several authors investigated the relationship between normal oscillations with cognitive function and behavioral states. The importance of "naps" is very well recognized in certain cultures and, indeed, brief periods of sleep (5-15 min) can improve cognitive performance. However, side naps that last longer than 30 min can result in a short period of impairment but produce better cognitive performance over longer periods. Early afternoon naps are most effective and can result in performance improvement revealing that the circadian time within which the nap occurs is very important (Lovato and Lack, 2010). Buzsáki, (1991) elaborated a model of memory trace formation based on neocortical-hippocampal interactions, proposing that during exploratory behavior, information is transmitted from neocortex to hippocampus through fast-firing granule cells projections to a specific population of CA3 pyramidal neurons. In fact, during the acquisition of memories (spatial and episodic), the hippocampus is initially engaged, but later the memory traces are migrated to the neocortex (Ribeiro *et al.*, 2007). Indeed, the immediate early genes expression is upregulated during REM sleep in cortical areas but not in the hippocampus (Ribeiro *et al.*, 2007). O'Neill and co-workers (2010) investigated the role of the hippocampus in episodic and spatial memories. The hippocampus is able to not only encode this type of memory, but also to consolidate it throughout interactions with the cortex during "reactivation" of the original network firing patterns during sleep and rest. These interactions could be coordinated by sharp wave/ripple events occurring in the hippocampus. There is a close relationship between sleep mechanisms and memory processes. During REM sleep, there is an increase on the transcription of genes linked to plasticity phenomena, allowing the occurrence of both long-term potentiation (LTP) and depotentiation in areas such as the hippocampus. Sleep spindles would be related to plasticity in the cortex, due to specific reactivation of hippocampal and cortical neuronal circuits. Interestingly, when there is a predominance of delta waves, a neuronal reactivation (in phase with delta activity) concomitant with high protein synthesis levels may have a crucial role to play in a long-lasting LTP (Poe *et al*, 2010).

Other authors have been investigating the sleep/awake EEG patterns during several types of situations. Miller (1995) studied EEG data acquired from truck drivers during sleep and wake period (driving) with the purpose of creating a database available internationally. Pavy Le-Traon & Roussel (1993) reviewed several studies about sleep during manned space flights and found that the most important disturbances occur because of changes in phase due to tasks that are required during the flight. The authors consider that environmental factors, such as microgravity, light-dark cycles and psychological elements, play a role and must be studied. Using an interesting approach to investigate the link between genetics and neurophysiology, Linkowski (1999) studied sleep in twins. Recording EEG during three consecutive nights using a small sample of both monozygotic and dizygotic young male twins, they found out that the twins had a variance in sleep stages that could be genetically determined. However, REM sleep variances apparently did not have a relationship with genetics. Teenagers have peculiar sleep schedules that are likely linked to brain "maturation". According to Feinberg & Campbell, (2010) the power on the delta (1-4 Hz) band declines between ages 11 and 12 years and falls by 65% by age 17 years. Theta power during NREM is reduced earlier. The group hypothesizes that during adolescence, the reorganization in the human brain, particularly frontal cortex, may contribute to these EEG changes. As this period is crucial, errors in brain plasticity may induce mental illness, such as schizophrenia.

Several investigators have focused on the study of sleep patterns in different species. Immediately prior to hibernation, REM sleep is not present if temperature is below 25°C and during deep hibernation animals are preferentially in NREM sleep. The hibernation is not homogenous through time and the power of the signal in the delta band is higher after arousal from hibernation and then reduced over time (Canguilhem & Boissin, 1996). Birds are frequently used to investigate auditory processing through the analysis of multiunit electrophysiological responses (Terleph *et al.*, 2006), but little is known about the occurrence of sleep in flying birds. Circumstantial evidence of sleep during flight indicates that similar to mammals, birds can exhibit slow-wave and REM sleep. Interestingly, slow wave sleep can occur in one or both hemispheres at a single time and REM sleep occurs only simultaneously in both hemispheres of the brain. Since the eye connected to the "awake" hemisphere remains open, it allows the bird to have navigation information during most of time during a flight (Rattenborg, 2006). In sum, the study of EEG sleep pattern in different species could one day allow a better understanding of sleep disturbances.

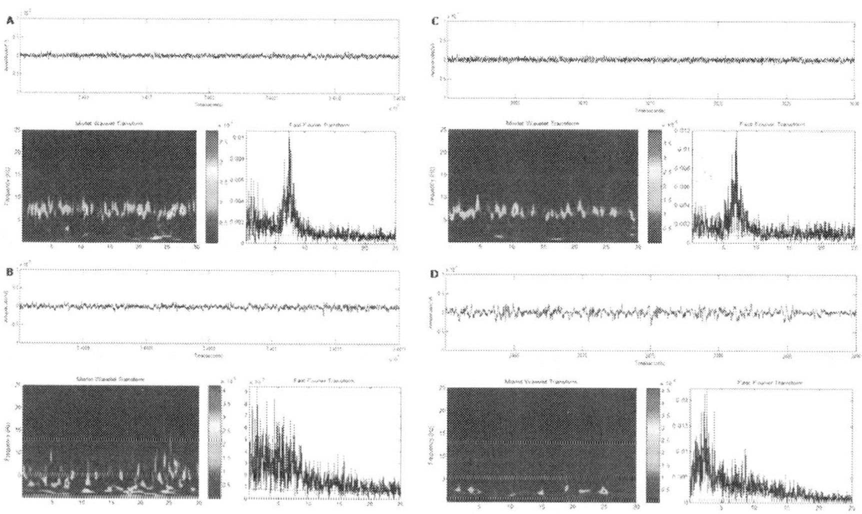

Fig. 1. Cortical electrocorticograms showing baseline electrical activity in Sprague-Dawley rats. The raw EEG (top), Morlet wavelet transform (bottom left), and FFT (bottom right) are being represented during the states of awake alert (exploratory behavior - A), awake non-alert (B - resting), REM sleep (C) and non-REM sleep (D). Note the sustained frequency on the theta band (4.1-8.0 Hz) during awake alert (scanning) and REM sleep. The dominant frequencies are shifted to the left during awake non-alert and much more during non-REM sleep.

3.2 Abnormal brain oscillatory synchronization

The abnormal changes found in EEG oscillations are highly linked to sleep disturbances, cognitive performance and syndromes like epilepsy. It is very important to keep regular sleep periods and a reduction of as little as 1.3 hrs may result in reductions in alertness (Bonnet and Arand, 1995). According to Newmark & Clayton, (1995), headaches and sleep problems are probably overlooked during medical evaluations during active duty. Sleep disturbances can be associated with depression (Vanbemmel, 1997) and interestingly, sleep deprivation can function as an antidepressant treatment in 40-60% of patients that suffer from depression (Hemmeter *et al.*, 2010). Although the mechanisms are still unclear, this phenomenon may help on the development of new antidepressants.

Among all situations that cause alterations of brain oscillatory patterns, brain damage is the most critical, leading to seizures and sleep disturbances. Shouse, da Silva, & Sammaritano (1996) pinpointed that seizures and inter-ictal events have circadian distribution, indicating that some arousal and sleep states are seizure-prone, while others are seizure resistant, both modulating seizure occurrence. Kotagal & Yardi (2008) pointed out that seizures during the sleep state are reported in approximately one third of epileptic patients. Both normal sleep pattern and sleep deprivation modulate the frequency of epileptiform discharges observed in the EEG and behavioral seizures do occur more frequently during NREM sleep.

Brain damage can be caused mechanically, chemically or even influenced by genetic factors. Blast is currently the major cause of battlefield injuries and death. Blast overpressure waves affect organs such the brain, auditory system, the gastrointestinal tract, and predominantly the lungs (Wightman and Gladish, 2001; DePalma *et al*, 2005; Garner and Brett, 2007; and Long *et al*, 2009). Unfortunately, there are no currently approved neuroprotective agents for use in ischemic stroke or traumatic brain injury. Recently, Vespa and co-workers (2010) showed that TBI can lead to electrographic SE, a state in which prolonged and uninterrupted seizures occur without recovery, for a period of 30 min or more. The identification of SE is essential in avoiding the development of epilepsy. Seizures are clinical manifestations of hypersynchronous and hyperexcitatory neuronal activity in a given neuronal network and can lead to brain damage and further "rewiring" that causes a chronic epileptic state, characterized by SRS (Shorvon, 2000). It is known that patients that suffer TBI may, at some point, develop SRS and latency to SRS is dependent on the degree of damage (Salazar *et al.*, 1995; Chen *et al.*, 2009; Lowenstein, 2009). It is very important to distinguish EEG traces characteristic of each state from seizures and seizure-like events. The clear identification of electrographic SE is essential to interfere and attempt to avoid the development of epilepsy.

Exposure to certain compounds can also induce SE and lead to brain damage. Exposure to organophosphorus agents (OP) can cause signs of seizures such as myoclonic movements, respiratory distress, and death (Engel, 1993; McDonough & Shih, 1997). OP compounds inhibit the enzyme acetylcholinesterase that normally degrades the neurotransmitter acetylcholine. When acetylcholinesterase is inhibited, the result is a cholinergic hyperactivation in brain areas such as piriform cortex and the medial septal area leading to increased glutamatergic drive in the piriform, entorhinal, and perirhinal cortices and the hippocampus, causing the expression of motor seizures and SE (Myhrer, 2007). This excessive glutamatergic drive can cause neuroexcitotoxicity (Wasterlain and Shirasaka, 1994). The overactivation of N-methyl-D-aspartate (NMDA; a type of glutamatergic receptor) immediately induces an influx of Ca^{2+}, leading to a series of molecular events that ultimately cause cell death (Delorenzo *et al.*, 2005). As one of the results of brain damage caused by SE, certain brain areas display neuroplastic changes (like axonal sprouting) in neuronal circuitry. The axonal sprouting in the hippocampus is hypothesized in the literature as one of the causes of epilepsy (Mello *et al.*, 1993; Okazaki *et al.*, 1995).

Although prolonged seizures lasting 30 min or more are characterized as SE (Sloviter, 1999), recently, Chen and Wasterlain (2006) proposed the term "impending status epilepticus" for seizures that last at least 5 min, pointing out such seizures should be treated immediately.

The use of animal models of SE is an excellent tool to study SE and its consequences. Approaches such as telemetry have greatly reduced the number of animals used and greatly refined such studies. Models such as seizures induced by systemic and intra-hippocampal pilocarpine (Turski *et al.*, 1983a; Cavalheiro *et al.*, 1991; Furtado *et al.*, 2002; Furtado *et al.*, 2011; Castro *et al.*, 2011), soman (McDonough *et al.*, 1986; Carpentier *et al.*, 1990; Petras, 1994; Shih and McDonough, 1997; Myhrer, 2007; de Araujo Furtado *et al.*, 2010; Figueiredo *et al.*, 2011), kainic acid (Ben-Ari *et al.*, 1979; Williams *et al.*, 2007) and electrical stimulation of the amygdala (Nissinen *et al.*, 2000) have brought answers to fundamental questions about the mechanisms of seizures and treatment options. SRS was found in animals experiencing SE induced by pilocarpine (Leite *et al.*, 1990; Mello *et al.*, 1993) and kainic acid (Pisa *et al.*, 1980; Cronin and Dudek, 1988; Hellier and Dudek, 1999) after a latent period. Also, self-sustaining SE and SRS can be provoked by uninterrupted electrical hippocampal stimulation (Lothman *et al.*, 1989; 1990), perforant path stimulation (Mazarati *et al.*, 1998; Mazarati *et al.*, 2002) and electrical stimulation of the amygdala (Nissinen *et al.*, 2000). Brain damage caused by OP (such as soman) can also lead to SRS. There are reports in the literature implying the occurrence of recurrent seizures in rats (McDonough *et al.*, 1986b) and a full characterization of soman-induced SRS is described by de Araujo Furtado *et al.*, (2010) using long-term EEG recording through telemetry.

Regardless of the fact that the discussion continues as to which brain changes lead to SRS, the occurrence of an initial insult may likely induce SRS (Sloviter, 1999). However, recent reports have shown that subjects that are challenged to a convulsive stimulus, but do not display SE, still have a probability of developing SRS much later (Navarro Mora *et al.*, 2009; Pernot *et al.*, 2009) suggesting that long-term video-EEG monitoring may be necessary in most studies in order to truly study epileptogenesis.

It is important to recognize that different patterns of seizures can be present after the brain receives a mechanical, electrical or chemical challenge. Although it is very complex, several seizure patterns have been found during the SE (Treiman *et al.*, 1990). Fig. 2 shows characteristic EEG during SE and a summary of recurrent seizure patterns and SRS are presented in the next section.

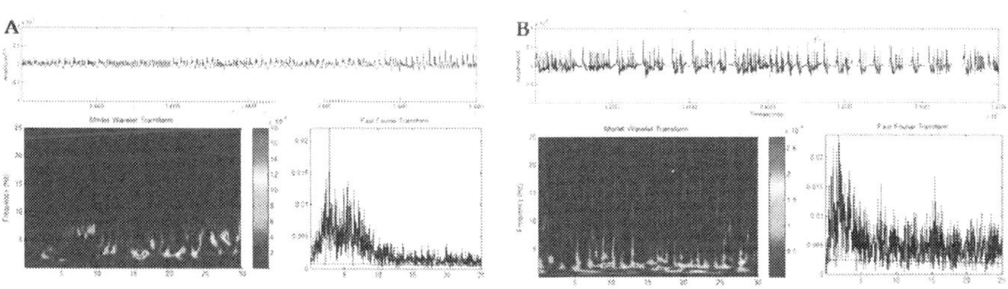

Fig. 2. Representative cortical electrocorticograms showing electrical activity during different periods after soman exposure. (A) 13 min after exposure. (B) 33 min after exposure. SE can last for several hrs and, even after treatment, recurrent seizures may occur (see next section).

3.2.1 Recurrent seizures

After the termination of SE, there is normally a period without seizures that can last from minutes to hours. Subsequently, subjects may display recurrent seizures that can induce additional brain damage. These seizures come however in different patterns, the type 1 pattern (Fig. 3A) is characterized by low frequencies between 0.8 and 1.4 Hz (delta band), with high amplitude spikes. The type 2 pattern also oscillated in the delta band, but faster than type 1, between 1.4 and 3.7. This pattern is characterized by high and low amplitude spikes (Fig. 3B). The type 3 pattern has frequencies oscillating in the theta band, between 4.8 and 5.4 Hz, with low spikes (Fig. 3C). The type 4 pattern is characterized by no spikes, but oscillates also in theta band, faster than type 3, between 5.5 and 6.5 (Fig. 3D). Long-term video-EEG monitoring may be necessary in most studies in order to detect epileptogenesis.

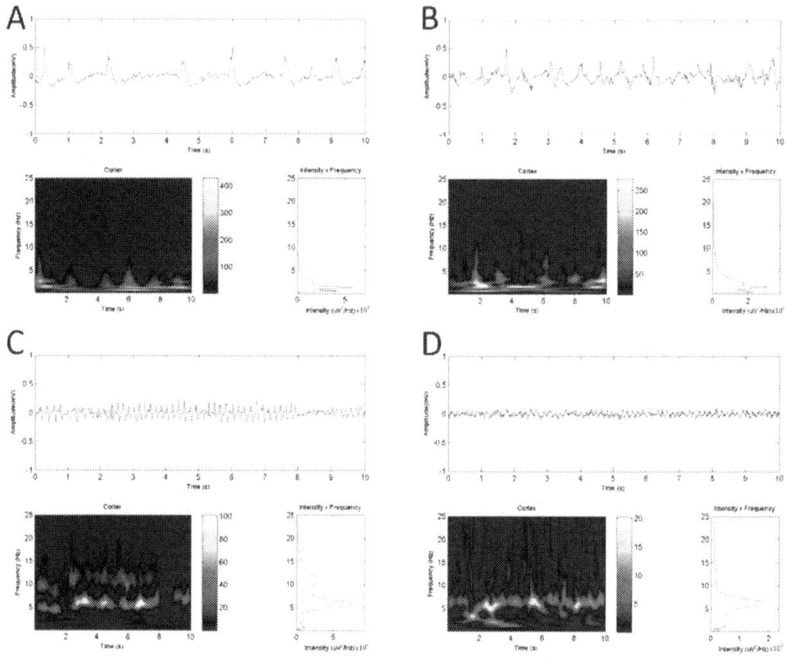

Fig. 3. Electrographic seizures patterns (10 sec) calculated and illustrated in wavelet transform analyses. A - Type 1 Pattern; B - Type 2 Pattern; C - Type 3 Pattern; D - Type 4 Pattern. The first fig (at the top) of each pattern shows the EEG (Amplitude x Time); the second fig (down left) of each pattern shows the frequencies in exact time (Frequency x Time); the third fig (down right) of each pattern shows the power of frequency (Intensity x Frequency).

3.2.2 Spontaneous recurrent seizures

Electrographic SRS are characterized by frequencies oscillating in the theta band (4.1 to 8 Hz) and are sustained during most of the duration of the seizure. From 25 sec up to 45 sec, there also appeared to be sustained oscillation in the alpha band (8.1 to 12 Hz) but with reduced power spectrum. Dominant frequencies of the delta band (0.1 to 4 Hz) also appeared mainly at the beginning of seizures, but were not sustained in the time (Fig. 4).

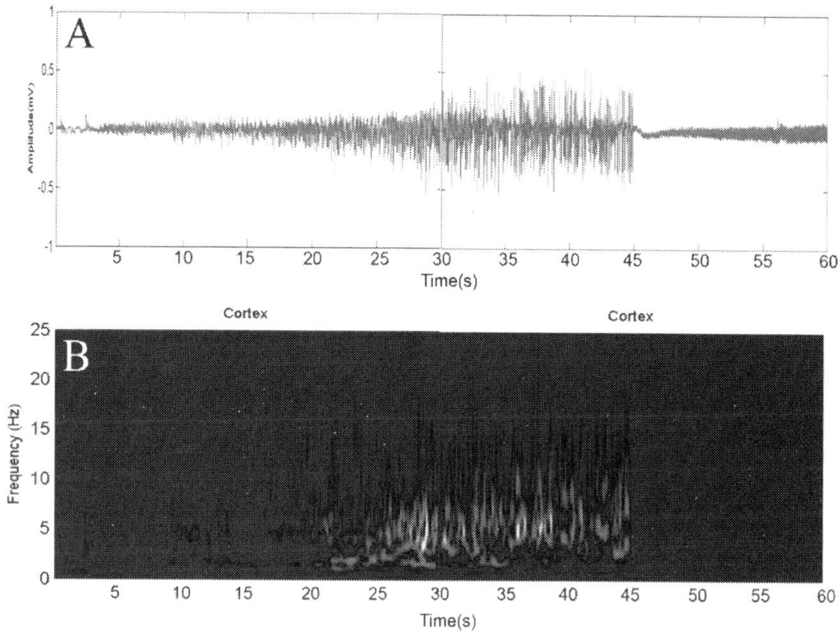

Fig. 4. Output of a representative SRS (60 sec.) wavelet transform spectral analysis. A - EEG (amplitude x time) of SRS; B - Frequency x time analyses of SRS; C- Intensity of frequencies analysis.

4. Assessment of the long-term EEG changes

The use of telemetry to capture continuous recordings has the advantage of allowing the detection of SRS and long term changes in circadian brain oscillations. However, telemetry results in a large accumulation of data. A large volume of data can result in analysis delay, frustration and poor EEG interpretation. Unique tools capable of performing efficient spectral analyses (Rossetti *et al.*, 2006; Romcy-Pereira *et al.*, 2008; Lehmkuhle *et al.*, 2009), seizure estimation, and spike detection (Saab and Gotman, 2005; White *et al.*, 2006; Casson *et al.*, 2007; Jacquin *et al.*, 2007; Hopfengärtner *et al.*, 2007) has been used in several studies on epilepsy. Artificial neural networks have proven to be the most reliable tool (Gabor *et al.*, 1996; Gabor, 1998; Nigam and Graupe, 2004; Kiymik *et al.*, 2004; Tzallas *et al.*, 2007; Srinivasan *et al.*, 2007; Patnaik and Manyam, 2008) but require tremendous computational power in order to be time effective when analyzing large data sets. Another alternative is the use of commercial software designed for seizure detection. However, most often, this type of software is "tuned" to specific parameters for human subjects, such as sleep stages and spike and wave activity. In some cases, these parameters must be changed between subjects, bringing bias to the analysis. Therefore, in several situations, the use of third-party software tools for the evaluation of large data sets (for example, EEG acquired during long-term pharmacological studies) may be contaminated by bias if the software was originally designed to address a dissimilar problem. However, several groups have invested time in creating tools that permit users, without previous programming experience, to run complex EEG analysis algorithms (Delorme and Makeig, 2004; Mørup *et al.*, 2007; Romcy-Pereira *et al.*, 2008; de Araujo Furtado *et al.*, 2009). Such tools are quite reliable, and some of them are now adjusted for large data sets with multiple parameters, such as EEG, EMG, temperature and gross motor activity.

4.1 Choosing the parameters of acquisition

Prior to the start of any experiment, it is fundamental to choose the proper parameters of acquisition to optimize further analysis. The objectives, maximum frequency of interest, duration of the experiment, number of channels and available disk storage are key factors in determining the sampling rate and pre-filtering options. Obviously, according to the Nyquist Theorem, the signal must be sampled at least twice the maximum frequency of interest to extract all of the information from the bandwidth and represent the original biopotential (Drongelen, 2006). For example, in order to observe massive oscillations such as hippocampal ripples (Buzsáki *et al.*, 1987; Buzsáki *et al.*, 2003; ~200 Hz) a sampling rate of over 1 KHz is recommended for practical purposes. Also, if one wants to verify whether electrographic seizures have a behavioral correlate or not, synchronous video should be recorded. The use of 2 EEG channels (250 Hz each) plus temperature (250 Hz), activity (0.1 Hz) and signal strength (16 Hz) recorded in a Data Systems International system (DSI, Arden Hills, MN) results in approximately 175 MB per day. If one performs a 30-day experiment, it will be necessary to reserve approximately 5.2 GB per subject. In this particular example, the animals were placed in individual cages, each positioned on AM radio receiving pads (RPC-1; Data Systems International - DSI, Arden Hills, MN) that detect signals from an implanted transmitter (F40-EET) and send them to an input exchange matrix. Each analog input matrix is capable of receiving input from up to four receivers. A PCI-card model number CQ2240 (Data Systems International - DSI, Arden Hills, MN) receives data input from an exchange matrix. The signal is sent to a computer and telemetry data (up to 16 animals) are recorded through Dataquest ART 4.1 (Acquisition software; Data Systems International - DSI, Arden Hills, MN). The DSI transmitter uses a voltage-controlled oscillator which converts the biopotential difference into a frequency signal. The biopotential channels are encoded in pulse-to-pulse intervals that are transmitted by the F40-EET as RF waves. The relationship between the transmitted interval in microseconds and the input signal in millivolts is described by the calibration entered into the Dataquest ART 4.1 in units of microseconds per millivolts. Attenuation of the signal is very low due to the close proximity of the transmitter to the receiver. The filtering at the device level for the system (implant and acquisition system) is described as less than 3dB attenuation at 1 Hz and 50 Hz in the case of the F40-EET. The filtering within the implanted transmitter is nominally 0.6 Hz (−3dB) for the high-pass filter and 60 Hz (−3dB) for the low-pass filter. It is generated by one-pole of a high-pass filtering and one-pole of low-pass filtering. The activity of each animal is derived from the strength of the signal. When the signal strength changes by a set amount, the data exchange matrix generates an activity count. The number of counts is proportional to both distance and speed of movement. However, the activity is a relative measure, not the distance traveled (de Araujo Furtado *et al.* (2009).

Also, when dealing with prolonged EEG recordings, usually the recordings are split in several files due to the operational system file size limitation. In this case, it is important to limit the file size (for example, 100 MB), so if a data corruption/loss occurs, there is still a chance to recover some or most of the EEG epochs. However, if the file size is too small (for example 1 MB), several files will be generated making copying of files to another unit for further analysis very slow.

4.2 Choosing the tools to analyze the EEG data

The objectives of the experiment will influence the tools used for EEG analysis. Parameters, such as changes in power spectra over time, seizure duration and frequency, and number of channels recorded are very important. For example, if more than one channel is recorded, then a coherence and cross-correlation analysis may be performed (electrodes must be bipolar to run cross-correlogram).

Also, the choice of using commercial EEG software or open source software (or a combination of both) will depend on one's budget and technical background. It is common to find commercial software that allows the processing of large datasets using relatively little memory, but it is not easy to find an open source code with this feature. The graphical user interface (GUI) is another important feature to take into account. Commercial software often includes a user-friendly GUI, while the open-source software GUI is often less functional for the implementation of useful tools. For example, several functions are normally run from the command line when dealing with open source software. Also, the open-source GUI is normally just used to semi-automate the use of certain functions or to visually screen biopotential recordings, such as the EEG. Commercial code is often more stable than open-source code which is constantly aggregated with new functions and therefore, more subject to unexpected errors. Thus, open-source software is not approved for clinical use and should be used only experimentally. User support is another important factor when choosing what type of tool one may use. Commercial software has dedicated personnel for user support, while the help provided by open-source code teams is dependent on its availability.

Open source software, like the EEGLAB (Delorme and Makeig, 2004) and Chronux Analysis Software (http://chronux.org), is able to open several different file types, while commercial software is restricted to handling a small number of formats. The European data format is open and very flexible (EDF; B Kemp *et al.* 1992; Bob Kemp and Olivan 2003). In fact, EEG MATLAB toolboxes (de Araujo Furtado *et al.*, 2009) can benefit from this open file format. Also, the number of functions present in open-source software is virtually unlimited, since one can always add new functions. Thus, the scientific community can always help to implement new analysis approaches. On the other hand, current commercial software is limited since the user cannot add new complex analysis options, since the source code is not available. Normally, the language adopted for open source software is MATLAB. Although it requires an initial investment in a MATLAB license, it still does not compare in terms of price to commercial code that does not have the same flexibility, and functions as MATLAB. Also, a compiled version of a MATLAB toolbox does not require MATLAB. Using MATLAB, one can test new tools that are not present yet in commercial software. Through open source software and MATLAB, one can create figures (in different formats) that are immediately suitable for publications. On the other hand, in commercial software, graphics can only be saved using specific formats. It is very clear that commercial EEG software and open-source software have advantages and disadvantages and the software selection for EEG analysis is usually not easy.

We record EEG, activity and temperature during the entire course of an experiment and for extended periods beyond SE. A set of MATLAB algorithms was developed (de Araujo Furtado *et al.*, 2009) to remove artifacts and measure the characteristics of long-term EEG recordings. The algorithms use short-time Fourier transforms to calculate the power spectrum of the signal for 2-sec intervals. The FFT can be represented by the expression:

$$X(k) = \sum_{j=1}^{N} x(j)\omega_N^{(j-1)(k-1)},$$

$$\text{where } \omega_N = e^{(2\pi i)/N}$$

The spectrum is then divided into the delta (1-4 Hz), theta (4.1-8 Hz), alpha (8.1-12 Hz), and beta (12.1-25 Hz) bands. Using the MATLAB function "robustfit.m", a linear fit to the power spectrum is used to indicate the likehood of normal EEG activity versus artifacts and high amplitude spike-wave activity. Changes in seizure frequency and duration over a prolonged period are a powerful indicator of the effects of potential neuroprotectants against seizures. The algorithm is very sensitive and, combined with further visual inspection, can give a reliable measurement of both SE duration and SRS frequency. Batch-processing is also used, which is a considerable advantage if a large number of subjects is used (such as in experimental pharmacology), because it increases the level of automation, allowing us to focus on other tasks, while the data is being processed.

Another way to evaluate spectral changes in the EEG signal is through the short-time Fourier transforms (STFT) that can be represented by the expression:

$STFT(t,w) = \int [x(\tau) - W\,(\tau - t)e^{-jw\tau}d\tau$, where W represents the sliding window used to divide the signal (Romcy-Pereira *et al.*, 2008). Normally, when the STFT of a signal is calculated, one can represent it in a spectrogram, where the power spectrum is calculated for different times (t), segmented by the window W. In essence, a spectrogram pictures the distribution of the energy of the signal in the time and in frequency domain. However the size and type of the time window are determinants in the analysis and one must keep in mind the limitations of the STFT: as the time resolution increases (shorter window), the accuracy in which the frequency component is measured is diminished. An alternative is the use of wavelets, but it takes a longer time to process these compared to FFT.

Among the several types of wavelets, the Morlet wavelet is one of the most used to create a time frequency representation of EEG signals that may have epileptiform patterns. The Morlet wavelet is represented according to the expression:

$w(f_0, t) = A\varphi \cdot e^{-t^{2}/2\sigma_t^2} \cdot e^{i2\pi f_0 t}$, where $\sigma_t = 1/2\pi\sigma_f$ is the time of the wavelet and σ_f is its frequency (Romcy-Pereira *et al* (2008).

The GUI shown in Fig. 5 simultaneously plots the EEG in the time domain, the FFT, Morlet wavelet transform, allowing the confirmation or rejection of seizures by the user. Although many artifacts are clipped automatically, the user has the chance to verify if artifacts are still present. Gross motor activity and temperature are compared with EEG changes.

It is very important to identify and, if possible, remove artifacts in the EEG recording. Either manually or semi-automatically, artifacts should be rejected prior to any interpretation of the results. Delorme and co-workers (2007) presented an elegant method that uses independent component analysis (ICA) decomposition as a tool to isolate different artifacts from the EEG, although muscle artifact detection was not very effective.

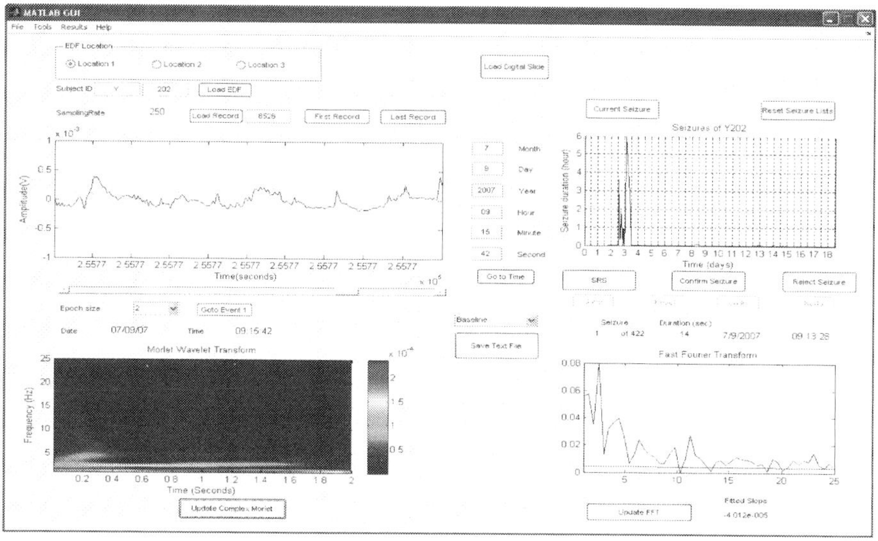

Fig. 5. Graphical user interface created using MATLAB that allows users to view various properties of EEG signal. Representative cortical electroencephalograms showing electrical activity during SE (B). Adapted from de Araujo Furtado and co-workers (2009).

As mentioned, when more than one channel is used, we can investigate the relationship between them. Connectivity between different brain circuits can be evaluated by determining the temporal relationship between brain signals from distinct brain regions. Cross-correlogram may be a better choice to analyze epileptiform patterns, when the propagation of temporal defined events has an important role. The coherence is preferred when the background activity between different areas is comparable (Drongelen, 2006).

According to Drongelen (2006), the coherence C between two different signals (x and y) can be defined as S_{xy} normalized by power spectra S_{xx} and S_{yy}, respectively. Then, in order to determine coherence, a number (without dimension) between 0 and 1, S_{xy} is squared. It can be represented by:

$$C(\omega) = \frac{|S_{xy}(\omega)^2|}{S_{xx}(\omega)S_{yy}(\omega)}$$

The cross-correlation R_{xy}, between two time series x and y, can be represented by:

$$R_{xy}(t_1 t_2 = E\{x(t_1)y(t_2)\}$$

However, the electrodes must be bipolar if ones decide to run a cross-correlogram, so the measurements on each channel will correspond to a better defined and small neuroanatomical area, something that does not happen with monopolar electrodes.

In summary, the choice of tools used for signal processing must be carefully evaluated, taking into account the goals and methodological limitations of the study. A reasonable background not only in neuroscience, but mathematics and computer programming may be necessary depending on the objectives.

5. Conclusions

The use of telemetry to record biopotentials like the EEG during long periods is fundamental to study the role of brain damage in epileptogenesis. Our group (de Araujo Furtado *et al.*, 2010) found and quantified SRS in rats exposed to the nerve agent soman, several days post-exposure. White and co-workers (2010) investigated the occurrence of spontaneous seizures in the kainate model through the use of a commercially available telemetry system (DSI). They were able to identify spikes and spike clusters, which occurred after the initial, prolonged seizure, but preceded the first spontaneous seizure, thus finding clues about the development of chronic epilepsy using the EEG as a powerful biomarker. An EEG telemetry system can allow the investigation of a phenomenon that without continuous monitoring would never be accurately studied. Still, one must be careful about the interpretation of results because the number of EEG channels limits the identification of the epileptic focus.

The identification and characterization of SRS, that occur after acute seizures induced by soman, emphasize the importance of quantifying SRS in studies where the objective is to find new therapeutics against soman-provoked seizures. It is known that exposure to soman can cause acute and chronic damage (Petras, 1994; Shih *et al.*, 2003), therefore, an ideal evaluation model must assess the neuroprotective effect of the therapeutic agent with both short-term and long-term EEG monitoring. However, it is very common to monitor the EEG for a time period of only 1–2 days post-exposure in the field of nerve agent studies. Obviously, this period is not enough to detect SRS and long-term morphological changes. Optimally, one should study the EEG changes over a period of several months (limited by the battery life of telemetry devices).

Among the limitations of telemetry, battery life is probably one of the most important. Also, an implantable telemetry system must be miniaturized in a way that the subject is not disturbed. Sealing of the transmitter plays a role, because if sealing is compromised it can ruin the device and consequentially the experiment. Several new technologies may address these limitations. New approaches that allow battery integration with the circuit/electrodes and the use of rechargeable batteries may be a great advantage (Budgett *et al.*, 2007). The lack of spatial resolution that is inherent in the EEG could be compensated by the use of arrays of multiple electrodes and the use of Bluetooth technology. Rechargeable batteries could permit one to run very long-term experiments (perhaps 1-2 years), studying epileptogenesis not only in animals that display acute seizures, but also on those that do not exhibit initial status epilepticus. Finally, the use of a semi-automated algorithm is a minimum requirement for data analysis in order to analyze continuous long-term EEG recordings in a time-efficient and accurate manner.

6. Disclosure statement

Material has been reviewed by the Walter Reed Army Institute of Research. There is no objection to its presentation and or publication. The opinions or assertions contained herein are the private views of the author, and are not to be construed as official or as reflecting true views of the Department of the Army or Department of Defense.

7. Acknowledgements

The Defense Threat Reduction Agency, Clinical Research Management, Inc and the National Research Council have provided financial and/or programmatic support. The technical assistance of Andy Zheng, Michael Addis, Keenan Bailey and Soma Chanda is gratefully acknowledged.

8. References

Akulinichev IT, Baevskii RM (1964) Use of radiotelemetry in space medicine. Vestnik Akademii meditsinskikh nauk SSSR 19:60-6.

Alsaadi TM, Thieman C, Shatzel A, Farias S (2004) Video-EEG telemetry can be a crucial tool for neurologists experienced in epilepsy when diagnosing seizure disorders. Seizure : the Journal of the British Epilepsy Association 13:32-4.

Bastlund JF, Jennum P, Mohapel P, Vogel V, Watson WP (2004) Measurement of cortical and hippocampal epileptiform activity in freely moving rats by means of implantable radiotelemetry. Journal of neuroscience methods 138:65-72.

Ben-Ari Y, Lagowska J, Tremblay E, Le Gal La Salle G (1979) A new model of focal status epilepticus: intra-amygdaloid application of kainic acid elicits repetitive secondarily generalized convulsive seizures. Brain Research 163:176-9.

Blanc C, Gravier H, Geier S (1967) Radiotelemetric recordings of the EEG of pilots in the course of flights of long duration. Revue Neurologique 117:222-5.

Bonnet MH, Arand DL (1995) We are chronically sleep deprived. Sleep 18:908-11.

Budgett DM, Hu AP, Si P, Pallas WT, Donnelly MG, Broad JWT, Barrett CJ, Guild S-J, Malpas SC (2007) Novel technology for the provision of power to implantable physiological devices. Journal of Applied Physiology (Bethesda, Md.: 1985) 102:1658-63.

Buzsáki G (1991) Network properties of memory trace formation in the hippocampus. Bollettino della Società Italiana di Biologia Sperimentale 67:817-35.

Buzsáki G, Buhl DL, Harris KD, Csicsvari J, Czéh B, Morozov a (2003) Hippocampal network patterns of activity in the mouse. Neuroscience 116:201-11.

Buzsáki G, Haas HL, Anderson EG (1987) Long-term potentiation induced by physiologically relevant stimulus patterns. Brain Research 435:331-3.

Caldwell JA, Lewis JA (1995) The feasibility of collecting in-flight EEG data from helicopter pilots. Aviation, Space, and Environmental Medicine 66:883-9.

Campbell IG (2009) EEG Recording and Analysis for Sleep Research In Current Protocols in Neuroscience

Canguilhem B, Boissin J (1996) [Is the animal in hibernal sleep awake?]. Neurophysiologie clinique = Clinical Neurophysiology 26:1-7.

Cantero JL, Atienza M (2005) The role of neural synchronization in the emergence of cognition across the wake-sleep cycle. Reviews in the Neurosciences 16:69-83.

Carpentier P, Delamanche IS, Le Bert M, Blanchet G, Bouchaud C (1990) Seizure-related opening of the blood-brain barrier induced by soman: possible correlation with the acute neuropathology observed in poisoned rats. Neurotoxicology 11:493-508.

Casson AJ, Yates DC, Patel S, Rodriguez-Villegas E (2007) Algorithm for AEEG data selection leading to wireless and long term epilepsy monitoring. Conference proceedings : ... Annual International Conference of the IEEE Engineering in Medicine and Biology Society. IEEE Engineering in Medicine and Biology Society. Conference 2007:2456-9.

Castro OW, Furtado MA, Tilelli CQ, Fernandes A, Pajolla GP, Garcia-Cairasco N (2011) Comparative neuroanatomical and temporal characterization of FluoroJadepositive neurodegeneration after status epilepticus induced by systemic and intrahippocampal pilocarpine in Wistar rats. Brain Research 1374:55.

Cavalheiro EA, Leite JP, Bortolotto ZA, Turski WA, Ikonomidou C, Turski L (1991) Long-term effects of pilocarpine in rats: structural damage of the brain triggers kindling and spontaneous recurrent seizures. Epilepsia 32:778-82.

Chen H-Y, Wu J-S, Hyland B, Lu X-D, Chen JJJ (2008) A low noise remotely controllable wireless telemetry system for single-unit recording in rats navigating in a vertical maze. Medical & Biological Engineering & Computing 46:833-9.

Chen JWY, Ruff RL, Eavey R, Wasterlain CG (2009) Posttraumatic epilepsy and treatment. Journal of Rehabilitation Research and Development 46:685-96.

Chen JWY, Wasterlain CG (2006) Status epilepticus: pathophysiology and management in adults. Lancet Neurology 5:246-56.

Cotugno M, Mandile P, D'Angiolillo D, Montagnese P, Giuditta A (1996) Implantation of an EEG telemetric transmitter in the rat. Italian Journal of Neurological Sciences 17:131-4.

Cronin J, Dudek FE (1988) Chronic seizures and collateral sprouting of dentate mossy fibers after kainic acid treatment in rats. Brain Research 474:181-4.

de Araujo Furtado M, Lumley L a, Robison C, Tong LC, Lichtenstein S, Yourick DL (2010) Spontaneous recurrent seizures after status epilepticus induced by soman in Sprague-Dawley rats. Epilepsia 51:1503-10.

de Araujo Furtado M, Zheng A, Sedigh-Sarvestani M, Lumley L, Lichtenstein S, Yourick D (2009) Analyzing large data sets acquired through telemetry from rats exposed to organophosphorous compounds: an EEG study. Journal of Neuroscience Methods 184:176-83.

Delorenzo RJ, Sun DA, Deshpande LS (2005) Cellular mechanisms underlying acquired epilepsy: the calcium hypothesis of the induction and maintainance of epilepsy. Pharmacology & Therapeutics 105:229-66.

Delorme A, Makeig S (2004) EEGLAB: an open source toolbox for analysis of single-trial EEG dynamics including independent component analysis. Journal of Neuroscience Methods 134:9-21.

Delorme A, Sejnowski T, Makeig S (2007) Enhanced detection of artifacts in EEG data using higher-order statistics and independent component analysis. NeuroImage 34:1443-9.

Dijk DJ, Duffy JF (1999) Circadian regulation of human sleep and age-related changes in its timing, consolidation and EEG characteristics. Annals of Medicine 31:130-40.

Dimpfel W, Spüler M, Borbe HO (1988) Monitoring of the effects of antidepressant drugs in the freely moving rat by radioelectroencephalography (tele-stereo-EEG). Neuropsychobiology 19:116-20.

Drongelen WV (2006) Signal processing for neuroscientists: an introduction to the analysis of physiological signals 1st ed. Academic Press.

Engel AK, Fries P, Singer W (2001) Dynamic predictions: oscillations and synchrony in top-down processing. Nature Reviews. Neuroscience 2:704-16.

Engel Jr J (1993) Surgical treatment of the epilepsies. New York: Ravel Press, Ltd.

Feinberg I, Campbell IG (2010) Sleep EEG changes during adolescence: an index of a fundamental brain reorganization. Brain and Cognition 72:56-65.

Figueiredo TH, Qashu F, Apland JP, Aroniadou-Anderjaska V, Souza AP, Braga MFM (2010) The GluK1 (GluR5) kainate / AMPA receptor antagonist LY293558 reduces soman-induced seizures and neuropathology. The Journal of Pharmacology and Experimental Therapeutics 336:303-12.

Fischler H, Frei EH (1963) Subminiature apparatus for radio-telemetering of EEG data. IEEE Transactions on Bio-medical Engineering 10:29-36.

Fitzgerald AL, Juneau P, Cain C, Southwick K (2003) Development of a quantitative method for evaluation of the electroencephalogram of rats by using radiotelemetry. Contemporary topics in laboratory animal science / American Association for Laboratory Animal Science 42:40-5.

Foote SL, Berridge CW, Adams LM, Pineda JA (1991) Electrophysiological evidence for the involvement of the locus coeruleus in alerting, orienting, and attending. Progress in Brain Research 88:521-32.

Frost Jr., J, Shumate W, Booher C, DeLucchi M (1975) The Skylab sleep monitoring experiment: methodology and initial results☆. Acta Astronautica 2:319-336.

Furtado MA, Castro OW, Del Vecchio F, Oliveira JAC de, Garcia-Cairasco N (2011) Study of spontaneous recurrent seizures and morphological alterations after status epilepticus induced by intrahippocampal injection of pilocarpine. Epilepsy & Behavior : E&B 20:257-66.

Furtado MD a, Braga GK, Oliveira J a C, Del Vecchio F, Garcia-Cairasco N (2002) Behavioral, morphologic, and electroencephalographic evaluation of seizures induced by intrahippocampal microinjection of pilocarpine. Epilepsia 43 Suppl 5:37-9.

Gabor AJ (1998) Seizure detection using a self-organizing neural network: validation and comparison with other detection strategies. Electroencephalography and Clinical Neurophysiology 107:27-32.

Gabor AJ, Leach RR, Dowla FU (1996) Automated seizure detection using a self-organizing neural network. Electroencephalography and Clinical Neurophysiology 99:257-66.

Gottesmann C (1992) Detection of seven sleep-waking stages in the rat. Neuroscience and Biobehavioral Reviews 16:31-8.

Graf MV, Kastin AJ (1984) Delta-sleep-inducing peptide (DSIP): a review. Neuroscience and Biobehavioral Reviews 8:83-93.

Gross BA, Walsh CM, Turakhia AA, Booth V, Mashour GA, Poe GR (2009) Open-source logic-based automated sleep scoring software using electrophysiological recordings in rats. Journal of Neuroscience Methods 184:10-8.

Gross DW, Dubeau F, Quesney LF, Gotman J (2000) EEG telemetry with closely spaced electrodes in frontal lobe epilepsy. Journal of Clinical Neurophysiology : official publication of the American Electroencephalographic Society 17:414-8.

Gross J, Schmitz F, Schnitzler I, Kessler K, Shapiro K, Hommel B, Schnitzler A (2004) Modulation of long-range neural synchrony reflects temporal limitations of visual attention in humans. Proceedings of the National Academy of Sciences of the United States of America 101:13050-5.

Hambrecht FT, Donahue PD, Melzack R (1963) A multiple channel EEG telemetering system. Electroencephalography and Clinical Neurophysiology 15:323-6.

Hellier JL, Dudek FE (1999) Spontaneous motor seizures of rats with kainate-induced epilepsy: effect of time of day and activity state. Epilepsy Research 35:47-57.

Helvey WM, Albright GA, Axelrod I (1964) A review of biomedical monitoring activities and report on studies made on f-105 pilots. Aerospace Medicine 35:23-7.

Hemmeter U-M, Hemmeter-Spernal J, Krieg J-C (2010) Sleep deprivation in depression. Expert Review of Neurotherapeutics 10:1101-15.

Herold N, Spray S, Horn T, Henriksen SJ (1998) Measurements of behavior in the naked mole-rat after intraperitoneal implantation of a radio-telemetry system. Journal of Neuroscience Methods 81:151-8.

Holter NJ, Generelli JA (1949) Remote recording of physiological data by radio. Rocky Mountain Medical Journal 46:747-51.

Hopfengärtner R, Kerling F, Bauer V, Stefan H (2007) An efficient, robust and fast method for the offline detection of epileptic seizures in long-term scalp EEG recordings. Clinical Neurophysiology : official journal of the International Federation of Clinical Neurophysiology 118:2332-43.

Jacobson B, Mackay RS (1957) A pH-endoradiosonde. Lancet 272:1224.

Jacquin A, Causevic E, John ER (2007) Automatic identification of spike-wave events and non-convulsive seizures with a reduced set of electrodes. Conference Proceedings: Annual International Conference of the IEEE Engineering in Medicine and Biology Society. IEEE Engineering in Medicine and Biology Society. Conference 2007:1928-31.

Kamp A (1984) Long-term supervised domiciliary EEG monitoring in epileptic patients employing radio telemetry and telephone telemetry. II. Radio telemetry system. Electroencephalography and Clinical Neurophysiology 57:584-6.

Kayama Y, Koyama Y (1998) Brainstem neural mechanisms of sleep and wakefulness. European Urology 33 Suppl 3:12-5.

Kemp B, Olivan J (2003) European data format "plus" (EDF+), an EDF alike standard format for the exchange of physiological data. Clinical neurophysiology : official journal of the International Federation of Clinical Neurophysiology 114:1755-61.

Kemp B, Värri A, Rosa AC, Nielsen KD, Gade J (1992) A simple format for exchange of digitized polygraphic recordings. Electroencephalography and Clinical Neurophysiology 82:391-3.

Kiymik MK, Subasi A, Ozcalik HR (2004) Neural networks with periodogram and autoregressive spectral analysis methods in detection of epileptic seizure. Journal of Medical Systems 28:511-22.

Kotagal P, Yardi N (2008) The relationship between sleep and epilepsy. Seminars in Pediatric Neurology 15:42-9.

Lapray D, Bergeler J, Dupont E, Thews O, Luhmann HJ (2008) A novel miniature telemetric system for recording EEG activity in freely moving rats. Journal of Neuroscience Methods 168:119-26.

Lee D, Hutt SJ, Forrest S, Hutt C (1964) Concurrent EEG and behavioural observations on freely moving children. Developmental Medicine and Child Neurology 6:362-5.

Lehmkuhle MJ, Thomson KE, Scheerlinck P, Pouliot W, Greger B, Dudek FE (2009) A simple quantitative method for analyzing electrographic status epilepticus in rats. Journal of Neurophysiology 101:1660-70.

Leite JP, Bortolotto ZA, Cavalheiro EA (1990) Spontaneous recurrent seizures in rats: an experimental model of partial epilepsy. Neuroscience and Biobehavioral Reviews 14:511-7.

Linkowski P (1999) EEG sleep patterns in twins. Journal of Sleep Research 8 Suppl 1:11-3.
Lothman EW, Bertram EH, Bekenstein JW, Perlin JB (1989) Self-sustaining limbic status epilepticus induced by "continuous" hippocampal stimulation: electrographic and behavioral characteristics. Epilepsy Research 3:107-19.
Lothman EW, Bertram EH, Kapur J, Stringer JL (1990) Recurrent spontaneous hippocampal seizures in the rat as a chronic sequela to limbic status epilepticus. Epilepsy Research 6:110-8.
Lovato N, Lack L (2010) The effects of napping on cognitive functioning. Progress in Brain Research 185:155-66.
Lowenstein DH (2009) Epilepsy after head injury: an overview. Epilepsia 50 Suppl 2:4-9.
Mazarati A, Bragin A, Baldwin R, Shin D, Wilson C, Sankar R, Naylor D, Engel J, Wasterlain CG (2002) Epileptogenesis after self-sustaining status epilepticus. Epilepsia 43 Suppl 5:74-80.
Mazarati AM, Wasterlain CG, Sankar R, Shin D (1998) Self-sustaining status epilepticus after brief electrical stimulation of the perforant path. Brain Research 801:251-3.
McCormick DA, Bal T (1997) Sleep and arousal: thalamocortical mechanisms. Annual Review of Neuroscience 20:185-215.
McDonough JH, Shih TM (1997) Neuropharmacological mechanisms of nerve agent-induced seizure and neuropathology. Neuroscience and Biobehavioral Reviews 21:559-79.
McDonough JH, Smith RF, Smith CD (1986)(a) Behavioral correlates of soman-induced neuropathology: deficits in DRL acquisition. Neurobehav Toxicol Teratol. 8:179-87.
McDonough JH, Smith RF, Smith CD (1986)(b) Behavioral correlates of soman-induced neuropathology: deficits in DRL acquisition. Neurobehavioral Toxicology and Teratology 8:179-87.
Meierkord H (1992) Clinical and neurophysiologic markers of epilepsy with frontal lobe seizures in a series of patients diagnosed by video-EEG-telemetry. Der Nervenarzt 63:485-91.
Mello LE, Cavalheiro EA, Tan AM, Kupfer WR, Pretorius JK, Babb TL, Finch DM (1993) Circuit mechanisms of seizures in the pilocarpine model of chronic epilepsy: cell loss and mossy fiber sprouting. Epilepsia 34:985-95.
Miller JC (1995) Batch processing of 10,000 h of truck driver EEG data. Biological Psychology 40:209-22.
Mohseni P, Najafi K, Eliades SJ, Wang X (2005) Wireless multichannel biopotential recording using an integrated FM telemetry circuit. IEEE Transactions on Neural Systems and Rehabilitation Engineering: a publication of the IEEE Engineering in Medicine and Biology Society 13:263-71.
Mong J a, Devidze N, Goodwillie A, Pfaff DW (2003) Reduction of lipocalin-type prostaglandin D synthase in the preoptic area of female mice mimics estradiol effects on arousal and sex behavior. Proceedings of the National Academy of Sciences of the United States of America 100:15206-11.
Mørup M, Hansen LK, Arnfred SM (2007) ERPWAVELAB a toolbox for multi-channel analysis of time-frequency transformed event related potentials. Journal of Neuroscience Methods 161:361-8.
Myhrer T (2007) Neuronal structures involved in the induction and propagation of seizures caused by nerve agents: implications for medical treatment. Toxicology 239:1-14.

Navarro Mora G, Bramanti P, Osculati F, Chakir A, Nicolato E, Marzola P, Sbarbati A, Fabene PF (2009) Does pilocarpine-induced epilepsy in adult rats require status epilepticus? PloS one 4:e5759.

Neihart N, Harrison R (2004) A low-power FM transmitter for use in neural recording applications. Conference Proceedings: Annual International Conference of the IEEE Engineering in Medicine and Biology Society. IEEE Engineering in Medicine and Biology Society. Conference 3:2117-20.

Newmark J, Clayton WL (1995) Persian Gulf illnesses: preliminary neurological impressions. Mil. Med. 160:505-7.

Nigam VP, Graupe D (2004) A neural-network-based detection of epilepsy. Neurological Research 26:55-60.

Nissinen J, Halonen T, Koivisto E, Pitkänen a (2000) A new model of chronic temporal lobe epilepsy induced by electrical stimulation of the amygdala in rat. Epilepsy Research 38:177-205.

Okazaki MM, Evenson DA, Nadler JV (1995) Hippocampal mossy fiber sprouting and synapse formation after status epilepticus in rats: visualization after retrograde transport of biocytin. The Journal of Comparative Neurology 352:515-34.

O'Keefe J, Burgess N, Donnett JG, Jeffery KJ, Maguire E a (1998) Place cells, navigational accuracy, and the human hippocampus. Philosophical transactions of the Royal Society of London. Series B, Biological Sciences 353:1333-40.

O'Keefe J, Speakman A (1987) Single unit activity in the rat hippocampus during a spatial memory task. Experimental brain research. Experimentelle Hirnforschung. Expérimentation Cérébrale 68:1-27.

O'Neill J, Pleydell-Bouverie B, Dupret D, Csicsvari J (2010) Play it again: reactivation of waking experience and memory. Trends in Neurosciences 33:220-9.

Pareti G, De Palma A (2004) Does the brain oscillate? The dispute on neuronal synchronization. Neurological Sciences : official journal of the Italian Neurological Society and of the Italian Society of Clinical Neurophysiology 25:41-7.

Patnaik LM, Manyam OK (2008) Epileptic EEG detection using neural networks and post-classification. Computer Methods and Programs in Biomedicine 91:100-9.

Pavy Le-Traon A, Roussel B (1993) Sleep in space. Acta Astronautica 29:945-50.

Peng S, Ma J, Yang C, Fang Z (2001) The development of multi-lead EEG telemetry and tele-monitoring system. Sheng wu yi xue gong cheng xue za zhi = J. Biomed. Eng.= Shengwu yixue gongchengxue zazhi 18:229-33.

Pernot F, Carpentier P, Baille V, Testylier G, Beaup C, Foquin A, Filliat P, Liscia P, Coutan M, Piérard C, Béracochea D, Dorandeu F (2009) Intrahippocampal cholinesterase inhibition induces epileptogenesis in mice without evidence of neurodegenerative events. Neuroscience 162:1351-65.

Petras JM (1994) Neurology and neuropathology of soman-induced brain injury: an overview. Journal of the Experimental Analysis of Behavior 61:319-29.

Pisa M, Sanberg PR, Corcoran ME, Fibiger HC (1980) Spontaneously recurrent seizures after intracerebral injections of kainic acid in rat: a possible model of human temporal lobe epilepsy. Brain Research 200:481-7.

Poe GR, Walsh CM, Bjorness TE (2010) Cognitive neuroscience of sleep. Progress in Brain Research 185:1-19.

Rattenborg NC (2006) Do birds sleep in flight? Die Naturwissenschaften 93:413-25.

Raymond AA, Gilmore WV, Scott CA, Fish DR, Smith SJ (1999) Video-EEG telemetry: apparent manifestation of both epileptic and non-epileptic attacks causing potential diagnostic pitfalls. Epileptic Disorders : International Epilepsy Journal with videotape 1:101-6.

Ribeiro S, Shi X, Engelhard M, Zhou Y, Zhang H, Gervasoni D, Lin S-C, Wada K, Lemos N a M, Nicolelis M a L (2007) Novel experience induces persistent sleep-dependent plasticity in the cortex but not in the hippocampus. Frontiers in Neuroscience 1:43-55.

Rizk M, Obeid I, Callender SH, Wolf PD (2007) A single-chip signal processing and telemetry engine for an implantable 96-channel neural data acquisition system. Journal of Neural Engineering 4:309-21.

Romcy-Pereira RN, Araujo DB de, Leite JP, Garcia-Cairasco N (2008) A semi-automated algorithm for studying neuronal oscillatory patterns: a wavelet-based time frequency and coherence analysis. Journal of Neuroscience Methods 167:384-92.

Rossetti F, Rodrigues MCA, Oliveira JAC de, Garcia-Cairasco N (2006) EEG wavelet analyses of the striatum-substantia nigra pars reticulata-superior colliculus circuitry: audiogenic seizures and anticonvulsant drug administration in Wistar audiogenic rats (War strain). Epilepsy Research 72:192-208.

Rothschild RM (2010) Neuroengineering tools/applications for bidirectional interfaces, brain-computer interfaces, and neuroprosthetic implants - a review of recent progress. Frontiers in Neuroengineering 3:112.

Saab ME, Gotman J (2005) A system to detect the onset of epileptic seizures in scalp EEG. Clinical neurophysiology : official journal of the International Federation of Clinical Neurophysiology 116:427-42.

Salazar AM, Schwab K, Grafman JH (1995) Penetrating injuries in the Vietnam war. Traumatic unconsciousness, epilepsy, and psychosocial outcome. Neurosurgery Clinics of North America 6:715-26.

Schnitzler A, Gross J (2005) Normal and pathological oscillatory communication in the brain. Nature Reviews. Neuroscience 6:285-96.

Schomer DL (2006) Ambulatory EEG telemetry: how good is it? Journal of Clinical Neurophysiology : official publication of the American Electroencephalographic Society 23:294-305.

Scott CA, Fish DR, Smith SJ, Free SL, Stevens JM, Thompson PJ, Duncan JS, Shorvon SD, Harkness WF (1999) Presurgical evaluation of patients with epilepsy and normal MRI: role of scalp video-EEG telemetry. Journal of Neurology, Neurosurgery, and Psychiatry 66:69 71.

Scremin OU, Shih TM, Li MG, Jenden DJ (1998) Mapping of cerebral metabolic activation in three models of cholinergic convulsions. Brain Research Bulletin 45:167-74.

Shih T-M, Duniho SM, McDonough JH (2003) Control of nerve agent-induced seizures is critical for neuroprotection and survival. Toxicology and Applied Pharmacology 188:69-80.

Shih TM, McDonough JH (1997) Neurochemical mechanisms in soman-induced seizures. Journal of Applied Toxicology 17:255-64.

Shorvon SD (2000) Handbook of Epilepsy Treatment. Blackwell Science, London.

Shouse MN, Silva AM da, Sammaritano M (1996) Circadian rhythm, sleep, and epilepsy. Journal of Clinical Neurophysiology: official publication of the American Electroencephalographic Society 13:32-50.

Singer W (1999) Neuronal synchrony: a versatile code for the definition of relations? Neuron 24:49-65, 111-25.

Sinton CM, McCarley RW (2004) Neurophysiological mechanisms of sleep and wakefulness: a question of balance. Seminars in Neurology 24:211-23.

Sloviter RS (1999) Status epilepticus-induced neuronal injury and network reorganization. Epilepsia 40 Suppl 1:34-39.

Srinivasan V, Eswaran C, Sriraam N (2007) Approximate entropy-based epileptic EEG detection using artificial neural networks. IEEE Transactions on Information Technology in Biomedicine: a publication of the IEEE Engineering in Medicine and Biology Society 11:288-95.

Terleph TA, Mello CV, Vicario DS (2006) Auditory topography and temporal response dynamics of canary caudal telencephalon. Journal of Neurobiology 66:281-92.

Timofeev I, Steriade M (2004) Neocortical seizures: initiation, development and cessation. Neuroscience 123:299-336.

Traub RD (2003) Fast Oscillations and Epilepsy. Epilepsy currents / American Epilepsy Society 3:77-79.

Treiman DM, Walton NY, Kendrick C (1990) A progressive sequence of electroencephalographic changes during generalized convulsive status epilepticus. Epilepsy Research 5:49-60.

Turski WA, Cavalheiro EA, Schwarz M, Czuczwar SJ, Kleinrok Z, Turski L (1983)(a) Limbic seizures produced by pilocarpine in rats: behavioural, electroencephalographic and neuropathological study. Behav. Brain Research 9:315-35.

Turski WA, Czuczwar SJ, Kleinrok Z, Turski L (1983)(b) Cholinomimetics produce seizures and brain damage in rats. Experientia 39:1408-11.

Tzallas AT, Tsipouras MG, Fotiadis DI (2007) Automatic seizure detection based on time-frequency analysis and artificial neural networks. Computational Intelligence and Neuroscience:80510.

Van der Weide H, Kamp A (1984) Long-term supervised domiciliary EEG monitoring in epileptic patients employing radio telemetry and telephone telemetry. I. Telephone telemetry system. Electroencephalography and Clinical Neurophysiology 57:581-3.

Vanbemmel a (1997) The link between sleep and depression: The effects of antidepressants on EEG sleep. Journal of Psychosomatic Research 42:555-564.

Vespa PM, McArthur DL, Xu Y, Eliseo M, Etchepare M, Dinov I, Alger J, Glenn TP, Hovda D (2010) Nonconvulsive seizures after traumatic brain injury are associated with hippocampal atrophy. Neurology 75:792-8.

Vreeland R, Collins C, Williams L, Yeager C, Gianascol A, Henderson J (1963) A subminiature radio EEG telemeter for studies of disturbed children. Electroencephalography & Clinical Neurophysiology 15:327-9.

Wasterlain CG, Shirasaka Y (1994) Seizures, brain damage and brain development. Brain & Development 16:279-95.Wei P, Ziaie B (2009) An optical microsystem for wireless neural recording. Conference Proceedings : ... Annual International Conference of the IEEE Engineering in Medicine and Biology Society. IEEE Engineering in Medicine and Biology Society. Conference 2009:5522-4.

11

An Efficient Adaptive Antenna-Impedance Tuning Unit Designed for Wireless Pacemaker Telemetry

Francis Chan Wai Po[1], Emeric de Foucauld[2], Jean-Baptiste David[2], Christophe Delavaud[2] and Pascal Ciais[2]
[1]*Institut Supérieur d'Electronique de Paris,*
[2]*CEA LETI MINATEC,*
France

1. Introduction

Since its first implantation into human body in 1958, pacemaker has known several evolutions [1-2] to become nowadays a vital cardiovascular device frequently prescribed to improve the quality of life for hearth failure patients. To increase the quality of service, pacemaker industry tends to integrate wireless telemetry technology into the medical device to allow home monitoring of the patient. Home monitoring technology challenges to analyse and to diagnose while the patient is sitting or sleeping at home.

The pacemaker radio communication module, designed to exchange data with an external base station, features new technologies including, but not limited, new architecture, low power design technique, acoustic wave filter co-integration, miniaturized antenna design, etc. The miniaturized antenna embedded on the pacemaker device is typically a narrow bandwidth high-Q antenna [3] easily detuned by unpredictable near field environmental factors [4-6]. The input impedance of the implanted antenna can vary due to the tissue (muscle, fat, skin, etc.) properties, thickness, and also the individual properties which differ from one person to another. In addition, the patient position and more generally the nearby objects may cause also change in the antenna input impedance. Mismatch of the antenna impedance significantly degrades the transmitter radiated output power, the receiver sensitivity, and therefore the power efficiency of the radio transceiver.

To highlight the possible random variability in the antenna input impedance that contributes to generate more or less important mismatch losses, precise characterization of the pacemaker antenna using different realistic human models is needed. In this way, electromagnetic simulations and measurements of the input impedance of the antenna immersed into homogeneous and heterogeneous human model were performed.

To guarantee the success of the wireless communication even in the presence of mismatch losses, traditional solution over specifies the design of the RF power modules consuming more energy at the expense of the battery lifetime. This solution is obviously not mandatory where a targeting lifetime at least greater than seven years is required for such implantable medical device. More suitable solution is focused on the addition of an adaptive antenna-impedance tuning unit to automatically match the antenna input impedance to the optimal impedance of the RF front-end radio communication module.

Most of existing antenna-impedance tuning units [7-15] operates iteratively to successfully adapt source and load impedances. However, iterative methods generally spend several hundred milliseconds to calibrate the system and are not well suited to low power pacemaker applications where energy is lost during the calibration as the proper state configuration of the system is not yet obtained.

The design of an energy efficient antenna-impedance tuning units based on a single step calibration method is proposed in this chapter to achieve a low power automatic matching process. The proposed method aims to extract the antenna complex impedance value in order to calculate the parameters of the network that match the extracted antenna impedance to the impedance of the RF power module at a selected frequency.

In this chapter, we describe briefly the pacemaker telemetry system, the design constraints and the limitations in section II. Since the pacemaker antenna is easily detuned by tissues, we challenge to characterize the impedance of the antenna immersed into different realistic human model in section III. In section IV, we propose a novel antenna impedance tuning method based on a single step process calibration to adapt automatically the antenna impedance to the optimal impedance of the front-end radio.

2. Pacemaker telemetry overview

Pacemaker industry is entering into the era of home monitoring technology. Home monitoring enables pacemaker's patients to be remotely followed-up via secured wireless or telephone networks as shown in Fig. 1. Depending on the patient's health status, the transfer of information could be done daily, weekly or monthly, and can be also triggered by the patient himself if he feels symptomatic. Home monitoring enhances patient safety and comfort, reduces pacing clinic visits and trips to the emergency room cutting down the overall healthcare costs and help the physicians better understand the patient's condition in less time.

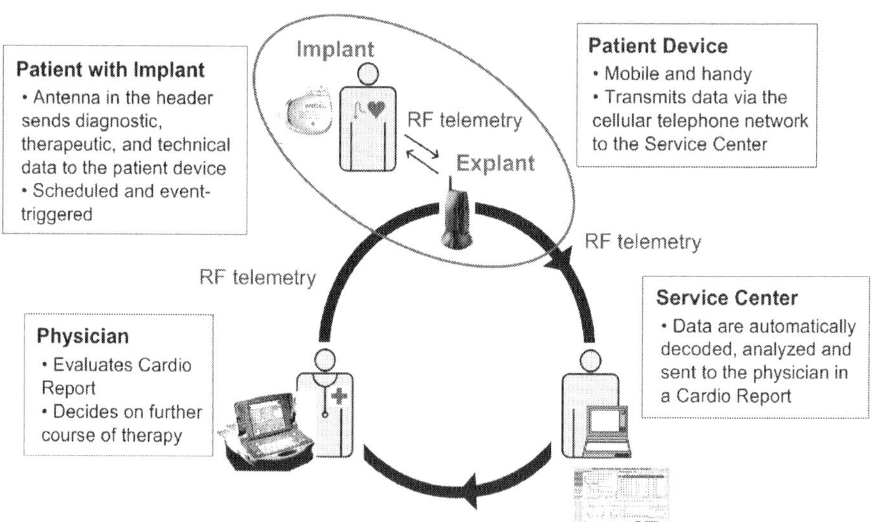

Fig. 1. Pacemaker home monitoring telemetry system

To allow home monitoring of the patient, it is necessary to integrate a wireless telemetry system into the medical device. Implantable pacemaker telemetry system provides a means for receiving downlink information from an external base station to the implanted medical device, and for transmitting uplink signals from the implanted device to the external unit.

2.1 Proposed wireless medical telemetry

Pacemaker microsystem typically embeds a controller, electrocardiogram (ECG) sensors and few analogue electronics blocs. In addition, the new generation device includes a wireless telemetry functionality which simplified bloc diagram is illustrated in Fig. 2. As the size of the final product should not be larger than its predecessor, it is necessary to tend towards a large scale integration of memory, controller, RF functionality including RF MEMS as well as analogue RF circuits.

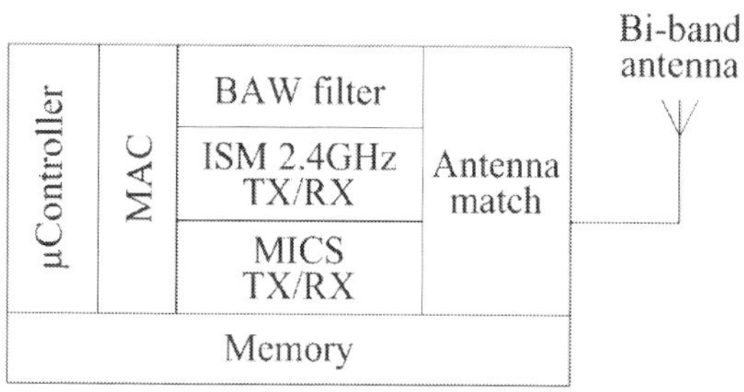

Fig. 2. Simplified bloc diagram of the pacemaker's wireless telemetry

The proposed wireless telemetry system integrates transceivers operating respectively at the Medical Implant Communication Service (MICS) frequency band and at the 2.4 GHz Industrial Medical Scientist (ISM) frequency band. The MICS 402-405 MHz frequency band is used to transmit short range secured data and for emergency link because only the exclusive MICS band is acknowledge as safe for medical devices by Food and Drug Administration (FDA). The ISM 2.4 GHz transceiver is dedicated for the implementation of a needed ultra low power wake up system and for transmitting data under higher equivalent isotropically radiated power (EIRP) to achieve the demanded increased communication range. In addition to the bi-band transceiver, a Bulk Acoustic Wave (BAW) filter and naturally a miniaturized loop antenna are embedded into the medical microsystem.

2.1.1 BAW Filter design and integration

The filter was implemented to address the high level risk of electromagnetic interferences in the widely used ISM 2.4 GHz frequency band using Solid Mounted Resonators (SMR). The resonators in SMR structures are realized on the top of an acoustic mirror structure based on the Bragg reflector principle [16]. The resonators layers were composed of classical couple AlN-Mo. In contrast to [17], the Bragg reflector was implemented using an exclusive dielectric stack composed of SiOC:H and SixNy. The acoustical performance of the fully dielectric stack is comparable to traditional SiO2-W reflectors. However, this fully dielectric configuration strongly reduces the electrical coupling between resonators, and ensures high

out-of-band rejection. Zero level packaging ensures a micro-cavity on the upper side of the resonator, thanks to a released bi-layer SiO2/BCB.
The filter is based on a double-lattice topology (Fig. 3 (a)) and series inductances of maximum 1nH can be added so as to increase slightly the bandwidth, or for matching considerations. The photography in Fig. 3 (b) shows the 2.4 GHz filter. The active area is 450x225μm², and the complete die is 1mm². 120μm diameter areas with a 150μm pitch were prepared for bumping as well as for probe testing.

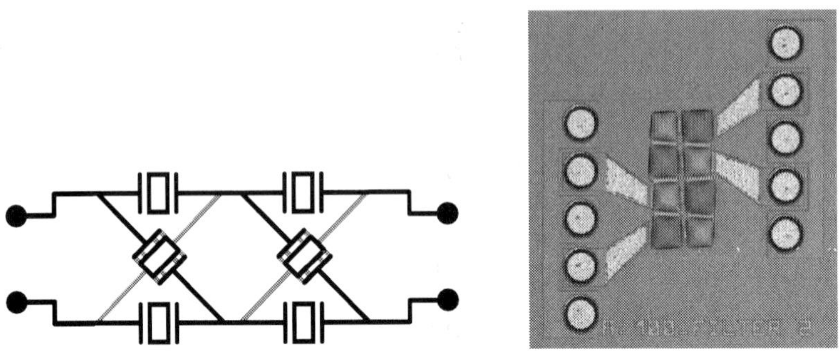

(a) (b)

Fig. 3. Double lattice BAW filter (a) topology (b) photography

Flip-chip on CMOS and LTCC technologies were studied for the integration of the filter. As illustrated in Fig. 4 (a), flip chip on CMOS integration approach exhibits limited performances for several reasons. The CMOS technology is based on a lossy substrate which give low performances interconnects. As consequences, wide pad bumps are strongly capacitive and minimum distance between bumps and pad ring gives long and lossy lines.

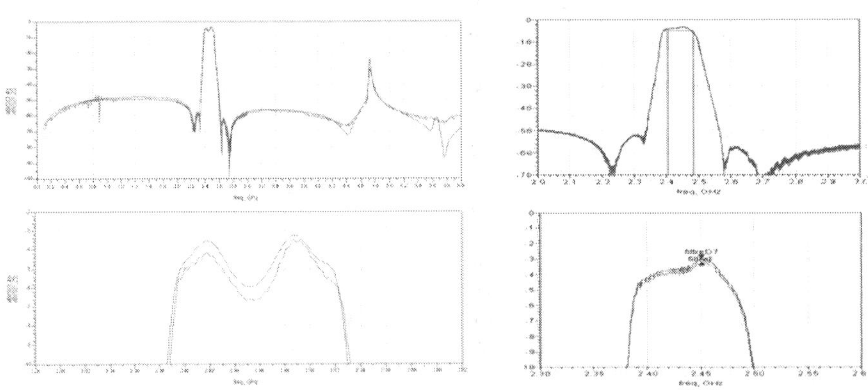

(a) (b)

Fig. 4. BAW filter responses (a) Flip chip on CMOS measurement and simulation (b) Stand alone BAW filter versus flip chip on LTCC

In order to get better performance in the antenna to CMOS link, an alternative design has been also investigated to assemble the BAW filter with the antenna matching network in a same LTCC die, leading to a SiP approach. The comparison between on-probe BAW measurement and the flip-chipped BAW on LTCC is illustrated in Fig. 4 (b) where the responses are very close each other. Less than 0.2 dB additional insertion loss is observed.

2.1.2 Miniaturized antenna

A miniaturized loop antennas for implanted medical device designed to operate at both MICS 402-405 MHz and ISM 2.4 GHz frequency bandwidths have been successfully fabricated [18-21]. As illustrated in Fig. 5, the designed rectangular loop antenna embedded in a titanium (σ=2.3×10^6 S/m) housing biocompatible pacemaker prototype is made of copper (σ=5.8×107 S/m) covered with a silicone layer (ε_r=2.8) for biocompatibility. The physical dimensions of the rectangular loop antenna are approximately equal to 29.5 mm width and 18 mm height.

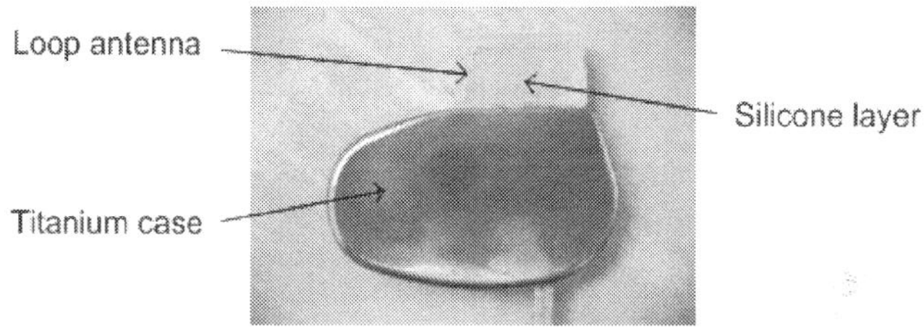

Fig. 5. Miniaturized loop antenna embedded in a pacemaker prototype

2.2 Transceiver design constraints and limitations

Medical devices require ultra low power, high performance transceiver. The design considerations of such transceivers are subjected to strong technical challenges which basic requirements [22] are as follows:

- Low power during communication is required since the battery power is limited. During communication sessions, current should be less than 6mA for most implantable device.
- Mostly in asleep mode, a designed ultra low power ISM 2.4 GHz receiver should periodically look for wakeup signal.
- As the size of the device should be continuously reduced, minimum external components is mandatory. High scale integration should also reduce significantly costs and increase the overall system reliability.
- Higher data rates, reliability are targeted.
- Good selectivity and interference rejection.
- Increase of the communication range greater than 2 meter range.

In such medical microsystem, over specify the system consumes more energy, reduces the battery lifetime and is therefore not mandatory to improve the limited communication range. Longer range implies the design of an automatic power optimized system. Thus, the integration of an automatic antenna tuning unit should contribute to improve the budget link by reducing the power losses due to impedance mismatch of the body affected small antenna.

3. Antenna input impedance characterization

The miniaturized high-Q loop antenna impedance is highly dependant on the close environment of this antenna. Due to the unpredictable near field tissues properties, its thickness variation or patient's position change, the antenna impedance can vary introducing some quite variable losses due to mis-adaptation. To address this problem, it can be advantageous to design a tunable matching network to improve the adaptation where the variability range of the network should be able to match the variation range of the antenna impedance to the optimal impedance of the front-end radio. Therefore, there is a first need that consists in the characterization of the variability in the antenna input impedance in order to decide of the matching topology. In so far as the approach is the same whatever the chosen frequency, we decide to focus our work considering the MICS frequency band.

3.1 Human body modeling

Generally, antenna impedance is characterized in homogeneous lossy dispersive fluids which simulate the average human body electrical properties. As impedance characterization requires to know the electromagnetic field behaviour in near antenna area, only reduced volume of these lossy materials is modelled. But, to accurately take into account the near field pacemaker antenna behaviour, different human tissues close to the implant have to be also considered. This will be done by using heterogeneous model with limited dimensions as multi-layered structures or as existing accurate human model of electromagnetic simulation tool.

3.1.1 Homogeneous model

The pacemaker implant is plunged in a dispersive and lossy liquid material with frequency dependent electrical properties. In order to characterize antenna pacemaker impedance in the 402-405 MHz MICS frequency band, the 450 MHz body tissue equivalent liquid is used. The target electrical parameters of this fluid (conductivity σ and real part of permittivity ε_r') are provided by the FCC [23], as given in Table 1.

	Permittivity (ε_r')	Conductivity (σ, S/m)
Target values	56.7	0.94
Measured values	56.2	0.95

Table 1. Body simulating liquid electrical properties at 450 MHz

In the electromagnetic simulation tool based on Finite-Integration Time-Domain (FITD) method (CST Microwave Studio) [24], the homogeneous liquid model is represented by a parallelepiped (15cm×11cm×3.4cm). The rectangular homogeneous block dimensions and the pacemaker inside it as illustrated in Fig. 6 (a) are optimized for the heterogeneous model. For the experimental setup in Fig. 6 (b), the pacemaker is plunged into a rectangular plastic recipient filled with homogeneous liquid and which dimensions are the same than the simulated one.

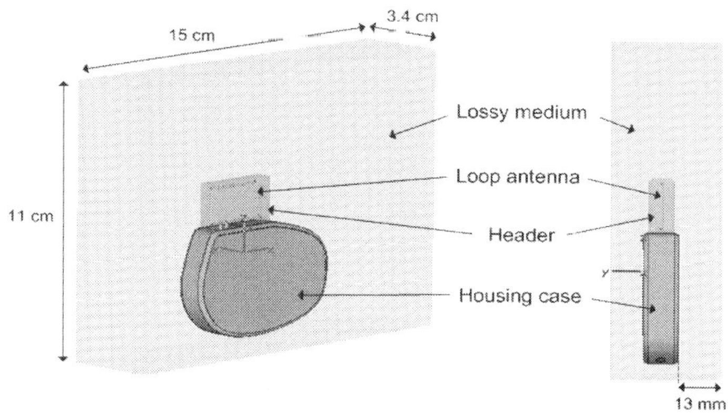

(a)

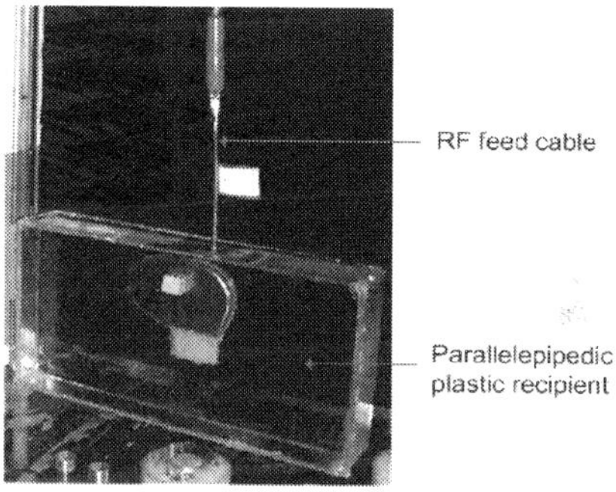

(b)

Fig. 6. Homogeneous model (a) simulated configuration (b) experimental set-up

3.1.2 Heterogeneous model

The implantable device is inserted in three heterogeneous models: the heterogeneous human model named Hugo which is the simulation tool human model [24], a multi-layered structure and a simple experimental setup made to validate simulated heterogeneous models, the "human + hand" model. Compared to previous homogeneous model, the main advantage of these heterogeneous models is the ability to carefully model all human tissues in near antenna area to accurately take into account the near field pacemaker antenna behaviour.

The pacemaker device is implanted in the pectoral of Hugo, in a limited volume sample of 11.2 x 6.4 x 11.6 cm^3 (Fig. 7 (a)). The voxel size of the human body model is the minimal voxel size of the simulation tool, i.e. 1 mm^3. The whole body phantom contains 44 different tissues, whose real part of permittivity (ε_r') and conductivity (σ) are taken from [24] at 450 MHz. The chosen limited sample obviously includes fewer tissues than the complete body model.

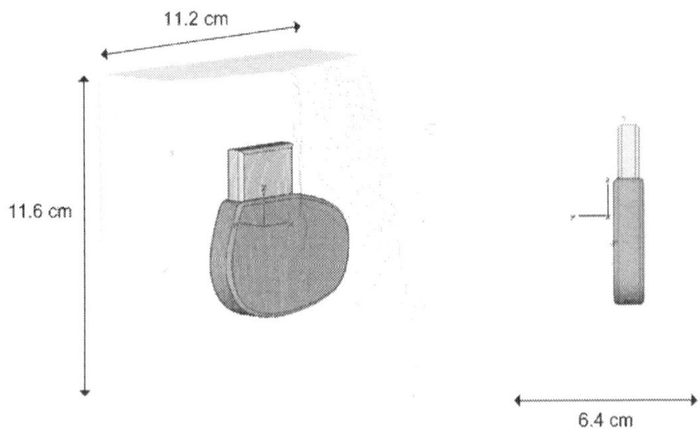

Fig. 7. Heterogeneous Hugo model

In order to easily design implanted antennas, multi-layered geometries which provide an acceptable model for the human body, were firstly proposed in [18]. Based on the real human body structure of the simulation tool, the heterogeneous multi-layered model used here (Fig. 8) is made of three layers (skin, fat, muscle) that have different thickness and different electrical properties. The thickness of the skin, fat and muscle tissues are respectively 4, 20 and 10 mm. The electrical properties of these three layers are taken from electrical data of human body phantom tissues and given in Table 2. The pacemaker is implanted in the fat layer just under the skin layer. The geometrical characteristics of the heterogeneous model, i.e. pacemaker position inside the rectangular block and dimensions of both layers and whole block, have been optimized in order to be in accordance with Hugo implant impedance.

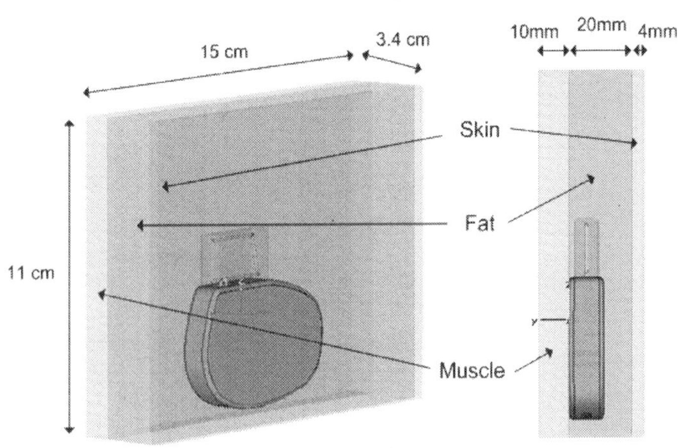

Fig. 8. Multi-layer heterogeneous model

Biological tissue	Permittivity (ε_r')	Conductivity (σ, S/m)
Fat tissue	5.560525	0.041934
Skin	45.753101	0.708836
Muscle	58.482101	0.851437

Table 2. Electrical data of human body phantom tissues

A simple experimental setup with a real human is also experimented. This one covers the pacemaker with his hand and puts it against his bust in exercising a strong pressure (Fig. 9). This setup has not the intention to replace an implantation in a realistic human body, but we will see in the next section that it constitutes a good approximation.

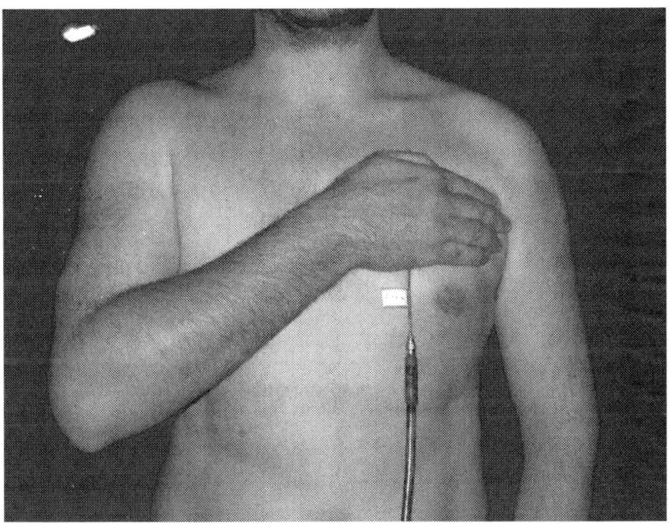

Fig. 9. "Human + hand" model

3.2 Results

The antenna input impedances characterized in homogeneous and heterogeneous models are respectively shown in Fig. 10 and Fig. 11. In homogeneous models, measured results with coaxial cable are systematically compared to simulated results with and without cable. In the configuration without cable, the loop antenna is fed by a lumped port which consists typically in a voltage applied between the two extremities of the loop. This configuration was used in order to simplify the numerical problem size to solve and thereby to reduce the total simulation time. Finally, only this simplified excitation setup will be used in accurate and heavy heterogeneous models because it allows fast simulation results to be obtained.

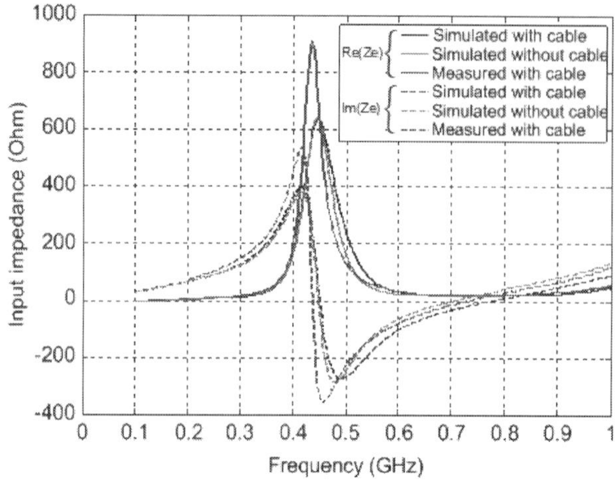

Fig. 10. Antenna impedance in homogeneous human models

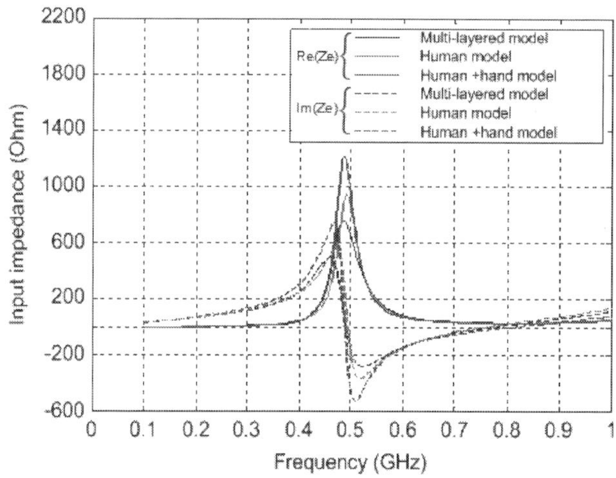

Fig. 11. Antenna impedance in heterogeneous human models

A global study of the impedance characteristics shows that the sensitivity of the antenna to the human tissues results in a shift of the resonant mode. As the MICS band is in the vicinity of this resonant frequency characterized by fast impedance variation, the shift of 50 MHz in frequency involves a huge shift in impedance levels (see Fig. 10 and Fig. 11); hence, while the values of real part of impedance in heterogeneous models are between 39 and 51 Ω, those in the homogeneous models are between 185 and 260 Ω. Similar discrepancies can be seen on imaginary part of impedance. These impedance random shifts are too significant to be neglected. To allow maximum power transfer between transceiver circuitry and antenna, it is necessary to design a variable matching network able to match automatically the wide range of antenna impedance to the front-end radio.

4. Single step antenna tuning unit

To address the problem due to impedance mismatch, many antenna impedance tuning units operating iteratively and/or using directional coupler to evaluate the quality of the link were investigated [7-15]. Since the use of a bulky additional coupler into the device is totally inacceptable and since iterative matching process spends time and consumes power to set the proper state of the network, we investigate on a novel coupler less method [25] solving the problems related to the impedance mismatch in a single iteration. The proposed solution detailed in this section is the first system able to match automatically in a single process both TX and RX matching networks. It reduces the power losses in transmission and in reception contributing to the optimization of the power efficiency of the transceiver itself.

4.1 Brief description

In general, the power consumption of radio communication modules is dominated by the power consumption of the power amplifier during the transmitting path and by the power consumption of the low noise amplifier during the receiving path. Since antenna impedance calibration procedure is done during the transmitting mode, in order to achieve low power antenna impedance tuning unit, it is necessary to reduce strongly the time required for the calibration.

Therefore, we propose an innovative single step antenna tuning unit concept which basic topology is illustrated in Fig. 12. A generic detector made of capacitor C_{det}, which advantageously replaces the usual bulky coupler, is inserted between the power module and the tunable matching network. The sensed signal v_1 and v_2 are attenuated for linearity issue, down converted to a lower intermediate frequency and analyzed by a processor. As described by the flow chart in Fig. 13, the processor exploits the magnitude and the phase of the sensed signals v_1 and v_2 to first calculate the impedance Z_1 and/or Z_2 located in the left and the right port of the detector, respectively. Finally, the extraction of the antenna input impedance exploits the well known deembedding techniques to calculate Z_{Ant} from Z_1 or Z_2. The obtained antenna input impedance value is used to directly calculate the parameters of the matching network that reach the proper state of the system at a selected frequency.

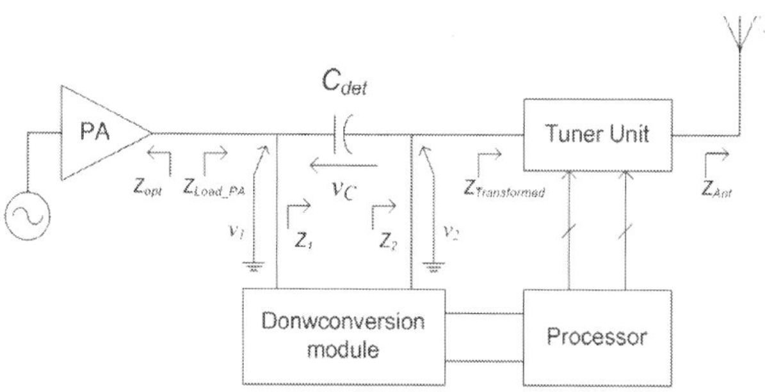

Fig. 12. Description of the proposed antenna tuning unit

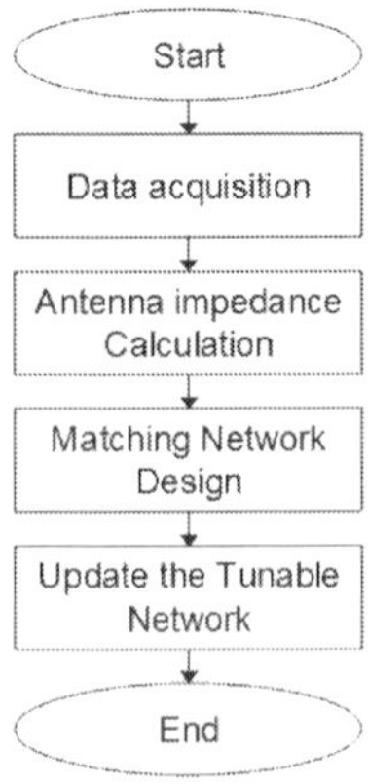

Fig. 13. Flow chart of the antenna tuning unit process

The success of the calibration with arbitrary source and load impedances is achieved with a single iteration. Since iteration is avoided, the matching time is strongly reduced by more than several hundred times compared to iterative optimization method to achieve high speed and low power consumption solution.

4.2 Proposed architecture and analysis

Here, we integrate the antenna tuning unit topology presented in Fig. 12 into the architecture of the MICS frequency band transceiver as illustrated in Fig. 14.

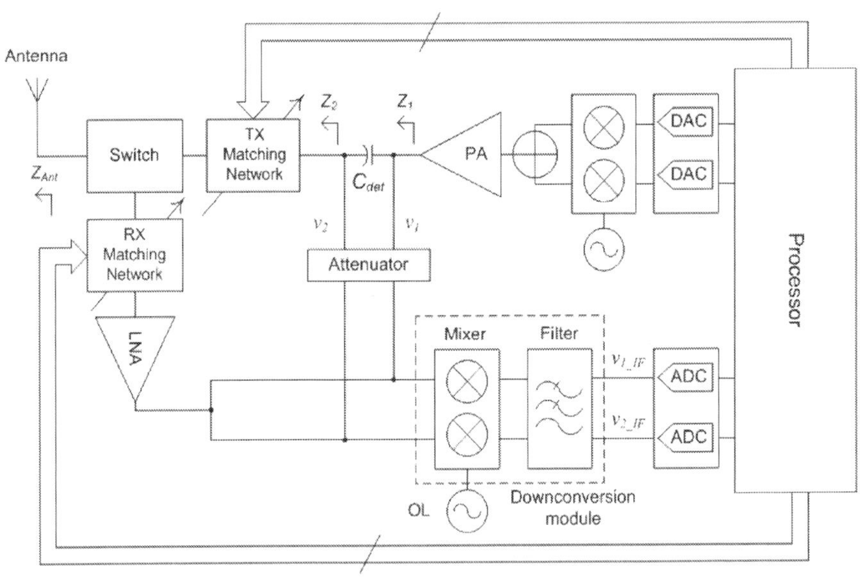

Fig. 14. Integration of the ATU into the architecture of the proposed MICS transceiver

The benefit of the proposed architecture is that the down conversion module and the baseband processor used for the design of the antenna tuning unit, as illustrated in Fig. 12 are already included into the MICS band transceiver [22]. Only minor extra hardware is therefore added for its implementation: a sensing module, an attenuator and tunable matching networks.

In addition to the TX tunable matching network, we insert a RX tunable matching network between the antenna and the front-end receiver in order to maximize the sensitivity of the receiver regardless of the value of the antenna impedance. Since the matching algorithm is able to match the extracted antenna impedance to the optimal impedance of the power amplifier, it is obviously possible to use the same program to match the antenna impedance to the input impedance of the low noise amplifier (LNA) optimizing the sensitivity of the receiver. This is to our knowledge the first antenna impedance tuning unit able to calibrate both the transmitter and the receiver in a same impedance matching process.

4.2.1 Sensing module

The sensing module made of a transmit capacitor C_{det} is inserted between the power amplifier and the TX tunable matching network. A capacitor is easy to integrate and its high quality factor advantageously limits the loss generated due to the sensing operation. However, the value of the capacitor C_{det} needs to be chosen carefully. To set the value of C_{det}, we analyze the impact of C_{det} on the degradation of the network transformation ratio and on the sensitivity of the detection.

As demonstrated in [26], the associated transformation quality factor Q of a network that matches a load resistance R_L to a source resistance R_S is

$$Q = \sqrt{\frac{R_S}{R_L} - 1} \qquad \text{if } R_S \geq R_L \tag{1}$$

$$Q = \sqrt{\frac{R_L}{R_S} - 1} \qquad \text{if } R_S \leq R_L \tag{2}$$

In the presence of the capacitor C_{det}, the expression of the equivalent source resistance is obtained exploiting the network series parallel transformation in Fig. 15.

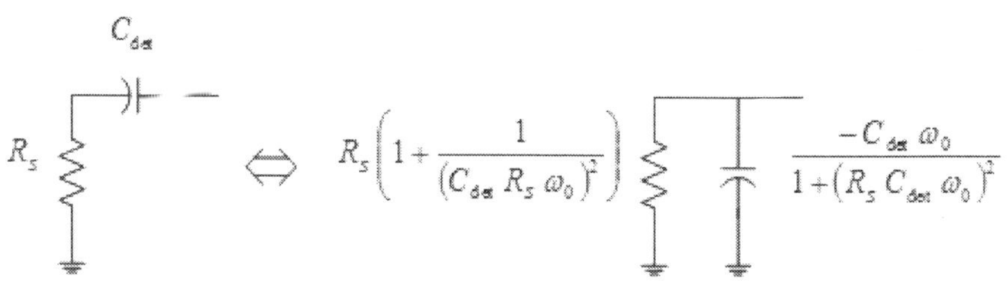

Fig. 15. Source equivalent resistance in the presence of C_{det}

The associated transformation quality factor Q of the network topology in the presence of C_{det} becomes

$$Q=\sqrt{\frac{R_S\left(1+\frac{1}{(C_{\text{det}}R_S\omega_0)^2}\right)}{R_L}-1}\qquad \text{if } R_S\left(1+\frac{1}{(C_{\text{det}}R_S\omega_0)^2}\right)\geq R_L \tag{3}$$

$$Q=\sqrt{\frac{R_L}{R_S\left(1+\frac{1}{(C_{\text{det}}R_S\omega_0)^2}\right)}-1}\qquad \text{if } R_S\left(1+\frac{1}{(C_{\text{det}}R_S\omega_0)^2}\right)\leq R_L \tag{4}$$

As demonstrated in [26], an increase of the transformation quality factor Q in (3) reduces the efficiency of a lossy matching network, whereas a decrease of Q in (4) offers a better efficiency. In order to limit the impact of C_{det} on the raise of Q in (3) and therefore on the degradation of the matching network efficiency, it is mandatory to set the C_{det} value greater than $1/(R_S\omega_0)$.

Moreover, as shown in Fig. 16, the sensing sensitivity depends on the value of C_{det}. In Fig. 16 (a), the range variation of the ratio v_2/v_1 is limited and centered around 1 and 0 for a strong and small value of C_{det}, respectively. An example of wide range variation of the ratio v_2/v_1 that provides a good sensitivity of the impedance sensing operation is illustrated in Fig. 16 (b) where C_{det} is equal to $1/(R_S\omega_0)$.

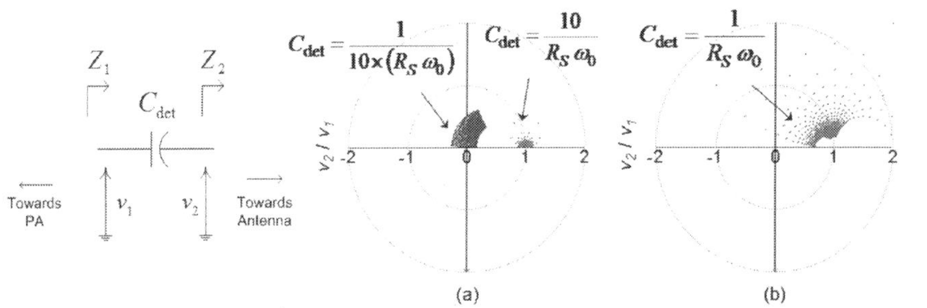

Fig. 16. Range variation of v2/v1 function of C_{det} value plotted in polar domain for $Re(Z_2) \in [10, 300]$ and $Im(Z_2) \in [-100, 100]$

A tradeoff between the sensitivity of the impedance sensing and the degradation of the association transformation quality factor, that could reduce lossy matching network efficiency, gives the expression of C_{det} as follow

$$C_{\text{det}}=\frac{2}{R_S\omega_0} \tag{3}$$

In this condition, neglecting the loss in capacitors and for R_S=100Ω , R_L=50Ω and Q_L=50, a well matched single stage matching network will achieve a power efficiency [27] ($\eta \approx 1-Q/Q_L$) of 98% and 97.55% without and with C_{det}, respectively. As the same, for R_S=50Ω, R_L=100Ω and Q_L=50, the power efficiency is this time improved from 98% to 98.45%.

4.2.2 Attenuator

An attenuator is inserted between the detection capacitor C_{det} and the down conversion module for linearity issue. Indeed, the magnitude of the signals v_1 and v_2 at the output of the power amplifier stage is large, whereas the input linearity of down conversion module made of mixer and channel filter is in general small. To avoid corruption of the wanted signals from undesirable harmonics generation, magnitude and phase errors due to AM/AM and AM/PM conversions in such nonlinear system, the attenuation value must be set so as to adapt v_1 and v_2 to the dynamic range of the down conversion module as shown in Fig. 17.

The 1-dB compression dynamic range $DR_{1\text{-}dB}$ of the down conversion module is the difference between the input 1-dB compression point *ICP1* and the sensitivity S_{min} of the donw conversion module. A back off is added to preserve the magnitude and phase integrity of the signals from AM/AM and AM/PM distortions. We obtain the dynamic range of the system as

$$DR = ICP1 - S_{\min} - Back\ off \tag{5}$$

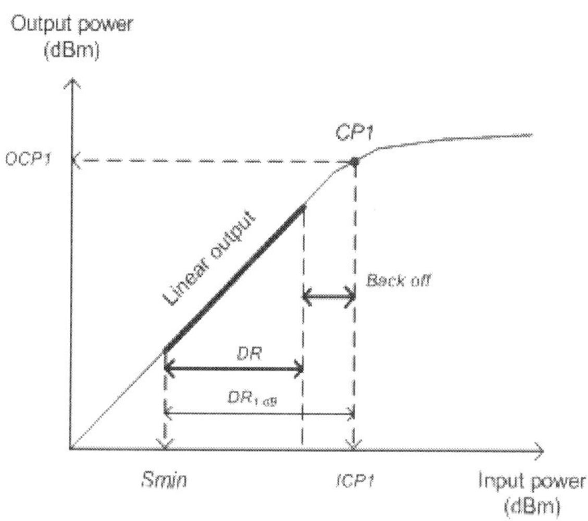

Fig. 17. Dynamic range of the down conversion module

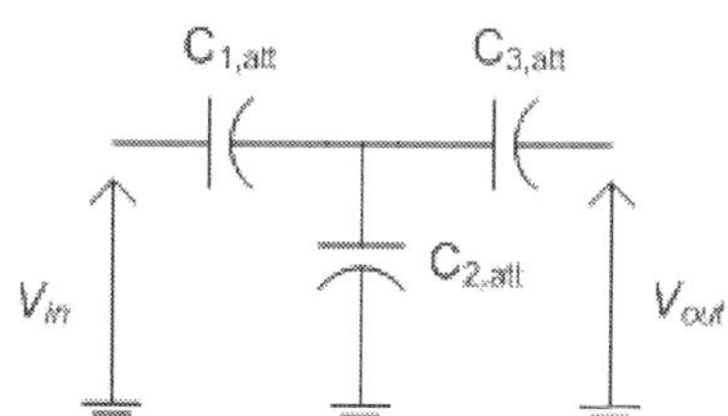

Fig. 18. Proposed capacitive attenuator

We basically implement a capacitive voltage divider as represented in Fig. 18 dedicated to the attenuation of v_1 and v_2. The value of the input capacitance $C_{1,att}$ is small enough to achieve good isolation, whereas the value of the shunted capacitor $C_{2,att}$ is strong and chosen to set the desired attenuation. $C_{3,att}$ is also small value capacitor and added to limit the impact the output load impedance on the attenuation.

4.2.3 Tunable matching network

The tunable matching network is needed for its ability to adapt a great number of load impedances or any change of load impedance to the source impedance. Single stage matching network ability to cover a wide range of impedance is relatively limited [28]. We prefer a generic low pass π matching network with complex load and source impedances as shown in Fig. 19. It is made of one fixed inductor and two variable capacitors made of diode varactors or bank of switched capacitors.

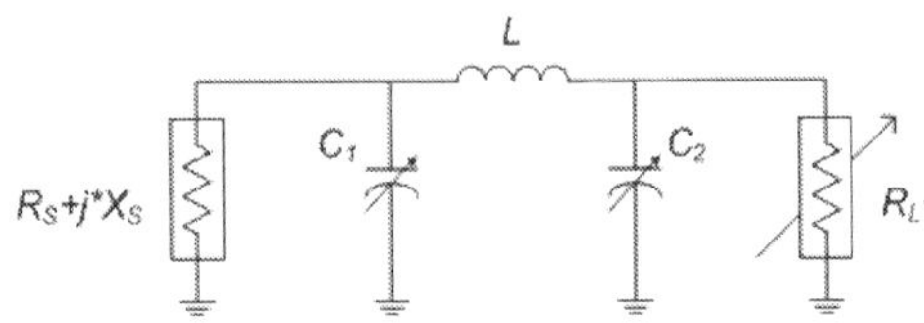

Fig. 19. Matching network with complex source and load impedances

As illustrated in Fig. 20, the ability of the network to match a load impedance range to the source impedance is strongly dependent on the inductance L value. Indeed, any normalized complex conjugate load impedance located in the dotted area can be matched to the source whereas any normalized impedance located in the forbidden region can not be adapted. As an example, let consider the poorly designed inductance L scenario in Fig. 20 (a). A part of the load impedance range, represented by the semicircular shape, is located in the forbidden region. To achieve the well-designed topology in Fig. 20 (b), the value of L must be set carefully.

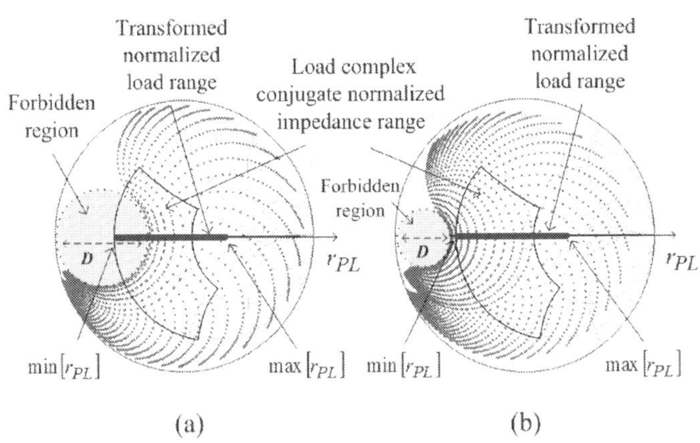

Fig. 20. Example of dynamic range of the impedance tuner (a) poorly inductance L designed scenario (b) well inductance L designed scenario

To facilitate the design of the inductance L value, we study the network in a real source and load impedance domain instead of complex source and load topology. A network transformation is computed and we obtain the matching network in Fig. 21 with real source and load impedances.

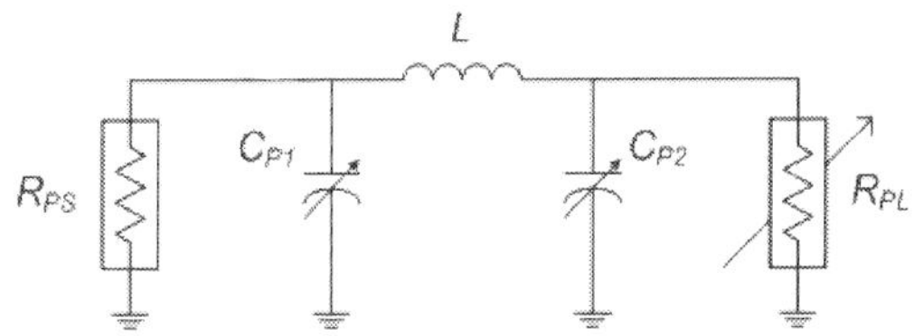

Fig. 21. Transformed matching network with real source and load impedances

The expression of the real source R_{PS} and real load R_{PL} are given by (6) and (7), respectively. The normalized real load impedance range varies from min(r_{PL}) and max(r_{PL}) as reported on the Smith charts in Fig. 20 by the blue bold lines.

$$R_{PS} = R_S\left(1+Q_S^2\right) \quad \text{where } Q_S = -X_S/R_S \tag{6}$$

$$R_{PL} = R_L\left(1+Q_L^2\right) \quad \text{where } Q_L = -X_L/R_L \tag{7}$$

As demonstrated in [27], at a given angular frequency ω, and neglecting the self resonant frequency of the elements, the forbidden circle where load impedance can not be matched to the source impedance has a diameter D function of the inductance L and given by

$$D = \left(\frac{L\omega}{R_{PS}}\right)^2 \tag{8}$$

Since r_{PL} should be outside the forbidden circle, the forbidden circle diameter should be smaller than

$$D_{\max} = \min\left(r_{PL}\right) = \frac{\min\left(R_{PL}\right)}{R_{PS}} \tag{9}$$

As a consequence, the value of the inductance L should be smaller than the inductance maximum value L_{max} which expression is

$$L_{\max} = \frac{R_{PS}}{\omega}\sqrt{\frac{\min\left(R_{PL}\right)}{R_{PS}}} \tag{10}$$

4.3 Matching processor algorithm

The architecture of the processor is illustrated in Fig. 22. It analyses the magnitude/phase information of the down converted signals v_{1_IF}, $v_{2\ IF}$ to extract the antenna input impedance Z_{Ant} used to calculate the proper state of the system. We detail in this section the steps of the algorithm that contribute to reach the goals. The impedances Z_1 and/or Z_2 are first calculated and de-embedded to extract the antenna input impedance Z_{Ant}. A novel matching network design algorithm presented in [27] is finally run to adapt the antenna input impedance to the front-end power module (power amplifier and low noise amplifier).

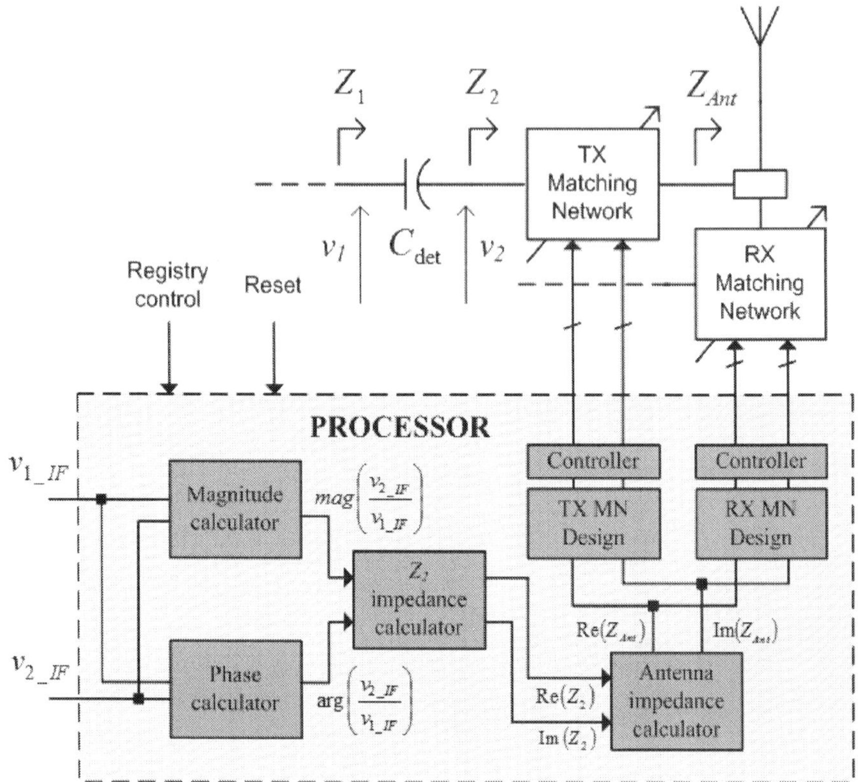

Fig. 22. Architecture of the ATU processor

4.3.1 Impedance calculation

Let consider the expression of $v_1(t)$ and $v_2(t)$ on the left and right terminals of C_{det} as

$$v_1(t) = A_1 \cos(\omega_0 t) \tag{11}$$

$$v_2(t) = A_2 \cos(\omega_0 t + \alpha) \tag{12}$$

where ω_0 is the angular carrier frequency, A_1 and A_2 are the magnitude of v_1 and v_2 respectively and α the phase shift.

The expression of the down converted signals $v_{1\_IF}(t)$ and $v_{2\_IF}(t)$ are

$$v_{1\_IF}(t) = B_1 \cos(\omega_{IF} t) \quad \text{with} \quad B_1 = K \times A_1 \tag{13}$$

$$v_{2\_IF}(t) = B_2 \cos(\omega_{IF}\, t - \alpha) \quad \text{with} \quad B_2 = K \times A_2 \tag{14}$$

From (11) (12) (13) and (14), we obtain the analytical expression for the voltage v_C across the detection capacitor C_{det} in the time domain as

$$v_{C\det}(t) = v_1(t) - v_2(t) = R\, \cos(\omega_0\, t - \sigma), \tag{15}$$

where,

$$R = \frac{1}{K}\sqrt{\left(B_1 - B_2 \cos(\alpha)\right)^2 + \left(B_2 \sin(\alpha)\right)^2} \tag{16}$$

and,

$$\sigma = \arctan\left(\frac{B_2 \sin(\alpha)}{B_1 - B_2 \cos(\alpha)}\right). \tag{17}$$

The impedance Z_1 at the left port of the detector C_{det} is

$$Z_1 = |Z_1| \times e^{j\times(\arg(Z_1))}, \tag{18}$$

where,

$$|Z_1| = \left|\frac{1}{jC_{\det}\omega_0}\right| \times \left|\frac{v_1}{v_{C\det}}\right| = \frac{B_1}{C_{\det}\,\omega_0 \sqrt{\left(B_1 - B_2 \cos(\alpha)\right)^2 + \left(B_2 \sin(\alpha)\right)^2}}, \tag{19}$$

and,

$$\arg(Z_1) = \sigma - \frac{\pi}{2}. \tag{20}$$

Similarly, we obtain the impedance Z_2 at the right port of the detection capacitor C_{det} as

$$Z_2 = |Z_2| \times e^{j\times(\arg(Z_2))}, \tag{21}$$

where,

$$|Z_2| = \frac{B_2}{C_{\det}\,\omega_0 \sqrt{\left(B_1 - B_2 \cos(\alpha)\right)^2 + \left(B_2 \sin(\alpha)\right)^2}}, \tag{22}$$

and,

$$\arg(Z_2) = \alpha + \sigma - \frac{\pi}{2}. \tag{23}$$

It is interesting to note that the impedances Z_1 and Z_2 at the ports of the detector are extracted with simplicity only from the magnitude B_1, B_2 and phase shift α of (v_{1_IF}, v_{2_IF}). The extraction of the antenna input impedance exploits the de-embedding techniques to calculate Z_{Ant} from Z_1 or Z_2. For better results, input parasitic capacitance from the attenuator could be taken into account during the process.

4.3.2 Matching network design

The matching design algorithm exploits a novel method for synthesizing an automatic matching network summarized in Fig. 23 and previously presented in [27] in order to match the antenna input impedance Z_{Ant} to the optimal impedance of the power amplifier Z_{opt} and to the input impedance of the low noise amplifier. This method transforms the load and source complex impedances to real source and load impedances for simplicity. The parameters of the networks that achieve the proper state of the system are calculated exploiting the Smith chart in a novel way achieving the process with simple analytical expressions. By reducing the complexity of the algorithm, we reduce the number of instructions, the time required to calculate the optimal configuration of the tunable matching networks and the power consumption of the antenna impedance calibration unit.

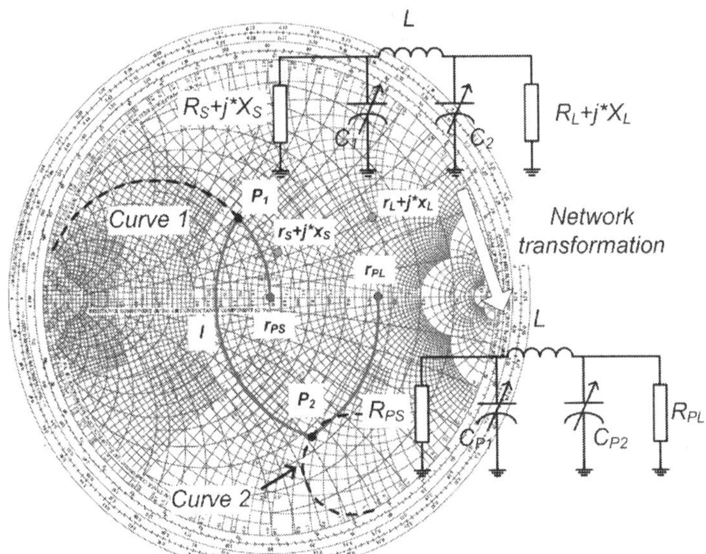

Fig. 23. Matching network design methodology presented in [27]

4.4 Results

A first experimental set-up of the antenna impedance tuning unit operating at the MICS 402-405 MHz frequency band was fabricated [29] as illustrated in Fig. 24. It includes the MICS frequency band demonstrator with only the TX low pass π tunable matching network, a microcontroller board and a pacemaker antenna immersed into a homogeneous human model liquid described in section III whose permittivity ε_r and conductivity σ are 56.2 and 0.95 S/m, respectively.

The demonstrator was made using a Flame Retardant 4 substrate (FR4) with a relative permittivity of 4.6, a dielectric loss tangent of 0.02 and a layer's thickness of 360 µm. The tunability of the low pass π matching network is realized by varactors which control voltages are decided by the microcontroller ADUC7026 from Analog Device. It is an ARM7TDMI based controller with a CPU that clocks up at 40MIPS. The signal carrier frequency is 403 MHz down converted to 256 kHz intermediate frequency and analyzed by the microcontroller for impedance matching consideration.

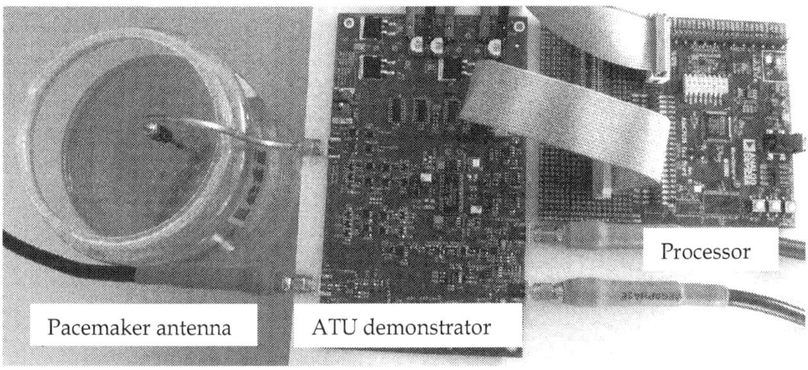

Fig. 24. ATU prototype including the pacemaker antenna

Fig. 25 shows two experimental reflection coefficient measurements. The first one plotted in Fig. 25 (a) was done before the calibration process in the presence of a detuned tunable low-pass π matching network. The second one illustrated in Fig. 25 (b) highlights a post-calibration reflection coefficient result up to -30 dB at the desired frequency of 403 MHz. As represented in Fig. 26, the proposed antenna tuning unit demonstrator spends no more than 900µs to realise the overall calibration process, including the data acquisition, the impedance calculation and the excecution of the matching network design algorithm.

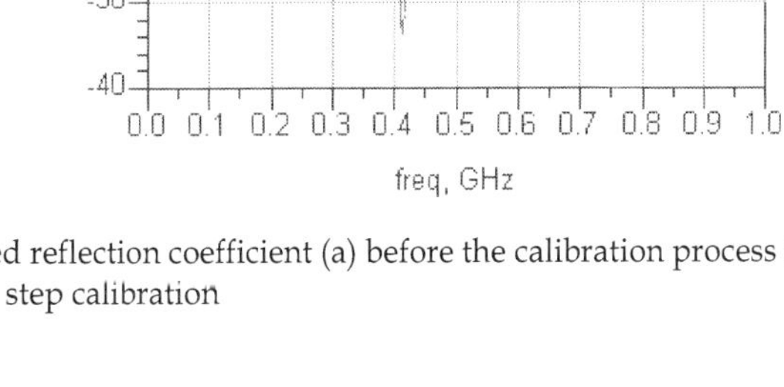

Fig. 25. Measured reflection coefficient (a) before the calibration process (a) after the proposed single step calibration

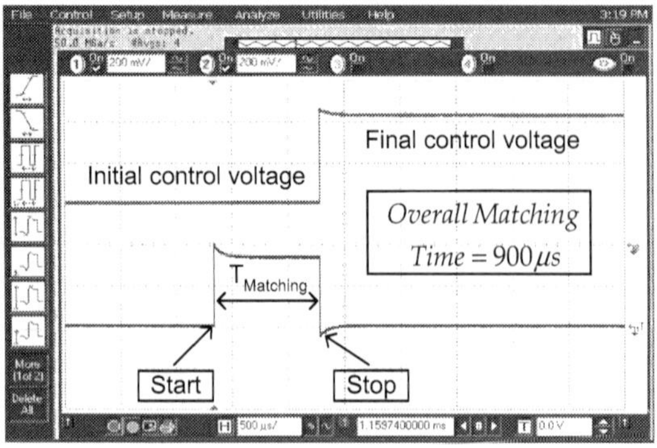

Fig. 26. Time Antenna calibration

5. Conclusion

New pacemaker tends to integrate a wireless telemetry system to allow home monitoring of the patient. The quality of service is strongly improved with an increase of safety, comfort and a reduction of cost. However, this challenge faces to a number of limitations like the need of low power high efficiency design, the degradation of the budget link while the antenna is immersed into the human body, etc. Indeed, it is demonstrated that the antenna impedance changes while immersed into human body causing mismatch of the antenna. To avoid antenna mismatch and reduction of the power efficiency of the radio link, we have proposed a new method to automatically match the antenna impedance to the front-end radio. This method operates in a single step to extract the antenna input impedance value exploited by a processor to match the antenna to the front-end radio both in transmission and reception. A demonstrator operating at the MICS 402-405 MHz frequency band was fabricated and an experimental set-up was presented. This prototype calibrates the system in less than 900µs with a 40MIPS clock processor to achieve a coefficient reflection S11 up to -30dB.

6. Acknowledgement

The authors would like to thank ELA Medical (SORIN Group) for supporting this work.

7. References

[1] Haddad, S.A.P., Houben, R.P.M., Serdijin, W.A (2006). The evolution of pacemakers, *IEEE Engineering in Medecine and Biology Magazine*, Vol. 25, Issue 3, pp. 38-48, Mars 2006

[2] Banbury, C.M. (1997). Surviving Technological Innovation in Pacemaker Industry 1959-1990, Garland Publishing Inc, ISBN 0815327967

[3] Wheeler, H.A. (1975). Small Antennas, *IEEE Transactions on Microwave Theroy and Techniques*, Vol. AP-23, No. 4, pp. 462-469, July 1975

[4] Boyle; K. (2003). The Performance of GSM 900 Antenna in the Presence of People and Phantom, *IEEE International Conference on Antennas and Propagation*, Vol. 1, pp. 35-38, March 2003

[5] Sadeghzadeh, R.A., McEwan, N.J. (1994). Prediction of Head Proximity Effect on Antenna Impedance Using Spherical Waves Expansions, *Electronics Letters*, Vol.6, No.4, pp. 844-847, August 1994

[6] Firrao, E.L., Ennema, A.J., Nauta, B., (2004). Antenna Behaviour in the Presence of Human Body, *15th Annual Workshop on Circuits, Systems and Signal Processing*, pp. 487-490, November 2004

[7] Song, H., Bakkaloglu, B., Aberle, J.T., (2009). A CMOS Adaptive Antenna-Impedance Tuning IC Operating in the 850 MHz to 2 GHz band, *IEEE International Solid-State Circuits Conference*, pp. 384-386, February 2009

[8] De Mingo, J., Valdovinos, A., Crespo, A., Navarro, D., Garcia, P., (2004). A RF Electronically Controlled Impedance Tuning Network Design and its Appliaction to an Antenna Input Impedance Matching System, *IEEE Transactions on Microwave Theory and Techniques*, vol. 52, no. 2, pp. 489-497, February 2004

[9] Sjöblom, P., Sjöland, H., (2005). An Adaptive Impedance Tuning CMOS Circuit for ISM 2.4 GHz Band, *IEEE Transactions on Circuits and Systems I: Regular Papers*, vol. 52, no. 6, pp. 1115-1124, June 2005

[10] Van Bezooijen, A., De Jongh, M.A., Chanlo, C., Ruijs, L.C.H., Van Straten, F., Mahmoudi, R., Van Roermund, H.M., (2008). A GSM/EDGE/WCDMA Adaptive Series LC Matching Network Using RF-MEMS Switches, *IEEE Journal on Solid-State Circuits*, vol. 43, no. 10, pp. 2259-2268, October 2008

[11] Firrao, E.L., Annema, A.J., Nauta, B., (2008). An Automatic Antenna Tuning System Using Only RF-Signal Amplitudes, *IEEE Transactions on Circuits and Systems II: Express Briefs*, vol. 55, no. 9, pp. 833-837, September 2008

[12] Song, H., Oh, S.H., Aberle, J.T., Bakkaloglu, B., Chakrabarti, C., (2007). Automatic Antenna Tuning Unit for Software-Defined and Cognitive Radio, *IEEE International Symposium on Antennas and Propagation*, pp. 85-88, June 2007

[13] Van Bezooijen, A., De Jongh, M.A., Van Straten, F., Mahmoudi, R., Van Roermund, A.H.M., (2010). Adaptive Impedance-Matching Techniques for Controlling L Networks, *IEEE Transactions on Circuits and Systems I: Regular Papers*, vol. 57, no. 2, pp. 495-505, February 2010

[14] Fu, J., Mortazawi, A., (2008). Improving Power Amplifier Efficiency and Linearity Using a Dynamically Controlled Tunable Matching Network, *IEEE Transactions on Microwave Theory and Techniques*, vol. 56, no. 12, pp. 3239-3244, December 2008

[15] Neo, E.W.C., Lin, Y., Liu, X., De Vreede, L.C.N., Larson, L.E., Spirito, M., Pelk, M.J., Buisman, K., Akhnoekh, A., De Graauw, A., Nanver, L.K., (2006). Adaptive Multi-Band Multi-Mode Power Amplifier Using Integrated Varactor-Based Tunable Matching Networks, *IEEE Journal on Solid-State Circuits*, vol. 41, no. 9, pp. 2166-2176, September 2006

[16] Lakin, K.M., McCarron, K.T., Rose, R.E. (1995). Solid Mounted Resonators and Filters, *IEEE International Ultrasonics Symposium*, vol. 2, pp. 905-908, November 1995

[17] Aigner, R. et al. (2003). Bulk Acoustic Wave Filters: Performance Optimization and Volume Manufacturing, IEEE MTT-S, pp. 2001-2004, 2003

[18] Kim J., Rahmat-Samii, Y. (2004). Implanted antennas inside a human body simulations, designs and characterizations, *IEEE Transactions on Microwave Theory and Techniques*, vol. 52, no. 8, pp. 1934-1943, August 2004

[19] Soontornpipit, P., Furse, C.M., Chung, Y.C., (2004). Design of Implantable Microstrip Antenna for Communication with Medical Implants, *IEEE Transactions on Microwave Theory and Techniques*, vol. 52, no. 8, pp. 1944-1951, August 2004

[20] Soontornpipit, P., Furse, C.M., Chung, Y.C., (2004). Miniaturized Biocompatible Microstrip Antenna Using Genetic Algorithm, *IEEE Transactions on Antennas and Propagation*, vol. 53, no. 6, pp. 1939-1945, June 2005

[21] Lee, C.M., Yo, T.C., Luo, C.H., Tu, C.H., Juang, Y.Z., (2007). Compact Broadband Stacked Implantable Antenna for Biotelemetry with Medical Devices, *Electronic Letters*, vol. 43, no. 12, pp. 660-662, June 2007

[22] Bradley P.D. (2006). An Ultra Low Power High Performance Medical Implant Communication System (MICS) transceiver for Implantable Devices, *IEEE Biomedical Circuits and Systems Conference*, pp. 158-161, November 2006

[23] Evaluating Compliance with FCC Guidelines for Human Exposure to Radiofrequency Electromagnetic Fields, Office Eng. Tech., FCC, Washington DC, FCC OET Bull. 65, Supp. C

[24] CST Microwave Studio, Computer System Technology, GmbH, Darmstadt, Germany

[25] Chan Wai Po, F., De Foucauld, E., Delavaud, C., Ciais, P., Kerhervé, E., (2008). A Vector Automatic Matching Network Designed for Wireless Medical Telemetry, *IEEE NEWCAS-TAISA joint Conference*, pp. 89-92, June 2008

[26] Yan, Y., Perreault, D.J. (2006). Analysis and Design of High Efficiency Matching Networks, *IEEE Transactions on Power Electronics*, vol. 21, no. 5, pp. 1484-1491, September 2006

[27] Chan Wai Po, F., de Foucauld, E., Morche, D., Vincent, P., Kerhervé, E. (2011). A Novel Method for Synthesizing an Automatic Matching Network and Its Control Unit, *IEEE Transactions on Circuits and Systems I: Regular paper*, vol. 58, Issue 11, November 2011

[28] Ludwig, R., Bogdanov, G., (2000). RF Circuit Design: Theory and Applications, 2nd edition Upper Saddle River, NJ: Prentice-Hall, 2000

[29] Chan Wai Po, F., de Foucauld, E., Vincent, P., Hameau, F., Morche, D., Delavaud, C., dal Molin, R., Pons, P., Pierquin, R., Kerhervé, E. (2009). A Fast and Accurate Automatic Matching Network Designed for Ultra Low Power Medical Applications, *IEEE International Symposium on Circuits and Systems*, pp. 673-676, May 2009

Part 5

Animal Telemetry

12

What Is the Proper Method to Delineate Home Range of an Animal Using Today's Advanced GPS Telemetry Systems: The Initial Step

W. David Walter[1], Justin W. Fischer[1], Sharon Baruch-Mordo[2] and Kurt C. VerCauteren[1]
[1]*USDA, APHIS, Wildlife Services, National Wildlife Research Center, Fort Collins, Colorado,*
[2]*Department of Fish, Wildlife, and Conservation Biology, & Graduate Degree Program in Ecology, Colorado State University, Fort Collins, Colorado, USA*

1. Introduction

The formal concept of an animal's home range, or derivations thereof, has been around for over half a century (Burt 1943). Within this time frame there have been countless published studies reporting home range estimators with no consensus for any single technique (Withey et al., 2001; Laver & Kelly 2008). Recent advances in global positioning system (GPS) technology for monitoring home range and movements of wildlife have resulted in locations that are numerous, more precise than very high frequency (VHF) systems, and often are autocorrelated in space and time. Along with these advances, researchers are challenged with understanding the proper methods to assess size of home range or migratory movements of various species. The most acceptable method of home-range analysis with uncorrelated locations, kernel-density estimation (KDE), has been lauded by some for use with GPS technology (Kie et al., 2010) while criticized by others for errors in proper bandwidth selection (Hemson et al., 2005) and violation of independence assumptions (Swihart & Slade 1985b). The issue of autocorrelation or independence in location data has been dissected repeatedly by users of KDE for decades (Swihart & Slade 1985a; Worton 1995, but see Fieberg 2007) and can be especially problematic with data collected with GPS technology.

Recently, alternative methods were developed to address the issues with bandwidth selection for KDE and autocorrelated GPS data. Brownian bridge movement models (BBMM), which incorporate time between successive locations into the utilization distribution estimation, were recommended for use with serially correlated locations collected with GPS technology (Bullard 1999; Horne et al., 2007). The wrapped Cauchy distribution KDE was also introduced to incorporate a temporal dimension into the KDE (Keating & Cherry 2009). Improvements were developed in bandwidth selection for KDE (e.g. solve-the-equation, plug-in; Jones et al., 1996; Gitzen et al., 2006) and biased random walk bridges were suggested as movement-based KDE through location interpolation (Benhamou & Cornelis 2010; Benhamou 2011). Other methods incorporated movement, habitat, and behavior components into estimates of home range that included model-supervised kernel smoothing (Matthiopoulos 2003) or mechanistic home-range models (Moorcroft et al., 1999). Finally, local convex hull nonparametric kernel method, which generalizes the minimum convex polygon method, was investigated for identifying hard boundaries (i.e. rivers, canyons) of home ranges but has not been evaluated with GPS datasets with >1,000 locations (Getz & Wilmers 2004; Getz et al., 2007). The multitude of advanced methods, lack of standardized procedures for setting input parameters, and advancements in theory makes it an arduous task for researchers to select the methods that best suit their needs.

As GPS technology advances so has the software available. Several researchers have summarized software available to analyze KDE, most often as extensions for Geographic Information System (GIS) software such as the Home Range Tools extension (Rodgers & Kie 2010) for ArcMap 9.x (ArcMap; Environmental Systems Research Institute, Redlands, CA; Lawson & Rodgers 1997; Kernohan et al., 2001). For details on software cost, operation systems compatibility, distributors, and bandwidth selection available for KDE see Larson (2001), however, some of these software have since been updated or lost technical support within the past several decades. Also in the past decade, the increased popularity of the freely available, open-source software Program R (R Foundation for Statistical Computing, Vienna, Austria; hereafter referred to as R) resulted in the development of R packages to estimate KDE home ranges. Estimates of BBMM home range can be calculated in R packages (BBMM, Nielson et al., 2011; adehabitat, Calenge 2006) and the independent Animal Space Use software (beta version 1.3; Horne et al., 2007). Here, we restricted our analyses to use of adehabitat (Calenge 2006) and ks (Duong 2007) R packages for KDE and package BBMM (Nielson et al., 2011) to calculate BBMM home range. We acknowledge that some estimation methods (e.g. LoCoH) or software (e.g. BBMM function in adehabitat) are absent from our analyses; however, our goal was not to provide a complete comparison of all methods, but rather to use freely available methods and software to highlight the challenges of estimating home range with large GPS datasets.

Our review detailed proposed methods to use on autocorrelated locations that are common in GPS datasets and explain the abilities of software, or lack thereof, to calculate home range of animals. Specifically, we focused on 4 key considerations researchers must address during the study design stage that include: 1) GPS collar function parameters, 2) bandwidth selection for KDE, 3) Brownian bridge movement models, and 4) comparison of methods to estimate home range. We used 5 large datasets collected on 2 terrestrial mammalian species [black bears (*Ursus americanus*), Florida panther (*Felis concolor coryi*)] and 3 avian species [black vulture (*Coragyps atratus*), turkey vulture (*Cathartes aura*), American White Pelicans (*Pelecanus erythrorhynchos*)] to explore relationships between the 4 key considerations outlined above (Table 1). When feasible, we will discuss the topic with examples and will suggest pertinent literature for additional details. Our attempt here is to assist researchers using GPS technology for home range analysis by recommending current methods to analyze data but is not intended to be a validation of any method described herein.

Species (sample size)	Number of locations: Mean (median)	Range (min–max)	GPS schedule
Black bear (n=10)	5,898 (5,577)	4,057–7,856	1 point per 15 min to 1 hr (variable season schedule)
Florida panther (n=10)	4,536 (3,370)	1,154–10,730	1 point per 15 min to 7 hr (variable collar schedule)
Black vulture (n=5)	7,257 (7,182)	5,690–9,477	1 point per 1 hr (dawn-dusk)
Turkey vulture (n=5)	8,078 (8,593)	2,377–11,455	1 point per 1 hr (dawn-dusk)
American White Pelican (n=10)	4,000 (3,399)	1,579–10,536	1 point per 1hr (dawn-dusk)

Table 1. Species, number of locations, and GPS collection schedule for datasets used for estimating size of home range.

2. GPS collar function parameters

Rapid development of GPS-based telemetry systems during the past two decades has led to numerous improvements in size, performance, and data transfer capabilities (Tomkiewicz et al., 2010). Potential disadvantages of GPS telemetry are substantial costs of GPS radiocollars, which often leads to smaller sample sizes and potentially inappropriate population-level inferences (Hebblewhite & Haydon 2010). In certain instances, manufacturers of GPS radiocollars may not understand the need of wildlife professionals and research objectives or the GPS technology may limit the desired data precision. Fix rates for GPS technology are beyond the control of manufacturers and, in some instances, related to movement rates (Dennis et al., 2010; Cappelle et al., 2011), habitats occupied (Lewis et al., 2007; Nielson et al., 2009), topographical ruggedness (D'Eon et al., 2002; Cappelle et al., 2011), type of battery power (e.g. solar vs. lithium; Cappelle et al., 2011), and temporal duration of the study (Kernohan et al., 2001). Here we discuss the nature, and the spatial and temporal context of the data collected that researchers need to consider when using GPS data for home range estimation.

2.1 Data truncation

Some GPS platform transmitter terminals lack the required precision needed for closely spaced points, truncating locations onto a grid of points thus eliminating accurate representation of animal location regardless of GPS accuracy (Fig. 1). Radiotelemetry and

GPS transmitter error has long been documented in wildlife research (D'Eon et al., 2002; Gilsdorf et al., 2008), however, manufacturer programmed or hardware limitation truncation of location coordinates is poorly understood. Truncation or rounding of decimal places will result in many duplicate locations for species that roost or den in the same location repeatedly. Most researchers are likely not aware of this issue that has significant implications to the final conclusions drawn from collection of GPS locations. Researchers need to know that truncated locations exist by some GPS radio-collars and that complications during data analysis and estimates of home range may result (see section 3.2). There are possible methods to address this issue (i.e. random generation of locations within a certain distance from duplicate locations), however, reliability of estimates of home range have not been evaluated.

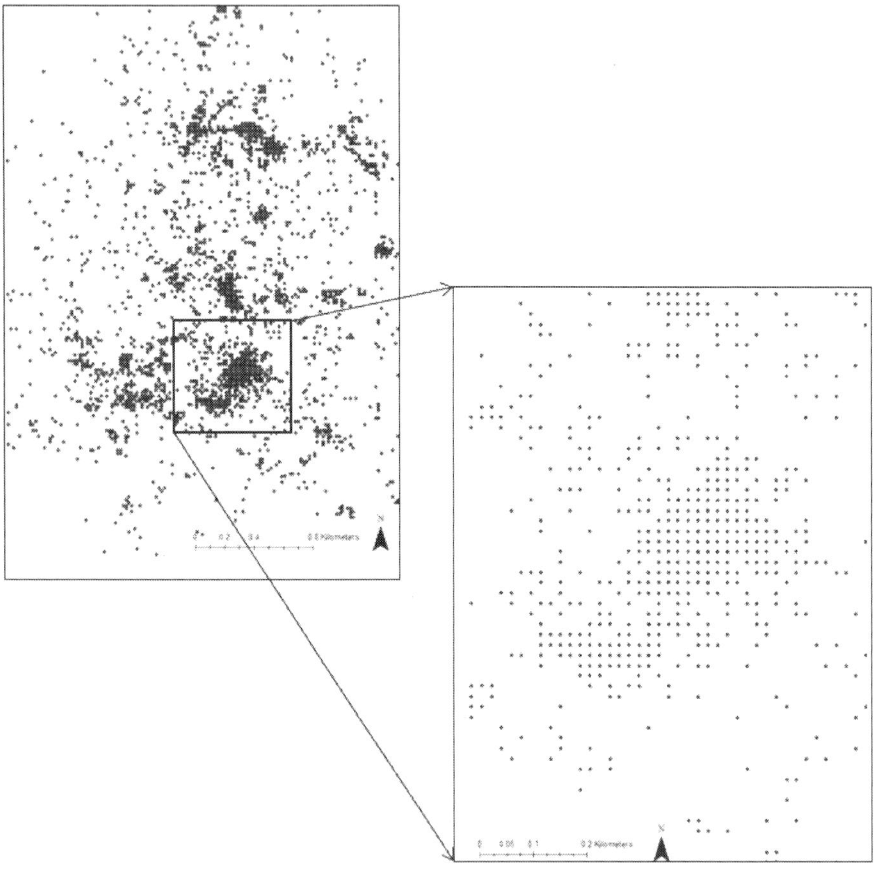

Fig. 1. Locations of a black vulture displaying the grid structure resulting from truncation of GPS coordinates.

2.2 Temporal context of data

When designing a study to analyze home ranges, time duration between successive locations is an important component to consider. Attempts at fix rates can be decreased to extend battery life for most GPS units or increased to identify detailed, real-time movements. Several manufactures provided the option of remotely downloading data to a server so locations are gathered weekly, approaching study animals within a certain distance to download locations, or store-on-board GPS units with drop-off mechanisms and VHF signals that researchers use to track and retrieve collars (Clark et al., 2006). Beyond the obvious trade-off between increased sampling effort and decreased battery life, seasonal and diel behavior of the species should be considered as it can greatly affect the resulting home range estimate depending on the data collection schedule used. For example, large data intervals can occur from failed GPS fixes or when the collar was programmed to turn off. Failed fixes can also occur for species fitted with solar-powered GPS collars that failed to charge the battery or for species that den or hibernate that had transmitters that were turned off to conserve battery life and to decrease duplicate locations. Therefore, depending on collection schedule, ecology of the species, and method of home range analysis, greater uncertainty can be associated with certain areas of the home range resulting in different levels of inference.

2.3 Spatial context of data

Various coordinate systems have been developed for different areas of the world that provides a common geographic framework to perform spatial analysis. Choosing the correct coordinate system for data analysis requires knowledge of the spatial distribution and extent of GPS points. Use of the geographic coordinate system (i.e. latitude, longitude) is recommended in cases of long distance movements and is often the default geographic collection method for GPS collar data. However, some home range software (e.g. BBMM package in R) requires input coordinate data to be in meters. This is challenging when global positioning system technology has been used to document movements of wildlife that migrate long distances (Mandel et al., 2008; Sawyer et al., 2009; Takekawa et al., 2010). For example, American White Pelicans captured in Louisiana, USA were tracked into southern Canada (D.T. King, National Wildlife Research Center, unpublished data). With such movements, a single American White Pelican could occupy 5 Universal Transverse Mercator (UTM) zones during migrations from southern to northern latitudes (Fig. 2). Therefore, BBMM analysis of home range of American White Pelican in the USA might be best depicted using Albers Equal Area or Lambert Conformal. Home range can be estimated for many animals within their respective UTM zone if GPS locations do not extend outside of more than one zone.

3. Bandwidth selection for kernel density estimation

In KDE, a kernel distribution (i.e. a three-dimensional hill or kernel) is placed on each telemetry location. The height of the hill is determined by the bandwidth of the distribution, and many distributions and methods are available (e.g. fixed versus adaptive, univariate versus bivariate bandwidth; for a complete review see Worton 1989; Seaman & Powell 1996). The study extent is then gridded with evaluation points in which different kernels are summarized to produce a utilization distribution across the area of interest. The resulting utilization distribution is therefore sensitive to the resolution of the evaluation grid, and more importantly, to the bandwidth selection (i.e. smoothing parameter) of the kernels.

Because GPS data are autocorrelated, they can pose difficulties in estimating the bandwidth (Gitzen et al., 2006) and violate the assumption of independence of locations that is inherent to KDE (Worton 1989). Therefore, although previous research on principles of bandwidth selection and selection of software is suitable for some datasets (e.g. VHF sampling protocols; Seaman et al., 1999; Gitzen et al., 2006; Kie et al., 2010), GPS datasets present additional challenges that need to be addressed (Amstrup et al., 2004; Hemson et al., 2005; Getz et al., 2007).

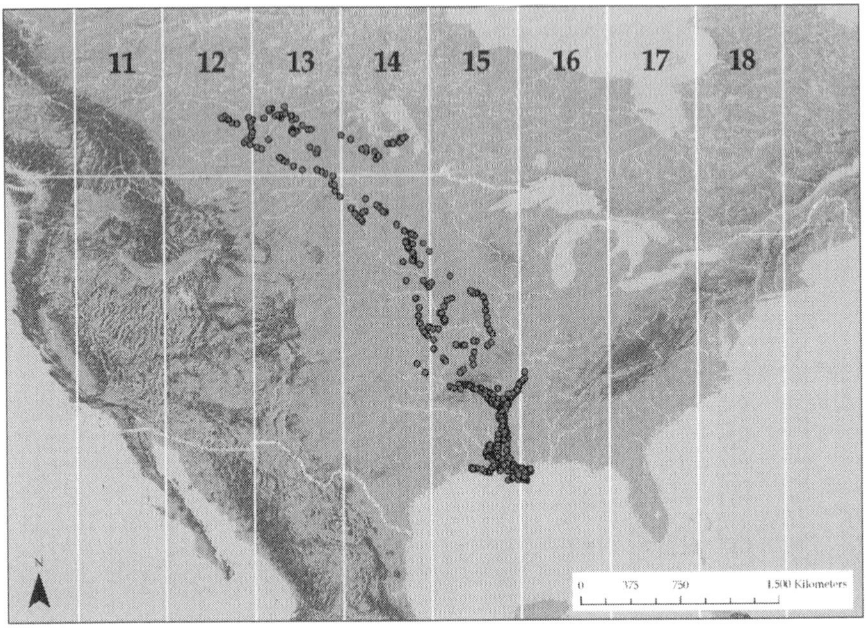

Fig. 2. Multiple Universal Transverse Mercator zones traversed by a migratory American White Pelican in the U.S.

3.1 Default (reference) bandwidth estimation

Datasets for avian and mammalian species can include as many as 10,000 locations and only the reference or default bandwidth (h_{ref}) was able to produce KDE in both Home Range Tools and adehabitat. Estimation with h_{ref} typically is not reliable for use on multimodal datasets because it results in over-smoothing of home ranges and multimodal distribution of locations is typical for most species (Worton 1995; Seaman et al., 1999). An important point to consider with previous investigations on bandwidth selection is that analyses used simulated data on only 10–1,000 locations for assessing reliability of h_{ref} (Seaman et al., 1999; Lichti & Swihart 2011). Still, results from simulated datasets and real-world examples concluded that h_{ref} should not be used on multimodal data typical for most mobile species (Worton 1995; Seaman & Powell 1996; Hemson et al., 2005). Our results confirmed that over-smoothing is considerable, especially for migratory avian species that migrate across vast geographic areas. For example, a turkey vulture that traversed from South Carolina to

Florida, USA, had a 95% home range calculated with h_{ref} that extended inland and into the Atlantic Ocean to areas locations were not even identified (J.W. Fischer, National Wildlife Research Center, unpublished data; Fig. 3).

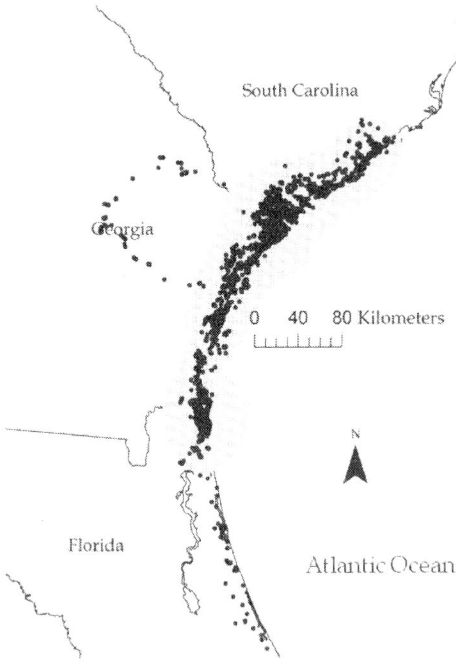

Fig. 3. Home range (yellow polygon) of a migratory turkey vulture from South Carolina to Florida, USA as estimated using KDE with h_{ref} bandwidth selection over-layed on actual GPS locations. Note that KDE occurs inland and into Atlantic Ocean where no GPS locations were collected.

An additional practical problem we encountered with h_{ref} in adehabitat is that the extent of the generated home range polygon was truncated or not generated at all because a greater extent for evaluation points needed to be specified. To work around this issue, we created an evaluation grid of increased extent and iteratively re-estimated the home range until a large enough extent was specified and all isopleth (i.e. probability contour) polygons were successfully created.

3.2 Least squares cross-validation bandwidth estimation

Both the least squares cross-validation (h_{lscv}) and bias crossed validation (h_{bcv}) have been suggested instead of h_{ref} in attempts to prevent over-smoothing of KDE (Rodgers & Kie 2010). However, h_{lscv} and h_{bcv} have been minimally evaluated on GPS datasets because previous literature only evaluated datasets collected on VHF sampling protocols or simulated data that included at most 1,000 locations and did not represent actual animal distributions (Worton 1995; Citzen et al., 2006; Lichti & Swihart 2011). Least-squares cross validation, suggested as the most reliable bandwidth for KDE (Worton 1989), was considered better than plug-in bandwidth selection (for description see 3.3) at identifying distributions with tight clumps of points but risk of failure increases with h_{lscv} when a distribution has a "very tight cluster of points" (Gitzen et al., 2006; Pellerin et al., 2008). Several of our species could be classified as having "very tight cluster of points" because American White Pelican locations were truncated to a grid with multiple overlapping points, vultures occupied the same roosts at dusk and dawn, or black bears rested in day beds. Considering that none of our datasets resulted in converged h_{lscv} or h_{bcv} estimates for home range calculation, our results on several species further supported the contention that h_{lscv} and h_{bcv} bandwidths are not suitable for GPS-derived datasets, unless convergence issues at sample sizes >1,000 locations and with clumped distributions can be resolved (Amstrup et al., 2004; Hemson et al., 2005). One way to address lack of convergence due to large datasets is subsampling (Avery et al., 2011) that can be used for crude estimates of home range using KDE with h_{lscv}. We conclude with others in cautioning against subsampling as it only serves to potentially remove important movement parameters or habitats used and will not result in the same estimate of home range size as the complete GPS dataset (Blundell et al., 2001; Pellerin et al., 2008; Rodgers & Kie 2010).

3.3 Plug-in bandwidth selection

Most first generation methods of bandwidth selection for density estimation (i.e. h_{lscv}, h_{bcv}) were developed before 1990 but advances in theory and technological capabilities has opened the door for second generation methods (Jones et al., 1996). Second generation methods, such as the smoothed bootstrap and plug-in methods (often combined into the solve-the-equation plug-in method; Jones et al., 1996), appear to be an improved alternative because of better convergence and reasonable tradeoffs between bias and variance compared to first generation methods (Jones et al., 1996; Duong & Hazelton 2003, but see Loader 1999). Debate about the appropriateness of second generation methods still exists with some claiming the estimates obtained with bivariate plug-in bandwidth selection ($h_{plug\text{-}in}$) performs poorly compared to first-generation methods (Loader 1999) while others showed it performed well even when analyzing dependent data (Hall et al., 1995).

Using $h_{plug\text{-}in}$ in ks, we were able to calculate KDEs for the sample GPS datasets on 3 avian species and 2 mammalian species where first generation methods (h_{lscv}) failed or generated a considerably over-smoothed KDE (h_{ref}). While home range polygons generated with $h_{plug\text{-}in}$ appeared fragmented, they may be appropriate when studying a species in highly fragmented landscapes such as urban areas. Based on our results and previous research, conclusions presented in Loader (1999) should be re-evaluated for analyses of large GPS dataset because sample size and clumping of locations has consistently failed using h_{lscv}, while $h_{plug\text{-}in}$ estimates converged for large multimodal datasets and resulted in reasonable estimates (Girard et al., 2002; Amstrup et al., 2004; Gitzen et al., 2006).

4. Brownian bridge movement models

The concept of BBMM is based on a Brownian bridge with the probability of being in an area dependent upon the elapsed time between the starting and ending locations (Bullard 1999; Horne et al., 2007). The BBMM "fills in" the space between sequential locations irrespective of the density of locations where the width of the Brownian bridge is conditioned only on the time duration between the beginning and ending locations for each pair of locations and GPS location error. As such, BBMM is able to predict movement paths that otherwise would not be observed with KDE methods. While some authors have suggested using ≤90% home range contours (Borger et al., 2006; Getz et al., 2007) to remove outliers or exploratory movements for KDE, increasing size of home range from 95% to 99% for BBMM does not over-smooth the utilization distribution but rather serves to more accurately define the area of use for some species (e.g. Fig. 4; Lewis 2007). Therefore, BBMM intuitively appears better suited for mammalian and avian species that migrate or travel long distances (Sawyer et al., 2009; Takekawa et al., 2010; J.W. Fischer, National Wildlife Research Center, unpublished data).

Fig. 4. Home range of an American White Pelican using 95% BBMM (outset) with 99% BBMM connecting potential used habitats in some areas of the home range (inset).

4.1 Time interval between locations

Although equal time intervals between successive relocations are not, in theory, a requirement of BBMM, the method uses a Brownian bridge to estimate the probability density that the animal used any particular pixel, given its relocations. The "shape" of the

Brownian bridge characterizing two successive relocations is adjusted as a function of the time lag separating these two relocations: if the time lag is short, the bridge will be narrower than if the time lag is long. Even though this approximation may be useful to account for movement constraints (e.g. an animal cannot move 20 km in two minutes), its implications may be problematic if the time lag between successive relocations is highly variable such as with relocations separated by time lags distributed over several orders of magnitude (e.g. days to weeks).
The variability in time lag between successive locations was important to consider for several of our species and resulted in size of home range 1.5 to 2 times larger when not accounting for time lag (Fig. 5). The GPS collars deployed on vultures were programmed to only turn on during the local dawn-dusk period, thus time lags occurred for black vultures (mean = 114 min ± 229 SD) and turkey vultures (mean = 103 min ± 162 SD) while on roost during nocturnal hours (Beason et al., 2010). Time lag was important for black bears (mean = 49 min ± 199 SD; Fig. 5a) due to screening and removal of position dilution of precision of GPS fixes and lack of GPS fixes for Florida panther (mean = 214 min ± 152 SD) in upland forest and cypress swamps. American White Pelican (mean = 359 min ± 1,633 SD; Fig. 5b) covered up solar panels of the GPS harness or occupied habitats that prevented the battery from maintaining a full charge thereby not allowing GPS data logging upon fix attempt (Cappelle et al., 2011). To improve results, we chose a crude approach to eliminate the top 1% of outliers of time difference such that 99% of the original data were included (O_{REM}). We estimated O_{REM} for each individual animal so inclusion criterion varied across individual for each species. After implementing O_{REM} that resulted in removal of locations, we re-calculated BBMM for black bear (Fig. 5c) and American White Pelican (Fig. 5d), that represented more realistic home ranges by only including time intervals ≤182 min and ≤69 hours for an individual black bear and American White Pelican, respectively.
We followed this method for all species and present the ratio of sizes of home range for the full dataset with all locations to a limited dataset after implementing O_{REM} (Table 2). An alternative approach could be to use the median distance between successive locations as suggested by Benhamou (2011). While O_{REM} may seem reasonable for some species and studies in eliminating large time differences and resulting in tighter home ranges, we caution researchers from using such an approach without considering its implications to the ecological questions at hand and prior to determining distribution of time differences with locations from each study animal.

Home range	Black bear	Florida panther	Pelican	Black vulture	Turkey vulture
50%	2.5 (1.3)	1.0 (0.04)	2.3 (2.3)	1.4 (0.4)	1.3 (0.5)
95%	2.2 (1.6)	1.0 (0.02)	1.6 (0.8)	1.3 (0.5)	1.1 (0.1)
99%	2.3 (1.7)	1.0 (0.04)	1.5 (0.8)	1.3 (0.4)	1.1 (0.2)

Table 2. Mean (SD) ratio (full/limited) of average 50%, 95%, and 99% home range areas calculated for each species using Brownian bridge movement models with full and limited datasets, where for the latter the top 1% outlier time intervals were removed.

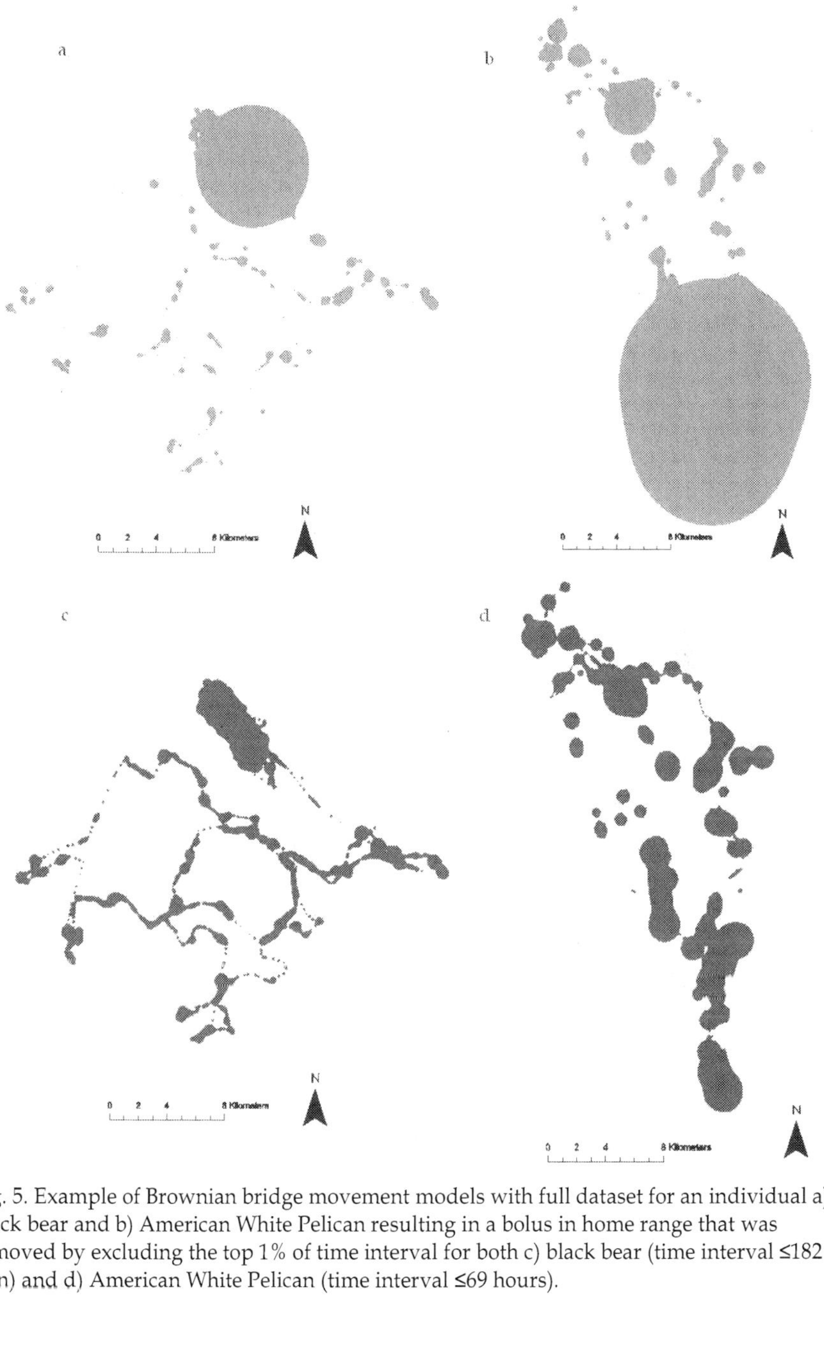

Fig. 5. Example of Brownian bridge movement models with full dataset for an individual a) black bear and b) American White Pelican resulting in a bolus in home range that was removed by excluding the top 1% of time interval for both c) black bear (time interval ≤182 min) and d) American White Pelican (time interval ≤69 hours).

5. Comparison of home range estimators

Use of BBMM or KDE is dependent on study objectives and should not be considered a similar method to an end result as previously suggested (Kie et al., 2010). Brownian bridge movement models were intended for data correlated in space and time to document the path followed and used by animals (Bullard 1999). Conversely, researchers have stressed the importance of using independent locations to accurately determine areas of use with KDE (Swihart & Slade 1985a; Worton 1989, but see Blundell et al., 2001). Animals that migrate several kilometers or avian species that cover large areas simply are not properly represented using traditional KDE and bandwidth selection common in available home range estimation software. Conversely, KDE with $h_{plug\text{-}in}$ would be better suited for less mobile species occupying patchy environments or small geographic areas because $h_{plug\text{-}in}$ is more conservative resulting in less smoothing than h_{lscv} (Gitzen et al., 2006). Use of $h_{plug\text{-}in}$ may also be an appropriate method compared to BBMM when the study focus is on resident or seasonal animal habitat use and exploratory movements are not of interest and should be excluded.

Species	$KDE_{href}/KDE_{plug\text{-}in}$	$KDE_{href}/BBMM$	$KDE_{plug\text{-}in}/BBMM$
50% contours			
Black bear	7.4 (6.9)	5.0 (7.7)	0.5 (0.3)
Florida panther	2.7 (0.5)	1.0 (0.5)	0.4 (0.1)
White pelican	39.6 (26.0)	15.6 (22.3)	0.3 (0.3)
Black vulture	26.4 (15.4)	2.1 (2.4)	0.1 (0.05)
Turkey vulture	14.9 (17.3)	1.4 (0.9)	0.1 (0.1)
95% contours			
Black bear	4.5 (2.9)	4.5 (6.4)	0.8 (0.6)
Florida panther	2.0 (0.4)	1.3 (0.4)	0.7 (0.1)
White pelican	13.5 (9.5)	10.4 (15.3)	0.5 (0.5)
Black vulture	6.8 (3.6)	1.7 (1.7)	0.2 (0.1)
Turkey vulture	6.9 (3.8)	1.9 (1.2)	0.3 (0.1)
99% contours			
Black bear	3.6 (1.8)	4.6 (6.1)	1.1 (0.9)
Florida panther	1.9 (0.4)	1.5 (0.5)	0.8 (0.2)
White pelican	8.8 (4.9)	9.1 (12.9)	0.7 (0.6)
Black vulture	5.4 (1.9)	1.7 (1.6)	0.3 (0.2)
Turkey vulture	5.7 (2.9)	2.4 (1.6)	0.4 (0.2)

Table 3. Mean (SD) ratio of 50%, 95%, and 99% isopleth home range areas calculated using fixed-kernel home range with default bandwidth (h_{ref}), fixed-kernel home range with plug-in bandwidth selection ($h_{plug\text{-}in}$), and the limited dataset for Brownian bridge movement models (BBMM) for black bears (n = 10), Florida panthers (n = 10), pelicans (n = 10), and black (n = 5) and turkey (n = 5) vultures equipped with GPS technology.

Ratios of home range areas varied considerably depending on size of home range estimated (50%, 95%, 99%), species studied, and method of home range analysis (Table 3). For all species, all KDE home ranges calculated with h_{ref} were from 2 to 40 times larger than $h_{plug\text{-}in}$ regardless of isopleth (Table 3). These differences were especially pronounced for avian species, and are likely a reflection of the challenges of the univariate kernel bandwidth estimator h_{ref} to capture the linear movement patterns generated by migratory American White Pelicans and black and turkey vultures, regardless of isopleth. Size of home range using KDE with h_{ref} would likely lead to over-smoothing between migratory locations (but see Blundell et al., 2001). Although we did not separate migratory and resident avian, differences in estimates likely would not be as considerable for avian species with minimal migratory movements. Conversely, we would expect greater differences in estimates for mammalian species that exhibit greater migratory movements such as seasonal migrations in mule deer (*Odocoileus hemionus*; Sawyer et al., 2009) and caribou (*Rangifer tarandus*; Bergman et al., 2000) that are not restricted by considerable roadways and development (i.e. Florida panther) or that occupy urban areas (i.e. black bears) that we assessed in our study. Our results support previous research on smaller datasets that even with serially correlated GPS locations, KDE with h_{ref} over-estimates size of home range compared to $h_{plug\text{-}in}$ (Table 3).

All isopleths of home ranges were only 1 to 16 times larger for KDE with h_{ref} than BBMM. The smaller difference in size of home range between KDE with h_{ref} and BBMM than KDE with h_{ref} and $h_{plug\text{-}in}$ is likely from the inherent nature of BBMM to identify pathways with Brownian bridges. Creating Brownian bridges across sequential GPS locations would be expected to result in larger size of home range than KDE with $h_{plug\text{-}in}$ that conservatively predicts a utilization distribution based on density of locations. Being that KDE has been known to over-smooth utilization distributions with h_{ref} and under-smooth with $h_{plug\text{-}in}$ (Gitzen et al., 2006), we expected BBMM to be in between the 2 bandwidth selections for KDE in size of home range.

Estimates of home range were more comparable for all species and isopleths between KDE with $h_{plug\text{-}in}$ and BBMM but $h_{plug\text{-}in}$ estimates were always smaller than BBMM with only one exception (Table 3). The minimal differences in size of home range between KDE with $h_{plug\text{-}in}$ and BBMM is likely only a reflection of identification of exploratory movements with BBMM. Similar to KDE with $h_{plug\text{-}in}$, BBMM conservatively creates a utilization distribution around areas of concentrated use but, unlike KDE with $h_{plug\text{-}in}$, also connects multiple areas of concentrated use. For example, a yearling black bear in an urban area of central Colorado, USA, exhibited exploratory movements that were identified with BBMM but not with KDE with $h_{plug\text{-}in}$ (Fig. 6). Actual size of home range for defining available habitats for analysis of resource selection may be more accurately depicted using KDE with $h_{plug\text{-}in}$ because it identified concentrated areas of use and not exploratory pathways that were not visited and are not necessary to an animal's fitness.

Across several avian and mammalian species, we identified similar general patterns of size and shape of home range for KDE with h_{ref} and $h_{plug\text{-}in}$ and BBMM. For example, 95% KDEs with h_{ref} (Fig. 7a) and KDE with $h_{plug\text{-}in}$ (Fig. 7b) bandwidths either over-smoothed or under-smoothed, respectively, size of home range of a Florida panther around agricultural habitats while BBMM (Fig 7c) identified a path around agricultural patches. Regardless of estimation method used, tradeoffs between depicting areas traversed or habitats occupied need to be considered in choosing KDE or BBMM. Use of KDE with h_{ref} or $h_{plug\text{-}in}$ may be alternatives to minimum convex polygon for resource selection studies to determine available resources under Type II or Type III study designs (Manly et al., 2002). Assessment of migration routes or commonly used travel corridors would be better represented by BBMM because bridges identify the pathways used by animals as they traverse their home range or explore new territories (Fig. 7c).

Wildlife derived GPS datasets require dedicated software and analysis tools for researchers to understand an animal's movements, behavior, and habitat use. The most well known program to calculate KDE (ArcView version 3.x) is not directly compatible with 64-bit computer operating systems and current extensions in the newer versions of ArcMap 9.x do not offer the flexibility in several components (i.e. batch-processing, bandwidth selection) afforded by earlier versions of ArcView 3.x, are unable to handle thousands of locations and overlapping coordinates (e.g. Home Range Tools), or were incorporated into the Geospatial Modelling Environment that requires ArcMap 10.x (i.e. Animal Movement Extension, Hawth's Tools; www.spatialecology.com). Furthermore, several studies have indicated that size of home range calculated with KDE differed with each program by as much as 20% for 95% contours (Lawson & Rodgers 1997; Mitchell 2006). Most home range programs require various input parameters or are programmed with defaults that should be considered prior to selecting the program that best suits the needs of the researcher (Lawson & Rodgers 1997; Mitchell 2006; Gitzen et al., 2006). Many new programs to estimate home range are comparable to the graphical user interface of ArcMap (e.g. Quantum GIS, www.qgis.org), require ArcMap and R (e.g. Geospatial Modelling Environment, www.spatialecology.com/gme), or considerably under-estimate home range and require further evaluation (BIOTA, www.ecostats.com; Mitchell 2006). To evaluate every program available would have been beyond the scope of our objectives, so we presented home range estimators in R that is freely available to all researchers.

Fig. 6. Home range of a yearling black bear using 95% plug-in with kernel density estimation (thick line) and exploratory movements with 95% BBMM (thin line) prior to dispersal in year 2.

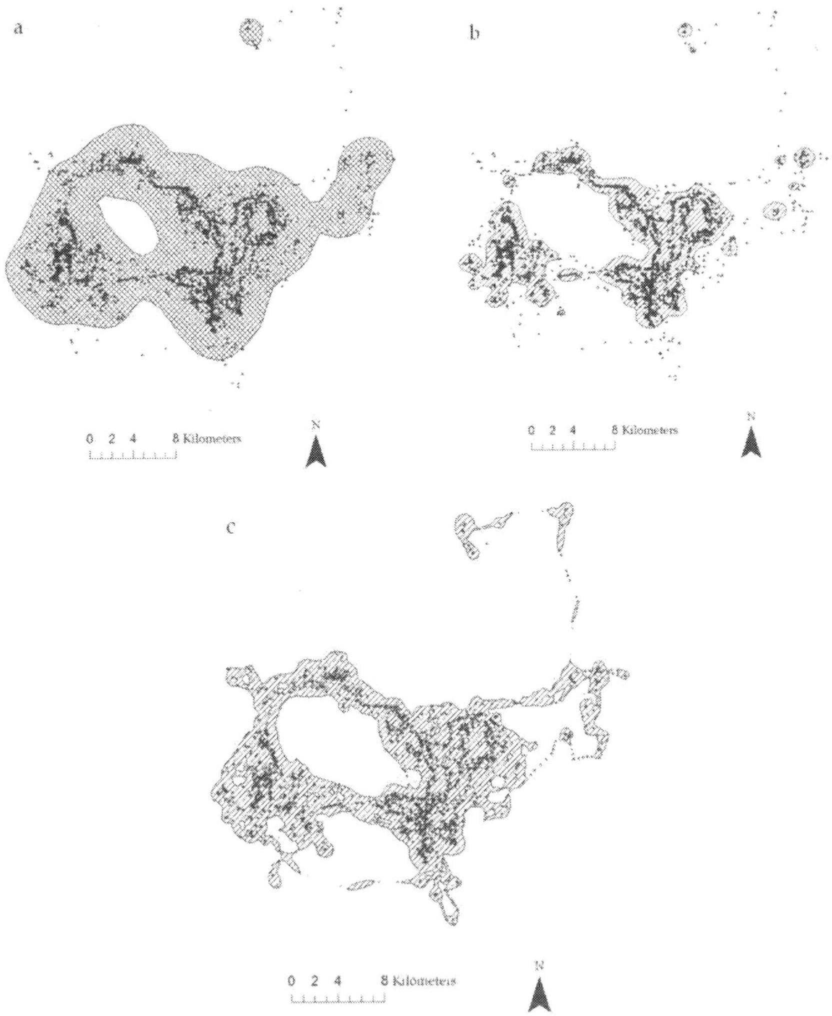

Fig. 7. Comparison of 95% estimates of panther home range derived from kernel density estimation with a) h_{ref} bandwidth selection and b) $h_{plug\text{-}in}$ bandwidth selection as well as c) a Brownian bridge movement model with GPS locations (•) in background.

6. Conclusions

Our goal was to assist researchers in determining the appropriate methods to assess size and shape of home range with a variety of species and movement vectors. Although we did not set out to assess the accuracy of methods, our results suggested that BBMM and $h_{plug\text{-}in}$ are more appropriate for today's GPS datasets that can have >1,000 locations seasonally and up to 10,000 locations annually over a 2-3 year collection period. Of equal importance, we were not able to generate KDE with h_{lscv} in Home Range Tools for ArcMap and, to our knowledge, no other software was suitable or reported to determine size of home range for both KDE with $h_{plug\text{-}in}$ and BBMM other than R. The next step of research should focus on alternate software that can be used to estimate size of home range with actual animal GPS datasets. Although all software would likely produce inconsistent home range sizes as previously indicated for earlier programs with VHF datasets (Lawson & Rodgers 1997; Mitchell 2006), the magnitude and reason for differences needs to be understood. Finally, continued assessment of accuracy of estimates of home range is necessary with simulated datasets that range from several thousand to 10,000 serial locations that have defined true utilization distributions to determine proper estimator for size of home range based on study objectives and to verify software reliability.

Further assessment of third generation methods (i.e. mechanistic home-range models, movement-based kernel density estimators) and development of user-friendly packages would be beneficial. As most third generation methods are in their infancy stages of development and evaluation, we are confident that home range estimation will continue to grow and evolve to offer researchers multiple choices for each study species. Undoubtedly, the debate over the proper technique to use should continue but we caution that ecology of the study animal, research objectives, software limitations, and home range estimators should be critically evaluated from the inception of a study (i.e. prior to ordering of GPS technology) to final estimation of size of home range.

7. Acknowledgment

Funding for this research was provided by the National Wildlife Research Center of the United States Department of Agriculture, Animal and Plant Health Inspection Service, Wildlife Services. We would like to thank Dave Onorato and the Florida Fish and Wildlife Conservation Commission for use of data on the Florida panther. We would like to thank Tommy King and the USDA/APHIS/WS National Wildlife Research Center Mississippi Field Station for data on American White Pelican. We would like to thank Michael Avery and the USDA/APHIS/WS National Wildlife Research Center Gainesville Field Station for data on black and turkey vultures. We would like to thank the USDA/APHIS/WS National Wildlife Research Center, Colorado State University, and the Colorado Division of Wildlife for use of black bear data.

8. References

Amstrup, S. C., McDonald, T. L. & Durner, G. M. (2004). Using satellite radiotelemetry data to delineate and manage wildlife populations. *Wildlife Society Bulletin*, Vol.32, No.3, pp. 661-679

Avery,M.L., Humphrey,J.S., Daughtery,T.S., Fischer,J.W., Milleson,M.P., Tillman,E.A., Bruce,W.E. & Walter,W.D., (2011). Vulture flight behavior and implications for aircraft safety. *Journal of Wildlife Management*, In press

Beason, R. C., Humphrey, J. S., Myers, N. E. & Avery, M. L. (2010). Synchronous monitoring of vulture movements with satellite telemetry and avian radar. *Journal of Zoology*, Vol.282, No.3, pp. 157-162

Benhamou, S. (2011). Dynamic approach to space and habitat use based on biased random bridges. *PLoS ONE*, Vol.6, No.1, pp. e14592

Benhamou, S. & Cornelis, D. (2010). Incorporating movement behavior and barriers to improve kernel home range space use estimates. *Journal of Wildlife Management*, Vol.74, No.6, pp. 1353-1360

Bergman, C. M., Schaefer, J. A. & Luttich, S. N. (2000). Caribou movement as a correlated random walk. *Oecologia*, Vol.123, No.3, pp. 364-374

Blundell, G. M., Maier, J. A. K. & Debevec, E. M. (2001). Linear home ranges: effects of smoothing, sample size, and autocorrelation on kernel estimates. *Ecological Monographs*, Vol.71, No.3, pp. 469-489

Borger, L., Franconi, N., De Michele, G., Gantz, A., Meschi, F., Manica, A., Lovari, S. & Coulson, T. (2006). Effects of sampling regime on the mean and variance of home range size estimates. *Journal of Animal Ecology*, Vol.75, No.6, pp. 1393-1405

Bullard, F. (1999). Estimating the home range of an animal: a Brownian Bridge approach. Thesis, University of North Carolina at Chapel Hill, Chapel Hill

Burt, W. H. (1943). Territoriality and home range concepts as applied to mammals. *Journal of Mammalogy*, Vol.24, No.3, pp. 346-352

Calenge, C. (2006). The package "adehabitat" for the R software: a tool for the analysis of space and habitat use by animals. *Ecological Modelling*, Vol.197, No.3-4, pp. 516-519

Cappelle, J., Iverson, S. A., Takekawa, J. Y., Newman, S. H., Dodman, T. & Gaidet, N. (2011). Implementing telemetry on new species in remote areas: recommendations from a large-scale satellite tracking study of African waterfowl. *Ostrich: African Journal of Ornithology*, Vol.82, No.1, pp. 17-26

Clark, P. E., Johnson, D. E., Kniep, M. A., Jerman, P., Huttash, B., Wood, A., Johnson, M., McGillivan, C. & Titus, K. (2006). An advanced, low-cost, GPS-based animal tracking system. *Rangeland Ecology & Management*, Vol.59, No.3, pp. 334-340

D'Eon, R. G., Serrouya, R., Smith, G. & Kochanny, C. O. (2002). GPS radiotelemetry error and bias in mountainous terrain. *Wildlife Society Bulletin*, Vol.30, No.2, pp. 430-439

Dennis, T. E., Chen, W. C., Koefoed, I. M., Lacoursiere, C. J., Walker, M. M., Laube, P. & Forer, P. (2010). Performance characteristics of small global-positioning-system tracking collars for terrestrial animals. *Wildlife Biology in Practice*, Vol.6, No.1, pp. 14-31

Duong, T. (2007). ks: kernel density estimation and kernel discriminant analysis for multivariate data in R. *Journal of Statistical Software*, Vol.21, No.7, pp. 1-16

Duong, T. & Hazelton, M. L. (2003). Plug-in bandwidth matrices for bivariate kernel density estimation. *Nonparametric Statistics*, Vol.15, No.1, pp. 17-30

Fieberg, J. (2007). Kernel density estimators of home range: smoothing and the autocorrelation red herring. *Ecology*, Vol.88, No.4, pp. 1059-1066

Getz, W. M., Fortmann-Roe, S., Cross, P. C., Lyons, A. J., Ryan, S. J. & Wilmers, C. C. (2007). LoCoH: nonparametric kernel methods for constructing home ranges and utilization distributions. *PLoS ONE*, Vol.2, No.2, pp. e207

Getz, W. M. & Wilmers, C. C. (2004). A local nearest-neighbor convex-hull construction of home ranges and utilization distributions. *Ecography*, Vol.27, No.4, pp. 489-505

Gilsdorf, J. M., VerCauteren, K. C., Hygnstrom, S. E., Walter, W. D., Boner, J. R. & Clements, G. M. (2008). An integrated vehicle-mounted telemetry system for VHF telemetry applications. *Journal of Wildlife Management*, Vol.72, No.5, pp. 1241-1246

Girard, I., Ouellet, J., Courtois, R., Dussault, C. & Breton, L. (2002). Effects of sampling effort based on GPS telemetry on home-range size estimations. *Journal of Wildlife Management*, Vol.66, No.4, pp. 1290-1300

Gitzen, R. A., Millspaugh, J. J. & Kernohan, B. J. (2006). Bandwidth selection for fixed-kernel analysis of animal utilization distributions. *Journal of Wildlife Management*, Vol.70, No.5, pp. 1334-1344

Hall, P., Lahiri, S. N. & Truong, Y. K. (1995). On bandwidth choice for density estimation with dependent data. *The Annals of Statistics*, Vol.23, No.6, pp. 2241-2263

Hebblewhite, M. & Haydon, D. T. (2010). Distinguishing technology from biology: a critical review of the use of GPS telemetry data in ecology. *Philosophical Transactions of the Royal Society B*, Vol.365, No.1550, pp. 2303-2312

Hemson, G., Johnson, P., South, A., Kenward, R., Ripley, R. & Macdonald, D. (2005). Are kernels the mustard? Data from global positioning systems (GPS) collars suggests problems for kernel home-range analyses with least-squares cross-validation. *Journal of Animal Ecology*, Vol.74, No.3, pp. 455-463

Horne, J. S., Garton, E. O., Krone, S. M. & Lewis, J. S. (2007). Analyzing animal movements using Brownian bridges. *Ecology*, Vol.88, No.9, pp. 2354-2363

Jones, M. C., Marron, J. S. & Sheather, S. J. (1996). A brief survey of bandwidth selection for density estimation. *Journal of the American Statistical Association*, Vol.91, No.433, pp. 401-407

Keating, K. A. & Cherry, S. (2009). Modeling utilization distributions in space and time. *Ecology*, Vol.90, No.7, pp. 1971-1980

Kernohan, B. J., Gitzen, R. A. & Millspaugh, J. J. (2001). Analysis of animal space use and movements, In: *Radio tracking and animal populations*, (J. J. Millspaugh & J. M. Marzluff (Eds.), pp. (125-166), Academic Press, San Diego

Kie, J. G., Matthiopoulos, J., Fieberg, J., Powell, R. A., Cagnacci, F., Mitchell, M. S., Gaillard, J.-M. & Moorcroft, P. R. (2010). The home-range concept: are traditional estimators still relevant with modern telemetry technology? *Philosophical Transactions of the Royal Society B*, Vol.365, No.1550, pp. 2221-2231

Larson, M. A. (2001). A catalog of software to analyze radiotelemetry data, In: *Radio tracking and animal populations*, (J. J. Millspaugh & J. M. Marzluff (Eds.), pp. (397-422), Academic Press, San Diego

Laver, P. N. & Kelly, M. J. (2008). A critical review of home range studies. *Journal of Wildlife Management*, Vol.72, No.1, pp. 290-298

Lawson, E. J. G. & Rodgers, A. R. (1997). Differences in home-range size computed in commonly used software programs. *Wildlife Society Bulletin*, Vol.25, No.3, pp. 721-729

Lewis, J. S. (2007). The effects of human influences on black bear habitat selection and movement patterns within a highway corridor. Thesis, University of Idaho, Moscow

Lewis, J. S., Rachlow, J. L., Garton, E. O. & Vierling, L. A. (2007). Effects of habitat on GPS collar performance: using data screening to reduce location error. *Journal of Applied Ecology*, Vol.44, No.3, pp. 663-671

Lichti, N. I. & Swihart, R. K. (2011). Estimating utilization distribution with kernel versus local convex hull methods. *Journal of Wildlife Management*, Vol.75, No.2, pp. 413-422

Loader, C. R. (1999). Bandwidth selection: classical or plug-in? *The Annals of Statistics*, Vol.27, No.2, pp. 415-438

Mandel, J. T., Bildstein, K. L., Bohrer, G. & Winkler, D. W. (2008). Movement ecology of migration in turkey vultures. *Proceedings of the National Academy of Sciences*, Vol.105, No.49, pp. 19102-19107

Manly, B. F. J., McDonald, L. L. & Thomas, D. L. (2002). *Resource selection by animals: statistical design and analysis for field studies* (2nd), Kluwer Academic Publishers, Dordrecht

Matthiopoulos, J. (2003). Model-supervised kernel smoothing for the estimation of spatial usage. *Oikos*, Vol.102, No.2, pp. 367-377

Mitchell, B. R. (2006). Comparison of programs for fixed kernel home range analysis, 5.4.2011, Available from: http://www.uvm.edu/~bmitchel/Publications/HR_Compare.pdf

Moorcroft, P. R., Lewis, M. A. & Crabtree, R. L. (1999). Home range analysis using a mechanistic home range model. *Ecology*, Vol.80, No.5, pp. 1656-1665

Nielson, R. M., Manly, B. F. J., McDonald, L. L., Sawyer, H. & McDonald, T. L. (2009). Estimating habitat selection when GPS fix success is less than 100%. *Ecology*, Vol.90, No.10, pp. 2956-2962

Nielson, R. M., H. Sawyer & T. L. McDonald. (2011). BBMM: Brownian bridge movement model for estimating the movement path of an animal using discrete location data, R package version 2.2, 21.4.2011, Available from: http://CRAN.R-project.org/package=BBMM

Pellerin, M., Said, S. & Gaillard, J.-M. (2008). Roe deer *Capreolus capreolus* home-range sizes estimated from VHF and GPS data. *Wildlife Biology*, Vol.14, No.1, pp. 101-110

Rodgers, A. R. & J. G. Kie. (2010). HRT: Home Range Tools for ArcGIS®, version 1.1, 24.4.2011, Available from: http://flash.lakeheadu.ca/~arodgers/hre/Draft%20HRT%20Users%20Manual%20Sep%2028%202010.pdf

Sawyer, H., Kauffman, M. J., Nielson, R. M. & Horne, J. S. (2009). Identifying and prioritizing ungulate migration routes for landscape-level conservation. *Ecological Applications*, Vol.19, No.8, pp. 2016-2025

Seaman, D. E., Millspaugh, J. J., Kernohan, B. J., Brundige, G. C., Raedeke, K. J. & Gitzen, R. A. (1999). Effects of sample size on kernel home range estimates. *Journal of Wildlife Management*, Vol.63, No.2, pp. 739-747

Seaman, D. E. & Powell, R. A. (1996). An evaluation of the accuracy of kernel density estimators for home range analysis. *Ecology*, Vol.77, No.7, pp. 2075-2085

Swihart, R. K. & Slade, N. A. (1985a). Testing for independence of observations in animal movements. *Ecology*, Vol.66, No.4, pp. 1176-1184

Swihart, R. K. & Slade, N. A. (1985b). Influence of sampling interval on estimates of home-range size. *Journal of Wildlife Management*, Vol.49, No.4, pp. 1019-1025

Takekawa, J. Y., Newman, S. H., Xiao, X., Prosser, D. J., Spragens, K. A., Palm, E. C., Yan, B., Li, F., Zhao, D., Douglas, D. C., Muzaffar, S. B. & Ji, W. (2010). Migration of waterfowl in the East Asian Flyway and spatial relationship to HPAI H5N1 outbreaks. *Avian Diseases*, Vol.54, No.s1, pp. 466-476

Tomkiewicz, S. M., Fuller, M. R., Kie, J. G. & Bates, K. K. (2010). Global positioning system and associated technologies in animal behaviour and ecological research. *Philosophical Transactions of the Royal Society B*, Vol.365, No.1550, pp. 2163–2176

Withey, J. C., Bloxton, T. D. & Marzluff, J. M. (2001). Effect of tagging and location error in wildlife radiotelemetry studies, In: *Radio tracking and animal populations,* (J. J. Millspaugh & J. M. Marzluff (Eds.), pp. (43–75), Academic Press, San Diego

Worton, B. J. (1995). Using Monte Carlo simulation to evaluate kernel-based home range estimators. *Journal of Wildlife Management*, Vol.59, No.4, pp. 794–800

Worton, B. J. (1989). Kernel methods for estimating the utilization distribution in home-range studies. *Ecology*, Vol.70, No.1, pp. 164–168

13

Quantifying Wildlife Home Range Changes

Trisalyn A. Nelson
Spatial Pattern Analysis and Research Laboratory,
Department of Geography, University of Victoria
Canada

1. Introduction

In wildlife research, telemetry data are often converted to home ranges. The concept of an animal's home range can be defined as the ". . . area traversed by the individual in its normal activities of food gathering, mating and caring for young" (Burt, 1943, pg. 351). The delineation and analysis of home ranges is common in wildlife research, and several reviews of home range studies exist (Harris et al., 1990; Laver & Kelly, 2008). Site fidelity (Edwards et al., 2009), population abundance (Trewhella et al., 1988), prey-predatory abundance (Village, 1982), impacts of human disturbance (Apps et al., 2004; Berland et al., 2008; Frair et al., 2008; Rushton et al., 2000; Thiel et al., 2008), feeding strategies (Hulbert et al., 1996) and ecological correlates of critical habitat (Tufto, 1996; Fisher, 2000) are examples of topics addressed using home range as the analysis unit.

Home ranges are typically delineated with polygons. Locations within the polygon are considered part of the animal's home range, and locations outside are not. As evidenced by the large number of home range studies, such binary approaches have been useful. However, landscape use by wildlife is spatially heterogeneous (Johnson et al., 1992; Kie et al., 2002). Edges (Yahner, 1988), disturbances (i.e., roads and forest harvesting) (Berland et al., 2008), and patch size (Kie et al., 2002) are just a few landscape features that cause heterogeneity in the geographic distribution of wildlife within home ranges. To account for spatial heterogeneity within a home range, core areas, defined as those used most frequently and likely to contain homesites, along with areas of refuge and dependable food sources (Burt, 1943) are sometimes delineated to create categories of habitat use (e.g., Samuel et al., 1985). Characterizing the spatial variation in wildlife distributions should improve our understanding of habitat use, especially in conjunction with the growing spatial extents of wildlife data sets.

Arguably, the two most common approaches to demarcating a home range are the minimum convex polygon and kernel density estimation (Harris et al., 1990). The minimum convex polygon tends to overestimate home range size by including all the unused areas between outermost locations and increasing in area with large sample sizes (Börger et al., 2006a; Katajisto & Moilanen, 2006). As such, kernel density estimation is often preferred when demarcating a home range (Seaman & Powell, 1996; Marzluff et al., 2004; Börger et al., 2006a; Laver & Kelly, 2008). Although used to delineate binary home ranges, kernel density estimation generates a surface of values within the home range, which is useful for characterizing spatial variability in wildlife intensity. Kernel density surfaces are often referred to as utilization distributions as they give values that indicate higher and lower utilization of locations by individuals.

Regardless of how the home range is calculated, there are benefits to converting point-based telemetry data to polygonal home ranges. First, unless telemetry data are collected at a very high temporal frequency, almost continuously, telemetry data represent a sample of locations visited by an individual. Conversion to a polygon is an attempt to represent the complete range of possible movements. Second, conversion to a utilization distribution has the additional benefit of being useful for integrating telemetry data with environmental data sets. Often stored within a Geographic Information System (GIS), many environmental data sets are represented using raster grids. A common example is elevation data sets, which are stored in grid cells, of varying size. Kernel density estimated values are also stored as grid cells enabling efficient integration of utilization distributions with other map-based data sets.

As telemetry data sets have grown in temporal extent, it has become useful to employ home ranges to assess wildlife movement and habitat use through time. Characterizing the temporal change in home ranges has been used to study seasonal movement (Georgii, 1980), relate home range size to population abundance (Lowe et al., 2003) and land use (Viggers & Hearn, 2005), and characterize the spatial interactions of predator and prey (Village, 1982). Typically, when quantifying home range change, areal sizes are compared (e.g., Lurz et al., 1997; Lowe et al., 2003; Edwards et al., 2009) or the proportions of areal overlap enumerated (e.g., Georgii, 1980; Atwood & Weeks, 2003). In a few examples, spatial-temporal patterns of home ranges are quantified in greater detail. For instance, the multi-temporal persistence of home ranges has been related to landscape disturbance (Berland et al., 2008). Two additional approaches were identified by Kie et al. (2010) as showing potential for identifying temporal changes in home ranges. The first approach uses mixed effect models to relate temporal variation in patterns of telemetry data to climate, habitat, and age/sex variables of deer (Börger et al., 2006b). The second considers spatial variation in habitat use (represented by utilization distributions, defined below) continuous in time and representative of four dimensions (latitude, longitude, elevation, and time) (Keating & Cherry, 2009). Using a product-kernel, temporal patterns in space use were characterized using a circular time scale. Improved approaches to wildlife data collection, such as satellite and global positioning system (GPS) collars, in combination with concerns over climate change and growing anthropogenic pressures on wildlife, have increased the number of possible multi-temporal wildlife research questions. Development of new analytical approaches has begun and must continue if high temporal resolution telemetry data can be used to their full potential.

Here, I present three novel approaches to quantifying spatial-temporal change in home ranges. The first method, Spatial Temporal Analysis of Moving Polygons (STAMP), uses topological relationships of home range polygons to quantify spatial-temporal patterns of home ranges. The second method detects statistically significant change between two kernel density-estimated surfaces, and is utilized to characterize statistical change in intensity of habitat use within home ranges. The third method, an integration of methods one and two, simultaneously quantifies both the spatial-temporal pattern and change in wildlife intensities within home ranges. Described below, the new methods are demonstrated on caribou (*Rangifer tarandus* caribou) data from western Canada, and their benefits are outlined and compared to traditional approaches. To begin, home range delineation and typical approaches to change detection are presented as the basis for comparison with these novel approaches.

2. Home range methods

2.1 Telemetry data

The methods presented and compared in this chapter are applied to data on the Swan Lake woodland caribou herd, located in the southern Yukon, near Swift River (60°10'N,

131°07'W), and northern British Columbia, east of Teslin Lake (59°59'N, 132°25'W). Data were collected using very high frequency (VHF) transmitters. In 2006, 128 telemetry locations were obtained from 27 animals. In 2007, 68 telemetry locations were obtained from 18 animals (Fig. 1).

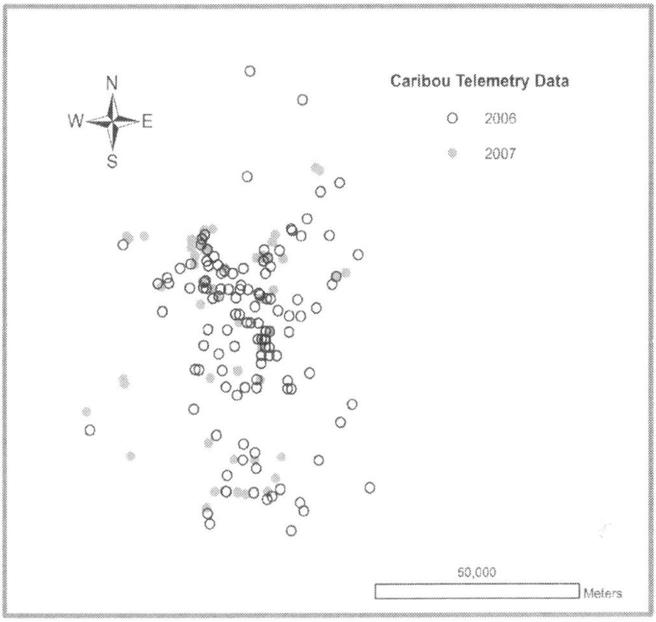

Fig. 1. Caribou telemetry data for 2006 and 2007.

2.2 Home range delineation and standard change analysis

Home ranges were delineated using kernel density estimation, a nonparametric approach for generating a continuous intensity surface (Seaman & Powell, 1996). Theoretically, the intensity $\lambda(z)$ of observations at each location z in a study area A is estimated using the kernel density estimator

$$\hat{\lambda}(z) = \frac{\text{the number of events in a neighbourhood centred on } z}{\text{area of the neighbourhood}} \tag{1}$$

A more exact estimate, $\hat{\lambda}_\tau(z)$, can be calculated using

$$\hat{\lambda}_\tau(z) = \left\{ \sum_{i=1}^{n} \frac{1}{\tau^2} k\left(\frac{(z - z_i)}{\tau} \right) \right\} \quad z \in A, \tag{2}$$

where z and A are defined as above, τ is the radius or bandwidth of a circular neighbourhood centred on z, $k()$ is the probability density function that is symmetric about

z, and z_i (i =1, ..., n), are the locations of n events. For home range delineation, the bandwidth size is typically selected via least-square cross-validation (LSCV) and a 95% threshold used to demarcate the home range boundary (Seaman & Powell, 1996; Seaman et al., 1999).

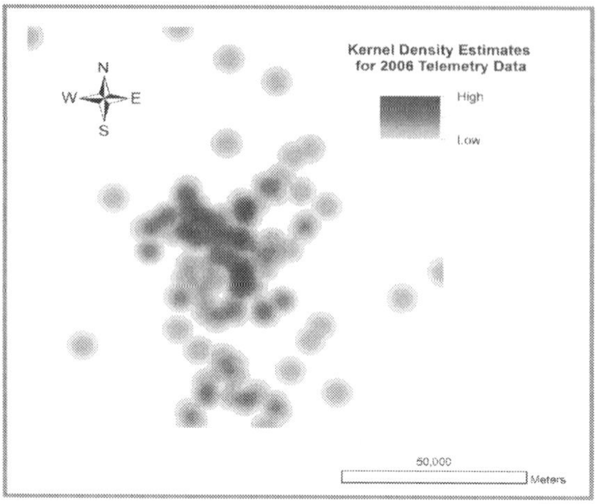

Fig. 2. Kernel density estimated surface generated from 2006 caribou telemetry data.

For the woodland caribou data, the bandwidth was defined as the mean LSCV for 2006 and 2007 data, which is 2.18 km (Fig. 2 and 3). For kernel-based change detection, it is beneficial to have consistent bandwidths (Bowman & Azzalini, 1997, pg. 114). The annual home range size was 1999.31 km^2 and 1231.28 km^2 in 2006 and 2007, respectively. Home ranges overlapped by 781.48 km^2 (31.91%) (Fig. 4).

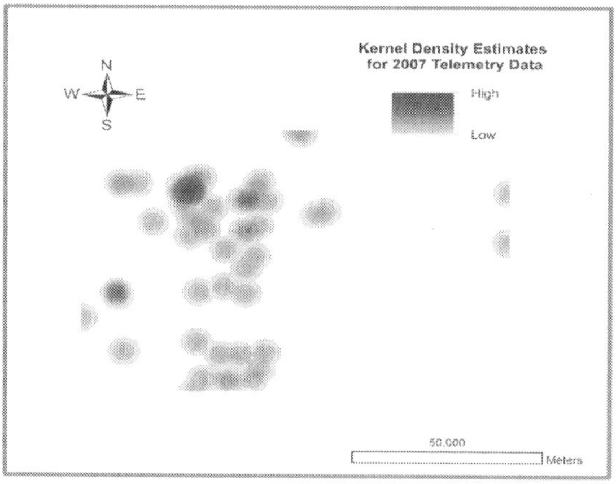

Fig. 3. Kernel density estimated surface generated from 2007 caribou telemetry data.

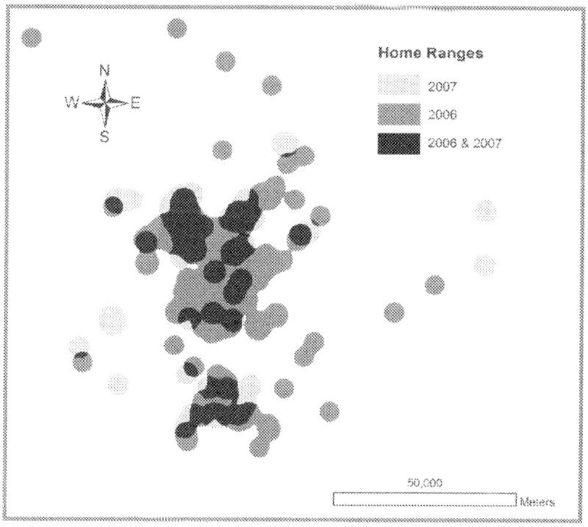

Fig. 4. Caribou home ranges for 2006 and 2007, generated using kernel density estimation.

3. Quantifying spatial-temporal change in home ranges

An overview of the three methods presented is provided in Fig. 5.

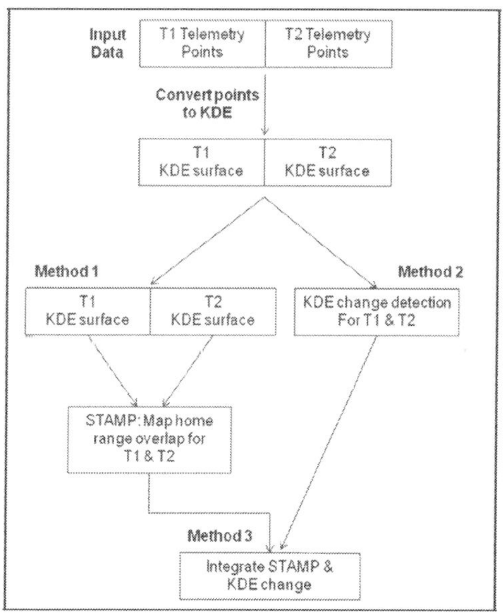

Fig. 5. An overview of the three methods presented: STAMP, kernel density estimation (KDE) change detection, and the integration of STAMP and KDE change detection. T1 and T2 indicate time period 1 and time period 2, respectively.

3.1 Spatial-temporal analysis of moving polygons (method 1)

STAMP employs topological relationships of polygons to characterize spatial-temporal patterns of home range change between two time periods (t and t+1) (Sadahiro, 2001; Sadahiro & Umemura, 2001; Robertson et al., 2007). By intersecting home range polygons for two time periods, within a GIS, polygon relationships may be used to categorize space-time patterns of change. New polygons are produced by the intersection, and each is classified based on the polygon state (home range or not) in both time periods and the space-time patterns of adjacent polygons. Polygons are assigned to one of five pattern categories: stable, disappearance, contraction, generation, and expansion (Fig. 6). Stable patterns are locations where the home range is present in t and t+1. In stable locations there is consistent habitat use or site fidelity (e.g., Edwards et al., 2009). Disappearance and contraction patterns indicate that a location is part of a home range in t but not t+1. Disappearance patterns are spatially isolated, as opposed to contraction patterns which are spatially adjacent to other home range areas that have changed in a different way. Generation and expansion patterns both indicate that a location was not part of a home range in t, but became part of a home range in t+1. While generation patterns are spatially isolated, expansion events are spatially adjacent to home range areas that have changed in other ways. Disappearance, contraction, generation, and expansion all indicate different types of home range drift (e.g., Edwards et al., 2009).

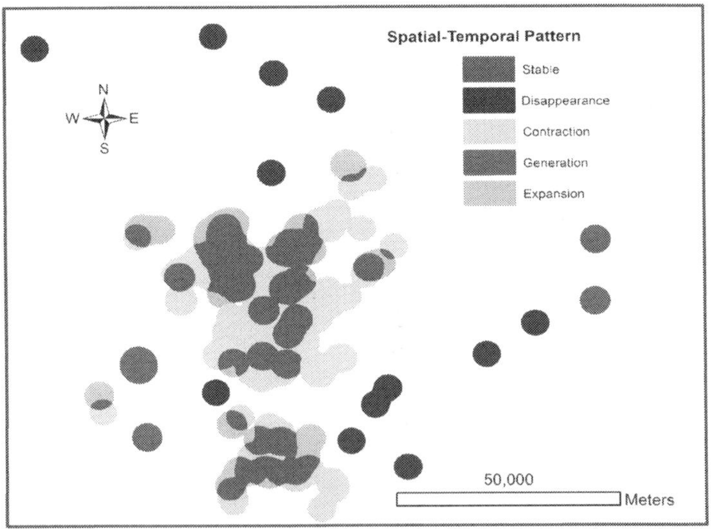

Fig. 6. Spatial-temporal patterns in 2006 to 2007 caribou home ranges. Spatial-temporal patterns are defined by STAMP or topological relationships between home range polygons.

For the Swan Lake caribou, all five spatial-temporal patterns were identified (Fig. 6, Table 1). Contraction was the dominant pattern (37.50%), while generation was least common (5.82%). Stable patterns occurred for 31.91% of the home range area, and expansion and disappearance occurred in similar proportions, 12.54% and 12.22% respectively.

	Spatial-Temporal Patterns	
	km^2	%
Stable	781.48	31.91
Disappearance	299.38	12.22
Contraction	918.45	37.50
Generation	142.63	5.82
Expansion	307.17	12.54
Total	2449.11	100.00

Table 1. Area and proportion of spatial-temporal patterns of home range change from 2006 to 2007.

Traditional methods demonstrate that the Swan Lake caribou's home range declined from 2006 (1999.31 km^2) to 2007 (1231.28 km^2). The STAMP analysis indicates that while a decline in home range area dominates, in some regions new habitat was used. For instance, Fig. 2 indicates that caribou were using new habitat to the east. In addition to providing a more complete spatial representation of space-time habitat use, the results of STAMP are mappable. Mapped spatial-temporal patterns can be related to additional data sets in order to evaluate hypotheses associated with home range change. For example, associations between resources and space-time patterns may be hypothesized and tested by integrating the spatial-temporal patterns with resource availability data.

3.2 Kernel density estimation change detection (method 2)

A method of change detection designed specifically for use with kernel density estimated surfaces is well suited to characterizing change in the intensity of habitat use within home ranges (Nelson et al., 2008). Kernel density estimation change detection identifies locations of statistically significant positive and negative changes, and enables the rate of change, considered significant, to vary spatially (Bowman & Azzalini, 1997, pp. 112-117). This method is a square root variance stabilizing transformation of the difference between two kernel density estimated surfaces, and is most appropriate for use when kernel estimates are generated using the same bandwidth (Bowman & Azzalini, 1997, pg. 114). The difference between the square root kernel density estimates at location *i*, for two time periods *t* and *t*+1, $change_{i\Delta t}$, is measured in terms of pooled standard deviations by calculating

$$change_{i\Delta t} = \frac{\sqrt{\hat{\lambda}_{i,t}} - \sqrt{\hat{\lambda}_{i,t+1}}}{\sqrt{se_t^2 + se_{t+1}^2}} \tag{3}$$

where $\hat{\lambda}_{i,t}$ is the kernel density estimate at location *i* in year *t*, and $\hat{\lambda}_{i,t+1}$ is the kernel density estimate at the same location in the following year. se_t and se_{t+1} are the standard errors in the respective years.

The standard error is a measure of the variance of the kernel function. Kernel density variance is dependent on the shape or curvature of the kernel, the search radius, and the total sample size. For traditional kernel density estimators, these parameters are invariant over space. Therefore, the standard error is a constant defined as

$$se = \sqrt{\frac{\left[\int (k(\mathbf{z}))^2 \, \mathrm{d}\mathbf{z}\right]^2}{4n\tau^2}} \tag{4}$$

where $k(z)$ is the Gaussian kernel with a mean of zero and a standard deviation of $\sqrt{2}$. Significant positive change ($\alpha = 0.05$) occurs at location i when $change_{i\Delta t} > 1.96$ and significant negative change occurs when $change_{i\Delta t} < -1.96$. Otherwise, no significant change is assumed to have occurred. Calculating $change_{i\Delta t}$ in this way does not produce an exact measure of statistically significant change. Kernel density estimators produce estimates, and the standard error or variance can be thought of as a confidence envelope around that value. Therefore, significant change is also estimated (Bowman & Azzalini, 1997, pg. 116; Fotheringham et al., 2002, pg. 205).

When change in the caribou home range is quantified as the intersection of two binary home ranges, 31.81% of the area is found to overlap, suggesting that change has occurred in 68.09% of the home range. However, when change is defined by statistical significance, only 31.39% of the area has changed and change can be categorized as increasing use (positive change, 5.39%) or decreasing use (negative, change 26.00%) (Fig. 7). By assessing change with statistical significance, and enabling the rate of significant change to vary over space, no change is identified near edges of the home range, where intensity values are small and/or zero. Changes in intensity, not captured with binary approaches, are emphasized.

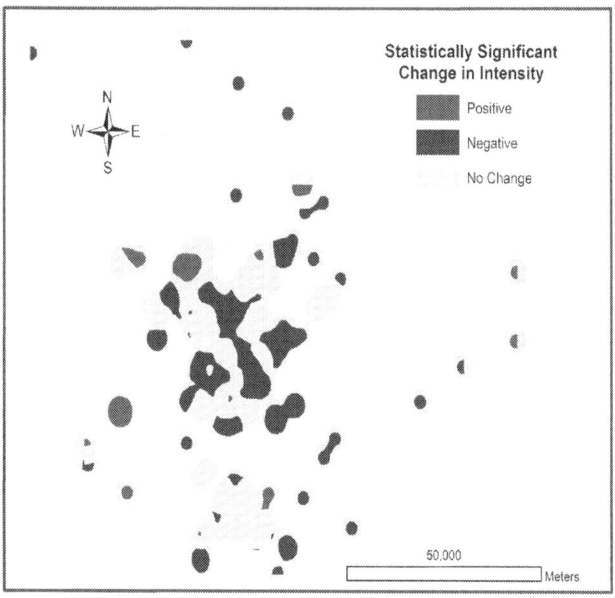

Fig. 7. Spatial-temporal change in 2006 to 2007 caribou home ranges. Change is defined as statistically significant variation in kernel density estimates generated from telemetry data. (The semicircles of positive and negative change are edge effects created by the software used for detecting change.)

As an example, when home ranges are binary, no change will be detected at a location associated with one telemetry point in the first time period and twelve in the second time period. The kernel approach, in contrast, has the potential to identify these as significant changes. As with STAMP, output of the kernel density approach is mappable, accounts for spatial variation in home range patterns, and integrates with other GIS data.

3.3 Integrating STAMP and kernel change approaches (method 3)

In the final method, STAMP and kernel density estimation change detection are integrated to characterize how wildlife intensity varies for different spatial-temporal home range patterns. The amount of statistically significant change in intensity can be determined for each spatial-temporal home range pattern. For disappearance and contraction, only negative change or decreasing use will occur; for generation and expansion, only positive change or increasing use will occur; and for stable patterns, both types of change may be present.
With the caribou data, stable patterns have both positive and negative change, and differentiating the types of change identifies how intensity of use is varying within areas used consistently through time (Table 2). In the caribou example, 3.73% and 12.99% of stable pattern areas had statistically significant positive and negative change, respectively. Given the general decline in home range areas, stable areas that have had an increased use, or no decline in use, may be the most important habitat for conservation.

	Positive Change		Negative Change		No Change		Total	
	km2	%	km2	%	km2	%	km2	%
Stable	29.17	3.73	101.52	12.99	650.79	83.28	781.48	100.00
Disappearance	0.00	0.00	83.58	27.92	215.80	72.08	299.38	100.00
Contraction	0.00	0.00	453.90	49.42	464.55	50.58	918.45	100.00
Generation	50.08	35.11	0.00	0.00	92.55	64.89	142.63	100.00
Expansion	52.75	17.17	0.00	0.00	254.42	82.83	307.17	100.00

Table 2. Area of statistically significant changes in kernel density estimates and the proportion of significant change for each spatial-temporal pattern of home range change from 2006 to 2007.

Integrating results of STAMP and kernel density change demonstrate that 27.92% of the area of disappearance patterns had statistically significant negative change, while 49.42% of contraction area was associated with negative change (Table 2). One might anticipate that the spatially isolated disappearance events would have more negative change, as these are locations within regions where habitat use has ceased. However, in the caribou example, disappearance is often associated with a single telemetry point in t followed by no use in t+1. Greater magnitude changes in intensity are occurring in central portions of the home range where many telemetry points are identified in t and in an area associated with contraction in spatial-temporal patterns.

4. Conclusion

Data on wildlife locations are increasingly detailed in both space and time. Conversion to binary home range maps has been useful. However, the methods presented here take advantage of greater data detail and enable new spatial-temporal research questions to be addressed. There is a general dearth of temporal methods for geographical data, and efforts are underway to develop new methods for space-time analysis that will likely have applications and benefits in wildlife and ecological studies (e.g., Rey & Janikas, 2006). Spatially explicit methods will be increasingly important as data sets continue to increase in size.

All the methods presented in this chapter are mappable and can be integrated with other GIS data sets. For instance, locations of change can be correlated to environmental variables (elevation or landscape fragmentation), resource selection functions (e.g., Boyce and McDonald, 1999), roads, or human disturbance data. Existing literature is useful for generating hypotheses on space-time home range patterns and changes in home range intensity. By quantifying observed patterns and integrating additional data, it is possible to determine if the patterns are different from or similar to our expectations. Linking patterns of change with additional data sets will enable testing of hypotheses on processes driving change.

Knowing where change is occurring is essential for conservation and management of wildlife and habitat. Methods that not only locate, classify, and quantify change, but that integrate change maps with data on environmental and human activities, are essential for conservation. The methods presented here are applicable to any wildlife research where home ranges are defined by kernel density estimation and two or more home ranges occur in a study area. While I have demonstrated approaches for detecting change between two time periods, these methods are also useful when comparing spatially overlapping home ranges of individuals or populations, such as analysis of predators and prey home ranges.

5. Acknowledgement

I am grateful to Mark Williams and the British Columbia Ministry of Environment for access to caribou data. This research is funded in part by the National Science and Engineering Research Council.

6. References

Apps, C.D., McLellan, B.N., Woods, J.G., & Proctor, M.F. (2004). Estimating grizzly bear distribution and abundance relative to habitat and human influence. *Journal of Wildlife Management*, Vol.68, No.1, (January 2004), pp. 138–152

Atwood, T.C., & Weeks, H.P. (2003). Spatial home-range overlap and temporal interaction in eastern coyotes: the influence of pair types and fragmentation. *Canadian Journal of Zoology*, Vol.81, No.9, pp. 1589–1597

Berland, A., Nelson, T., Stenhouse, G., Graham, K., & Cranston, J. (2008). The impact of landscape disturbance on grizzly bear habitat use in the Foothills Model Forest, Alberta, Canada. *Forest Ecology and Management*, Vol.256, No.11, (November 2008), pp. 1875–1883

Börger, L., Franconi, N., De Michele, G., Gantz, A., Meschi, F., Manica, A., Lovari, S., & Coulson, T. (2006a). Effects of sampling regime on the mean and variance of home range size estimates. *Journal of Animal Ecology*, Vol.75, No.6, (November 2006), pp. 1405–1493

Börger, L., Franconi, N., Ferretti, N., Meschi, F., De Michele, G., Gantz, A., & Coulson, T. (2006b). An integrated approach to identify spatio-temporal and individual-level determinants of animal home range size. *American Naturalist*, Vol.168, No.4, (October 2006), pp. 471–485

Bowman, A., & Azzalini, A. (1997). *Applied Smoothing Techniques for Data Analysis: The Kernel Approach.* Claredon Press, Oxford

Boyce, M.S., & McDonald, L.L. (1999). Relating populations to habitats using resource selection functions. *Trends in Evolution and Ecology,* Vol.14, No.7, (July 1999), pp. 268-272

Burt, W.H. (1943). Territoriality and home range concepts as applied to mammals. *Journal of Mammalogy,* Vol.24, No.3, (August 1943), pp. 346-352

Edwards, M.A., Nagy, J.A., & Derocher, A.E. (2009). Low site fidelity and home range drift in a wide-ranging, large Arctic omnivore. *Animal Behaviour,* Vol.77, No.1, (January 2009), pp. 23-28

Fotheringham, A.S., Brunsdon, C., & Charlton, M. (2002). *Geographically Weighted Regression: The Analysis of Spatially Varying Relationships.* John Wiley & Sons Ltd, London

Fisher, D.O. (2000). Effects of vegetation structure, food and shelter on the home range and habitat use of an endangered wallaby. *Journal of Applied Ecology,* Vol.37, No.4, (August 2000), pp. 660-671

Frair, J.L., Merrill, E.H., Beyer, H.L., & Morales, J.M. (2008). Thresholds in landscape connectivity and mortality risks in response to growing road networks. *Journal of Applied Ecology,* Vol.45, No.5, (October 2008), pp. 1504-1513

Georgii, B. (1980). Home range patterns of female red deer (*Cervus elaphus L.*) in the Alps. *Oecologia,* Vol.47, No. 2, pp. 278-285

Harris, S., Cresswell, W.J., Forde, P.G., Trewhella, W.J., Woollard, T., & Wray, S. (1990). Home-range analysis using radio-tracking data—a review of problems and techniques particularly as applied to the study of mammals. *Mammal Review,* Vol.20, No.2/3, (June 1990), pp. 97-123

Hulbert, I.A.R., Iason, G.R., Elston, D.A., & Racey, P.A. (1996). Home-range sizes in a stratified upland landscape of two lagomorphs with different feeding strategies. *Journal of Applied Ecology,* Vol.33, No.6, (December 1996), pp. 1479-1488

Johnson, A.R., Wiens, J.A., Milne, B.T. & Crist, T.O. (1992). Animal movements and population dynamics in heterogeneous landscapes. *Landscape Ecology,* Vol.7, No.1, pp. 63-75

Katajisto, J., & Moilanen, A. (2006). Kernel-based home range method for data with irregular sampling intervals. *Ecological Modelling,* Vol.194, No.4, (April 2006), pp. 405-413

Keating, K., & Cherry, S. (2009). Modeling utilization distributions in space and time. *Ecology,* Vol.90, No.7, (July 2009), pp. 1971-1980

Kie, J.G., Bowyer, T., Nicholson, M.C., Boroski, B.B., & Loft, E.R. (2002). Landscape heterogeneity at differing scales: effects on spatial distribution of mule deer. *Ecology,* Vol.83, No.2, (February 2002), pp. 530-544

Kie, J.G., Matthiopoulos, J., Fieberg, J., Powell, R.A., Cagnacci, F., Mitchell, M.S., Gaillard, J.-M., & Moorcroft, P.R. (2010). The home-range concept: are traditional estimators still relevant with modern telemetry technology? *Philosophical Transactions of the Royal Society B,* Vol.365, pp. 2221—2231

Laver, P.N., & Kelly, M.J. (2008). A critical review of home range studies. *Journal of Wildlife Management,* Vol.72, No.1, (January 2008), pp. 290-298

Lowe, C.G., Topping, D.T., Cartamil, D.P., & Papastamatiou, Y.P. (2003). Movement patterns, home range, and habitat utilization of adult kelp bass *Paralabrax clathratus* in a temperate no-take marine reserve. *Marine Ecology Progress Series,* Vol.256, (July 2003), pp. 205-216

Lurz, P.W.W., Garson, P.J., & Wauters, L.A. (1997). Effects of temporal and spatial variation in habitat quality on red squirrel dispersal behaviour. *Animal Behaviour*, Vol.54, No. 2, (August 1997), pp. 427–435

Marzluff, J.M., Millspaugh, J.J., Hurvitz, P., & Handcock, M.S. (2004). Relating resources to a probabilistic measure of space use: forest fragments and Steller's Jays. *Ecology*, Vol.85, No.5, (May 2004), pp. 1411-1427

Nelson, T.A., Duffus, D., Robertson, C., & Feyrer, L.J. (2008). Spatial-temporal patterns in intra-annual gray whale foraging: Characterizing interactions between predators and prey. *Marine Mammal Science*, Vol.24, No.2, (April 2008), pp. 356–370

Rey, S.J., & Janikas, M.V. (2006). STARS: Space-time analysis of regional systems. *Geographical Analysis*, Vol.38, No.1, (January 2006), pp. 67–86

Robertson, C., Nelson, T.A., Boots, B., & Wulder, M.A. (2007). STAMP: spatial-temporal analysis of moving polygons. *Journal of Geographical Systems*, Vol.9, No.3, (September 2007), pp. 207–227

Rushton, S.P., Barreto, G.W., Cormack, R.M., MacDonald, D.W., & Fuller, R. (2000). Modelling the effects of mink and habitat fragmentation on the water vole. *Journal of Applied Ecology*, Vol.37, No.3, (June 2000), pp. 475–490

Sadahiro, Y. (2001). Exploratory method for analyzing changes in polygon distributions. *Environment and Planning B: Planning Design*, Vol.28, pp. 595–609

Sadahiro, Y., & Umemura, M. (2001). A computational approach for the analysis of changes in polygon distributions. *Journal of Geographic Systems*, Vol.3, No.2, (May 2001), pp. 137–154

Samuel, M.D., Pierce, D.J., & Garton, E.O. (1985). Identifying areas of concentrated use within the home range. *Journal of Animal Ecology*, Vol.54, No.3, (October 1985), pp. 711-719

Seaman, D.E., & Powell, R.A. (1996). An evaluation of the accuracy of kernel density estimators for home range analysis. *Ecology*, Vol.77, No.7, (October 1996), pp. 2075–2085

Seaman, D.E., Millspaugh, J.J., Kernohan, B.J., Brundige, G.C., Raedeke, K.J., & Gitzen, R.A. (1999). Effects of sample size on kernel home range estimates. *Journal of Wildlife Management*, Vol.63, No.2, (April 1999), pp. 739–747

Thiel, D., Jenni-Eiermann, S, Braunisch, V., Palme, R., & Jenni, L. (2008). Ski tourism affects habitat use and evokes a physiological stress response in capercaillie *Tetrao urogallus:* a new methodological approach. *Journal of Applied Ecology*, Vol.45, No.3, (June 2008), pp. 845–853

Trewhella, W.J., Harris, S., & McAllister, F.E. (1988). Dispersal, distance, home-range size and population density in the red fox (*Vulpes vulpes*): a quantitative analysis. *Journal of Applied Ecology*, Vol.25, No. 2, (August 1988), pp. 423–434

Tufto, J., Andersen, R., & Linnell, J. (1996). Habitat use and ecological correlates of home range size in a small cervid: the roe deer. *Journal of Animal Ecology*, Vol.65, No.6, (November 1996), pp. 715–724

Viggers, K.L., & Hearn, J.P. (2005). The kangaroo conundrum: home range studies and implications for land management. *Journal of Applied Ecology*, Vol.42, No.1, (February 2005), pp. 99–107

Village, A. (1982). The home range and density of kestrels in relation to vole abundance. *Journal of Animal Ecology*, Vol.51, No.2, (June 1982), pp. 413–428

Yahner, R.H. (1988). Changes in wildlife communities near edges. *Conservation Biology*, Vol.2, No.4, (December 1988), pp. 333–339

14

Use of Telemetry Data to Investigate Home Range and Habitat Selection in Mammalian Carnivores

Marina Silva-Opps and Sheldon B. Opps
Animal Movement and Resource Selection Research Group, University of Prince Edward Island, Charlottetown, Prince Edward Island, Canada

1. Introduction

Management of mammalian carnivore populations, whether to conserve a threatened species or to control the abundance of a noxious one, requires a basic understanding of the ecology and behaviour of a given species. Habitat selection and home range are fundamental processes in the ecology and behaviour of most animals, explaining why most researchers generally investigate them when assessing a species' needs. Presumably, species should have a higher fitness in habitats that they select or allow them to accomplish basic activities such as foraging and reproduction. Once habitats can be ordered by their relative preference, they can be evaluated as to their relative importance in terms of fitness (Garshelis, 2000). Wildlife managers and conservation biologists can, then, make decisions regarding any habitat modification or population control requirement that may be needed to deal with the species in question.

The assessment of either habitat selection or home range requires the collection of data on the animals' use of space. In theory, different approaches can be used to obtain the data needed to assess habitat selection and home range patterns. One approach may be to obtain the data by following an animal in order to observe its movements and habits. However, this approach is likely to prove very difficult, particularly in areas with thick vegetation or where the animal is active at night or when dealing with a species with secretive habits. There is also the risk that the close proximity of humans could affect the animal's behaviour resulting in an unrealistic outcome of the study or possibly having a negative effect on the studied animal, like interfering with the hunting success in mammalian carnivores. Another approach may involve obtaining data from transect surveys (Buckland et al., 1993). These surveys record animals in the vicinity of a set of sampling lines or points and therefore tend to yield relatively few sightings, particularly for rare species living in inaccessible environments. Telemetry is without any doubt the most common method to quantify either habitat selection or home range patterns, especially in mammalian carnivore species. Telemetry is a tool or technique used to research wild animal species in the field in order to gain a thorough understanding of that population and its dynamics as well as to identify any potential threats to its survival (White & Garrott, 1990). It is typically used to gather data from distant, inaccessible locations, or when data collection would be dangerous or difficult for a variety of reasons. Wildlife telemetry concerns the use of telemetry techniques to remotely locate wild species and obtain ecological, behavioural and physiological data. It was in the 1960s, when telemetry, specifically radio-telemetry, was first used to study terrestrial wildlife (Craighhead, 1982; Hebblewhite & Haydon, 2010). Since then, wildlife telemetry has contributed significantly to our understanding of fundamental ecological and behavioural processes of many animal species (e.g., Johnson et al., 2006). Advances in wildlife telemetry have made it possible to acquire detailed data on animal' space use, including habitat selection, home-range size, movement metrics as well as migration timing and routes. Since many wildlife species are secretive and difficult to observe, telemetry has become a valuable tool to learn more about their respective life-histories.

Human attitudes vary worldwide towards mammalian carnivore species. The overlap in space-use with human populations results in competition for habitats and resources which is at the heart of most of the conflicts between mammalian carnivore species, especially canids, and humans (Sillero-Zubiri & Switzer, 2004). For instance, canids tend to prey upon a range of livestock, game stock and threatened wildlife, and some of the large-bodied size species may also attack, and on rare occasions, deadly harm humans. Human–carnivore conflicts are among the major causes of population decline in many species (Treves & Karanth, 2003) and can be particularly controversial when the resources concerned have economic value (e.g., livestock) and the carnivore species involved have a high conservation profile (Graham et al., 2005). This is usually the case of large-bodied size carnivore species that usually have extensive space requirements, low reproductive rates and are persecuted by humans (Matthiae & Stearns, 1981). But, while these carnivore species are declining globally, others have not only managed to survive, but to become abundant. Many medium-bodied size generalist carnivores have been able to expand their geographic ranges because they are capable of using human-use areas and anthropogenic resources (Harris & Smith, 1987; Prange et al., 2004). For instance, red foxes (*Vulpes vulpes*) and coyotes *(Canis latrans)* may occur not only in rural areas, but also in suburban and occasionally more densely populated urban areas (Atkinson & Shackleton, 1991; Gibeau, 1998; Grinder & Krausman, 2001; Lewis et al., 1999).

In this study, we will consider the use of telemetry data to investigate habitat selection and home-range patterns of two mammalian carnivore species. Although both species occur in human-dominated landscapes, their interactions with humans are very distinct, resulting in very different abundance levels and conservation status. However, in both cases, investigations of habitat selection and home-range patterns are fundamental initial steps in the management of their populations. In the following Section 2, we will briefly define key concepts that will be used in this chapter. In Case Study 1 (Section 3), we will use telemetry data to investigate habitat selection and home range of the red fox in Prince Edward Island, Canada. In this case, the species is benefiting from its interaction with human populations. Our objective for Case Study 1 is to show how telemetry data can be used to elucidate the effects of fox-feeding (anthropogenic food resources provided to foxes by humans) on habitat selection and home-range patterns. In Case Study 2 (Section 4), telemetry data will be used to investigate habitat selection and home range patterns of the African wild dog (*Lycaon pictus*) in Mkhuze Game Reserve, South Africa. Contrary to the red fox, the interaction with humans has had detrimental effects on African wild-dog populations in South Africa and other parts of Africa. Our objective for Case Study 2 is to illustrate the use of telemetry data to assess the success of the establishment part of a reintroduction program of a endangered or threatened carnivore species. For purposes of comparison, we have tried to use the same approaches, methods and data-analysis procedures for both case studies whenever possible. However, differences in abundance levels and current status of red foxes and African wild dogs, as well as data collection, needed sometimes the use of different approaches to achieve the objectives set out for each case study. Section 5 concludes the chapter and comments on the use of radio-telemetry and other similar technologies in ecology and wildlife management.

2. Basic concepts

Habitat refers to a distinctive set of physical environmental factors that a species uses for its survival and reproduction (Block & Brennan, 1993). The semantic and empirical distinctions between the terms habitat *use* and habitat *selection* are often unclear (Hall et al., 1997). Habitat *selection* carries a connotation of understanding complex behavioral and environmental processes that habitat *use* does not; habitat-use patterns are the end result of habitat-selection processes. *Use* of habitat is the way in which an individual or species exploits habitats to meet its life history needs (Block & Brennan, 1993). The study of habitat-use patterns describes the actual distribution of individuals across habitat types (Hutto, 1985). *Selection* of habitat is the process by which an animal actually chooses habitat (Johnston, 1980). In other words, habitat *selection* refers to a hierarchical process of behavioral responses that may result in the disproportionate *use* of habitats to influence survival and fitness of individuals (Block & Brennan, 1993; Hutto, 1985). *Use* is considered selective if habitat is used disproportionately compared with its *availability*, the latter being the amount of that habitat *accessible* to the animal. In field studies, however, where the *availability* of habitat is variable, habitat selection is the use of habitat relative to its availability in the environment and is conditional on the availability of all habitats to the animal. It is important to distinguish between the terms *accessible* and *available* because it may be possible that certain habitats, within a given landscape, are available to an animal (or species), but they may not be accessible. Use-availability studies inherently assume that study animals have free and equal access to all habitats considered to be available, implying that at any given moment each studied animal should be able to use any available habitat (Garshelis, 2000). This assumption may stand if use and availability are measured for each animal individually, but it may be violated when data from different animals are pooled together and the available habitat is considered to be same for all when it is not the case. For instance, use and availability may be considered to be the same when all animals move as a pack or in cases when there is significant overlap in their home ranges. However, differences between use and availability may occur when not all animals have the same habitat types within their home ranges (Garshelis, 2000). Differences between use and availability may also occur when not all animals have free or equal access to all areas within their home ranges.

Habitat-selection scales are often assumed to be a function of home-range sizes (e.g., Chamberlain et al., 2003; McLoughlin et al., 2002, 2004; Rettie & Messier, 2000). Thus, an important concept associated with habitat selection is home range. Burt (1943) first defined home range as the area traversed by an individual when performing normal activities such as foraging, mating and caring for young. However, this definition has been challenged because the word "normal" is difficult to interpret and lacks a temporal component (Cavallini, 1996; White & Garrott, 1990). A less ambiguous, and more popular, definition of the home range of an animal is the limited area within which it can be found during a specified time period (Harris et al., 1990; Kernohan et al., 2001). According to this definition, a home range can be flexible, varying with season and overlapping with conspecifics (Harris et al., 1990), making the concept of home range particular useful for habitat selection studies. In contrast, a territory, a term commonly used interchangeably with home range, is defined as an area that is occupied by an individual or group to the exclusion of other animals of the same species (Börger et al., 2008; Burt, 1943; Mech, 1970). Animals may or may not be territorial, but will still have a home range.

Quantifying an animal's home-range size and shape allows researchers to gain information on foraging behaviour and inter- and intraspecific interactions (Harris et al., 1990). It is also useful for investigating animal-habitat relationships such as habitat selection (e.g., Johnson, 1980). For instance, Johnson (1980) proposed a habitat selection classification system that involves the notion of home range. Johnson's (1980) classification system is based on a hierarchical order of selection: 1st-order selection of a species' geographic range from the global pool, 2nd-order selection of home ranges from the geographic range, 3rd-order selection of habitat within home ranges (e.g., *core areas*), and 4th-order selection of structures, variables or conditions within habitats. The term *core area* refers to those areas within the home range where individuals are found with greater probability (Börger et al., 2008; Kaufmann, 1962; White & Garrott, 1990). Thus, core areas are locations of concentrated use within home ranges (Kaufmann, 1962) that contain important resources such as den sites and quality foraging areas (Ewer, 1968). Although core areas may contain similar landscape elements as the whole home-range area, the importance of a given habitat type can vary between "core areas" and "home-range size". While home ranges of different animals have been found to overlap (e.g., Kolb, 1986; Lovari et al., 1994), overlap of the core areas does not commonly occur (Samuel et al., 1985). Thus, the identification of core areas is important when studying intraspecific interactions or when investigating animal-habitat relationships (Samuel et al., 1985).

Another important factor that must be taken into consideration when investigating habitat selection patterns is that many resources used by wild species occur heterogeneously across the landscape, linking the concept of habitat selection with the ideas of space-use and scale. For instance, the process of habitat selection in mammalian carnivores has increasingly been studied as a hierarchical, multi-scale process, in which selection of habitat features is accomplished at progressively smaller scales (Orians & Wittenberger, 1991; Rettie & Messier, 2000; Schaefer & Messier, 1995). An organism selects a home range in which to live, and then it makes decisions about the use of different habitats within this home range in which fundamental activities such as foraging will be performed (Johnson, 1980). Rettie & Messier (2000) proposed that animal selection patterns that are governed by an avoidance of factors that tend to limit individual fitness dominate at the larger spatial scales, while less important limiting factors influence habitat selection patterns at smaller spatial scales. If Rettie & Messier's (2000) hypothesis holds true, then processes occurring at the larger spatial scales exert the most influence on species habitat selection. One may then predict that habitat quantified at the largest spatial scales would explain or describe the most variability in species habitat selection.

3. Case study 1: The red fox

The red fox is a generalist species that can occur in a variety of habitats, including forest, tundra, agricultural land, desert and urban areas. Several studies, however, have shown that this species tends to be more abundant in mixed mosaic habitats such as those characterizing human-altered landscapes (Ables, 2009; Catling & Burt, 1995; Lloyd, 1975). In Prince Edward Island (Canada), the red fox was the largest mammalian carnivore species until the arrival of coyotes during the early 80s. Although no studies have assessed the abundance of red foxes on Prince Edward Island, it is commonly known that they occur throughout the whole province, including urban areas. Regardless of its widespread distribution, little is known about the home range, habitat selection, behaviour and population dynamics of red foxes in Prince Edward Island.

The red fox is an opportunistic species with a diverse diet that has allowed it to survive in natural and human-altered landscapes (Dell'Arte et al., 2007). Eating habits of red foxes vary, but normally they include entire mice, voles, birds and rabbits. However, the importance of each prey varies depending on habitat type, regional prey availability and anti-predator behavior (Dell'Arte et al., 2007; MacDonald, 1977). Additionally, studies have found that anthropogenic food items can sometimes play an important role in the diet of red foxes (e.g., Contesse et al., 2004; Newsome et al,. 2010). Another relevant characteristic of red foxes is that their interactions with humans can take different forms. In areas where they are potential carriers of the rabies virus, red foxes are considered nuisance animals and are usually subject to population control even though these operations are generally unsuccessful (Smith & Harris, 1991). In Prince Edward Island, especially within and near Prince Edward Island National Park, red foxes are considered charismatic animals and many residents and tourists feed them throughout the year. Red foxes are fed by humans inhabiting houses or cottages located near the park, as well as by tourists on roadsides. Little is known about the consequences of this activity on red fox population occurring within Prince Edward Island National Park. However, it has been postulated that because humans feed these animals in the park, red foxes tend to select road and human-use habitats, rather than natural habitats for foraging, thus increasing the probability of being accidentally killed by vehicles.

In this study, we determined habitat selection and home range of red foxes occurring in Prince Edward Island National Park using radio-telemetry data. Specifically, we examined the use of radio-telemetry data to elucidate the importance of human-use areas and fox-feeding in habitat selection and home range patterns of red foxes.

3.1 Study site

Prince Edward Island is situated in the Gulf of the St. Lawrence and encompasses an area of about 5,660 km^2 (Weighs, 1995). Prior to the 17th century, Prince Edward Island was covered by tree species characteristic of the Acadian Forest region, such as sugar maple (*Acer saccharum*), yellow birch (*Betula alleghaniensis*) and beech (*Fagus grandifolia*) (Round Table on Resource Land Use and Stewardship, 1997). Since the arrival of European colonizers about three centuries ago, anthropogenic activities such as urbanization, forestry, and agriculture have altered the natural habitats of the island. Although the peak of deforestation occurred in the early 1900s, it is the intensive exploitation for agriculture that have occurred during the last century that have resulted in most of the major transformation of the natural habitats of Prince Edward Island (Johnston, 2000). Currently, the forests of Prince Edward Island are composed of species such as white spruce (*Picea glauca*), balsam fir (*Abies balsamea*), and trembling aspen (*Populus tremuloides*) (Round Table on Resource Land Use and Stewardship, 1997). It is possible to assume that these changes in the structure and composition of vegetation have been followed by significant alterations in the distribution and abundance of natural resources for mammalian species occurring in Prince Edward Island.

The study site selected for this study was located in Stanhope (543 ha; 46°25′E; 63°06′N), Prince Edward Island National Park (Fig. 1). Although situated within the park, Stanhope is surrounded by private houses and cottages, many of them inhabited throughout the whole year. It encompasses forest patches, marshes, shrubs, ponds, dunes, beaches, roads, agricultural fields, and human-use areas (about 0.30 human dwellings per ha). Although we do not possess quantitative data regarding fox-feeding intensity in Stanhope, anecdotal information and personal observations clearly indicate that fox-feeding is a common activity in Stanhope, with residents setting out food for foxes throughout the whole year and many tourists feeding these animals during the touristic season (i.e., summer).

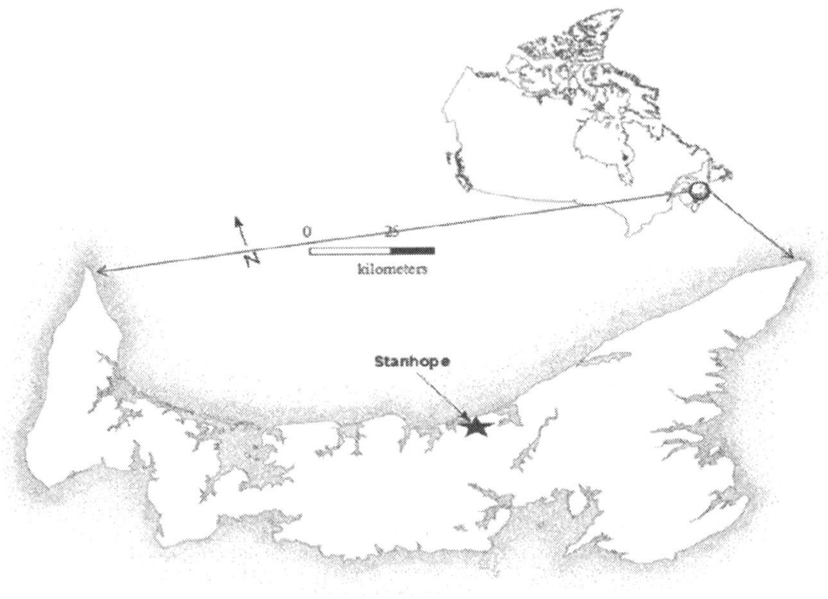

Fig. 1. Map of Prince Edward Island (Canada) in relation to Canada indicating the location of the study site (Stanhope) with a star. The scale-bar refers to Prince Edward Island only.

3.2 Data collection and analysis

Radio-telemetry data were obtained between April and September 2004. Trapping efforts were conducted from February to March 2004. Large Havahart single door box-traps (106.7 cm length x 38 cm width x 38 cm height) made from a combination of tensile wire mesh and steel were set within the study site in areas where red foxes or their tracks had been observed. Traps were baited with food for human consumption or wild meat and were checked every day. Captured foxes were anesthetized using Xylazine/Ketamine (1:10 mg/kg) and Atipamezole (1 mg per 10 mg of Xylazine; Animal Care Protocol, University of Prince Edward Island 03-043), and then radio-collared (TS-37 Telemetry Solutions; 50 g). The radio-telemetry procedure used in this study followed recommendations made by White & Garrott (1990). During the less active periods (morning and early afternoon), animal locations were estimated by one observer who recorded 2-3 azimuths within 15-min intervals over a period of 1 hr. During the active periods (late afternoon and early evening), simultaneous triangulation was performed by 2-3 observers within 15-min intervals over a period of 1 hr. In addition, we also conducted 8-hr intensive (1 location every 15 min) telemetry sessions (sequential locations) twice per month (one in the afternoon: 13:00 to 21:00 and one during the night: 21:00 p.m. to 05:00 a.m.). These telemetry sessions were subjected to weather conditions, thus sometimes they were shorter than 8 hr. Tracking was done on foot using hand-held Yagi antennas and portable receivers (R-1000; Communications Specialists, Inc.). Triangulation angles were maintained between 30° and 150° (Gese, 2001). About 50% of radio-tracking locations were taken with the animal in view of the observers. Bearings were plotted immediately using LOAS 2.1 (Ecological Software Solutions 2003) to determine the accuracy of the locations. For the purposes of this study, we have not looked for statistical independence of locations (e.g., Swihart & Slade, 1985), but rather for their biological independence, using a minimum time interval between successive locations long enough to allow any radio-collared animal to cross entirely its home range. Repeated observations on the same individuals, as is the case with radio-telemetry locations, are often assumed to give rise to constant within-group correlation structures (i.e., lack of independence in the data). Although some ecologists and wildlife managers think that correlation structures represent a problem for the analysis and interpretation of wildlife telemetry data (Hansteen et al., 1997), others suggest that much can be learned by studying the causes and consequences of correlation structures in telemetry data. If a large time interval between successive locations is possible and/or the calculation of home-range size is the main goal of the study, strict adherence to the collection of non-autocorrelated data may be necessary. However, it may be difficult to translate autocorrelated data into an independent form and still retain a sample size that is adequate for the home-range size to reach an asymptote. Thus, the goals of most home-range or habitat selection studies require the collection of data which are dependent to some degree. This was the case in this study.

Habitat variables were determined using 2000 Prince Edward Island aerial photographs (1: 17500; Prince Edward Island Department of Agriculture and Forestry) of the study site, and complemented with field observations to update any land-cover changes. ArcView GIS (version 3.3; Environmental Systems Research Institute, Inc., ESRI) was used to map animal locations obtained from radio-telemetry monitoring sessions and to assign to each location a habitat cover-type. Habitat was classified into 1 of 10 cover-types: agriculture (hay fields and pasture), forest (mature white spruce and hardwood forest), water or aquatic systems (frozen during winter; including ponds and saltwater bodies), dunes, beaches, roads (mostly paved), human-use areas (residential areas, recreational areas, parking lots), abandoned fields, marshes, and shrubs.

Habitat selection was examined by comparing use and availability of habitat types within the study area using the Neu Method (Neu et al., 1974). The Neu method is a straightforward application of the χ^2 goodness-of-fit test, and is usually used to compare observed counts of animals in each habitat with the counts expected if habitats were used in proportion to their availability. The method involves the calculation of confidence intervals (Bonferroni Z-statistic) around the expected proportions to determine whether the observed proportion of usage in each habitat is significantly different from expected. The usage of a particular habitat type was defined as the ratio between animal locations in each habitat type and the total number of locations recorded in the study area. Expected usage of a habitat type was defined as the ratio of the area of the particular habitat type to the total area of the study site. The study-site area was defined at the home-range spatial scale using the smallest rectangle that included all 95% fixed-kernel home-ranges (see below for more information about the fixed-kernel home-range method), and at the core-area spatial scale using the smallest rectangle that included all the 50% fixed-kernel home ranges (sensu Kazmaier et al., 2001). This corresponds to a design-2 analysis of habitat selection according to Johnson (1980) because individuals could be identified using radio-telemetry data. ArcView GIS (version 3.3; ESRI) was used to calculate all the study site areas, as well as the availability of the different habitat types comprised within each study site.

Data on home-range size and core-areas were analyzed using the Animal Movement SA version 2.0 in ArcView (version 3.3; ESRI). The minimum number of locations required to accurately assess the home-range size of each animal was estimated by plotting cumulative home-range sizes against the number of locations (i.e. asymptotic home-range; Phillipps & Catling, 1991). The minimum convex polygon (MCP; Mohr, 1947) and the 95% fixed-kernel (Seaman & Powell, 1996) methods were used to determine home-range areas. The 100% MCP was utilized because it is the most commonly reported method in the literature (Harris et al., 1990), and therefore allows for some comparison with other studies. The 95% fixed-kernel method, while not without problems, has shown the best performance in simulation trials of home-range estimators that also included MCP. The 50% fixed-kernel method was used to estimate the size and shape of the core-areas or centers of activity within home-ranges. Fixed-kernel analyses were performed with a bandwidth calculated using least-squares cross validation (Powell, 2000; Seaman et al., 1999). The overlap area in home-ranges between two individuals was estimated using ArcView (version 3.3; ESRI).

3.3 Results

Amongst the five adult red foxes captured in Stanhope, sufficient data to calculate home-range sizes were only obtained for three individuals (Table 1). Asymptotic home-range was achieved with 140 locations for both females, and with 40 locations for the male. Using the 100% MCP method, home-ranges varied between 105.7 ha and 168.8 ha while the 95% fixed-kernel method resulted in home-ranges that varied between 77.4 ha and 131.3 ha (Table 1; Fig. 2). The 50% fixed-kernel method resulted in core-area values that ranged between 7.4 ha and 13.2 ha, representing about 10% of each animal's home-range (Fig. 2). Home ranges of all three foxes overlapped to some extent, with the greatest overlap (63 ha) occurring between F3 and M2. The overlap in home ranges between F1 and M2 was 8.6 ha while between F3 and F1 was 3.2 ha.

	F1 (♀)	**F3 (♀)**	**M2 (♂)**
Telemetry locations recorded	172	368	63
100% Minimum convex polygon (ha)	121.6	168.8	105.7
95% Fixed-kernel (ha)	99.5	131.3	77.4
50% Fixed-kernel (ha)	13.2	10.5	7.4

Table 1. Radio-telemetry data collected from three red foxes captured in Stanhope, Prince Edward Island National Park (Prince Edward Island, Canada).

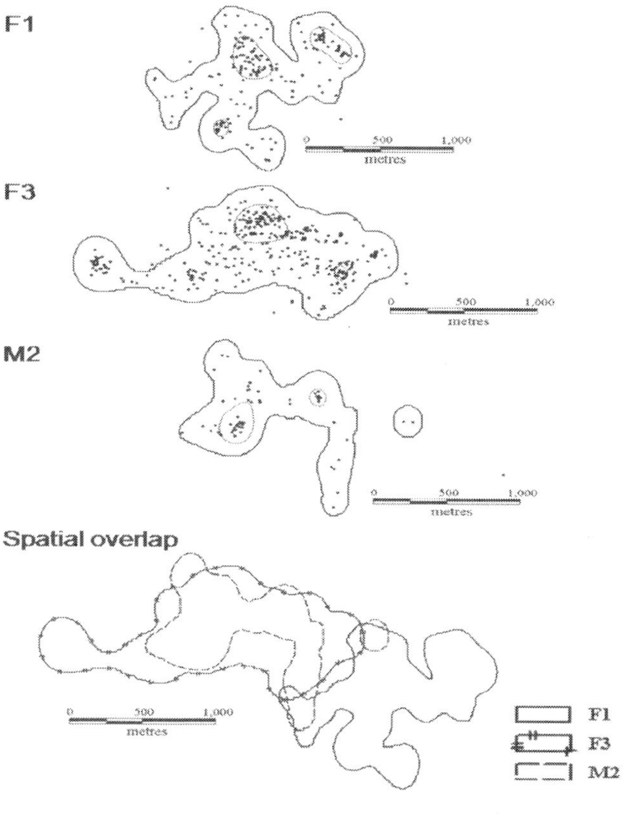

Fig. 2. Home range (95% fixed kernel analysis) and core areas (50% fixed kernel analysis) of F1, F3, and M2. Core areas are contained within the home range boundary. Animal locations are indicated by solid black circles. Spatial overlap of the home ranges of the radio-tracked red foxes in Stanhope is shown in the bottom panel.

All three red foxes used all available habitats in Stanhope, except for the abandoned field habitat. At the home-range spatial scale, red foxes selected for agricultural fields, dunes, roads, and human-use areas, while forest, marsh, and water habitat were used less than expected based on their availability (Table 2). No significant preference was observed for beach habitat. At the core-area spatial scale, red foxes selected only for dunes and roads, while beach, forest, marsh, and water habitats were used less than expected based on their availability. No significant preference was observed for human-use, agriculture and shrub habitats at this spatial scale.

Habitat	Observations (# locations)	Habitat Use proportion Average	SD	Expected Use proportion	Preference
Home-range Level					
Human-use	300	0.517	0.077	0.114	+
Dune	86	0.148	0.054	0.053	+
Road	64	0.110	0.048	0.033	+
Agriculture	31	0.053	0.034	0.005	+
Beach	41	0.071	0.039	0.100	0
Shrub	15	0.026	0.024	0.003	0
Marsh	1	0.002	0.006	0.109	0
Forest	39	0.067	0.038	0.503	-
Water	3	0.005	0.011	0.060	-
Abandoned Field	0	0	0	0.019	-
Core-Area Level					
Dune	67	0.249	0.056	0.118	+
Road	16	0.172	0.036	0.084	+
Human-use	103	0.369	0.062	0.394	0
Shrub	8	0.035	0.026	0.028	0
Agriculture	11	0.012	0.007	0.008	0
Beach	18	0.089	0.048	0.161	-
Forest	27	0.067	0.028	0.142	-
Marsh	1	0.003	0.004	0.01	-
Water	1	0.003	0.008	0.054	-

Table 2. Comparisons of use and availability of various habitat types in Stanhope (Prince Edward Island National Park) based on telemetry data from three red foxes. Habitat types are shown in order of preference. Comparisons were made using the Neu Method and Bonferroni confidence intervals. Preference was determined with Bonferroni confidence intervals (a = 0.001) placed on use. "+" indicates used more than expected; "-" indicates used less than expected; "0" use according to availability or non-significant difference between expected and available.

3.4 Discussion

Although home-ranges and core areas of red foxes inhabiting the study site were comparable to values observed in studies conducted in other parts of North America and Europe (e.g. Adkins & Stott, 1998; Voigt & Macdonald, 1984), they were at the lower end of the spectrum for this species. There are several possible explanations for these results. It is possible that our findings reflect the habitat requirements and movement patterns of foxes during the kit-rearing season when foxes are involved in cub rearing and lactation (especially females) and need to stay close to their dens (e.g. Saunders et al., 1995). If this is true, it is possible to assume that home ranges and core areas obtained during this study are underestimations of values at other times of the year. This hypothesis was supported by the fact that one of the females (F3) was observed rearing three pups and receiving help from the male (M2). This observation would also explain the considerable overlap in home range areas found between F3 and M2. Another possible explanation for our findings is that the small home ranges observed in this study are the result of the aggregated distribution of anthropogenic food sources. It has been shown that the distribution of non-territorial, solitary carnivores tend to become more aggregated when anthropogenic resources are concentrated into a few patches, resulting in smaller and more stable home ranges (Joshi et al., 1995). Alternatively, it is possible that home ranges were small because Stanhope supports a high density of red foxes due to high fox-feeding levels. Small home ranges would allow foxes to cover their territories in a relatively short time to maintain exclusive rights to the areas and reduce intraspecific competition (Baker et al., 1998). Although this has not been investigated yet, anecdotal information suggests that there may be a correlation between fox numbers and the overabundance of anthropogenic resources within certain sectors of Prince Edward Island National Park. Observations made by wardens from the park suggest that red-fox abundance in Stanhope has actually increased during the last years. Although it is logical to expect that deaths caused by vehicles can reduce foxes abundance in the park, they can also incite an increase in the reproductive output or productivity of the fox population. Some predator species compensate for high mortality levels resulting from exploitation (e.g., trapping, hunting, etc.) by increasing their litter size or reproductive output (e.g., van Deelen & Gosselink, 2006). Although an accidental death caused by a vehicle is not the same than exploitation, it may contribute to the adverse effects that other human activities in the area or nearby (e.g., tourism, trapping, farming) may have on the red-fox population inhabiting the study site.

Red foxes are typically considered habitat generalists, and their adaptability to marginal or degraded ecological conditions has been a key factor in allowing them to survive in fragmented landscapes and human-dominated areas. However, this does not necessarily mean that they do not have preferences for certain habitat types. For instance, red foxes did not show much preference for habitats such as forests, abandoned fields, and shrubs, in which they would normally have to hunt for prey such as small mammals. In this study, we found that red foxes used both human-use areas and dune habitats during the study period which corresponds to the kit-rearing season for this species. Our analyses also indicate that in Prince Edward Island, red foxes seem to avoid forests even though this habitat is the most available habitat type. Red foxes showed a preference for dune habitats in the study site at both large (home range) and small (core area) spatial scales, providing support for anecdotal information that suggest that it is in the dunes where their dens are located. The granular and sandy composition of dune habitats likely provides suitable habitat for excavation of dens. In addition, dune habitats are protected within the national park, thus limiting their access to humans.

Our analyses also showed that the value of certain habitat cover types to red foxes varies with the spatial scale at which habitat-selection is investigated. For instance, even though red foxes used human-use areas at the large spatial scale (home range), they did not significantly select for this habitat at the small spatial scale (core area). At the small spatial scale, our results indicated that foxes selected for dunes and roads. In our study site, foxes use roads to move between different habitat cover-types and to obtain food. Fox-feeding along roads is a common human activity during the kit-rearing season. Indeed, it is very common to see many red foxes of all ages sitting along the roads waiting for humans to feed them. During the kit-rearing season, although humans inhabiting cottages and houses still set out food for foxes, these animals must find "foraging" along the roads more efficient. During this season, it is not only easy to obtain food along the roads without too much effort, but roads are situated very close to the dunes where it is suspected that their dens are located. Parental care is particularly demanding in terms of food resources, so it may be more energetically efficient to stay close to the dens. Thus, our findings provide evidence suggesting that anthropogenic food resources are important for foxes at both small and large spatial scales. It is, thus, possible to use our findings as indirect evidence supporting the idea that fox-feeding is altering the way that red foxes use habitats in the study site, and possibly other areas of Prince Edward Island National Park where fox-feeding is common.

4. Case study 2: The African wild dog

The African wild dog is a highly endangered carnivore (IUCN 2006) that has showed significant declines in population numbers over the last century, especially during the last 35-45 years (Woodroffe et al., 1997). Like much of Africa, the agricultural and economic development of South Africa led to the local extinction or extirpation of large predators in all but the most uninhabitable areas (e.g., Kruger National Park and north-east KwaZulu-Natal). Apart from rainforest areas and deserts, African wild dogs (herein called wild dogs) were historically distributed throughout much of sub-Saharan Africa (Fanshawe et al., 1991; Monod, 1928; Schaller, 1972). Now, however, they have been extirpated from most of their range, being confined to a few areas in southern Africa where human population density remains low. According to Fanshawe et al. (1997), there is about 3,000-5,500 wild dogs left in 600-1,000 packs, more than half of which are found in southern Africa. Unfortunately, most of these populations are too small to be considered viable in the long-term. For instance, it is commonly accepted that the only viable population of wild dogs in South Africa occurs in Kruger National Park (Fanshawe et al., 1991).

The principal threats to wild dogs are pressures resulting from human activities and infectious diseases. Both of these are mediated by habitat fragmentation, which increases contact between wild dogs, humans and domestic dogs. Wild dogs are intensely social animals, spending almost all of their time in close association with one other. Hunting in packs, each member achieves a higher foraging success than it would if it hunted alone (Creel & Creel, 1995). Packs may be as small as a pair, or number as many as 49 adults, yearlings and pups. Studies have shown that wild dogs live at very low densities, and are rare even when they live in large well-protected habitats where prey may be abundant, making these animals unusually susceptible to the loss and fragmentation of natural habitats (Woodroffe & Ginsberg, 1997). Growing human populations have caused wild-dog habitat to become increasingly fragmented or discontinuous, as large tracts of land have been taken over for livestock grazing and cultivation. In addition, wild dogs have been persecuted and their prey has been depleted. Like other large- and medium-bodied size mammalian carnivore species, wild dogs do kill livestock under some circumstances, and have therefore been shot, snared and poisoned in most livestock areas. Overall, the combination of all these factors has resulted in wild dog populations to become increasingly isolated in fragments of habitats with low human population densities.

Species reintroduction is a tool for conservation and wildlife management (Griffith et al., 1989) that may sometimes offer the only chance of survival for highly endangered or threatened species (Hayward et al., 2007a, 2007b). In the interest of improving the current status of the African wild dog, efforts are underway to reintroduce wild-dog packs into several parks and reserves of South Africa, including Mkhuze Game Reserve (IUCN Wild Dog Advisory Group, 2005; Lindsey et al., 2004; Lines, 2006; Mills et al., 1998; Wells & Richmond, 1995). Mkhuze Game Reserve (~ 360 km^2) was established in 1912 and forms part of iSimangaliso Wetland Park (World Heritage Site formerly called the Greater St.

Lucia Wetland Park) which is approximately 3,320 km^2. Regardless of its small size, Mkhuze Game Reserve supports a very diverse mammalian community that includes four of the five big-game animals expected to occur in the area: leopard (*Panthera pardus*), African elephant (*Loxodonta africana*), black rhinoceros (*Diceros bicornis*), and buffalo (*Syncerus caffer*). Wild dogs were present in Mkhuze Game Reserve until the 1930s. In this game reserve, the reintroduction of wild dogs began in 2005 as part of the Priority Species Monitoring Project. In 2004, thirteen wild dogs originating from two other South African conservation areas (Marakele National Park and Madikwe Game Reserve) were placed together in two adjoining bomas in Mkhuze Game Reserve with the purpose of bonding all the animals into one pack. Boma construction was fundamental to ensure animals were exposed to electrified fencing (Mkhuze Game Reserve is surrounded by electric fencing), habituated to game vehicles, allowed to settle, become accustomed to radio-collars and other conspecifics within a new social group, and finally ensure that territorial bonds were relaxed so they remained at the release location (Hayward et al., 2007a, 2007b).

Although a variety of methods are used to assess the success of a species reintroduction program, a common recommended first step in most of these methods is to demonstrate that the species is adapting well to its new habitat during the establishment phase of the reintroduction (Hayward et al., 2007a, 2007b). Researchers generally accomplish this first step by examining habitat selection and home-range patterns, as the reestablishment of species in areas where they formerly occurred is often influenced by the suitability of habitats at proposed release sites (IUCN, 1998; Wolf et al., 1998). Without high quality habitats that provide adequate food, water and suitable places to forage and breed, reintroduction programmes have a low chance of success (Griffith et al., 1989; Hayward et al., 2007a, 2007b).

The main objective of this study was to examine how telemetry data can be used to quantify habitat selection and home-range patterns of a wild-dog pack during the establishment phase of a reintroduction program. We also expected that a better knowledge of the home range and habitat-selection patterns of reintroduced animals will help identify what resources and habitats are essential for the survival of wild dogs in small reserves or parks such as Mkhuze Game Reserve.

4.1 Study site

Mkhuze Game Reserve is located between 32°06′25″ to 32°56′46″ E and 26°51′26″ to 28°29′07″ S in the subtropical zone (Fig. 3). The game reserve receives about 1,200 mm of rain annually, 60% of which falls in the summer. Mkhuze Game Reserve comprises a diverse array of habitat types, including grasslands, lakes and pans, wetlands, savannahs, thickets, woodlands and forests (van Rooyen, 2004). Two types of grasslands characterize the game reserve: lebombo-wooded grasslands and floodplains. Lebombo-wooded grasslands are mostly found on sandy soils near the bordering Lebombo Mountains but can also be present on soils composed of clay. The game reserve also includes several freshwater pans that although are mostly permanent bodies of water, may also undergo seasonal changes such as regular flooding and inundation (Van Rooyen, 2004). Although thickets and savannahs occur in various parts of the game reserve, most of the area is occupied by woodlands and forests. Woodlands have a discontinuous canopy while forests, also known as closed-woodlands, have a continuous canopy that commences at an elevation of 5 m or greater above the ground (Hockey et al., 2005)

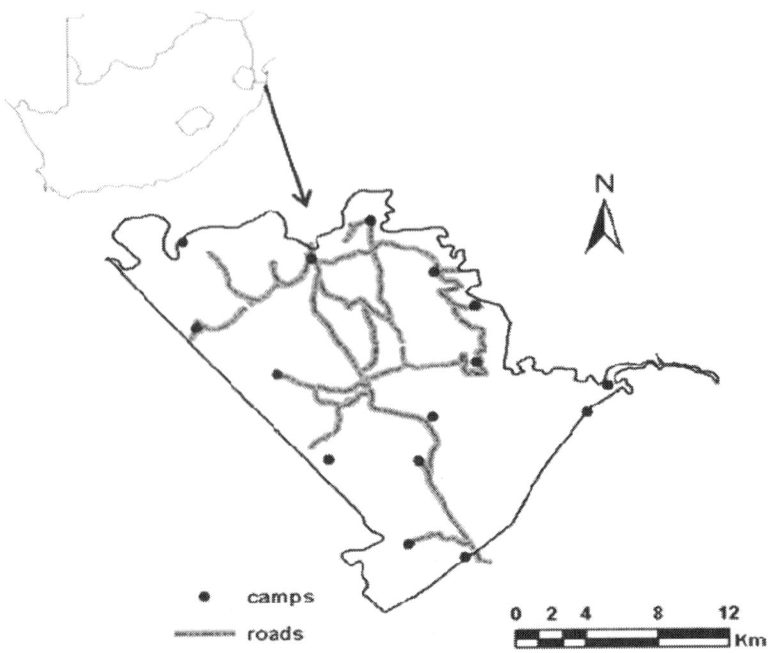

Fig. 3. Map of Mkhuze Game Reserve in relation to South Africa showing the main camps (solid dots) and roads (dashed lines) traversing the game reserve. The scale-bar refers to Mkhuze Game Reserve only.

4.2 Data collection and analysis

Radio-telemetry data of wild dogs were obtained from the Priority Species Monitoring Project of the Mkuze Game Reserve. As part of this monitoring project, two African wild dogs belonging to a pack reintroduced in 2005 were radio-collared and tracked from December 2006 to June 2008. Although only one animal usually needs to be tracked when following a wild-dog pack, two animals were tracked in this case to ensure data collection success in case of death or malfunctioning of a collar. For the purpose of this study, we only used the radio-tracking data from the animal for which more data were collected. The Animal Care Protocol used in this study followed the guidelines of the American Society of Mammalogists (Gannon et al., 2007) and was approved by both Ezemvelo KwaZulu-Natal Wildlife Conservation and iSimangaliso Wetland Park Authority. Animals were darted with a combination of fentanyl and xylazine to minimize capture and handling stress. Once animals were immobilized, radio-collars (with activity and mortality signals as well as anti-snare plates; Model V5C181; width = 40 mm, circumference = 420 mm, weight ~ 420 g; Sirtrack radio-collars) were attached to them. The radio-telemetry procedure used in this study followed White & Garrott (1990). Radio-collared animals were tracked as a pack using Telonics aerials (Telonics, Arizona, USA) and Sirtrack receivers (Sirtrack, Hastings, New

Zealand). In order to reduce disturbance during the early stages of this wild-dog reintroduction program, the pack was located only twice daily (once at dawn and once at dusk). Geographic coordinates (latitude, longitude) of radio-tracking locations were recorded using a Garmin-GPS unit (± 0.30 m). Three types of radio-tracking locations or sightings were recorded in this study: A-sightings consisted of a close and accurate radio-tracking location where the pack was seen directly; B-sightings represented the presumed location of the close, but elusive, pack where a strong signal was recorded but the landscape prevented direct viewing; and C-sightings resulted from three compass bearings and a computer-tabulated triangulation. Triangulation angles were maintained between 40° and 150°. About 80% of radio-tracking locations were taken with the animal in view of the observers (i.e., 80% of locations were A-sightings). The software LOAS 2.1 (Ecological Software Solution 2003) was used to estimate the actual locations. Statistical independence of radio-telemetry data was not an issue for this study since only two sightings were recorded per day. Data on home-range size and core-areas were analyzed using the Animal Movement SA version 2.0 in ArcView (version 3.3; ESRI). The minimum number of locations required to accurately assess the home-range size of the pack was estimated by plotting cumulative home-range sizes against the number of locations (i.e., asymptotic home-range; Philipps & Catling, 1991). Similar to Case Study 1, home-range values were calculated using the 100% minimum convex polygon (MCP) and the 95% fixed Kernel method while the 50% fixed-kernel method was used to estimate size and shape of the core-areas or centers of activity within home-ranges.

Habitat variables were determined using a digitized map (aerial photographs of the study area were not available) of the habitat types comprised within Mkuze Game Reserve. ArcView GIS (version 9.3 and 3.3; Environmental Systems Research Institute, Inc., ESRI) was used to map animal locations obtained from radio-telemetry monitoring sessions and to assign to each location a habitat type. Two habitat classification systems were used to examine habitat selection patterns. First, we used a broad classification system that separated the habitats encompassed within Mkhuze Game Reserve into six types: woodland, forest, thicket, river floodplain (includes seasonal stream habitats), *Terminalia sericea* savannah and other habitats (includes human-use areas, roads, etc). Most mammal species move throughout their home range and as they encounter different components and combination of features of their habitats they also make different selections. Thus, our second classification system involved a more refined classification that attempted to separate certain habitats (i.e., woodlands and forests) in categories that were perhaps a little bit more relevant to wild dogs inhabiting southern South Africa (Woodroffe & Ginsberg, 1997). Eleven habitat types were used for this second classification system: *Acacia nilotica* low-closed woodland, Acacia tall-open woodland, *Acacia tortillis* low-open woodland, dry-closed woodland, Lebombo wooded-grassland, low-thicket, open-woodland, river floodplain (includes seasonal stream habitats), riverine forest, *Terminalia sericea* savannah and other habitats (includes human-use areas, roads, etc). Similar to Case Study 1, habitat selection was examined by comparing use and availability of habitat types (using both habitats classification systems) within Mkhuze Game Reserve using the Neu Method (see Section 3.2.2).

4.3 Results

When all the radio-telemetry locations (n = 847) were plotted on the map of the Mkhuze Game Reserve, they appeared scattered throughout the entire reserve, although the number of radio-telemetry observations were higher near the southern border of the reserve (Fig. 4). A 100% MCP yielded a home range of 383.9 km² while the 95% fixed-kernel method resulted in a home-range of 377.8 km². Thus, both 100% MCP and 95% fixed-kernel methods resulted in home-range sizes that were larger than the game reserve (~360 km²). In terms of centers of activity, the 50% fixed-kernel method resulted in a core-area of 103.6 km², representing about 29% of the total area covered by the game reserve.

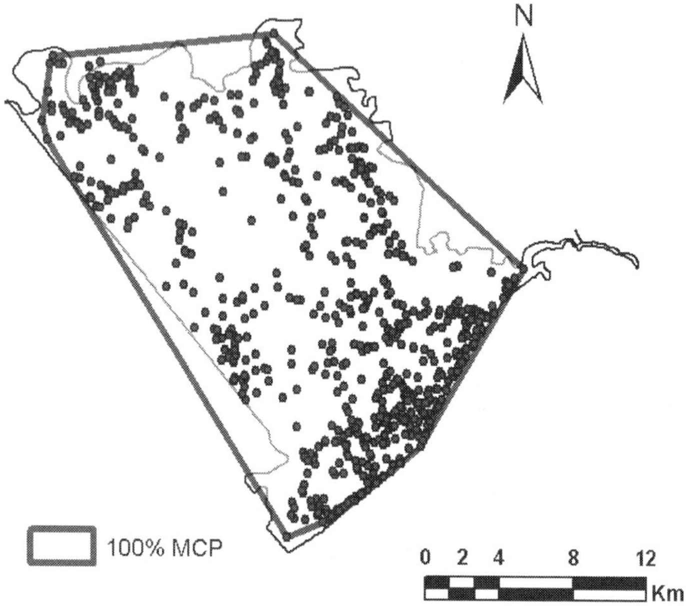

Fig. 4. Map of the Mkhuze Game Reserve showing 847 radio-tracking locations collected from a wild-dog pack. The solid line represents the 100% MCP home-range of the wild-dog pack calculated in this study.

Using the broad habitat classification system, wild dogs selected only for one habitat, *Terminalia sericea* savannah habitats while thicket habitat types and river floodplains were used less than expected based on their availability (Table 3). Using the most refined habitat classification system, our analyses indicated that out all woodland habitat types, *Acacia nilotica* low-closed woodland was the most important for wild dogs. Using this same classification system, it was also found that wild dogs clearly selected for *Terminalia sericea* savannah habitats (Table 3). These analyses also showed that the habitats that were used less than expected based on their availability were thicket habitat types, river floodplains and riverine forest. No significant preference was observed for any of the other habitat types.

Habitat	Observations (# locations)	Habitat Use proportion		Expected Use proportion	Preference
		Average	SD		
Broad Habitat Classification System					
Terminalia sericea savannah	155	0.187	0.048	0.093	+
Woodland habitat types	279	0.336	0.058	0.379	0
Forest habitat types	269	0.324	0.056	0.291	0
Other habitats	10	0.012	0.013	0.014	0
Low-thicket habitat	49	0.059	0.029	0.096	-
River floodplains & streams	68	0.082	0.034	0.127	-
Refined Habitat Classification System					
Terminalia sericea savannah	155	0.187	0.039	0.093	+
Acacia nilotica low-closed woodland	134	0.161	0.037	0.049	+
Acacia tall-open woodland	106	0.128	0.033	0.160	0
Acacia tortillis low-open woodland	49	0.059	0.024	0.064	0
Dry-closed woodland	122	0.147	0.035	0.167	0
Lebombo-wooded grassland	52	0.063	0.024	0.071	0
Open-woodland	72	0.087	0.028	0.084	0
Other habitats	10	0.014	0.013	0.014	0
Low-thicket habitat	49	0.059	0.024	0.096	-
River floodplains & streams	68	0.082	0.027	0.127	-
Riverine forest	13	0.016	0.013	0.076	-

Table 3. Comparisons of use and availability of various habitat types of an African wild dog pack reintroduced to Mkhuze Game Reserve based on telemetry data. Habitat types are shown in order of preference. Comparisons were made using the Neu Method and Bonferroni confidence intervals. Preference was determined with Bonferroni confidence intervals (a = 0.001) placed on use. "+" indicates used more than expected; "-" indicates used less than expected; "0" use according to availability or non-significant difference between expected and available.

4.4 Discussion

An important requisite for the success of any reintroduction program of mammalian carnivores is the elimination of the factors that initially caused the decline of the species. As previously mentioned the main factors explaining the decline of wild dogs in Africa include killing by humans, reduced prey availability, competition with other carnivores, loss and fragmentation of habitats, as well as infectious diseases. The wild-dog pack reintroduced into Mkhuze Game Reserve in 2005 was seen in this game reserve only until June 2008. Although it is suspected that some pack members moved out of the reserve onto neighbouring conservation parks or reserves, other individuals were found dead within or nearby Mkhuze Game Reserve. Possible causes for the deaths of these animals include snares, predation, hunting injuries and infectious diseases that are still occurring in the study area (personal communication, Mkhuze Game Reserve staff and veterinarians). Thus, the analyses discussed below contribute to a forensic-like study that we hope can provide some insights into the factors that may have played a role in the failure of this wild-dog reintroduction program.

Several studies have suggested that a major reason why very few wild-dog reintroduction programs have succeeded to produce viable populations is because the game reserves were too small to include the whole home range of this species. Our findings provide support for this argument. In this study, the reintroduced wild-dog pack had a home range that was larger than the boundaries of the game reserve, indicating that these animals needed to use not only the entire reserve but also adjacent areas. Moreover, the center of activities (i.e., core areas) of the reintroduced wild-dog pack represented ~29% of the whole game reserve. Interestingly, most of the telemetry locations recorded in this study were situated in the southern region of the game reserve (Fig. 3). Different factors may be attracting wild dogs to this part of the game reserve and its neighbouring habitats. First, there is a private-game reserve (Phinda Game Reserve) that presents a similar wildlife diversity (including wild dogs) than that of Mkhuze Game Reserve, with the addition of lions. Wild dogs are social animals, so it is possible that they were interacting with conspecific animals occurring in the private game reserve. Second, the habitats preferred by wild dogs are more abundant in the southern border of the game reserve. In this study, we found that the wild-dog pack selected for *Terminalia sericea* savannah (3,334 ha) and *Acacia nilotica* low closed woodland (1,742 ha) habitats. These two habitats only represent ~14% of the whole game reserve, with most of the *Terminalia sericea* savannah habitat being located at the southern border of the reserve. Conservation efforts and future wild-dog reintroduction programs should consider the protection and restoration of these two habitat types in other parts of the Mkhuze Game Reserve.

Another factor that may have contributed to the failure of this wild-dog reintroduction may be competition for prey with other mammalian predators. Several studies have shown that wild dogs will avoid areas with high prey density if competition (or mortality due to) with predators such as hyaenas and lions is high (Creel & Creel, 1996; Mills & Gorman, 1997). In Mkhuze Game Reserve, there are no lions, but hyaenas are abundant. Thus, it is possible that although some habitats were available to wild-dogs, in practical terms, they were not accessible to them. For example, we found that one of the habitat types that wild dogs preferred was low closed woodlands dominated by *Acacia nilotica,* small bushes and deciduous tree species. This type of habitat is ideal for antelope species such as impala and nyala, but it may be sometimes too dense to prevent wild-dogs pack hunting coordination to be effective. However, *Terminalia sericea* savannah, the other habitat type preferred by wild dogs, is characterized by dense vegetation. Although hunting should theoretically be more efficient in this habitat type because the ability of other competitor species (e.g., hyaena) to locate and steal prey from wild-dog packs is reduced, *Terminalia sericea* savannah only represents ~9% of the total game reserve. Other studies have found that wild dogs preferred deciduous and thorn woodlands (Creel & Creel, 2002) as well as forest and open-woodland (Andreka, 1996). In this study, we found that river floodplain, riverine forest and woodland habitats dominated by tall *Acacia* trees were avoided by wild dogs. Low-thicket habitats can be dense in many areas of Mkhuze Game Reserve. Although many avian and small-bodied mammalian species may benefit from dense vegetation, large-bodied herbivores (common prey of wild dogs) are usually not able to find sufficient grazing area in this type of habitat. This may explain why wild-dogs tended to avoid low-thicket habitats in the game reserve.

Two decades ago, a successful reintroduction of a mammalian carnivore species in Africa was considerable unfeasible. Today, however, sufficient evidence exists suggesting that planned and well-documented reintroductions of mammalian carnivores are possible (Hayward et al., 2007a, 2007b). In part, this is because the results of other reintroductions (successful and unsuccessful) are being published and peer-reviewed at more frequent intervals, so other reintroduction attempts can benefit from these experiences. In this case study, we analyzed telemetry data from an unsuccessful wild-dog pack reintroduction and learned a few key issues regarding the species' needs that must be considered in future reintroductions, especially in small game reserves.

5. Conclusions and future directions

The examination of habitat selection and home range patterns is an essential first step in the management of any wildlife species whether they are abundant, rare or endangered. The main goal of this chapter was to demonstrate how radio-telemetry data could be used to provide previously unavailable insights into the habitat selection and home range patterns of two mammalian carnivore species inhabiting human-dominated landscapes. In Case 1, the use of radio-telemetry data helped us to show that the presence of anthropogenic food sources in human-use areas and along roads is altering home range and habitat-selection patterns of red foxes inhabiting Prince Edward Island National Park (Prince Edward Island, Canada). In Case 2, radio-telemetry data were used to quantify home range and habitat-selection patterns of a wild-dog pack reintroduced in Mkhuze Game Reserve, South Africa. In this case, our analyses not only helped us to quantify these patterns, but also to provide some insights into the reasons why this wild-dog reintroduction program failed. Radio-telemetry data clearly showed that the game reserve was smaller than the home-range of the wild dog pack and that the two habitat types that are preferred by the wild dogs only represent 9% of the total area of the reserve.

The advent of satellite technology, such as global positioning systems (GPS), has allowed wildlife researchers to collect telemetry data on a temporal scale that was not previously practical. Observations can now be obtained many times per day for many months with GPS devices. Although GPS applications have certainly transformed wildlife telemetry, they are not without problems. GPS-collars can be very expensive and experience failures in the field during data collection and trade-offs between GPS location collection intervals and unit longevity lead generally to fewer monitored individuals and shorter study durations compared with radio-telemetry (Frair et al., 2010; Gau et al., 2004; Hebblewhite et al., 2007). Another problem associated with GPS-telemetry is that a decreased interval between recorded locations results in an increased level of autocorrelation in the resulting data. Although some researchers consider that autocorrelation in telemetry data is not a problem, others still disagree with this statement and argue that is really necessary to account for GPS errors in wildlife telemetry studies (Frair et al., 2010). In contrast with GPS telemetry, radio-telemetry is inexpensive, accuracy is adequate for many types of investigations and it is possible to carry out studies for a relatively long time period. For instance, if the budget for the investigation is low, the use of radio-telemetry technology may be the only choice. This is the case of many developing areas of the world where ecologically-sensitive issues are present and is often very difficult for researchers or wildlife managers to acquire GPS-collars. Another important advantage of radio-telemetry technology is that radio-collars can be implemented on almost all animals for which GPS telemetry devices are too heavy. Having said this, it is important to mention that radio-telemetry technology can be time-consuming and limited by weather conditions. Thus, interpretations should be constrained within the accuracy and precision of the equipment and personnel involved in collecting the radio-telemetry data.

It is clear that emerging technologies such as GPS-telemetry open new avenues in wildlife telemetry and ecological research because they can provide more detailed information regarding fine-grain movement patterns. Ultimately, however, technologies are just tools in the hands of researchers. The choice of a given telemetry technology should be based on the kind of questions that one is trying to answer or investigate. In this chapter, the key focal points of our case studies were very specific, have clear conservation/management applications and dealt with medium-bodied size carnivore species. Additionally, in both case studies, the study areas were small which facilitated field work and our ability to track all collared animals daily without much effort. Therefore, in both case studies examined here, radio-telemetry technology was more than adequate to identify the habitat types that were avoided or preferred by the carnivore species under investigation. Clearly, the advent of GPS technology will allow ecologists and wildlife managers to develop more sophisticated and rigorous methods to assess home range and habitat-selection patterns. However, what is really needed at this point is to develop new methods or approaches to extract a maximal amount of information from data obtained from less-sophisticated technology such as radio-telemetry.

6. Acknowledgments

This research was supported by research discovery grants to M. Silva-Opps and S. Opps from the Natural Sciences and Engineering Research Council of Canada, a contract from Parks Canada and a grant from the Faculty of Science of the University of Prince Edward Island. We are grateful to Karen Johnson and the staff of the Prince Edward Island National Park for their help during the red-fox radio-tracking sessions. We also thank the Prince Edward Island Department of Agriculture and Forestry for providing digital information on Prince Edward Island forests. We are indebted to the iSimangaliso Wetland Park Authority, the personnel of the Priority Species Monitoring Project, the Operation Wallacea and Xander Conbrin for providing radio-telemetry data of the African wild dog. Finally, we are thankful to Eva Jenkins and the staff of the Mkhuze Game Reserve for their work and logistic support during African wild-dog radio-tracking sessions.

7. References

Ables, E.D. (2009). Ecology Of The Red Fox In North America, In: *The Wild Canids: Their Systematics, Behavioral Ecology and Evolution,* M. Fox, (Ed.), 216-236, ISBN 978-1929242641,Van Nostrand Co., New York

Adkins, C.A. & Stott, P. (1998). Home Ranges, Movement and Habitat Associations of Red Foxes *Vulpes vulpes* in Suburban Toronto, Canada. *Journal of Zoology,* Vol. 244, pp. 355-346, ISSN 1469-7998

Andreka, G. E. (1996). Spatial Utilization, Habitat Selection and Population Status of the Wild Dog (*Lycaon pictus*) Population in Hluhluwe Umfolozi Park. Master's thesis, University of Natal, Pietermaritzburg, South Africa

Atkinson, K. T. & Shackleton, D.M. (1991). Coyote, *Canis latrans,* Ecology in a Rural-Urban Environment. *Canadian Field-Naturalist,* Vol. 105, pp. 49-54, ISSN 0008-3550

Baker, P.J.; Robertson, C.P.J.; Funk, R.M. & Harris, S. (1998). Potential Fitness Benefits of Group Living in the Red Fox, *Vulpes vulpes. Animal Behaviour,* Vol. 56, pp. 1411-1424, ISSN 1095-8228

Beyer, H.L.; Haydon, D.T.; Morales, J.M.; Frair, J.L.; Hebblewhite, M.; Mitchell, M. & Matthiopoulos, J. (2010). The Interpretation of Habitat Preference Metrics Under Use-Availability Designs. *Philosophical Transactions of the Royal Society Series B*, Vol. 365, pp. 2245-2254, ISSN 1471-2970

Börger, L.; Dalziel, B.D. & Fryxell, J.M. (2008). Are there General Mechanism of Animal Home Range Behaviour? A Review and Prospects for Future Research. *Ecology Letters,* Vol. 11, pp. 637-650, ISSN 1461-0248

Buckland, S.T.; Anderson, D.R.; Burnham, K.P. & Laake, J.L. (1993). *Distance Sampling: Estimating Abundance of Biological Populations.* Chapman and Hall, ISBN 0-412-42660-9, London, England

Blakesley, J.A.; Franklin, A.B. & Gutierrez, R.J. (1992). Spotted Owl Roost and Nest Site Selection in Northwestern California. *Journal of Wildlife Management,* Vol. 56, pp. 388-392, ISSN 1937-2817

Block, W.M. & Brennan, L.A. (1993). The Habitat Concept in Ornithology: Theory and Applications, In: *Current Ornithology Volume 11,* D.M. Power (Ed.), 35-91, Springer-Verlag, ISBN 9780306445507, New York, US

Burt, W.H. (1943). Territoriality and Home Range Concepts as Applied to Mammals. *Journal of Mammalogy*, Vol. 24, pp. 346-352, ISSN 1545-1542

Catling P.C. & Burt, R.J. (1995). Why are Red Foxes Absent from some Eucalypt Forests in Eastern New South Wales? *Wildlife Research,* Vol. 22, pp. 535-546, ISSN 10353712

Cavallini, P. (1996). Variation in the Social System of the Red Fox. *Ethology, Ecology & Evolution,* Vol. 8, pp. 323-342, ISSN 1828-7131

Chamberlain, M.J.; Conner, L.M.; Leopold, B.C. & Hodges, K.M. (2003). Space Use and Multi-Scale Habitat Selection of Adult Raccoons in Central Mississippi. *Journal of Wildlife Management,* Vol. 67, pp. 334-340, ISSN 1937-2817

Chapin, T.G.; Harrison, D.J. & Phillips, D.M. (1997). Seasonal Habitat Selection by Marten in an Untrapped Forest Preserve. *Journal of Wildlife Management,* Vol. 61, pp. 707-717, ISSN 1937-2817

Contesse, P.; Hegglin, D.; Gloor, S.; Bontadina, F. & Deplazes, P. (2004). The Diet of Urban Foxes (*Vulpes vulpes*) and the Availability of Anthropogenic Food in the City of Zurich, Switzerland. *Mammalian Biology,* Vol. 69, pp. 81-95, ISSN 1618-1476

Creel, S. & Creel, N.M. (1995). Communal Hunting and Pack Size in African Wild Dogs, *Lycaon pictus. Animal Behaviour,* Vol. 50, pp. 1325–1339, ISSN 1095-8282

Creel, S. & Creel, N.M. (1996). Limitation of African Wild Dogs by Competition with Larger Carnivores. *Conservation Biology*, Vol. 10, pp. 526-538, ISSN 1523-1739

Creel, S. & Creel, N.M. (2002). *The African Wild Dog: Behavior, Ecology, and Conservation.* Princeton University Press, ISBN 978-0691016542, Princeton, New Jersey, US

Craighead, F. C. (1982). *Track of the Grizzly.* Random House, ISBN 978-0871563224, New York, US

Dell'Arte, G.L.; Laaksonen, T.; Norrdahl, K. & Korpimäki, E. (2007). Variation in the Diet Composition of a Generalist Predator, the Red Fox, in Relation to Season and Density of Main Prey. *Acta Oecologica,* Vol. 31, pp. 276-281, ISSN 1146-609x

Ewer, R.F. (1968). *Ethology of Mammals.* Logos Press, ISBN 978-0236308569, London, England

Fanshawe, J. H.; Frame, L.H. & Ginsberg, J.R. (1991). The Wild Dog—Africa's Vanishing Carnivore. *Oryx,* Vol. 25, pp. 137-146, ISSN 1365-3008

Fanshawe, J. H.; Ginsberg, J.R.; Sillero-Zubiri, C. & Woodroffe, R. (1997). The status and distribution of remaining wild dog populations, In: *The African Wild Dog – Status Survey and Conservation Action Plan*, R. Woodroffe; Ginsberg, J. & Macdonald, D., (Eds.), 11-57, IUCN/SSC Canid Specialist Group, ISBN 2-8317-0418-g, Gland, Switzerland

Frair, J.L.; Fieberg, J.; Hebblewhite, M.; Cagnacci, F.; DeCesare, N.J. & Pedrotti, L. (2010). Resolving Issues of Imprecise and Habitat-biased Locations in Ecological Analyses Using GPS Telemetry Data. *Philosophical Transactions of the Royal Society B*, Vol. 365, pp. 2187-2200, ISSN 1471-2970

Gaillard, J.-F.; Hebblewhite, M.; Loison, A.; Fuller, M.; Powell, R.; Basille, M. & van Moorter, B. (2011). Habitat-performance Relationships: Finding the Right Metric at A Given Spatial Scale. *Philosophical Transactions of the Royal Society Series B*, Vol. 365, pp. 2255-2265, ISSN 1471-2970

Gannon, W. L. ; Sikes, R.S. & The Animal Care and Use Committee of the American Society of Mammalogists. (2007). Guidelines of the American Society of Mammalogists for the Use of Wild Mammals in Research. *Journal of Mammalogy*, Vol. 88, pp. 809-823, ISSN 1545-1542

Garshelis, D.L. (2000). Delusions in habitat evaluation: measuring use, selection and importance, In *Research Techniques in Animal Ecology: Controversies and Consequences*, L. Boitani & Fuller, T.K. (Eds.), 111-164, Columbia University Press, ISBN . 0231113412, New York, US

Gau, R.J.; McLoughlin, P.D.; Case, R.L.; Cluff, H.D.; Mulders, R. & Messier, F. (2004). Movements of Subadult Male Grizzly Bears in the Central Canadian Arctic. *Canadian Field-Naturalist*, Vol. 118, pp. 239–242, ISSN 0008-3550

Gese, E.M. (2001). Monitoring of Terrestrial Carnivore Populations, In: *Carnivore Conservation*, Gittleman, J.L.; Funk, S.M.; MacDonald, D.W. & Wayne, R.K., (Eds.), 372-396, Cambridge University Press, ISBN 9780521665377, Cambridge, England

Gibeau, M. L. (1998). Use of Urban Habitats by Coyotes in the Vicinity of Banff Alberta. *Urban Ecosystems*, Vol. 2, pp. 129-139, ISSN 1573-1642

Graham, K.; Beckerman, A.P. & Thirgood, S. (2005). Human-predator-prey Conflicts: Ecological Correlates, Prey Losses and Patterns of Management. *Biological Conservation*, Vol. 122, pp. 159-171, ISSN 0006-3207

Griffith, B.; Scott, J.M.; Carpenter, J.W. & Reed, C. (1989). Translocation as a Species Conservation Tool: Status and Strategy. *Science*, Vol. 245, pp. 477-480, ISSN 1095-9203

Grinder, M. I. & Krausman, P.R. (2001). Home Range, Habitat Use, and Nocturnal Activity of Coyotes in an Urban Environment. *Journal of Wildlife Management*, Vol. 65, pp. 887-898, ISSN 1937-2817

Hall, L.S.; Krausman, P.R. & Morrison, M.L. (1997). The Habitat Concept and a Plea for Standard Terminology. *Wildlife Society Bulletin*, Vol. 25, pp. 173-182, ISSN 0091-7648

Hansteen, T.L.; Andreassen, H.P. & Ims, R.A. (1997). Effects of Spatiotemporal Scale on Autocorrelation and Home Range Estimators. *Journal of Wildlife Management*, Vol. 61, pp. 280-290, ISSN 1937-2817

Harris, S. & Smith, G.C. (1987). Demography of Two Fox (*Vulpes vulpes*) Populations. *Journal of Applied Ecology*, Vol. 24, pp. 75-86, ISSN 1365-2664

Harris, S.; Cresswell, W.J.; Forde, P.G.; Trewhella, W.G.; Woollard, T. & Wray, S. (1990). Home Range Analysis Using Radio-Tracking Data – A Review of Problems and Techniques Particularly as Applied to the Study of Mammals. *Mammal Review*, Vol. 20, pp. 97-123, ISSN 1365-2907

Hayward, G.D.; Hayward, P.H. & Garton, E.O. (1993). Ecology of Boreal Owls in the Northern Rocky Mountains, U.S.A. *Wildlife Monograph,* Vol. 124, pp. 1-59, ISSN 1938-5455

Hawyard, M.W.; Adendorff, J.A.; O'Brien, J.; Sholto-Douglas, A.; Bissett, C.; Moolman, L.C.; Bean, P.; Fogarty, A.; Howarth, D.; Slater, R. & Kerley, G.I.H. (2007a). Practical Considerations for the Reintroduction of Large, Terrestrial, Mammalian Predators Based on Reintroductions to South Africa's Eastern Cape Province. *Open Conservation Biology Journal,* Vol. 1, pp. 1-11, ISSN 1874-8392

Hawyard, M.W.; Adendorff, J.A.; O'Brien, J.; Sholto-Douglas, A.; Bissett, C.; Moolman, L.C.; Bean, P.; Fogarty, A.; Howarth, D.; Slater, R. & Kerley, G.I.H. (2007b). The Reintroduction of Large Carnivores to the Eastern Cape, South Africa: An Assessment. *Oryx,* Vol. 41, pp. 205-214, ISSN 1365-3008

Hebblewhite, M. & Haydon, D.T. (2010). Distinguishing Technology from Biology: A Critical Review of the Use of GPS Telemetry Data in Ecology. *Philosophical Transactions of the Royal Society B,* Vol. 365, pp. 2303-2312, ISSN 1471-2970

Hebblewhite, M.; Percy, M. & Merrill, E.H. (2007). Are all Global Positioning System Collars Created Equal? Correcting Habitat-induced Bias Using three Brands in the Central Canadian Rockies. *Journal of Wildlife Management,* Vol. 71, pp. 2026-2033, ISSN 1937-2817

Hockey, P.A.R.; Dean, W.R.S. & Ryan, P.G. (2005). Roberts' Birds of Southern Africa, Trustees of the John Voelcker Bird Book Fund, ISBN 9780620340533, Cape Town, South Africa

Hutto, R.L. (1985). Habitat Selection by Nonbreeding, Migratory Land Birds, In: *Habitat Selection in Birds,* M.L. Cody, (Ed.), 455-476, Academic Press, ISBN 9780121780814, New York, US

IUCN (1998). *IUCN Guidelines for Re-introductions.* IUCN/SSC Re-introduction Specialist Group (Ed.), Information Press, ISBN 2-8317-0448-0, Oxford, UK

IUCN. (2006). *IUCN Red List of Threatened Species.* IUCN, Gland, Switzerland, 15.05.2010, Available from http://www.iucnredlist.org

IUCN Wild Dog Advisory Group. (2005) *Principles and Guidelines for the Management of the South African Wild Dog Metapopulation,* IUCN/SSC Canid Specialist Group (ED.), NO ISBN, Gland, Switzerland

Johnson, D. (1980). The Comparison of Usage and Availability Measurements for Evaluating Resource Preference. *Ecology,* Vol. 61, pp. 65-71, ISSN 0012-9658

Johnson, D.S.; Thomas, D.L.; ver Hoef, J.M. & Christ, A. (2008). A General Framework for the Analysis of Animal Resource Selection from Telemetry Data. *Biometrics,* Vol. 64, pp. 968-976, ISSN 1541-0420

Johnston, I.G. (2000). *Changes in the Island Landscape.* Brigus Books, ISBN NONE, Darmouth, Nova Scotia, Canada

Joshi, A.R.; Smith, J.L. & Cuthbert, F.J. (1995). Influence of Food Distribution and Predation Pressure on Spacing Behavior in Palm Civets. *Journal of Mammalogy,* Vol. 76, pp. 1205-1212, ISSN 1545-1542

Katnik, D.D. (1992). Spatial Use, Territoriality and Summer-autumn Selection of Habitat in an Intensively Harvested Population of Martens on Commercial Forestland in Maine. Master's Thesis, University of Maine, Maine, US

Kaufmann, J.H. (1962). Ecology and Social Behavior of the Coati, *Nasua narica*, on Barro Colorado Island, Panama. *University of California Publications in Zoology*, Vol. 60, pp. 95-222, ISSN 0068-6506

Kazmaier, R.E.; Hellgren, C & Ruthven, D.C. (2001). Habitat Selection by the Texas Tortoise in a Managed Thornscrub Ecosystem. *Journal of Wildlife Management*, Vol. 65, pp. 653-660, ISSN 1937-2817

Kernohan, B.J.; Gitzen, R.A. & Millspaugh, J.J. (2001). Analysis of Animal Space Use and Movements, In: *Radiotracking and Animal Populations*, J.J. Millspaugh & Marzluff, J.M., (Eds.), 126-166, Academic Press, ISBN 978-0-12-497781-5, San Diego, US

Kolb, H.H. (1986). Some Observations on the Home Range of Vixens (*Vulpes vulpes*) in the Suburbs of Edinburgh. *Journal of Zoology*, Vol. 210, pp. 636-639, ISSN 1469-7998

Lewis, J. C.; Sallee, K.L. & Golightly, R.T., Jr. (1999). Introduction and Range Expansion of Nonnative Red Foxes *(Vulpes vulpes)* in California. *American Midland Naturalist* Vol. 142, pp. 372-381, ISSN 1938-4238

Lindsey, P. A.; Du Toit, J.T. & Mills, M.G.L. (2004). Area and Prey Requirements of African Wild Dogs under Varying Habitat Conditions: Implications for Reintroductions. *South African Journal of Wildlife Research*, Vol. 34, pp. 77-86, ISSN 0379-4369

Lines, R. (2006). African Wild Dog Introductions into Smaller Fenced Reserves: A Metapopulation Management Strategy, *Report Wild Dog Project, Namibia,* pp. 1-28, Namibian Nature Foundation, Namibia

Lloyd, H.G. (1975). The Red Fox in Britain, In: *The Wild Canids: Their Systematics, Behavioral Ecology and Evolution,* M. Fox, (Ed.), 207-215, ISBN 978-1929242641,Van Nostrand Co., New York, US

Lovari, S.; Valier, P. & Lucchi, R.M. (1994). Ranging Behaviour and Activity of Red Foxes in Relation to Environmental Variables in a Mediterranean Mixed Pinewood. *Journal of Zoology,* Vol. 232, pp. 323-339, ISSN 1469-7998

Manly, B. (1974). A Model for Certain Types of Selection Experiments. *Biometrics*, Vol. 30, pp. 281-294, ISSN 1541-0420

Manly, B.F.J.; McDonald, L.L.; Thomas, D.L.; McDonald, T.L. & Erickson, W.P. (2002). *Resource Selection by Animals*, Kluwer Academic Publishers, ISBN 9781402006777, Norwell, Massachusetts, US

Matthiae, P. E. & Stearns, F. (1981). Mammals in Forest Islands in Southeastern Wisconsin, In: *Forest Island Dynamics in Man-Dominated Landscapes*, R. L Burgess & Sharpe, D.M., (Eds.), 55-66, Springer-Verlag, ISBN 978-0387905846, New York, US

MacDonald, D.W. (1977). On Food Preference in the Red Fox. *Mammal Review*, Vol. 7, pp. 7-23, ISSN 1365-2907

McLoughlin, P.D.; Walton, L.R.; Cluff, H.D.; Paquet, P.C. & Ramsay, M.A. (2004). Hierarchical Habitat Selection by Tundra Wolves. *Journal of Mammalogy*, Vol. 85, pp. 576–580, ISSN 1545-1542

Mills, M. G. L. & Gorman, M.L. (1997). Factors Affecting the Density and Distribution of Wild Dogs in The Kruger National Park. *Conservation Biology*, Vol. 11, pp. 1397-1406, ISSN 1523-1739

McLoughlin, P.D.; Case, R.L.; Gau, R.J.; Cluff, H.D.; Mulders, R. & Messier, F. (2002). Hierarchical Habitat Selection by Barren-ground Grizzly Bears in the Central Canadian Arctic. *Oecologia*, Vol. 132, pp. 102–108, ISSN 1432-1939

Mech, L.D. (1970). *The Wolf: Ecology and Behavior of an Endangered Species*. Natural History Press, ISBN 9780385086608, Garden City, New Jersey, US

Mills, M. G. L.; Ellis, S.; Woodroffe, R.; Maddock, A.; Stander, P.; Rasmussen, G.; Pole, A.; Fletcher, P.; Bruford, M.; Wildt, D.; Macdonald, D.W. & Seal, U. (1998). Population and Habitat Viability Analysis for the African Wild Dog (*Lycaon pictus*) in Southern Africa, *UCN/SSC Conservation Breeding Specialist Group workshop report, Pretoria*, ISBN 2-8317-0418-g, pp. 1-182, Gland, Switzerland

Monod, T. (1928). Sur la Presence au Sahara du *Lycaon pictus* (Temm.). *Bulletin de la Société Zoologique de France*, Vol. 53, pp. 262-264, ISSN 0037-962x

Mohr, C.O. (1947). Table of Equivalent Populations of North American Small Mammals. *American Midland Naturalist*, Vol. 37, pp. 223-249, ISSN 1938-4238

Neu, C.W.; Byers, C.R. & Peek, J.M. (1974). A Technique for Analysis of Utilization Availability Data. *Journal of Wildlife Management*, Vol. 38, pp. 541-545, ISSN 1937-2817

Newsome, S.D.; Ralls, K.; Van Horn, C.; Fogel, M.L. & Cypher, B.L. (2010). Stable Isotopes Evaluate Exploitation of Anthropogenic Foods by Endangered San Joaquin Kit Fox (*Vulpes macrotis mutica*). *Canadian Journal of Zoology*, Vol. 91, pp. 1313-1321, ISSN 1480-3283

Orians, G.H. & Wittenberger, J.F. (1991). Spatial and Temporal Scales in Habitat Selection. *American Naturalist, Supplement* Vol. 137, pp. 29-49, ISSN 1537-5323

Philipps, M. & Catling, P. (1991). Home Range and Activity Patterns of Red Foxes in Nadgee Nature Reserve. *Wildlife Research*, Vol. 18, pp. 677-686, ISSN 1035-3712

Prange, S.; Gehrt, S.D. & Wiggers, E.P. (2004). Influences of Anthropogenic Resources on Raccoon (*Procyon lotor*) Movements and Spatial Distribution. *Journal of Mammalogy*, Vol. 85, pp. 483-490, ISSN 1545-1542

Potvin, F.; Lowell, K., Fortin, M.J. & Belanger, L. (2001). How to Test Habitat Selection at the Home Range Scale: A Resampling Random Windows Technique. *Ecoscience*, Vol. 8, pp. 399-406, ISSN 1195-6860

Powell, R.A. (2000) Animal Home Ranges and Territories and Home Range Estimators, In: *Research Techniques in Animal Ecology: Controversies and Consequences*, L. Boitani & Fuller, T, (Eds.), 65-110, Columbia University Press, ISBN 0-231-11341-2, New York, US

Rettie W.J. & Messier, F. (2000). Hierarchical Habitat Selection by Woodland Caribou: Its Relationship to Limiting Factors. *Ecography*, Vol. 23, pp. 466-478, ISSN 1600-0587

Round Table on Resource Land Use and Stewardship, Cultivating Island Solutions. (1997). *Prince Edward Island Round Table on Resource Land Use and Stewardship*, Prince Edward Island Government Publication, Charlottetown, Canada.

Samuel, M.D.; Pierce, D.J. & Garton, E.O. (1985). Identifying Areas of Concentrated Use Within the Home Range. *Journal of Animal Ecology*, Vol. 54, pp. 711-719, ISSN 1365-2656

Saunders, G.; Coman,B.; Kinnear, J. & Braysher, M. (1995). *Managing Vertebrate Pests: Foxes*, Australian Government Service Publication, Canberra, Australia

Schaefer, J.A. & Messier, F. (1995). Habitat Selection as a Hierarchy: The Spatial Scales of Winter Foraging by Muskoxen. *Ecography,* Vol. 8, pp. 333-344, ISSN 1600-0587

Schaller, G.B. (1972). *The Serengeti Lion: a Study of Predator-prey Relations,* University of Chicago Press, ISBN 9780226736402, Chicago, US

Seaman, D.E. & Powell, R.A. (1996). An Evaluation of the Accuracy of Kernel Density Estimators for Home Range Analysis. *Ecology,* Vol. 77, pp. 2075-2085, ISSN 0012-9658

Seaman, D.E.; Millspaugh, J.J.; Kernohan, B.J.; Brundige, G.C.; Raedeke, K.G. & Gitzen, R.A. (1999). Effects of Sample Size on Kernel Home Range Estimates. *Journal of Wildlife Management,* Vol. 63, pp. 739-747, ISSN 1937-2817

Sillero-Zubiri, C. & Switzer, D. (2004). Management of Wild Canids in Human-dominated Landscapes, In: *Canids: foxes, wolves, jackals and dogs – Status Survey and Conservation Action Plan,* C. Sillero-Zubiri; Hoffmann, M. & Macdonald, D.W., (Eds.), 257-266, IUCN Publications Services, ISBN 2831707862, Gland, Switzerland

Smith, G.C. & Harris, S. (1991). Rabies in Urban Foxes (Vulpes vulpes) in Britain: The Use of a Spatial Stochastic Simulation Model to Examine the Pattern of Spread and Evaluate the Efficacy of Different Control Regimes. *Philosophical Transactions of the Royal Society B,* Vol. 334, pp. 459-479, ISSN 1471-2970

Swihart, R.K. & Slade, N.A. (1985). Influence of Sampling Interval on Estimates of Home-range Size. Journal *of Wildlife Management,* Vol. 49, pp. 1019-1025, ISSN 1937-2817

Thomas, D.L. & Taylor, J. (1990). Study Designs and Tests for Comparing Resource Use and Availability. *Journal of Wildlife Management,* Vol. 54, pp. 322-330, ISSN 1937-2817

Treves, A. & Karanth, K.U. (2003). Human-carnivore Conflict Perspectives on Carnivore Management Worldwide. *Conservation Biology,* Vol. 17, pp. 1491-1499, ISSN 1523-1739

van Deelen, T.R. & Gosselink, T.E. (2006). Coyote survival in a Row-crop Agricultural Landscape. *Canadian Journal of Zoology,* Vol. 84, pp. 1630-1636, ISSN 1480-3283

Van Rooyen, N. (2004). Vegetation Types and Wildlife Re-establishment in the Greater St Lucia Wetland Park, *Report to Greater St Lucia Wildlife Park Authority,* KwaZulu-Natal, South Africa

Voigt, D.R. & MacDonald, D.W. (1984). Variation in the Spatial and Social Behaviour of the Red Fox, *Vulpes vulpes. Acta Zoologica Fennica,* Vol. 171, pp. 261-265, ISSN 0001-7299

Weighs, J. (1995). *Facts about Canada, its provinces and territories,* H.W. Wilson Press, ISBN 9780824208646, New York

White, G.C. & Garrott, R.A. (1990). *Analysis of Wildlife Radio-tracking Data,* Academic Press, ISBN 9780127467252, San Diego, US

Woodroffe, R. & Ginsberg, J.R. (1997). Past and Future Causes of Wild Dogs' Population Decline, In: *The African Wild Dog – Status Survey and Conservation Action Plan,* R. Woodroffe; Ginsberg, J. & Macdonald, D., (Eds.), 63-64, IUCN/SSC Canid Specialist Group, ISBN 2-8317-0418-g, Gland, Switzerland

Wolf C. M.; Garland, T., Jr. & Griffith, B. (1998). Predictors of Avian and Mammalian Translocation Success: Reanalysis with Phylogenetically Independent Contrasts. *Biological Conservation,* Vol. 86, pp. 243–255, ISSN 0006-3207

15

Telemetry as a Tool to Study Spatial Behaviour and Patterns of Brown Bears as Affected by the Newly Constructed Egnatia Highway – N. Pindos - Greece

Mertzanis G. et al.*
NGO "Callisto" - Wildlife and Nature Conservation Society, Thessaloniki, Greece

1. Introduction

Throughout the world, traffic volumes have increased markedly in the past two decades (United Nations 1992) and the increasing area occupied by recently constructed roads is affecting wildlife populations in the EU from 1990 to 1998 circa 33.000 ha of landscape (10ha daily) have been used and occupied for transportation infrastructure development purposes. The average surface of undisturbed (by transportation infrastructure) continuous landscape ranges from 20 km2 in Belgium to 600 km2 in Finland with an EU average of 130 km2 (EEA, 2001). For many mammal populations, the main demonstrated impact of roads to date has been in terms of increased disturbance or mortality. Avoidance of otherwise suitable habitats in close proximity to roads has been shown to occur for brown bears *(Ursus arctos)* and wolves (*Canis lupus*) in the U.S.A. (McLellan and Shackleton 1988, Mace et al. 1996, Mech et al. 1988). For some mammal species, roads have been shown to act also as a considerable barrier to dispersal (Mader 1984). Roads can therefore have a significant effect in fragmenting wildlife populations and eventually lead them to local extinction (Fahrig and Merriam 1994). Increased awareness of environmental problems caused by infrastructure construction has moved engineers, ecologists and policy makers to develop planning concepts to deal with the impacts on nature and landscape. If avoidance of a certain project is not feasible, mitigation measures can be undertaken as a second planning concept.
In this general context of invasive roading and large scale transportation infrastructure development Greece has not "escaped". The "Egnatia" highway project of modern times was planned to connect the western part of the country with the eastern and serve as a trade route between the EU, through Italy and Greece, and the Orient. With funds allocated by the EU (Cohesion Funds) and the Hellenic Government, the modern Egnatia, only partly follows the route of its predecessor "Via Egnatia" from the Roman times (as of Rome's first

---

* Mazaris Ant.[1], Sgardelis St.[1], Aravidis El.[4], Giannakopoulos Al.[3], Godes C.[2], Riegler S.[2], Riegler A.[2] and Tragos Ath.[2]
1 Department of Ecology, School of Biology, Aristotle University, Thessaloniki, Greece,
2 NGO "Callisto" - Wildlife and Nature Conservation Society, Thessaloniki, Greece,
3 University of Aegean, Environmental Studies Dept, Lab. of Biodiversity & Management, Xenia Hills, Mytilini, Greece,
4 Development Agency of Thessaloniki Prefecture, Thessaloniki, Greece.

imperial roads), and is a 670 km long and 24.5m (+/- 5m) wide highway, thus making it one of the largest construction projects in Europe and part of the TENT (Trans-European Network Transportation). This highway actually connects Greece with all neighbouring countries and service 5 ports, 6 airports and 36% of the country's total population.
Throughout its course in northern Greece, the highway crosses also the Pindus mountain range, cutting through natural areas, which are of outstanding importance for biodiversity and several priority species of the Hellenic mammal fauna and avifauna (i.e. bear (*Ursus arctos)*, wolf (*Canis lupus*) etc. see maps 1 & 2) as well as for priority habitat types, according to E.U. Directive 92/43 "(i.e. pinus nigra forests 9530*) but also for being one of the last strongholds of the brown bear (Ursus arctos) in the southern Balkans. (see photos 1,2&3).

Photo 1., 2. and 3. Construction of the Egnatia highway

With only 290-350 bears remaining in Greece and the expected detrimental impact of the highway on natural habitats, bear population structure and movement patterns of the NE Pindus brown bear sub-population the NGO's were alerted and made several notifications to the competent authorities. In the very beginning hardly any mitigation measures were foreseen along the 37 km most critical highway stretch cutting through core brown bear habitat with a bear indigenous population estimated approximately at 80 ind . It is only after NGO's strong pressure that the revised highway EIA study finally incorporated the construction of a number of additional mitigation measures such as: tunnels, wildlife underpasses, green bridge and viaducts that are expected to prevent serious habitat fragmentation and population disruption of the indigenous large mammal species. Additional mitigation measures included a ban on hunting in a 2+2 km corridor along the highway, the construction of noise barriers, adequate fencing and the appropriate ecological landscaping of areas affected by the construction of the highway.
It is important to note that the above measures were taken only after a Council of the State verdict issued in 1997 and postulating the least environmentally costly alignment of this highway stretch (regarding especially bear populations and habitat), obliging EGNATIA ODOS A.E. (the construction supervisor) to carry out a revised EIA study for this most compromising (for the brown bear) 37km highway stretch and to incorporate additional mitigation measures such as: 13 tunnels (8.85 km), 11 bridges (2.64 km), 1-2 green bridges and 5 - 9 wildlife underpasses, thus mitigating about 31% of the 37km highway stretch. (photo 4.)

Photo 4. Partial view of the mitigated Egnatia Highway

Moreover in compliance to the relevant articles of the relevant EIA study, a special monitoring and research project was set-up and launched in 3 phases and in cooperation between the highway construction supervisor (EGNATIA ODOS A.E.) and specialized NGO's. The aim of this project was to monitor and assess the highway's impact on big mammals and their habitats prior and during highway construction as well as during highway operation. In compliance with the Joint Ministerial Decision for the 37km stretch Panagia - Grevena (4.1) of the Egnatia highway, the two phases (2003-2009) of the project were carried out in cooperation with three NGO's ("Arcturos", "Callisto" & Hellenic Ornithological Society) and two Universities (Aristotle University of Thessaloniki and University of Thessaly, comprising 4 Faculty departments). The two phases of the project were co-financed by the EGNATIA ODOS S.A. and the E.U. (DGREGIO). Implementation of the third phase is still on paper.It is worth mentioning that the implementation of this project was an integrated part of the environmental terms and provisions of the revised EIA study, the ex-ante part being of outstanding importance. The aim of the overall project was to evaluate the status of brown bear and wolf populations in the study area prior to and during the planned construction of the 37 km Egnatia highway stretch. The final objective of the project was a comparative evaluation of the effectiveness of the mitigations measures versus the status and ecological requirements of the targeted species in the study area. The required multilevel approach of this project encompassed several disciplines such as: Genetics, Ecology, Forestry, Wildlife management, provided by the aforementioned parties.

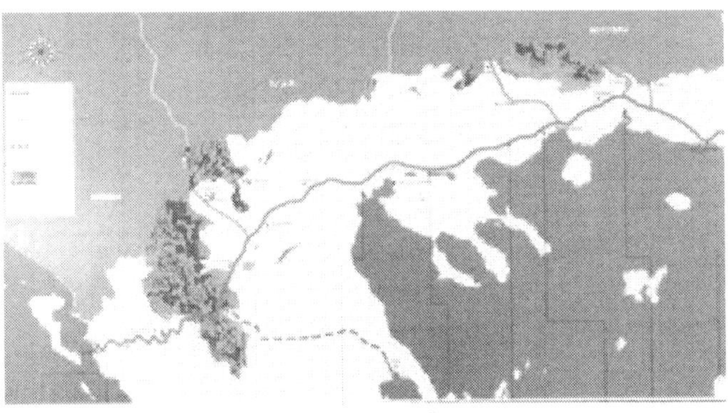

Map 1. Brown bear (Ursus arctos) distribution versus Egnatia highway total alignment (Greece)

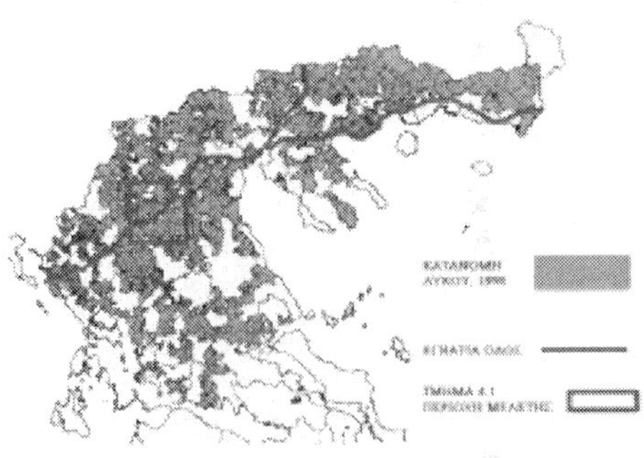

Map 2. Wolf (Canis lupus) distribution versus Egnatia highway total alignment (Greece)

To date the two first phases of the project (prior to construction 2002-2005 and during highway construction 2006-2009) have been completed. Due to lack of financial resources on behalf of the state authorities and the construction supervisor (EGNATIA ODOS A.E.) the third phase (monitoring of highway impact during construction) scheduled for 2009 has been delayed. Nevertheless and after three (3) traffic fatalities with two bear victims on the monitored highway stretch and which occurred within the first 4 months of the highway operation (between June and September 2009), further pressure was put from NGO's upon state authorities in order to replace the inappropriate highway fence with a bear proof fence. The fence was replaced in 2009 and 2010 although not keeping full standards recommendations (see photos).

Photo 5. First bear traffic fatality on Egnatia highway

Photo 6. New bear proof fence

Photo 7. Old inappropriate fence destroyed by bears highway crossings

Photo 8. New fence permeability problems due to inadequate standards (missing of the upper bent part)

The main objectives of the study were to investigate behavioral changes of the brown bears in response to the road as a disturbance factor in terms of :

- Potential changes in habitat use range
- Potential differences in movement distance (mean and max)
- Potential differences in movement patterns
- Habitat suitability conditions and status in relation to bear presence and activity.

2. Study area

The project area extends over almost 1000km^2 of a mixed forest and agricultural ecosystem and is located in the north-western part of Greece, in Pindos mountain range. Of this area 43.23% are forests, 31.11% are meadows (pasture lands), 19.47% agricultural lands, whereas human settlements occupy 3.69% of the total area. Major forest vegetation types comprise oak (*Quercus sp.*), black Pine (*Pinus nigra*) and beech (*Fagus sp.*) (see photos 1 & 2). The area is characterized by a mosaic of dense forests, openings and small scale cultivations. Altitude ranges between 500m -2.200 m. Specific sampling pressure was given to the sector that was more directly influenced by the highway construction works and which covers a surface of 160 sq.km. This surface includes the total length of the highway segment (37 km) in a "buffer zone" of 2+2 km width. The current alignment of the newly constructed Egnatia Motorway (total length 670 km), which is one of the largest transportation infrastructures projects in Europe and part of the TENT, cuts through the study area over a 50km stretch. In the total study area the overall highway mitigation measures comprise: 20 tunnels (16.465 km), 12 bridges (2.84 km), 1 green bridge (50m), 7 wildlife underpasses, and 59 culverts have been placed thus mitigating about 38,6% of the 50 km highway segment. The wider study area extends over 5.229 km^2 and there are 48.293 inhabitants (9.56 id/ km^2).

Photo 9. and 10. Two different aspects of the study area: mixed coniferous and deciduous forests and oak forests with openings and small scale cultivations

3. Materials and methods

3.1 Telemetry protocol

Over a three 3 year bear monitoring period (2007-2009) during the project's second phase, field work has focused on satellite telemetry combined to systematic collection of bear signs of presence and activity. An additional monitoring protocol was developed using thermo-sensitive, IR and conventional pre-programmed video and photo cameras.

In total twenty two (22) adult and sub-adult brown bears have been fitted with GPS/GSM radiocollars: eighteen (15) males and seven (7) females. Bears were trapped from April to mid May and from September to mid-October in 2007 and 2008 within a buffer zone of 10 kilometres along the Egnatia Highway stretch 4.1 (routing from "Grevena to Metsovo"). We captured bears using Aldrich foot snares (Johnson and Pelton 1980) and immobilized bears with a zolazepam-tiletamine /medetomidine combination and reversed with atipamezole (Riegler et al. 2009). Body measurements were recorded and a premolar was extracted to determine bear age (Stoneberg and Jonkel 1966).

Photo 11., 12., 13. and 14. Bears equiped with radio-collars - radio-collars types: Simplex, Tellus GSM

Bears were fitted with Televilt/Followit Simplex, Tellus, Tellus GSM and Tensyx GPS collars with remote drop-offs. GPS collars were fitted with devices such as VHF transmitter, mortality -activity sensors and were programmed to record a location every 60 minutes. During the denning period we programmed each GPS-receiver to obtain a location fix twice a day. For Simplex and Tellus collars data were remotely downloaded from the ground four times monthly using a RX-900 Receiver (Televilt TVP Positioning AB, Lindesberg, Sweden). Tellus/GPS-GSM collars worked via cell phone coverage and data were downloaded through internet every 8 hours via Televilt-Followit server.

3.2 Home range size

We calculated home ranges with Arc View 3.2.a and the Home Range Extension (A. R. Rodgers and A. P. Carr, Ontario Ministry of Natural Resources) using the minimum convex polygon (100%MCP), 95%MCP, Fixed Kernel method and 50% contours of activity for core areas (areas of high intensity of use). The 100% MCP estimates were used to facilitate comparisons between studies and regions. Fixed Kernel Method range analysis was performed because, in addition to estimating range size, it reveals range use patterns, using a smoothing factor determined by least squares cross validation (LSCV) (Seaman and Powell 1996). We ignored autocorrelation within the data because the data continued to exhibit a high degree of dependence even when using extended fix intervals (24 hr; e.g., Reynolds and Laundre´ 1990, Rooney et al. 1998, De Solla et al. 1999). We tested collars GPS accuracy in the field and the mean error was 30m (Giannakopoulos et al. 2010).

Data gathered from the aforementioned methods were mainly used to identify bear presence as well as bear movements patterns and spatial behavior versus the highway alignment and especially in correlation to two main factors:

- the disturbance related to the construction phase
- the location of the different mitigation measures

3.3 Habitat use – movement distances - movement patterns – habitat suitability

More specifically data analyses were used in order to test whether the highway construction phase affected:

(a) the dispersal ability, (b) preferences on habitat use and (c) distributional patterns of the species.

To estimate **potential changes in habitat use range** we estimated home range polygons (95% Kernel core area). Additionally group home range estimates were based on home range size. We also calculated min distance of polygons from road using t-test and ANOVAs. Data were organized and grouped according to the sex of the individuals and the seasons. Adequate data to perform statistical analyses were found for males in spring and summer and for females in summer.

The analysis was repeated for males and females and for data collected at different seasons

To estimate **potential changes in movement distances** we analyzed day and night movement distances but also home ranges of each individual (estimated by using Kernel based methods) to examine whether the distance from the highway is an important indicator of the quality or quantity of brown bears activity levels. Mean and maximum moving distances according to the time of activity and distance from the highway were examined as well as variations in mean direction with respect to the distance from highway (angular analysis of point patterns). We used ANOVAs and the analysis was repeated for males and females and for data collected on daytime or at night.

To estimate **potential changes in movement patterns** angular analysis of point patterns (changes in mean direction with respect to the distance from road) was performed according to the following protocol:

- we used point records to describe movement patterns
- we grouped moment pattern data into 4 categories in relation to distance from the highway (0-2000m, 2000-4000m, 4000-6000m & >6000m)
- we used circular stats (*Rayleigh's Mean Direction test*) to test differences in direction

To **assess habitat suitability** in relation to bear presence and prediction of use of a certain point (or area) of the HR, we used a series of digital sources to derive potential predictor variables (land use, topographical, vegetation). In addition, 17 variables were calculated by using neighbourhood statistics techniques. The significance of distance from highway and of the former predictor variables upon species distribution and habitat use were assessed by using Generalized Linear Models (GLM), Logistic Regression (LR) and Regression and Classification Trees (CART). Relative abundance - (Generalised Linear Models)(Naves et. al., 2003, Wiegandet al., 2004, Nielsen et al., 2006).

For each bear habitat pixel we calculated the following parameters using neighbourhood statistics:

- Average altitude within a 5 pixels radius from the central pixel. This variable allows to characterize the altitude of the central pixel based not only on its proper value but also on the values of the neighboring pixels as for the pixel selection by a bear depends also on its accessibility which is related to the altitudinal variation (ruggedness).
- Average altitude within a 20 pixels radius from the central pixel.
- Altitude coefficient of variance within a radius of 5 pixels from the central pixel. This variable allows the quantification of altitude variance in a wider area.
- Altitudes range within a 5 pixel radius from the central pixel. This variable examines the max and min altitude differences in an area and functions as an indicator of selection or avoidance of movement in the given area.
- Average slope value within a 5 pixels radius from the central pixel.
- Coefficient of variance of the average slope value within a 5 pixels radius from the central pixel.
- Coefficient of variance of the average slope value within a 25 pixels radius from the central pixel.
- Slope range values within a 5 pixels range from the central pixel.
- Slope range values within a 15 pixels range from the central pixel.
- Slope range values within a 25 pixels range from the central pixel.
- Vegetation types variability index within a 5 pixels radius from the central pixel. Vegetation types variability was calculated after Shannon's (H) index as follows:

$$H' = \sum_{i=1}^{S} p_i \cdot \ln p_i$$

Where: *H* the Shannon's index value

- p_i: is the relative abundance of each vegetation type, which is calculated from the percentage of occurrence of the characteristics of a given vegetation type compared to overall vegetation characteristics within in the same pixel.
- *S* the number of vegetation types.

- Shannon (vegetation) diversity index within a 10 pixels radius from the central pixel.
- Shannon (vegetation) diversity index within a 5 pixels radius from the central pixel.
- Number of different vegetation types within a 5 pixels radius from the central pixel.
- Number of different vegetation types within a 10 pixels radius from the central pixel.
- (%) of contribution of the dominant vegetation type over the total number of recorded vegetation types within 5 and 10 pixels radius from the central pixel.
- (%) of contribution of 2nd and 3rd rank vegetation type over the total number of recorded vegetation types within 5 and 10 pixels radius from the central pixel.

Bear telemetry data sets were incorporated on these pixel maps. For each map pixel with a bear radiolocation we extracted all relevant information related to topographic and vegetation characteristics, distances from the highway and the values of all neighborhood statistics variables as described above. It is important to note that in a random pixel of the study area there may be more than one radiolocation indicating bear presence. This may be attributed to selection and repetitive use (by one or more bears) of a given pixel due to its specific attributes and characteristics. Therefore it is interesting to investigate the effect of pixels attributes upon the probability of their use by bears (preference/avoidance) but also the frequency of their use. For this we have developed prediction models focusing on various characteristics related to spatial behavior and presence of bears, according to two main approaches:

- To what extent the selected variables allow prediction of abundance of bear presence in given areas. This allows to identify which variables contribute most in the selection of most frequently used/visited habitat units by bears.
- prediction models emphasized only on the presence or absence of bears in each pixel without taking into account the frequency of use (stationary of transitional) of each pixel.

For the first approach we used General Linear Models (GLM) which allow the development of linear relations between the dependent variable and a group of categorized or qualitative factors but also with continuous variables (covariates) through specific operational connection functions (Quinn and Keough, 2002). These models allow a non-normal distribution of the dependent variable. We used Pearson's correlation coefficient to investigate the correlation degree between all variables. In total 15 variables were kept in our analysis. Their utility to predict abundance of bear presence over the study area was examined. Of them, two (vegetation types and aspect) were introduced in the model as "factors" and the rest as "covariates" (continuous numeric variables).

The possibility of implementation of those models and their prediction efficiency in bear presence abundance and habitat pixels use according to the explanatory variables, was evaluated following different statistical tests such as: likelihood-ratio chi-square test, Deviance, Pearson Chi-Square statistics (Quinn and Keough, 2002).

For the second approach we developed a Logistic Regression model (LR) which is only applied in the case of binary data (presence/absence). We used a logic function to interrelate the key variable (presence and bear activity) with the group of descriptive variables. We performed a group of diagnostic tests such as Hosmer-Lemeshow goodness-of-fit statistic, improvement of chi-square test in order to examine the suitability and efficiency of the model as a predictor tool for bear presence or absence in a given pixel of the study area.

Additionally we developed Classification Trees (CT) by using bear presence and absence as the dependent variable and we examined probable classification rules for the explanatory (descriptive variables). Here again we performed a group of diagnostic tests in order to examine the efficiency of the produced rules from the aforementioned analysis. This type of analysis is based on artificial intelligence methods (machine learning techniques principle) (Vayssieres κ.α. 2000, De'ath & Fabricius 2000, Thuiller κ.α. 2003, Mazaris κ.α. 2006).

4. Results

Telemetry data from the twenty two (22) radio-collared bears of the sample have yielded up to **42,849** GPS radiolocations. Part of the sampled radiolocations in relation to the highway alignment and the highway buffer corridor and the study area are shown on map 3.

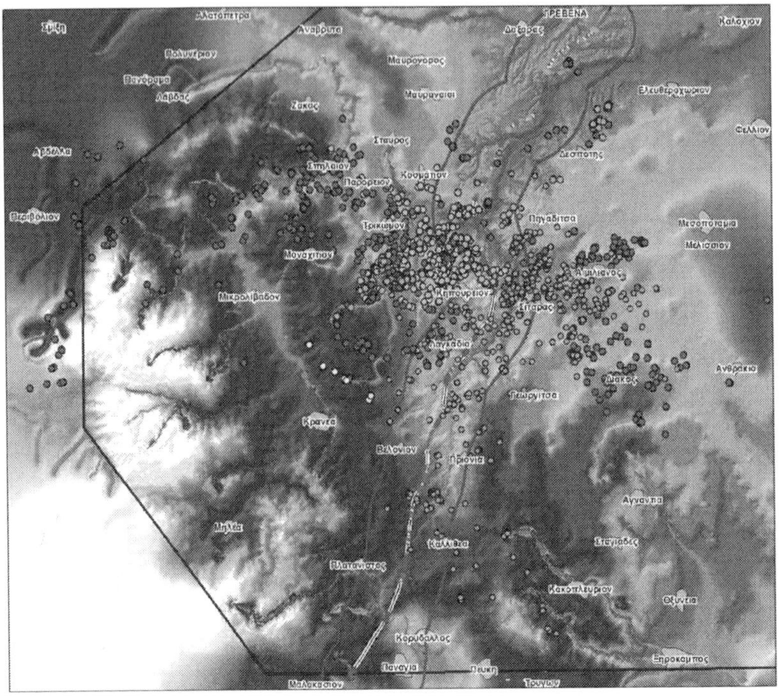

Map 3. Radiolocations of seven (7) different bears from the sample in the study area

4.1 Home range

The annual average MCP100 home range of all bears of the sample was 213,77 ± 35,8 (SE) and ranged from 58,13 - 362,12 Km^2 (Table 1). The mean MCP100 for males (n=5) was 271.075 Km^2 ± 26.12 and for females (n=3) 118.245 Km^2 ± 48.85. The male annual home-ranges were significantly larger than female using also the other three estimating methods: 95%MCP, Fixed Kernel Method 95% and Core Areas 50% (Mann–Whitney U test: Z=--2,236, P=0.025).

Home range sizes of males (n=5) differ significantly between all seasons (Friedman test, Monte-Carlo simulation for exact P<0.05). Home range sizes of females (n=3) did also differ significantly between all seasons only for MCP100 and FKM (Friedman test, Monte-Carlo simulation for exact $P<0.05$). Males home range sizes were significantly larger than females with all estimate methods (Kruskal-Wallis test: MCP100: $\chi^2=11$, $P=0.012$, MCP95: $\chi^2=10.76$, $P=0.013$, FK95: $\chi^2=9.6$, $P=0.022$ and CA50: $\chi^2=9.33$, $P=0.025$).(Giannakopoulos et al.2011). (see also table 1 and 2).

In addition we found that the bears (2 males and 2 females) who kept collars more than one year seemed to maintain the same territories. Moreover the spatial patterns and distribution of home ranges between males and females were delineated in most of the cases by natural barriers and landmarks such as rivers, big streams, county roads and in some cases according with the topographic complexity (Giannakopoulos et al. subm.).

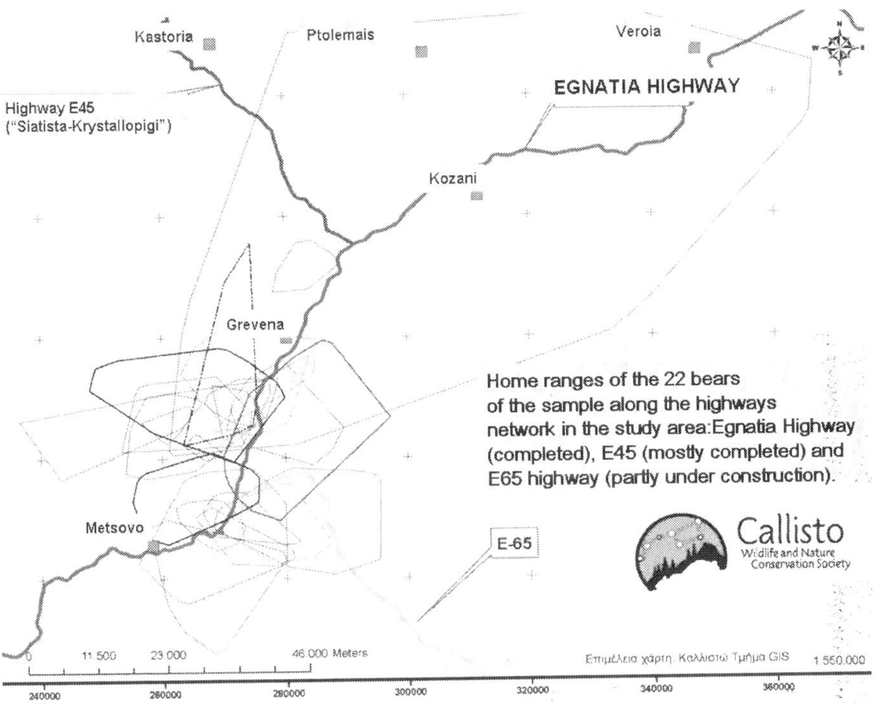

Map 4. Home ranges of 22 bears of the sample versus highways network in the study area

Sex	Age	N	Gps Lo	MCP100	MCP95	FKM	CA50
Males	Adult	5	22083	271±26,1	200±14,5	130±15,1	30±4,2
Females	Adult	3	15502	118±48,8	72±28,2	39±13	7±3,2

Table 1. Annual home range sizes of GPS collared bears (2007-2009) estimated with (MCP100, MCP95, FKM and CA50) in Northeastern Pindos mountains Greece (n=8)

Data from the above table (1) refer only to the bears of the sample (males and females) that have kept their collar for an entire year cycle. A more analytical presentation of data on seasonal home range sizes on the overall sample are presented in table (2).

From map (4) we observe a high level of home range overlap among most bears. Fifty-nine of the 82 possible pairings of bears indicated overlapping areas according to the MCP95 and FK methods. For areas of high intensity of use (CA50) 40.24% pairings of bears indicated overlapping areas (Giannakopoulos et al. subm.).

Bear	Sex	Spring MCP100	Summer MCP100	Autumn MCP100	Winter MCP100
MELIS	MALE	159,641	251,34	178,094	-
AL PATSINO	MALE	34,657	-	-	-
KOYTALAINOS	MALE	153,127	54,46	-	-
TETRADAKTYLOS	MALE	194,729	45,646	-	-
STRATIGOS	MALE	22,054	48,908	-	-
KALLISTO	FEMALE	13,1	-	-	-
KATERINA	FEMALE	7,09*	28,457	54,729	7,459
TOBIAS	MALE	148,126	64,061	119,532	17,46
MONAXH	FEMALE	-	-	26,171	0
ALEKA	FEMALE	1,381*	38,18	204,066	1,744
KAPETANIOS	MALE	190,297	322,4	207,807	22,789
KLEOPATRA	FEMALE	75,004	50,473	30,542	2,035
ARIS	MALE	59,076	39,424	-	-
DIAS	MALE	21,662	46,594	-	-
SOFOKLIS	MALE	196,023	337,71	14,74	-
HLIAS	MALE	170,466	248,97	76,969	7,861
LIGNOS	MALE	195,927	140,053	53,447	28,349
PETHEROS	MALE	174,917	155,129	147,834	54,901
TYXERH	FEMALE	-	54,764	9,197	-
POLIMYLOS	MALE	2.684	731,68	992,101	126,409

Table 2. Seasonal Home ranges (km^2) for Brown bears (n=20) in Northeastern Pindos mountain range in Greece, 2007-2009

4.2 Potential changes in habitat use amplitude and range

Regarding the **potential changes in habitat use amplitude and range (surface units)** in relation to the distance from the highway, the results of our analysis demonstrated that the size of the habitat units (within spring and summer male bears home range) significantly increased with the distance from the highway while their number (of used habitat units) decreased as the distance from highway increased.

The differences between the number of habitat units and their size (surface) used inside the home range in relation to distance from the highway were statistically significant in all cases of males bears in spring and summer (spring: F=5.419, P<0.01; summer: F=6.52, P<0.01) and for females in summer (F=18.735; P<0.01). An example of this differentiation is given on fig.1 in the case of the male bears of the sample.

More specifically in the case of all male individuals of the sample the number of used habitat units (perceived through clustered radiolocations) is significantly higher as their surface size decreases and subsequently their distance from the highway decreases as well (spring: x^2=96.63, P<0.01; summer: x^2= 20.204, P<0.01). This means that larger ranges in surface and limited distinct ranges (in clustered radiolocations) were observed as the distance from the highway increases.

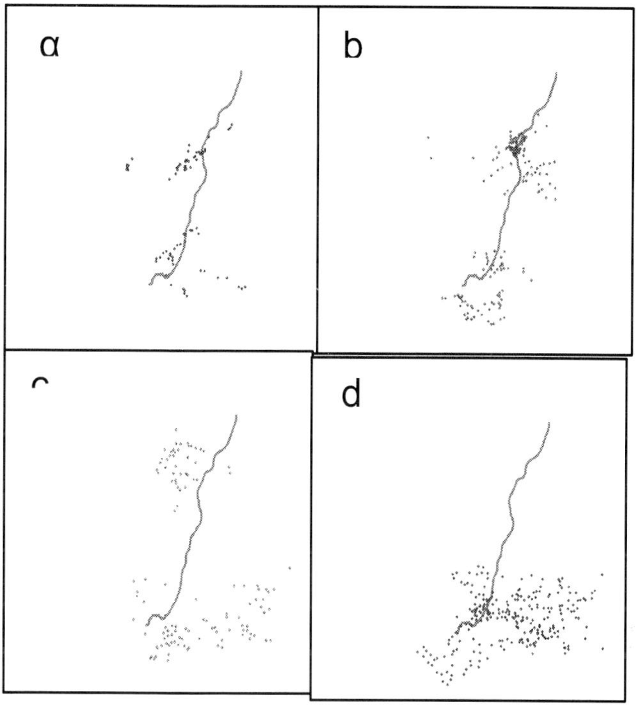

Fig. 1. Distribution of habitat units clusters (from a to d) for male bears in spring. Diagrams from **a** to **d** correspond to different increment units of activity areas (surfaces) within the home range

4.3 Potential differences in movement distance and patterns

Regarding **potential differences in movement distance and patterns:** we found no statistically significant differences in dispersal patterns of bears with respect to the time (hour-daytime/night time) of activity and/or distance from the highway. Analyses showed no statistically significant differences between the maximum and minimum distances travelled by male and female individuals during the day or night (in most of the cases up to $P>0.05$) in relation to the distance from the highway. Nevertheless significant differences were observed in specific cases when bears movements were studied individually and seasonally but even in these cases there was not enough evidence of a specific pattern regarding spatial behavior of the bears versus the distance of the highway. No significant differences were observed between the average and maximum distances travelled by bears in relation to their distances from the highway under construction. Similarly, we found only limited evidence to support an effect of the highway upon bears movement angles when approaching the highway corridor.

4.4 Habitat suitability

Regarding **habitat suitability** analyses in relation to bear presence and habitat use: *distance from highway* was recognized as one of the statistically significant variables affecting both analyses: the relative *abundance* (GLM) (table 3) and the *bear presence/absence* (LR) (table 4) thus influencing in both scenario cases the selection and the frequency of use of the different sites (habitat units) within the study area and in relation to the presence of the highway under construction. Bears seem to appear more often at distant sites from the highway. For the first analysis: **bear abundance and frequency of habitat pixels use,** of the set of 13 variables selected, seven (7) could be used as reliable prediction tools. Results of this analysis are presented in table (3).

Variables	Wald Chi-Square	P-value	Wald statistic	P-value
Aspect	80,444	0.000	65,844	0.000
Distance from road.	288,652	0.000	1196,691	0.000
Mean altitude within 1.5km radius.	21,683	0.000	15,199	0.000
CV of altitude within 1.5km radius	23,198	0.000	7,810	0.005
CV of mean slope within 1.5km radius	19,902	0.000	16,071	0.000
CV of mean slope within 7.5km radius	104,065	0.000	181,321	0.000
Diversity of vegetation types within 1.5km radius	8,961	0.003	60,570	0.000

Table 3. General Linear Models parameters as predictors of bear abundance in relation to the presence of the highway

For P values < 0.01, the related variables are considered to effectively contribute in the prediction model. We notice that vegetation types, altitude and aspect are recognized as important variables for the prediction of areas (habitat units) with more abundant/frequent bear presence and use. We also notice that the slope variance in neighbouring pixels also plays a role in the spatial distribution of the signs of presence. As stated above distance from the highway is the key variable with high statistical value in the model thus influencing site selection by bears. The negative value of the related coefficient indicates that the number of the most frequent bear occurrences in specific sites increases as the distance from the highway decreases.

Our analysis showed that there are no specific habitat parameters close to the highway corridor that hinder bears movements. Bears utilize the same habitat types within the overall landscape but move in a much more "conservative" pattern (in terms of duration and habitat surface used) when found in proximity of the highway corridor.

The second analysis regarding **presence/ absence** data (by means of LR & CART- *predictive accuracy of models which was high*) demonstrated a series of topographical and vegetation characteristics (habitat features) as important predictors for bear presence or absence. Here again **distance from highway** was recognized, as mentioned above, as one of the critical factors affecting the presence of an animal in a given point (pixel) of its home range. According to table (4) we may notice that a group of variables remains effective in the model for the prediction of bear presence in pixels with specific characteristics. We once again notice the importance of "altitude" and "slope" and their range of variations as prediction indicators. It comes out that the combination of landscape ruggedness with the characteristics of certain vegetation types and the distance from the highway influence selection or avoidance by bears of a given pixel (habitat unit).

Variable	Coefficient	Wald	Level of importance
Average altitude within 5 pixels radius.	-0,004	15,199	0,000
Altitude coefficient variation within 5 pixels radius.	0,067	7,810	0,005
Average slope within 5 pixels radius.	0,039	58,315	0,000
Average slope coefficient variation within 5 pixels radius.	-0,003	16,071	0,000
Average slope coefficient variation within 15 pixels radius.	-0,015	181,321	0,000
Vegetation types variability	-0,098	0,641	0,423
Vegetation Type		23,492	0,001
Type (1)	-1,207	7,244	0,007
Type (2)	-1,112	11,511	0,001
Type (3)	-1,102	11,466	0,001
Type (4)	-1,117	8,990	0,003
Type (5)	-1,186	13,805	0,000
Type (6)	-,957	5,891	0,015
Type (7)	-,585	2,712	0,100
Distance from highway	-0,000114	1196,691	0,000
Aspect		65,844	0,000
Slope	-0,007	10,344	0,001
Number of different vegetation types within a 5 pixel radius	-0,477	60,570	0,000
(%) of contribution of dominant vegetation type within a 5 pixels radius	-0,005	0,682	0,409
(%) of contribution of the 2nd rank vegetation type within a 5 pixels radius	0,001	0,611	0,435
(%) of contribution of the 3rd rank vegetation type within a 5 pixels radius	0,003	1,978	0,160

Table 4. Results from the LR analysis for the prediction model on bear presence/absence.

The negative sign of variable "distance from highway" indicates that presence or absence of bears decreases as distance from the highway increases. In a recent study by Roever et al. (2008) it was found that grizzlies showed a relatively high frequency of occurrence in areas nearby forest roads despite the relatively high mortality probability rate in these areas (also McLellan, 1998, Benn and Herrero, 2002, Johnson κ.α., 2004 και Nielsen κ.α., 2004). But this phenomenon might also be related to other parameters such as:

α) the type of data used in the analysis
β) a possible adaptive "shift" in bears behavior.

In our case we may have two possible explanations:

1. the topography of our study area allows bears to approach and use sectors in the immediate vicinity of the highway under construction in order to move towards other important sectors such as denning areas, high food availability areas etc. We have to bear in mind that this is a fraction of the whole picture, as at a wider scale (including our study areas) there might be bears avoiding completely the highway sector or moving at longer distances.
2. More frequent bear occurrence and use of pixels in the vicinity of the highway maybe related to the fact that bears do valorize small surface habitat units due to the fact that they still remain attractive. It is also likely that bears are waiting for the appropriate moment to cross the highway and therefore are attempting to locate more appropriate crossing points.(Mace κ.α., 1996). The highway as an artificial barrier is a stress factor and is likely to induce a certain modification in bears spatial behavior exposing a limitation of movements combined to an opportunistic mobility related to the most favorable low disturbance conditions.

The **CRT analysis** showed also that the variable "distance from highway" was used to separate two central "branches" of the classification tree in the early analysis stages. Two differentiated branches are defined according to a limit value of 4.996 m of distance from the highway. When this distance is <4.996 m then a combination of topographic characteristics in relation to high slope values and medium altitude values are characterizing the pixels used by bears.

In the second case d > 4.996 m, vegetation types but also certain combinations of topographic characteristics define the habitat use patterns in each pixel. It also came out from this analysis that pixels at a distance > 8.434m have lower use frequencies by the sampled bears.

5. Conclusions-discussion

A general conclusion would be that the presence of the highway under construction and the distance from it in relation to bear presence, abundance and activity is an interrelated and dynamic system in which telemetry is the most appropriate technique to approach and understand it.

The following behavioral patterns in relation to bear activity, movements and habitat use have been identified:

- High in number and small surfaced clusters of bear activity and movements appear when the animals are located at close distance from the highway, whereas less clusters in number and on larger surfaces appear when the animals are located at a longer distance from the highway.
- This differentiation which in the first case appears fragmented in time and space and in the second case continuous and more expanded maybe related to the disturbance factor of the highway under construction upon bears activity and spatial behavior or in a more pronounced habitat fragmentation problem close to the highway due to its degradation because of the construction woks.
- For male individuals which yielded a larger data set, we have observed that the number of activity and habitat use clusters increases with the fragmentation degree of the larger zones of used habitat. Therefore we may conclude that it is not some different habitat features that hinder bear habitat use when close to the highway but more the fact of a quantitative and qualitative reduction and fragmentation of the habitat units in most probably relation to highway construction.

- Distance from the highway does not seem to influence independently bear habitat selection activity and abundance (presence/absence), but co-acts in synergy with other habitat characteristics.
- Findings from all three models agree on the importance of the "distance from the highway" as a critical variable for the prediction of bears spatial behavior in relation to the highway. Therefore the new highway represents a critical parameter that significantly affects distribution, habitat use, movement selection and frequency of occurrences of brown bears.
- The frequent presence of brown bears within the vicinity of the road network highlights the need for direct and effective protection measures in the area. (i.e adequate and appropriate fencing).

Considering previous results we suggest that animal (bear) activity is not reduced but rather qualitatively affected by the existence of the highway.

Overall we suggest that the new highway functions as a critical landscape parameter (barrier) that seems to significantly affect distribution, habitat use, movement patterns and frequency of occurrences of brown bears.

The results of our study will essentially contribute in further adjustment of mitigation measures along the highway as well as in close monitoring of their efficiency during highway operation in the critical areas.

6. Acknowledgements

Telemetry research was possible in the framework of the two "Monitoring projects on impact evaluation of Egnatia highway construction (stretch 4.1 "Panagia-Grevena" and stretch "Panagia-Metsovo") on large mammals in the area of Grevena-Ioannina and Trikala (2006-2009). This project was co-funded by EGNATIA ODOS SA, Hellenic Ministry of Environment, Planning & Public Works and the EU (DG Regio). We thank the Forestry Services of Kastoria, Grevena & Kalambaka for forestry data provision and the NGO CALLISTO field team : Sp. Galinos, M.Petridou, H. Pilidis, Y. Tsaknakis and local assistant Y.Lazarou for their precious help. Special thanks go also to Dr. John Beecham, from Idaho Fish & Wildlife Service, U.S and to Yorgos Iliopoulos for their help and advice.

7. References

Austin, M. P. 2002. Spatial Prediction of Species Distribution. an Interface Between Ecological Theory and Statistical Modelling. Ecological Modelling 157:101-118.

Benn, B., Herrero, S., 2002. Grizzly bear mortality and human access in Banff and Yoho National Parks, 1971–1989. Ursus 13, 213–221.

Bergman, C. M., J. A. Schaefer, and S. N. Luttich. 2000. Caribou Movement as a Correlated Random Walk. Oecologia 123:364-374.

Bontadina, F., H. Schofield, and B. Naef-Daenzer. 2002. Radio-Tracking Reveals That Lesser Horseshoe Bats (Rhinolophus Hipposideros) Forage in Woodland. Journal of Zoology 258:281-290.

Debeljak, M., S. Dzeroski, K. Jerina, A. Kobler, and M. Adamic. 2001. Habitat Suitability Modelling for Red Deer (Cervus Elaphus L.) In South-Central Slovenia With Classification Trees. Ecological Modelling 138:321-330.

Dettki, H., R. Lφfstrand, and L. Edenius. Modeling habitat suitability for moose in coastal northern Sweden: empirical vs. process-oriented approaches. AMBIO 32[8], 549-556. 2003.

Death, G. and Fabricius. K. E., 2000. Classification and Regression Trees: a Powerful Yet Simple Technique for Ecological Data Analysis. Ecology 81:3178-3192.

Franco, A. M. A., J. C. Brito, and J. Almeida. 2000. Modelling Habitat Selection of Common Cranes Grus Grus Wintering in Portugal Using Multiple Logistic Regression. Ibis 142:351-358.

Giannakopoulos Al., Akriotis T., Mertzanis Y.(2011) : Spatio-temporal interactions in relation to social behaviour of Brown bears in Greece (submitted.)

Glenz, C., A. Massolo, D. Kuonen, and R. Schlaepfer. 2001. A Wolf Habitat Suitability Prediction Study in Valais (Switzerland). Landscape and Urban Planning 55:55-65.

Gros, P. M. and M. Rejmanek. 1999. Status and Habitat Preferences of Uganda Cheetahs: an Attempt to Predict Carnivore Occurrence Based on Vegetation Structure. Biodiversity and Conservation 8:1561-1583.

Guisan, A., J. P. Theurillat, and F. Kienast. 1998. Predicting the Potential Distribution of Plant Species in an Alpine Environment. Journal of Vegetation Science 9:65-74.

Guisan, A. and N. E. Zimmermann. 2000. Predictive Habitat Distribution Models in Ecology. Ecological Modelling 135:147-186.

Hastie, L. C., S. L. Cooksley, F. Scougall, M. R. Young, P. J. Boon, and M. J. Gaywood.2003. Characterization of Freshwater Pearl Mussel (Margaritifera Margaritifera) Riverine Habitat Using River Habitat Survey Data. Aquatic Conservation-Marine and Freshwater Ecosystems 13:213-224.

Heithaus, M. R., L. M. Dill, G. J. Marshall, and B. Buhleier. 2002. Habitat Use andForaging Behavior of Tiger Sharks (Galeocerdo Cavier) in a Seagrass Ecosystem. Marine Biology 140:237-248.

Hirzel, A. H. and R. Arlettaz. 2003. Modeling Habitat Suitability for Complex Species Distributions by Environmental-Distance Geometric Mean. Environmental Management 32:614-623.

Hirzel, A. H., J. Hausser, D. Chessel, and N. Perrin. 2002. Ecological-Niche Factor Analysis: How to Compute Habitat- Suitability Maps Without Absence Data? Ecology 83:2027-2036.

Hirzel, A. H., V. Helfer, and F. Metral. 2001. Assessing Habitat-Suitability Models With a Virtual Species. Ecological Modelling 145:111-121.

Huettmann, F. and J. Linke. 2003. An Automated Method to Derive Habitat Preferences of Wildlife in Gis and Telemetry Studies: a Flexible Software Tool and Examples of Its Application. Zeitschrift Fur Jagdwissenschaft 49:219-232.

Jerina, K., M. Debeljak, S. Dzeroski, A. Kobler, and M. Adamic. 2003. Modeling the Brown Bear Population in Slovenia - a Tool in the Conservation Management of a Threatened Species. Ecological Modelling 170:453-469.

Johnson, C. J., K. L. Parker, D. C. Heard, and M. P. Gillingham. 2002. Movement Parameters of Ungulates and Scale-Specific Responses to the Environment. Journal of Animal Ecology 71:225-235.

Johnson, C.J., Boyce, M.S., Schwartz, C.C., Haroldson, M.A., 2004. Modeling survival: application of the multiplicative hazards model to Yellowstone grizzly bear. J. Wildl. Manage. 68, 966–978.

Jones, P. F., R. J. Hudson, and D. R. Farr. 2002. Evaluation of a Winter Habitat Suitability Index Model for Elk in West-Central Alberta. Forest Science 48:417-425.

Kobler, A. and M. Adamic. 2000. Identifying Brown Bear Habitat by a Combined Gisand Machine Learning Method. Ecological Modelling 135:291-300.

Le Pape, O., F. Chauvet, S. Mahevas, P. Lazure, D. Guerault, and Y. Desaunay. 2003. Quantitative Description of Habitat Suitability for the Juvenile Common Sole (Solea Solea, L.) In the Bay of Biscay (France) and the Contribution of Different Habitats to the Adult Population. Journal of Sea Research 50:139-149.

Mace, R.D. Waller, J.S. Manley, T.L. Lyon L.J. and Zuuring, H. 1996. Relationships among grizzly bears, roads and habitat in the Swan Mountains, Montana, Journal of Applied Ecology 33, 1395–1404.

McLellan, B.N., 1998. Maintaining viability of brown bears along the southern fringe of their distribution. Ursus 10, 607–611.

Manderson, J. P., B. A. Phelan, C. Meise, L. L. Stehlik, A. J. Bejda, J. Pessutti, L. Arlen, A. Draxler, and A. W. Stoner. 2002. Spatial Dynamics of Habitat Suitability for the Growth of Newly Settled Winter Flounder Pseudopleuronectes Americanus in an Estuarine Nursery. Marine Ecology-Progress Series 228:227-239.

Massolo, A. and A. Meriggi. 1998. Factors Affecting Habitat Occupancy by Wolves in Northern Apennines (Northern Italy): a Model of Habitat Suitability.Ecography 21:97-107.

Matthiopoulos, J. 2003. Model-Supervised Kernel Smoothing for the Estimation of Spatial Usage. Oikos 102:367-377.

Mazaris, D. A., Matsinos, G. Y., Margaritoulis, D., 2006. Analyzing the profiles of nest site selection of loggerhead sea turtles. A case study of the island of Zakynthos, W-Greece. Journal of Experimental Marine Biology and Ecology 336, 157 - 162

Mauritzen, M., A. E. Derocher, O. Wiig, S. E. Belikov, A. N. Boltunov, E. Hansen, and G. W. Garner. 2002. Using Satellite Telemetry to Define Spatial Population Structure in Polar Bears in the Norwegian and Western Russian Arctic. Journal of Applied Ecology 39:79-90.

Mcgrath, M. T., S. Destefano, R. A. Riggs, L. L. Irwin, and G. J. Roloff. 2003. Spatially Explicit Influences on Northern Goshawk Nesting Habitat in the Interior Pacific Northwest. Wildlife Monographs1-63.

McLoughlin, P. D., H. D. Cluff, R. J. Gau, R. Mulders, R. L. Case, and F. Messier. 2002. Population Delineation of Barren-Ground Grizzly Bears in the Central Canadian Arctic. Wildlife Society Bulletin 30:728-737.

Miller, J. and J. Franklin. 2002. Modeling the Distribution of Four Vegetation Alliances Using Generalized Linear Models and Classification Trees With Spatial Dependence. Ecological Modelling 157:227-247.

Mladenoff, D. J., T. A. Sickley, and A. P. Wydeven. 1999. Predicting Grey Wolf Landscape Recolonization: Logistic Regression Models Vs. New Field Data. Ecological Applications 9:37-44.

Naves, J., Wiegand, T., Revilla, E., and Delibes. M., 2003., Endangered species balancing between natural and human constrains: the case of brown bears (Ursus arctos) in northern Spain Conservation Biology 17:1276-1289.

Nielsen, E.S., Boyce M.S. and Stenhouse, G.B., 2006. A habitat-based framework for grizzly bear conservation in Alberta. Biological Conservation, 130, 217-229

Nielsen, S.E., 2005. Habitat ecology, conservation, and projected population viability of grizzly bears (Ursus arctos L.) in west-central Alberta, Canada. Ph.D. Thesis. Department of Biological Sciences, University of Alberta, Edmonton, Alberta.

Patthey, P. 2003. Habitat and corridor selection of an expanding red deer (Cervus elaphus) population.

Peeters Ethm and J. J. P. Gardeniers. 1998. Logistic Regression as a Tool for Defining Habitat Requirements of Two Common Gammarids. Freshwater Biology 39:605-615.

Quinn, G.P., Keough, M.J., 2002. Experimental Design and Data Analysis for Biologists. Cambridge University Press, Cambridge;

Riegler S., Riegler Ar., Mertzanis Y., Giannakopoulos Al., Tragos Ath: Recovery times s in brown bears in greece using zolazepam-tiletamine/medetomidine/ketamine and Atipamezole, Ursus (in prep.).

Roever, C.L., Boyce, M.S., Stenhouse, G.B. 2008. Grizzly bears and forestry II: Grizzly bear habitat selection and conflicts with road placement. Forest Ecology and Management 256, 1262–1269.

Robertson, M. P., C. I. Peter, M. H. Villet, and B. S. Ripley. 2003. Comparing Models for Predicting Species' Potential Distributions: a Case Study Using Correlative and Mechanistic Predictive Modelling Techniques. Ecological Modelling 164:153-167.

Rondinini, C. and C. P. Doncaster. 2002. Roads as Barriers to Movement for Hedgehogs. Functional Ecology 16:504-509.

Schadt, S., E. Revilla, T. Wiegand, F. Knauer, P. Kaczensky, U. Breitenmoser, L.Bufka, J. Cerveny, P. Koubek, T. Huber, C. Stanisa, and L. Trepl. 2002.Assessing the Suitability of Central European Landscapes for the Reintroduction of Eurasian Lynx. Journal of Applied Ecology 39:189-203.

Schmitt, F. G. and L. Seuront. 2001. Multifractal Random Walk in Copepod Behavior. Physica a-Statistical Mechanics and Its Applications 301:375-396.

Seoane, J., J. Vinuela, R. Diaz-Delgado, and J. Bustamante. 2003. The Effects of Land Use and Climate on Red Kite Distribution in the Iberian Peninsula. Biological Conservation 111:401-414.

Stoner, A. W. and R. H. Titgen. 2003. Biological Structures and Bottom Type Influence Habitat Choices Made by Alaska Flatfishes. Journal of Experimental Marine Biology and Ecology 292:43-59.

Thuiller, W., Araujo, M. B. and Lavorel. S., 2003. Generalized Models Vs. Classification Tree Analysis: Predicting Spatial Distributions of Plant Species at Different Scales. Journal of Vegetation Science 14:669-680.

Vayssieres, M. P., Plant, R. E. and Allen-Diaz, B. H. 2000. Classification Trees: an Alternative Non-Parametric Approach for Predicting Species Distributions. Journal of Vegetation Science 11:679-694.

Wiegand, T., Knauer, F., Kaczensky, P., and Naves, J., 2004. Expansion of brown bears (Ursus arctos) into the eastern Alps: a spatially explicit population model. Biodiversity and Conservation 13:79-114. 2004.

Yee, T. W. and N. D. Mitchell. 1991. Generalized Additive-Models in Plant Ecology. Journal of Vegetation Science 2:587-602.

Zaniewski, A. E., A. Lehmann, and J. M. C. Overton. 2002. Predicting Species Spatial Distributions Using Presence-Only Data: a Case Study of Native New Zealand Ferns. Ecological Modelling 157:261-280.

16

Combining Radio and PIT-Telemetry to Study the Large and Fine-Scale Movements of Stocked and Wild Brown Trout (*Salmo trutta* L.) in a Northeastern Stream, Portugal

Amílcar A. T. Teixeira[1] and Rui M. V. Cortes[2]

[1]*Polytechnic Institute of Bragança, School of Agriculture, Mountain Research Centre*

[2]*University of Trás-os-Montes, Centre for the Research and Technology of Agro-Environmental and Biological Sciences*

Portugal

1. Introduction

Stream-resident salmonid movements have been the subject of numerous studies and their behaviour is relatively well-known (Harcup et al., 1984; Heggenes, 1988). For example, brown trout (*Salmo trutta*) is described as a sedentary species based on the behaviour displayed, often associated to the strong site attachment to a territory or home range (Bridcut & Giller, 1993; Armstrong & Herbert, 1997). Other salmonids like brook (*Salvelinus fontinalis*) (Roghair & Dolloff, 2005) and cutthroat trout (*Oncorhynchus clarki*) (Hegennes et al., 1991) showed similar behaviour. However, there are studies reporting a wide range of movements for brown (Meyers et al., 1992; Young, 1994), cutthroat (Hilderbrand & Kershner, 2000) and brook (Gowan & Fausch, 1996) trout populations. Trout behaviour can be modified by natural (*e.g.* fish density, food availability) and especially by man induced factors (*e.g.* environmental degradation, harvest and stocking) responsible for major threats of wild populations (Laikre et al., 2000). Indeed, stocking of hatchery-reared brown trout is a management tool commonly used to improve the recreational fishing (Cowx, 1999). This activity is responsible for a sudden artificial increase of fish density in a particular area. Negative impacts on wild populations, such as genetic contamination, competition, predator attraction and disease transmission were often referred (White et al., 1995; Einum & Fleming, 2001; Weber & Fausch, 2003) and are potentially amplified with the dispersal failure, since many hatchery-reared trout tend to remain near of the stocking site (Cresswell, 1981; Aarestrup et al., 2005). There are also contradictory results, as reported by Bettinger & Bettoli (2002) where stocked trout dispersal reached over 12 km in the downstream direction, just 24 hours after their release. Cortes et al. (1996) found for Portuguese salmonid streams that, during three successive years (2000 to 2003), less than 20% of stocked brown trout remained in the stream segment, one month after the release. However, in this study a mark-recapture method was used that did not allow to assess the main causes of the fish depletion and was not appropriate for the observation of fish behaviour. In fact, a wide variety of techniques, grouped as capture dependent (*e.g.* mark-recapture, telemetry) and independent (*e.g.* visual observation) methods, were used for the investigation of the spatio-temporal behaviour of freshwater fish (Lucas & Baras, 2000), although the comparisons and the validity of some results have been questioned (Gowan & Fausch, 1996). Recent technology and the development of a set of techniques (e.g. passive integrated- PIT, acoustic, radio and electromyogram- EMG transmitters), broadly referred as biotelemetry, enabled new information for researchers in basic and applied ecology, namely related with a better understanding of the physiology, behaviour and energetic status of free-living animals (Cooke et al., 2004). Radiotelemetry has been widely used, providing a high-resolution, in temporal and spatial scale, of information at individual level. Despite of the high costs of individual radio-tags and the detection equipment that restrict the number of tagged fishes, different studies were made to evaluate the home range of target species, like diel (Belanger & Rodriguez, 2001) and seasonal movements (Burrell et al., 2000), the influence of environmental factors (Ovidio et al., 1998) and the efficacy of fishways (Scruton et al., 2002). On the other hand, passive integrated transponder (PIT) technology has been developed for monitoring the individual movements of free-ranging fish for tracking (Prentice et al., 1990a; Armstrong et al., 1996; Greenberg & Giller, 2000), even small aquatic animals in shallow waters, involving low equipment costs and the possibility of addressing numerous questions in fields of animal behaviour, habitat use and population dynamics not covered by radiotelemetry (Roussel et al., 2000, Quintella et al., 2005). The indefinite life span and high tag retention with no apparent effects on growth and survival of tagged animals are other advantages mentioned to the PIT telemetry (Ombredane et al., 1998; Bubb et al., 2002). Several improvements occurred in the PIT technology throughout the last decades. Initially, stationary systems were used to evaluate the migration and survival of fish passing through fishway orifices (Prentice et al., 1990b; Castro-Santos et al., 1996) or streamwide antennae (Barbin-Zydlewski et al., 2001). In recent years, different types of portable equipments, like the flat-bed antenna design (Armstrong et al., 1996), the multipoint decoders connected to several flat-bed antennae (Riley et al., 2003) and the portable antenna (Roussel et al., 2000; Coucherousset et al., 2010), were developed and adapted to assess the behaviour of local populations in shallow streams. However, there is a lack of studies combining both radio and PIT telemetry technologies to study the behaviour of trout populations and this possibility is important to enhance the data quality.

The objective of the present study was to evaluate the spatial and temporal behaviour of wild and hatchery-reared brown trout populations in a stream of northeastern Portugal after stocking. Radio and PIT telemetry technologies were combined in order to study the movements of these sympatric populations. Radiotelemetry was used for large-scale continuous monitoring of individual fish and detailed information on movements was obtained at two distinct temporal scales: day-by-day and hourly diel cycles. Complementarily, PIT telemetry allowed a fine-scale approach considering the microhabitat use and activity pattern of each tagged fish in a confined area. This information was relevant to analyse the efficiency of stocking, the evolution of stocked fish condition and the potential impacts on the wild populations in order to define the most appropriate management measures for the Portuguese salmonid streams.

2. Material and methods

The study was carried out in summer and autumn of 2002 and 2005 in a salmonid stream, the Baceiro River, tributary of the Douro River, located in the Montesinho Natural Park, northeastern Portugal (Figure 1).

2.1 Study area

The Baceiro River is a third-order stream, approximately 25 km long, mean annual discharge of 1.93 $m^3.s^{-1}$ and mean gradient of 4%, subjected to a reduced human pressure and a land use cover dominated by oak (*Quercus pyrenaica* Willd.) forests and also some meadows and planted chestnut (*Castanea sativa* Mill.) and *Pinus* spp., which contributes to the low impact on water composition (conductivity < 70 $\mu S.cm^{-1}$, dissolved oxygen > 9 $mg.l^{-1}$, alkalinity < 25 mg $HCO_3^-.l^{-1}$, hardness < 15 mg $CaCO_3.l^{-1}$, NO_3^- < 0.5 $mg.l^{-1}$, PO_4^{3-} < 0.1 $mg.l^{-1}$). This stream is characterized by a constrained channel, gravel-pebble over sand streambed and riparian vegetation is well developed and dominated by alder (*Alnus glutinosa* (L.) Gaertn.), although willow (*Salix salvifolia* Brot. and *S. atrocinerea* Brot.), poplar (*Populus nigra L.*) and ash (*Fraxinus angustifolia* Vahl) trees are also present. The stream width ranged between 5 m in the riffle to 12 m in the pool habitats, with maximum depth of 3 m. During summer (late) and autumn (early), the water temperature ranged from 5.0 to 19.0 °C and discharge from 0.05 to 2.1 $m^3.s^{-1}$ (the last after a storm event). It is important to mention that, during 2005, an extremely dry period was observed in the region and the stream became intermittent during a part of the summer. In the stream segment, the fish community consisted almost exclusively of wild brown trout populations and few numbers of nase (*Pseudochondrostoma duriense* Coelho) and Iberian chub (*Squalius carolitertii* Doadrio). Otter (*Lutra lutra* L.), water snakes (*Natrix maura* L. and *Natrix natrix* L.) and heron (*Ardea cinerea* L.) were the natural predators found in this stream.

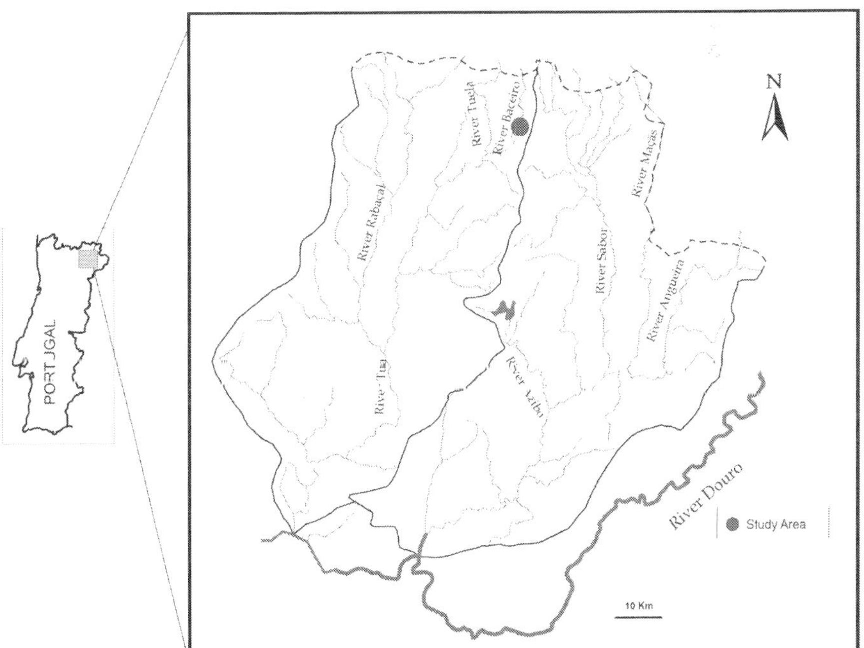

Fig. 1. Map of study area in the Baceiro River, a salmonid stream located in the Douro basin.

2.2 Field survey: Radio-tagging and tracking procedures

Fish activity and movements were monitored using a sequential scanning receiver- Lotek Eng. Inc. SRX_400 and a hand-held directional Yagi antenna (flexible elements) (Figure 2). Two different microprocessor coded radio transmitters (Lotek Engineering Ltd.) were used for the experiments carried out during 2002 and 2005. In the first and exploratory experiment, from 15 to 28 October 2002, one non-resident (from Sabor stream belonging to the contiguous watershed) native (330 mm total length, L_T) and one stocked brown trout (270 mm L_T) were tagged using a MCFT-3KM model (18 mm long x 7.3 mm diameter, 1.4 g in water) with 14 warranty life days and 5.00 sec. of signal burst rate. The transmitters operated with two codes (10 and 11) at the same frequency (149.420 MHz) and were attached (adding 0.5g, in air), alongside the base of the dorsal fin (Figure 3). The fish were previously anesthetized with 2-phenoxy-ethanol solution (0.25 mg.l^{-1}) and the radio-tags externally attached with nylon cords, which passed through the body muscles (inside of a hypodermic needle) to plastic plates cushioned with foam on the two sides of the fish to minimise scale damage.

Fig. 2. Radiotelemetry monitoring session in the Baceiro river (summer 2005).

This previous study allowed to set the methodology for the 2nd experiment, which was conducted from 16 September to 18 November 2005 and a MCFT-3D model used with the following characteristics: 61 warranty life days, 5.00 sec. of signal burst rate, 29 mm long x 10.3 mm diameter and weight of 2.1g in water. They operated with six different codes (001 to 006) at the same frequency (149.460 MHz) and were externally attached on six hatched-reared brown trout (size range 255-277 mm in total length, L_T, mean 265 ± 0.745 S.D. mm). Stocked trout were tagged according to the methodology defined, and maintained during one day in the hatchery to recover from the surgical procedures (Figure 3). After this period, fish were conditioned and transported in aerated tanks and, subsequently, released in the stream.

Fig. 3. Trout radio-tagging procedures and recover period of stocked trout in fishfarms, located near of Baceiro River.

The habitat unit selected for the release of stocked trout was 210 m long by 9.0 m mean width by 2.5 m of maximum depth, comprising all representative microhabitats of stream segment. Temperature (thermometer, accuracy of 0.1 °C) and water column velocity (Valeport flowmeter, accuracy of 0.01 $m.s^{-1}$) were daily measured (Figure 4) and stream discharge determined near the stocking site. Velocity at 0.6 of total depth was considered as the mean water column velocity when the depth was less than 0.75 m. At deeper points the readings were averaged at 0.2 and 0.8 of total depth.

Fig. 4. Measuring temperature (°C) and water column velocity ($m.s^{-1}$) in the Baceiro River (summer 2005).

The fish were monitored and located at least once a day until the end of their transmitter's battery life during the whole study period (14 days in 2002 and 64 days in 2005). Net daily journeys were registered, which were defined as the distance between locations at two consecutive days. During 2005, the fish were also monitored hourly for a partial diel cycle (from 06.00 a.m. to 24.00 p.m.) for eight days (week periodicity). Such registrations took place on 23 and 30 September, on 7, 14, 21 and 28 October and on 4 and 12 November. All tracks were conducted along the stream banks and the potential disturbance of fish activity minimized. To measure the trout movements, yellow fluorescent marks were sprayed on the stream bank (alder branches or rocks were selected) at regular intervals of 25 meters. The identification of a fish position was registered after the detection of the maximum signal strength for at least 1 min. The positions of each fish were used to determine the dispersal (defined as the distance travelled by individual fish from the stocking site), the daily home range (D.H.R., the difference between the most upstream and most downstream positions), and the total distance moved (T.D.M., the sum of all displacements detected). Non-parametric Mann-Whitney *U*-tests were performed to detect statistical differences between native and stocked fish dispersal in 2002 and between stocked trout for dispersal, D.H.R. and T.D.M. throughout 2005. Spearman rank order correlations (r_S) were made to assess the significant relationship between the dispersal of stocked fish and two relevant environmental variables: water temperature and discharge. All statistical analyses were performed using STATISTICA 7.0 package (Statsoft, 2004).

2.3 Field survey: PIT-tagging and monitoring design

The Passive Integrated Transponder (PIT) technology is composed of PIT tags, which are internally implanted in the fish, and one or several antennae connected to a transceiver. The PIT tag is detected and their individual code recorded when a tagged fish passed within the read range of the antenna. The fish detection is recorded when the transceiver energizes the tag by sending an electric current through the antenna, which emits an electromagnetic signal captured by the circuit board of the PIT tag that sends their individual code back to the transceiver (Riley et al., 2003; Gibbons & Andrews, 2004). The PIT technology used was based on a multi-point decoder (MPD) unit (UKID Systems Ltd, Preston, U.K.). This unit consists of DC integrated MPD/antenna multiplexer (8-channel) powered by a 24 V (18 Ah) rechargeable lead-acid battery pack, which provided more than 24 hours of continuous use, and eight black circular panel antennae connected to the PIT–tag reader by cable lengths of 10 m. Each panel antenna (22 mm deep and 300 mm in diameter) operates at a frequency of 134 kHz. Two distinct PIT tags (UKID Systems) were used in this study: 1) 12.0 mm long x 2.1 mm in diameter (122IJ) (defined as Type I) and 2) 34 mm (L) x 4 mm (D) (Type II) (344GL), with detection ranges of approximately 90 mm and 300 mm, respectively. This system enables logging up to 1000 time-stamped events from an onboard Real Time Clock and the Battery Backed-up Memory. In order to reduce the number of repetitive events, resulting from a fish that remained over the same antenna, a data repeated filter precluded the repeat reading of the same tag code within each 25 seconds period. The identification data (ID) output was further downloaded from MPD (via RS232) to a personal computer. The battery pack and the MPD was safeguard by a special enclosure (Peli-Plastic case) (Figure 5). A Casper Handheld reader was used when fish were captured and a unique identification required.

A stream segment (30 m long by a width ranging from 3 to 10 m), with riffle and pool habitats, was selected in the Baceiro stream. Before PIT telemetry experiment, the aquatic habitat was assessed based on transects (starting point randomly chosen), made perpendicular to the stream, with intervals of 5 m throughout each stream segment. Point measurements were done at 0.5 m intervals across each transect for the variables of total depth, surface velocity (measured 10 cm below the surface), bottom velocity (10 cm above the streambed) and mean water column velocity (0.6 of total depth), substrate composition and cover. Substrate composition was classified according to a modified Wentworth scale, adopting the following categories: 1) organic detritus; 2) silt and sand (< 2 mm); 3) gravel (2-16 mm); 4) pebble (17- 64 mm); 5) cobble (65- 256 mm); 6) boulder (> 256 mm) and 7) bedrock. Cover types were divided into five categories: 1) objects > 15 cm (substrate emerging from the streambed); 2) overhanging vegetation; 3) roots, undercut banks and submerged woody debris; 4) surface turbulence and 5) no cover. Total depth was directly measured with a stick meter and the velocities were measured with a Valeport electronic flowmeter. The following characteristics were determined for the available habitat: mean total depth of 40 cm (maximum depth= 90 cm); maximum water column velocity detected near the riffle zone of 0.90 $m.s^{-1}$; substrate composition dominated by sand, cobbles and boulders; main cover for fish provided by undercut banks and boulders. Water temperature ranged from 12 to 19 °C. Between 12 August and 30 September 2005, the entire stream reach section selected was closed with stop nets. Previously to the beginning of the experiments, the study area was depleted of fish through several electrofishing sweeps (Hans Grassl ELT60 DC, 1.5W, 300/600 volts) and biometric data of local trout population recorded. Twenty-five resident native trout, distributed into three size classes (Table 1), were marked with 12 mm PIT tags and the adipose fin clipped.

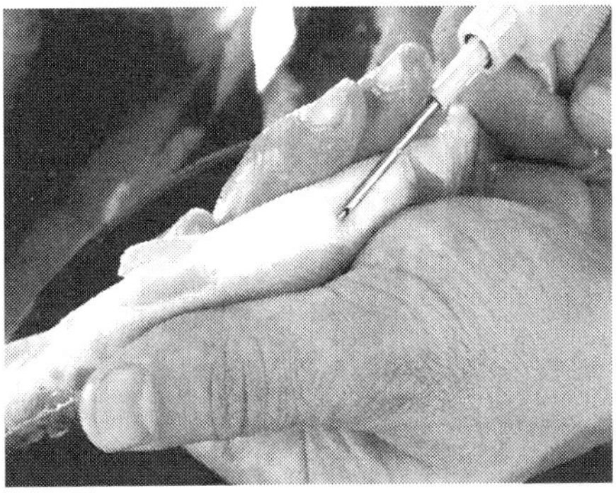

Fig. 5. PIT equipment (battery-pack and multi-point decoder- MPD) unit and PIT tagging procedures.

After a recovery period of two hours, the wild trout population was released into the blocked stream reach. At the same time, a sympatric condition was promoted in the confined area adding a total of fifty PIT tagged stocked trout using transponders Type I and II (Table 1). Before tagging, individual fish were anesthetized with a solution of 2-phenoxy-ethanol (0.25 $ml.l^{-1}$) and the abdominal region disinfected (Betadine®). A sterilised needle linked to a special tagging gun was used for surgical implantation of the Type I tag in the fish peritoneal cavity (Figure 5). The Type II tag was manually implanted through an incision of approximately 4 mm made in the midventral line, without suturing the incision.

The MPD unit, the antennae installation and the data acquisition were made following a similar design described in Riley et al. (2003) and Teixeira & Cortes (2007), using a random distribution of antennae, changing their position every two days (Figure 6). During the study period the dry weather conditions verified and the values of microhabitat measurements were assumed constant for every two days. Biometric data of both sympatric populations were obtained five weeks after stocking through an electrofishing survey and unique identification codes obtained for all tagged fish.

Trout Group	Fish Number	L_T (cm)	M (g)	K*	Tag ratio ** (%)
1) Stocked					
Type I PIT tag	25	22.3 ± 1.6	126.7 ± 28.2	1.12 ± 0.08	0.08 ± 0.02
Type II PIT tag	25	23.2 ± 1.3	146.2 ± 24.9	1.16 ± 0.07	0.85 ± 0.17
2) Native					
A) < 15.0	8	13.3 ± 1.2	23.5 ± 6.7	1.00 ± 0.07	0.10 ± 0.03
B) 15.0-20.0	8	17.0 ± 1.2	48.6 ± 9.8	0.98 ± 0.08	0.22 ± 0.04
C) > 20.0	9	22.0 ± 1.9	108.9 ± 30.3	0.97 ± 0.04	0.46 ± 0.15

* $K = 100(M.\ L_T^{-b})$, *where* M- trout mass (g); L_T- total lenght (cm); b- alometric coefficient
** 100.(tag mass).(trout mass)$^{-1}$

Table 1. Mean ± standard deviation (S.D.) of total length (L_T), mass (M), Fulton's condition factor (K) and tag ratio of the pit-tagged brown trout in the Baceiro stream, during summer 2005.

Fig. 6. PIT-tagged trout passing over an antenna, during field experiment in the Baceiro River (summer 2005).

The analyses of movement and activity patterns of stocked and native trout populations were based on the non-repeated data (the continuous repeated records of each fish in the same antenna were not considered) recorded by the MPD unit during the five weeks of the sampling period. Non-metric multidimensional scaling (NMDS) analysis, an ordination method based on a rank order of Bray-Curtis similarities, was applied to non-repeated frequency to detect the behaviour differences between native and stocked trout. The NMDS was computed using the log transformed [log (x+1)] data. A multivariate analysis of similarities- one-way ANOSIM test, as a nonparametric randomization approach, was then applied to the Bray-Curtis similarity matrix to test the statistical differences between the two considered groups. These analyses were performed through the package PRIMER 5 (Clarke & Gorley, 2001). The relationship between the microhabitat variables and stocked and wild trout were assessed through a canonical correspondence analysis (CCA), a method of direct gradient analysis, where the ordination of objects (stocked and native fish) is based on species data (fish positions) and on environmental information associated (Jongman et al., 1987). Two CCA's were performed for two distinct periods: 1) first week- the adaptation period of stocked fish to wild environment; 2) from the 2nd to the 5th week, considering the post-adaptation period. This analysis was performed using the CANOCO software package (ter Braak & Smilauer, 1998). Data were standardized for microhabitat variables and log transformed [log (x+1)] for the non-repeated frequency data of the detected fish in all antennae positions. Only those variables with a variation inflation factor (VIF) of less than 20 were included to avoid multicollinearity (ter Braak, 1986). In addition, a Monte Carlo permutation test (199 permutations) was performed to test the significance of the axes. The fish activity was analysed based on the antennae non-repeated frequency data for the tagged trout populations, considering the following classes for *1)* native trout: A< 15.0; B- 15.0 to 20.0; C> 20.0 cm using Type I PIT tags and *2)* stocked brown trout: Type I and Type II PIT tags. Polynomial regressions were fitted to the data. Trout activity pattern was analyzed over 24-hours cycles, but discriminated for dawn, day, dusk and night periods. The influence of distinct detection range of the two types of PIT tags (only for stocked fish) and the ontogenetic variation of native trout was assessed. The differences between the trout classes for the defined periods were assessed using non-parametric Mann-Whitney *U*-tests (data did not fit to the assumptions of normality- Bartlet test). These *U*-tests were also performed for the comparisons between size (total length, L_T), mass (M) and the Fulton's condition factor (K) of stocked and native trout. A significant level of $P< 0.05$ was accepted.

3. Results

3.1 Radio-telemetry analysis

A distinct movement pattern was detected comparing stocked and native brown trout (Mann-Withney *U*-test, $P< 0.001$), from the radiotelemetry survey carried out in autumn 2002 (Figure 7). An initial stationary behaviour of stocked trout (for five days remaining in the stocking site) was replaced by their migration in a downstream direction, and at the end of 14 days (transmitter battery life) the fish were located in a small pool, 1,500 m from the stocking site. The magnitude of the displacement was correlated with the increase of stream discharge (Spearman correlation $r_S> 0.85$, $P< 0.01$). Conversely, wild trout remained near the stocking site hiding under a fallen tree, in spite of the non-residency status. It was only detected a downstream movement of 200 m coinciding with a sudden rainstorm, which raised the water level by 1 m. Nevertheless, after this period, the wild trout followed the upstream migration and travelled to feeding zones (90 m from stocking site) near a riffle/run habitat.

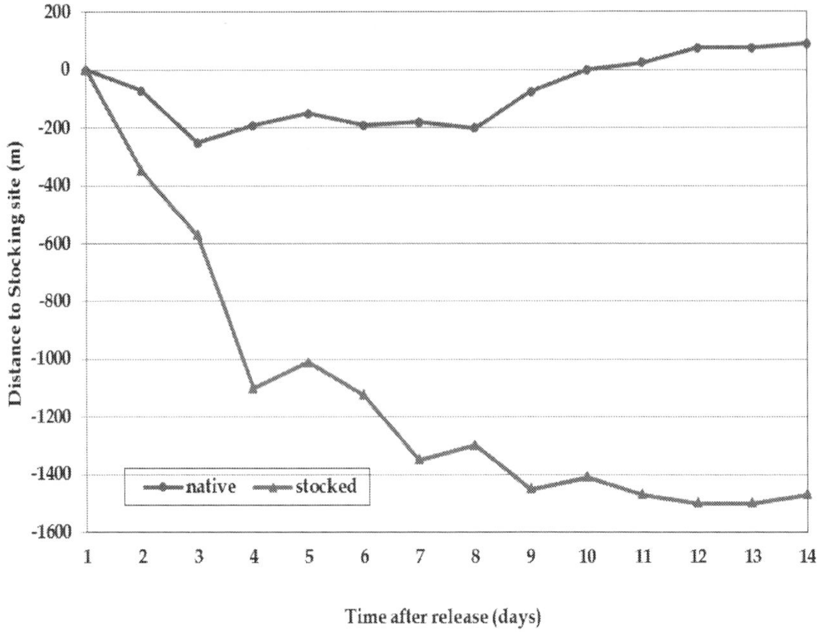

Fig. 7. Dispersal of one stocked and one native brown trout after being released in the Baceiro stream, on 15 October 2002. Symbols are daily positions of radio-tagged trout for 14 days (transmitter battery life).

Of the experiment conducted during summer/autumn of 2005 with six radio-tagged stocked trout, four individuals (T1, T3, T5 and T6) were tracked during the entire study period (64 days) and trout T2 and T4 signals were missed early, respectively on the 27th of October (after 42 days) and on the 31st of October (after 46 days) (Figure 8). Individual movements of stocked radio-tagged trout released in the Baceiro stream exhibited different patterns: a wide-range of displacements was recorded, and at the end of the registration period, the displacement of fish from the stocking site (dispersal) varied from 0 to 4,500 meters (Table 2).

Trout code	Total Length L_T (cm)	Mass (g)	Days tracked	Total Dispersal (m)
T1	26.8	223.5	64	0
T2	26.5	193.5	42	-350
T3	26.5	228.5	64	-4500
T4	25.5	178.4	46	-200
T5	27.7	209.6	64	-1025
T6	26.0	171.3	64	-1125

Table 2. Characteristics of stocked radio-tagged trout in the Baceiro stream (September to November 2005).

showed the incisions to be healed up and only two stocked trout had signs of tag expulsion. At the same time, only 28% (Type I tags) and 32% (Type II) of stocked fish survived, reaching a minimum of 4% at the end of the study (7th week). On the other hand, 92% of native tagged fish remained alive in the study area. Furthermore, the variables *K* and *M* (only for Type II- PIT tagged fish) displayed a significant decrease (Mann-Whitney *U*-tests, $P < 0.05$) for the stocked fish and smaller size classes (A and B) of native trout. The CCA's ordinations (Figure 10 and 11) showed a similar relationship between the microhabitat variables and stocked and native trout for the two defined periods (eigenvalues of 0.472 and 0.177 for the 1st period and 0.228 and 0.124 for the 2nd one), and the first two axes explained, respectively, 63.8% and 65.0% of the variation relating to trout populations and the environmental variables. The Monte Carlo randomization test detected for both CCA's showed significant results for the sum of all eigenvalues (199 permutations, $P < 0.05$). For both CCA's a set of variables (*e.g.* total depth, dominant and subdominant substrate, aquatic cover, overhanging vegetation, distance to riffle and the distance to the nearest streambank) presented a similar importance that contributed to the distribution of stocked and native trout along the sympatric period and no substantial differences were detected between the initial adaptation period (1st week) and the remaining weeks.

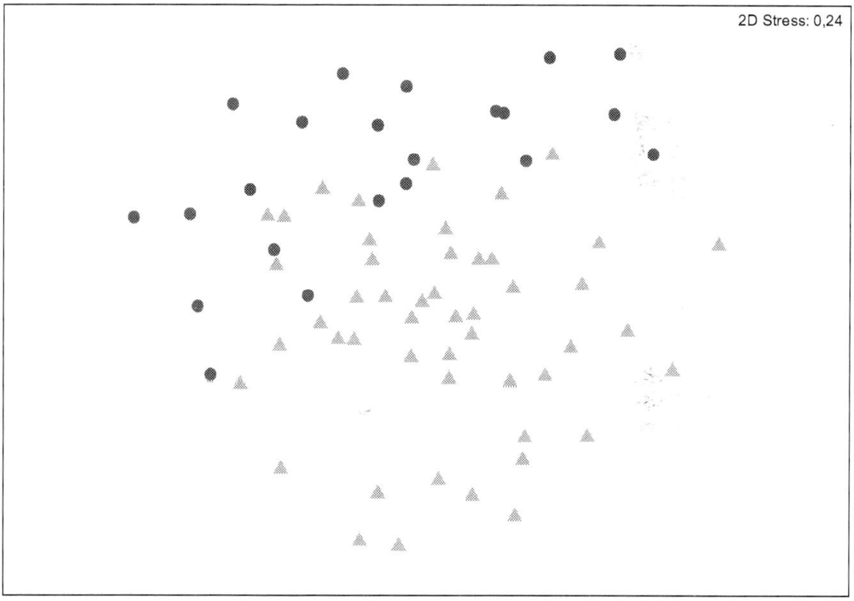

Fig. 9. NMDS ordination of stocked and native brown trout in the Baceiro stream (summer 2005). Ordination was based on a matrix of pair-wise Bray-Curtis similarities coefficients constructed from non-repeated records, log transformed (Log[x+1]). Symbols: ● = native trout; ▲ = stocked trout.

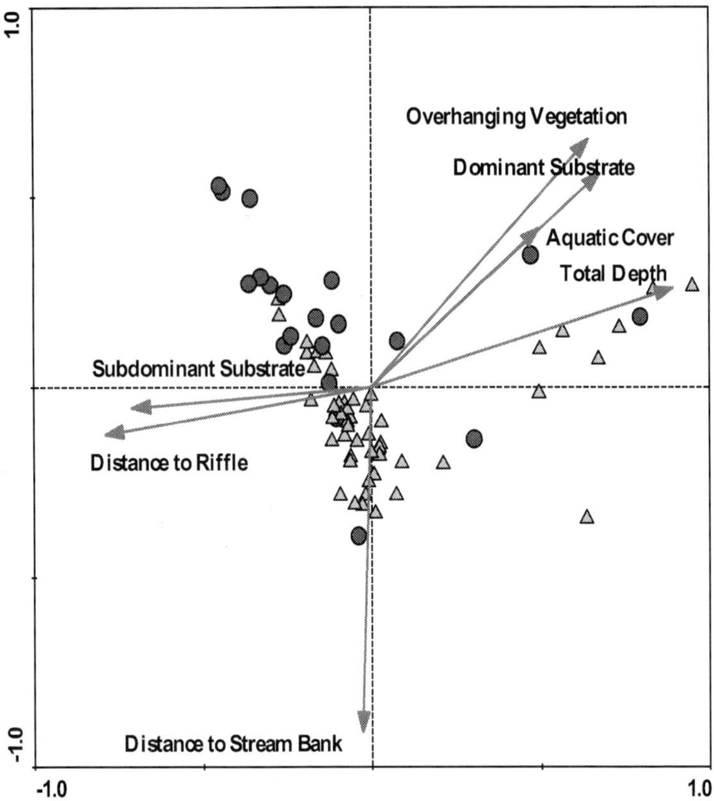

Fig. 10. CCA ordination diagrams of the 1st week for the Baceiro stream: distribution of native and stocked trout according to the selected microhabitat variables for the two first axes. The arrows represent the microhabitat variables and the symbols are the trout identification: *A)* arrows- total depth ; aquatic cover; overhanging vegetation; distance to riffle; distance to the stream bank; dominant and subdominant substrate; *B)* Symbols:● = native trout; △ = stocked trout. The length of the arrow is a measure of the importance of the environmental variable and the arrowhead points at the direction of increasing influence.

Comparatively, a greater proportion of the overall movements recorded for the dominant native trout occurred during the day period but no obvious activity pattern was detected among fish of same class. The diel activity pattern of trout varied substantially between both populations and with the type of PIT tags used. A significantly higher number of movements (62% of total non-repeated records) was detected by the MPD unit between Type II PIT-tagged stocked trout and the remained groups for every diel period (dawn, day, dusk and night) defined (*U*-tests, $P < 0.05$). Despite of the distinct detection range of the PIT tags, the Type I- PIT tagged stocked trout movements were also significantly different from all native trout classes, except for adult native fish during the dawn period (*U*-tests, P< 0.05). The activity rhythm pattern of both stocked fish groups took place mainly at dawn and day and to a lesser extent at night periods. This activity pattern was roughly adopted by adult native trout, which differed significantly compared with the smaller size classes, precisely for dusk and night periods (*U*-tests, P< 0.05). Complementary analyses, based on the polynomial regressions (Figure 12), confirmed the distinct behaviour displayed by dominant trout (C Class > 20.0 cm), more active during the daylight period, related to the smaller native classes (A and B classes ≤ 20.0 cm), showing higher mobility during dusk and night periods. In fact, a temporal segregation was observed and probably dependent on the high density (three times more) promoted in the confined area as a result of the stocking experiment established.

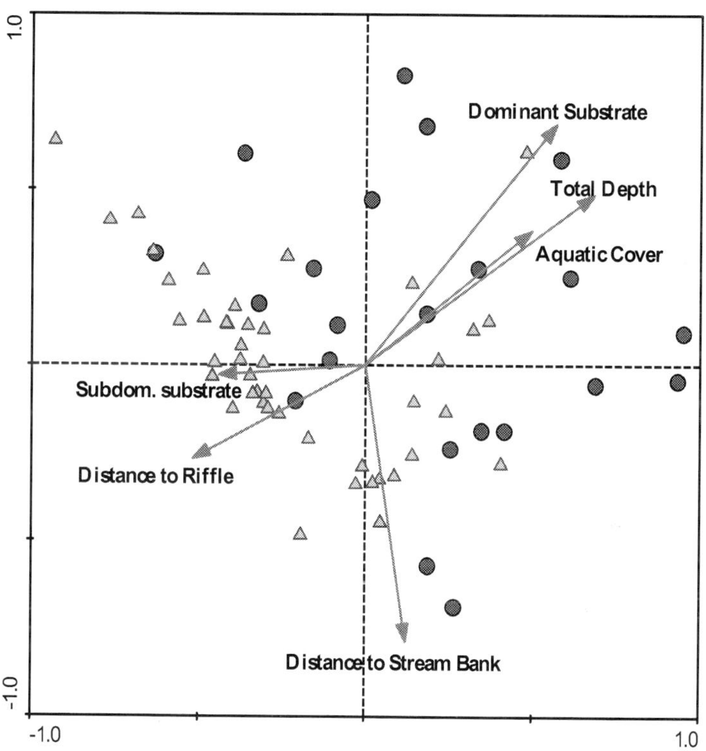

Fig. 11. CCA ordination diagrams of the 2nd to 5th week for the Baceiro stream: distribution of native and stocked trout according to the selected microhabitat variables for the two first axes. The arrows represent the microhabitat variables and the symbols are the trout identification: *A)* arrows- total depth ; aquatic cover; overhanging vegetation; distance to riffle; distance to the stream bank; dominant and subdominant substrate; *B)* Symbols: ● = native trout; ▲ = stocked trout. The length of the arrow is a measure of the importance of the environmental variable and the arrowhead points at the direction of increasing influence.

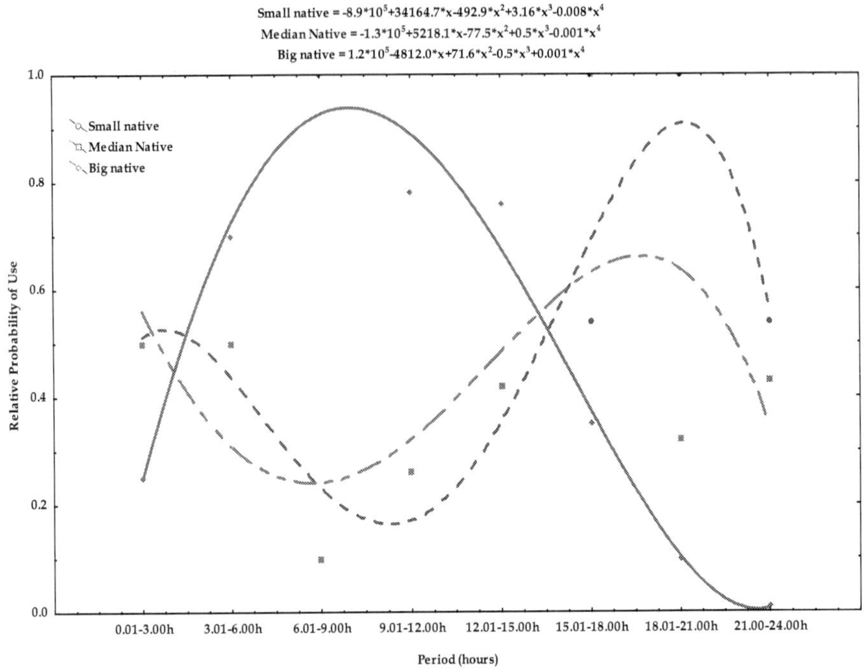

Fig. 12. Activity pattern based on polynomial regressions, performed for native trout, considering the different size classes: A) small < 15.0 cm; B) median 15.0-20.0 cm; C) big > 20.0 cm) using PIT Telemetry technology relative to eight diel periods and three hours classes in the Baceiro stream, during summer 2005. The dependent variable represents the relative probability of use (standardized to a 0-1 scale).

The comparisons between polynomial regressions calculated for the native size classes and stocked brown trout (Figures 12 and 13), showed similar behaviour only for the bigger individuals (dominant native and stocked trout) in spite of the increased probability of spatial competition and agonistic events. However, the morphological (fin deformities, hyperbuoyancy), physiological (stress response) and behavioural (lack of social hierarchy, weak territorial behaviour) characteristics presented by many stocked trout could explain their potentially disadvantageous performance in relation to dominant wild fish. The higher density referred for the PIT experiment established, did not affect the body condition of dominant native trout and contribute to explain the superior capacity to explore the available resources, namely in terms of feeding and resting activities. This pattern was not observed for smaller native trout and for stocked trout populations that showed a significant decrease in the body condition during the five weeks experiment.

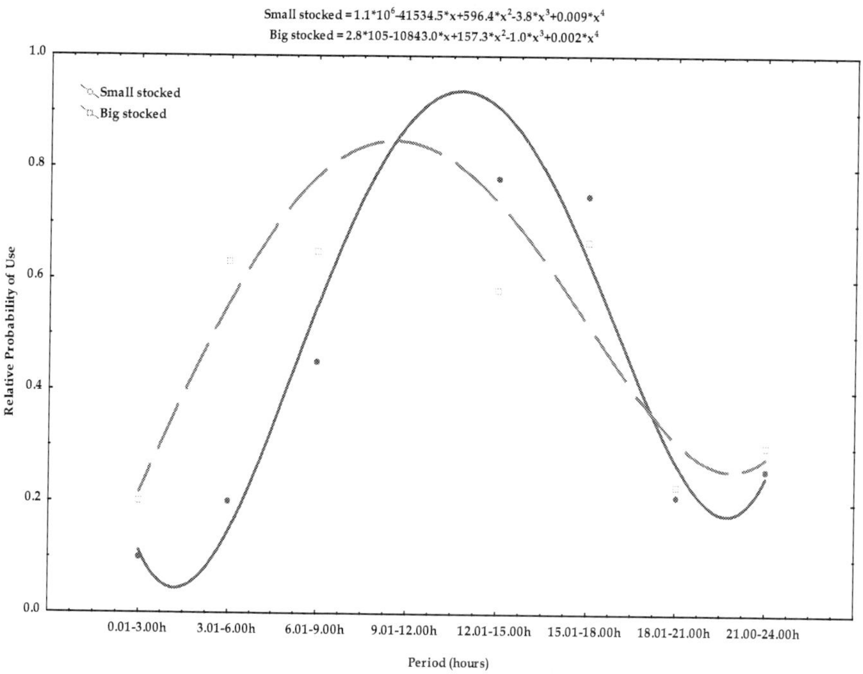

Fig. 13. Activity pattern based on polynomial regressions, performed for stocked trout: small- Type I PIT-tags; big- Type II PIT tags) using PIT Telemetry technology relative to eight diel periods and three hours classes in the Baceiro stream, during summer 2005. The dependent variable represents the relative probability of use (standardized to a 0-1 scale).

4. Discussion

Native brown trout showed a significantly less dispersal behaviour than stocked trout. However, caution should therefore be taken in the interpretation of this result since only two fish were considered in the exploratory experiment. Nevertheless, the limited movement exhibited by native fish was also identified in several studies (Knouft & Jutila, 2002; Maia, 2003), although, as referred by Bunnel et al. (1998), it may be function of the size of the habitat that provides adequate feeding and resting zones. These authors mentioned that brown trout movement varied among individuals of a same population, but most fish moved within a single continuous riffle/run-pool sequence in a diel cycle. In opposition to the resident trout movement, strictly related with the energetic cost/benefit ratio, Bachman (1984) found an erratic behaviour for the recently stocked trout. According to this study, confirmed by personal observations, hatchery-reared brown trout displayed a typical behaviour acquired in raceway tanks and moved constantly, leading to an excessive expenditure of energy in the swimming activity and agonistic encounters, which contributed to poor growth and survival rates in the wild environment. Stocked radio-tagged trout in the Baceiro stream showed a clear tendency to dispersal in downstream direction, although they exhibited distinct distance ranges. The dispersion of stocked brown trout is relatively well documented in the literature and, similarly to the present study, distinct individual movements were also found including stationary (maintaining the position near the stocking site) and mobile (ranging from upstream to downstream migrations) behaviour in the same stocked trout population (Cresswell, 1981). For example, Aarestrup et al. (2005) found that four brown trout left the study area whereas the remaining fish (*n*= 46) were stationary. However, in our study it was observed a decline in the water flow that conditioned the potential displacement of fish during the radio-telemetry study (32 days). Different factors can be associated with the downstream dispersal and often the harsh environmental conditions like higher levels of discharge originate the referred fish mobility (Ovidio et al., 2000), which was confirmed now. However, the river regulation (e.g. rapid fluctuations in flow resulted from hydroelectric peaking operations), water temperature regimes, different variables of physical habitat (e.g. channel slope, presence of coarse substrate particles, woody debris and roots functioning like potential cover refuges) and fish condition contribute to distinct migration behaviour of stocked fish in the natural environment. On the other hand, the influence of tagging implantation on fish movement was minimized, since external attachment of radio-transmitters and a low body/transmitter weight ratio was used, according to Brown et al. (1999). In the present study, the total distance moved (mean= 203 m) by stocked trout over the partial diel cycle considered (from 06.00 to 24.00 h) averaged about two times the length of home ranges (mean 82 m). However, total distance moved and home ranges are probably underestimated, since it was not possible to conduct registrations during a part of the night (from 00.00 to 06.00 h) and comparisons with other studies must be analysed taking into account this situation. The daily home ranges (minimum of 40 m for T4 and maximum of 118 m for T3) observed for stocked brown trout in the Baceiro stream are within the range of values observed for the same species by Young (1999) in a south-eastern Wyoming river (mean of 41 m), Ovidio et al.(2002) in a Belgian stream (8-480 m; mean 48 m), Knouft & Spotila (2002) in a Pennsylvania stream (20-2000 m) and Maia (2003) in a north-western Portuguese river (Vade River, 0-300m), excluding the migratory behaviour caused by spawning activity linked to reproduction. However, D.H.R. mentioned in the literature corresponded to resident trout and, because these fishes have a consistent fidelity to their home range or territory (Bunnel et al., 1998), it would be expected that non-resident fish, like stocked trout used in this study, had a superior mobility justifying greater dispersal, distance moved and home range, either in seasonal and diel scale analyses. Probably the dry climate during 2005 and the low discharge observed linked to high water temperatures recorded during the initial post-stocking period have restricted the movement of stocked fish. Stocked trout were shown to be more active during the day periods than during the night period in the Baceiro stream and can be related to the feeding habits acquired in the fishfarms. Brown trout is a visual feeder and the foraging efficiency decreases as light intensity declines (Fraser & Metcalfe, 1997; Klemetsen, 2003), but nocturnal (Clapp et al., 1990) and crepuscular (Bunnel et al., 1998) feeding patterns were also reported. However, the tendency of stocked trout in the Baceiro stream must be confirmed in complete (24 h) diel cycles.

Complementary analyses based on PIT-telemetry showed that only 30% of stocked fish survived five weeks after their release in the stream reach, while 92% of native trout were recaptured alive for the same period, considering the confined area of the experiment. Poor stocked brown trout survival rates were also reported in several studies (Pedersen et al.,

2003; Aarestrup et al., 2005). The significant decrease in the condition of stocked brown trout suggested a lower ability to explore the available resources. In fact, the inefficient behaviours displayed by hatchery-reared fish contributed to a lesser adaptation to wild environment when compared with native trout. For example, higher aggression levels (Deverill et al., 1999), lack of social dominance structures (Jenkins, 1971), lower efficiency at feeding on wild prey (Olla et al., 1994), higher metabolic rates (Ersbak & Haase, 1983) and reduced swimming ability are reported for stocked salmonids. On the other hand, the hatchery-reared fish are more vulnerable to angling and natural predation ((Ludwig et al., 2002; Jacobsen, 2005) and higher mortality rates are associated near large stocked fish releases (Marnell, 1985). Observations from the stream bank revealed, during the experimental periods, a reduced fright response of stocked trout to human presence, confirming their potential weakness to avoid natural predation. In fact, most of the Portuguese northeastern salmonid streams supported growing populations of otter (*Lutra lutra* L.) and the higher number of spraints (4 PIT tags were detected) observed on stream banks suggested the higher mortality detected, mainly on stocked fish.

Stocked trout movements, for larger and even for smaller PIT tagged fish, were greater than for every native trout class defined. These fishes displayed an activity pattern more intense during day-light hours, namely during the dawn period. Normally, hatchery-reared trout are more active than wild fish (McLaren, 1979) and the higher mobility pattern showed during day-light hours in this study was, probably, related to the rearing environment (feeding habits in the hatchery) and the increasing ability of fish to detect food as light intensity increases (Fraser & Metcalfe, 1997). Furthermore, these results are according to the exploratory experiments made over two weeks in the previous year and confirmed the lack of a capacity to define a territory and a non-cost-effective behaviour, also detected by other authors (Bachman, 1984). In fact, the importance of habitat variables for both populations was similar during the 5 weeks suggesting that the stocked fish did not change their strategy in terms of habitat use. Hatchery-reared fish occupied habitats away from the stream banks, mainly, without aquatic cover (*e.g.* boulders, roots) and overhanging vegetation (shading). Other studies confirmed the distinct behaviour between wild and stocked salmonids based on the referred variables (Magoulick & Wilzback, 1997). Obviously, the different habitat use and the less concealment behaviour (Bachman, 1984) of stocked trout relative to wild fish increase their visibility and the vulnerability to avian and aquatic predators. A low influence of PIT tag surgical implantation in the fish peritoneal cavity was reported on different studies, with regard to survival, growth, swimming performance and general behaviour (Riley et al. 2003). During this study, trout were recaptured five weeks after their release in the stream, and healing was completed, without signs of inflammation or necrosis in the tissues, suggesting that the behaviour of both sympatric populations was not affected by the tagging procedures. Furthermore, only two stocked fish presented signs of tag expulsion, in spite of the incisions not having been closed with sutures for both 12 and 34 mm PIT tags used. However, low tag loss rates for PIT tags were also recorded for brown trout (4%, after seven months) and other salmonid species (0-2 %, 3 to 4 months) (Ombredane et al., 1998). Differences between the detection range of both PIT tags used (9 cm for 12 mm long vs. 30 cm for 34 mm PIT tags) produced a distinct amount of information (approximately three times more for 34 mm PIT tags) on fish behaviour confirmed by the number of repeated and non-repeated records, but higher mortality rates were found when the larger PIT tags are implanted in the smaller (< 15.0 cm) fish, in previous experiments conducted in the hatchery. However, caution should be taken in the interpretation of data, since a low proportion of area (eight panel antennae) was sampled for every diel cycle. This limitation was reported in several studies using PIT telemetry technology and further improvements are needed to increase the detection range of PIT reading units. With regard to the experimental design of this study, protocols combining a superior number of stationary flat-bed antennas and MPD units covering, at the same time period, the entire stream reach selected, and the use of portable antenna technology will improve the quality of data acquisition related to the small-scale movements by sympatric stocked and native trout populations.

5. Conclusion

The combination of the different methodologies used, *i.e.* radio and PIT-telemetry, allowed a better understanding of the movement patterns and spatial distribution of stocked and native trout through intensive tracking of a small number of radio-tagged fish over a short time scale and continuous monitoring of movements and microhabitat use by PIT-telemetry. As pointed out by Ovidio et al. (2009) gaps in the fish behaviour can be closed using complementary methodologies. This study also confirmed previous observations following distinct methodologies (*e.g.* snorkelling, electrofishing), which detected, just one month after, a low proportion of stocked brown trout in the stream segment where they had been released (Cortes et al., 1996; Teixeira et al., 2006). The potential negative impacts of stocking on wild population seemed to be limited in time and space and were demonstrated by the monitoring of fish movement (*e.g.* radiotelemetry), since a high dispersion was registered, mainly in downstream direction, of the majority of stocked fish. The rapid decrease of stocked fish condition, the variation of hydrological parameters and the vulnerability to predation were factors that contributed to the low efficiency of the stocking programs. For these reasons, stocking of brown trout as a management tool for supplementing the recreational fisheries in rivers must be questioned based on the reduced adaptation of stocked trout to wild environment. However, in specific conditions it could be a cost-effective option, namely if catchable-size trout were used and applied to selected areas where angling pressure is intense. It is possible that a greater proportion of stocked trout never adopt the adequate behaviour that normally is displayed by native trout. Probably the minor adaptation of hatchery-reared fish to the wild environment is more visible when stocking is made recurring to fish of superior size/age ($> 1^+$). Although Pedersen et al. (2003) had found a higher survival and adaptation of smaller brown trout (0^+) over a period of 11 months, a longer time is needed to fish reach the legal catch size for anglers and, as referred by Aarestrup et al. (2005), stocking with trout over the legal size limit could be the correct management tool for supplementing the recreational fisheries. Finally, it is important to consider alternative management techniques with low ecological risks like the improvement of the fish habitat and protective measures (*e.g.* catch-and-release, better management and angling regulations), to promote a superior biogenic capacity of the aquatic system and assure the conservation and/or exploitation of self-sustainability of wild trout populations.

6. Aknowledgments

We wish to thank Ângelo Saraiva, Tiago Martins and Paula Escalda for their field assistance. Thanks also to Rogério Rodrigues, Graça Barreira, Julieta Sampaio and Augusto Maia from

Forestry Governmental Services and the hatchery personnel at Marão and Castrelos Trout Hatchery.

7. References

Aarestrup, K., Jepsen, N., Koed, A. & Pedersen, S. (2005). Movement and mortality of stocked brown trout in a stream. *Journal of Fish Biology* 66: 721-728.

Armstrong, J.D., Braithwaite, V.A. & Rycroft, P. (1996). A flat-bed passive integrated transponder antenna array for monitoring behaviour of Atlantic salmon parr and other fish. *Journal of Fish Biology* 48: 539-541.

Armstrong, J.D. & Herbert, N.A. (1997). Homing movements of displaced stream-dwelling brown trout. *Journal of Fish Biology* 50: 445-449.

Bachman, R.A. (1984). Foraging behaviour of free-ranging wild and hatchery brown trout in a stream. *Transactions of the American Fisheries Society* 113: 1-32.

Barbin-Zydlewski, G., Haro, A., Whalen, K.G. & Mccormick, S.D. (2001). Performance of stationary and portable passive transponder detection systems for monitoring of fish movements. *Journal of Fish Biology* 58: 1471-1475.

Belanger, G. & Rodriguez, M.A. (2001). Homing behaviour of stream-dwelling brook charr following experimental displacement. *Journal of Fish Biology* 59: 987-1001.

Bettinger, J.M. & Bettoli, P.W. (2002). Fate, dispersal and persistence of recently stocked and resident rainbow trout in a Tennessee tailwater. *North American Journal of Fisheries Management* 22: 425-432.

Bridcut, E.E. & Giller, P.S. (1993). Movement and site fidelity in young brown trout *Salmo trutta* populations in a southern Irish stream. *Journal of Fish Biology* 43: 889-899.

Brown, R.S., Cooke, S.J., Anderson, W.G. & Mckinley, R.S. (1999). Evidence to challenge the "2% rule" for biotelemetry. *North American Journal of Fisheries Management* 19: 867-871.

Bubb, D.H., Lucas, M.C., Thom, T.J. & Rycroft, P. (2002). The potential use of PIT telemetry for identifying and tracking crayfish in their natural environment. *Hydrobiologia* 483: 225-230.

Bunnel, D.B. Jr, Isely, J.J., Burrell, K.H. & Van Lear, D.H. (1998). Diel movement of brown trout in a southern Appalachian river. *Transactions of the American Fisheries Society* 127: 630-636.

Burrell, K.H., Isely, J.J., Bunnell Jr, D.B., Van Lear, D.H. & Dolloff, C.A. (2000). Seasonal movement of brown trout in a Southern Appalachian River. *Transactions of the American Fisheries Society* 129: 1373-1379.

Castro-Santos, T., Haro, A. & Walk, S. (1996). A passive integrated transponder (PIT) tag system for monitoring fishways. *Fisheries Research* 28: 253-261

Clapp, D.F., Clark, R.D. Jr & Diana, J.S. (1990). Range activity, and habitat of large, free-ranging brown trout in a Michigan stream. *Transactions of the American Fisheries Society* 119: 1022-1034.

Clarke, K.R. & Warwick, R.M. (1994). *Change in marine communities: An approach to statistical analysis and interpretation.* Natural Environment Research Council. London. 144 pp.

Clarke, K.R. & Gorley, R.N. (2001). *Primer v5: User Manual/Tutorial.* PRIMER-E Plymouth.

Cooke, S.J., Hinch, S.G., Wikelski, M., Andrews, R.D., Kuchel, L.J., Wolcott, T.G. & Butler, P.J. (2004). Biotelemetry: a mechanistic approach to ecology. *Trends in Ecology and Evolution* 19: 334-343.

Cortes R.M.V., Teixeira A. & Pereira C. (1996). Is supplemental stocking of brown trout (*Salmo trutta*) worthwhile in low productive streams? *Folia Zoologica* 45: 371-381

Cowx, I.G. (1999). An appraisal of stocking strategies in the light of developing country constraints. *Fisheries Management and Ecology* 6: 21-34

Cresswell, R. (1981). Post-stocking movements and recapture of hatchery-reared trout into flowing waters - a review. *Journal of Fish Biology* 18: 429-441.

Cucherousset, J., Roussel, J.M., Keeler, R., Cunjak, R.A. & Stump, R. (2005). The use of two new portable 12-mm PIT tag detectors to track small fish in shallow streams. *North American Journal of Fisheries Management* 25: 270-274.

Cucherousset, J., Britton J.R., Beaumont W.R.C., Nyqvist M., Sievers K. & Gozlan R.E. (2010). Determining the effects of species, environmental conditions and tracking method on the detection efficiency of portable PIT telemetry. *Journal of Fish Biology* 76: 1039–1045

Deverill, J.E., Adams, C.E. & Bean, C.W. (1999). Prior residence, aggression and territory acquisition in hatchery-reared and wild brown trout. *Journal of Fish Biology* 55: 868-875.

Einum, S. & Fleming, I.A. (2001). Implications of stocking: Ecological interactions between wild and released salmonids. *Nordic Journal of Freshwater Research* 75: 56-70.

Ersbak, K. & Haase, B.L. (1983). Nutritional deprivation after stocking as a possible mechanism leading to mortality in stream stocked brook trout. *North American Journal of Fisheries Management* 3: 142-151.

Fraser, N.H. & Metcalfe, N.B. (1997). The costs of becoming nocturnal: feeding efficiency in relation to light intensity in juvenile Atlantic salmon. *Functional Ecology* 11: 385-391.

Gibbons, J.W. & Andrews, K.M. (2004). PIT tagging: simple technology at its best. *Bioscience* 54: 447-454.

Gowan, C. & Fausch, K.D. (1996). Mobile brook trout in two high-elevation Colorado streams: Re-evaluating the concept of restricted movement. *Canadian Journal of Fisheries and Aquatic Sciences* 53: 1370-1381.

Greenberg, L.A. & Giller, P.S. (2000). The potential of flat-bed passive integrated transponder antennae for studying habitat use by stream fishes. *Ecology of Freshwater Fish* 9: 74-80.

Harcup, M.F., Williams, R. & Ellis, D.M. (1984). Movements of brown trout, *Salmo trutta* L., in the River Gwyddon, South Wales stream. *Journal of Fish Biology* 24: 415-426.

Heggenes, J. (1988). Effect of experimentally increased intraspecific competition on sedentary adult brown trout (*Salmo trutta*) movement and stream habitat choice. Canadian Journal of Fisheries and Aquatic Sciences 45: 1163-1172.

Heggenes, J., Northcote, T.G. & Peter, A. (1991). Seasonal habitat selection and preferences by cutthroat trout (*Oncorhynchus clarki*) in a small, coastal stream. *Canadian Journal of Fisheries and Aquatic Sciences* 117: 1364-1370.

Hilderbrand, R.H. & Kershner, J.L. (2000). Movement patterns of stream-resident cutthroat trout in Beaver Creek, Idaho-Utah. *Transactions of the American Fisheries Society* 129: 1160-1170.

Jacobsen, L. (2005). Otter (*Lutra lutra*) predation on stocked brown trout (*Salmo trutta*) in two Danish lowland rivers. *Ecology of Freshwater Fish* 14: 59-68.

Jenkins, T.M. (1971). Role of social behaviour in dispersal of introduced rainbow trout (*Salmo gairdneri*). *Journal of Fisheries and Resources Board of Canada* 28: 1019-1027.

Jongman, R.H.G., ter Braak, C.F.J. & Van Tongeren, O.F.R. (eds) (1987). *Data analysis in community and landscape ecology*. Pudoc, Wageningen.

Klemetsen, A., Amundsen, P.A., Dempson, J.B., Jonsson, B., Jonsson, N., O'Connel, M.F. & Mortensen, E. (2003). Atlantic salmon *Salmo salar* L., Brown trout *Salmo trutta* L. and

Arctic charr *Salvelinus alpinus* (L.): A review of aspects of their life histories. *Ecology of Freshwater Fish* 12: 1-59.

Knouft, J.H. & Spotila, J.R. (2002). Assessment of movements of resident stream brown trout, *Salmo trutta* L., among contiguous sections of stream. *Ecology of Freshwater Fish* 11: 85-92.

Laikre, L. (ed.) (2000). *Conservation genetic management of brown trout (Salmo trutta) in Europe.* Fair Project Report CT97 3882: 91 pp.

Lucas, M.C. & Baras, E. (2000). Methods for studying spatial behaviour of freshwater fishes in natural environment. *Fish and Fisheries* 1: 283-316.

Ludwig, G.X., Hokka, V., Sulkava, R. & Ylonen, H. (2002). Otter *Lutra lutra* predation on farmed and free-living salmonids in boreal freshwater habitats. *Wildlife Biology* 8: 193-199.

Magoulick, D. & Wilzbach, M. (1997). Microhabitat selection by native brook trout and introduced rainbow trout in a small Pennsylvania stream. *Journal of Freshwater Ecology* 12: 607-614.

Maia, C.F.Q. (2003). *Estratégias de ciclo de vida das populações de truta, Salmo trutta* L., *na bacia hidrográfica do Rio Lima.* PhD Dissertation. Oporto University. 166 p. (In portuguese).

Marnell, L.F. (1985). Impacts of hatchery stocks on wild fish populations. In: *Fish culture in fisheries management.* Stroud, R.H. (ed.). American Fisheries Society. Fish Culture Section and Fisheries Management Section. Bethesda. 339-348 pp.

McLaren, J.B. (1979). Comparative behaviour of hatchery-reared and wild brown trout and its relation to intergroup competition in a stream. Ph. D. dissertation, Pennsylvania State University, University Park.

Meyers, L.S., Thuemler, T.F. & Kornely, G.W. (1992). Seasonal movements of brown trout in northeast Wisconsin. *North American Journal of Fisheries Management* 12: 433-441.

Olla, B.L., Davis, M.W. & Ryer, C.H. (1994). Behavior deficits in hatchery-reared fish: potential effects on survival following release. *Aquaculture Fisheries Management* 25: 19-34.

Ombredane, D., Baglinière, J.L. & Marchand, F. (1998). The effects of Passive Integrated Transponder tags on survival and growth of juvenile brown trout (*Salmo trutta* L.) and their use for studying movement in a small river. *Hydrobiologia* 371: 99-106.

Ovidio, M., Baras, E., Goffaux, D., Birtles, C. & Philippart, J.C. (1998). Environmental unpredictability rules the autumn migration of brown trout (*Salmo trutta* L.) in the Belgian Ardennes. *Hydrobiologia* 371/372: 263-274.

Ovidio, M., Philippart, J.C. & Baras, E. (2000). Methodological bias in home range and mobility estimates when locating radio-tagged trout, *Salmo trutta,* at different time intervals. *Aquatic Living Resources* 13: 449-454.

Ovidio, M., Baras, E., Goffaux, D., Giroux, F. & Philippart, J.C. (2002). Seasonal variations of activity pattern of brown trout (*Salmo trutta*) in a small stream, as determined by radio-telemetry. *Hydrobiologia* 470: 195-202.

Ovidio, M, Detaille A., Bontinck C. & Philippart J.C. (2009). Movement behaviour of the small benthic Rhine sculpin Cottus rhenanus (Freyhof, Kottelat & Nolte, 2005) as revealed by radio-telemetry and pit-tagging. *Hydrobiologia* (2009) 636:119–128

Pedersen, S., Dieperink, C. & Geertz-Hansen, P. (2003). Fate of stocked trout *Salmo trutta* L. in Danish streams: survival and exploitation of stocked and wild trout by anglers. *Ecohydrology & Hydrobiology* 3: 39-50.

Prentice, E.F., Flagg, T.A. & McCutcheon, C.S. (1990)a. Feasibility of using implantable passive integrated transponder (PIT) tags in salmonids. American Fisheries Society Symposium 7: 317-322.

Prentice, E.F., Flagg, T.A., McCutcheon, C.S. & Brastow, D.F. (1990)b. PIT-Tag monitoring systems for hydroelectric dams and fish hatcheries. American Fisheries Society Symposium 7: 323-334.

Quintella, B.R., Andrade, N.O., Espanhol, R. & Almeida, P.R. (2005). The use of PIT telemetry to study movements of ammocoetes and metamorphosing sea lampreys in river beds. *Journal of Fish Biology* 66: 97-106.

Riley, W.D., Eagle, M.O., Ives, M.J., Rycroft, P. & Wilkinson, A. (2003). A portable passive integrated transponder multi-point decoder system for monitoring habitat use and behaviour of freshwater fish in small streams. *Fisheries Management and Ecology* 10: 265-268.

Roghair, C.N. & Dolloff, C.A. (2005). Brook trout movement during and after recolonization of a naturally defaunated stream reach. *North American Journal of Fisheries Management* 25: 777-784.

Roussel, J.M., Haro, A. & Cunjak, R.A. (2000). Field test of a new method for tracking small fishes in shallow rivers using passive integrated transponder PIT technology. *Canadian Journal of Fisheries and Aquatic Sciences* 57: 1326-1329.

Scruton, D.A., McKinley, R.S., Kouwen, N., Eddy, W. & Booth, R.K. (2002). Use of telemetry and hidraulic modelling to evaluate and improve fish guidance efficiency at a louve rand bypass system for downstream-migration Atlantic salmon (*Salmo salar*) smolts and kelts. *Hydrobiologia* 483: 83-94.

Statsoft Inc. 2004. *STATISTICA (Data Analysis Software System)*. Version 7. www.statsoft.com. Tulsa, USA.

Teixeira A., Cortes R.M.V. & Oliveira D. (2006). Habitat Use by Native and Stocked Trout (*Salmo trutta* L.) In Two Northeast Streams, Portugal. *Bulletin Française de la Pêche et la Pisciculture* 382: 1-18.

Teixeira A. & Cortes R.M.V. (2007). Pit Telemetry as a Method to Study the Habitat Requirements of Fish Populations. Application to Native and Stocked Trout Movements. *Hydrobiologia* 582:171-185.

ter Braak, C.J.F. (1986). Canonical correspondence analysis: a new eigenvector technique for multivariate direct gradient analysis. *Ecology* 67: 1167-1179.

ter Braak, C.J.F. & Smilauer, P. (1998). *CANOCO- Reference manual and user's guide to Canoco for Windows: Software for Canonical Community Ordination (version 4)*. Microcomputer Power, Ithaca, NY, USA.

Weber, E.D. & Fausch, K.D. (2003). Interactions between hatchery and wild salmonids in streams: differences in biology and evidence for competition. *Canadian Journal of Fisheries and Aquatic Sciences* 1018-1036.

White, R.J., Karr, J.R. & Nehlsen, W. (1995). Better roles for fish stocking in aquatic resource management. In: *Uses and Effects of Cultured Fish in Aquatic Ecosystems,* Schramm, H.L. Jr. & Piper, R.G. (eds.), 527-547, American Fisheries Society, Bethesda, Maryland.

Young, M.K. (1994). Mobility of brown trout in south-central Wyoming streams. *Canadian Journal of Zoology* 72: 2078-2083.

Young, M.K. (1999). Summer diel activity and movement of adult brown trout in high-elevation streams in Wyoming, U.S.A. *Journal of Fish Biology* 54: 181-189.

17

Sea Turtle Research

I-Jiunn Cheng
Institute of Marine Biology,
National Taiwan Ocean University, Keelung, Taiwan
Republic of China (ROC)

1. Introduction

1.1 Definition

Telemetry includes an array of techniques that allow remote monitoring, measurement and recording or reporting of information. It was first used in weather research and has expanded quickly to other disciplines. Relatively accurate measurements without direct observer participation allow some important research that was impossible to conduct in the past. This has an important implication for study of life history traits of species that migrates long-distances, such as sea turtles. The ocean habitat, wide distribution ranges and movement across political boundaries all create difficulties for direct study of sea turtle behavior. Telemetry can overcome these obstacles and is a cost-effect tool for behavioral ecology.

1.2 Importance to sea turtle researches

1.2.1 Life history trait studies

Animal migrations, especially long-distance movements, are to explore for resources across substantial temporal and spatial scales. They are often adaptations for avoiding seasonal depletion of local resources in order to survive and reproduce in suitable environments (Alerstan et al., 2003; Southwood and Avens, 2010). Sea turtle hatchlings, because of high predation pressure in nearshore waters and otherwise unsuitable habitats near nesting beaches, must migrate (actually they must "drift") after leaving their nests to suitable nursery grounds (Bolten, 2003). In addition, sea turtles evolved from freshwater turtles (Pritchard, 1997). Thus, even though these giant reptiles have successfully invaded the ocean, they must still return to their natal beaches to nest (called "natal homing"; Carr, 1967). Therefore, migrations play substantial roles in the survival of sea turtle populations.

Sea turtles are ocean-wide, long-distance migrating reptiles that spend more than 95% of their time at sea. Except for leatherbacks, olive ridleys, flatbacks and some loggerheads, hatchlings spend their early lives drifting in the ocean (often referred to as "the lost years"; e.g. Bolten, 2003; Carr, 1967). After 5 to 7 years in the open ocean, they migrate into food-rich nearshore waters and feed along the bottom (Carr, 1967; Plotkin, 2003). Some food-rich areas, such as coral reefs, seagrass beds and nearshore fishing grounds are the sites favorable for juvenile sea turtles (e.g. Hawkes et al., 2006). Due to the developmental shift in nutrient requirements and other needed conditions for growth, sea turtles often exhibit an ontogenetic shift in habitat (Crouse et al., 1987). In addition, different species may stay in different habitats. For example, green, hawksbill, olive ridley, flatback and some loggerhead turtles migrate into nearshore waters when they advance from hatchling to juvenile status, while leatherbacks and some loggerhead turtles remain in the open ocean until adulthood (Bolten, 2003). Therefore, understanding the population dynamics of these giant reptiles requires detailed information for each life stage.

1.2.2 Energy and material transformation among ecosystems

Sea turtles are important in the dynamics of material and energy in the ocean, especially in nearshore ecosystems. Even though the migration of sea turtles is resource-driven (Plotkin, 2003), they can transfer the energy and material they have gathered by feeding hundreds to thousands of miles away to their nesting beaches and nearshore waters. The materials are deposited in the form of excretion, feces and eggs, providing resources for the local ecosystem (Bjorndal and Jackson, 2003). Also, they can transfer the materials and energy from feeding during their post-nesting migrations to their foraging and resting areas in the form of excretion and feces (e.g. Bjorndal and Jackson, 2003).

1.2.3 Sea turtle conservation

Sea turtles appeared in the world more than one hundred million years ago. Due to their large body size, fast swimming speed and scales and scutes armor, they thrived through the age of dinosaurs and the radiation of mammals until two hundred years ago. The ancient character of sea turtles raises great interest in understanding their phylogeny, adaptive evolution, distribution and migratory behavior. Furthermore, the high commercial value and development of their nesting beaches for human recreation and housing projects, the losses they sustain to fisheries by-catch, the effects of pollution, the ingestion of marine debris and other human impacts have resulted in severe depletion of these once abundant marine reptiles (Hutchinson and Simmonds, 1992). The endangered status of sea turtles stresses the importance of understanding how they migrate from one life-stage habitat to the next, migrations being among the most vulnerable phases of their lives. Adequate knowledge of migrations is critical for design and adoption of effective conservation measures. The puzzles of migration can be largely solved through the application of telemetry tools, along with other techniques such as genetic markers of relationship (e.g. Bolten et al., 1998).

2. History of sea turtle telemetry studies

2.1 Initiation ages

Sea turtles are endangered or vulnerable species according to the list of the World Conservation Union (IUCN, 2003). They are difficult to track because a majority of their lives is spent in the ocean. In addition, the conservation status forbids extensive sampling and sacrifice of live specimens. Thus, the life history of sea turtles has remained largely unknown for a long period of time. In the past, Dr. Carr used helium balloons (Carr and Schroder, 1967) and flipper tagging (Carr, 1980) to track the whereabouts of sea turtles in the ocean, but without much success. The problems remained unsolved until the late 1970s when satellite telemetry techniques were first applied to wildlife studies (Stonburner, 1982;

Taillade, 1992). Solutions to the mysteries of sea turtle movement in the ocean have begun to emerge.

The first publications on satellite telemetry were by Timko and Kolz (1982) and Stoneburner (1982), based on studies conducted in 1979. The tags they used, designed to study the migrations of polar bears, reported to Nimbus satellites. Despite the cumbersome tags involved, the success of their work strongly encouraged researchers to apply satellite telemetry to sea turtle migratory behavior worldwide.

2.2 Early generation of satellite telemetries

The early generation of satellite tags was heavy and large, such as the Telonics ST-6 and ST-14 PTT. All the data were processed by the Argos system (Taillade, 1992). They only provides locations based on Doppler analyses, date and time of the data collection, location class, dive duration and on-site temperature. The accuracy and confidence limits of each location were determined based on how many transmitted data the satellites received during the passover period and were referred to a location class (LC). The most accurate LC (LC 3) has an estimated precision <150 m when at least four messages are received during a satellite pass. The worst available location class has only one message during a passover, with no estimate of location accuracy (LC Z; Argos, 1996). The relatively low accuracy of the location data and the diving behavior of sea turtles, only surfacing briefly for breath (e.g. Lutcavage and Lutz, 1997), resulted in small data volumes with high uncertainties. Despite these shortfalls, the widespread application of this technique allows us a thorough understanding of the behavior and distribution of animals, especially those most difficult to observe in the past. For example, by deploying 7 Argos-linked satellite PTTs (platform terminal transmitters) on green turtles that nested on Wan-an Island, Penghu Archipelago, Taiwan from 1994 till 1996, Cheng (2000) found that they migrate to coastal waters in Northeast Asia after their nesting seasons.

2.3 Radio and sonic telemetries

Distinct from satellite tags are directional radio and sonic telemetry and ultrasonic-pinger tracking. Directional radio and sonic telemetry have been used widely to track terrestrial animals such as rabbits, raccoons and striped skunks (e.g. Cochran et al., 1963), and also birds (e.g. Fuller et al., 1988). However, application of these techniques to sea turtle migration study is very limited. Because positions of animals are determined by triangulation, radio telemetry can only be applied in areas where three receivers can be set up. Thus, most studies on sea turtles are limited either to the coastal zone during short-term studies of movements between nesting visits to the shore (e.g. Dizon and Balazs, 1982) or to estuarine environments (e.g. Brauna et al., 1997) where the detection range is less than 5 km. Ultrasonic pinger tracking involves attaching a pinger to the trailing edge of a sea turtle's dorsal carapace, and then locating its position by listening with a hydrophone from a boat. Theoretically, the receiver can detect signals within 1 to 2 km. In practice, however, due to the attenuation of the sound and contamination of the sound by noise from waves, turbulence, marine organisms, etc., the signal can only be heard clearly within 100 to 200 m. Thus, this system, like radio tracking, works better for very short-range studies, such as diel migration in foraging grounds or coastal movements. (e.g. Addison et al., 2002). The labor-intensive aspect and the short range of detection have curtailed extensive development of these telemetry systems.

2.4 Diving behavior studies

Since 1980, researchers have turned their attention to the study of sea turtle diving behavior. This is based on the general interest in animal behavior and to serve conservation purposes Techniques have indeed been developed to record turtle diving behaviors. Time-Depth Recorders (TDRs) have been used for this purpose since the late 80's (Eckert et al., 1986; Hays et al., 2001). A TDR contains pressure and light sensors and a clock. Thus, one can calculate the depth and record the diving behavior of a sea turtle during the course of monitoring. A TDR is a self-recording device without transmitting function, so the instrument and data must be retrieved before the dive sequences can be analyzed. This limits application mainly to the study of diving behavior for short durations in narrow geographic areas, such as the intervals between nestings (e.g. Cheng, 2009).

2.5 Advancement in satellite tag performances

For satellite telemetry studies, the advances of computer techniques in the 1990s enabled development of satellite tags that are smaller, lighter and with greater battery capacity. These improvements allow application of satellite tags to a wider range of both species and ages for longer tracking durations. For example, Shaver and Rubio (2008) used satellite tags to study the migration of the "head-strated" olive ridleys. They confirmed that nearshore areas close to the release points of the "head started" turtles are their main foraging grounds. In addition, the migration behaviors of the "head started" release turtles were similar to those of wild-born turtles. Recently, Wyneken et al. (2008) used miniature satellite tags to track small juvenile loggerhead turtles, discovering the migration of the hatchlings during their "lost years" proposed by Carr (1967).

Advances in tag performance include addition of new sensors. Thus, more information on the life history traits can be measured. Among the most useful and widely used are pressure sensors, which enable us to characterize the diving behavior of the tagged animal along the migration route. We can now view sea turtle migration patterns in three, rather than two, dimensions. An important example is the SDR (Satellite Depth Recorder) produced by Wildlife Computer Inc. Depth sensors require extended recording, enabled by the SPLASH, MK-10 tags and SRDL (Satellite Relay Data Logger) produced by the Sea Mammal Research Unit. Other sensors attached to turtles and reporting via satellite tags include IMASEN (Inter-MAndibular Angle SENsor), which is used to understand the foraging behavior of a sea turtle during migration (e.g. Fossette et al., 2008), and a body temperature logger, which is used to understand how large sea turtles like leatherbacks maintain body temperatures suitable for survival in both warm tropical and cold polar waters (Casey et al., 2010). These improvements in data collection provide more complete understanding of sea turtle life history traits other than simple migration routes in the wild. After review of more than 130 relevant publications over 20 years, Godley et al. (2008) confirmed that detailed information on sea turtle life history traits in the ocean can be gathered through this technique. However, the limit on the available storage space on the environmental polar orbiting satellites curtails the detailed information provided from the sensors themselves.

2.6 GPS satellite telemetries

A new technique emerged in late 2000 – the GPS (global positioning system) satellite tag. This advance acts as the stepping stone to a new era of telemetry studies. GPS was developed in the early 1970s to overcome the limitations of navigation systems and mainly was used for military defense purposes at that time. A code (i.e. SA; Selective Availability) added by the US government resulted in poor resolution (± 100 m) for the civilian purposes. Lifting of the SA interference in 2000 increased the accuracy of GPS positions substantially (< ± 10 m). This enables us to apply GPS to the study of animal behavior more widely. Despite this improvement, the application of GPS to marine organisms, especially those emerging briefly for breath like sea turtles, is still impossible. Each geographic location determined by the GPS device requires confirmation from at least 6 satellites, which takes about 3 minutes to complete. The breath duration of sea turtles is equal to or less than 90 seconds. Thus, the GPS can only be applied to general oceanographic studies, such as buoy tracking. Only in recent years has the development of Fastloc technology allowed combining GPS with satellite telemetry technology. According to a document available from Widllfie Computer Inc. (www.wildlifecomputers.com), this software can acquire position signals within 10 mS. This makes possible the study of sea turtle movement on fine scales, such as home-range studies during the inter-nesting interval (e.g. Schofield et al., 2009).

2.7 Underwater video camera--Crittercam

In recent years, underwater video camera systems have been introduced to "visualize" an animal's behavior in the water by attaching the camera to the carapace aligned toward the head. This system is called "Crittercam" and has been funded mostly by the National Geographic Society. Seminoff et al. (2006) used this system to determine that there are six different diving patterns and three foraging strategies of the green sea turtle. Furthermore, they found that sea turtles may conduct different types of activities during the same dive. Thus, one has to interpret diving behavior with caution. Because this system provides more information than the TDR, it provides us new interpretations of the diving behavior of sea turtles in the wild. However, due to the expense of the instruments and lack of transmission capability, Crittercam has to be retrieved and the data downloaded. Therefore, application of this technique to the diving behavior of sea turtles is still limited.

3. Retrievable recording studies

3.1 Time-Depth Recorders (TDRs)

Retrievable recording instruments are self recording devices without data transmitting ability. They are mainly used for the study of animal diving behavior. The most important instrument in sea turtle research is the TDR.

Sea turtles spend more than 95% of their time in the ocean, and their migration behaviors are not simply swimming in surface water and recordable in just 2-dimentions. Rather, they dive during their migrations; thus, migrations are three-dimensional movements. Similarly to marine mammal activity, how sea turtles adapt to changes of water temperature and pressure when diving is an interesting physiological question. For example, Boye (1997) discussed the relationships among foraging depth, lung oxygen content, dive duration, water temperature and the size of sea turtles. TDR has been used widely to record the diving behavior of sea turtles since late 80's (e.g. Eckert et al., 1986; Hays et al., 2000a), enhancing our understanding of sea turtle diving substantially.

3.2 Dive patterns

Based on the high frequency of TDR sampling (1 second or less per sample) the pattern of each dive can be represented graphically. Basically, six diving patterns have been identified, U, V, W, S (include inverse S), shallow and "others". U dives are mainly used during rest intervals or for moving along the seabed (Cheng, 2009); V dive are mainly used for traveling or exploring the environment (Hochscheid, et al., 1999); W dives are commonly considered as foraging dives during which turtles spend time in a food patch (Fossette et al., 2008); S dives are apparently related to energy conservation (Hochscheid et al., 1999); shallow dives are mainly used for swimming in near-surface waters (Houghton et al., 2002); and "others" are dives that combine more than one dive type. The high resolution of the diving pattern allows us to explain what turtles really do during diving periods, including the diel variability of the behavior (Storch et al., 2005). This instrument has used to study the diving behavior of immature hawksbill (van Dam and Diez , 1996), wild hawksbill turtles (Storch et al., 2005), gravid leatherback turtles during the inter-nesting interval (Eckert et al. , 1986; Southwood et al., 2005), green turtles (Hays et al., 2004) and loggerhead turtles (Houghton et al., 2002). It is generally found that most gravid females conduct resting U-dives during the inter-nesting intervals, decreasing this dive type and switching to shallow dives a few days prior to nesting events, apparently searching for the proper nesting beach (Cheng, 2009). Recently, a new device has emerged on the market, the G5 tag. It is a miniature tag, 8 mm long and 1.3 g weight in the water. This instrument has been used to study the diving behavior of jellyfish (Hays et al., 2008). It may enable us to study the diving behavior of turtle hatchlings after they enter the sea.

3.3 Long-term migration studies

Only a few researchers have employed TDR tags to conduct long-term migration studies that include pre-nesting, inter-nesting and post-nesting periods (e.g. Rice and Balazs, 2008). A requirement for conducting such TDR studies is that researchers must understand the whereabouts of sea turtles in detail. Then they can determine when and where to retrieve the TDR. Based on the results of the above studies, one can clearly define the diving behavior and the physiological significance of different dive patterns, as well as the responses of sea turtles to the temporal and spatial variations of both food availability and hydrodynamic features. This has made an indelible contribution to the understanding of the diving behavior of sea turtles.

4. Non-retrievable telemetry studies

4.1 Satellite telemetry studies

Non-retrievable telemetry instruments use an antenna to transmit data they have collected via radio to a boat or shore station or via radio to a satellite and from the satellite to a ground receiver. They do not require having the instrument in hand to download the data. Therefore, they can be used to determine movement patterns across wide geographic areas and under varied environmental condition. Due to the size limit of this chapter, I will only focus on the instruments most widely used to date such as satellite telemetry.

There are two kinds of satellite tag; the conventional satellite PTT (platform terminal transmitter) tag and Pop-up Archival Transmitting (PAT) tags. Each tag is designed for a specific purpose and provides slightly different information.

4.2 Conventional satellite telemetries

A conventional satellite PTT transmits its data to a satellite at frequency determined by the user, e.g. 6 h on (transmitting) and 6 h off (not transmitting). Because radio signals cannot be transmitted under water, there is a salt-water switch installed on the tag that stops transmission of signals 5 seconds after the sensor is covered by the water, in most cases when the sea turtle starts to dive. It allows transmission when the turtle surfaces. Combining the salt-water switch with intermittent transmissions maximizes tag performance and extends battery life significantly. Because sea turtles are air breathing, this kind of tag enables us to track their migrations in detail.

Sea turtles are capital breeders, investing heavily in their beach deposits of eggs (Southwood and Avens, 2010). They must use hydrodynamic features effectively in order to arrive at nesting destinations at suitable seasons, reduce unnecessary costs and increase their fitness. However, both genetic and tagging studies show that sea turtles migrate several hundreds to thousands miles to both forage and nest (Bowen et al., 1995; Cheng, 2000), even crossing entire oceans (Bolten et al., 1998; Hughes et al., 1998). There is much evidence also showed that, except for a few species like flatbacks (*Natator depressa*), sea turtle species have widespread distributions in the oceans (Bowen et al., 1992). Thus, use of environmental information to determine their migration routes is essential to the survivor of their populations. Studies have shown that currents, fronts, winds, Earth's magnetic field variations, bathymetric features, path integrations and more factors are important influences determining the migratory navigation of sea turtles (Plotkin, 2003).

Many studies have shown that the highly migratory species tend to use surface currents to conduct their long-distance movements (e.g. across the ocean) (Bolten et al., 1998). From a physiological ecology point of view, swimming with the current can reduce energy expenditure. However, it is not easy to prove this argument. Usually, in addition to the migratory routes of animals, researchers also need the current trajectories or related information to determine the relationships. One may misinterpret the relationship if the two parameters are evaluated on the different scales. For example, when examining the overlap of migration routes tracked by the satellite telemetry with surface chlorophyll distributions in Atlantic, Hays et al. (2002) found no apparent relationship between the post-nesting migration of green turtles from Ascension Island and surface currents. It is possible that the scale of measurement for chlorophyll is much larger than that of the migration routes of the turtles. In other cases, the relationship is more straightforward. For example, Hawkens et al. (2006) combined satellite telemetry with surface currents and chlorophyll distribution, revealing that larger loggerhead turtles in the Atlantic migrate to the coastal waters, while smaller ones remain in the open ocean.

4.3 Study the diving behavior with satellite telemetries

Some researchers try to expand the function of conventional PTTs by using the dive duration to judge the diving behavior (e.g. Godley et al., 2003). However, due to the fact that this instrument does not provide detailed information on dives (see TDR functions in the previous section), researchers can only evaluate the diving behaviors in different waters. The application of this device to study diving behavior is quite limited.

Adding pressure sensors to satellite tags is a substantial improvement. In addition to the position data provided by conventional satellite tags, pressure data allows us to study sea turtle diving behavior during oceanic migration. Two of the most widely used combinations are the SDR (Satellite Depth Recorder) and SRDL (Satellite Relay Data Logger), already mentioned. However, due to the limited space available in the satellite to store data for transmission, not all the collected data are processed and send to the user. SDR only provides the percentage of time a sea turtle stays in a specific water depth. It does not describe the full diving behavior, but it does reveal the water depths where sea turtles explore most frequently. Howell et al. (2010) used SDR-10 and SDR-16 tags to track loggerhead turtles captured as longline by-catch in the mid-Pacific. They found that the seasonal diving behavior of these immature turtles is related to hydrodynamic features such as eddies and the depth of the mixing layer.

Sea Mammal Research Unit selects the five most representive positions in a dive profile from SRDL (Satellite Relay Data Logger) data and provides them to the user. One can then reconstruct the dive profile based on those five positions. By using this device, Hays et al. (2004) found that, once leatherbacks migrated well out into Atlantic Ocean, they go deeper and deeper the longer away from the nesting beaches. They suggested that this behavior was related to foraging activities. Hamel et al. (2008) deployed SRDLs to study the inter-nesting diving behavior of six olive ridley turtles offshore from Northern Australia and found that they spent most of the time resting on the seabed and decreased dive durations a few days prior to each nesting event.

In recent years, these instruments reporting to satellites have been used extensively to study the diving behavior of sea turtles during their post-nesting phase, even their whole migration periods. Among sea turtles, leatherbacks are the best candidates. This is because leatherbacks make cross-ocean migrations. They nest on tropical beaches and forage in sub-polar waters. Their exclusive food items - jellyfish – are distributed widely in the open ocean; from pole to pole and from surface to several hundred even a thousand meters depth. Thus, the study of their diving behaviors can provide long-term and rich information on their life history traits. López-Mendilaharsu et al. (2009) conducted a long-term study of leatherback turtles with SDRL, confirming the high use area for nesting in South Africa and the relationship between the dive depth and the concentration of zooplankton.

4.4 Dichotomous development in satellite tracking devices

The emergence of GPS satellite telemetry creates a new dimension in the study of animal behavior. For example, by combining GPS satellite telemetry with the local marine environmental data, Schofield et al. (2010) determined the home range of nesting loggerhead turtles at Zakynthos Island, Greece. Furthermore, they found that the females would adjust their home range and nesting beaches slightly, depending on weather conditions, to maintain the maximum fitness of the population.

There has been a dichotomous development in satellite tracking devices after emergence of GPS technology. Despite their fine-scale position resolution, GPS satellite tags are not equipped with pressure sensors, and thus provide no diving information. On the other hand, even though SDR or SRDL does provide good dive information it still relies on the Argos system to determine positions. There is an urgent need to combine these techniques to provide comprehensive information on 3-D behavior of sea turtles in the ocean. Furthermore, despite the improvements in tag performance, a major drawback is the limitation on power supply. The water-tight design of the satellite tag does not allow battery replacement. Thus, if the antenna has not broken during operation, the lifetime of the tag depends mainly on battery life. Even though the manufacturer uses lithium batteries, saltwater switches and pre-set transmitting intervals to extend tag lifetime, scarcely any telemetry study lasts more than 2 years. Some researchers try to extend their tag life by using 2 batteries instead of one or by refrigerating tags to protect the batteries. Still, tags cease transmission once their batteries are drained. The remigration interval of sea turtles usually lasts from 2 to 7 or more years, which is much longer than the battery lifetime. Therefore, the understanding of life history traits throughout the period before remigration will be limited. One solution to this problem is to use solar-battery satellite tags. This tag is still in the protocol stage at this writing. The other solution is to invent a hydrodynamically rechargeable battery.

4.5 Pop-up PAT tags

PAT tags are designed to track the large-scale movements and behavior of fish and other animals which do not spend enough time at the surface to allow the use of real-time satellite tags (http://www.wildlifecomputers.com/technologies.aspx?ID=4). In sea turtle research, PAT tags are used to study survivorship. A PAT must detach from the animal and surface before the data it collected (e.g. temperature, depth, light level) can be transmitted to a satellite. Thus, the length of attachment is a compromise between the requirements for the tag to release properly and the need for long-term attachment. The interval should also allow for operation of a break-away link should the animal become entangled (Epperly et al., 2007). PATs are usually used to determine the post-hooking survival rate of marine turtles interacting with fishing gear such as longlines. Sasso and Epperly (2007) deployed them on 15 by-caught loggerhead turtles in the North Atlantic Ocean and found that lightly hooked turtles may not suffer any additional mortality after release. Despite these important functions, the major drawback of PAT tags is that they only transmit signals when they surface, thus providing only one position datum (the tag surface position).

5. Multi-disciplinary telemetry studies

5.1 Combination the satellite telemetries with oceanographic features

Multi-disciplinary telemetry studies combine telemetering devices with other techniques, sensors and oceanographic instruments for sea turtle research. With advances in image processing in recent years, we can combine migration route data with oceanographic features like chlorophyll distribution, sea surface height, temperature, salinity, etc. Then, the influence of oceanographic features on sea turtle behaviors becomes graphically evident. Saba et al. (2008) found that ENSO, by influencing the abundance of major food sources, specifically jellyfish for leatherback turtles, determines the number in the nesting population in the next year; warm El Niño years had decreased nesting populations, while cold La Niña years had greater nesting populations.

Recently, the focus of telemetry studies has shifted to the relationship between sea turtle migration and currents. From the physiological point of view, migration routes of sea turtles are influenced by the distance to food sources (Godley et al., 2003). For example, in order to save energy on long-distance trips, sea turtles may divide migration routes into several sections and feed during the migration to reduce the energy depletion and replenish body energy reserves (Alerstan et al., 2003).

5.1.1 Qualitative evaluation the relationship between oceanographic features and migration behavior

Physical features in the ocean, such as tidal currents can influence the migratory behavior of sea turtles. Alerstan et al. (2003) believed that currents can be either beneficial or negatively impact the long distance migration of sea turtles. Some recent studies even estimate qualitatively the extent of current influence on the migration of sea turtles. For example, in a recent review paper, Sale and Luschi (2009) pointed out that sea turtles adjust their migration speed and direction to overcome the influence of currents to reach their destinations. Recently, Hay's research team fitted buoy tracks and particle drifts in the ocean into a Lagrangian drifter model. They compared the model results with satellite tracking trajectories of turtles, distributions of foraging areas, nesting sites and a genetic map to prove that, after hatchling green turtles enter the sea, they drift with the current to their distant foraging ground. Then, with the aid of surface current, they return to the vicinity of their birth places to forage after reaching the size of immature juveniles (Hays et al., 2010).

5.1.2 Quantitative evaluation the relationship between oceanographic features and migration behavior

In addition to qualitative studies, some researchers try to determine quantitatively the influence of current on the migration behavior of sea turtles. Most such studies are done by fitting the migration data to numerical current models and determining their relationship. The first publication of a model for turtle trajectories was done by Graper et al. (2006). They found that leatherback turtles in the Atlantic Ocean swim either with, against or across the current and forage in the dynamically active areas. They also suggested that the current has a noticeable influence on the migration behavior of sea turtles. Cheng and Wang (2009) compared the satellite tracking results from the post-nesting migration of green turtles from Wan-an Island, Penghu Archipelago, Taiwan, with the current strength and direction on each monitoring position from a sb-ADCP derived current model. They proved that the tidal current in Taiwan Straits does influence the migration behavior of green turtles: some migrated with the current to save energy; some migrated against the current, possibly using it as directional cue, while others were deflected by the current. In addition, even though they were able to adjust their speeds and directions when deflected by the current, they were not able to compensate completely for the deflection. Kobayash et al. (2011) compared the satellite telemetry from 34 by-caught loggerheads from pondnets in I-Lan County, Taiwan, with oceanographic features (e.g. NOAA Pathfinder sea surface temperature (SST), AVISO altimetry products - sea surface height, geostrophic u- and v-component, SeaWiFS ocean colour, bathymetry) and Earth magnetic-field data from the IGRF-10 model (total force, declination, inclination) and found that the East China Sea is their main region of congregation, and they prefer to stay on the edges of eddies. Sea turtles migrate in the ocean in three dimensions, sometimes diving down to hundreds of meters, and current strength and direction may be different at different depths. The above quantitative studies assumed that the animal swims entirely in the surface water, which is not true. Thus, there is a need to include diving data in the numerical models, as well as the migration speed, in order to determine the "true" influence of ocean currents on the migration of sea turtle.

In addition to satellite telemetry, combinations of other instruments have also been used to discover sea turtle migration patterns and diving behaviors. By combining TDR and electrocardiograph studies, Southwood et al. (1999) confirmed the increase in heart rate while leatherback turtles are air breathing during surface emergence. Makawski et al. (2006) used ultrasonic pinger with TDR recording and found that the home range of immature green turtles in offshore Florida waters is related to the distribution of seagrass meadows. They forage there during daytime and rest as well as avoid predators there in the night. All these results emphasize the importance of multi-disciplinary approaches for acquiring full understanding of the life history traits of sea turtles.

6. Telemetry studies for sea turtle conservation

6.1 By-catch post-release survivorship studies

Sea turtles spend the majority of their lives in the sea, only emerging on beaches to nest. Despite the intense conservation efforts on the beaches, some populations have still declined to the edge of extinction. Results of population stochastic model analyses, such as elastic and deterministic models (e.g. Heppell et al., 1998), show that fisheries by-catch is the major source of mortality. Therefore, understanding of the interaction between the sea turtles and fisheries is the key to solving the conservation problem. Telemetry, especially satellite telemetry, can be a useful tool for this purpose. Pop-up PAT tags described in the previous section were used to determine the post-release survivorship of by-caught turtles. Snoody and Williard (2010) combined satellite telemetry results and evaluated plasma biochemistry of post-release Kemp's ridley and green turtles caught in gillnets and found that entanglement by the fishery can disrupt the homeostasis of physiological functions, reducing their survivorship.

6.2 Identification of the "hot spot" regions in the ocean

In addition to study of the interaction of sea turtle migrations and diving behavior with fishing gear, the aggregation of sea turtles in the open ocean identified by satellite telemetry (so called "hot spots") can also act as a focal point for conservation measures. Polovina et al. (2006) used SDR and oceanographic features (chlorophyll and geostrophic current) to prove that oceanic regions, specifically the KEBR (Kuroshio Extension Bifuration Region), represent an important forage habitat for loggerheads. They suggested that conservation efforts should focus on identifying and reducing threats to the survivorship of loggerhead turtles in that region of the North Pacific. Kobayash et al. (2011) trackedg 34 by-caught loggerheads carrying conventional satellite PTT tags that had been released near eastern Taiwan. They found that loggerhead hotspot areas are on the continental shelf next to the Yangtze River and in coastal and pelagic areas next to Taiwan, China, Japan, and South Korea. They noted that this area is also intensively fished, primarily by boats from China. The incidental or targeted takes of loggerhead turtles by these and other fisheries over the continental shelf need detailed investigation. Recently, GPS satellite telemetry was also apply to this issue. For example, Schofield et al. (2010) used GPS satellite tags to determine in fine scale the home range of loggerhead turtles nesting in Greece during their inter-nesting interval. The improvement in accuracy of the positions provides important information for delimiting and adjusting marine protected areas.

6.3 Application of the GIS (geographic information system)

With the popularization of GIS (geographic information system) since 2000, researchers have tried to combine the migration data from this technique with relevant physical, chemical and biological oceanographic information, and to determine their relationships, basically using mapping. For example Halpin et al. (2006) developed the OBIS-SEAMAP (Ocean Biogeographic Information System-Spatial Ecological Analysis of Marine Megavetebrate Animal Population) system in 2002, and they post the migration routes of marine animals at large scales on ocean and weather feature maps in order to understand the dynamics of animal populations. That not only serves research on animal biogeography, but acts as a reference tool for resource management, marine conservation and popular science education. Despite the fact that this system is still in the promotion stage, many research teams have published their results using this system.

6.4 Global climate change effects

The effect of global climate changes on living organisms and ecosystems has become one of the major scientific and social issues in recent years. For the marine environment, the rise in temperature will change wind patterns and influence both marine productivity and the survival of sea turtle populations (Reina et al., 2009). Besides, global climate change will also influence surface current patterns. This will influence the foraging behavior of sea turtles and the quality of their nesting environments, influencing the migration routes and behaviors of sea turtles (Hawkes et al., 2009). Thus, long-term application of satellite telemetry and relevant ocean features will provide valuable information on how sea turtles come to cope with the ever changing environment. Because the influence of global climate change is more pronounced in higher latitude regions than at lower latitudes, the leatherback turtle appears to be an excellent candidate for this kind of study. Leatherback turtles forage near the polar region and nest in tropical continents (López-Mendilaharsu et al., 2009).

7. Biologging

7.1 Definition

Biologging is a miniature self-recording device that attaches to an animal, records its behavior, physiological condition and nearby environmental information (Rutz and Hays, 2009). The collected data either transmits via antenna or is stored and decoded after the device is retrieved. Because it is not necessary to observe the animal directly, these devices are usually used to study animal behaviors that are difficult to track, especially those of endangered species.

7.2 New tools to study the behavioral ecology of the animal

Biologging research started in the 1960s' and 1970s' (Koyman, 2004) and has expanded substantially in the last 20 years. With the advances of computer technologies, these devices have become lighter and smaller, while their function improved greatly and memory capacity (e.g. allowing increased sampling frequency). The sensors on the device, such as oxygen content, pH, stomach temperature meters, have also increased substantially. In addition, the development of software to analyze the large quantity of data allows scientists to conduct more sophisticated research on the behavior of large animals, and to an extent on small animals as well (e.g. jellyfish; Lilley et al., 2009). With more accuracy in the data and improvement in the software to analyze the relevant environmental information, the researchers can obtain important details of animal behavior in the wild. These kinds of device act as diaries that faithfully record the animal's activities during the deployment period and lead to possible explanations. Therefore, an entire field has opened in biologging research (e.g. Rutz and Hays, 2009). For example, Hochscheid et al. (2010) found, based on the diving data from SRDL, that the extended surface drifting period of the loggerheads in the Mediterranean is related to breathing and the absorption of solar energy to assist in digestion and to increase body temperature for deep dives.

Biologging-related research has increased substantially since the First International Symposium on Biologging Science in 2003. Because biologging systems allow us to record much unnoticed behavior, it cans both determine the relationship between the animal behavior and the environment and bring new explanatory power to the field of behavioral ecology (Cheng, 2010). Sea turtles are oceanic migratory animals and are difficult to track directly. Thus, one can use biologging data to obtain much greater understanding of sea turtle behavior in the wild.

8. Conclusion

Sea turtles are ocean-wide, long-distance migrating reptiles that spend more than 95% of their time at sea. The study of migratory behavior is important to demographic studies, dynamics of marine ecosystem and conservation measures of these marine reptiles . Telemetry devices developed since the late 70's, enhancing our understanding of sea turtle migratory mechanism substantially. In addition to conventional satellite tags, directional radio and sonic telemetry and ultrasonic-pinger were also developed in 1980's. However, the low resolution and labor-intense efforts limited their developments. The retrievable device—TDR developed since 1980's enables us to interpret the diving behavior of sea turtle in great detail. With the advancement of computer technologies, the new generation of non-retrievable satellite tags allows more sensors add to the satellite tags, thus enhance the tag performance. The combination of the oceanographic instruments with the satellite telemetries allows researchers to conduct multi-disciplinary approach to study the sea turtle migratory behavior, both qualitatively and quantitatively. These approaches allow us to conduct proper conservation measures in the ocean. The miniature, high resolution and multi-function telemetry tags emerges the biologging concept and may bring new explanatory power to the field of behavioral ecology.

9. Acknowledgements

Author thanks the students and assistants from Marine Ecology and Conservation Laboratory at Institute of Marine Biology, National Taiwan Ocean University, Taiwan for their assistants in the field works. Author especially thanks Mr. George H. Balazs, from Pacific Islands Fisheries Science Center, National Marine Fisheries Services, NOAA, US for his selfless introduce into this field and provides all the necessary assistants. The telemetry studies in Taiwan were mainly supported by grants from National Science Council, Department of Forestry, Council of Agriculture and I-Mei Environmental Protection Foundation.

10. References

Addison, DS, JA. Gore, J. Ryder, and K. Worley. "Tracking Post-nesting Movements of Loggerhead Turtles (*Caretta caretta*) with Sonic and Radio Telemetry on the Southwest Coast of Florida, U.S.A.," Marine Biology 141 (2002): 201-205.

Alerstan, T, A. Hedenström, and S. Akesson. "Long-distance Migration: Evolution and Determinants," Oikos 103 (2003): 247-260.

Argos. User's Manual. Version 1.0 January 1996. Service Argos, Inc. Toulouse, France, 1996.

Bjorndal, KA, and JBC. Jackson. "Chap. 10. Roles of Sea Turtles in Marine Ecosystems: Reconstructing the Past," In The Biology of Sea Turtles, Vol. II, edited by Lutz, PL, JA. Musick, and J. Wyneken, 259-273. New York: CRC Press, 2003.

Bolten, AB. "Chap. 9. Variation in Sea Turtle Life History Patterns: Neritic vs. Oceanic Developmental Stages." In The Biology of Sea Turtles, Vol. II, edited by Lutz, PL, JA. Musick, and J. Wyneken, 243-257. New York: CRC Press, 2003.

Bolten, AB, KA. Bjorndal, HR. Martins, T. Dellinger, MJ. Biscotto, SE. Encalada, and BW. Bowen. "Transaltanic Developmental Migrations of Loggerhead Sea Turtles Demonstrated by mtDNA Sequence Analysis," Ecological Application 8 (1998): 1-7.

Bowen, BW, AB. Melyan, JP. Ross, CJ. Limpus, GH. Balazs, and JC. Avise. "Global Population Structure and Natural History of the Green Turtle (*Chelonia mydas*) in Terms of Matriarchal Phylogeny," Evolution. 46 (1992): 865-881.

Bowen, BW, FA. Abreu-Grobois, GH. Balazs, N. Kamezaki, CJ. Limpus, and RJ. Ferl. "Trans-Pacific Migrations of the Loggerhead Sea Turtle Demonstrated With Mitochondrial DNA Markers," Proceedings of National Academy of Science USA 92 (1995):3731-3734.

Boye, JL. "The Behavioural and Physiology Ecology of Diving," TREE 266 (1997): 213-217.

Brauna, J, SP. Epperly, and JA. Collazo. "Evaluation of a sonic Telemetry System in Three Habitats of an Estuarine Evironment," Journal of Experimental Marine Biology and Ecology 212 (1997): 111–121.

Carr, A. So Excellent a Fishe: A Natural History of Sea Turtles. Scribner Publishers. New York, 1967.

Carr, A. "Some Problems of Sea Turtle Ecology." American Zoology 20 (1980): 489-498.

Carr, A, and RE. Schroder. "Caribbean Green Turtle, Imperiled Gift of the Sea," National Geographic Journal. 131 (1967): 876-890.

Casey, JJ, JJ. Garner, SS. Garner, and AS. Williard. 2010. "Diel Foraging Behavior of Gravid Leatherback Sea Turtles in Deep Waters of the Caribbean Sea," Journal of Experimental Biology 213 (2010): 3961-3971.

Cheng, I-J. Post-nesting Migrations of Green Turtle (*Chelonia mydas*) at Wan-An Island, Penghu Archipelago, Taiwan," Marine Biology 137 (2000): 747-754.

Cheng, I-J. "Changes in Diving Behaviour During the Internesting Period by Green Turtles," Journal of Experimental Marine Biology and Ecology 381 (2009): 18-24.

Cheng, I-J. Green Turtle—Follow the Sea Turtle Professor to Search for Green Turtle. Taiwan: Morning Star Publishing Co. 2010.

Cheng, IJ, YH. Wang. "Influence of Surface Currents on Post-nesting Migration of Green Sea Turtles Nesting on Wan-an Island, Penghu Archipelago, Taiwan," Journal of Marine Science and Technology 17(4) (2009): 306-311

Cochran, WW, and RD. Lord Jr. "A Radio-tracking System for Wild Animals," Journal of Wildlife Management 27(1) (1963): 1963: 9-24.

Crouse, DT, LB. Crowder, and H. Caswell. "A Stage-Based Population Model for Loggerhead Sea Turtles and Implications for Conservation," Ecology 68 (1987):1412–1423.

Van Dam, RP, and CE. Diez. "Diving Behavior of Immature Hawksbill (*Eretmochelys imbricate*) in a Caribbean Cliff-wall Habitat," Marine Biology 127 (1996): 171-178.

Dizon, AE, and GH. Balazs. "Radio Telemetry of Hawaiian Green Turtles at Their Breeding Colony," Marine Fisheries Review 44 (1982): 13-20.

Eckert, SA, DW. Nellis, KL. Eckert, and GL. Kooyman. "Diving Patterns of Two Leatherback Sea Turtles (*Dermochelys coriacea*) During Internesting Intervals at Sandy Point, St. Croix, U.S. Virgin Islands," Herpetologica 42(3) (1986): 381-388.

Epperly, SP, J. Wyneken, J. Flanagan, CA. Harms, and B. Higgins. "Attachment of Popup Archival Transmitting (PAT) Tags to Loggerhead Sea Turtles (*Caretta caretta*)," Herpetological Review 38(4) (2007): 419-425.

Fossette, S, P. Gaspar, Y. Handrich, Y. Le Maho, and J-Y. Georges. "Dive and Beak Movement Patterns in Leatherback Turtles *Dermochelys coriacea* During Internesting Intervals in French Guiana," Journal of Animal Ecology 77 (2008): 236-246.

Fuller, MR, WS. Seegar, and LS. Schueck. "Routes and Travel Rates of Migrating Peregrine Falcons *Falco peregrinus* and Swainson's Hawks *Buteo swainsoni* in the Western Hemisphere," Journal of Avian Biology 29(4) (1988): 433-440.

Gaspar, P, JY. Georges, S. Fossette, A. Lenoble, S. Ferraroli, and YL. Maho. "Marine Animal Behaviour: Neglecting Ocean Currents Can Lead us Up the Wrong track," Proceedings of the Royal Society B, 3623 (2006): 1-5.

Godley, BJ, AC. Broderick, F. Glen, and GC. Hays. "Post-nesting Movements and Submergence Patterns of Loggerhead Marine Turtles in the Mediterranean Assessed by Satellite Tracking," Journal of Experimental Marine Biology and Ecology 287 (2003): 119-134.

Godley, BJ, JM. Blumenthal, AC. Broderick, MS. Cyone, MH. Godfrey, LA. Hawies, and MJ. Witt. "Satellite Tracking of Sea Turtles: Where Have We Been and Where Do We Go Next?" Endangered Species Research 4 (2008): 3-22.

Hamel, MA, CR. McMahon, CJA. Bradshaw. "Flexible Inter-nesting Behaviour of Generalist Olive Ridley Turtles in Australia," Journal of Experimental Marine Biology and Ecology 359 (2008): 47-54.

Halpin, PN, AJ. Read, BD. Best, KD. Hyrenbach, E. Fujioka, MS. Coyne, LB. Crowder, SA. Freeman, and C. Spoerri. "OBIS-SEAMAP: Developing a Biogeographic Research Data Commons for the Ecological Studies of Marine Ammals, Seabirds, and Sea Turtles," Marine Ecology Progress Series 316 (2006): 239-246

Hawkes, LA, AC. Broderick, MS. Coyne, MF. Godfrey, L-F. Lopez-Jurado, P. Lopez-Suarez, SE. Marino, N. Vero-Cruz and BJ. Godley. "Phenotypically Linked Dichotomy in Sea Turtle Foraging Requires Multiple Conservation Approaches," Current Biology 16 (2006): 990-995.

Hays, GC, JD. Metcalfe, and AW. Walne. "The Implications of Lung-regulated Buoyancy Control for Dive Depth and Duration," Ecology 85(4) (2004): 1137-1145.

Hays, GC, R. Adams, AC. Broderick, BJ. Godley, DJ. Lucao, JD. Metacalfe, and AA. Prior. 2000. "The Diving Behavior of Green Turtles at Ascension Island," Animal Behavior 59 (2000): 577-586.

Hays, GC, AC. Broderick, F. Glen, BJ. Godley, and WJ. Nichols. "The Movements and Submergence Behaviour of Male Green Turtles at Ascension Island," Marine Biology 139 (2001): 386-399.

Hays, GC, TK. Doyle, JR. Houghton, MKS. Lilley, JD. Metcafle, and D. Righton. 2008. "Diving Behaviour of Jellyfish Equipped with Electronic Tags," Journal of Plankton Research 30 (2008): 325-331.

Hays, GC, S. Fossette, KA. Katselidis, P. Mariani, G. Schofield. "Ontogenetic Development of Migration: Lagrangian Drift Tajectories Suggest a New Paradigm for Sea Turtles," Journal of Royal Society of Interface 7 (2010): 1319-1327.

Heppel, SS, CJ. Limpus, DT. Crouse, NB. Frazer, and LB. Crowder. "Population Model Analysis for the Loggerhead Sea Turtle, *Caretta caretta*, in Queensland," Wildlife Research 23(2) (1998): 143 - 161.

Hoscheid, S, BJ. Godley, AC. Broderick, and RP. Wilson. "Reptilian Diving: Highly Variable Dive Patterns in the Green Turtle *Chelonia mydas*," Marine Ecology Progress Series 185 (1999): 101-112.

Hochscheid, S, F. Bentivegna, A. Hamza, and GC. Hays. 2010. "When Surfacers Do Not Dive: Multiple Significance of Extended Surface Times in Marine Turtles," Journal of Experimental Biology 213 (2010): 1328-1337.

Houghton, JDR, AC. Broderick, BJ. Godley, JD. Metcalfe, and GC. Hays. "Diving Behaviour During the Internesting Interval for Loggerhead Turtle *Caretta caretta* Nesting in Cyprus," Marine Ecology Progress Series 237 (2002): 63-78.

Howell, EA, PH. Dutton, JJ. Polovina, H. Bailey, DM. Parker, and GH. Balazs. "Oceanographic Influences on the Dive Behavior of Juvenile Loggerhead Turtles (*Caretta caretta*) in the North Pacific Ocean," Marine Biology 157 (2010):1011–1026.

Hughes, GR, P. Luschi, R. Mencacci, and F. Papi. "The 7000-km Oceanic Journey of a Leatherback Turtle Tracked by Satellite," Journal of Experimental Marine Biology and Ecology 229 (1998): 209-217.

Hutchinson, J, and M. Simmonds. "Escalation of Threats to Marine Turtles," Oryx 26 (1992): 95-102.

IUCN, 2003. 2003 IUCN Red List of Threaten Species. International Union for Nature and Natural Resources Conservation.

Kobayash, DR, I-J. Cheng, DM. Parker, JJ. Polovina, N. Kamezaki, and GH. Balazs. "Loggerhead Turtle (*Caretta caretta*) Movement off the Coast of Taiwan: Characterization of a Hotspot in the East China Sea and Investigation of Mesoscale Eddie," ICES Journal of Marine Sciemce 68(4) (2011): 704-718.

Liew, H-C, and E-H. Chan. "Biotelemetry of Green Turtles (*Chelonia mydas*) in Pulau Redang, Malaysia, During the Internesting Period," Biotelemetry XII (1992).

Lilley, MKS, JDR. Houghton, and GC. Hays. "A Review of Distribution, Extent of Inter-annual Variability and Diet of the Bloom-forming Jellyfish Rhizostoma in European Waters,"Journal of Marine Biology Association United Kingdom 89 (2009): 39-48.

López-Mendilaharsu, M, CFD. Rocha, P. Miller, A. Domingo, and l. Prosdocimi. "Insights on Leatherback Turtle Movements and High Use Areas in the Southwest Atlantic Ocean," Journal of Experimental Marine Biology and Ecology 378 (2009): 31-39.

Lutcavage, ME, and PL. Lutz. "Diving Physiology." In The Biology Of Sea Turtles, edited by Lutz, PL, and JA. Musick, 277-296. Boca Raton: CRC Press, 1997.

Plotkin, P. "Chap. 8. Adult migrations and habitat use," In The Biology of Sea Turtles, Vol. II, edited by Lutz, PL, JA Musick, and J. Wyneken. 205-240, New York: CRC Press, 2003.

Pritchard, PCH. "Chap. 1. Evolution, Phylogeny and Current Status." In The Biology of Sea Turtles, edited by Lutz PL, and JA. Musick. 1-28, New York: CRC Press, 1997.

Rice, MR, and GH. Balazs. "Diving Behavior of the Hawaiian Green Turtle (*Chelonia mydas*) During Oceanic Migration," Journal of Experimental Marine Biology and Ecology 356 (2008): 121-127.

Rutz, C, and GC. Hays. "New Frontiers in Biologging Science," Biology Letter 5 (2009):289–292.

Saba, VS, GL. Shillinger, AM. Swithenbank, BA. Block, JR. Spotila, JA. Musick, and FV. Paladino. 2008. "An Oceanographic Context for the Foraging Ecology of Eastern Pacific Leatherback Turtles: Consequences of ENSO," Deep-Sea Research I, 55 (2008): 646-660.

Sale, A, and P. Luschi. "Navigational Challenges in the Oceanic Migrations of Leatherback Sea Turtle," Proceedings of Royal Society B 276 (2009): 3737–374

Sasso, CR, and SP. Epperly. "Survival of Pelagic Juvenile Loggerhead Turtles in the Open Ocean," Journal of Wildlife Management 71(6) (2007): 1838-1835.

Schofield, G, CM. Bishop, KA. Katselidis, P. Dimopoulos, JD. Pantis, and GC. Hays. 2009. "Microhabitat Selection by Sea Turtles in a Dynamic Thermal Marine Environment," Journal of Animal Ecology 78 (2009): 14–22.

Schofield, G, VJ. Hobson, MKS. Lilley, KA. Katselidis, CM. Bishop, P. Brown, and GC. Hays. "Inter-annual Variability in the Home Range of Breeding Turtles: Implications for Current and Future Conservation Management," Biological Conservation 143 (2010):722–730

Seminoff, JA, TT. Jones, and GJ. Marshall. "Underwater Behavior of Green Turtles Monitored With Vedio-time-recorders: What's Missing from Dive Profile?" Marine Ecology Progress Series 322 (2006): 269-280.

Shaver, DJ, and C. Rubio. "Post-nesting Movement of Wild and Head-started Kemp's Ridley Sea Turtles *Lepidochelys kempii* in the Gulf of Mexico," Endangered Species Research 4 (2008): 43-55.

Snoddy, JE, and AS Williard. "Movements and Post-release Mortality of Juvenile Sea Turtles Released from Gillnets in the Lower Cape Fear River, North Carolina, USA," Endangered Specie Research 12 (2010): 235–247.

Southwood, A, and L. Avens. "Physiological, Behavioral, and Ecological Aspects of Migration in Reptiles,' Journal of Comparative Physiology B 180 (2010):1–23.

Southwood, AL, RD. Andrew, ME. Lutcage, FV. Paladino, NH. Wes, RH. George, and DR. Jones. "Heart Rate and Diving Behavior of Leatherback Sea Turtles in the Eastern Pacific Ocean," Journal of Experimental Biology 202 (1999): 1115 1125.

Southwood, AL, RD. Andrews, FV. Palodino, and DR. Jones. "Effects of Diving and Swimming Behavior on Body Temperature of Pacific Leatherback Turtles in Tropical Seas," Physiology, Biochemistry and Zoology 78(2) (2005): 285-297.

Stoneburner, DL. 1982. "Satellite Telemetry of Loggerhead Sea Turtle Movement in the Georgia Bight," Copeia (1982): 400-408.

Storch, S, R. Pwilson, Z-M. Hills-Starr, and D. Adolung. "Cold-blooded Divers: Temperature-dependent Dive Performance in the Wild Hawksbill Turtle *Eretmochelys imbricate*," Marine Ecology Progress Series 293 (2005): 263-271.

Taillade, M. "Chap. 21. Animal tracking by satellite." In Wildlife Telemetry, Remote Monitoring and Tracking of Animals, edited by Priede, IG, and SM. Swift, 149-160. New York: Ellis Horwood Ltd., 1992.

Timko, RE, and AL. Kolz. "Satellite Sea Turtle Tracking," Marine Fishery Review 44(4) (1982): 19-24.

Wyneken, J, SV. Madrak, M. Salmon, and J. Foote. "Migratory Activity by Hatchling Loggerhead Sea Turtle (*Caretta caretta*): Evidence for Divergence Between Nesting Groups," Marine Biology 156 (2008): 171-181.

18

Movements and Habitat Use by Lake Sturgeon (*Acipenser fulvescens*) in an Unperturbed Environment: A Small Boreal Lake in the Canadian Shield

Terry A. Dick[1], D. Block[2] and Dale Webber[3]
[1]*Department of Biological Sciences, University of Manitoba, Winnipeg, Manitoba*
[2]*Department of Highways, Province of Manitoba*
[3]*Vemco, Division of Amirix, Halifax Nova Scotia*
Canada

1. Introduction

The order Acipenseriformes, belonging to a group of basal Acthopterygian fishes (Choudhury and Dick 1998), has two living families (Acipenseridae and Polyodontidae), 6 genera, and 26 species worldwide (Nelson and Paetz, 1992; Nelson 1994). The Acipenseridae are old with the fossil record of sturgeon like fish dating back 100 million years to the upper Cretaceous (Harkness and Dymond 1961, Fogle 1975, Pearce 1986, Mecozzi 1988, Choudhury and Dick 1998). Fossils of an extinct family, the chondrosteidae, are dated from the lower Jurassic to the lower Cretaceous (Scott and Crossman 1998). Other authors state that sturgeon species are primitive relicts of the Devonian period 300 million years ago (Glover 1961, Ono et al. 1983, Houston 1987). Choudhury and Dick (1998) suggest that acipenserids diversified within a narrow time frame and lapsed into a subsequent long period of morphological stasis.

The lake sturgeon has the most local names of all North American sturgeon species. These names include: rock, common, red, ruddy, Ohio, stone, shell-back, bony, freshwater, smooth-back, rubbernose, black, dogface, bull-nosed and Great Lakes sturgeon (Harkness and Dymond 1961, Williams and Vondett 1962, Scott and Crossman 1998), Pearce 1986, Mecozzi 1988).

The decline of sturgeon populations throughout the world (Bemis and Findeis, 1994) and in North America is well documented. Population numbers plummeted around the turn of the 20th century as a result of over-fishing (Prince, 1905, Dick et al. 1998). The continued decline of populations across Canada is due to a variety of factors including habitat loss, continued fishing pressure in the form of commercial, sport, and subsistence fisheries. Consequently, the Committee on the Status on Wildlife in Canada (COSEWIC) raised major concerns on the status of the species and a report was written for Canada by Dick et al. (2006a). Considerable effort has gone into sturgeon research over the past two decades and since then the understanding of lake sturgeon biology and habitat use has improved, facilitating the possible rehabilitation of some populations. The Manitoba records on lake sturgeon population declines are relatively complete because there are good historical records for lake sturgeon harvests from commercial fisheries (Prince, 1905; Bajkov and Neave, 1930; Baldwin et al. 1979, Choudhury et al. 1990), and the aboriginal communities have a strong knowledge base and a long fishing and cultural connection to sturgeon (Holzkamm and Wilson, 1988; Dick et al. 2002).

Information on lake sturgeon (*Acipenser fulvescens*) in North America was first compiled by Dick and Choudhury (1992). A considerable amount of new data has been accumulated since the early 1990s on lake sturgeon in North America and in Canada (Dick et al. 2006b). This document clearly shows that the national trends for lake sturgeon populations are a general decrease in numbers with some of the decline attributed to environmental perturbation. However, not all declines are due to environmental perturbations, for example, the recent decision by the Province of Quebec to reduce the commercial fishery quota on what was considered viable stocks indicates that commercial fishing still has a major impact on a few sturgeon populations (Dick et al. 2006a). Furthermore, continued fishing of any sort on numerous sturgeon stocks across Canada will have a detrimental affect on their chances of survival. According to current information there are atleast six distinct genetic stocks across Canada, therefore rehabilitation programs will be limited by restrictions on the transfer of stocks across major watersheds (Ferguson and Duckworth, 1997; Ferguson et al. 1993).

Today, a substantial amount of information is available on the general state of most lake sturgeon populations across Canada and the United States, the natural fragmentation of sturgeon populations, and how to retrospectively view lake sturgeon distributions. We also have some idea of what constitutes "good" sturgeon habitat, the habitat by juvenile sturgeon in natural systems (Chiasson et al. 1997; Barth et al. 2009), and new information on genetic diversity and rare phenotypes of lake sturgeon in a Canadian contex (Ferguson and Duckworth 1997; Ferguson et al. 1993).

The objectives of this study were to develop methods to study movements and habitat use by lake sturgeon, especially subadults and juveniles and develop tags that provide data on specific activities such as feeding. This study was designed to collect data on lake sturgeon movements and then to attempt to define habitat by describing substrate and currents in the vicinity of their movements. The Pigeon River was chosen because there was a relatively confined population in Round Lake, which would allow for fine scale movements to be assessed without the complications of immigration and emigration. Most of the data on which this chapter is based is from research conducted in Round Lake, Manitoba, Canada and from the laboratory of T. Dick at the University of Manitoba. No attempt was made in this chapter to provide a complete literature review of lake sturgeon as this has been published elsewhere (Dick et al. 2006b).

Round Lake study area: Round Lake is located on the Pigeon River which flows from Family Lake to Lake Winnipeg (Fig. 1). It is a small isolated lake in eastern Manitoba, Canada that was never commercially fished and consequently has remained a relatively unperturbed and an important reference lake for lake sturgeon studies. The study area included the Pigeon River in the vicinity of Round Lake, areas upstream from the lake to the first set of falls, Grant Falls, and downstream of the lake to the first set of falls. Round Lake has a typical boreal lake fish species compositions plus lake sturgeon. The fish species composition in Round Lake is illustrated in Fig. 2. Diets of fish species collected from Round Lake are presented in (Fig. 3) and lake sturgeon consumed mostly mayflies, clams and amphipods (based on the gavage method, see Dick (2004). Lake sturgeons are about 10% of the fish community based on catch per unit effort.

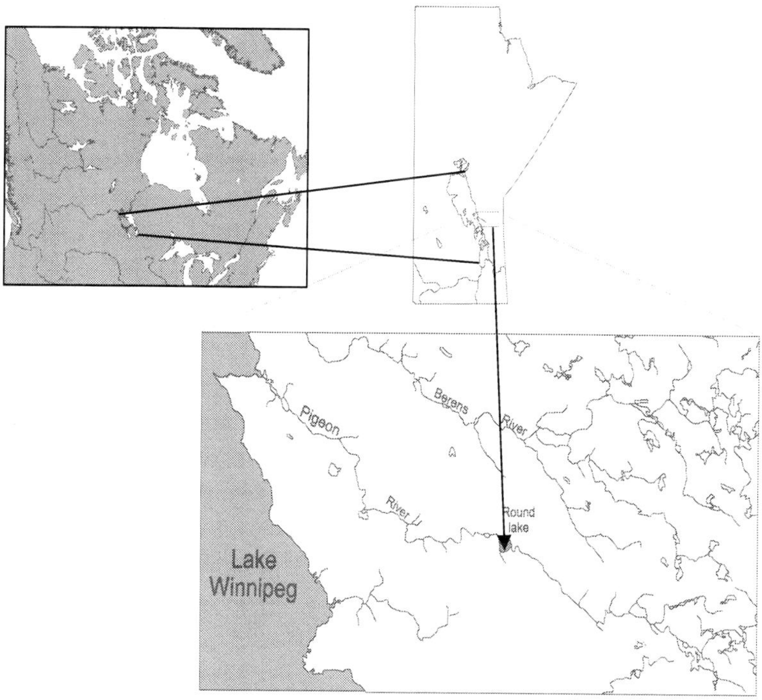

Fig. 1. Map of the Pigeon River, from Family Lake to Lake Winnipeg.

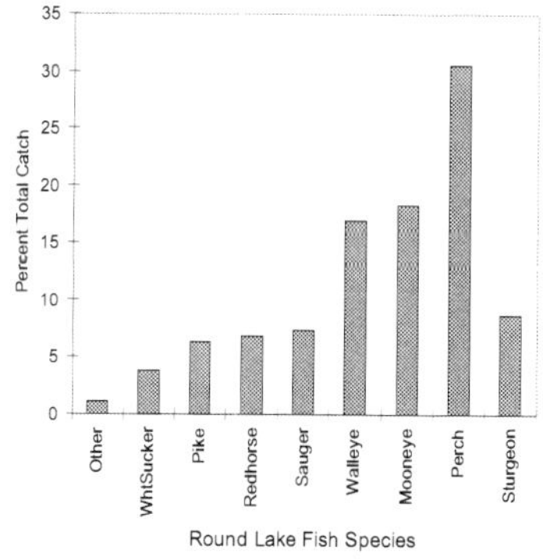

Fig. 2. The composition of fish species in Round Lake.

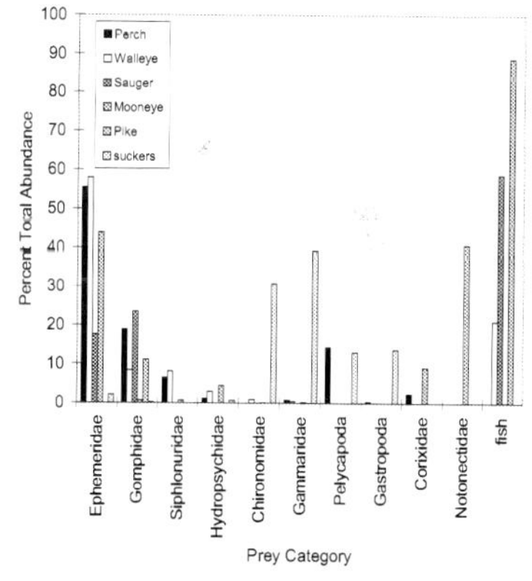

Fig. 3. The abundance of prey items in the stomach contents of each individual species of fish in Round Lake.

2. Telemetry technologies

2.1 Comparison of radio and acoustic tag technologies

Radio and acoustic telemetry were the two methods used to study animal movements but there are differences in their applications and the type of data acquired. Acoustic signals must be received underwater while radio signals are received in the air. Data from radio tags can be received from boats, airplanes and through the ice and is best for large scale studies where animals move considerable distances but is usually less precise in terms of location and is also labour intensive, especially the way we applied it. Both types of tags provide repeat data. Acoustic receivers are more precise (especially the VRAP system of Vemco Ltd.) and tags can measure variables such as depth and temperature, and are good for fine scale studies. Initially acoustic tags were large and the equipment was expensive and cumbersome to handle due to bulk and weight. More recently tags and receivers have been constructed that are reduced in size and the life of the tags has increased. Both radio and acoustic tags can be detected with mobile receivers but precision in locating animals is lower, for both systems, and there are usually fewer observations.

Gill nets were used to capture all lake sturgeon. Three different nets were used: 30 cm stretched mesh, 22.5 cm stretched mesh and a standard gang with six panels (3.1, 5, 6.9, 8.8, 10.6, 12.5 cm stretched mesh). Fish were brought to shore and placed on a damp canvas sheet. Weight, length was recorded and on a few fish a pectoral fin ray was removed to establish a size to age relationship.

This following section deals with a comparison between the two technologies. Both radio and acoustic tags were attached externally to the dorsal fin. For short term studies over days or a few months, external tags are adequate but for longer term studies of several years internally implanted tags are necessary. Radio tags were obtained from Lotek, Missassauga, Ontario, Canada and the acoustic tags were obtained from Vemco Ltd. (Halifax, Nova Scotia). Two types of acoustic tags were used. Large fish were tagged with V16 pressure tags, the remaining fish were tagged with V8 position tags. Pressure tags transmitted information on swimming depth as well as positional information. The V8 tags transmitted positional data. The tag weight to body weight ratio for both radio and acoustic telemetry was less than 1% for all fish. A piece of neoprene was placed between the tag and the dorsal fin and a piece of neoprene was placed on the opposite side of the fin for support of the attachment wires. Two hypodermic needles, spaced apart the length of the tag, were pushed through the neoprene backing and then through the dorsal fin of the fish. The attachment wires were fed through the tag, through the second piece of neoprene, and then through the needles. The needles were then pulled out pulling the attachment wires through the fin and the neoprene on the opposite side of the fin. The attachment wires were pulled snug and several knots were tied to secure the tag. Excess wire was removed using wire cutters. Later, a 40 gauge neoprene was used between the tag and the fin instead of the foam and neoprene also replaced the foam and plastic backing on the opposite side. This method gave a tighter fit for the tag when tested by hand, however there was no tag loss using either method. The radio tags were manufactured by Lotek Engineering, Missassauga, Ontario, Canada. All tools were sterilized before use and salt was applied to the tagged area after the procedure to reduce infection. Lake sturgeons, after attaching external tags, were held in a holding net placed in the lake at a depth of 2.0 meters. Fish remained inactive for periods of 20 to 40 minutes but as soon as normal swimming behaviour was observed they were released.

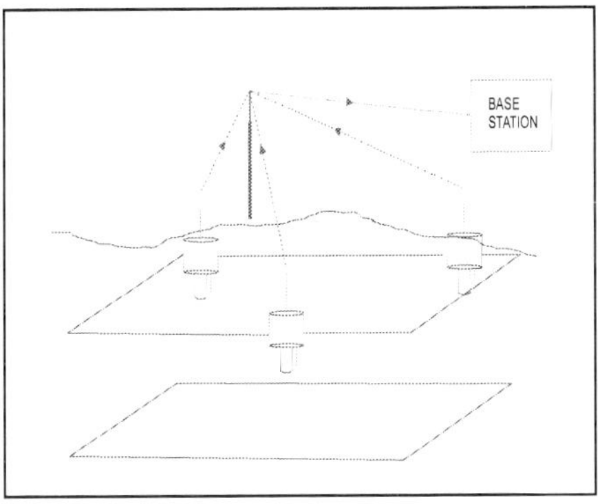

Fig 4. Diagram of the Vemco (VRAP) system.

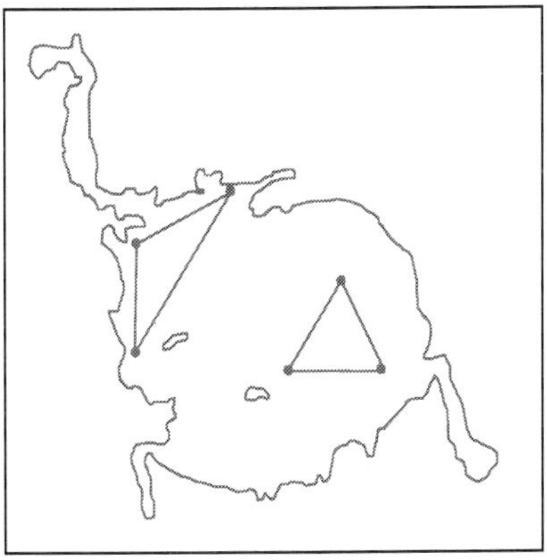

Fig. 5. Location of the two acoustic arrays in Round Lake.

Precise positioning of lake sturgeon was done using two radio linked acoustic positioning arrays (VRAP, Vemco Ltd.). Each array consisted of a base station which communicated with each of three buoys anchored in the lake (Fig. 4). Each buoy contained an acoustic transmitter, an omnidirectional hydrophone, and a VHF modem.

Buoy location was determined using survey techniques and having an understanding of the lake morphometry so that there was a clean line of site between receivers so that a tag signal was picked up by atleast two receivers. Test tags determined if a signal could not be picked up by a receiver due to an under water obstruction, such as a boulder, and if the receiver was obstructed it was re-positioned. The chosen positions covered 80% of the surface area of the lake. Figure 5 shows the distribution of the two 3-receiver arrays.

2.2 Telemetry data

Telemetry data analysis and presentation was done using Idrisi for Windows (Clark University, MA). Some maps were created in Idrisi for Windows. Acoustic telemetry data was imported from the VEMCO system program.

Determination of depth selection and substrate selection was done by hand. Seven days were selected for analysis. Selection was based on movements to include the widest possible range of movement patterns. Days 206 and 221 were selected for sturgeon 4014. Days 210 and 222 were selected for sturgeon 4015. Days 206, 211 and 219 were selected for sturgeon 4017. For each location on each day bottom depth was determined.

Swimming depth minus bottom depth was calculated to determine all locations in which the fish was in contact with the substrate. All values of 1 or less were included. All figures and comments pertaining to substrate selection only include locations in which a fish was in contact with the bottom. Other location statements and figures used all the positional data available.

Radio tags: These tags were attached externally to the dorsal fin. Initially, a piece of foam was placed between the tag and the dorsal fin and a piece of foam and a plastic backing were placed on the opposite side of the fin for support of the attachment wires. Details on tag attachment are outlined above.

A total of 20 radio tags were used and lake sturgeons were tracked periodically by boat (Table 1). When a signal was received the exact location of the fish was determined by circling the area until the signal was strong enough to trigger the code on the receiver. The locations were plotted on a map of the lake by visual triangulation with known points on land. A GPS location was recorded. Fig. 6A shows the total movements of all lake sturgeon in Round Lake fitted with radio tags. Twenty lake sturgeons were monitored over a three year period. The main patterns of movements over the deeper areas of the lake related to the flow of the river through the lake.

ID	Total (cm)	Fork(cm)	Weight(g)	Age
code 33	140	129	21000	-
code 31	129	121	13200	-
code 64	144	138	25970	-
code 63	132	122	14900	-
code 75	123	110	10185	-
code 65	122	112	9870	-
code 60	47	41	499	-
code 66	47	42	485	-
code 68	55	49	734	5
code 70	62	55	1202	7
code 72	50	45	551	-
code 32	114	106	8700	-
code 56	107	98.5	7120	34
code 51	66	60.5	2272	-
code 41	99	91	5350	-
code 42	114	109	9945	-
code 43	119	112	11596	-
code 40	135	122	14470	-
code 55	124	116	12840	
code 45	104	99	7920	

Table 1. Biological data for the radio tagged lake sturgeon.

Acoustic telemetry: Figure 6B illustrates the overall movements of nine tagged lake sturgeon in Round Lake in July and August 1997 using acoustic telemetry and provides details on each tagged fish (Table 2). Figs. 4 and 5 illustrate an array configuration and the base station (VRAP system) and the relative positions of two arrays. The main patterns trends are related to the deeper areas of the lake and related to the flow of the river into, through and out of the lake. Since stationary receivers were used we had the opportunity to run transects to determine if boat activity influenced lakes sturgeon movements as there have been concerns that boat activity may affect lake sturgeon movements.

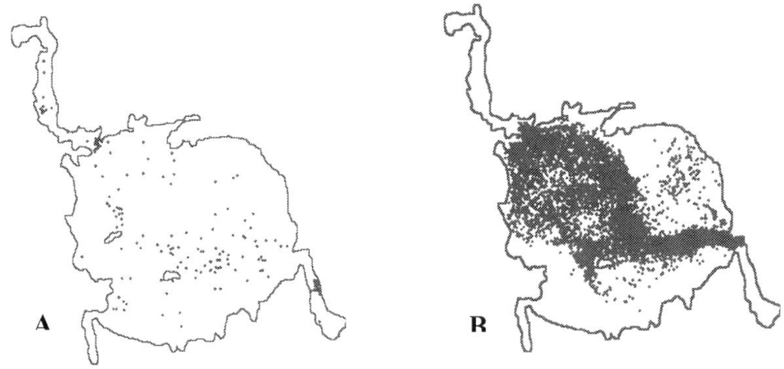

Fig. 6. A) Total movements of lake sturgeon in Round Lake using radio telemetry, B) Total movements of lake sturgeon in Round Lake Round Lake using acoustic telemetry

A series of transects were run at the same time each day on the acoustic tagged sturgeon to test the hypothesis that boat activity affected lake sturgeon movements. The results showed that movements of lake sturgeon during periods when boat transects were run do not differ from the sturgeon movements when no boat was on the water (Fig. 5). Lake sturgeon 4014 was located at the inlet and in the middle of the lake with and without boat activity. Lake sturgeon 4015 was located at the inlet with and without boat activity. Lake sturgeon 4017 was located generally in the area of the outlet with and without boat activity.The swimming depth of lake sturgeon during periods when the boat was on the water did not change from depths of lake sturgeon directly prior to when the boat was on the water (Figs.7 and 8). Lake sturgeon swimming depth changed often but was not correlated with presence or absence of boat activity. Mean depths were similar for times when boat transects were being run and times immediately prior to boat activity. We conclude that boat activity had no impact on lake sturgeon movements in our study and the lack of correlation between boat activity and lake sturgeon movements may relate to lake depth. By contrast, the application of radio tags and a mobile receiver in a shallow (2-3m) prairie river did affect lake sturgeon movements (Dick, unpubl. data). Clearly the type of aquatic system one is working in needs to be assessed, for impacts of boats and other anthropogenic activities, to be certain that abnormal sturgeon movements are not being recorded.

Number	Total length(cm)	Fork Length(cm)	Weight(g)	Age
4010	54	48	632	-
4013	49	44	572	-
4011	49	45	562	-
4012	48	43	506	4
4014	143	128	16900	-
4015	125	117	13250	-
4016	138	126	14750	31
4017	119	113	11620	-
4009	101	95	6790	22

Table 2. Lake sturgeon data for the acoustic tagged fish.

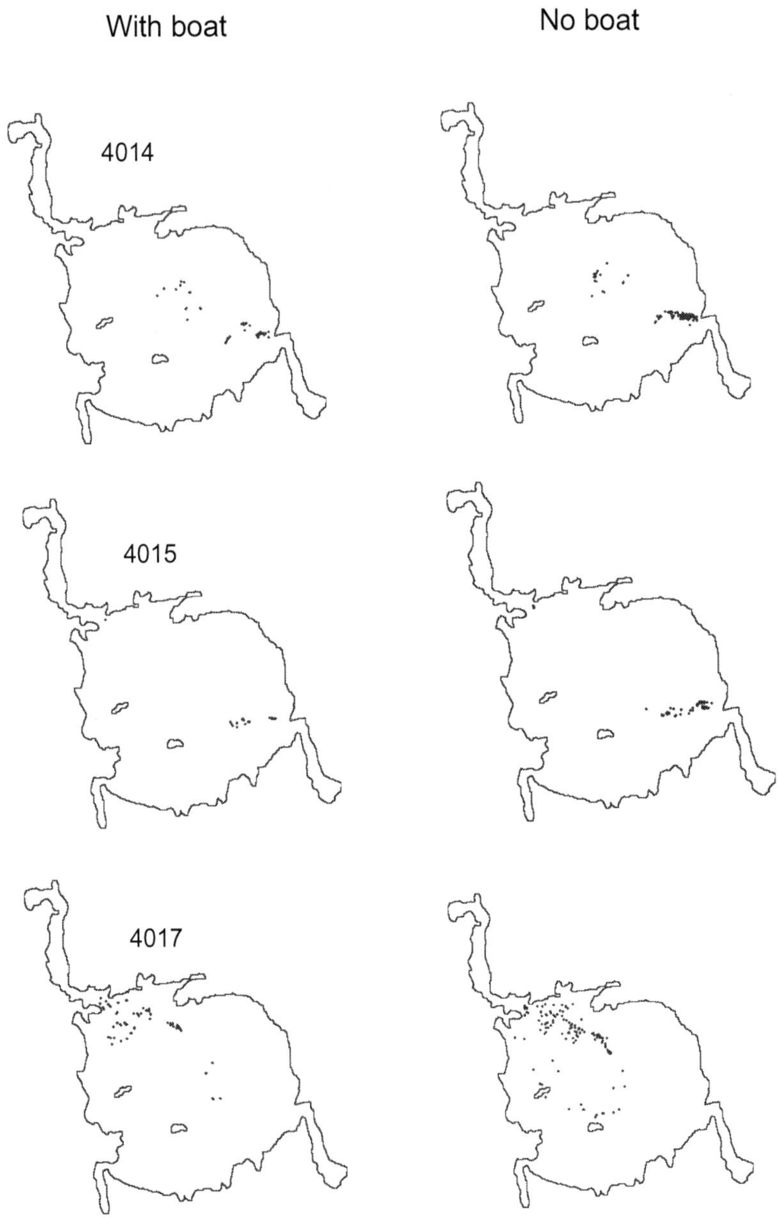

Fig. 7. Movement of lake sturgeon during movements of the boat and during times when no boat was on the lake

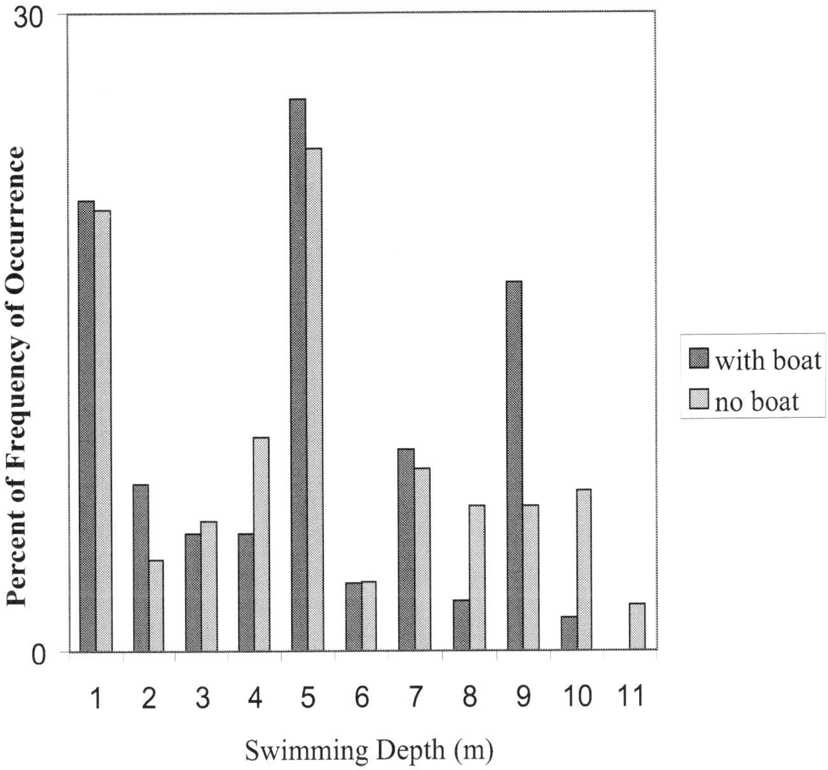

Fig. 8. Depth selection of lake sturgeon with and without boat activity

The major difference between radio and acoustic telemetry in freshwater is the receiving systems for the radio system can be above the surface of the water while acoustic telemetry receivers requires the more dense water to transmit the signal. This allows the former to be detected by aircraft as well as on the water surface but is labour intensive. A weakness of the acoustic system is bubbles in the water column interfere with transmission of the signal while a major advantage is that repeated collection of signals by well placed receivers can save considerable time and provide a much better indication of frequency of use of an area. Acoustic tags can also provide depth data.

We conclude that while there is a place for both types of tags, radio tags work best below rapids and waterfalls where there are usually plenty of air bubbles and in small stretches of rivers where there are dramatic current shifts, some air bubbles and up welling currents. Acoustic technology allows repeated measures but is scale limited due to the distance that the signal can be received. However, the Vemco VRAP system it is highly useful for relatively small aquatic systems with well defined boundaries, little or no emigration from the system and where accuracy to a few metres is important to describe habitat use, especially when pressure sensors are used to collect depth data on individual fish.

3. Sturgeon habitat assessment

3.1 Lake substrates

There are two main types of equipment now available for bottom classification but reviewers differ on the quality of bottom categorisation. The RoxAnn classification is based on energy calculations for first and second echosounder returns and the QTC view (version 5) calculates first echo shape parameters. QTC view provides automatic classifications and confidence estimates, while the RoxAnn relies on arbitrary manual calibration. The QTC bottom classes generally have consistent grain size and texture properties and follow grain size trends but RoxAnn classes are difficult to define. Both the RoxAnn and two versions of the QTC -View, series 5 were used to assess substrate.

Depth and Substrate Hardness: Substratum information was collected using an American Pioneer V digital sonar system and a Trimble Pro XR submeter Global Positioning System. Sonar data was collected using a 120 kHz - 12 degree transducer. Information collected included depth, bottom hardness, and roughness. Bottom hardness is an interval measure of the magnitude of the sonar ping return signal. Larger byte range values indicate a harder substrate.

The QTC-View Series 5 classification system is based on the principle that the shape of an echo sounder's first echo discriminates seabeds or substrates. For example, the acoustical signal of a smooth, simple, muddy seabed absorbs a high amount of energy and exhibits a low degree of backscatter resulting in an echo trace with a relatively narrow peak and no tail. Energy reflected from a rough, complicated, gravel seabed exhibits a high degree of backscatter. This results in an echo with a wide peak and a tail. The QTC-View series collected all echos and then post-processes the data in QTC IMPACT. The echo and GPS data is merged and the poor quality echos are filtered out. After echo digitization and preprocessing, the datum is analyzed by algorithms which characterize the waveform by using energy and spectral components to generate a digital string of over 100 shape descriptors. This series of numbers constitutes a description of the echo shape. Statistical analysis determines the most useful elements or series of elements to best discriminate echo shape.

The depth and substrate was collected and calculation of available habitat was done on Idrisi for windows. A frequency distribution was created using the data from each pixel on the hardness and depth images. For most of the mapping ArcMap, digital elevation models and/or kriging were used.

Sediment Analysis: Thirty-seven sediment grabs were collected so that comparisons could be made between sonar data and the sediment type. A substrate type; silt, sand, cobble, etc., could be related to hardness values, ranging from 90-145. Sampling sites were selected so that all possible substrate types were collected. Transects were run across the depth gradient in the lake running from the shallow sandy areas to the deeper silt/clay areas. Current was considered when selecting sample sites. Areas of high and low current were sampled (see section on current profiles).

Buoys were placed at the spot to be sampled. The location of each sample was recorded using a GPS unit. An Eckman dredge was dropped at the buoyed site and the sample retrieved. The sample was placed in a bag and kept cool until it could be tested in the laboratory.

The total sample at each site was divided into three parts. 100 ml was taken for particle size analysis, 100 ml was taken for invertebrate sampling and the remaining portion (if any) was frozen.

Laboratory analyses: Gravel and larger particle sizes were separated individually by hand, sieve analysis was used to separate the portion of the sample in the very fine sand to gravel categories, and settling velocity was used for silt and clay particle sizes.

The sample was placed in a tray and mixed thoroughly. The sample was added to water and dispersent (Calgon-sodium hexametaphosphate), mixed, and let sit overnight. The sample was then mixed, frozen, thawed and mixed again. The process was repeated a second time to ensure that the particles were completely separated. After the sample was separated thoroughly by the above mentioned process the silt and clay particles were removed from the sand and gravel particles. The sample was wet sieved through a 4 phi sieve to remove the silt and clay from the sample. The sediment left in the 4 phi sieve was placed in a beaker and the sediment falling through the sieve was stored in a separate container. The fine particles and larger particles were then treated separately.

Sand samples were placed into a pyrite beaker and allowed to dry in the oven until the sample was completely dry. A pestle and mortar were used to break up any chunks formed by the drying process. The total sample was weighed and placed in the top of a series of sieves ranging from -1.5 phi to 4 phi (0.5 phi intervals). The sieves were then placed into a Ro-tap shaker and then shaken for ten minutes. The material left in each sieve was weighed and recorded.

Silt/clay samples were placed in a 4000 ml graduated cylinder. Water was added to the cylinder to make the total solution 4000 ml. The solution was then shaken thoroughly and allowed to settle for the appropriate amount of time necessary to separate silt from clay. Five phi (1/32 mm) particles are the largest size category and were removed first. Five phi particles fall at a rate of 4 mm/second. The 4000 ml suspension is 500 mm high therefore the suspension was allowed to settle for 6 minutes and 15 seconds to allow all 1/32 mm particles to fall the full length of the cylinder. The supernatant (water and particles smaller than 1/32 mm) was siphoned off and saved. The process was repeated twice more to remove any smaller particles that would settle from the bottom portion of the cylinder. The remaining precipitant after the third siphon was dried and weighed as the silt category. The siphoned water was also dried and weighed as the clay category.

The particle size classification used was Cummins (1962) modification of the Wentworth Scale. Thirty-seven sediment grabs were taken and analysed from Round Lake. GPS locations for the sediment grabs were compared to hardness values from the Round Lake map at the same GPS location to obtain a system of classifying hardness values obtained by sonar.

Telemetry data analysis: Data was presented in maps using Idrisi for Windows (Clark University, MA). Some maps were created in Idrisi for Windows. Acoustic telemetry data was imported from the Vemco system program.

Determination of depth selection and substrate selection was done by hand. Seven days were selected for analysis. Selection was based on movements to include the widest possible range of movement patterns. Days 206 and 221 were selected for sturgeon 4014.

Days 210 and 222 were selected for sturgeon 4015. Days 206, 211 and 219 were selected for sturgeon 4017 (Table 2). For each location on each day bottom depth was determined. Swimming depth minus bottom depth was calculated to determine all locations in which the fish was in contact with the substrate. All values of 1 or less were included. All figures and comments pertaining to substrate selection only include locations in which the fish was in contact with the bottom. Other location statements and figures use all positional data available.

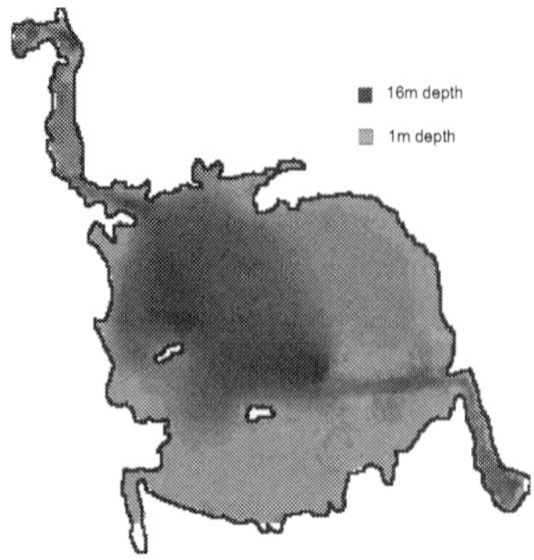

Fig. 9. Digital elevation model of Round Lake.

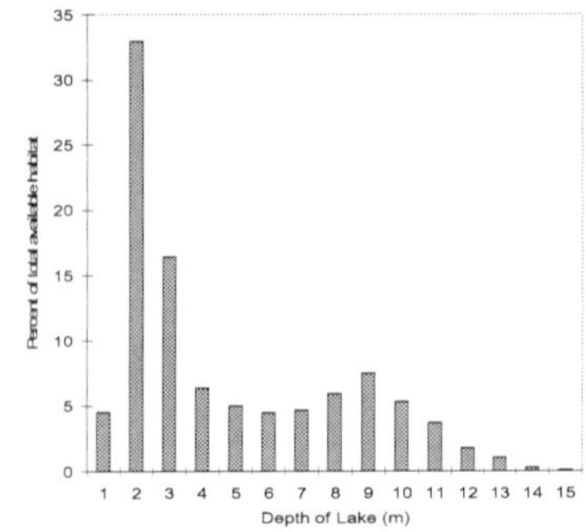

Fig. 10. Depth availability in Round Lake

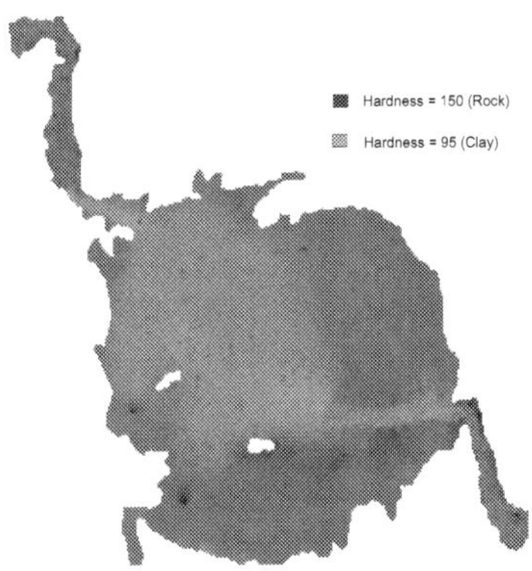

Fig. 11. Hardness map of Pigeon River at Round Lake obtained from sonar data.

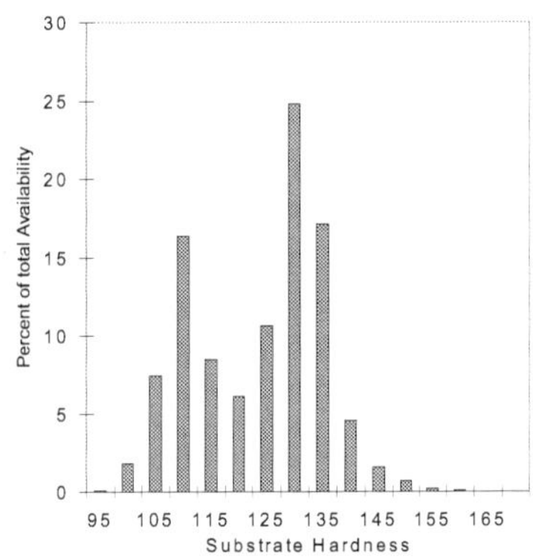

Fig. 12. Hardness (substrate) availability in Round Lake.

Substrate and Depth: Maximum depth of Round Lake is 16m. A depth map of Round Lake is shown in Fig. 9. Two deep holes, one off the Northeast corner of each island, are found in the lake. The general structure is bowl shaped. Depth availability is shown in Fig. 10. Two and three meters depths are available 33 and 16% respectively. Seven, 8, and 9 meter depths are available 5, 6, and 8% respectively.

Substrate hardness of the lake is shown in Fig. 11. Substrate was generally related to depth. The deeper areas of the lake had softer substrates with a high percentage of silt. The shallow sections along the shoreline to about 10m depth had sandy substrates. Cobble and rock substrate predominated in areas of high flow at the inlet and outlet. Availability of substrate hardness was 11, 25, and 17 percent for hardness values of 125 (coarse sand), 130 (gravel), and 135 (medium sand) respectively (Fig. 12). Substrate hardness of 110 (fine sand) had a frequency of 16 percent.

Phi	Particle Size (mm)	Category	Hardness
9	<0.0039	clay	95
5,6,7,8	0.0039 - 0.0625	silt	100
4	0.00625 - 0.125	Very fine sand	105
3	0.125 – 0.25	Fine sand	110
2	0.25 – 0.5	Medium sand	115
1	0.5 - 1	Coarse sand	120
0	1 – 2	very coarse sand	125
-1,-2,-3	2 – 16	gravel	130
-4,-5	16 - 64	Pebble	135
-6,-7	64 - 256	Cobble	140
-8	>256	Boulder	145

Table 3. Sediment classification scheme for Round Lake.

Thirty-seven sediment grabs were taken to compare with the hardness values obtained from the sonic data. Table 3 lists the substrate classification given to each range of hardness values. Hardness values range from 95 (clay) to 150 (rock, see Fig. 11).

4. Lake sturgeon movements

The biological data for the nine lake sturgeon tagged with acoustic tags are listed in Table 2. The nine fish were tracked for 27 days and 15,446 locations were obtained. Movements ranged from individuals that were mostly sedentary to highly mobile individuals. Daily movements were variable between fish as well as by the same fish on different days. Figure 13 shows the locations of fish 4015 on four separate days. Movement was confined to the inlet to Round Lake on day 210. Movement increased on days 211 and 212 and covered most of the lake. Movement on day 220 was restricted to the river outlet.
A comparison of the movements of juvenile and adult lake sturgeon is shown in Fig. 14. Movements of the juvenile fish were focused at the inlet and outlet and in the deep hole (~16 m). Movements of the subadult and adult lake sturgeon were also associated with the inlet and outlet but the movements were more widespread around the lake. The channel where water entered the lake was a preferred site as was the outlet from the lake. Figure 15 shows the swimming depth of sturgeon 4014 on day 206 relative to the bottom depth. Note the day 206 is based on January 1 being day 1. Sturgeon 4014 was on the bottom 30% of all locations on day 206. During the hours from midnight to 5 AM sturgeon 4014 was in the water column the majority of the time. From 5 AM to 11 PM more time was spent on the bottom. After 11 PM lakes sturgeon movements shifted to the water column. Figure 16 shows sturgeon 4015 on day 221 where 53% of all locations were on the bottom on day 221. Sturgeon 4017 on day 211 was on the bottom for the entire day but periodically swam to the surface (Fig. 17). Figure 18 shows the overall distribution of each lake sturgeon fitted with a pressure tag and the total distribution of all fish on the bottom and in the water column.

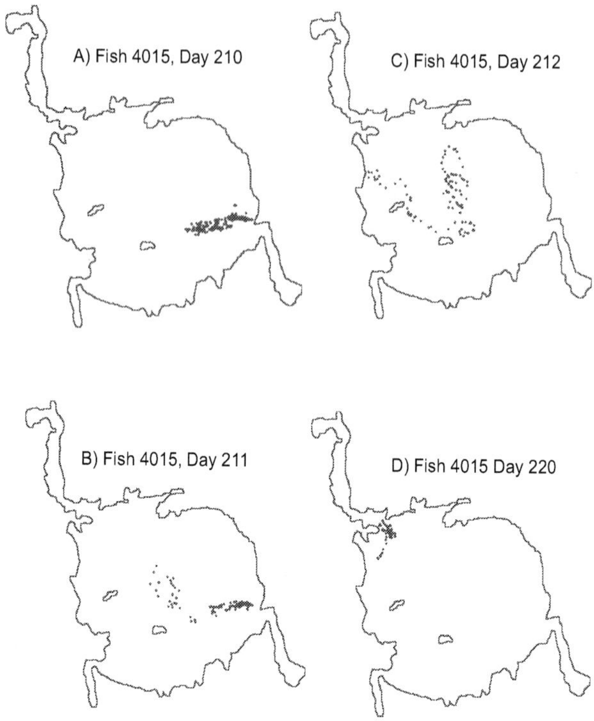

Fig. 13. Movements of lake sturgeon 4015 on four separate days.

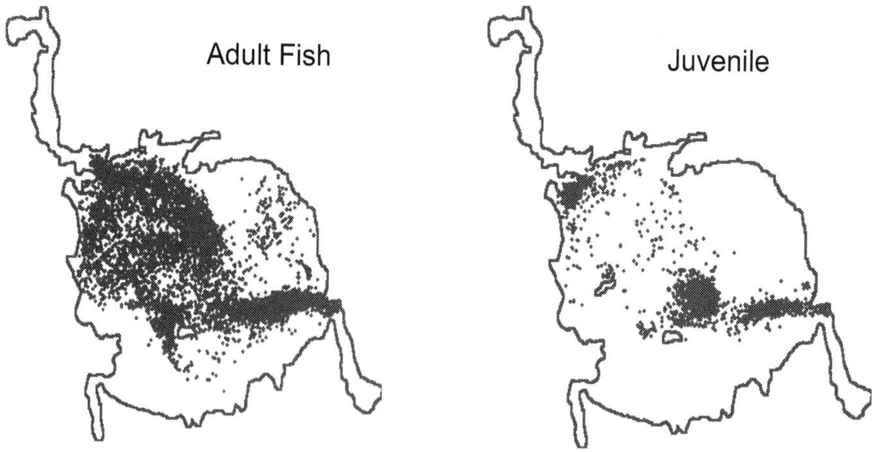

Fig. 14. Comparison of the movements of adult and juvenile sturgeon in Round Lake

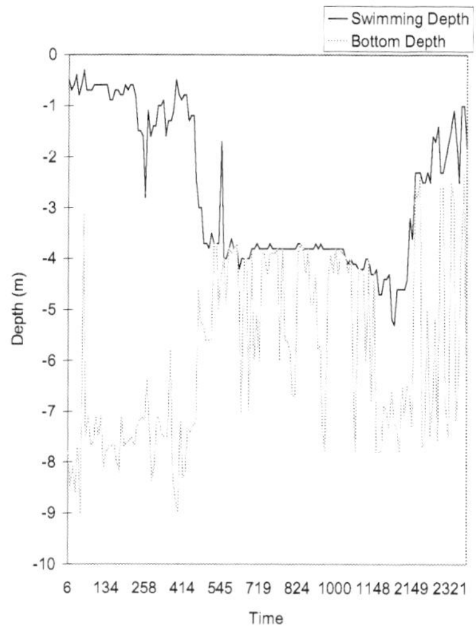

Fig. 15. A comparison of swimming depth and bottom depth of the lake for sturgeon 4014 on day 206.

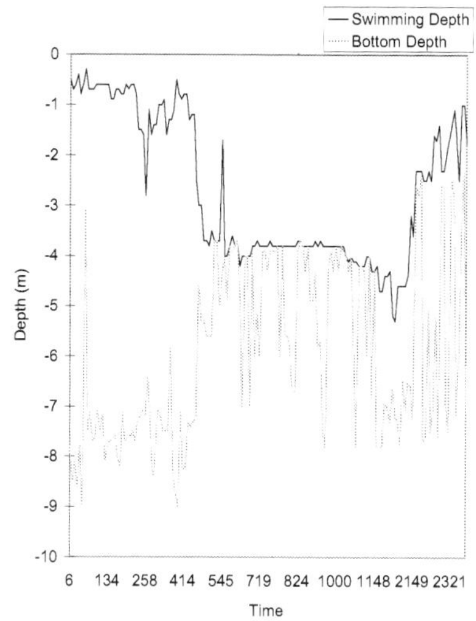

Fig. 16. A comparison of swimming depth and bottom depth of the lake for sturgeon 4014 on day 221.

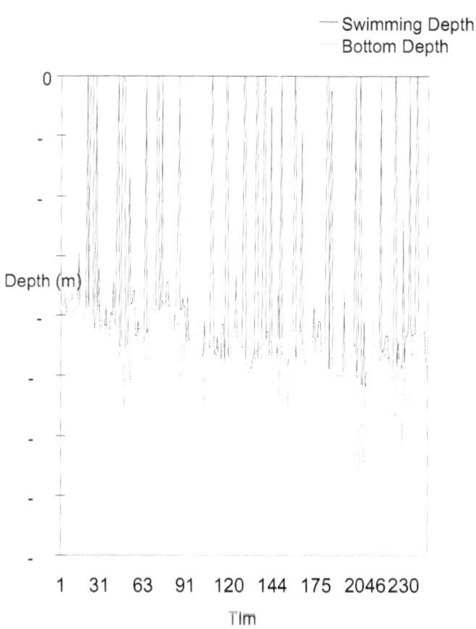

Fig. 17. A comparison of swimming depth and bottom depth of the lake for sturgeon 4017 on day 211.

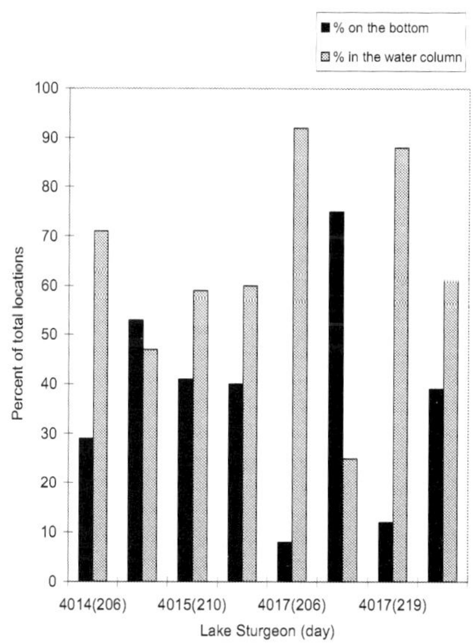

Fig. 18. Time spent in the water column and on the lake bottom for sturgeon 4014, 4015 and 4017 combined total.

Figure 20 shows substrate selection of sturgeon 4014, 4015, 4017 from the 7 day sample. Substrate with a hardness value of 110 was selected 53% of all locations.

Overall, lake sturgeons were located on the bottom 39% and in the water column 61% of the locations on the 7 day sample (day 215 based on January 1 being day 1).

The amount of time spent at the surface varied with time of day. The majority of locations < 1m occurred between the hours of 8 PM and 8 AM (Fig. 19).

The selection of depth was analysed from two perspectives. Figure 21 shows the overall depth selection of the three lake sturgeon tagged with depth tags. Thirty percent of all locations were less than two meters. Sixty-six percent were less than four meters. Figure 22 shows the depth selection of the three lake sturgeon including only the locations in which they were in contact with the substrate during the 7 day sample. Seven, 8, and 9 meter depths were selected 11, 31, and 21 percent respectively. Figure 23 shows movements of lake sturgeon 4014. It spent 70% of the time in the water column at the inlet on day 206 and on day 221 lake sturgeon 4014 spent 47% of the time in the water column.

Figure 24 shows movements of lake sturgeon 4015 on day 210. It spent 59% of its time in the water column at the inlet of the river. Lake sturgeon 4017 (Fig. 25) spent 60% of the time in the water column on days 206 and 222, 25% on day 211, and 88% on day 219. On days 211 and 219, sturgeon 4017 covered most of lake, including areas around the inlet and outlet.

The use of depth tags eliminates the guess work of whether a fish was on the bottom or in the water column at each position. Comparisons were made in this study among telemetry position, depth and substrate using data from depth tags. Substrate, depth and current were the three primary environmental variables measured.

Lake sturgeon movements ranged from sedentary to highly active. Movements in the areas of the inlet and outlet, areas of higher flow rate were quite common as well as movements in the deeper areas and along the natural flow of the river. Movements along the shorelines were rare. Along the shorelines the water is shallow, there is little flow, and the substrate is primarily sandy. Movements of smaller and larger fish were similar but larger fish moved greater distances. Nevertheless, juvenile fish appear to use most of the same habitat as the larger fish. Movements for both were related to the inlet and outlet and the deeper part of the lake.

The larger lake sturgeon spent a significant amount of time in the water column and at the surface. We do not know what juveniles were doing concerning depth selection because they were too small to be fitted with tags with pressure sensors. The amount of time in the water column by the larger fish suggests these fish were feeding on organisms drifting with the current. A majority of the records on movement were near the inlet and outlet where drift nets recovered insects and the occasional small fish.. Extensive lake sturgeon activity was noted where insects were carried by the current, were floating on the surface, or were emerging i.e. mayflies. High sturgeon activity in some areas was also correlated with clam beds.

The timing of movements in the water column and at the surface was correlated to light intensity. Lake sturgeon spent more time at the surface at night than during the day, when more time was spent on the bottom.

Based on the comparison of substrate selection and substrate availability lake sturgeon were found over fine sand, cobble, and rock substrate at higher frequencies than the proportion of this substrate in the lake. Coarse sand and gravel substrates were selected at a lower frequency than their proportions in the lake.

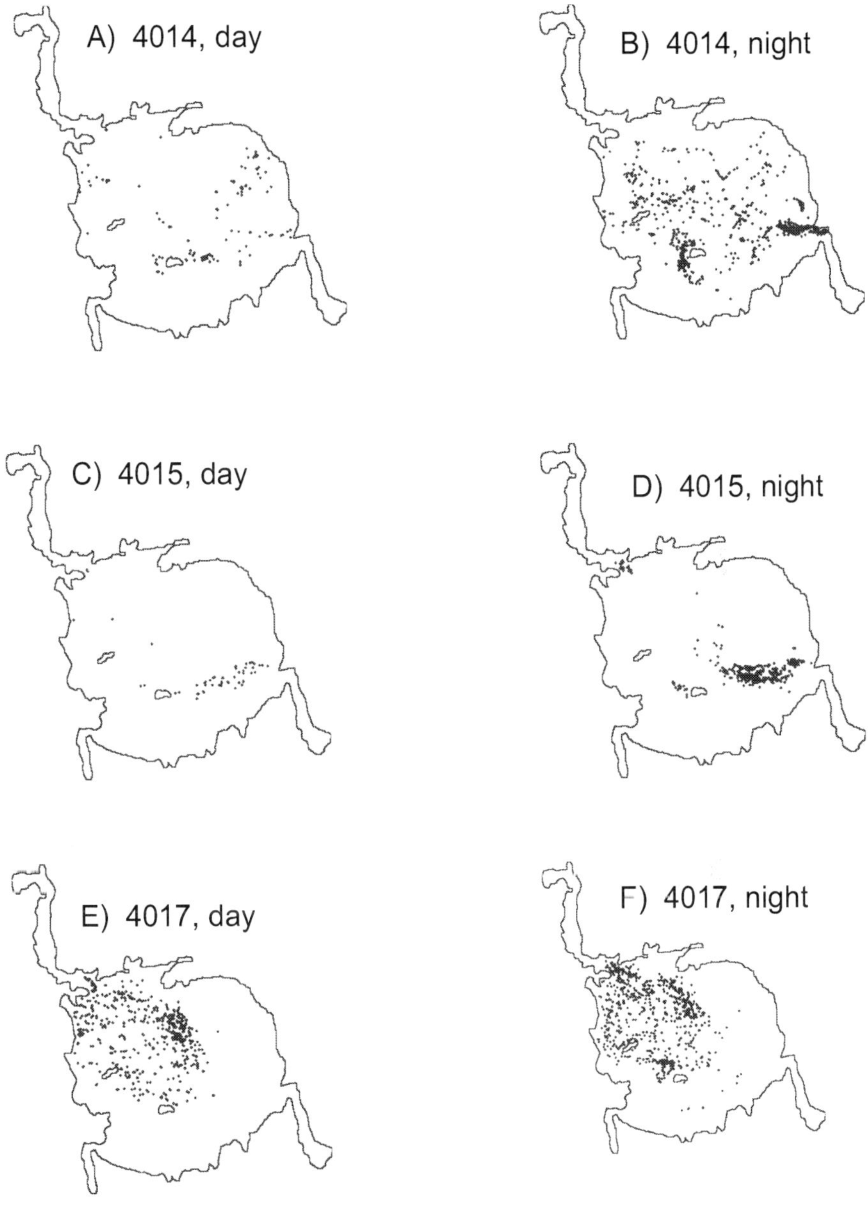

Fig. 19. Day and night comparison of time spent at the surface for sturgeon 4014, 4015, and 4017.

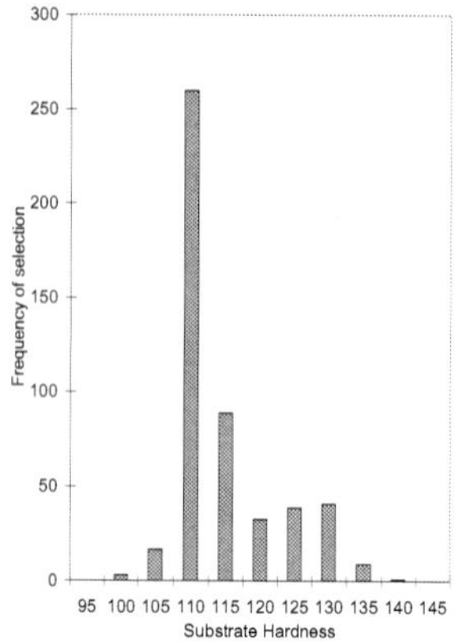

Fig. 20. Substrate selection by lake sturgeon in Round Lake (see Table 3)

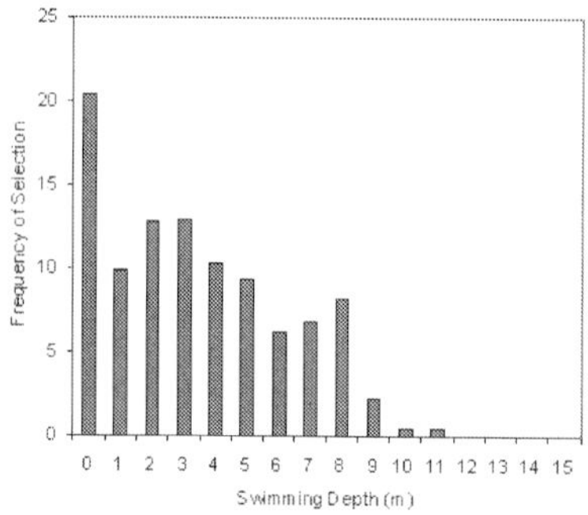

Fig. 21. Overall depth selection by lake sturgeon in Round Lake.

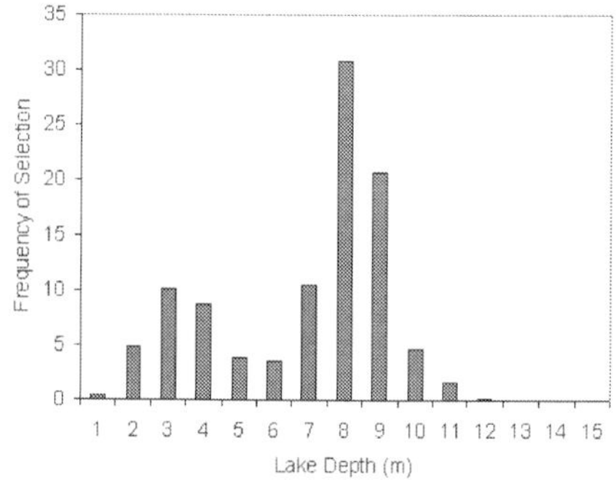

Fig. 22. Depth selection by lake sturgeon when in contact with the substrate.

Hexagenia (Ephemeridae) is a common prey item of lake sturgeon and silt and clay substrates are the preferred habitats. By contrast clams were often found in sandy substrates. While invertebrates were not common in the sieved substrates mayflies are a major food source for most fish species in the lake. Similarly, mayflies were a major food item of lake sturgeon, based on stomach contents which was verified by gavage. It appears in this system that mayflies are a major food source but competition for this food source by most fish species in the lake may make this food item a potentially limiting factor. Similar observations have been reported by others (Choudhury et al.. 1995; Chiasson et al. 1997).

The selection of depth based on horizontal and vertical movements of lake sturgeon seems to be related to current. Lake sturgeon tended to stay in the water column more often in areas of high flow such as the inlet and outlet. Since the study took place in mid summer and this activity was not related to spawning behaviours or movement related to fall/winter migrations the majority of movements are likely related to feeding behaviour.

Fig. 23. Movements and depth selection of lake sturgeon 4014.

Fig. 24. Movements and depth selection of lake sturgeon 4015.

Fig. 25. Movements and depth selection of lake sturgeon 4017.

5. Current profiling

Since lake sturgeon movements and substrate were being evaluated in Round Lake and there was evidence that currents had a role in their distribution we evaluated current distribution in the lake. Figure 26A illustrates the cross sections of the river and lake where data was collected for current profiling and Fig. 26B identifies transects for which data was presented and discussed in the text.

Current profiling was done with the RDI Workhorse (Acoustic Doppler Current Profiler). This system was initially designed for stationary applications but its use was broadened to include total discharge measurements of streams and rivers and to measure currents in the areas where fish moved. This can be done from small moving boats.

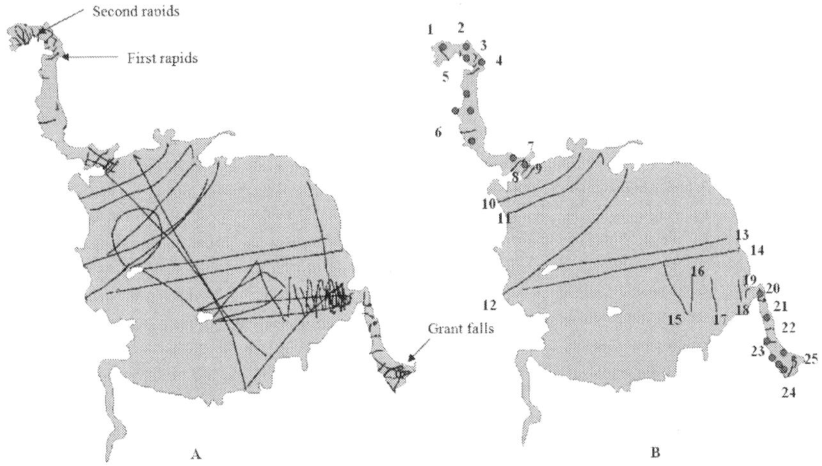

Fig. 26. Transects for the current profile measurements in the Pigeon River at Round Lake. A) all transects throughout the lake and B) includes transects where current profiles are presented in this report with additional transects and current profiles also shown tagged lake sturgeon where in these areas for extended periods of time. Red dots = location of radio tagged lake sturgeon

Data collection focused in the areas of greatest activity in the Pigeon River in and around Round Lake because lake sturgeon tagged with radio and sonar tags moved short distance upstream to Grant Falls and downstream to the second rapids (Fig. 26A).

Current profiles: Current profiles were taken in 1997, 2000, 2001. Movements of lake sturgeon in regions of the Pigeon River above and below Round Lake were determined with radio tags and sites where more transects were run are illustrated in Fig. 26A. Figure 26B outlines selected cross sections, some of which are discussed below. The current cross sections shown in Fig. 27 is above the second rapids on the Pigeon River downstream of Round Lake and the graph below the velocity magnitude is the boat or ship track that also indicates the direction and relative magnitude of the current. Note current is measured across a body of water and in the water column in units referred to as cells. The cells are coloured and represent the current in a cell. Each cell is coloured in the graph (see velocity magnitude) and is ~20 cm but cell size may vary depending on depth at the sampling point.

The stick ship tract directly below illustrates the ship tract across the river (red) and the blue lines shows relative current flows and direction along the transect. The top of the ship tract is the right side looking downstream, unless otherwise described. Figure 27 (transect 1) has a current ranging from 0.250-1.0 m/sec and while lake sturgeon moved through this area they spent most of their time on the right side in back eddies separated from the main flow by a ridge on the bottom. The current in this area was between 0.25 and 0.750 m/sec. In the area of transect 2 (Fig. 26B) lake sturgeon moved through this region but did not remain in the area. The strongest current encountered throughout this section of the Pigeon River was up to 2 m/sec. The river was shallow about 1.5 m at the narrowest section of the river with turbulence and air bubbles (the reason for the large numbers of blank spaces i e. no data).

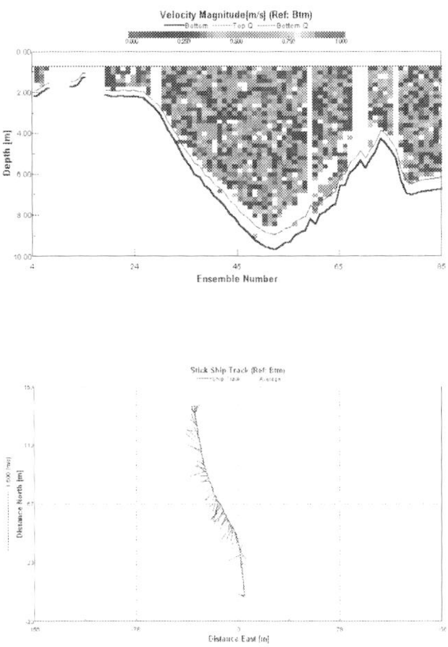

Fig. 27. Pigeon River ship transect 1 (see Fig. 26B).

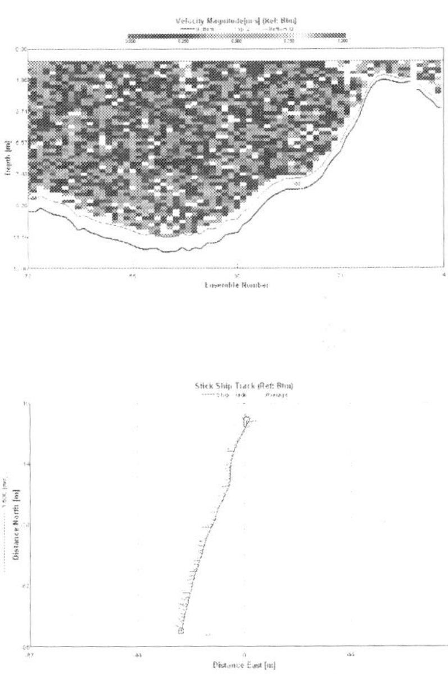

Fig. 28. Pigeon River ship transect 8 (see Fig. 26B).

The current was slightly lower on the left side (looking downstream) and deeper but this was off the main flow. Transects 7, 8 and 9 are from a region of the river where considerable lake sturgeon activity was recorded (Fig. 14). It is apparent from the boat track of Fig. 28 that a small back eddy occurs on the right side (looking downstream). From the acoustic tag data there was extensive movement throughout this area indicating that lake sturgeon movements in currents up to 1 m/sec were routine. Figure 29 illustrates a transect from a region of Round Lake with high lake sturgeon activity and where currents ranged from 0.00 to 0.250 m/sec. Transects 15 (Fig.26B) represents an area of Round Lake where flow from the river entering Round Lake starts to slow. Most of the current in the river bed is 0.5 m/sec. Figure 30 (transect 16) illustrates the river bottom and shallow area with macrophytes on the right side. Macrophytes have a similar affect on the equipment as air bubbles and as result the quality of the data is reduced. From the ship track in transect 16 the main flow of the river is becoming apparent and in Fig. 30 there is some evidence for a back eddy on the right side. This back eddy becomes more pronounced in transect 17 (not shown) but declines in transect 18 (Fig. 26B) and the current in both transect 17 and 18 increases to be predominantly 0.7 m/sec. Figure 31 (transect 19) illustrates that the strongest current occurs at the point the river enters the lake and the current across the entire river changes its direction as it passes over rocks on the right side. The majority of the current in Fig. 31 (transect 19) and transect 20 is between 0.7 and 1.0 m/sec. Transect 25 below Grant Falls has current ranging from 0.7 to 1.0 m/sec. This was also a region of the Pigeon River where spawning lake sturgeons were found.

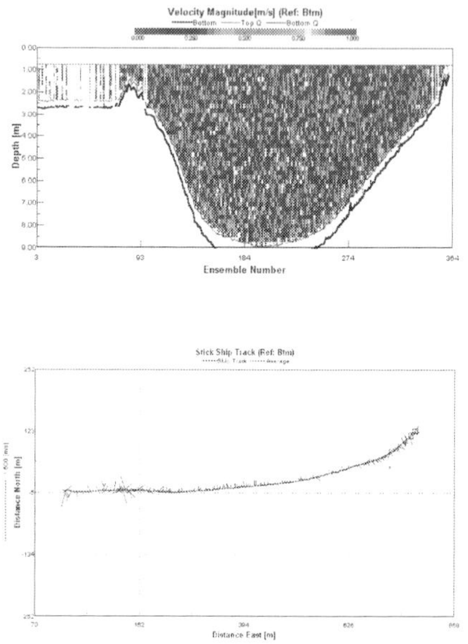

Fig. 29. Pigeon River ship transect 10 (see Fig. 26B).

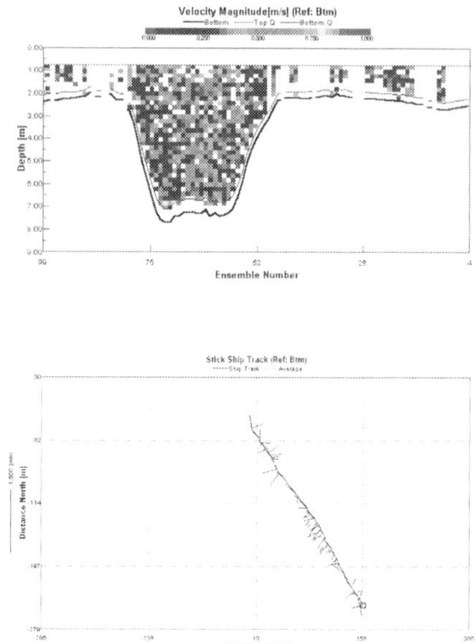

Fig. 30. Round Lake ship transect 16 (see 26B).

Correlation of lake sturgeon movements with current profiles: The overall frequency of movement of all acoustically tagged lake sturgeon is shown in Fig. 14 and it clearly indicates that activity is concentrated at the inlet and outlets to Round Lake. In the area of the inlet activity is concentrated in the main river channel as it enters the lake. The current at transect 19 (Fig. 26B) is up to 1.0 m/sec but this area is frequented by both large and small sturgeon (Fig. 14). It is worth noting that the current close to the contour of the river bed is < 1.0m/sec so lake sturgeon might be moving through these areas. Figure 14 shows that the smallest sturgeon also concentrated much of their activity in the deepest part of the lake and the main river channel entering the lake (Figs. 9 and 14). By contrast the largest sturgeon spent proportionally less time in the deepest hole in the lake suggesting there may be some segregation of habitat, at the fine scale. It was also noteworthy that the smaller lake sturgeon frequented the area to the left of the outlet from Round Lake, again suggesting that there may be some differences in habitat use between small and large lake sturgeon (Fig. 14).

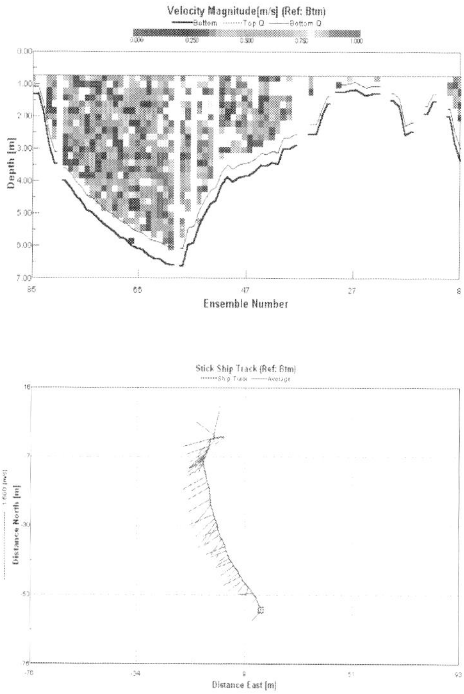

Fig. 31. Round Lake ship transect 19 (see 26B).

Interestingly while the larger sturgeon utilized this region they were more offshore. The larger sturgeon were concentrated at the outlet (Fig. 14) where currents were 0.25 to 0.5m/sec (Fig. 26B, transects 7, 8 and 9). These currents are below those noted for transect 9 at the inlet to Round Lake. Clearly there is more to the habitat requirements of juvenile lake sturgeon than a certain level of current. It is also apparent that the larger sturgeon frequented areas of the lake where currents were very low (Fig 26B, transect 12) but the ship track suggests a slight amount of counter flow (eddy) in this area. However, there was very little activity by smaller sturgeon in this area of the lake. The larger acoustically tagged lake sturgeon frequently ventured into the river, upstream and downstream from the lake but did not remain in these areas for extended periods of time as they always returned to the lake. None of the tagged lake sturgeon moved out of the area, either due to strong site fidelity or because this region of the Pigeon River is physically isolated due to rapids and small waterfalls.

Generally, the smallest lake sturgeon remained in slower flowing water and tended to frequent areas less used by large sturgeon in both deep and shallow regions of the lake. Unlike the larger sturgeon the small sturgeons were rarely located in water under 1 meter. Larger lake sturgeon can move through water with currents as high as 2m/sec but generally frequent areas with currents less than 1m/sec and if situated in the river tend to locate in the back eddies rather than in the main current. Current undoubtedly plays a role in defining lake sturgeon habitat but it is only one of several variables.

6. Sturgeon feeding tags

6.1 Background

Lake sturgeon movements in the field are readily identified using different tagging systems but establishing feeding behaviour is somewhat more complicated because one can not observe feeding directly as lake sturgeon generally do not feed at the surface. However, results reported in this chapter clearly revealed that lake sturgeon spend a significant proportion of time in the water column and were likely feeding on drift concentrated at the inlet and outlet of the lake, and emerging insects in the lake. Consequently a key question was could a sensor be developed to document lake sturgeon feeding? From previous studies on the histology of larval lake sturgeon we knew that there were extensive pressure receptors inside the mouth of lake sturgeon (Dick, unpubl. data). From other observations it was apparent that lake sturgeon utilized the branchial chamber to not only sense and feel the food but also to clean and to expel food with considerable force if the food was found to be unacceptable (Dick, unpubl. data). Furthermore, since lake sturgeons extend their mouth to feed we hypothesized that this may change the pressure inside the branchial chamber. We also knew that lake sturgeon extended the mouth with and without feeding.

Branchial pressure ranges from 50-150 pascals for restrained animals and no studies had attempted to relate branchial pressure to various levels of metabolic activity. We expect pressure to be correlated to oxygen consumption but our initial question was to determine if we could measure differences in the branchial chamber of lake sturgeon. Since lake sturgeon feed by sucking in prey and water this action should result in large pressure pulses interrupting rhythmic ventilation pressure pulses. It should be possible to distinguish mouth movements associated with feeding, coughing etc. The objective was to build a prototype tag to test the feasibility of a pressure tag to monitor branchial chamber pressure and use this as a measure of feeding activity. Previous reports by Webber et al. (2001a) and Webber et al. (2001b) describe the application of pressure tags to measure swimming speeds of fish.

6.2 Methods

Lake sturgeon used in this study were cultured at the University of Manitoba and subdued with tricaine methanol sulfonate (MS-222). The pressure sensor is a proprietary design with a cannula (PE 160) attached to the positive port, inserted under the tegument and into the parabranchial cavity under the opercular flap such that most of the cannula was not exposed to the environment. The tip of the cannula did not interfere with the movement of the gill filaments. The pressure sensors were powered by a standard bridge voltage (+10v), amplified and sampled at 69Hz. The pressure sensors were calibrated against a column of water of known density at the beginning and end of each experiment. Pressure signals were digitized by a MACLAB data acquisition system (AD Instruments Ltd.) and stored on disk. The resolution of the sensor was 1.85 pascals digital value^{-1} or 0.0189 cm freshwater at 4°C. The prototype sensor was designed to be attached by wires to the receiver to obtain physiological data. The second sensor was designed to transit the signal directly to a receiver. The experimental setup for the study is shown in Fig. 32

6.3 Results

The original experiments utilized direct wiring from the sensor and the data are represented by the Analog to Digital conversion (A/D) of the A/D board in the PC (Fig. 33).

Fig. 32. Initial set up to collect data from sensor.

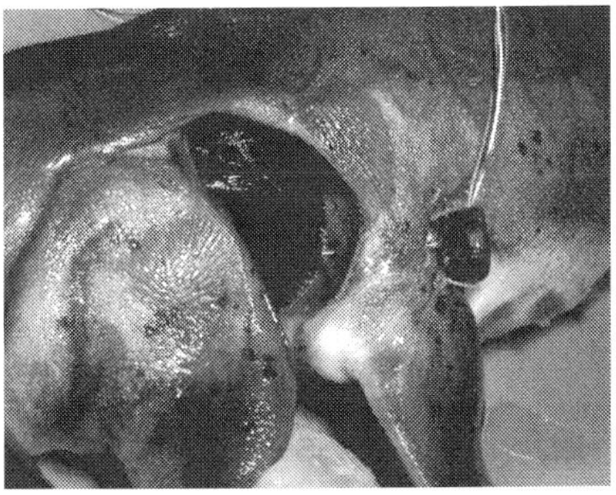

Fig. 33. Sensor on pectoral fin and cannula inserted into the branchial chamber with cannula visible.

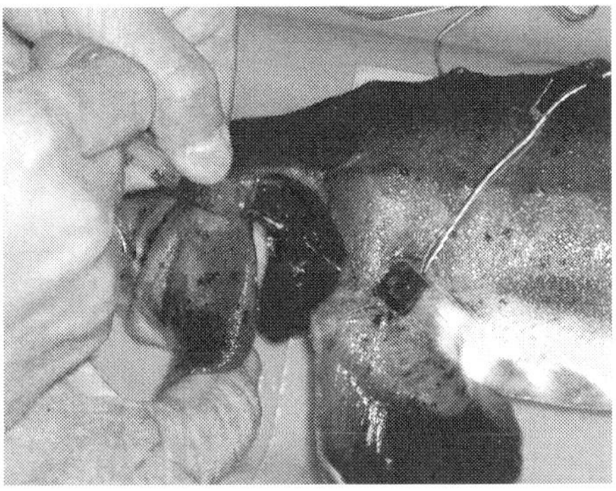

Fig. 34. Flushing cannula with syringe to remove air bubbles.

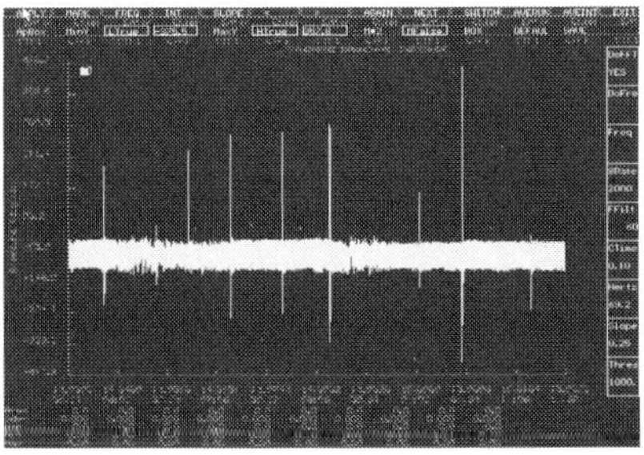

Fig. 35. Branchial pressure at 15°C. Note occasional negative values.

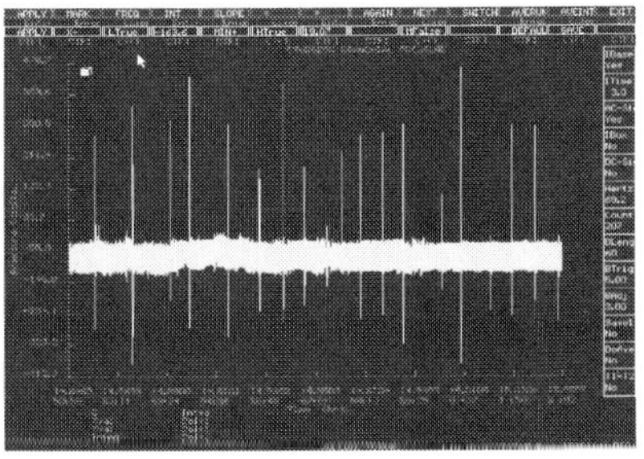

Fig. 36. Branchial pressure at 22°C.

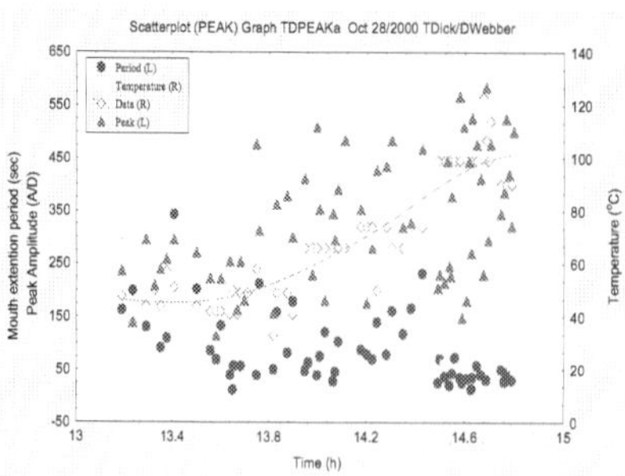

Fig. 37. Ability to rapidly alter branchial frequency.

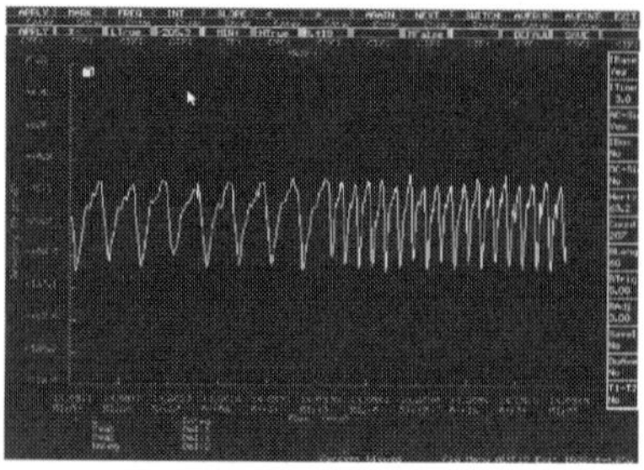

Fig. 38. Direct observation of changing frequency due to stress.

Approximately 1 cm of water pressure is equivalent to 40-50 A/D. The method to attach the wiring to the body wall is illustrated in Fig. 33. Figure 33 illustrates the sensor attached to the fish with the opercle lifted to observe the end of the cannula inside the branchial chamber. Figure 34 illustrates the priming of the cannula and the removal of air bubbles. For the majority of the time, data from the opercular cavity had a regular pattern exhibiting consistent amplitude and frequency (Figs. 35 and 36). However, peaks varied in amplitude in both positive and negative directions. Peak amplitude was approximately 5.5 cm (230 AD) at 15°C and increased to 9.5 cm (400 AD at 22°C) and the period ranged from 150 sec at 15°C to 40 sec at 22°C (Fig. 37). The peak amplitude and frequency increased with temperature (Fig. 35 at 15°C and Fig. 36 at 20°C). Figures 36 and 37 illustrate how quickly an individual can alter the opercular frequency in response to activity, metabolism and stress. Figure 38 demonstrates the changing opercular frequency of lake sturgeon as a result of stress. Figures 39 and 40 illustrate that immediately after a large pressure pulse (feeding peak) the regular breathing movements were larger than the preceding ones. Regular pulses increased in frequency and amplitude in response to temperature. Amplitude (green diamond) increased from 2 cm (45 AD) to 2.5 cm (110 AD) (Fig. 42).

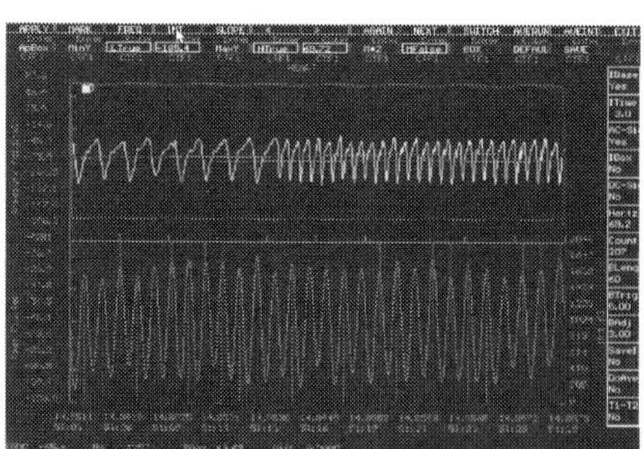

Fig. 39. Regular breathing movements are higher immediately after feeding.

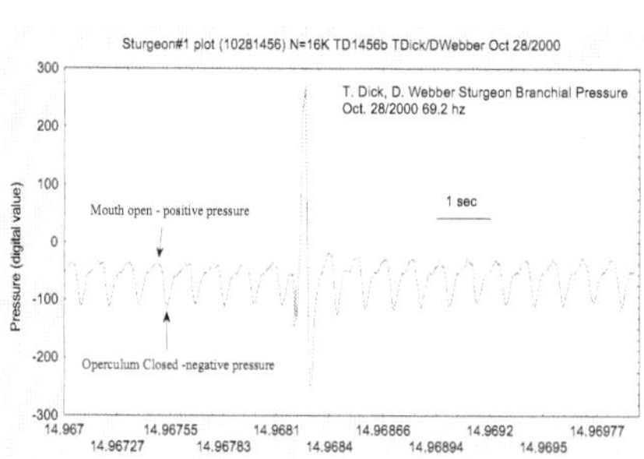

Fig. 40. Feeding pulse is followed by rapid change to normal pulse.

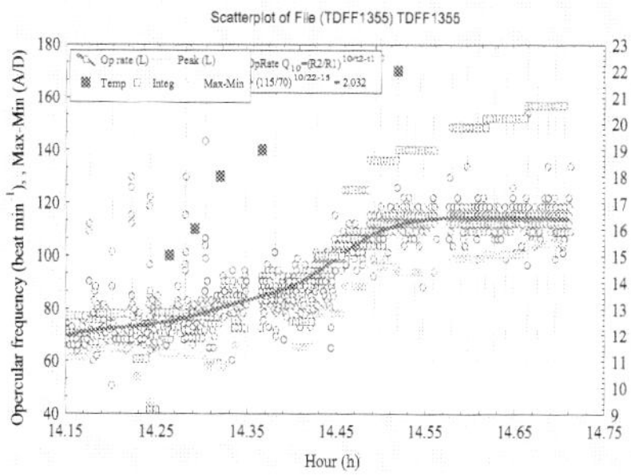

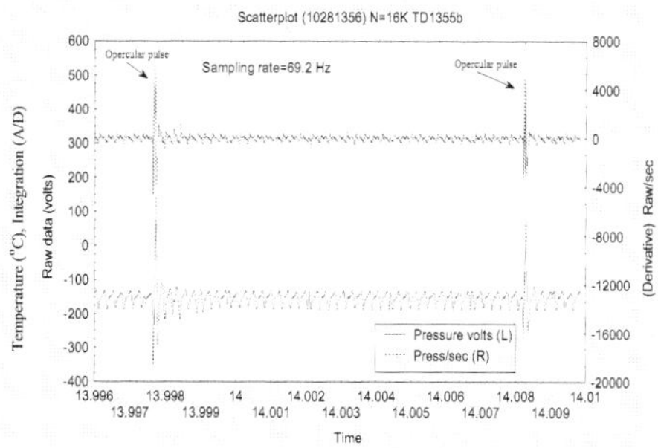

Fig. 41. Increase in frequency and amplitude due to temperature.

Fig. 42. High correlation between pressure and voltage changes.

It was decided to build a prototype tag to test the feasibility of a pressure tag to monitor branchial chamber pressure from 12 to 22°C. Frequency (blue circles) increased from 70 to 115 opercular beats^{-1} (Fig. 42). The calculated Q_{10} for frequency was 2.03, which describes the general response of most metabolic processes with temperature. The increase in amplitude and frequency was due a metabolic increase in routine metabolic rate. There was a high correlation between pressure in the branchial chamber and voltage changes (Fig. 41). When the TELEPLAY.EXE was used to integrate branchial pressure waveform as an AC neg-pos-neg waveform the integration (red squares) was highly correlated to temperature. Frequency of pulses was highly correlated to both integration (Fig. 43) and amplitude (Fig. 44).

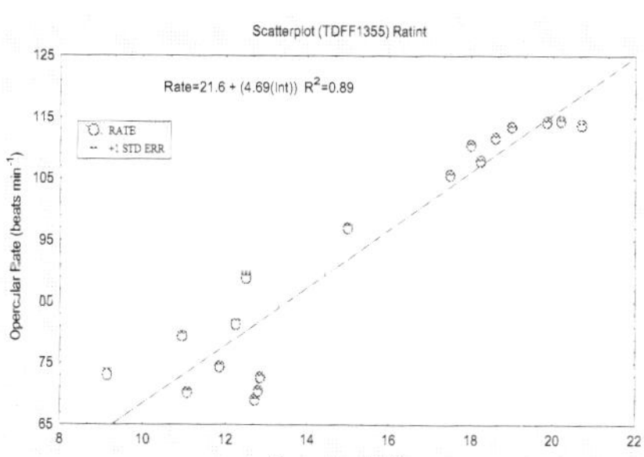

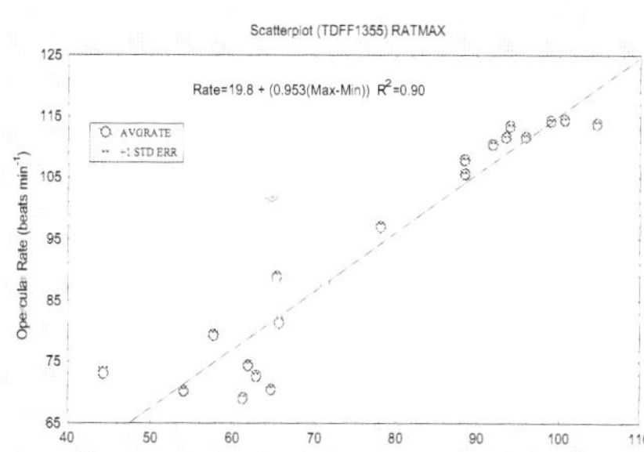

Fig. 43. Frequency of pulses correlated to integration.

Fig. 44. Frequency of pulses highly correlated to amplitude

The feeding pressure tag (Fig. 45) was tested under laboratory conditions (Fig. 46). A major challenge was determining how to stabilize the cannula and how to attach it to the lake sturgeon. Several methods to attach the tag were attempted, including drilling holes through the scutes and attaching to the dorsal surface of pectoral fin (Fig. 47) and attached to the pectoral fin (Fig. 48). Two methods were tested for placement of the cannula to monitor pressure, 1) attached to the tegument and under the opercle and 2) inserted through the cartilage at the base of the pectoral fin (Figs. 33 and 34).

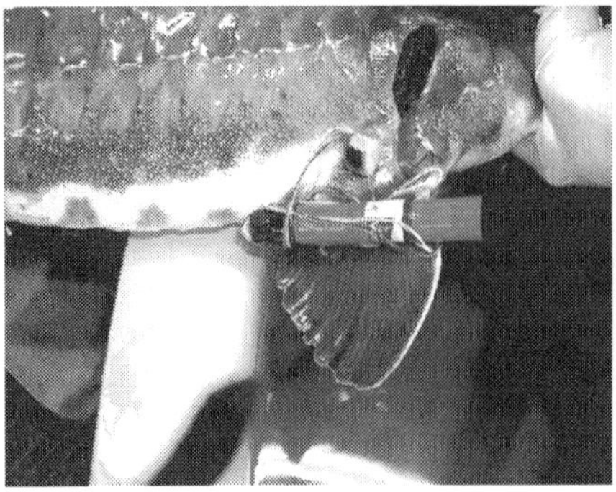

Fig. 45. Tag attached to pectoral fin.

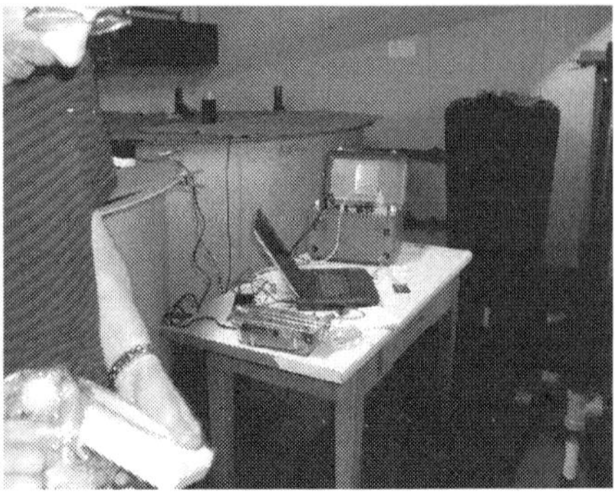

Fig. 46. Collection of data from tag in tank.

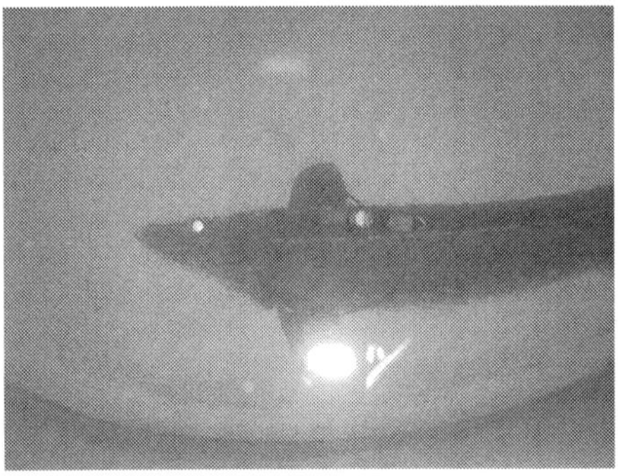

Fig. 47. Tag attached to dorsal scutes.

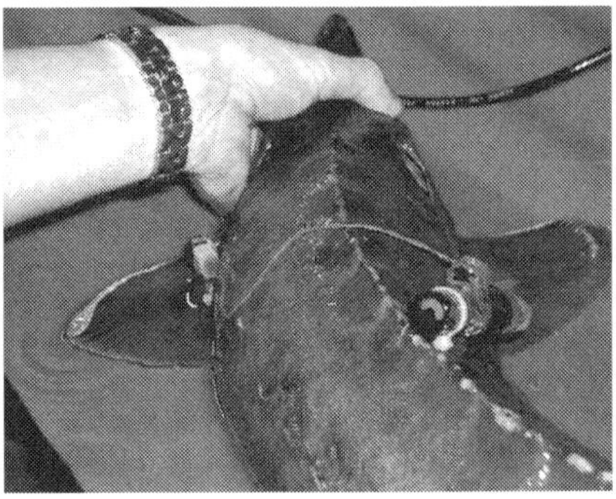

Fig. 48. Tag attached to right pectoral fin and connected to sensor situated on the left pectoral fin.

The feeding sensor pressure tag gave identical results to the data collected from the prototype experimental data. The major problem was attachment of the tag as the longest time for attachment was 12 days. The best location was on the surface of the pectoral fin and surprisingly there was little influence on normal use of the fin by lake sturgeon in a tank. Attaching the tag to the scutes was the least effective as the sharp boney scutes severed both wire and heavy fishing line with ease. Once the tag was not firmly attached the cannula was dislocated and either became clogged with mucous or was outside the branchial chamber and was unable to measure any pressure changes. There was no evidence of infection when the cannula was inserted through the tegument and the cartilage and once the cannula was removed there was no infection. The point at which the cannula was inserted was undetectable within 2 weeks of its removal.

6.4 Discussion

Ventilation was characterized by alternating positive and negative pressure pulses whose amplitude and frequency were very constant when activity and temperature were stable.

Positive pulses were always associated with opening of the mouth and negative pressure with closing of the mouth. Amplitude of these rhythmic pulses generally ranged from 50 to 100 pascals for all lake sturgeon. We also observed that all fish periodically made rapid mouth movements that resulted in considerably larger pressure pulses (800 pascals) compared to the rhythmic ventilations pulses described previously. These pulses were caused by the sudden projection of the jaw approximately 3-4 cm outward form the mouth. Pressure amplitude was often an order of magnitude greater when compared to ventilation pulse pressure. This is interpreted as instances of feeding or feeding attempts. Temperature influences all variables as integral and max-min pressure and frequency of ventilation on pulses increased with temperature. As well, amplitude and period of feeding pulses increased with temperature.

Although we did not measure MO_2 (oxygen consumption) directly the data on integration of branchial pressure and an AC waveform indicates that integration and amplitude can be used to predict MO_2 (energy budgets) sturgeon in nature. This information could be combined with temperature and feeding data to predict seasonal growth rates, etc.

We have developed a specialized feeding tag for lake sturgeon that functions under laboratory conditions. Inserting the cannula through the cartilage above the pectoral fins had a minimal affect on the fish; however, we have yet to find a satisfactory method to hold the tag securely to the fish for more than 12 days. Internal placement of the tag is not an option as the wires would then have to come from the tag through the body wall to the sensor. The prototype tag weighed 46 gm in air and the next stage of development will be to reduce the weight of the tag size considerably (we are already using depth tags that have a much lower weight than the V16s). Even the prototype tag can be attached to large lake sturgeon (over 25 kg) and the preferred attachment site will likely be the pectoral fin. The next tags will have to weigh less than 15 gm in air, be more streamed lined to reduce resistance and mode of attaching to the boney fins rays will need to accommodate self tightening strap.

7. Summary

Lake sturgeon (*Acipenser fulvescens*) in Canada in the early 1900s were reduced to remnant populations over most of their historic range and extirpated from much of the Great Lakes and Lake Winnipeg. Populations continued to decline over the next 100 years due to commercial fishing pressure, hydroelectric and other industrial developments. This led in the early 2000s to the Committee on the Status of Endangered Wildlife in Canada recommending that lake sturgeon be listed as threatened or endangered in various regions of Canada. Most of the current research on lake sturgeon is related to environmental assessment for hydroelectric developments from perturbed areas where populations are low. The purpose of this research was to study a lake sturgeon population in an unperturbed system, the Pigeon River at Round Lake on the west side of Lake Winnipeg, Manitoba, Canada. Round Lake is a small isolated lake with a typical fish community found in the boreal region of Canada. The size of the sturgeon population relative to other fish species in the lake was determined by randomly set standard gang gillnets and all sturgeon caught were tagged with external and PIT tags and returned to the wild. Lake sturgeon comprised about 10% of the total population of fish. The main food item of lake sturgeon was mayflies and a detailed stomach analyses indicates that mayflies are important food for several other fish species. Since we were interested in determining how lake sturgeon, from juvenile to adults, utilized their environment a comprehensive study was undertaken. Round Lake was mapped using sonar technology to establish substrate types and current profiles were described at the inlet and outlet to the lake, and in the lake. The substrate map, based on roughness/smoothness and hardness/softness, were correlated with substrate types i.e. silt, fine sand, fine and coarse gravel, cobble, and rock.

Lake sturgeons were tagged using radio and acoustic tags. Radio tags were more useful to study movements in the river due to the high flows and air bubbles in the water but were limited because of the high labour input to track individual fish. Some of the acoustic tags had both temperature and pressure sensors and the application of the VRAP acoustic system (Vemco, Canada) enabled us to obtain 3-D positioning of individual fish in real time. Results from the lake sturgeon movement studies using acoustic tags showed that there was individual variation with some fish spending most of their time on the bottom while others spent up to 75% of their time in the water column. The amount of time spent in shallow and deep water and over substrate types was determined. The movements of large (over 5 kg) and small lake sturgeon (< 2 kg) often overlapped but there was a tendency to frequent different areas i.e. smaller lake sturgeon frequented the deeper parts of the lake but were also found in shallow sections near the main flow. The most frequently used sites by both groups of lake sturgeon were near the inlet and outlet from the lake where currents were up to 1m/sec. Larger lake sturgeon moved through regions of the river where currents were up to 2m/sec. Lake sturgeon were more active over substrates consisting of fine sand, cobble, and rock.

The conventional view is that lake sturgeons are primarily a bottom feeder. However, we noted that lake sturgeon fitted with pressure sensors moved up and down the water column and spent more time in the water column than previously thought based on a review of the literature. We noted that this movement was usually correlated with emerging mayflies and postulated we were likely observing a feeding event. This led to the development of a pressure tag with the potential to record feeding events in sturgeon by measuring branchial chamber pressure. The pressure sensor consists of a cannula (PE 160) attached to the positive port, inserted under the tegument and into the parabranchial cavity under the opercular flap such that most of the cannula was not exposed to the environment. The tip of the cannula did not interfere with the movement of the gill filaments. The resolution of the sensor was 1.85 pascals digital value^{-1} or 0.0189 cm freshwater at 4°C. The prototype sensor was designed to be attached by wires to the receiver to obtain physiological data. The second sensor was designed to transit the signal directly to a receiver. The reason for providing this example of sensor development (feeding in this case) is that with 3-D movement studies, using a VRAP system or the more recent VPS (Vemco Ltd.), researchers are not only able to record fine scale fish movements but with new sensors like the pressure sensor can pose new questions and drive technology, especially sensor technology, in new directions.

8. Acknowledgments

T. Dick acknowledges financial support for these studies from a Natural Sciences and Engineering Council of Canada operating grant and from the Department of Fisheries and Oceans Canada, Environment Canada, Manitoba Hydro and Manitoba Model Forest. T. Dick also thanks elder Henry Letander, Sagkeeng First Nations, Fort Alexander, Manitoba for advice on lake sturgeon and companionship in the field. We thank Dr. M. Papst (Department of Fisheries and Oceans Canada) and Keith Kristopherson (Fisheries Branch,

Province of Manitoba) for encouragement and logistical support. We thank Ph.D student Kate Gardiner for help with the illustrations. We also thank contractors Paul Coolie (substrate mapping) and Maria Begout (acoustic tag studies) for helping with the collection of data and some of the analysis.

9. References

Bajkov,A.D. and F. Neave. 1930. The sturgeon and sturgeon industry of Lake Winnipeg. *In*: Canadian Fisheries Manual. National Publications Ltd. Gardenville, Quebec. 43-47.

Baldwin, N.S., R.W. Saalfeld, M. A. Ross and H.J. Buettner. 1979. Commercial fish production in the Great Lakes 1867- 1977. pp. 6,30,31,70,84-85, 124-125, 158-159. IN: Gr. Lakes Fish. Comm. TGech. Rep. 3. Available from www.gflc.org/databases/commercial/commerc.php

Barth, C.C., S.J. Peake, P.J.Allen and W.G. Anderson. 2009. Habitat utilization of juvenile lake sturgeon, *Acipenser fulvescens,* in a large Canadian river J. Appl. Ichthyol. 215: 18-26.

Bemis, W.E. and E.K. Findeis. 1994. The sturgeons' plight. Nature 370: 602.

Chiasson, W.B., D.L.G. Noakes and F.W.H. Beamish.1997. Habitat, benthic prey and distribution of juvenile lake sturgeon (*Acipenser fulvescens*) in northern Ontario rivers. Can. J. Fish. Aquat. Sci. 54: 2866-2871.

Choudhury, A., R. Bruch, and T.A. Dick. 1995. Helminths and food habits of lake sturgeon, *Acipenser fulvescens* from the Lake Winnebago system, Wisconsin. The American Midland Naturalists 135: 274-282.

Choudhury, A. and T. A. Dick. 1998. Historical biogeography of sturgeons (Osteichthyes: Acipenseridae): a synthesis of phylogenetics, palaeontology and palaeography. Journal of Biogeography 25: 623-640.

Choudhury, Anindo, Terry A. Dick, Harry L. Holloway, and Chris Ottinger. 1990. The lake sturgeon - *Acipenser fulvescens* (Chondrostei, Acipenseridae) in Canada: Preliminary studies on parasitofauna and immunological parameters. 1990 Interbasin Biota Transfer Study Program Proceedings (Eds., J.A. Leitch and D. J. Christensen), North Dakota Water Resources Research Institute, Fargo, North Dakota, 121-133.

Cummins, K.W. 1962. An evaluation of some techniques for the collection and analysis of benthic samples with special emphasis on lotic waters. American Midland Naturalist, 67(2): 177 501.

Dick, T. A. R. R. Campbell, N. E. Mandrak, B. Cudmore, J. Reist, J. Rice, P. Bentzen and P. Dumont. 2006a. Update COSEWIC status report on lake sturgeon, *Acipenser fulvescens*. 154 p.

Dick, T. A., S.R. Jarvis, C.D. Swatzky and D.B. Stewart. 2006b. The lake sturgeon, An annotated bibliography. Can. Tech. Rep. Fish Aquat. Sci. iv + 252 p.

Dick, T.A. 2004. Lake sturgeon studies in the Pigeon and Winnipeg rivers and biota indicators. Report prepared for Manitoba Hydro and Manitoba Model Forest. 445p

Dick, Terry, Henry Letander, Kim Morriseau and Chris Paci. 1998. Namay an northern resource in crisis, In: Issues in the north (Eds. Jill Oakes and Rick Riewe), Canadian Polar Institute and Department of Native Studies, University of Manitoba, Vol. III: 181-190.

Dick, T.A. and A. Choudhury. 1992. The lake sturgeon *Acipenser fulvescens* (Chondrostei: Acipenseridae): annotated bibliography. Can. Tech. Report Fisheries and Aquatic Sciences No. 1861. 69p.

Dick, Terry A. and Bryan Macbeth. 2002. The importance of First Nations community participation in determining the status of species at risk. *In*: Native Voices in Research (*Eds*. J. Oakes, R. Riewe, K. Wilde, and A. Dubois), Native Studies Press, University of Manitoba, Winnipeg.

Ferguson, M.M. and G.A. Duckworth. 1997. The Status and Distribution of Lake Sturgeon, *Acipenser fulvescens*, in the Canadian Provinces of Manitoba, Ontario, and Quebec: a Genetic Perspective. Environmental Biology of Fishes, 48: 299-309.

Ferguson, M.M., L. Bernatchez, M. Gatt, B.R. Konkle, S. Lee, M. Malott and R.S McKinley. 1993. Distribution of mitochondrial DNA variation in lake sturgeon (*Acipenser fulvescens* from the Moose River basin, Ontario, Canada. J. Fish. Biol. 43: 91-101.

Fogle , N.E. 1975. Michigan's oldest fish. Mich. Nat. Res. 44(1): 32-33.

Glover, C.R. 1961. The sturgeon in Pennsylvania. Penn. Angler, Jan. 1961: 3.

Harkness, W.J.K., and J.R. Dymond. 1961. The lake sturgeon, the history of its fishery and problems of conservation. Ont. Dept Land. For. Fish Wildl. Br. 121p.

Houston, J.J. 1987. Status of the lake sturgeon, *Acipenser fulvescens*, in Canada. Can. Field Nat. 101(2): 171-185.

Holzkmann, T.E., and Wilson, Chief W. 1988. The sturgeon fishery of the Rainy River Ojibway Bands,. *In* Smithsonian Institution (ed.) Smithsonian Columbus Quincentenary Program "Seeds of the past" ("Raices del Pasado"). Smithsonian Institution, Washington. p. 1-10.

Holzkmann, T.E. 1987. Sturgeon utilization by the Rainy River Ojibwa Bands. *In* W. Cowan (ed.) Papers of the Eighteenth Algonquin Conference, Carlton University, Ottawa. p. 155-163

Mecozzi, M. 1988. Lake sturgeon (*Acipenser fulvescens*). Wis. Dept Nat. Res. Bur. Fish. Manage. PUBL-FM-704 88. 6p.

Nelson, J.S. and M.J. Paetz. 1992. The fishes of Alberta (2nd ed.). The University of Calgary Press and the University of Alberta Press, Canada. [Pagination unknown]

Nelson, J.S. 1994. Fishes of the World. 3rd edition. John Wiley and Sons Inc. New York. 600p.

Ono, R.D., J.D. Williams, and A. Wagner. 1983. p. 29-33 & 232-233. In Vanishing fishes of North America. Stone Wall Press Inc.

Pearce, W.A. 1986. Methuselah of freshwater fishes - the lake sturgeon. Conservationist 41(3): 10-13.

Prince, E.E. 1905. The Canadian sturgeon and caviare (sic) industruies. Can. Sess. Pap. 22: Spexc. Append. Rep.: liii-lxx.

Scott, W.B. and E.J. Crossman. 1998. Freshwater Fishes of Canada. Galt House Publications Ltd. Oakville, Ontario, 82-95.

Webber, D.M., Boutilier, R.G, Kerr, S.R., and Smale, S. M. (2001a) Caudal differential pressure as a predictor of swimming speed and power output of cod (Gadus morhua). J. Exp. Biol. 20, 3561-3570.

Webber, D.M., McKinnon, G.P., and Claireaux, G. (2001b) Calibrating differential pressure to swimming speed in the European sea bass, Dicentrarchus labrax. . In Electronic Tagging and Tracking in Marine Fishes. (eds. J. R. Sibert and J. L. Nielsen), pp.297-314. Kluwer Academic Publishers.

Williams, J.E., and H.J. Vondett. 1962. The lake sturgeon, Michigan's largest fish. Mich. Dept Conserv. Fish Div. Pamph. 35: 6p.

19

Radiotracking of Pheasants (*Phasianus colchicus* L.): To Test Captive Rearing Technologies

Marco Ferretti, Francesca Falcini, Gisella Paci and Marco Bagliacca
Veterinary college, University of Pisa
Italy

1. Introduction

The common pheasant is a species that comes from Asia: its natural geographical distribution includes the central western and eastern areas of Asia, from Caucaso to Formosa island. It has been largely introduced in Europe: in Italy since Roman age, in most of central western and eastern Europe between 500 and 800 B.C.; much later it has been introduced also in North America, Hawaii islands, New Zealand and in many other countries (Cramp & Simmons, 1980; Hill & Robertson, 1988; Johnsgard, 1986). In Italy the populations of pheasant are composed of hybrids coming from subspecies of "*Phasianus colchius*" part of "*colchius*" group, "*mongolicus*" and "*torquatus*" and from the two subspecieses of "*Phasianus versicolor*" (Brichetti, 1984). At the present, the nominal subspecies can be considered extinct in Italy: the last stocks, probably extinct or genetically contaminated by captive reared pheasants released for hunting purposes, survived until the end of last century in Tuscany, Basilicata, Calabria and some other small areas of the north Italy. It is difficult to establish the consistency of the Italian population of this species, because its distribution is not known and because generally data density are missing. The Italian population is constituted by more or less isolated sub-populations, preserved in Protected Areas (PA) and in few hunting areas. The groups of animals, which are in free hunting territories, cannot be considered real populations because these groups are not self-sustaining, but they are artificially re-constituted year after year by regular restocking with new pheasants, breeders or young ones, captive reared or wild ones captured in no hunting areas during the winter months (Santilli & Bagliacca, 2008).

1.1 Rearing technique of breeders

The breeders are selected by the farmers within the same hatching group on vivacity of temperament, origin, health, body development, size and feather condition. The weight and growing speed are so very important. The restocking, which is carried out by the farmers during January and February, is the formation of harems constituted by one male and 5-6 females, or colonies of breeders constituted by 8-10 males and 40-50 females. The breeders are raised in outside little ground pens (1 or more pheasant/sq.m) or in cages. The wild females lay approximately 15-20 eggs and the best farmed hens up to 80-100 eggs. The top of the output of the wild animals is recorded between the second and the third year of activity.

At the end of the reproductive season, the farmer who uses farm pheasants adapted to the breeding, eliminate his own breeders selling them as subjects "ready to be hunted". The farmer who uses breeding pheasants coming from the wild keeps them for 2-3 years. For this purpose the farmer chooses the most prolific and strong subjects and moves them into different and big aviaries, where they will recover their strength in view of the following reproductive season. The eggs of the pheasant, that have an average weight of 33 g., have a smooth shell and a changeable plain color from the light brown to the grayish - green. The reproduction is usually between March and July. The eggs are picked once - twice a day, and after the discarding of the defective ones, are preserved in special drawers or in simple bowls containing fine sand, at a temperature below 18°C - 20°C no longer than 7-10 days, in rooms, with or without air changing. Before being incubated the eggs are disinfected by formaline fumigation, ozone, UV rays, washing or nebulization of disinfectant. The incubation period lasts for 23-25 days and can be natural or artificial. In the natural incubation the eggs are hatched in varying numbers from 6 to 24, rarely by the pheasants, most of the times by hens. The artificial incubation is the most widespread and it is carried out in the same incubators used for poultry. The hatching takes average 24 hours and it is obtained in specific machines where the eggs are moved for the last 3 days of incubation. The pheasant chicks, hatched from the egg, remain 8-24 hours into the hatching machines, to totally dry up and to take a rest.

1.2 Rearing technique of growing pheasants

The breeding of the growing pheasants starts with the so called warm stage that takes about 3/5 weeks. The chicks are kept in well ventilated areas with a decreasing temperature from 37,6°C during the first 3 days, to approximately 21°C at the end of the third/fourth week.

In natural incubation the warm stage is carried out, by maternal warmth and in artificial incubation by artificial heaters, all over the shed or localized, the so called substitutes of the mother. For this purpose different equipment can be used: hot batteries (multi shelves heating cages in which 50 - 60 chicks can stay per shelf) or radiant heaters suspended on the top of simple control circles (circular box in wood, plastic net or other, till the capacity of 500-600 little pheasants, equipped with gas heater, electric heater or infrared rays lamps put to the right height to guarantee the correct temperature at the pheasant level). In this first stage, the animals are submitted to the most of the vaccinations and treatments. Around day 21, the chicks raised for the repopulating operations are submitted to a transition stage. The animals from internal rooms, where the temperature never goes down 21°C, start to go to external grass parks, shaded and sheltered from winds. After 30 days, the so called cold stage starts and the chicks are placed in big breeding aviaries (between some hundreds sq.m to a few hectares) in which they have to get used to the external environment. These aviaries are localized in flat pieces of land or with little slope, loose with good drainage and totally enclosed by wire mesh supported by chestnut cement poles. The complete feed, pellets or crumbles, are replaced, partially or totally by rations containing cereal grains, but also vegetables (e.g. salad, nettle, alfalfa and so on) to ensure proper fiber intake. When the pheasants are 60-70 days old can reach the territory of release. These pheasants, however, must stay, for a period of acclimatization (there they will prepare and exercise the functions required by free-living) in special aviaries with grass shrub and tree vegetation. These special aviaries must be prepared in the releasing areas.

1.3 Problems related to traditional rearing

The major problems associated with traditional methods of farming have arisen with the uncritical application of criteria of domestic poultry production to the rearing of game. This approach has favored the most domestic characteristics, the productivity in captivity is therefore greatly increased, both for direct selection and for the natural, often unconscious, breeding selection. Another effect was to reduce pheasant genetic variability that the original group of subjects had. In addition, the reproducers, have been identified among pheasants producing the best performance in captivity and, consequently, has increased exponentially the selection of subjects suitable for captive breeding. The genotype of the pheasants that were most productive in the rearing has thus spread rapidly in all breeders and from them into the wild. The farms became more intensive over time, as a result of increased demand for captive birds. Stocking density was greatly increased, especially through the use of devices that limited the aggressiveness, and the extensive phase, represented by the finisher period spent in the aviaries that replicate the wild environment, has worsened, reducing time and going to a progressive degradation of the environment. The arboreal vegetation, as required by pheasants roost for the night, was eliminated from nearly all the farms, because his presence made more difficult to manage the aviaries and did not allow to achieve low and cheaper structures. The herbaceous vegetation, suitable for the pheasants and planted inside the aviaries for food and mimicry, has been reduced since plant cultivation inside the aviaries is difficult and expensive; seeds suitable for pheasants has been almost completely abandoned and remained only the species useful for camouflage and natural weed of reduced interest for pheasant nutrition (Bagliacca et al., 1994). At the same time the high density and the constant use of farm breeders , with the culling of the subjects with imperfect plumage (pecked), determined the increase of the aggressiveness in the farm pheasants. Discarding the pheasants which were injured not only chooses the most aggressive animals, but also chooses those with the most beautiful plumage (bright and intense colors) (Bagliacca et al., 1996). Since it is known that the characteristics of the plumage are secondary sexual characteristics associated with the level of sex hormones, with this choice, preference was given automatically to animals more aggressive, which occupy the highest positions in the scale of the pecking order and which are the subjects with the greater performances (higher ovarian efficiency and deposition rates). The use of mechanical devices to control aggression has become so indispensable in almost all farms. The application of various models of antipecking devices (such as beak guards, blinkers, or ring-beak bite) completely alters the behavior during captivity. These systems in fact hamper the functionality of the bill, preventing contact with the object of the same pecking, counter the complete closing, or block the direct frontal view needed to catch or flight. Diets normally used in rearing, rich in energy, protein and low in fiber, differ from those that the pheasants can find into the wild. In captive rearing concentrate diets also allow the weaker subject to reach the reproductive age. Concentrate diets thus contribute to the selection of domestication or captive rearing, with clear negative consequences on the genetics of animals whose aim is the wildlife. Concentrate diets also do not allow a proper development of the caeca, necessary for the use of poor food in nature. The adaptation of the digestive system to the diluted diets (poor in nutrients and rich in fiber), typical of pheasants living in the wild, needs at least 30 days (Bagliacca et al. 1994, 1996).

1.4 Considerations on restocking of wild pheasants

The term restocking is defined as the release of individuals of a species still existing in the habitat, but with a reduced population levels. This type of intervention, using farm subjects, is widespread in many areas of the Hunting Italian Districts (HTD) and in most of them is the only technique used for management. As summarized by Meriggi (1998), the use of captive animals have a wide range of negative effects:

- prevent the formation of proper management and conservative mentality of the hunters;
- require large investments of money, which could be used for the improvement of the environment;
- create high concentrations of individuals who may cause damage to the habitat, the predators attraction, consequent to the high concentration of pheasants can also affect natural populations and epidemics outbreaks can involve the releasing places;
- can cause the lost of the local populations which are genetically replaced by the captive reared animals.

Regarding in particular the captive pheasants, several studies have shown that these animals have a poor attitude to settle in the wild (Cocchi et al., 1998). In particular, a study conducted in a protected area in the province of Florence, with radio collared pheasants (Papeschi & Petrini, 1993), showed that the captive pheasants had a significantly lower survival rates than the wild translocated (from another PA), especially during the first month after release, while the wild translocated showed surprising survivals of about 80% even after 10 months from release.

1.5 The attempt to reduce the problems of restocking with captive pheasants

In Italy the first attempt to reduce the problem related to the release of farm pheasants was done by the Regional Agency for Development and Innovation in Tuscany Agriculture (ARSIA). Together with leading experts in the field, the Agency produced a "Guideline for the breeding of galliformes fitted for restocking and reintroduction" (Dessi Fulgheri et al., 1998). This work analyzed the different breeding techniques showing that the quality of the animal produced is deeply influenced by the different choices and technologies adopted by the farmers. Almost simultaneously data on an experimental trial conducted in Province of Siena, on the farm of Casabianca were published by Santilli & Mazzoni Della Stella (1998). These data demonstrated the possibility to use pheasants captured inside the PA as reproducers in the farm, although with some objective difficulties. Behavioral tests (Santilli et al., 2004) were also made on the progeny of these animals. The different origin of the pheasants subjected to behavioral tests showed differences attributable to the different genetic origin of the animals. Both experimental groups were in fact kept in the same rearing conditions from hatch. It appeared that natural selection, which acted on wild pheasant reproducers, was able to select a population of pheasants characterized by a different behavior than the population obtained from captive pheasant reproducers in which acted the farm selection. Although the behavior is a character modulated by the experiences (influenced by training) and received with the imprinting, the offspring of the farm pheasants reacted differently from the offspring of the pheasants catch into the PA. Another interesting study (Bagliacca et al., 2007), in some ways preparatory to the use of the wild pheasants as reproducers in the farms, showed that there are genetic differences between pheasants from different wild origin (PA) and different breeding farms. This latest study brings to the indication to use wild pheasants reproducers captured from no far areas to those where the offspring will be released. The experience of Siena at the end of 90 years has been replicated and implemented, on an ongoing basis over time, from the farm of Casentino (Province of Arezzo), in collaboration with the Florence HTD (Fronte et al., 2005).

The data from this experience confirmed that farm reproducers show significantly higher production than those of wild captured. It is therefore evident that the use of wild pheasants as reproducers in intensive farms is not a quantitatively convenient choice, despite the improvement observed in the subsequent years of captivity. A proposed good compromise in terms of productivity was the use of the offspring of the wild captured pheasants as the a farm pheasant reproducers. These subjects, while retaining most of the genetic traits of wildness that distinguishes the parental generation, did not show production significantly different compared to those of the farm pheasants. Finally, in 2003, ARSIA produced the disciplinary for the production of "Quality Pheasants”. The main elements shown were to restore conditions more similar to those observed in the wild in the farm growing. In particular, the following traits were considered essentials:

- to supply diets with low protein and energy content and high fiber content with the aim to promote a "functional exercise" of the digestive system of birds, at least during the final stage of rearing (finisher period);
- to guarantee a minimum height of the aviaries which is essential to promote bird flight learning;
- to guarantee the presence of trees or perching facilities for the pheasants;
- to decrease the density to a level which allows the presence of feeding vegetation species and refuge vegetation species;
- to forbid the use devices or drugs with the aim to control pecking;
- to reduce temporally the so called warm phase which is a totally artificial period;

Experiments on the survival of pheasants produced following this disciplinary, have been carried out by two different research groups. Improved survivals were observed by Ciuffreda et al. (2007) in respect to the traditional farm pheasants and different dispersion behaviors were observed by Bagliacca et al. (2008). The use of quality pheasants improves significantly the restocking results, but gives problems for the structure of the wild populations that game manager want to preserve. Paradoxically, while the poor quality of pheasants, which are produced by intensive farming, guarantee a low genetic risk (they are unable to survive for long time), the quality pheasants, if genetically different from the local ones, may represent a real risk for the self-reproducing wild local populations. These last are in fact able to survive in large number until the next breeding season and can alter the genotype of the local pheasants, even in surrounding areas (secondary irradiation). Until now the breeding techniques suggested to the game producers has obliged them to reduce the so called warm phase, not considering the effect of this artificial period on the imprinting on pheasants. The use of hens for the hatching of pheasant eggs, or only for the adoption of the pheasant chicks, has been defined a technique that improves the ability to adapt to the natural life of the offspring out from the farm (Game Conservancy 1994). It remains to prove the feasibility of using this technique for producing pheasants in contexts other than amateur or incidental, that is, with a project that is "economical. "

2. The case study example

Studies have repeatedly emphasized the limited survival of pheasants reared using traditional methods compared to the wild one, mainly in relation to the inefficient behavior versus the predators and the reduced capacity utilization of natural foods. These inefficient behavior do not happen in pheasants reared by parents who show the typical attitude of defense. The need for technical improvement of the animals, immediately after hatching (imprinting phase, during the so called warm phase), has been poorly evaluated, especially for the production of pheasants for the restocking of wild populations.

The purpose of this study was therefore to measure the effects related to the use of brooding hens after the hatch for the growing of pheasants, compared to the artificial rearing of the growing pheasants under gas heater after hatch (during the warm phase). The real effect of the proposed new technology must be consequently evaluated measuring the comparative survival rates in nature, as well as the habitat use and the characteristics of the home range of the pheasants after their release into the wild.

2.1 Materials and methods

At the end of March 2008, 32 wild pheasants were transferred to the State Forestry Corps breeding division of Bieri (Province of Lucca) from various PA of the Florence HTD. To capture the pheasants, "falling baskets" (cages) were placed at random throughout the entire PA territories: the birds were attracted by grain nearby and below the baskets. When the birds went to peck at the feed, they triggered the release mechanism, making the basket fall. The captured pheasants, 7 males and 25 females, were used to produce eggs for artificial hatching.

2.1.1 Experimental pheasant production

The pheasant reproducers caught in the PA were placed in an aviary (5x8 x h 3 meters). It had an almost full outer wooden screen to disturb the birds as little as possible. Inside, there was a plastic net (h 1.5 meter) below the roof to protect the birds from injuring themselves in a potential attempt to escape through the roof. Wooden screens were also provided to guarantee pheasant to hide when workers entered to collect the laid eggs. In the first few days, 2 males and 1 female died for trauma, bringing the total number of birds down to 6 males and 24 females. The collected eggs were incubated in accordance with standard methods. Near to the aviary for the captured pheasants, another aviary was constructed for hens to be forced into brooding (Game Conservancy 1994). The pheasants chicks hatchd in the incubator were then forcedly adopted by the hens and raised for 60 days, 6-15 pheasants/hen.

2.1.2 Release zones

The experiment was conducted in two small PA where reared pheasants can be released ("Zone di Rispetto Venatorio" - ZRV) in the Province of Florence. The first, "Leccio Poneta" in Strada in Chianti, had an area of 176 hectares; the second, "Le Bartaline," in Panzano in Chianti, had an area of 184 hectares (Figure n. 2).

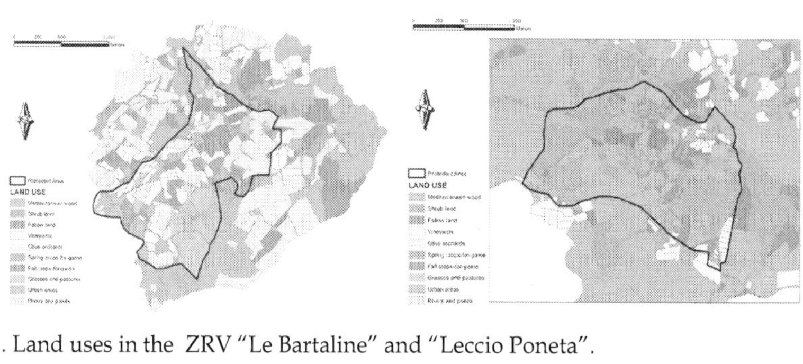

Fig. 1. Land uses in the ZRV "Le Bartaline" and "Leccio Poneta".

Both ZRV have a very similar assortment of environmental characteristics, natural vegetation, as well as trees and shrubs, mainly of the Mediterranean variety. The former zone is characterized by the presence of common broom (*Cytisus scoparius*), wild blackberry (*Rubus ulmifolius*), bay laurel (*Laurus nobilis*), heather (*Erica arborea*) and blackthorn (*Prunus spinosa*) growing at the edges of roads and fields. The latter zone consists of small stone pine forests (*Pinus pinea*), downy oak (*Quercus pubescens*), turkey oak (*Quercus cerris*), holm oak (*Quercus ilex*), wild cherry (*Prunus avium*) and black alder (*Alnus glutinosa*). Small farmers practicing "traditional" or organic agriculture are the only farms present in the ZRC, most of them characterized by small fields. The major crops are grapes (*Vitis vinifera*) and olives (*Olea europea*), while herbaceous plants are very often left uncultivated. Both ZRC are also characterized by natural boundaries separating the different plots of land. Rather than fences, there are borders of uncultivated land, farm roads, hedges, and trees, widely exploited by small game for shelter and feeding (Simonetta, 1975). Fruit trees including common fig (*Ficus carica*), wild cherry (*Prunus avium*), white and black mulberry (*Morus alba* and *Morus nigra*) and common hazel (*Corylus avellana*) are randomly widespread in the ZRC. There is no artificial irrigation equipment in the ZRC but there are abundant small rivers, streams and lakes. Each year; the HTD of Florence, which manage the public wildlife institutions on behalf of the Province of Florence; and the ZRV Management Committee, through cooperation landowners, seed the so-called "crops to be lost for game" (plots of no-harvested food crops) on special strips of land. In the Spring, a mixture of sorghum (*Sorghum vulgare*), rapeseed (*Brassica napus*) and sunflower (*Helianthus annuus*) are sown. In the Fall, a combination of broad bean (*Vicia faba*), hard and common wheat (*Triticum durum* and *Triticum aestivum*) are sown. This makes the area more suitable to both sedentary and migrating wild birds. In these ZRC, the hunting guards and landowners of the HTD perform constant monitoring of the game population in addition to predator activity (censuses and, if necessary, capture and slaughter). In both ZRV there are fenced areas fitted for pheasants acclimatization and equipped with anti-cat device on the outside fence. The fenced area in ZRV "Leccio Poneta," has an area of 3 hectares, and in "Le Bartaline" has an area of 9 hectares. Within the fenced areas there are also two acclimatization aviaries where the pheasants can be placed before being released. In both the ZRV there are also artificial feeding points which are regularly inspected and refilled (mainly troughs) inside and outside the fenced areas, 6 in "Leccio Poneta" and 3 in "Le Bartaline".

2.1.3 Pheasants under study

A total of 117 pheasants were evaluated for about 100 days, regarding their survival and behavior in nature: 57 of which were traditionally bred (29 males and 28 females) **Control**, and the remaining 60 were adopted and raised by hens (30 males and 30 females), **Hen**. Before being placed in the acclimatization aviaries in either ZRV, the following parameters were measured in the pheasants :

- **Live weight:** a technical balance (±1g) with a box, the weight of which was known, was used for weighing each bird;
- **Tarsus length:** a Vernier caliper (0.2 mm error) was used to measure the length of the tarsus (the measurement was carried out externally, from the talocrural joint (ankle) to the distal trochlea of the tarsometatarsus.
- **Tarsus Diameters:** the measurement, always taken with the Vernier caliper, was taken at the midpoint of the right tarsometatarsus, noting the longitudinal diameter - **minimum diameter** and the transverse diameter (just before the spur with males) **maximum diameter**;

- **Spur Length:** the transverse diameter or tarsus including the spur was taken by the Vernier caliper in the males;
- **Remiges Length:** a metal tape measure was used to externally measure the distance between the bird hand and the longest primary flight feather.

Radio collars (TW3 Biotrack + ½AA cell) were supplied to 40 pheasants (20 from the Hen group and 20 from the Control group) while the remaining 77 (40 from the Hen group and 37 from the Control group) were provided with numbered and differently colored ponchos (Figure 2). The frequencies of all tags ranged between 151,045 and 151,975 MHz. (crystal modulation radios, maximum instability ±4.2 MHz).

Fig. 2. Pheasants with mounted radio collar (left) and poncho + radio collar (right).

The radiotags did not affect the animals' survival as the weight of the radio (with cell, antenna and collar) was well below 3% of the animals' own weight (Perez et al., 2004). The radio was always attached to the neck (Bardi et al., 1983), eliminating the potential risk of diseases and/or injury caused by the other types of fixing. Once all the measurements had been taken and the radio transmitters had been fixed on all the pheasants, they were placed in the acclimatization aviary: a tunnel-shaped, 30*3 m, entirely constructed of soft plastic square mesh netting to prevent head injuries during attempts to escape. The pheasants remained in the aviaries for 24 hours in order to test the proper working of their tags, and to ensure that the attached collar did not create problems for the pheasants. Only 114 pheasants were released due to damage occurred during handling for collar supplying or measuring.

2.1.4 Localization techniques

The radio tagged pheasants were monitored through radio-tracking (Godfrey & Bryant, 2003), the poncho equipped pheasants were monitored by direct sighting through the aid of binoculars and then by telescope. A portable radio receiver with a modulation ranging from 151,000 to 151,999 MHz was used to localize the radio signals (Biotrack Sica-receiver). The operator could select the desired frequency on the receiver and then identify and locate each pheasant. A Yaghi, four element, manual antenna (a characteristically directional antenna) was used to locate the signal's direction of the tag. Having a small number of birds, most of the radio localization were made via direct sighting; triangulation was rarely used. All locations were made from late September to early April, 2 or 3 times a week, and always from the early morning until early afternoon. A GPS (Global Positioning System) on a handheld device (Garmin eTrex Legend navigator) was used to record the direct sighting localization. The data were then transferred on a geo-referencing program (ArcGIS ®-ESRI), which had been previously loaded with the maps of the ZRV through a specific software (GPS-Utility ltd. 1998-2006). The geographical coordinates of points on the earth's surface obtained by satellites orbiting the earth (Betti et al., 2001), in our study were saved as Northeast Cartesian coordinates (Gauss-Boaga), referring to the reference system ROMA 1940 (Galetto & Spalla, 1995). when the pheasants was not clear to the observer (did not succeed in direct observation of the pheasant) a triangulation obtained with a single worker was used to obtain the fix. The observer, made the first detection, quickly moved to a second point of listening in order to minimize the possible pheasant movement, and then to calculate the pheasant triangulation as precise as possible (Hessler et al. 1970; Warner & Etter, 1983). The two identified directions were manually reported on the regional technical maps (1:10,000) using a still rule and a pencil. If an animal was not seen or triangulated more than twice in the same place, direct sighting was always used the next time, to verify the conditions of the subject (death or not). All locations were analyzed for survival, dispersion, home range and land use. The locations obtained through triangulation were manually entered into the geo-referencing program, in the same file where the direct locations were automatically transferred. Cards were also used, together with the GPS devices to complete the daily data collection; frequency of tag or poncho number, time, habitat where the pheasant was observed, weather conditions and other features were recorded for each pheasant in the cards.

2.1.5 Data processing

The two groups, **Hen** and **Control**, were studied in many ways over time from late September to early April. Data on biometrics measurement (live weight, tarsus length, diameters, spur length, and remiges length), recorded before release, were submitted to variance analysis in relation to the two groups and different sex (SAS 2002). Survival rates were analyzed using the Kaplan-Meier method, which allows to follow the survival pattern over time and probabilistically classify the missing animals in relation to tag, group, sex and within the different ZRV of release (Efron 1988, Lee 1980, Petrini 1995, Pollock et al. 1989a, Pollock et al. 1989b, SAS 2002). In particular, when the animal was checked alive or changed its position in two consecutive sightings, it was coded as alive, whereas if the poncho or the radiotag was found, with the remains or not, the birds was coded as dead. Animals sighted up to a certain period and then no longer detected, were consequently considered "missing" (probabilistically live/dead), and considered alive only up until the last time they were seen. The causes of death of the animals were only recorded and not submitted to statistical analysis, due to the little number of necroscopies. The maximum distances reached from the point of release calculated on GIS (ArcGIS ®- ESRI) were submitted to variance analysis in relation to tag, group and sex within the different release ZRV (nested model; SAS, 2002). The home range of each subject was determined using the Hawth's Tool GIS (ArcGIS ®- ESRI), evaluating the Minimum Convex Polygon or maximum area (MCP) obtained by joining the outermost points where each subject had been detected. The MCP was determined only for pheasants with a radio collar that had been observed at least 5 different times. The MCP areas were then subjected, as in the previous cases, to variance analysis (SAS 2002). The land use maps, in digitized format, were produced by a preliminary process of photo-interpretation, then verified by a location scout view into the field to identify the crops that were not identifiable through aerial photos or were changed, and to correctly define the polygon vectors. The ten environmental types summarized and categorized were: woods, shrub area, uncultivated fields, vineyards, olive orchards, Spring crops for game, winter crops for game, grassland and pastures, urban areas (such as cities and construction sites) and river and ponds. The environmental composition of each home range, and the type of environment assigned to each location were obtained using Hawth's Tool GIS (ArcGIS ®- ESRI). The environmental availability was calculated from random points used like centers of circles with an area equal to the average pheasant home range, calculated for each ZRV (Fearer & Stauffer 2004). Two criteria were used to evaluate the use of available habitat through the Composition Analysis (Aebisher et al. 1993; Manly et al. 2002; Pendleton et al. 1998):

1. The home range choice = home range composition in relation to the composition of the available habitat, equal to:

$$\frac{\dfrac{\text{Surface area of a single type of environment in the home range}}{\text{Home range (MCP) surface area}}}{\dfrac{\text{Surface area of a single type of environment in the study area}}{\text{Study surface area}}}$$

2. The choice in the home range = the number of fixes in a particular habitat relative to how often that habitat appears in the home range, equal to:

$$\frac{\dfrac{\text{Total number of localization of a subject in a single type of environment}}{\text{Total number of localization of a subject}}}{\dfrac{\text{Surface area of a single type of environment in the home range}}{\text{Home range surface area}}}$$

The environmental choices (log transformed) were then submitted, as in the previous case, to variance analysis for more categorical factors (Pendleton et al. 1998; SAS 2002). If there was an available habitat in the home range not being used by the animal, zero values were converted to 0.01% before the log transformation. (Aebisher et al. 1993).

2.2 Results and discussion

The morphological characteristics, survival rates, use of the fenced acclimatization area, pheasant home range surfaces and dispersion (distances from the releasing points) and pheasant land uses, were opportunely summarized in tables and figures and separately discussed.

2.2.1 Morphological characteristics

The live weights, the tarsus length and diameter, the remiges length, the tarsus diameter and the spur + tarsus diameter, for each thesis, mean ± standard deviation, are shown in the Table n. 1 and Table n. 2.

group:		Control – n. 29		Hen - n. 30	
Live weight mean	g	1,235 ± 23.2	A	960 ± 21.7	B
Tarsus length	cm	8.53 ± 0.083	ns	8.50 ± 0.078	ns
Remiges length	cm	23.8 ± 0.170	A	22.7 ± 0.159	B
Tarsus diameter min	mm	6.93 ± 0.101	a	6.59 ± 0.095	b
Tarsus diameter max	mm	10.2 ± 0.169	A	8.84 ± 0.158	B
Spur + tarsus diameter	mm	18.6 ± 0.290	A	14.6± 0.269	B

Table 1. Male morphologic characteristics (means ± st.dev), different letters show differences per p<0.05 if cursive or p<0.01 if capital.

group:		Control - n. 28		Hen - n. 30	
Live weight	g	945 ± 16.9	**A**	749 ± 17.2	**B**
Tarsus length	cm	7.44 ± 0.174	ns	7.43 ± 0.177	ns
Remiges length	cm	21.7 ± 0.118	ns	21.3 ± 0.131	ns
Tarsus diameter min	mm	5.92 ± 0.092	ns	5.69 ± 0.094	ns
Tarsus diameter max	mm	8.42 ± 0.112	**A**	7.68 ± 0.114	**B**

Table 2. Female morphologic characteristics (means ± st.dev); different letters show differences per p<0.01.

From the observation of the tables, we can see great differences in the live weights, remiges length, tarsus diameters and spur length between the males bearing to the two groups. However, also in the females, the average larger sizes were measured in the Control group, even if only the differences between the body weights reached the minimum significant level. these results show that the maximum pheasant growth rate can be obtained only with the totally controlled rearing conditions used by the standard technology while the use of natural brooding does not allow the pheasant chicks to reach their maximum potential growth.

2.2.2 Survival rates

The results of the survival rates (Table n. 3) showed difference survivals in relationship to the different rearing technique; the pheasants of the group Hen showing an improvement of their survival rates, either with poncho or radio tags (90.0% *vs.* 57.1% and 35.0% *vs.* 21.1%, respectively).

			Poncho tag	Chi square Tests		Radio tag	Chi square Tests		Both tags	Tests	
Control	Released/Dead	n	35/15	Log-rank=5.50* P=0.02	Wilkoxson=4,07* P=0.04	19/15	Log-rank=1.34 P=0.24	Wilkoxson=1,80 P=0,18	54/30	Log-rank=5 50* P=0.02	Wilkoxso5.48* P=0.02
	Survived	%	**57.1**			**21.1**			**44.4**		
Hen	Released/Dead	n	40/4			20/13			60/17		
	Survived	%	**90.0**			**35.0**			**71.7**		
Both	Released/Dead		75/19			39/28			114/47		
	Survived		**74.4**			**28.2**			**58.8**		
	Chi square Test		Log-rank 1.14* P= 0.02 Wilkoxson 0.23 P- 0.63								

Table 3. Survival rates of the reared pheasants: effect of different rearing and tag (* show significant differences between percentages).

Survival rates of the pheasants bearing a poncho was higher than the survival rates of the radio tagged pheasants. Surely the survival rates of the poncho tagged pheasants were deeply overestimated (not every dead pheasant can be found). For this reason ponchos can be used only for the comparison between different groups with equivalent subjects and cannot be used to evaluated absolute survival rates. However, also the survival rates estimated with the radio-tagged pheasants were very high, either in the Control or in the Hen group. Several factors hardly influences the survival rates of the captive reared pheasants (e.g. the use of nasal blinders or not, the age of the access to the flying pens and so on) and both our groups of pheasants were reared expressly with the aim of their future wild release. The Graphic n. 1 shows very well how the mortality of the Control group was higher than the Hen group after the release and how this phenomenon increased differently during the observation period.

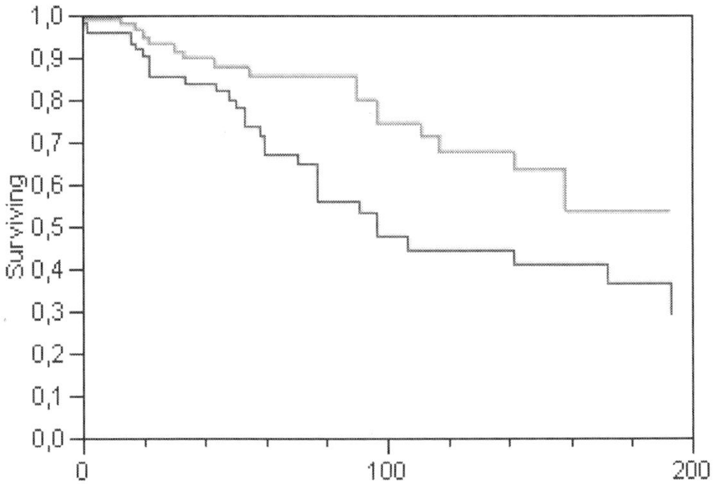

Fig. 3. Survival rates of the two groups with the Kaplan-Meier method (SAS 2002)

2.2.3 Effect of the fenced acclimatization area

The position of the pheasants were arbitrary studied in two periods (the month of release and the 5th mouth after release), see Table 4a. Differences were evidenced in relation to sex and group, as well as by ZRV. In the "Le Bartaline" ZRV during the month after their release, the females of the Control group remained inside the fenced acclimatization area more than the Hen group, the same trend was shown by the males but differences did not reach the statistic significance. In the "Leccio Poneta" ZRV, on the contrary, during the month after their release the dispersion did not differ between thesis.

The month of release			Males	Test		Females	Test		Both	Test	
ZRV Leccio Poneta - pheasant fixes within the fenced areas											
Control outside/total	n		11/37	Log-rank=1.89 P=0.17	Wilkoxson=1.87 P=0.17	20/53	Log-rank=0.01 P=0.98	Wilkoxson=0.01 P=0.98	31/90	Log-rank=0.84 P=0.36	Wilkoxson=0.84 P=0.36
Control fence use	%		**70.27**			**62.26**			**65.56**		
Hen outside/total	n		20/45			15/40			35/85		
Hen fence use	%		**55.56**			**62.50**			**58.82**		
ZRV Le Bartaline											
Control outside/total	n		10/48	Log-rank=3.10 P=0.08	Wilkoxson=2.92 P=0.08	5/31	Log-rank=8.48 P<0.01	Wilkoxson=6.61 P<0.01	15/79	Log-rank=9.43 P<0.01	Wilkoxson=8.70 P<0.01
Control fence use	%		**79.17**			**83.87**			**81.81**		
Hen outside/total	n		3/39			0/38			3/77		
Hen fence use	%		**92.31**			**100.00**			**96.10**		

Table 4a. Contingency tables of the use of the acclimatization fenced area in the two ZRV the month after release.

During the 5th month, see Table 4b, in the "Le Bartaline" ZRV the trend changed: the pheasants of the Control group remained more in the fenced area than the Hen group (the comparison within female was not possible due to a lack of fixes for Control females). The same trend was shown in the "Leccio Poneta" ZRV but, again the differences did not reach the significant level. This can be explained by the smaller size of the acclimatization fenced area of the Leccio Poneta ZRV and the generally better environment of the acclimatization fenced area in Le Bartaline ZRV (olive orchards, crops for game, shrubs land and little woods).

The results of the use of the fenced acclimatization areas of both ZRV are summarized in Table 5. As expected the fenced acclimatization areas is less used after 5 months than during the month following the pheasant release (high significant differences are shown for the Hen group, while the differences within the males of the Control group did not reach the statistical significance). The clear effect of dispersion which characterizes the 5th month (significant for both the group, but more evident in the Hen group than in the Control group and more clear for females than for males) show that with the approaching of the reproductive season the fenced area is abandoned by most females (the fenced area can be a good nesting only for few females) but the presence of pheasants in the fenced areas remains high in both sexes, probably for the presence of the strips of crops for game and of the supplementary feed feeders.

the 5th months after release			Males	Test		Females	Test		Both	Test	
ZRV Leccio Poneta											
Control	outside/total	n	8/18	Log-rank=1.81 P=0.18	Wilkoxson=1.80 P=0.18	19/33	Log-rank=1.06 P=0.30	Wilkoxson=1.05 P=0.31	27/51	Log-rank=2.56 P=0.11	Wilkoxson=2.54 P=0.11
	fence use	%	**55.56**			**42.42**			**47.06**		
Hen	outside/total	n	12/18			19/27			31/45		
	fence use	%	**33.33**			**29.63**			**39.58**		
ZRV le Bartaline											
Control	outside/total	n	6/21	Log-rank=9.19** P<0.01	Wilkoxson=8.84**P<0.01	-			6/21	Log-rank=6.78** P<0.01	Wilkoxson=6.62**P<0.01
	fence use	%	**71.43**			-			**71.43**		
Hen	outside/total	n	15/20			8/16			23/36		
	fence use	%	**25.00**			**50.00**			**36.11**		

Table 4b. Contingency tables of the use of the acclimatization fenced area in the two ZRC the 5th month after release.

Control group			Males	Test		Females	Test		Both	Test	
The month of release	outside/total	n	21/85	Log-rank=1.61 P=0.20	Wilkoxson=1.65 P=0.20	25/84	Log-rank=7.66** P<0.01	Wilkoxson=7.81** P<0.01	46/169	Log-rank=7.73** P<0.01	Wilkoxson=7.94** P<0.01
	fence use	%	**75.29**			**70.24**			**72.78**		
the 5th month	outside/total	n	14/39			19/33			33/72		
	fence use	%	**64.10**			**42.42**			**54.17**		

Table 5a. Contingency tables of the use of the acclimatization fenced areas in the Control group.

the different behavior shown by the Hen group and the Control group can be explained by the imprinting needed to find food, received by the Hen group but not received by the Control group and the greater antipredator capacity of the Hen group than the Control group.

	Hen group		Males	Test		Females	Test		Both	Test	
The month of release	outside/total	n	61/84	Log-rank=20.7** P<0.01	Wilkoxson=20.6**P<0.01	63/78	Log-rank=23.1** P<0.01	Wilkoxson=23.2**P<0.01	38/162	Log-rank=42.8** P<0.01	Wilkoxson=42.9**P<0.01
	fence use	%	**72.62**			**80.77**			**76.54**		
5 month later	outside/total	n	5/41			57/73			54/81		
	fence use	%	**46.75**			37.21			**43.14**		

Table 5b. Contingency tables of the use of the acclimatization fenced areas in the Hen group.

2.2.4 Pheasant Home range surfaces and dispersion

There were not differences between the home range surfaces and dispersion (distances from the releasing points) of the two groups (Table 6 and 7). The similarity between the home-range sizes of the two groups can be well appreciated in Figure 4 and 5. This result is very interesting for the pheasants gamekeeper choices. In similar environments these parameters can be used as reference parameter to plan releasing points or for the creation of a new correctly dimensioned PA or to establish efficient networks of supplementary artificial feeders.

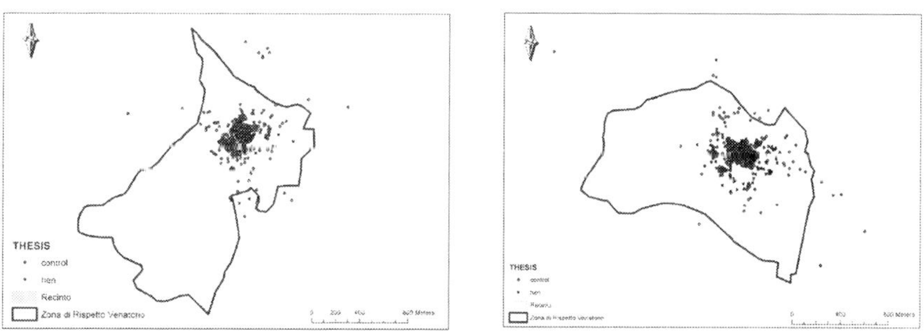

Fig. 4. Animals observations (fixes) by different groups within the two ZRV

ZRV	group Hen		group Control	
	pheasants	avg - st.dev	pheasants	avg - st.dev
Le Bartaline	9	369 ± 191.5	9	401 ± 196.7
Leccio Poneta	10	408 ± 157.9	11	447 ± 279.8

Table 6. Average Max distances from the release sites (meters ± std.dev).

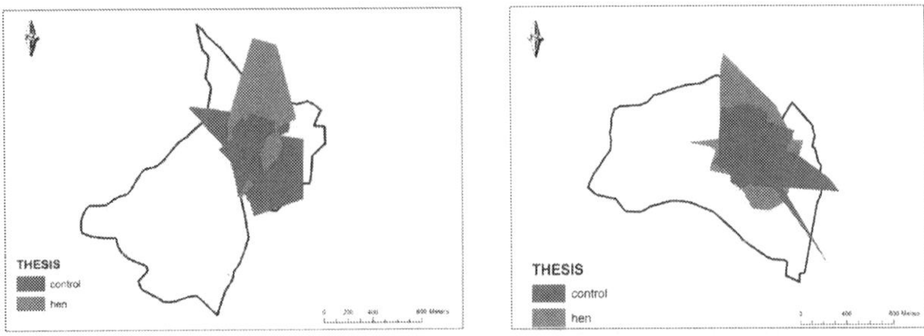

Fig. 5. Animals home ranges (MCP) by thesis inside the two Protected Areas

ZRV	group Hen		group Control	
	pheasants	avg - st.dev	pheasants	avg - st.dev
Le Bartaline	9	11.1 ± 8.26	9	10.1 ± 8.06
Leccio Poneta	10	12.9 ± 11.92	11	12.9 ± 7.59

Table 7. Average Home Range areas (MCP) (hectare ± std.dev).

2.2.5 Pheasant land use

The data concerning the pheasant land uses (considering both the ZRV), referring to both sexes, are shown in Table 8.

"Le Bartaline" & ZRV "Leccio Poneta"	Hen	Control	Overall values
	home range uses		
Woods	0.945^{abc}	0.883^{abc}	0.917^{ab}
Shrubs area	0.881^{abc}	0.777^{abc}	0.833^{bc}
Uncultivated fields	2.010^{a}	1.920^{ab}	1.970^{ab}
Vineyards	0.397^{cd}	0.399^{cd}	0.397^{cd}
Olive orchards	0.805^{abc}	0.705^{bcd}	0.760^{bc}
Spring crops for game	1.620^{ab}	2.630^{ab}	2.130^{ab}
Winter crops for game	2.900^{a}	3.810^{a}	3.370^{a}
Grasses and pastures	0.484^{bcd}	0.314^{cd}	0.406^{cd}
Urban areas	0.073	0.273^{cd}	0.164^{d}
River and ponds	0.015^{d}	0.019^{d}	0.017^{d}
Standard error of means	0.0938	0.0899	0.0646

note: Least square means > 1 show larger incidences of the land use in the home range than in the study area; Least square means < 1 show smaller incidences of the land use in the home range than in the study area; Land uses bearing different superscripts differ within the same column per $p<0.05$;

Table 8. Land uses in the pheasant home range (MCP) in respect to the overall land uses (analysis carried out on log-values, Aebischer et al., 1993).

The winter crops-for-game, the spring crops-for-game, the fallow lands and the wood were more represented within the home ranges of both group of pheasants. However the home ranges of the Hen group were characterized by a greater presence of shrub land and olive orchards. The home ranges of the Control group were characterized by a greater presence of shrub land. In general these results confirmed the great importance of crops for game. Winter crops for game in this experiment represented old crops, since they were seeded the year before the release of the pheasants (wheat, broad beans and oats). In this phenological state these crops are able to provide feeding but also good protection and hiding places for the pheasants. There were not evident differences between the different crops for game. We note, however, that the Hen group preferred a greater number of types.
The presence of pheasants fixes in the different land uses, referring to both sexes, are shown in Table 9.

ZRV Le Bartaline & ZRV Leccio Poneta	Hen	Control	Overall values
	choices in the home range		
Woods	5.356^{ab}	5.628^{a}	5.497^{a}
Shrubs area	1.456^{abc}	1.738^{abc}	1.597^{bcd}
Uncultivated fields	6.226^{a}	5.388^{ab}	5.797^{a}
Vineyards	0.830^{c}	0.597^{cd}	0707^{d}
Olive orchards	0.945^{bc}	1.098^{bc}	0.981^{bcd}
Spring crops for game	3.916^{abc}	4.208^{ab}	4.067^{ab}
Winter crops for game	2.176^{abc}	3.858^{ab}	3.047^{ab}
Grasses and pastures	0.937^{bc}	1.008^{bc}	0.970^{cd}
Urban areas (biased)	0.016^{de}	0.015^{de}	0.015^{de}
River and ponds (biased)	0.016^{de}	0.015^{de}	0.015^{de}
Standard error of means	0.1067	0.0988	0.0720

note: Least square means > 1 show greater number of fix in the land use than the incidence of the land use in the home range; Least square means < 1 show smaller number of fix in the land use than the incidence of the land use in the home range; Land uses bearing different superscripts differ within the same column per $p<0.05$;

Table 9. Land use location of the pheasant fixes in respect to the land use incidence in the MCP (analysis on log-values, Aebischer et al., 1993).

The fix locations of the pheasants within their home range showed that wood, uncultivated fields and crops for-game were the most frequented within the home range. No fix was observed during the trial in the artificial areas (extractive, construction sites and urban areas) or river and ponds. Considering only the Control group the shrubs area, the olive orchards and the grasses and pastures acquire greater importance while in the Hen group the majority of fix were found in the uncultivated fields; followed by both types of crops for game and the shrubs area. Also in this case the importance of the uncultivated fields and the crops for game were confirmed by the pheasant fixes. The preference for the woods was explained by their reduced dimensions (several small woods) which allowed the pheasants to find perches for the night and refuges for the day.

2.3 Conclusion

The high survival rates of the pheasants, reared according to the disciplinary rules set forth for the production of pheasants to be released in the wild as part of game repopulating programs, can be further increased with the adoption of the technique of mother fostering applied to the artificially hatched pheasants chicks. With the aim to estimate the future survival of the pheasants to be released, the simple evaluation of the morphological traits is of reduced or none interest; in our case, the brooded pheasants were worse than the artificially heated one. Radio tracking is not the only methodology to check the survival rates of the pheasants after release. The efficiency of radio tracking pheasants can be greatly increased by the simple use of ponchos which did not cause any increase of the research costs, on condition to tests groups with similar numbers. The increase of the production costs of hen brooded pheasants, mainly space and man working time, however, must be evaluated on the positive effect on survivals linked with the use of this technology. The same problem concerns the positive results obtained with the adaptation of pheasants to be released in fenced areas located in the releasing sites with the presence of artificial feeding and crops-for-game.

3. References

Aebischer, N.J.; Robertson, P.A. & Kenword, R.E. (1993). Compositional analysis of habitat use from animal radio-tracking data. *Ecology* 74 (5): 1313-1325.

Bagliacca, M.; Paci, G.; Marzoni, M.; Santilli, F. & Calzolari G. (1994). Diete a basso e alto contenuto di fibra per fagiani in accrescimento. *Annali della Facoltà di Medicina Veterinaria di Pisa*. 46: 367-375.

Bagliacca, M.; Santilli, F. & Marzoni M. (1996). Valutazione del volo dei fagiani. Nota 1: ripetibilità delle caratteristiche dell'involo misurate in voliera. *N=K Ricerche di Ecologia Venatoria* 2: 3-8.

Bagliacca, M.; Cappuccio, I.; Paci, G. & Valentini A. (2007). Problemi genetici nella produzione in allevamento di fagiani (*Phasianus colchicus* L.) di qualità - in Lucifero & Genghini (editors) *Valorizzazione agro-forestale e faunistica dei territori collinari e montani*. Ist. Naz. Fauna Selv. Min. Pol. Agr. Alim. e For., Ed. Grafiche 3B Toscanella di Dozza (BO): 135-154.

Bagliacca, M.; Falcini, F.; Porrini, S.; Zalli, F.& Fronte B. (2008). Pheasant hens (Phasianus colchicus L.) of different origin. Dispersion and habitat use after release. *Italian Journal of Animal Science* (7): 321-333.

Bardi, A.; Bendini, L.; Coppola, F.; Fasola, M. & Spina F. (1983). *Manuale per l'inanellamento degli uccelli a scopo di studio*. Ed. INBS, Bologna.

Betti, B.; Casella, B.; Manzino, A.; Pinto, L.; Spalla, A. & Tornatore B. (2001). Trattamento dei dati GPS e datum altimetrico. *Bollettino SIFET*, supplemento al n. 2: 39-54.

Brichetti, P. (1984). Distribuzione attuale dei Galliformi (Galliformes) in Italia. In: *Biologia dei Galliformi*. F. Dessì-Fulgheri & T. Mingozzi (EDS). Università della Calabria, Arcavacata: 15-27.

Ciuffreda, M.; Ballerini, C.; Berti, A.; Binazzi, R.; Cilio, A.; Ferretti, M.; Giannelli, C.; Nesti, V.; Papeschi, A.; Rastelli, V.; Silli, M.A.; Zaccaroni, M. & Dessì Fulgheri, F. (2007). Alcuni fattori che influenzano la riuscita dei ripopolamenti di fagiano comune (*Phasianus colchicus*). in Lucifero & Genghini (editors) *Valorizzazione agro-forestale e faunistica dei territori collinari e montani.* Ist. Naz. Fauna Selv. Min. Pol. Agr. Alim. e For., Ed. Grafiche 3B Toscanella di Dozza (BO): 135-154.

Cocchi, R.; Riga, F. & Toso, S. (1998). *Biologia e gestione del Fagiano.* Documento Tecnico n° 22. INFS.

Cramp, S. & Simmons, K.E.L. (Eds) (1980). *Handbook of the birds of Europe, the Middle East and North Africa.* Vol 2: Hawks to bustard. Oxford University Press.

Dessì Fulgheri, F.; Papeschi, A.; Bagliacca, M.; Mani, P. & Mussa P.P. (1998). *Linee guida per l'allevamento di galliformi destinati al ripopolamento e alla reintroduzione.* Ed. Regione Toscana - Arsia.

Efron, B. (1988). Logistic regression, survival analysis and the Kaplan-Meier curve. *Journal of the American Statistical Association.* 83: 414-425.

Fearer, T.M. & Stauffer, D.F. (2004). Relationship of ruffed grouse *Bonasa umbellus* to landscape characteristics in southwest Virginia, USA. - *Wildlife Biology* 10: 81-89.

Fronte, B.; Porrini, S.; Ferretti, M.; Zalli, F.; Bagliacca, M. & Mani, P. (2005). Performance riproduttive in condizioni di cattività di fagiani (*Phasianus colchicus*) di origine selvatica in allevamento. *Annali Facoltà Medicina Veterinaria di Pisa,* 58: 177-218.

Galletto, R. & Spalla, A. (1995). I sistemi informativi territoriali per la gestione del territorio e dell'ambiente. In: *Il telerilevamento e i sistemi informativi territoriali nella gestione delle risorse ambientali.* Lussemburgo: 21-30.

Game Conservancy (1994). *Gamebird Rearing.* - Game Conservancy Limited. UK.

Godfrey, J.D. & Bryant, D.M. (2003). Effect of radio transmitters on energy expenditure of takahe. in: Williams M. (Comp): *Conservation application of measuring energy expenditure of New Zealand birds: assessing habitat quality and costs of carrying radio transmitters.* Science for conservation 214: 69-81.

Hessler, E.; Tester, J.R.; Sniff, D.B. & Nelson, M.M. (1970). A biotelemetry study of survival of penrearend pheasants released in selected habitats. *Journal of Wildlife Management 34: 267-274.*

Hill, D.A. & Robertson, P.A. (1988). *The pheasant: ecology, management and conservation.* Blackwell Scientific Publ., Oxford.

Johnsgard, P.A. (1986). *The phesant of the world.* Oxford University Press. Oxford.

Lee, E.T. (1980). *Statistical Method for Survival Data Analysis.* Lifetime Learning Publications, Belmont, CA.

Manly, B.F.; McDonald, L.; Thomas, D.L.; McDonald, T.L. & Erickson, W.P. (2002). *Resource selection by animals: statistical design and analysis for field studies.* Kluwer academic publishers.

Meriggi, A. (1998). Interventi diretti sulle popolazioni di animali selvatici. Immissioni. Metodi e tecniche di immissione. In: Simonetta, A. M. & Dessì-Fulgheri F. editors, *Principi e tecniche di gestione faunistico-venatoria,* Greentime: 59-74.

Papeschi, A. & Petrini, R. (1993). Predazione su fagiani di allevamento e selvatici immessi in natura. *Supplemento Ricerca Biolologia della Selvaggina,* 21: 651-659.

Pendleton, G.W.; Titus, K.; Degayner, E.; Flatten, C. J. & Lowell, R.E. (1998). Compositional Analysis and GIS for Study of Habitat Selection by Goshawks in Southeast Alaska. *Journal of Agricultural, Biological, and Environmental Statistics* 3(3): 280-295.

Perez, J.A.; Alonso, M.E.; Gaudioso, V.R.; Olmedo, J.A.; Diez, C. & Bartolome, D. (2004). Use of Radio-Tracking Techniques to Study a Summer Repopulation with Red-Legged Partridge (*Alectoris rufa)* Chicks. *Poultry Science* 83: 882- 888.

Petrini, R. (1995). Il metodo Kaplan-Meier per l'analisi quantitativa della sopravvivenza degli animali in natura: applicazione ad uno studio sul fagiano. *Supplemento Ricerca Biolologia della Selvaggina* 23: 177-183.

Pollock, K.H.; Winterstein, S.R.; Bunk, C.M. & Curtis, P.D. (1989a). Survival analysis in telemetry studies: the staggerd entry design. *Journal of Wildlife Management* 53: 7-15.

Pollock, K.H.; Winterstein, S.R. & Conroy, M.J. (1989b). Estimation and analysis of survival distribution for radio-tagged animals. *Biometrics* 45: 99-109.

Santilli, F. & Mazzoni Della Stella, R. (1998). Allevamento di fagiani catturati nelle Zone di Ripopolamento e Cattura della provincia di Siena. *Habitat* 85: 28-32.

Santilli, F.; Mazzoni Della Stella, R.; Mani, P.; Fronte, B.; Paci, G. & Bagliacca, M. (2004). Differenze comportamentali fra fagiani di ceppo selvatico e di allevamento. *Annali Facoltà Medicina Veterinaria di Pisa* 57: 317-326

Santilli, F. & Bagliacca, M. (2008). Factors affecting pheasant *Phasianus colchicus* harvesting in Tuscany, Italy. *Wildlife Biology* 14 (3): 281-287.

SAS (2002). JMP Statistical and Graphic Guide. In: *SAS* Institute Inc. (Ed.). Cary NC USA.

Simonetta, A. (1975). *Ecologia*. Ed. Boringhieri, Torino.

Warner, R.E. & Etter, S.L. (1983). Reproduction and survival of radio-marked hen ring-nacked pheasants in Illinois. *Journal of Wildlife Management* 47: 369-375.

20

The Use of Acoustic Telemetry in South African Squid Research (2003-2010)

Nicola Downey, Dale Webber, Michael Roberts, Malcolm Smale, Warwick Sauer and Larvika Singh
Bayworld Centre for Research and Education
South Africa

1. Introduction

The South African chokka squid, *Loligo reynaudii* is found along the coast of South Africa, from Southern Namibia in the west to Port Alfred in the east (Augustyn, 1991). Inshore spawning, however, is limited to the South Coast between Plettenberg Bay and Port Alfred (Figure 1) (Augustyn, 1990). As it is these inshore spawning aggregations that are targeted by the squid jigging fishery (Sauer et al., 1992), an in depth knowledge of the spawning process is essential to the development of effective management strategies for this fishery. In addition squid catches are determined to a large extent by the successful formation and size of these aggregations. As a result, the majority of research on the chokka squid has focused on inshore spawning, i.e. environmental effects on spawning (Augustyn, 1990, Roberts, 1998, 2005; Roberts & Sauer, 1994; Roberts & van den Berg, 2002, 2005; Sauer et al. 1991, 1992), the impact of fishing on spawning concentrations (Hanlon et al., 2002; Oosthuizen et al., 2002a; Sauer, 1995; Schön et al. 2002), biological studies (Augustyn 1990; Lipinski & Underhill, 1995; Melo & Sauer, 1999; Olyott et al., 2006; Roel et al., 2000; Sauer & Lipinski, 1990; Sauer, 1995; Sauer et al., 1992, 1999), life cycle (Augustyn, 1990, 1991; Olyott et al. 2007; Roberts & Sauer, 1994), feeding on the spawning grounds (Augustyn, 1990; Sauer & Lipinski, 1991; Sauer & Smale, 1991, 1993; Sauer et al., 1992), spawning behaviour (Hanlon et al, 1994, 2002; Sauer, 1995; Sauer & Smale, 1993; Sauer et al. 1992, 1993, 1997; Shaw & Sauer, 2004), the inshore spawning environment (Augustyn, 1990; Roberts, 1998, 2002; Roberts & Sauer, 1994; Roberts and van den Berg, 2002; Sauer et al. 1991, 1992), the location of spawning grounds (Augustyn, 1990; Roberts, 1995; Roberts & Sauer, 1994; Sauer, 1995; Sauer et al., 1992, 1993), predation on spawning grounds (Hanlon et al. 2002; Roberts, 1998; Sauer & Smale, 1991, 1993; Smale et al., 1995, 2001), migration / movement on spawning grounds (Augustyn, 1990, 1991; Lipinski et al. 1998; Roberts & Sauer, 1994; Sauer & Smale, 1993) and paralarval development (Oosthuizen & Roberts, 2009; Oosthuizen et al. 2002b; Roberts & van den Berg, 2002; Vidal et al. 2005).

A number of these studies have, however, been limited by certain factors. The inshore spawning grounds extend from ~20 to 70 m. Diving observations are only possible up to a depth of 30 m, are limited in terms of the amount of time that can be spent underwater and are highly dependent on water visibility. Many of these limitations can be overcome by the use of underwater cameras, however, the issue of water visibility remains. Not only has the development of acoustic telemetry systems allowed researchers to overcome many limitations, it has also opened up new avenues of research.

Initial telemetry experiments, conducted in 1993 and 1994 (Sauer et al., 1997), made use of a four buoy radio-linked acoustic positioning system and simple acoustic transmitters. The use of this then "unorthodox technique" (Sauer et al., 1997) led to the discovery that the formation of spawning aggregations and mating behaviours is well organized in time and space. The advancement of telemetry systems has enabled researchers to apply this technique to many different areas of research. This chapter describes and compares the various telemetry systems used in South African squid research from 2003 to date. These studies aimed to:

1. further our knowledge of inshore (20-70 m) spawning behaviour
2. determine the effect of upwelling and turbidity events on spawning
3. investigate movement on the inshore spawning grounds
4. investigate nocturnal behaviour
5. monitor the presence and movement of predators on the inshore spawning grounds
6. investigate movement on the deep spawning grounds (71-130 m)

Also described are the types of transmitters used and the various transmitter attachment techniques developed, which are dependent on the species being tagged.

2. The chosen study site for acoustic telemetry squid research

Kromme Bay (St Francis Bay, South Africa, Figure 1) forms part of the main squid spawning grounds on the south coast of South Africa, and is a commonly used spawning area. Relatively sheltered from south-westerly swells and winds, with a gentle-sloping seabed (Birch, 1981) consisting mainly of rippled coarse sand (Roberts, 1998), this area is an ideal study site for squid acoustic telemetry experiments. The annual November squid fishery closed season provides an ideal opportunity to conduct such studies, as the potential impact of boat anchors on instrumentation, as well as intense commercial fishing on spawning aggregations, are avoided.

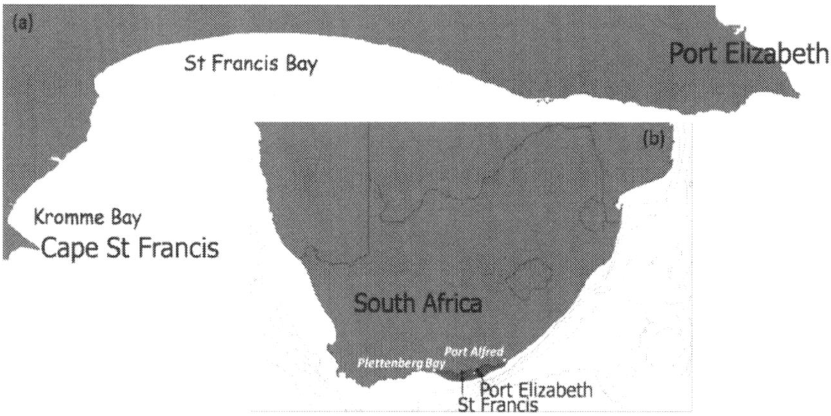

Fig. 1. Maps of (a) the study site, Kromme Bay, (b) the main spawning grounds (shaded area) between Plettenberg Bay and Port Alfred

3. Passive tracking telemetry systems

Passive tracking involves the use of stationary or fixed receivers to monitor the movement of acoustically tagged animals in a particular area. South African researchers made use of two such systems, namely VR2 receiver arrays and the VRAP system. All acoustic telemetry equipment mentioned throughout this section and following sections was purchased from Vemco, Ltd, Canada.

3.1 VR2 receivers

VR2 receivers (Figure 2) are single frequency autonomous omnidirectional underwater units. Transmitters send out a series of pings, known as a 'pulse train', which are detected by the receivers. When all the pings are recognised in sequence, the 'pulse train' is then recorded as a signal detection by the VR2. The transmitter ID code, date and time of detection as well as any other received information (depth/temperature) are stored in the internal memory. Once the receiver has been recovered the data is downloaded using a VR PC interface and a computer running VR2PC software. Receiver ranges vary depending on the power output of the transmitters as well as local factors and environmental conditions (Singh et al., 2009).

Fig. 2. VR2 receiver deployed in Kromme Bay

3.2 VRAP system

The VRAP (Vemco Radio-linked Acoustic Positioning) system (Figure 3) is comprised of three buoys and a computer base station. The three buoys are controlled from the base station by way of line-of-sight radio modems. Each buoy has a hydrophone which receives acoustic transmitter signals. The information received is then transmitted to the base station where a VRAP computer software programme calculates the position of the transmitter, based on the arrival time of the signal at each buoy. Each detected signal, as well as the position of the three buoys, is plotted in real-time on the computer monitor and stored in a database for playback and analysis at a later date (Figure 4). A number of studies have shown the VRAP system to calculate transmitter position with an accuracy of 1 to 3 m (Bégout Anras et al., 1999; Klimeley et al., 2001; Zamora & Moreno-Amich, 2002 as cited in Jadot et al., 2006; Aitken et al., 2005), within the buoy triangle, with accuracy decreasing outside of the array.

Fig. 3. One of the three VRAP buoys deployed in Kromme Bay

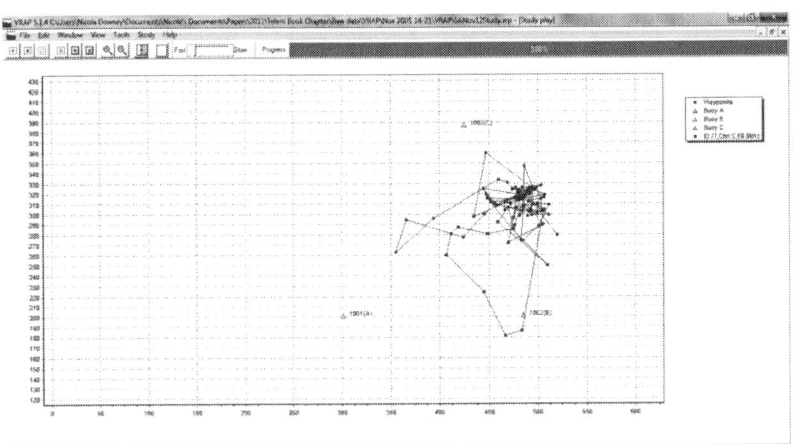

Fig. 4. A single animal track, recorded by the VRAP Buoys, and played back using VRAP software. The smaller triangles in the diagram denote the position of the buoys in the equilateral triangular formation

3.3 Passive tracking studies

Four experiments using VR2 receiver were performed in Kromme Bay during the November 2003-2006 squid fishery closed seasons. In addition to the VR2 receiver arrays, the VRAP system was deployed in November 2005 and 2006.

3.3.1 VR2 study

Each year researchers searched for an active spawning aggregation. Diver observations confirmed the presence of egg beds, the footprint of these aggregations. VR2 receivers were then deployed 500 m apart, in a hexagonal array, on and around these egg beds. Initial range tests showed the receiving range of the VR2 receivers to be <500 m in Kromme Bay. It was therefore decided to deploy receivers 500 m apart to allow for an overlap in receiving ranges. In 2004, an additional VR2 receiver was deployed on a spawning site off Cape St Francis. The position of these arrays can be seen in Figure 5. Depending on the thermal conditions of the water column (Singh et al., 2009) the hexagonal configuration allowed an area of up to 1.28 km^2 to be monitored. Each receiver was deployed 5 m above the seabed using a hollow-core polypropylene rope tensioned with a subsurface buoy. The mooring was anchored to the seabed with a 50 kg weight. During each study temperature data were collected using an array of Star-oddi Starmon mini underwater temperature recorders deployed at depths of 9, 14, 18, 21, and 24 m. This thermistor array (Figure 5) recorded temperature hourly. Hourly wind data, recorded at Port Elizabeth (Figure 1) airport, for 2003-2006 were obtained from the South African Weather Services. Wind data were filtered using an UNH Lanczos filter (weighted 73), and stick vector plots generated.

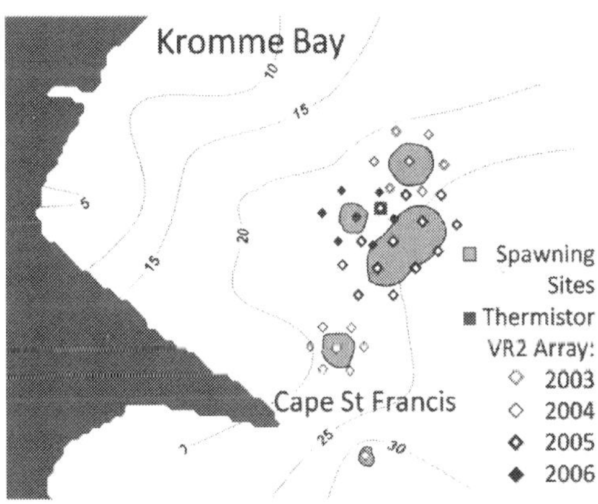

Fig. 5. The positions of the hexagonal VR2 receiver arrays (2003-2006) and the thermistor array overlaid on the bathymetry (contour lines).

3.3.2 VRAP study

VRAP buoys were deployed in the centre of the VR2 receiver arrays (Figure 6) in a 300 m equilateral triangle. This configuration allowed for optimal buoy performance. Each buoy was anchored to the seabed with two 50 kg weights. The hydrophone cable was run down the hollow-core polypropylene rope used to attach the buoy to the weights. The omnidirectional hydrophone was positioned approximately 5 m above the seabed.

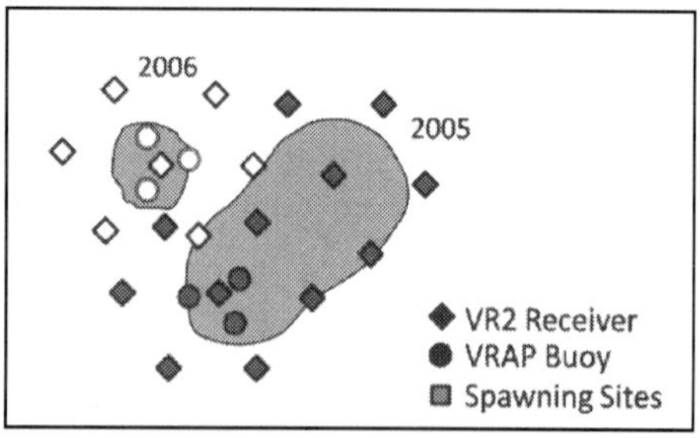

Fig. 6. The positions of the triangular VRAP arrays (2005 & 2006) within the VR2 receiver arrays.

3.3.3 Transmitter attachment

A total of 45 squid and eight predators were tagged over the four experiments. The predators tagged included three ragged tooth sharks (*Carcharias taurus*), three shorttail stingrays (*Dasyatis brevicaudata*) and two smooth hound sharks (*Mustelus mustelus*). Details of the acoustic transmitters used are given in Table 1. For those animals that were tagged with transmitters without pressure sensors, only presence-absence data were collected. Transmitters with pressure sensors provided both depth and presence-absence data.

Year	Transmitter type	Min off-time (s)	Max off-time (s)	Pressure sensor	Number of animals tagged	Male	Female
2003	V8SC-2H-R256	10	35	No	4 (*L. reynaudii*)	2	2
2004	V9P-6L-S256	30	90	Yes	12 (*L. reynaudii*)	6	6
	V16-5H-R04K	35	109	No	3 (*C. taurus*)	Unknown	
	V16-5H-R04K	35	109	No	1 (*D. brevicaudata*)	Unknown	
	V16-5H-R04K	35	109	No	1 (*M. mustelus*)	Unknown	
2005	V9P-6L-S256	30	90	Yes	23 (*L. reynaudii*)	13	10
	V9P-2H-S256	20	60	Yes	1 (*D. brevicaudata*)		1
	V9P-2H-S256	20	60	Yes	1 (*M. mustelus*)		1
2006	V9P-6L-S256	30	90	Yes	6 (*L. reynaudii*)	4	2
	V9P-2H-S256	20	60	Yes	1 (*D. brevicaudata*)		1

Table 1. Details of acoustic transmitters used in the VR2 and VRAP studies

Squid were caught, using jigs (Figure 7), and tagged with V9 acoustic transmitters (Figure 8a). The modification of transmitters for attachment and the tagging process have been described in detail in Downey et al. (2010). Two-18-guage hypodermic needles were glued to the surface of each transmitter, to allow for attachment to the squid (Figure 8a). The length of the needles was dependent on the sex and size of the animal tagged. Hypodermic needles with a length of 17 mm were used for males and needles with a length of 14 mm for the smaller "sneaker" males and females. Each year squid were caught within the hexagonal array of VR2 receivers. Once the animals were removed from the water and their sex determined they were placed on a damp cloth (Figure 9a). Using an applicator specifically designed for this purpose (Figure 8b), a transmitter with the appropriate needles length was inserted into the mantle cavity (Figure 9a). A protective sheath covered the hypodermic needles during insertion (Figure 8b).

Fig. 7. A chokka squid, *Loligo reynaudii*, caught on a jig

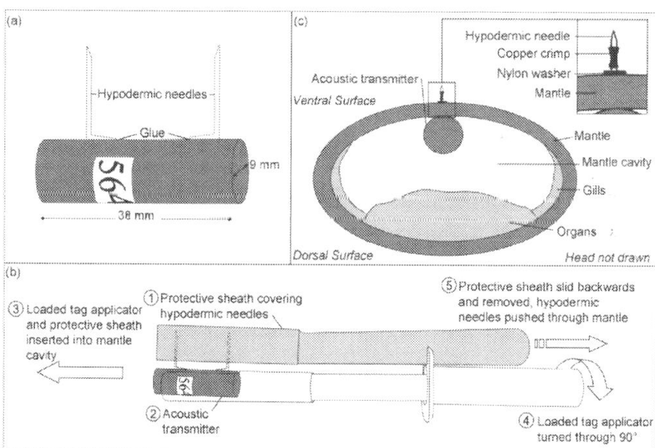

Fig. 8. Tagging instrumentation (taken directly from Downey et al. (2010)): (a) the attachment of hypodermic needles to an acoustic transmitter, (b) the specially designed tag applicator used to tag *L. reynaudii*, and (c) the placement of the acoustic transmitter within the mantle of the squid, on the ventral side, to avoid piercing organs with the hypodermic needles

The applicator was initially held sideways and once inserted was turned 90° and the protective sheath removed (Figure 8b). After pushing the hypodermic needles through the mantle (Figure 9b), nylon washers were pushed onto the ends of the needles (Figures 8c and 9c) followed by copper crimps (Figures 8c and 9d and e). The tagged squid was then placed in a bin containing seawater or held alongside the boat (Figure 9f), depending on sea conditions, to recover. Once normal fin-beating had resumed, the animal was released within the array of VR2 receivers.

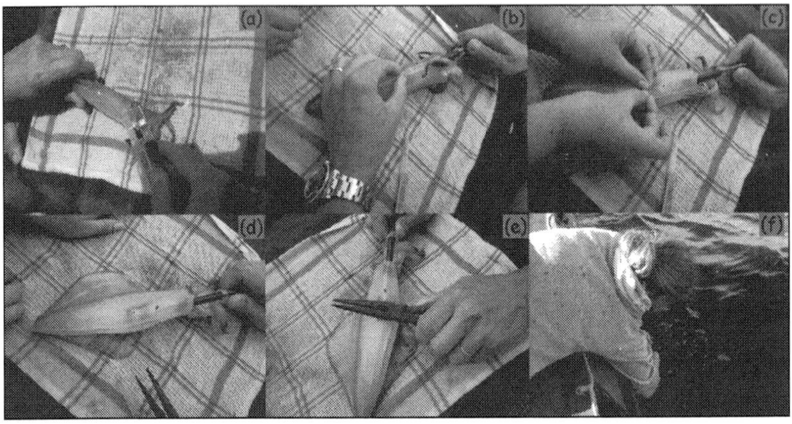

Fig. 9. Attaching a transmitter to a squid (taken directly from Downey et al. (2010)): (a) a transmitter is inserted beneath the mantle using the applicator; (b) the apparatus is turned through 90°, the protective applicator sheath removed, and the hypodermic needles pushed through the mantle. (c) Nylon washers are pushed onto the ends of the hypodermic needles and (d) a metal cylinder slipped over each hypodermic needle, (e) the metal cylinders are crimped using long-nose pliers, and (f) the squid are held submerged alongside the boat until strong swimming ability is displayed (fin beating). Only then is the animal released on the capture site

Predators were tagged with V16 pingers (2004) and V9 sensor acoustic transmitters (2005 & 2006). The transmitters were modified for attachment by gluing a stainless steel trace (Figure 10) to the surface of the transmitter. Predators were either tagged by divers who used a Hawaiian sling (modified spear), to embed the stainless steel trace into the muscle alongside the fin, by wrapping the transmitter in bait and feeding it to the predator, or by surgical implantation. By using the feeding technique, the likelihood of transmitter loss due to merely falling off was avoided, however transmitters can be regurgitated. Surgical implantation, although more invasive, removes the possibility of transmitter loss.

3.3.4 VR2 data analysis

To correct time-drift of individual VR2 receiver clocks, VR2 data files were time-corrected using a program created by Dale Webber of Vemco. The VR2 data was analysed separately for each year. To measure spawning intensity the number of hours each squid was present on the spawning site, expressed as a percentage of the total number of hours of passive tracking, was plotted. The presence-absence of individual squid was determined by plotting transmitter detections at the spawning site, bottom temperature, and wind data against date and time. To determine significant differences in mean depth by day vs. night for male, female, and all squid combined, as well as mean depth for males vs. females by day and night, duplicate data, i.e. single detections recorded by more than one VR2 receiver, were removed and the total number of successfully detected transmissions for each sex per day and night calculated. The data for each sex were separated into depth categories, and the percentage of detections recorded in each depth category by day and night plotted. Two-sample, two-tailed t-tests were used to identify significant differences. To analyse diurnal patterns at the spawning sites, the percentage of transmissions successfully detected per hour in a typical 24-h period were plotted, separately for males and females, using the data from which duplicates had been removed. The plots generated and the results of this analysis are given in Downey et al., (2010).

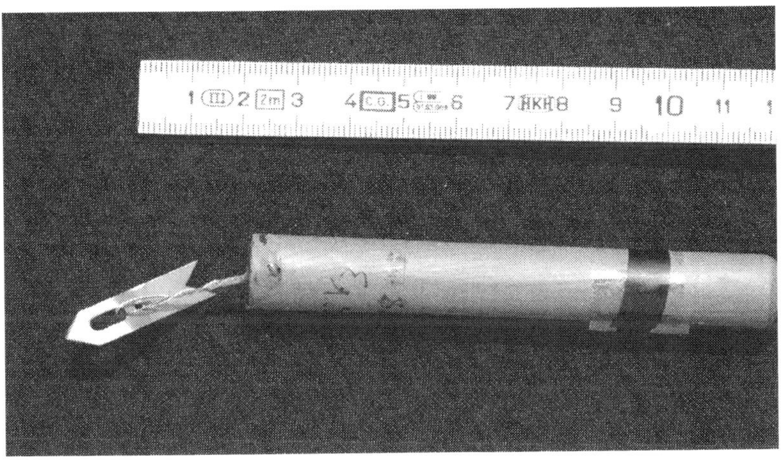

Fig. 10. A V16 pinger with a stainless steel trace attached to allow for external attachment.

The analysis of the VR2 data showed three general presence–absence behaviours to be found at chokka squid spawning sites (Downey et al., 2010). They are, as given in Downey et al., (2010): (i) arrival at dawn and departure after dusk, (ii) a continuous and uninterrupted presence for a number of days, and (iii) a presence interrupted by frequent but short periods of absence. These authors also concluded that , in contrast to the findings of earlier studies, a core aggregation of squid occasionally remains on active spawning sites at night. At dawn, more squid arrive at the spawning site and the size of the aggregation increases, resulting in a dense aggregation by day. Shortly after dusk, spawning pairs break apart, and some squid leave the spawning site. Those squid remaining at a spawning site at night search for prey throughout the water column and in the benthos, whereas lone females deposit egg strands. The authors also found that movement between the spawning sites continues at night. Their VR2 study confirmed previous observations that the initial formation of spawning aggregations, before the deposition of the first egg strand, is triggered by upwelling.

To investigate presence-absence of predators on the monitored spawning sites, the VR2 data was analysed per year. Signal detections from all tagged squid (grouped), the tagged predators (individually) and surface and bottom temperatures were plotted. The position of predators in the water column, in relation to squid, was analyzed by plotting all squid depth data (grouped), predator depth data (individually) and surface and bottom temperatures. Plots were generated only for those days predators were present.

The results of the predator study are as yet unpublished. This study, however, showed predators moved to and from the spawning sites a number of times, despite the continual presence of squid. The presence of predators on the spawning sites appeared to be strongly linked to surface temperature. When temperatures were stable at ~18 °C, predators remained on the spawning sites for long periods. When surface temperatures increased, predators either moved to the surface and left the spawning site shortly thereafter or immediately moved off.

3.3.5 VRAP data analysis

Invalid positional fixes were identified by their large distance from previous and successive fixes, whereas these were close in proximity. For each squid monitored by the VRAP system daily plots, separating day vs. night movement, were generated using Arcview GIS software. This allowed analysis of horizontal movement at the individual level as well as the identification of patterns in movement. Similarly depth over time was plotted for each individual. Depth data recorded by the VRAP system was not analyzed in great detail as the analysis of the VR2 receiver depth data was fairly comprehensive. The distance between two consecutive points, when the time between consecutive detections was less than 10 minutes, was used to calculate swimming speed. The distance (d) between two consecutive locations was calculated in Microsoft Excel using Equasion 1:

$$\begin{aligned} d=&\text{acos}(\cos(\text{radians}(90-\text{Latitude1})).\cos(\text{radians}(90-\text{Latitude2}))+ \\ &\sin(\text{radians}(90-\text{Latitude1})).\sin(\text{radians}(90-\text{Latitude2})). \\ &\cos(\text{radians}(\text{Longitude1}-\text{Longitude2}))).R \end{aligned} \tag{1}$$

The value 6371 km was used for the radius of the earth (R). This formulae made use of latitudes and longitudes in decimal degrees. Swimming speed was calculated by dividing the distance between two consecutive detections by the number of seconds taken to move between the two points ($m.s^{-1}$). Average swimming speeds were then calculated. As these results are as yet unpublished and data is still being analysed, only the initial analysis and findings are reported here.

At night males appeared to move around the spawning site, covering a larger surface area, compared to females. This was possibly due to the males' main nocturnal activity being feeding, whereas females often continue to deposit eggs, using stored spermatophores for fertilization. On occasion however, males would also spend a number of hours in one specific area of the site, possibly resting. Both sexes spent time concentrated in one area for a number of hours during the day. Average swimming speed for males at night was calculated as 0.25 $m.s^{-1}$, compared to 0.22 $m.s^{-1}$ for females. These slight differences are possibly a result of the different nocturnal activities. Average swimming speed for males during the day (0.21 $m.s^{-1}$) was slower than that calculated for females (0.24 $m.s^{-1}$). The 1993/1994 telemetry studies (Sauer et al., 1997) also reported males to swim more slowly than females when part of a spawning aggregation. The swimming speeds reported by these authors were however, slower than those observed in this study (0.18 $m.s^{-1}$ for females and 0.14 $m.s^{-1}$ for males). No predators were detected by the VRAP system.

4. Active tracking telemetry system

Active or manual tracking involves monitoring the movement of acoustically tagged animals from a vessel. South African researchers made use of the VR100 system for active tracking.

4.1 VR100 receiver

The manual tracking study discussed here made use of a VH110 directional hydrophone and a VR100 receiver. This general purpose, splash-resistant receiver is designed for tracking animals from vessels. The hydrophone is held in the water, either manually or by attachment to the side of the boat. The hydrophone detects transmitter signals and the VR100 records the ID Code, date, time, other received information (depth/temperature) and GPS location of the detections. This information can then be downloaded to a computer for viewing or analysis.

4.2 Active tracking studies

As part of a project investigating deep spawning (71-130 m) in *Loligo reynaudii*, a phenomenon researchers as yet know very little about, the movement of squid on the deep spawning grounds was monitored using the above-mentioned manual tracking system. As it is difficult to find and identify active spawning aggregations deeper than 60 m, using the two fixed telemetry systems previously described would not be feasible. This study was conducted during the November 2010 squid fishery closed season.

4.2.1 Tagging of animals

Using the jigging fishing method (Figure 7), squid at depths >60 m can only be caught at night, using powerful lights to attract them to the surface. For the manual tracking study, squid were caught from an 8 m inflatable boat anchored next to a chokka boat. The two boats were close enough for the chokka boat lights to attract squid to the area around the smaller boat. Two squid were caught in this manner, on separate nights, and tagged with V9TP-6L continuous sensor transmitters. Details of the transmitters used are given in Table 2. Animals were tracked (Figure 11) from the time of tagging to shortly after sunrise. The tagging method and instrumentation used was the same as that described for the VR2 and VRAP studies.

Year	Transmitter type	Min period (ms)	Max period (ms)	Pressure sensor	Temperature sensor	Frequency (kHz)	Sex
2010	V9TP-6L	450	1050	Yes	Yes	63	Male
	V9TP-6L	450	1050	Yes	Yes	75	Sneaker male

Table 2. Details of acoustic transmitters used in the VR100 tracking study

4.2.2 VR100 data analysis

The VR100 data was manually examined, using Microsoft Excel, for erroneous depth and/or temperature data. Erroneous data were identified by their large difference from previous and successive values, whereas these were similar. Those data entries containing errors were removed before plotting. Depth and temperature data were plotted against date and time, allowing for analysis of the vertical movement of squid on the deep spawning grounds. Depending on the strength of received signals, a strong signal indicating the tagged animal to be in close proximity, VR100 GPS coordinates were integrated into Arcview GIS. This allowed for an analysis of the horizontal movement of tagged squid on the deep spawning grounds.

As this is an ongoing study, only initial findings are discussed here. The large male remained in the upper 40 m of water from the time of release until just before sunrise. As the sky turned pink in the east (dawn) the squid quickly moved to the bottom, where it remained until tracking was terminated. Similarly the sneaker male remained at depths 40 to 80 m from the time of release until dawn when it too moved to the bottom, remaining there until the termination of tracking. Both animals remained on the midshelf, directly off Cape St Francis point (Figure 1), with the large male covering an area ~ 3.311 km^2 and the sneaker male an area of ~ 1.29 km^2. Both animals moved continuously until settling on the bottom at sunrise, where they remained fairly still. During these movements the tagged squid were exposed to water temperatures of 15 to 19 °C, and 11 °C when settling on or near the bottom.

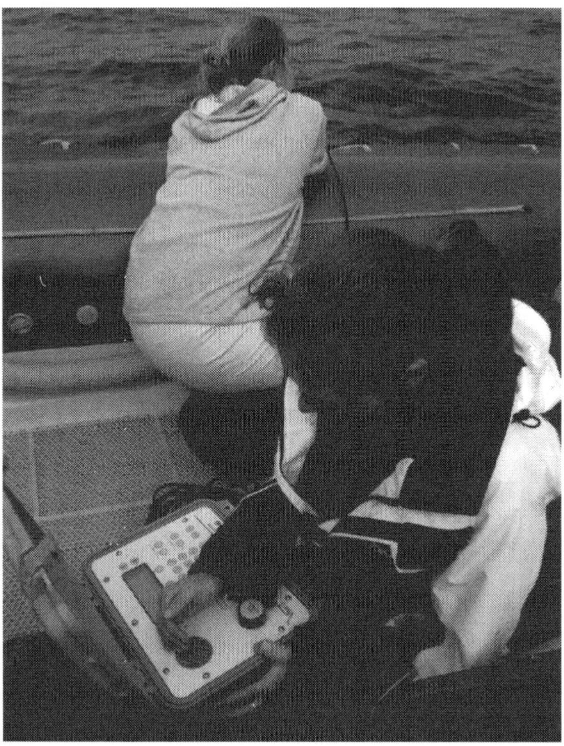

Fig. 11. Active tracking using a VH110 directional hydrophone, held in the water, and a VR100 receiver

5. Comparison of the various telemetry systems

Each of the systems described here (VR2 receiver arrays, VRAP system and VR100 manual tracking system) have various advantages and disadvantages. VR2 receiver arrays are ideal for studying movement and behaviour on a spawning site (Downey et al. 2010), homing behaviour (Mitamura et al., 2005), movement in a river (Carr et al., 1997) or straight (Welch et al., 2004) and movement within a marine reserve (Egli & Babcock, 2004), to name a few examples. These receivers allow researchers to monitor a large area (depending on the number of receivers used) continuously and for long periods of time. Depending on the study area, the geometry of the array can be selected to maximize coverage in critical sites, providing information on the entering and exiting of a specific area (Egli & Babcock, 2004). Range tests can be used to determine the maximum and minimum receiver ranges at a specific location and using specific transmitters (Singh et al., 2009). Placing the VR2 receivers in such a way that the receiver ranges of individual VR2s overlap, maximises the likelihood of a tagged animal being detected when in the area. VR2 receivers can be used to determine direction of animal movement to a certain degree, depending on the design of the array and the study site itself. These receivers are however, more often used to collect presence-absence data and it is not known where in the array the animal is situated. As the VR2 receiver is programmed to work on a single frequency, there is a limit to the number of transmitters that can be introduced into the system at one time. As previously mentioned and as described by Singh et al., (2009), transmitters send out a series of pulses known as a 'pulse train'. Only when all the pings are recognised in sequence by the receiver, is the pulse recorded as a signal detection. The overlapping of 'pulse trains' from two or more transmitters results in no signals being detected. As the number of transmitters in a system increases, so it is possible for the number of successful detections to decrease. However, as the data can only be downloaded once the receiver is retrieved, it is not possible to discern how many transmitters are present in the area using the VR2 receivers. It is therefore necessary to use a VR100 to monitor 'system saturation' (Singh et al., 2009) before introducing more tagged animals into the system. Another method to reduce the number of signal collisions is to programme transmitters with longer off times. However, the speed with which the study species moves needs to be taken into consideration, to prevent an animal moving through an array too quickly to be detected.

The VRAP system differs from the VR2 receiver array in that data recorded is transmitted to a land-based station and the movement of tagged animals in the study area can be observed in real-time. In addition, the direction of movement and location of a tagged animal within the array can be monitored and recorded. One major disadvantage of the VRAP system when compared to the VR2 receiver array is the size of the area that can be monitored. In the study discussed here, the 300 m equilateral triangular configuration resulted in the buoy triangle covering an area of ~ 400 m^2. As previously mentioned, accuracy decreases outside of the buoy triangle. In addition, when a transmitter is directly behind a buoy, no position can be calculated (Aitken et al., 2005). Shadow zones (areas along parabolas behind each buoy) also exist. Two positions are calculated for transmitters in this area. The VRAP software assumes the calculated position closest to the last valid position fix is correct and this value is plotted. As for the VR2 receiver arrays, it is also possible for 'system saturation' to result in a decreased number of successfully detected signals. As the VRAP system is used to monitor tagged individuals in real-time however, the number of tagged animals present within the area can be observed before introducing more tagged individuals. The

VRAP system has been used to study the search behaviour of fish towards bait (Vabø et al., 2004) and food (Løkkeborg et al., 2000), activity patterns, home-range size and habitat utilization (Jadot et al., 2006) and behaviour and energetics (Aitken et al., 2005).

Manual tracking is more labour-intensive and manpower-demanding (Jadot et al., 2006) than the passive or fixed telemetry systems, which require more logistical support (boats, divers etc.). Tagged animals can be tracked for a number of hours, possibly days, unlike the VR2 and VRAP systems which can track animals for weeks or even months. It is only possible to track one animal at a time however, the animal can be followed and tracked wherever in the area it moves. Manual tracking has been used to study daily movements, habitat use and submergence intervals in turtles (Brill et al., 1995), estuarine movement patterns (Almeida, 1996), movement patterns and trajectories of crabs (Carr et al., 2004) and the behaviour and mortality of caught-and-released bonefish (Cooke & Phillip, 2004), to name a few examples.

A number of studies have made use of multiple telemetry systems, for example Jadot et al. (2006) and Acolas et al. (2004) both made use of the VRAP and manual tracking systems. Comparing the different telemetry systems available to researchers can aid in determining which system will be most favourable for a particular study. However, as each system has its limitations, using two or even three simultaneously would be the most beneficial. For example the use of the VR2 receiver arrays and VRAP system simultaneously in this study has enabled the study of not only presence-absence related topics but also movement and swimming speed on the spawning sites.

To conclude, a number of telemetry systems are available to researchers. The type of system, transmitters and hydrophones used are dependent not only the species studied but also the key questions or focus areas of the study. Our research has shown that not only can a number of telemetry systems be used simultaneously to great benefit, but telemetry systems can also be used to monitor species interactions as well as environmental effects on behaviour.

6. References

Acolas, M.L., Bégout Anras, M.L., Véron, V., Jourdan, H., Sabatié, M.R. & Baglinière, J.L. (2004). An assessment of the upstream migration and reproductive behaviour of allis shad (*Alosa alosa* L.) using acoustic tracking. *ICES Journal of Marine Science*, Vol.61, (December 2004), pp. 1291-1304, ISSN 1054-3139

Aitken, J.P., O'Dor, R.K. & Jackson, G.D. (2005). The secret life of the giant Australian cuttlefish *Sepia apama* (Cephalopoda): Behaviour and energetics in nature revealed through radio acoustic positioning and telemetry (RAPT). *Journal of Experimental Marine Biology and Ecology*, Vol.320, (June 2005), pp. 77-91, ISSN 0022-0981

Almeida, P.R. (1996). Estuarine movement patterns of adult thin-lipped grey mullet, *Liza ramada* (Risso) (Pisces, Mugilidae), observed by ultrasonic tracking. *Journal of Experimental Marine Biology and Ecology*, Vol.202, (September 1996), pp. 137-150, ISSN 0022-0981

Augustyn, C.J. (1990). Biological studies on the chokker squid *Loligo vulgaris reynaudii* (Cephalopoda; Myopsida) on spawning grounds off the south-east coast of South Africa. *South African Journal of Marine Science*, Vol.9, (June 1990), pp. 11-26, ISSN 0257-7615

Augustyn, C.J. (1991). The biomass and ecology of chokka squid *Loligo vulgaris reynaudii* off the west coast of South Africa. *South African Journal of Zoology*, Vol.26, No.4, (October 1991), pp. 164-181, ISSN 0254-1858

Birch GF. (1981). Bathymetry and geomorphology of the Cape Seal to Cape Recife inner shelf. *Transactions of the Geological Society of South Africa*, Vol.84, pp. 233–237, ISSN 0371-7208

Brill, R.W., Balazs, G.H., Holland, K.N., Chang, R.K.C., Sullivan, S. & George, J.C. (1995). Daily movements, habitat use, and submergence intervals of normal and tumor-bearing juvenile green turtles (*Chelonia mydas* L.) within a foraging area in the Hawaiian islands. *Journal of Experimental Marine Biology and Ecology*, Vol.185, (February 1995), pp. 203-218, ISSN 0022-0981

Carr, J.W., Lacroix, G.L., Andersons, J.M. & Dilworth, T. (1997). Short communication: Movements of non-maturing cultured Atlantic salmon (*Salmo salar*) in a Canadian River. *ICES Journal of Marine Science*, Vol.54, (December 1997), pp. 1082-1085, ISSN 1054-3139

Carr, S.D., Tankersley, R.A., Hench, J.L., Forward, R.B. Jr., Leittich, R.A. (2004). Movement patterns and trajectories of ovigerous blue crabs *Callinectes sapidus* during spawning migration. *Estuarine, Coastal and Shelf Science* Vol.60, (August 2004), pp. 567-579, ISSN 0272-7714

Cooke, S.J. & Philipp, D.P. (2004). Behaviour and mortality of caught-and-released bonefish (*Albula* spp.) in Bahamian waters with implications for a sustainable recreational fishery. *Biological Conservation*, Vol.118, (August 2004), pp. 599-607, ISSN 0006-3207

Downey N.J., Roberts, M.J. & Baird, D. (2010). An investigation of the spawning behaviour of the chokka squid *Loligo reynaudii* and the potential effects of temperature using acoustic telemetry. *ICES Journal of Marine Science*, Vol.67, (March 2010), pp. 231-243, ISSN 1054-3139

Egli, D.P. & Babcock, R.C. (2004). Ultrasonic tracking reveals multiple behavioural modes of snapper (*Pagrus auratus*) in a temperate no-take marine reserve. *ICES Journal of Marine Science*, Vol.61, (August 2004), pp. 1137-1143, ISSN 1054-3139

Hanlon, R.T., Smale, M.J. & Sauer, W.H.H. (1994). An ethogram of body patterning behaviour in the squid *Loligo vulgaris reynaudii* on spawning grounds in South Africa. *Biology Bulletin*, Vol.187, (December 1994), pp. 363-372, ISSN 1062-3590

Hanlon, R.T., Smale, M.J. & Sauer, W.H.H. (2002). The mating system of the squid *Loligo vulgaris reynaudii* (Cephalopoda, Mollusca) off South Africa: Fighting, guarding, sneaking, mating and egg laying behaviour. *Bulletin of Marine Science*, Vol.71, No.1, (January 2002), pp. 331-345, ISSN 0007-4977

Jadot, C., Donnay, A., Acolas, M.L., Cornet, Y. & Bégout Anras, M.L. (2006). Activity patterns, home-range size, and habitat utilization of *Sarpa salpa* (Teleostei: Sparidae) in the Mediterranean Sea. *ICES Journal of Marine Science*, Vol.63, (January 2006), pp. 128-139, ISSN 1054-3139

Lipinski, M.R., Hampton, I., Sauer, W.H.H. & Augustyn, C.J. (1998). Daily net emigration from a spawning concentration of chokka squid (*Loligo vulgaris reynaudii* d'Orbigny, 1845) in Kromme Bay South Africa. *ICES Journal of Marine Science*, Vol.55, (April 1998), pp. 258-270, ISSN 1054-3139

Lipinski, M.R. & Underhill, L.G. (1995). Sexual maturation in squid: Quantum or continuum. *South African Journal of Marine Science*, Vol.15, (June 1995), pp. 207-223, ISSN 0257-7615

Løkkeborg, S., Skajaa, K. & Fernö, A. (2000). Food-search strategy in ling (*Molva molva* L.): Crepuscular activity and use of space. *ICES Journal of Marine Science*, Vol.247, (April 2000), pp. 195-208, ISSN 1054-3139

Melo, Y.C. & Sauer, W.H.H. (1999). Confirmation of serial spawning in the chokka squid *Loligo vulgaris reynaudii* off the coast of South Africa. *Marine Biology*, Vol.135, (November 1999), pp. 307-313, ISSN 0025-3162

Mitamura, H., Arai, N., Sakamoto, W., Mitsunaga, Y., Tanaka, H., Mukai, Y., Nakamura, K., Sasaki, M. & Yoneda, Y. (2005). Role of olfaction and vision in homing behaviour of black rockfish *Sebastes inermes*. *Journal of Experimental Marine Biology and Ecology*, Vol.322, (September 2005), pp. 123-134, ISSN 0022-0981

Olyott, L.J.H., Sauer, W.H.H. & Booth, A.J. (2006). Spatio-temporal patterns in maturation of the chokka squid (*Loligo vulgaris reynaudii*) off the coast of South Africa. *ICES Journal of Marine Science*, Vol.63, (July 2006), pp. 1649-1664, ISSN 1054-3139

Olyott, L.J.H., Sauer, W.H.H. & Booth, A.J. (2007). Spatial patterns in the biology of the chokka squid, *Loligo vulgaris reynaudii* on the Agulhas Bank, South Africa. *Reviews in Fish Biology and Fisheries*, Vol.17, No.2-3, (August 2007), pp. 159-172, ISSN 0960-3166

Oosthuizen, A. & Roberts, M.J. (2009). Bottom temperature and *in situ* development of chokka squid eggs (*Loligo vulgaris reynaudii*) on the deep spawning grounds, South Africa. *ICES Journal of Marine Science*, Vol.66, (October 2009), pp. 1967-1971, ISSN 1054-3139

Oosthuizen, A., Roberts, M.J. & Sauer, W.H.H. (2002a). Temperature effects on the embryonic development and hatching success of the squid *Loligo vulgaris reynaudii*. *Bulletin of Marine Science*, Vol.71, No.2, (September 2006), pp. 619-632, ISSN 0007-4977

Oosthuizen, A., Roberts, M.J. & Sauer, W.H.H. (2002b). Early post-cleavage stages and abnormalities identified in the embryonic development of chokka squid eggs *Loligo vulgaris reynaudii*. *South African Journal of Marine Science*, Vol.24, (June 2002), pp. 379-382, ISSN 0257-7615

Roberts, M.J. (1998). The influence of the environment on chokka squid *Loligo vulgaris reynaudii* spawning aggregations: Steps towards a quantified model. *South African Journal of Marine Science*, Vol.20, (December 1998), pp. 267-284, ISSN 0257-7615

Roberts, M.J. (2005). Chokka squid (*Loligo vulgaris reynaudii*) abundance linked to changes in South Africa's Agulhas Bank ecosystem during spawning and the early life cycle. *ICES Journal of Marine Science*, Vol.62, No.1, (February 2005), pp. 33-55, ISSN 1054-3139

Roberts, M.J. & Sauer, W.H.H. (1994). Environment: the key to understanding the South African chokka squid (*Loligo vulgaris reynaudii*) life cycle and fishery? *Antarctic Science*, Vol.6, No.2, (June 1994), pp. 249-258, ISSN 0954-1020

Roberts, M.J. & van den Berg, M. (2002). Recruitment variability of chokka squid (*Loligo vulgaris reynaudii*) - Role of currents on the Agulhas Bank (South Africa) in paralarvae distribution and food abundance. *Bulletin of Marine Science*, Vol.71, No.2, (September 2002), pp. 691-710, ISSN 0007-4977

Roberts, M.J. & van den Berg, M. (2005). Currents along the Tsitsikamma coast, South Africa, and potential transport of squid paralarvae and ichthyoplankton. *African Journal of Marine Science*, Vol.27, No.2, (October 2005), pp. 375-388, ISSN 1814-232X

Roel, B.A., Cochrane, K.L. & Field, J.G. (2000). Investigation into the declining trend in chokka squid *Loligo vulgaris reynaudii* catches made by South African trawlers. *South African Journal of Marine Science,* Vol.22, (June 2000), pp. 121-135, ISSN 0257-7615

Sauer, W.H.H. (1995). The impact of fishing on chokka squid *Loligo vulgaris reynaudii* concentrations on inshore spawning grounds in the South-Eastern Cape, South Africa. *South African Journal of Marine Science,* Vol.16, (December 1995), pp. 185-193, ISSN 0257-7615

Sauer, W.H.H., Goschen, W.S., & Koorts, A.S. (1991). A preliminary investigation of the effect of sea temperature fluctuations and wind direction on catches of chokka squid *Loligo vulgaris reynaudii* off the Eastern Cape, South Africa. *South African Journal of Marine Science*, Vol.11, (December 1991), pp. 467-473, ISSN 0257-7615

Sauer, W.H.H. & Lipinski, M.R. (1990). Histological validation of morphological stages of sexual maturity in chokker squid *Loligo vulgaris reynaudii* D'Orb (Cephalopoda; Loliginidae). *South African Journal of Marine Science,* Vol.9, (June 1990), pp. 189-200, ISSN 0257-7615

Sauer, W.H.H. & Lipinski, M.R. (1991). Food of squid *Loligo vulgaris reynaudii* (Cephalopoda: Loliginidae) on their spawning grounds off the Eastern Cape, South Africa. *South African Journal of Marine Science,* Vol.10, (June 1991), pp. 193-201, ISSN 0257-7615

Sauer, W.H.H., McCarthy, C, Smale, M.J. & Koorts, A.S. (1993). An investigation of the egg distribution of the chokka squid, *Loligo vulgaris reynaudii,* in Krom Bay, South Africa. *Bulletin of Marine Science,* Vol.53, No.3, (November 1993), pp. 1066-1077, ISSN 0007-4977

Sauer, W.H.H., Melo, Y.C. & de Wet, W. (1999). Fecundity of the chokka squid *Loligo vulgaris reynaudii* on the southeastern coast of South Africa. *Marine Biology,* Vol.135, (November 1999), pp. 315-319, ISSN 0025-3162

Sauer, W.H.H., Roberts, M.J., Lipinski, M.R., Smale, M.J., Hanlon, R.T., Webber, D.M. & O'Dor, R.K. (1997). Choreography of the squid's "nuptial dance". *Biology Bulletin,* Vol.192, (April 1997), pp. 203-207, ISSN 1062-3590

Sauer, W.H.H. & Smale, M.J. (1991). Predation patterns on the inshore spawning grounds of the squid *Loligo vulgaris reynaudii* (Cephalopoda: Loliginidae) off the south-eastern cape, South Africa. *South African Journal of Marine Science,* Vol.11, (December 1991), pp. 513-523, ISSN 0257-7615

Sauer, W.H.H. & Smale, M.J. (1993). Spawning behaviour of *Loligo vulgaris reynaudii* in shallow coastal waters of the south-Eastern Cape, South Africa, In: *Recent Advances in Fisheries Biology,* Okutani, T., O'Dor, R.K. & Kobodera, T., pp. 489-498, Tokai University Press, Tokyo

Sauer, W.H.H., Smale, M.J. & Lipinski, M.R. (1992). The location of spawning grounds, spawning and schooling behaviour of the squid *Loligo vulgaris reynaudii* (Cephalopoda: Myopsida) off the Eastern Cape coast, South Africa. *Marine Biology,* Vol.114, (September 1992), pp. 97-107, ISSN 0025-3162

Schön, P., Sauer, W.H.H. & Roberts, M.J. (2002). Environmental influences on spawning aggregations and jig catches of chokka squid *Loligo vulgaris reynaudii*: a 'black box' approach. *Bulletin of Marine Science*, Vol.71, No.2, (September 2002), pp. 783-800, ISSN 0007-4977

Shaw, P.W. & Sauer, W.H.H. (2004). Multiple paternity and complex fertilisation dynamics in the squid *Loligo vulgaris reynaudii*. *Marine Ecology Progress Series*, Vol.270, (April 2004), pp. 173-179, ISSN 0171-8630

Singh, L., Downey, N.J., Roberts, M.J., Webber, D.M., Smale, M.J., van den Berg, M.A., Harding, R.T., Engelbrecht, D.C. & Blows, B.M. (2009). Design and calibration of an acoustic telemetry system subject to upwelling events. *African Journal of Marine Science*, Vol.31, No.1, (May 2010), pp. 355-364, ISSN 0257-7615

Smale, M.J., Sauer, W.H.H. & Hanlon, R.T. (1995). Short Communications: Attempted ambush predation on spawning squids *Loligo vulgaris reynaudii* by benthic pyjama sharks, Poroderma africanum, off South Africa. *Journal of the Marine Biological Association of the United Kingdom*, Vol.75, (August 1995), pp. 739-742, ISSN 0025-3154

Smale, M.J., Sauer, W.H.H. & Roberts, M.J. (2001). Behavioural interactions of predators and spawning chokka squid off South Africa: towards quantification. *Marine Biology*, Vol.139, (December 2001), pp. 1095-1105, ISSN 0025-3162

Welch, D.W., Ward, B.R. & Batten, S.D. (2004). Early ocean survival and marine movements of hatchery and wild steelhead trout (*Oncorhynchus mykiss*) determined by an acoustic array: Queen Charlotte Strait, British Columbia. *Deep-Sea Research II*, Vol.51, (March-May 2004), pp. 897-909, ISSN 0967-0645

Vabø, R., Huse, G., Fernö, A., Jørgensen, T., Løkkeborg, S. & Skaret, G. (2004). Simulating search behaviour of fish towards bait. *ICES Journal of Marine Science*, Vol.61, (December 2004), pp. 1224-1232, ISSN 1054-3139

Vidal, E.A.G., Roberts, M.J. & Martins, R.S, (2005). Yolk utilization, metabolism and growth in reared *Loligo vulgaris reynaudii* paralarvae. *Aquatic Living Resources*, Vol.18, (October 2005), pp. 385-393, ISSN 0990-7440

Part 6

Military Telemetry

21

Error Separation Techniques Based on Telemetry and Tracking Data for Ballistic Missile

Huabo Yang, Lijun Zhang and Yuan Cao
National University of Defense Technology
China

1. Introduction

An intercontinental ballistic missile (ICBM) is a ballistic missile with a long range (some greater than 10000 km) and great firepower typically designed for nuclear weapons delivery, such as PeaceKeeper (PK) missile (Shattuck, 1992), Minutesman missile (Tony C. L., 2003). Due to the long-distance flight, the requirement for navigation system is rigorous and only gimbaled inertial navigation system (INS) is presently competent, such as the advanced inertial reference sphere (AIRS) used in the PK missile (John L., 1979), yet the strapdown inertial navigation system is generally not used on the intercontinental ballistic missile because of the poor accuracy (Titterton & Weston, 1997). The gimbaled inertial navigation system typically contains three single-degree-of-freedom rate integrating gyros, three mutually perpendicular single-axis accelerometers, a loop system and other auxiliary system, providing an orientation of the inertial navigation platform relative to inertial space. Due to system design and production technology there exist a lot of errors referred as guidance instrumentation systematic errors (IEEE Standards Committee, 1971; IEEE Standards Board, 1973), which have an important effect on impact accuracy of ballistic missile. Before the flight of ballistic missile, the guidance instrumentation systematic errors are need to calibrate, and then the calibration results are used to compensate the instrumental errors, which has been discussed in depth by Thompson (Thompson, 2000), Eduardo and Hugh (Eduardo & Hugh, 1999), Jackson (Jackson, 1973), Coulter and Meehan (Coulter & Meehan , 1981). Some content discussed has been issued as IEEE standard (IEEE Standards Committee, 1971; IEEE Standards Board, 1973).

However, the guidance instrumentation systematic errors cannot be completely compensated by using the calibration results. Therefore, flight test of ballistic missile is usually performed to qualify the performance. Because of different objectives of test or some other reasons specific testing trajectory is sometimes adopted, and herein the flight test cannot reflect the actual situation of ballistic missile in the whole trajectory. Consequently, it is necessary to analyze the landing errors resulted from guidance instrumentation systematic errors in the specific trajectory and convert them into those landing errors in the case of the whole trajectory.

In fact, there are many factors affecting the impact accuracy of ballistic missile, such as gravity anomaly, upper atmosphere, electromagnetic force, etc. Forsberg and Sideris has taken into account the effect of gravity anomaly and presented the analysis method (Forsberg & Sideris, 1993). The effect of upper atmosphere and electromagnetic force is considered by Zheng (Zheng, 2006), but these error factors are so small compared to guidance instrumentation systematic errors that they are capable of not being considered when analyzing the impact accuracy. The analysis of guidance instrumentation systematic errors is generally performed using telemetry data and tracking data. Telemetry data are the angular velocity and acceleration information measured by inertial navigation system on the ballistic missile and transmitted by telemetric equipment, while tracking data are those information measured by radar and optoelectronic device in the test range. It is generally considered that the telemetry data contain instrumentation errors while tracking data contain systematic errors and random measurement errors of exterior measurement equipment, which is independent of instrumentation errors (Liu et al, 2000). Comparison of telemetry data and tracking data is used to obtain the velocity and position errors resulted from guidance instrumentation systematic errors. It is noticeable that the telemetry data are measured in the inertial coordinate system and exclude gravitational acceleration information while tracking data usually measured in the horizontal coordinate system. The conversion of two types of data into identical coordinate system is necessary.

Maneuvering launch manners are commonly adopted such as road-launched and submarine-launched manners to improve the viability and strike capacity for ballistic missile. Maneuvering launch ballistic missile especially for submarine-launched ballistic missile is often affected by ocean current, wave, and vibration environment, etc. Obviously, there are measurement errors in the initial launch parameters including location and orientation parameters as well as carrier's velocity. Theoretical analysis and numerical simulation indicate that initial launch parameter errors are equivalent in magnitude to the guidance instrumentation systematic errors (Zheng, 2006; Gore,). Since the landing errors due to initial launch parameter errors and guidance instrumentation systematic errors are coupled, the error separation procedure for those two types of errors must be performed using telemetry and tracking data.

The error separation model can be simplified as a linear model using telemetry and tracking data (Yang et al, 2007). It is noted that the linear model is directly obtained by telemetry and tracking data and is independent of the flight of ballisitc missile. The remarkable features of this linear model is high dimension and collinearity, which is a severe problem when one wishes to perform certain types of mathematical treatment such as matrix inversion. These categories of problem can be treated many advanced methods, such as improved regression estimation (Barros & Rutledge, 1998; Cherkassky & Ma, 2005), partial least square (PLS) method (Wold et al, 2001), and support vector machines (SVM) (Cortes & Vapnik, 1995), however, these analysis methods are of no interest in this chapter. This chapter mainly focuses on the modeling of separation of instrumentation errors based on telemetry and tracking data and presents a novel error separation technique.

2. Calculation of difference between telemetry and tracking data

Telemetry and tracking data are known as important information sources in the error separation procedure. Two key problems are needed to be solved when computing the difference between telemetry and tracking data, since they are described in different coordinate systems. One is to convert the telemetry and tracking data into the same coordinate system, the other is to subtract the gravitational acceleration from tracking data or to add gravitational acceleration into telemetry data. The difference between telemetry and tracking data can be reckoned in either launch inertial coordinate system or launch coordinate system. A typical method is to convert the tracking data into launch inertial coordinate system and then to subtract the gravitational acceleration. In fact, guidance instrumentation systematic errors are contained in the telemetry data while initial launch parameter errors are generated in the case of the conversion for tracking data and the computation of gravity acceleration, so the sources of them are absolutely different.

The apparent velocity and position in the launch inertial coordinate system can be computed as follows.

1. Transformation matrix

The transformation matrix from geocentric coordinate system to launch coordinate system can be represented by

$$\mathbf{C}_e^g = \mathbf{M}_2[-(90^0 + A_T)]\mathbf{M}_1[B_T]\mathbf{M}_3[-(90^0 - \lambda_T)]$$
$$= \begin{bmatrix} -\sin A_T \sin\lambda_T - \cos A_T \sin B_T \cos\lambda_T & \sin A_T \cos\lambda_T - \cos A_T \sin B_T \sin\lambda_T & \cos A_T \cos B_T \\ \cos B_T \cos\lambda_T & \cos B_T \sin\lambda_T & \sin B_T \\ -\cos A_T \sin\lambda_T + \sin A_T \sin B_T \cos\lambda_T & \cos A_T \cos\lambda_T + \sin A_T \sin B_T \sin\lambda_T & -\sin A_T \cos B_T \end{bmatrix} \quad (1)$$

where subscript e denotes geocentric coordinate system and superscript g denotes launch coordinate system; A_T, B_T, λ_T are astronomical azimuth, latitude and longitude, respectively. Also, the transformation matrix relating launch coordinate system to launch inertial coordinate system is given by

$$\mathbf{C}_g^a = \mathbf{A}^T\mathbf{B}^T\mathbf{A} \quad (2)$$

with

$$\mathbf{A} = \begin{bmatrix} \cos A_T \cos B_T & \sin B_T & -\sin A_T \cos B_T \\ -\cos A_T \sin B_T & \cos B_T & \sin A_T \sin B_T \\ \sin A_T & 0 & \cos A_T \end{bmatrix}, \mathbf{B} = \begin{bmatrix} 1 & 0 & 0 \\ 0 & \cos\omega_e t & \sin\omega_e t \\ 0 & -\sin\omega_e t & \cos\omega_e t \end{bmatrix} \quad (3)$$

where superscript a denotes launch inertial coordinate system, ω_e is the earth rate, t is the in-flight time.

2. Radius vector from earth center to launch site

The radius of prime vertical circle of launch site is given by

$$N_0 = \frac{a_e(1-\alpha_e)}{\sqrt{1-(2\alpha_e - \alpha_e^2)\sin^2 B_0}} \quad (4)$$

where a_e is the earth semimajor axis, α_e is the earth flattening, B_0 is the geodetic latitude. Ignoring higher-order terms yields

$$N_0 = a_e(1 + \alpha_e \sin^2 B_0) \quad (5)$$

Thus, the components of launch site in the geocentric coordinate system are written as

$$\mathbf{R}_{0e} = \begin{bmatrix} (N_0 + H_0)\cos B_0 \cos \lambda_0 \\ (N_0 + H_0)\cos B_0 \sin \lambda_0 \\ \left(N_0\left(1-\alpha_e^2\right) + H_0\right)\sin B_0 \end{bmatrix} \quad (6)$$

where λ_0 , B_0 , H_0 are the geodetic longitude, geodetic latitude and geodetic height of launch site, respectively. Using coordinate transformation we can write the radius vector from earth center to launch site in the launch coordinate system as

$$\mathbf{R}_{0g} = \mathbf{C}_e^g \mathbf{R}_{0e} \quad (7)$$

3. Earth rate

The components of earth rate expressed in the launch coordinate system are given by

$$\boldsymbol{\omega}_{eg} = \mathbf{C}_e^g \begin{bmatrix} 0 \\ 0 \\ \omega_e \end{bmatrix} = \omega_e \begin{bmatrix} \cos B_T \cos A_T \\ \sin B_T \\ -\cos B_T \sin A_T \end{bmatrix} \quad (8)$$

The angular velocity of launch coordinate system with respect to launch inertial coordinate system is the earth rate, so earth rate expressed in the launch inertial coordinate system is given by

$$\boldsymbol{\omega}_{ea} = \mathbf{C}_g^a \cdot \boldsymbol{\omega}_{eg} \quad (9)$$

4. Gravitational acceleration

The radius vector from earth center to center of mass of missile in the launch coordinate system is given by

$$\mathbf{r}_g = \mathbf{R}_{0g} + \boldsymbol{\rho}_g \quad (10)$$

where $\boldsymbol{\rho}_g$ is the missile location provided by tracking data.

The gravitational acceleration taking into account the J_2 term in the launch coordinate system is given by

$$\mathbf{g}_g = g_r \cdot \frac{\mathbf{r}_g}{|\mathbf{r}_g|} + g_\omega \cdot \frac{\boldsymbol{\omega}_{eg}}{\omega_e} \quad (11)$$

where

$$g_r = -\frac{\mu}{r_g^2} \cdot [1 + J_2 \cdot (\frac{a_e}{r_g})^2 \cdot (1 - 5\sin^2 \phi)] \quad (12)$$

$$g_\omega = -2\frac{\mu}{r_g^2} \cdot J_2 \cdot (\frac{a_e}{r_g})^2 \cdot \sin \phi \quad (13)$$

and the geocentric latitude ϕ can be computed as follows

$$\phi = \arcsin \frac{\mathbf{r}_g \cdot \boldsymbol{\omega}_e}{\left| \mathbf{r}_g \cdot \boldsymbol{\omega}_e \right|} \tag{14}$$

Hence, gravitational acceleration in the launch inertial coordinate system is written as

$$\mathbf{g}_a = \mathbf{C}_g^a \cdot \mathbf{g}_g \tag{15}$$

5. Calculation of apparent velocity and position of tracking data
The tracking apparent velocity is given by

$$\mathbf{W}_{\text{tra}}^a(t) = \mathbf{C}_g^a(t) \cdot \mathbf{V}_g(t) + \boldsymbol{\Omega}_\omega^a \cdot \mathbf{C}_g^a(t) \cdot \left(\mathbf{R}_0 + \boldsymbol{\rho}_g \right) - \mathbf{V}_{0a} - \int_0^t \mathbf{g}_a(\tau) d\tau \tag{16}$$

with

$$\boldsymbol{\Omega}_\omega^a = \begin{bmatrix} 0 & -\omega_{eaz} & \omega_{eay} \\ \omega_{eaz} & 0 & -\omega_{eax} \\ -\omega_{eay} & \omega_{eax} & 0 \end{bmatrix} \tag{17}$$

where $\omega_{eax}, \omega_{eay}, \omega_{eaz}$ are three components of $\boldsymbol{\omega}_{ea}$, respectively; $\mathbf{V}_g$ and $\boldsymbol{\rho}_g$ are the velocity and position of missile in the launch coordinate system provided by tracking data, respectively. $\mathbf{V}_{0a}$ is the initial velocity of launch site with respect to launch coordinate system due to earth rotation, written as

$$\mathbf{V}_{0a} = \boldsymbol{\omega}_{ea}(0) \times \mathbf{R}_{0a} \tag{18}$$

Likewise, the tracking apparent position is given by

$$\mathbf{W}_{\text{tra}}^a(t) = \mathbf{C}_g^a(t) \cdot \left(\mathbf{R}_0 + \boldsymbol{\rho}_g \right) - \mathbf{R}_{0a} - \mathbf{V}_{0a} \cdot t - \int_0^t \int_0^u \mathbf{g}_a(\tau) d\tau du \tag{19}$$

6. Calculation of apparent velocity and position of telemetry data
The telemetric apparent velocity can be obtained by the integration of telemetric apparent acceleration, given by

$$\mathbf{W}_{\text{tele}}^a(t) = \int_0^t \dot{\mathbf{W}}_{\text{tele}}^a(\tau) d\tau \tag{20}$$

Integrating Eq.(20) gives the telemetric apparent position

$$\mathbf{W}_{\text{tele}}^a(t) = \int_0^t \mathbf{W}_{\text{tele}}^a(\tau) d\tau \tag{21}$$

7. Calculation of difference between telemetry and tracking data
The difference between telemetry data and tracking data is obtained by subtracting synchronous tracking data and compensation from telemetry data, namely, we can have the difference between telemetry velocity and tracking velocity, $\delta \mathbf{X}_v(t)$, and the difference between telemetry velocity and tracking velocity, $\delta \mathbf{X}_r(t)$.

3. Separation model of guidance instrumentation systematic errors

There are many reasons influencing the landing errors of ICBM, which can be fallen into two categories: 1) guidance instrumentation systematic errors, and 2) initial launch parameter errors. Guidance instrumentation systematic errors primarily consist of accelerometer, gyroscope and platform systematic errors. Before the flight test ground calibration test is usually performed for inertial navigation system and then the estimates of instrumentation error coefficients are compensated in flight, which can reduce the landing errors and the difference between telemetry and tracking data effectively. However, because of the residual between the calibrated values and the actual values of instrumentation errors, the separation of the behaved values of the instrumentation error coefficients from telemetry and tracking data is need to perform.

3.1 Model of guidance instrumentation systematic errors

Since the determination of error model is correlated with the performance of inertial platform, there are many error coefficients required to separate for inertial platform with high accuracy while a minority of primary error terms for general inertial platform with poor accuracy. The gyroscope error model of inertial platform is given by

$$\begin{cases} \dot{\alpha}_x(t) = k_{g0x} + k_{g11x}\dot{W}_x(t) + k_{g12x}\dot{W}_z(t) \\ \dot{\alpha}_y(t) = k_{g0y} + k_{g11y}\dot{W}_y(t) + k_{g12y}\dot{W}_x(t) \\ \dot{\alpha}_z(t) = k_{g0z} + k_{g11z}\dot{W}_z(t) + k_{g12z}\dot{W}_y(t) \end{cases} \tag{22}$$

and accelerometer error model is given by

$$\begin{cases} \Delta_x(t) = k_{a0x} + k_{a1x}\dot{W}_x(t) \\ \Delta_y(t) = k_{a0y} + k_{a1y}\dot{W}_y(t) \\ \Delta_z(t) = k_{a0z} + k_{a1z}\dot{W}_z(t) \end{cases} \tag{23}$$

Where $\dot{\alpha}_x, \dot{\alpha}_y, \dot{\alpha}_z$ are angular velocity drifts of three gyroscopes, respectively; $\dot{W}_x, \dot{W}_y, \dot{W}_z$ are apparent accelerations of vehicle; $k_{g0x}, k_{g0y}, k_{g0z}$ are zero biases of three gyroscopes, $k_{g11x}, k_{g11y}, k_{g11z}$ are proportional error coefficients, $k_{g12x}, k_{g12y}, k_{g12z}$ are first-order error coefficients; $k_{a0x}, k_{a0y}, k_{a0z}$ are zero biases and $k_{a1x}, k_{a1y}, k_{a1z}$ are proportional error coefficients of three accelerometers. Model of guidance instrumentation systematic errors contains 15 error coefficients in total.

The accurate velocity, position and orientation information of ballistic missile are not available due to the errors resulted from maneuvering of ballistic missile and measurements, which generates the initial launch parameter errors. The initial launch parameter errors primarily consist of geodetic longitude, geodetic latitude, geodetic height, astronomical longitude, astronomical latitude and astronomical azimuth errors of launch site, and initial velocity errors of ballistic missile about three directions, amounting to 9 terms.

3.2 Separation model of instrumentation errors

Guidance instrumentation systematic errors can affect telemetric apparent acceleration so as to affect apparent velocity and position. Without regard to the calculation error of gravitational force, the velocity and position errors of trajectory are the errors of apparent velocity and position respectively. The apparent acceleration error arisen from guidance instrumentation systematic error is represented by

$$\delta\dot{\mathbf{W}} = \dot{\mathbf{W}}_p - \dot{\mathbf{W}}_a = \dot{\mathbf{W}}_p - \mathbf{M}_3(-\alpha_z)\mathbf{M}_2(-\alpha_y)\mathbf{M}_1(-\alpha_x)\cdot(\dot{\mathbf{W}}_p - \mathbf{\Delta}) \quad (24)$$

where $\dot{\mathbf{W}}_p$ is the apparent acceleration measured by inertial navigation platform, $\dot{\mathbf{W}}_a$ is the real apparent acceleration; $\mathbf{M}_3(\cdot)$, $\mathbf{M}_2(\cdot)$, $\mathbf{M}_1(\cdot)$ are the rotation matrices about z, y, x axis, respectively; α_x, α_y, α_z are the drift angles along the three directions, which are assumed as small values; $\mathbf{\Delta}$ is the error vector measured by accelerometer. Since the true value of $\dot{\mathbf{W}}_a$ is not available, the substitution of $\dot{\mathbf{W}}_a$ is generally obtained by converting the tracking data. Thereby $\delta\dot{\mathbf{W}}$ is the difference of apparent acceleration between telemetry and tracking data. Neglecting the second-order term, Eq.(24) is changed to

$$\delta\dot{\mathbf{W}} = \dot{\mathbf{W}}_p - \begin{bmatrix} 1 & -\alpha_z & \alpha_y \\ \alpha_z & 1 & -\alpha_x \\ -\alpha_y & \alpha_x & 1 \end{bmatrix} \cdot (\dot{\mathbf{W}}_p - \mathbf{\Delta}) \quad (25)$$

Rearranging Eq.(25) and ignoring the second-order small values yield

$$\delta\dot{\mathbf{W}} = \begin{bmatrix} 0 & -\dot{W}_{pz} & \dot{W}_{py} \\ \dot{W}_{pz} & 0 & -\dot{W}_{px} \\ -\dot{W}_{py} & \dot{W}_{px} & 0 \end{bmatrix} \begin{bmatrix} \alpha_x \\ \alpha_y \\ \alpha_z \end{bmatrix} + \mathbf{\Delta} \quad (26)$$

where $\dot{W}_{px}$, $\dot{W}_{py}$, $\dot{W}_{pz}$ are the components of $\dot{\mathbf{W}}_p$; α_x, α_y, α_z are the drift angles of gyroscope and obtained by integrating Eq.(22)

$$\begin{bmatrix} \alpha_x \\ \alpha_y \\ \alpha_z \end{bmatrix} = \int_0^t \begin{bmatrix} \dot{\alpha}_x \\ \dot{\alpha}_y \\ \dot{\alpha}_z \end{bmatrix} dt = \int_0^t \begin{bmatrix} k_{g0x} + k_{g11x}\dot{W}_{ax} + k_{g12x}\dot{W}_{ay} \\ k_{g0y} + k_{g11y}\dot{W}_{ay} + k_{g12y}\dot{W}_{ax} \\ k_{g0z} + k_{g11z}\dot{W}_{az} + k_{g12z}\dot{W}_{ay} \end{bmatrix} dt \quad (27)$$

By the accelerometer error model, we can have

$$\begin{bmatrix} \Delta_x \\ \Delta_y \\ \Delta_z \end{bmatrix} = \begin{bmatrix} k_{a0x} + k_{a1x}\dot{W}_{ax} \\ k_{a0y} + k_{a1y}\dot{W}_{ay} \\ k_{a0z} + k_{a1z}\dot{W}_{az} \end{bmatrix} \quad (28)$$

Note that $\dot{W}_{ax}, \dot{W}_{ay}, \dot{W}_{az}$ are the apparent accelerations in the launch inertial coordinate system, unfortunately we cannot obtain the measurements in practice. Since the values of $\dot{W}_{px}, \dot{W}_{py}, \dot{W}_{pz}$ are given by the telemetry data, so we can approximately substitute $\dot{W}_{px}, \dot{W}_{py}, \dot{W}_{pz}$ for $\dot{W}_{ax}, \dot{W}_{ay}, \dot{W}_{az}$ during the error separation process. Hence, Eqs.(27) and (28) can be rewritten respectively as

$$\begin{bmatrix} \alpha_x \\ \alpha_y \\ \alpha_z \end{bmatrix} = \int_0^t \begin{bmatrix} \dot{\alpha}_x \\ \dot{\alpha}_y \\ \dot{\alpha}_z \end{bmatrix} dt = \int_0^t \begin{bmatrix} k_{g0x} + k_{g11x}\dot{W}_{px} + k_{g12x}\dot{W}_{py} \\ k_{g0y} + k_{g11y}\dot{W}_{py} + k_{g12y}\dot{W}_{px} \\ k_{g0z} + k_{g11z}\dot{W}_{pz} + k_{g12z}\dot{W}_{py} \end{bmatrix} dt \tag{29}$$

$$\begin{bmatrix} \Delta_x \\ \Delta_y \\ \Delta_z \end{bmatrix} = \begin{bmatrix} k_{a0x} + k_{a1x}\dot{W}_{px} \\ k_{a0y} + k_{a1y}\dot{W}_{py} \\ k_{a0z} + k_{a1z}\dot{W}_{pz} \end{bmatrix} \tag{30}$$

Herein we select $\mathbf{D} = \begin{bmatrix} k_{g0x} & k_{g0y} & k_{g0z} & k_{g11x} & k_{g11y} & k_{g11z} & k_{g12x} & k_{g12y} & k_{g12z} & k_{a0x} & k_{a0y} & k_{a0z} & k_{a1x} & k_{a1y} & k_{a0z} \end{bmatrix}^T$, then apparent acceleration error $\delta\dot{\mathbf{W}}$ and instrumentation error coefficients $\mathbf{D}$ are written in linear relation as

$$\delta\dot{\mathbf{W}} = \mathbf{S}_a \cdot \mathbf{D} \tag{31}$$

where $\mathbf{S}_a$ is the environmental function matrix of apparent acceleration, given by

$$\mathbf{S}_a = \begin{bmatrix} \mathbf{S}_e \cdot \mathbf{S}_{Ag} & \mathbf{S}_{Aa} \end{bmatrix} \tag{32}$$

where

$$\mathbf{S}_e = \begin{bmatrix} 0 & \dot{W}_{zp} & -\dot{W}_{yp} \\ -\dot{W}_{zp} & 0 & \dot{W}_{xp} \\ \dot{W}_{yp} & -\dot{W}_{xp} & 0 \end{bmatrix}, \quad \mathbf{S}_{Aa} = \begin{bmatrix} 1 & 0 & 0 & \dot{W}_{px} & 0 & 0 \\ 0 & 1 & 0 & 0 & \dot{W}_{py} & 0 \\ 0 & 0 & 1 & 0 & 0 & \dot{W}_{pz} \end{bmatrix},$$

$$\mathbf{S}_{Ag} = \begin{bmatrix} t & 0 & 0 & W_{xp} & 0 & 0 & W_{yp} & 0 & 0 \\ 0 & t & 0 & 0 & W_{yp} & 0 & 0 & W_{xp} & 0 \\ 0 & 0 & t & 0 & 0 & W_{zp} & 0 & 0 & W_{yp} \end{bmatrix}$$

Integrating Eq.(31) gives the apparent velocity error

$$\delta\mathbf{W}(t) = \int_0^t \mathbf{S}_a(\tau)dt \cdot \mathbf{D} = \mathbf{S}_v(t)\mathbf{D} \tag{33}$$

where $\mathbf{S}_v(t)$ is the environmental function matrix of instrumental error of apparent velocity. Taking the integration of Eq.(33) again gives the apparent position error

$$\delta\mathbf{W}(t) = \int_0^t \mathbf{S}_v(\tau)dt \cdot \mathbf{D} = \mathbf{S}_r(t)\mathbf{D} \tag{34}$$

where $\mathbf{S}_r(t)$ is the environmental function matrix of instrumental error of apparent position. In the actual situation, the apparent velocity and position error models with the consideration of random errors are represented by

$$\delta\mathbf{W}(t) = \mathbf{S}_v(t)\mathbf{D} + \boldsymbol{\varepsilon}_v$$
$$\delta\dot{\mathbf{W}}(t) = \mathbf{S}_r(t)\mathbf{D} + \boldsymbol{\varepsilon}_r \tag{35}$$

where $\boldsymbol{\varepsilon}_v$ and $\boldsymbol{\varepsilon}_r$ are the random errors. It is seen from Eq.(35) that the separation model of instrumentation errors can be simplified as a linear model.

Actually, the apparent velocity and position errors are computed by the telemetry and tracking data. When taking no account of the random errors, the tracking data can be considered as the true values of ballistic data.

4. Error separation model of initial launch parameters

The initial launch parameter errors not only affect the apparent position and velocity and stress of ballistic missile, but also the airborne computer guidance calculation. The mechanism of initial errors is analyzed thereinafter.

4.1 Effect to landing error of ballistic missile caused by initial errors

1. Effect to trajectory in the geocentric coordinate system

The localization and orientation parameters directly determine the foundation of coordinate system. When the launch inertial coordinate system $O_a - x_a y_a z_a$ changes to $O_a' - x_a' y_a' z_a'$, the base of controlling the attitude motion will also change. At this point, the reference plane $O_a - x_a z_a$ controlled by pitch angle changes to $O_a' - x_a' z_a'$ plane, simultaneously the reference plane $O_a - x_a y_a$ controlled by yaw angle changes to $O_a' - x_a' y_a'$ plane. Due to the noncoincidence of the two pairs of planes, the shape and azimuth of the in-flight trajectory are not the same with respect to the "real earth". Also, the location of trajectory is determined by the initial localization and orientation parameters. Therefore, the position of landing point of ballistic missile in the geocentric coordinate system will offset the objective point when the parameters are not error-free, in despite of taking no account of other error factors.

2. Effect to the initial velocity of missile in the launch inertial coordinate system

The launch site coordinate $\boldsymbol{R}_{0a}$ and the earth rate ω_{ea} are determined by the initial localization and orientation parameters, which affect the initial velocity and stress of ballistic missile.

In the case of maneuvering launch, the initial missile velocity in the launch inertial coordinate system is given by

$$\boldsymbol{V}_{0a} = \boldsymbol{\omega}_{ea} \times \boldsymbol{R}_{0a} + \boldsymbol{V}_s^a \tag{36}$$

where $\boldsymbol{V}_s^a$ is the carrier's instantaneous velocity with respect to the ground. Obviously, the initial velocity is largely related to the initial localization and orientation parameters and the velocity of carrier. When these parameters are with errors, the initial velocity of missile is in error.

3. Effect to the stress of missile

The acceleration of gravity of missile is determined by the angular velocity of the Earth and the coordinates of launch point in the launch inertial coordinate system and launch coordinate system. Due to the difference of stress of missile, the flight height and velocity are different, which indirectly causes the variation of thrust and aerodynamic forces. When computing the thrust forces, the effect of atmospheric pressure is considered, which is known as a function of height. At the same time, the calculation of thrust vector is related to the deflection angle of rudder, of which calculation is also affected by the height. In addition, the aerodynamic coefficients, velocity head and velocity are related to the height.

4. Effect to airborne guidance calculation

At present, the real velocity and position are commonly adopted for the calculation of guidance. Firstly, the integration of the apparent acceleration measured is performed to obtain apparent velocity; secondly, the real velocity and position are computed by the recursion formulas according to the computed apparent velocity and acceleration of gravity. When the true velocity and position satisfy the cut-off equations, the engines of missile shut down.

When there exist localization and orientation errors, on the one hand, the guidance coordinate system is different from the actual flight coordinate system, thereby the fact that the cut-off equations are satisfied cannot ensure that the missile hit the target; on the other hand, the initial values of recursion formulas involved real velocity and position and the calculation of gravitational acceleration are different from those of actual conditions, which induces that the computed real velocity and position don't agree with those under the actual situations.

For the closed-loop guidance case, the required commanded missile velocity is determined by the onboard computer in real time. Specifically, the required velocity is a function of current velocity and position of missile, location of launch point and target point, angular velocity of the Earth and orientation parameters, that is

$$\boldsymbol{V}_{aR} = \boldsymbol{V}_{aR}(\boldsymbol{V}_a, \boldsymbol{R}_a, \boldsymbol{R}_{obj}, \boldsymbol{R}_{0a}, \omega_{ea}, \lambda_T, B_T, A_T) \tag{37}$$

It is obvious that the errors of localization and orientation parameters directly influence the calculation of required velocity and the cut-off of missile.

4.2 Sources of errors of initial localization and orientation parameters

In fact, the telemetry data should reflect the acceleration information of ballistic missile provided that the guidance instrumentation systematic errors are not taken into account. Tracking data are obtained in the horizontal coordinate system by measurement devices and then converted into geocentric coordinate system. Since the precise data in the local horizontal coordinate system are available, the tracking data measured in the geocentric coordinate system don't contain the initial errors and are precise.

The difference between telemetry and tracking data is generally reckoned in the launch inertial coordinate system. The launch inertial coordinate system is determined by the initial location and orientation parameters, and the launch inertial coordinate system is inaccurate if those parameters are with errors. It is necessary to convert the tracking data in the geocentric coordinate system into the launch inertial coordinate system. The location parameters are required for the calculation of initial velocity and position while orientation parameters are demanded for the calculation of the Euler angle mapping the geocentric coordinate system into launch inertial coordinate system, which generates the initial location and orientation parameter errors. The conversion of the tracking data is described as follows:

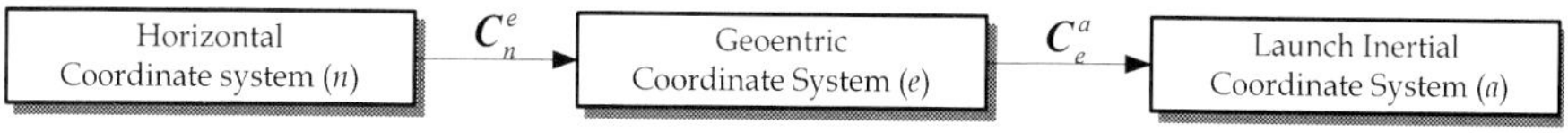

Fig. 1. The conversion of tracking data.

where C_n^e is the rotation matrix mapping horizontal coordinate system to geocentric coordinate system. The precise Euler angles are available since the geodetic coordinates of the observation station are accurate. However, there are errors in the Euler angles of rotation matrix C_e^a and then the orientation errors are introduced.

4.3 Relationship between initial orientation errors and alignment errors of platform

Before work the levelling and aligning are need to perform for inertial platform. For the maneuvering-launch-based missile, there may exist errors in the process of levelling and aligning for onboard platform system.

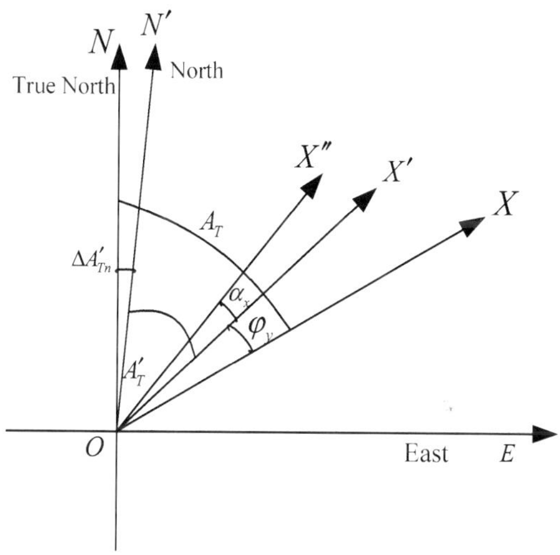

Fig. 2. The relationship between orientation errors and alignment errors of platform.

As shown in Fig.2, N is true north direction, N' is north direction measured by the vehicle, and $\Delta A'_{Tn}$ is the northing error. X is the ideal direction of fire, X' is the direction contaminated by alignment error φ_y, X'' is the actual direction provided by INS due to the platform drift angle α_x. In fact, telemetry data provides the apparent acceleration information measured in the frame involved in X'' axis while tracking data provides the information measured in the frame involved in X axis. Therefore, the azimuth from X direction to true north direction is given by

$$A_T = A'_T + \Delta A'_{Tn} + \varphi_y \tag{38}$$

and the initial azimuth error is defined as

$$\Delta A_T' = \Delta A_{Tn}' + \varphi_y \tag{39}$$

The above analysis gives an indication of linear correlation between the northing error and alignment errors of INS. Similarly, the relationship between astronomical latitude and levelling error is linear correlation.

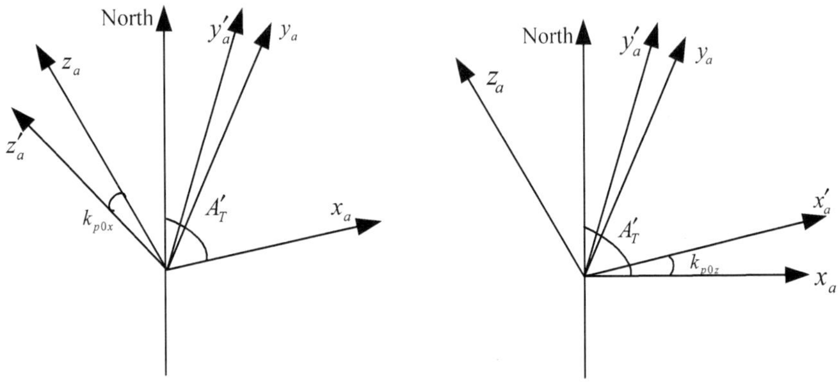

Fig. 3. The relationship between levelling errors and orientation parameters.

As can be seen in Fig.3, x_a, y_a, z_a are the coordinate axes of launch inertial frame, k_{p0x} and k_{p0z} are the levelling errors along x_a' and z_a' axes, respectively. Thus, the levelling errors can be converted into the astronomical latitude errors in the following form

$$\begin{aligned} \Delta B_p &= -k_{p0x} \sin A_T' - k_{p0z} \cos A_T' \\ \Delta \lambda_p &= k_{p0x} \cos A_T' - k_{p0z} \sin A_T' \end{aligned} \tag{40}$$

It is shown from the above analysis that the relationship between initial errors and levelling and alignment errors of guidance instrumentation systematic errors is linear correlation. Therefore, those errors cannot be separated merely using the telemetry and tracking data. Thereinafter the levelling and alignment errors are not included in the simulated cases.

4.4 Preliminary analysis of tracking data

In order to obtain the tracking data with sufficient precision, the incorporated measurement of multiple observation stations is generally used. It is pointed out in the previous section that the horizontal coordinate system of observation station is known exactly and the mapping relation with the geocentric coordinate system can be precisely described. To simplify the definition, the tracking velocity in the geocentric coordinate system is denoted by $\mathbf{V}_e$, and the position vector from the earth center expressed in the geocentric coordinate system is denoted as $\mathbf{r}_e$. Obviously, provided that the random errors of exterior devices are not taken into account, then both $\mathbf{V}_e$ and r_e are precise. The tracking velocity $\mathbf{V}_e$, consisting of three terms is written as

$$\mathbf{V}_e = \mathbf{V}_{eg} + \mathbf{V}_{es} + \mathbf{V}_{ew} \tag{41}$$

where $\mathbf{V}_{eg}$ is the incremental velocity due to gravitational acceleration, $\mathbf{V}_{es}$ is the velocity of maneuverable carrier, $\mathbf{V}_{ew}$ is the tracking apparent velocity which has removed the effect of the gravity forces and initial velocity of carrier.
The position vector $\mathbf{r}_e$ is given by

$$\mathbf{r}_e = \mathbf{r}_{eg} + \mathbf{r}_{es} + \mathbf{r}_{ew} + \mathbf{R}_{0e} \tag{42}$$

where $\mathbf{r}_{eg}$ is the incremental position due to gravitational acceleration, $\mathbf{r}_{es}$ is the incremental position due to the velocity of maneuverable carrier, $\mathbf{r}_{ew}$ is the apparent tracking position getting rid of the effect of gravity force and initial velocity of carrier, $\mathbf{R}_{0e}$ denotes the radius vector of origin of north-east-down coordinate system in the geocentric coordinate system.

4.4.1 Analysis of tracking data in the launch coordinate system

The tracking missile position in the launch coordinate system can be written in vector form

$$\boldsymbol{\rho}_g = \mathbf{C}_e^g \cdot \mathbf{r}_e - \mathbf{R}_{0g} \tag{43}$$

with

$$\mathbf{C}_e^g = \mathbf{M}_2(-\frac{\pi}{2} - A'_T)\mathbf{M}_1(B'_T)\mathbf{M}_3(-\frac{\pi}{2} + \lambda'_T) \tag{44}$$

and

$$\mathbf{R}_{0g} - \mathbf{C}_e^g(\lambda'_l, B'_T, A'_T)\begin{bmatrix} (N_0 + H'_0)\cos B'_0 \cos \lambda'_0 \\ (N_0 + H'_0)\cos B'_0 \sin \lambda'_0 \\ \left[N_0\left(1 - e^2\right) + H'_0\right]\sin B' \end{bmatrix} \tag{45}$$

where λ'_T, B'_T, A'_T are the orientation parameters contaminated by random errors, H'_0, B'_0, λ'_0 are localization parameters contaminated by random errors.
The tracking velocity expressed in the launch coordinate system is represented by

$$\mathbf{V}_g = \mathbf{C}_e^g \cdot \mathbf{V}_e \tag{46}$$

The initial errors are introduced due to the localization and orientation parameters contaminated by random errors when computing transformation matrix $\mathbf{C}_e^g$ and position vector $\mathbf{R}_{0g}$, although precise $\mathbf{V}_e$ and $\mathbf{r}_e$ are available.

4.4.2 Effect of maneuverable carrier's velocity

The carrier's velocity is generally expressed in the body frame and the measurement is denoted as $\mathbf{V}_s'$, which is represented in the north-east-down (NED) coordinate system by

$$\mathbf{V}_s^n = \mathbf{M}_2(A_s)\mathbf{M}_3(-\varphi_s)\mathbf{M}_1(-\gamma_s)\mathbf{V}_s' \tag{47}$$

where A_s is the flight-path angle, which is measured from the north and is clockwise about the body axes , is positive; φ_s is the pitch angle, upward direction is positive; γ_s is the roll angle, and is clockwise about the body axes, is positive. Herein assume A_s, φ_s and γ_s are known exactly. Letting $\mathbf{C}_n^g = \mathbf{M}_2(-A_T')$, thus,

$$\mathbf{V}_s^a = \mathbf{C}_g^a \cdot \mathbf{V}_s^g = \mathbf{C}_g^a \cdot \mathbf{C}_n^g \cdot \mathbf{V}_s^n \tag{48}$$

where $\mathbf{C}_n^g$ is coordinate transformation matrix relating horizontal coordinate system to launch coordinate system. It is seen that the carrier's velocity is related to the launch azimuth. The carrier's velocity is known as a portion of initial velocity of missile, yet the tracking velocity and position reflect the real velocity and position of missile if the random errors are not taken into account, therefore, the tracking velocity contains the information of the carrier's velocity.

The position variation of missile due to the initial velocity is represented by

$$\mathbf{r}_s^a = \mathbf{C}_g^a \cdot \mathbf{r}_s^g = \mathbf{C}_g^a \cdot \mathbf{V}_s^g \cdot t = \mathbf{C}_g^a \cdot \mathbf{C}_n^g \cdot \mathbf{V}_s^n \cdot t \tag{49}$$

It follows from Eq.(36) that the carrier's velocity is contained in the initial velocity of missile and the incurred position variation is also contained in the tracking data.

4.5 Separation model of initial errors

It follows from the foregoing analysis that the guidance instrumentation systematic errors are contained in the telemetry data while the initial errors are primarily introduced during the data processing for tracking data. Therefore, the separation of these two types of errors can be performed respectively. The difference between telemetry and tracking data is written in the following form

$$\delta\mathbf{X} = \begin{bmatrix} \mathbf{W}_{\text{tele}}^a(t) - \mathbf{W}_{\text{tra}}^a(t) \\ \dot{\mathbf{W}}_{\text{tele}}^a(t) - \dot{\mathbf{W}}_{\text{tra}}^a(t) \end{bmatrix} = \begin{bmatrix} \left(\mathbf{W}_{\text{tele}}^a(t) - \mathbf{W}_{\text{tra0}}^a(t)\right) - \left(\mathbf{W}_{\text{tra}}^a(t) - \mathbf{W}_{\text{tra0}}^a(t)\right) \\ \left(\dot{\mathbf{W}}_{\text{tele}}^a(t) - \dot{\mathbf{W}}_{\text{tra0}}^a(t)\right) - \left(\dot{\mathbf{W}}_{\text{tra}}^a(t) - \dot{\mathbf{W}}_{\text{tra0}}^a(t)\right) \end{bmatrix} \tag{50}$$

where $\mathbf{W}_{\text{tele}}^a$ and $\dot{\mathbf{W}}_{\text{tele}}^a$ are apparent velocity and position provided by telemetry data, respectively; $\mathbf{W}_{\text{tra}}^a$ and $\dot{\mathbf{W}}_{\text{tra}}^a$ are apparent velocity and position provided by tracking data, respectively; $\mathbf{W}_{\text{tra0}}^a$ and $\dot{\mathbf{W}}_{\text{tra0}}^a$ are the tracking information which don't contain the initial errors. The term on the right-hand side of Eq.(50) comprises two parts of information, one is the effect of guidance instrumentation systematic errors, and the other is the effect of initial errors. Thus, the difference between the telemetry data and tracking data can be rewritten as

$$\delta\mathbf{X}=\begin{bmatrix}\mathbf{W}_{\text{tele}}^{a}(t)-\mathbf{W}_{\text{tra0}}^{a}(t)\\ \underset{\cdot}{\mathbf{W}}_{\text{tele}}^{a}(t)-\underset{\cdot}{\mathbf{W}}_{\text{tra0}}^{a}(t)\end{bmatrix}-\begin{bmatrix}\mathbf{W}_{\text{tra}}^{a}(t)-\mathbf{W}_{\text{tra0}}^{a}(t)\\ \underset{\cdot}{\mathbf{W}}_{\text{tra}}^{a}(t)-\underset{\cdot}{\mathbf{W}}_{\text{tra0}}^{a}(t)\end{bmatrix}\equiv\delta\mathbf{X}_{I}-\delta\mathbf{X}_{P} \tag{51}$$

where $\delta\mathbf{X}_I$ is the difference of telemetry data and tracking data due to guidance instrumentation systematic errors, and $\delta\mathbf{X}_P$ is the difference of telemetry data and tracking data due to initial errors.

Define the initial errors as

$$\mathbf{P}_a=\mathbf{P}'-\mathbf{P} \tag{52}$$

where $\mathbf{P}'$ are the known binding values of initial launch parameters consisting of 9 terms mentioned above, $\mathbf{P}$ is the unknown true value.

Recalling Eqs.(16) and (19) gives $\mathbf{W}_{tra}^{a}(t)$ and $\underset{\cdot}{\mathbf{W}}_{tra}^{a}(t)$

$$\mathbf{W}_{\text{tra}}^{a}(t)=\mathbf{C}_{g}^{a}(t)\cdot\mathbf{V}_{g}(t)+\mathbf{\Omega}_{\omega}^{a}\cdot\mathbf{C}_{g}^{a}(t)\cdot\left(\mathbf{R}_0+\boldsymbol{\rho}_g\right)-\mathbf{V}_{0a}-\int_0^t\mathbf{g}_a(\tau)d\tau \tag{53}$$

$$\underset{\cdot}{\mathbf{W}}_{\text{tra}}^{a}(t)=\mathbf{C}_{g}^{a}(t)\cdot\left(\mathbf{R}_0+\boldsymbol{\rho}_g\right)-\mathbf{R}_{0a}-\mathbf{V}_{0a}\cdot t-\int_0^t\int_0^u\mathbf{g}_a(\tau)d\tau du \tag{54}$$

The tracking position in the launch inertial coordinate system can be written as

$$\boldsymbol{\rho}_a=\mathbf{C}_{g}^{a}(t)\cdot(\mathbf{R}_0+\boldsymbol{\rho}_g)-\mathbf{R}_{0a}=\mathbf{C}_{g}^{a}(t)\cdot\mathbf{r}_g-\mathbf{R}_{0a} \tag{55}$$

and the tracking velocity expressed in the launch inertial coordinate system is given by

$$\mathbf{V}_a=\mathbf{C}_{g}^{a}(t)\cdot\mathbf{V}_g=\mathbf{C}_{g}^{a}(t)\cdot\mathbf{C}_{e}^{g}\cdot\mathbf{V}_e \tag{56}$$

where $\mathbf{r}_e$ and $\mathbf{V}_e$ are the error-free tracking position and velocity expressed in the geocentric coordinate system.

By the definition of transformation matrix, we can have

$$\mathbf{C}_{g}^{a}\cdot\mathbf{C}_{e}^{g}=\left(\mathbf{M}_3(B_T')\mathbf{M}_2(A_T')\right)^T\mathbf{M}_1(-\omega_{0e}t)\mathbf{M}_3(B_T')\mathbf{M}_2(-\frac{\pi}{2})\mathbf{M}_1(B_T')\mathbf{M}_3(-\frac{\pi}{2}+\lambda_T') \tag{57}$$

Simplifying the Eq.(57) results in

$$\mathbf{C}_{e}^{a}=\mathbf{C}_{g}^{a}\cdot\mathbf{C}_{e}^{g}=\mathbf{M}_2(-A_T')\mathbf{M}_3(-B_T')\mathbf{M}_2(-\frac{\pi}{2})\mathbf{M}_3(-\frac{\pi}{2}+\lambda_T'-\omega_{0e}t) \tag{58}$$

Substituting Eq.(58) into Eqs. (55) and (56) yields the tracking apparent velocity

$$\mathbf{W}_{\text{tra}}^{a}(t)=\mathbf{C}_{e}^{a}(t)\cdot\mathbf{V}_e+\boldsymbol{\omega}_{e}^{a}\times\left(\mathbf{C}_{e}^{a}(t)\cdot\mathbf{r}_e\right)-\mathbf{V}_{0a}-\int_0^t\mathbf{g}_a(\tau)d\tau \tag{59}$$

and the tracking apparent position

$$\underset{\cdot}{\mathbf{W}}_{\text{tra}}^{a}(t)=\mathbf{C}_{e}^{a}(t)\cdot\mathbf{r}_e-\mathbf{R}_{0a}-\mathbf{V}_{0a}\cdot t-\int_0^t\int_0^u\mathbf{g}_a(\tau)d\tau du \tag{60}$$

Taking the total differentiation of Eq.(59), thus apparent velocity error is given by

$$\begin{aligned}\delta\mathbf{X}_{Pv} &= \Delta\left(\mathbf{C}_e^a(t)\cdot\mathbf{V}_e(t)+\boldsymbol{\omega}_e^a\times\left(\mathbf{C}_e^a(t)\cdot\mathbf{r}_e\right)-\mathbf{V}_{0a}-\int_0^t\mathbf{g}_a(\tau)d\tau\right)\\ &= \Delta\left(\mathbf{C}_e^a(t)\cdot\mathbf{V}_e(t)\right)+\Delta\left(\boldsymbol{\omega}_e^a\times\left(\mathbf{C}_e^a(t)\cdot\mathbf{r}_e\right)\right)-\Delta\mathbf{V}_{0a}-\Delta\int_0^t\mathbf{g}_a(\tau)d\tau\end{aligned} \tag{61}$$

Similarly, taking the total differentiation of Eq.(60) gives apparent position error

$$\begin{aligned}\delta\mathbf{X}_{\mathbf{Pr}} &= \Delta\left(\mathbf{C}_e^a(t)\cdot\mathbf{r}_e-\mathbf{R}_{0a}-\mathbf{V}_{0a}\cdot t-\int_0^t\int_0^u\mathbf{g}_a(\tau)d\tau du\right)\\ &= \Delta\left(\mathbf{C}_e^a(t)\cdot\mathbf{r}_e\right)-\Delta\mathbf{R}_{0a}-\Delta\mathbf{V}_{0a}\cdot t-\Delta\int_0^t\int_0^u\mathbf{g}_a(\tau)d\tau du\end{aligned} \tag{62}$$

4.5.1 Error analysis of apparent velocity

It follows From Eq.(61) that the tracking apparent velocity is related to initial localization and orientation parameters, initial velocity and the calculation of attraction. To separate the initial errors, the relationship between them is needed to be analyzed. Four terms contained in Eq.(61) are taken into account as follows.

1. First term

The first term on the right-hand side of Eq.(61) can be written in expended form

$$\delta\mathbf{X}_{pv1} = \Delta\mathbf{C}_e^a(t)\cdot\mathbf{V}_e(t) = \left(\frac{\partial\mathbf{C}_e^a}{\partial\lambda_T'}\Delta\lambda_T'+\frac{\partial\mathbf{C}_e^a}{\partial B_T'}\Delta B_T'+\frac{\partial\mathbf{C}_e^a}{\partial A_T'}\Delta A_T'\right)\cdot\mathbf{V}_e(t) \tag{63}$$

where

$$\frac{\partial C_e^a}{\partial\lambda_T'} = \begin{bmatrix} -\cos(\lambda_T'-\omega_e t)\sin A_T'+\sin(\lambda_T'-\omega_e t)\sin B_T'\cos A_T' & -\cos(\lambda_T'-\omega_e t)\sin B_T'\cos A'-\sin(\lambda_T'-\omega_e t)\sin A_T' & 0\\ -\sin(\lambda_T'-\omega_e t)\cos B_T' & \cos(\lambda_T'-\omega_e t)\cos B_T' & 0\\ -\cos(\lambda_T'-\omega_e t)\cos A_T'-\sin(\lambda_T'-\omega_e t)\sin B_T'\sin A_T' & \cos(\lambda_T'-\omega_e t)\sin B_T'\sin A_T'-\sin(\lambda_T'-\omega_e t)\cos A_T' & 0 \end{bmatrix}$$

$$\frac{\partial C_e^a}{\partial B_T'} = \begin{pmatrix} -\cos(\lambda_T'-\omega_e t)\cos B_T'\cos A_T' & -\sin(\lambda_T'-\omega_e t)\cos B_T'\cos A_T' & -\sin B_T'\cos A_T'\\ -\cos(\lambda_T'-\omega_e t)\sin B_T' & -\sin(\lambda_T'-\omega_e t)\sin B_T' & \cos B_T'\\ \cos(\lambda_T'-\omega_e t)\cos B_T'\sin A_T' & \sin(\lambda_T'-\omega_e t)\cos B_T'\sin A_T' & \sin B_T'\sin A_T' \end{pmatrix}$$

$$\frac{\partial C_e^a}{\partial A_T'} = \begin{bmatrix} -\sin(\lambda_T'-\omega_e t)\cos A_T'+\cos(\lambda_T'-\omega_e t)\sin B_T'\sin A_T' & \sin(\lambda_T'-\omega_e t)\sin B_T'\sin A_T'+\cos(\lambda_T'-\omega_e t)\cos A_T' & -\cos B_T'\sin A_T'\\ 0 & 0 & 0\\ \sin(\lambda_T'-\omega_e t)\sin A_T'+\cos(\lambda_T'-\omega_e t)\sin B_T'\cos A_T' & \sin(\lambda_T'-\omega_e t)\sin B_T'\cos A_T'-\cos(\lambda_T'-\omega_e t)\sin A_T' & -\cos B_T'\cos A_T' \end{bmatrix}$$

Therefore, $\delta\mathbf{X}_{pv1}$ can be rewritten as follows

$$\delta\mathbf{X}_{pv1} = \begin{bmatrix}\frac{\partial\mathbf{C}_e^a}{\partial\lambda_T'}\cdot\mathbf{V}_e & \frac{\partial\mathbf{C}_e^a}{\partial B_T'}\cdot\mathbf{V}_e & \frac{\partial\mathbf{C}_e^a}{\partial A_T'}\cdot\mathbf{V}_e\end{bmatrix}\cdot\mathbf{P}_t \tag{64}$$

where $\mathbf{P}_t \equiv [\Delta\lambda_T' \quad \Delta B_T' \quad \Delta A_T']^T$.

2. Second term

The second term on the right-hand side of Eq.(61) can be written in expended form

$$\delta\mathbf{X}_{pv2} = \Delta\left(\boldsymbol{\omega}_e^a \times (\mathbf{C}_e^a(t)\mathbf{r}_e)\right) = \Delta\boldsymbol{\omega}_e^a \times (\mathbf{C}_e^a(t)\mathbf{r}_e) + \boldsymbol{\omega}_e^a \times \Delta(\mathbf{C}_e^a(t)\mathbf{r}_e)$$
$$= \left(\frac{\partial \boldsymbol{\omega}_e^a}{\partial \lambda_T'}\Delta\lambda_T' + \frac{\partial \boldsymbol{\omega}_e^a}{\partial B_T'}\Delta B_T' + \frac{\partial \boldsymbol{\omega}_e^a}{\partial A_T'}\Delta A_T'\right) \times (\mathbf{C}_e^a(t)\mathbf{r}_e) + \boldsymbol{\omega}_e^a \times \left(\frac{\partial \mathbf{C}_e^a}{\partial \lambda_T'}\Delta\lambda' + \frac{\partial \mathbf{C}_e^a}{\partial B_T'}\Delta B_T' + \frac{\partial \mathbf{C}_e^a}{\partial A_T'}\Delta A_T'\right)\mathbf{r_e} \quad (65)$$

where

$$\frac{\partial \boldsymbol{\omega}_e^a}{\partial \lambda_T'} = 0\,,\quad \frac{\partial \boldsymbol{\omega}_e^a}{\partial B_T'} = \omega_e \begin{pmatrix} -\sin B_T' \cos A_T' \\ \cos B_T' \\ \sin B_T' \sin A_T' \end{pmatrix}, \text{ and } \frac{\partial \boldsymbol{\omega}_e^a}{\partial A_T'} = \omega_e \begin{pmatrix} -\cos B_T' \sin A_T' \\ 0 \\ -\cos B_T' \cos A_T' \end{pmatrix}.$$

Thus, Eq.(65) can be rewritten as follows

$$\delta\mathbf{X}_{pv2} = \left[\boldsymbol{\omega}_e^a \times \frac{\partial \mathbf{C}_e^a}{\partial \lambda_T'}\mathbf{r}_e \quad \frac{\partial \boldsymbol{\omega}_e^a}{\partial B_T'} \times (\mathbf{C}_e^a(t)\mathbf{r}_e) + \boldsymbol{\omega}_e^a \times \frac{\partial \mathbf{C}_e^a}{\partial B_T'}\mathbf{r}_e \quad \frac{\partial \boldsymbol{\omega}_e^a}{\partial A_T'} \times (\mathbf{C}_e^a(t)\mathbf{r}_e) + \boldsymbol{\omega}_e^a \times \frac{\partial \mathbf{C}_e^a}{\partial A_T'}\mathbf{r}_e\right]\mathbf{P}_t \quad (66)$$

3. Third term

At launch, launch coordinate system coincides with launch inertial coordinate system, so the initial velocity expressed in the launch inertial coordinate system can be substituted for the initial velocity expressed in the launch coordinate system.

The third term on the right-hand side of Eq.(61) can be written in expended form

$$\begin{aligned}
\delta\mathbf{X}_{Pv3} &= -\Delta\mathbf{V}_{0a} = -\Delta\left(\boldsymbol{\omega}_e^a(0) \times \mathbf{R}_{0a}\right) - \Delta\left(\mathbf{C}_n^a(0)\cdot\mathbf{V}_s^n\right) \\
&= -\left(\frac{\partial \boldsymbol{\omega}_e^a}{\partial \lambda_T'}\Delta\lambda_T' + \frac{\partial \boldsymbol{\omega}_e^a}{\partial B_T'}\Delta B_T' + \frac{\partial \boldsymbol{\omega}_e^a}{\partial A_T'}\Delta A_T'\right) \times \mathbf{R}_{0a} \\
&\quad -\boldsymbol{\omega}_e^a \times \left(\frac{\partial \mathbf{R}_{0a}}{\partial \lambda_T'}\Delta\lambda_T' + \frac{\partial \mathbf{R}_{0a}}{\partial B_T'}\Delta B_T' + \frac{\partial \mathbf{R}_{0a}}{\partial A_T'}\Delta A_T' + \frac{\partial \mathbf{R}_{0a}}{\partial \lambda_0'}\Delta\lambda_0' + \frac{\partial \mathbf{R}_{0a}}{\partial B_0'}\Delta B_0' + \frac{\partial \mathbf{R}_{0a}}{\partial H_0'}\Delta H_0'\right) \\
&\quad -\left(\frac{\partial \mathbf{C}_n^a(0)}{\partial \lambda_T'}\Delta\lambda_T' + \frac{\partial \mathbf{C}_n^a(0)}{\partial B_T'}\Delta B_T' + \frac{\partial \mathbf{C}_n^a(0)}{\partial A_T'}\Delta A_T'\right)\mathbf{V}_s^n - \mathbf{C}_n^a(0)\cdot\Delta\mathbf{V}_s^n
\end{aligned} \quad (67)$$

Similarly, Eq.(67) can be rewritten in the form

$$\begin{aligned}
\delta\mathbf{X}_{Pv3} &= -\left[\boldsymbol{\omega}_e^a \times \frac{\partial \mathbf{R}_{0a}}{\partial \lambda_0'} \quad \boldsymbol{\omega}_e^a \times \frac{\partial \mathbf{R}_{0a}}{\partial B_0'} \quad \boldsymbol{\omega}_e^a \times \frac{\partial \mathbf{R}_{0a}}{\partial H_0'}\right]\cdot\mathbf{P}_s \\
&\quad -\left[\frac{\partial \boldsymbol{\omega}_e^a}{\partial \lambda_T'} \times \mathbf{R}_{0a} + \boldsymbol{\omega}_e^a \times \frac{\partial \mathbf{R}_{0a}}{\partial \lambda_T'} \quad \frac{\partial \boldsymbol{\omega}_e^a}{\partial B_T'} \times \mathbf{R}_{0a} + \boldsymbol{\omega}_e^a \times \frac{\partial \mathbf{R}_{0a}}{\partial B_T'} \quad \frac{\partial \boldsymbol{\omega}_e^a}{\partial A_T'} \times \mathbf{R}_{0a} + \boldsymbol{\omega}_e^a \times \frac{\partial \mathbf{R}_{0a}}{\partial A_T'}\right]\mathbf{P}_t \\
&\quad -\left[\frac{\partial \mathbf{C}_n^a(0)}{\partial \lambda_T'}\mathbf{V}_s^n \quad \frac{\partial \mathbf{C}_n^a(0)}{\partial B_T'}\mathbf{V}_s^n \quad \frac{\partial \mathbf{C}_n^a(0)}{\partial A_T'}\mathbf{V}_s^n\right]\mathbf{P}_t - \mathbf{C}_n^a(0)\cdot\mathbf{P}_v
\end{aligned} \quad (68)$$

where $\mathbf{C}_n^a(0) = \mathbf{C}_n^g(0)$, $\mathbf{P}_s \equiv [\Delta\lambda_0' \quad \Delta B_0' \quad \Delta H_0']^T$, $\mathbf{P}_v \equiv \left[\Delta V_{sx} \quad \Delta V_{sy} \quad \Delta V_{sz}\right]^T$.

4. Fourth term

Because the telemetry data don't contain the effect of gravitational acceleration, the effect of gravitational acceleration of tracking data is necessary to drop when computing the difference between telemetry data and tracking data. Integrating gravitational acceleration one can obtain the velocity and perform the integration again to obtain the position. It is noted that the tracking data is used to calculate the gravitational acceleration. It follows from the previous section that the gravitational acceleration in the launch inertial coordinate system is given by

$$\mathbf{g}_a = g_r \frac{\mathbf{C}_e^a \cdot \mathbf{r}_e}{r} + g_\omega \frac{\mathbf{C}_e^a \cdot \boldsymbol{\omega}_{e0}}{\omega_e} = \mathbf{C}_e^a \cdot \left(g_r \frac{\mathbf{r}_e}{r} + g_\omega \frac{\boldsymbol{\omega}_{e0}}{\omega_e} \right) \tag{69}$$

By examining Eq.(69) we can find that the main reason introducing the computational error of gravitational acceleration is that there exist errors in the Euler angles of transformation matrix $\mathbf{C}_e^a$, whereas the bracketed term on the right-hand side of Eq.(69) is error-free. It is noted that

$$\sin\varphi_e = \frac{\mathbf{r}_a \cdot \boldsymbol{\omega}_{ea}}{r\omega_e} = \frac{(\mathbf{C}_e^a \mathbf{r}_e) \cdot (\mathbf{C}_e^a \boldsymbol{\omega}_{e0})}{r\omega_e} = \frac{(\mathbf{C}_e^a \mathbf{r}_e)^T (\mathbf{C}_e^a \boldsymbol{\omega}_{e0})}{r\omega_e} = \frac{\mathbf{r}_e \cdot \boldsymbol{\omega}_{e0}}{r\omega_e} \tag{70}$$

which can be computed exactly, thus, the error of gravitational acceleration is given by

$$\Delta\mathbf{g}_a = \Delta\mathbf{C}_e^a \cdot \left(g_r \frac{\mathbf{r}_e}{r} + g_\omega \frac{\boldsymbol{\omega}_{e0}}{\omega_e} \right) = \begin{bmatrix} \frac{\partial \mathbf{C}_e^a}{\partial \lambda_T'} \mathbf{g}_e & \frac{\partial \mathbf{C}_e^a}{\partial B_T'} \mathbf{g}_e & \frac{\partial \mathbf{C}_e^a}{\partial A_T'} \mathbf{g}_e \end{bmatrix} \mathbf{P}_t = \mathbf{G}_g \cdot \mathbf{P}_t \tag{71}$$

where $\mathbf{g}_e = \left(g_r \frac{\mathbf{r}_e}{r} + g_\omega \frac{\boldsymbol{\omega}_{e0}}{\omega_e} \right)$.

The error of tracking apparent velocity is given by

$$\delta\mathbf{X}_{Pv4} = -\int_0^t \Delta\mathbf{g}_a(\tau) d\tau \cdot \mathbf{P}_t = -\int_0^t \mathbf{G}_g(\tau) d\tau \cdot \mathbf{P}_t \tag{72}$$

4.5.2 Error analysis of apparent position

Recalling Eq.(62) gives apparent position error

$$\begin{aligned} \delta\mathbf{X}_{\mathbf{Pr}} &= \Delta\left(\mathbf{C}_e^a(t) \cdot \mathbf{r}_e - \mathbf{R}_{0a} - \mathbf{V}_{0a} \cdot t - \int_0^t \int_0^u \mathbf{g}_a(\tau) d\tau du \right) \\ &= \Delta\left(\mathbf{C}_e^a(t) \cdot \mathbf{r}_e \right) - \Delta\mathbf{R}_{0a} - \Delta\mathbf{V}_{0a} \cdot t - \Delta\int_0^t \int_0^u \mathbf{g}_a(\tau) d\tau du \end{aligned} \tag{73}$$

In the similar manner four terms contained in Eq.(73) are analyzed as follows.

1. First term

The first term on the right-hand side of Eq.(73) can be written in expended form

$$\delta\mathbf{X}_{Pr1} = \Delta\mathbf{C}_e^a \cdot \mathbf{r}_e = \left(\frac{\partial \mathbf{C}_e^a}{\partial \lambda_T'} \Delta\lambda' + \frac{\partial \mathbf{C}_e^a}{\partial B_T'} \Delta B_T' + \frac{\partial \mathbf{C}_e^a}{\partial A_T'} \Delta A_T' \right) \cdot \mathbf{r}_e \tag{74}$$

Rearranging Eq.(74) gives

$$\delta\boldsymbol{X}_{Pr1} = \begin{bmatrix} \frac{\partial \boldsymbol{C}_e^a}{\partial \lambda_T'} \cdot \boldsymbol{r}_e & \frac{\partial \boldsymbol{C}_e^a}{\partial B_T'} \cdot \boldsymbol{r}_e & \frac{\partial \boldsymbol{C}_e^a}{\partial A_T'} \cdot \boldsymbol{r}_e \end{bmatrix} \cdot \boldsymbol{P}_t \tag{75}$$

2. Second term

The second term on the right-hand side of Eq.(73) can be written in expended form

$$\begin{aligned}\delta \mathbf{X}_{Pr2} &= -\Delta \mathbf{C}_e^a \cdot \mathbf{R}_{0e} - \mathbf{C}_e^a \cdot \Delta \mathbf{R}_{0e} \\ &= -\left(\frac{\partial \mathbf{C}_e^a}{\partial \lambda_T'} \Delta \lambda' + \frac{\partial \mathbf{C}_e^a}{\partial B_T'} \Delta B_T' + \frac{\partial \mathbf{C}_e^a}{\partial A_T'} \Delta A_T' \right) \cdot \mathbf{R}_{0e} \\ &\quad - \mathbf{C}_e^a \cdot \left(\frac{\partial \mathbf{R}_{0e}}{\partial \lambda_0'} \Delta \lambda_0' + \frac{\partial \mathbf{R}_{0e}}{\partial B_0'} \Delta B_0' + \frac{\partial \mathbf{R}_{0e}}{\partial H_0'} \Delta H_0' \right)\end{aligned} \tag{76}$$

It follows from the previous section that

$$\mathbf{R}_{0e} = \begin{bmatrix} (N_0 + H_0')\cos B_0' \cos \lambda_0' \\ (N_0 + H_0')\cos B_0' \sin \lambda_0' \\ \left[N_0 \left(1 - e^2\right) + H_0' \right] \sin B_0' \end{bmatrix} \tag{77}$$

Therefore, we can have that

$$\frac{\partial \mathbf{R}_{0e}}{\partial \lambda_0'} = \begin{pmatrix} -\cos B_0' \sin \lambda_0' [H_0' + a_e(1 + \alpha_e \sin^2 B_0')] \\ \cos B_0' \cos \lambda_0' [H_0' + a_e(1 + \alpha_e \sin^2 B_0')] \\ 0 \end{pmatrix} \tag{78}$$

$$\frac{\partial \mathbf{R}_{0e}}{\partial B_0'} = \begin{pmatrix} -\cos \lambda_0' \sin B_0' [a_e + H_0' - \frac{1}{2} a_e \alpha_e (1 + 3\cos 2B_0')] \\ -\sin \lambda_0' \sin B_0' [a_e + H_0' - \frac{1}{2} a_e \alpha_e (1 + 3\cos 2B_0')] \\ \cos B_0' [a_e + H_0' - 2a_e \alpha_e - \frac{3}{2} a_e \alpha_e (-1 + 2\alpha_e)(1 - \cos 2B_0')] \end{pmatrix} \tag{79}$$

$$\frac{\partial \mathbf{R}_{0e}}{\partial H_0'} = \begin{pmatrix} \cos B_0' \cos \lambda_0' \\ \cos B_0' \sin \lambda_0' \\ \sin B_0' \end{pmatrix} \tag{80}$$

Thus, Eq.(76) can be rewritten as

$$\delta \mathbf{X}_{Pr2} = -\begin{bmatrix} \frac{\partial \mathbf{C}_e^a}{\partial \lambda_T'} \mathbf{R}_{0e} & \frac{\partial \mathbf{C}_e^a}{\partial B_T'} \mathbf{R}_{0e} & \frac{\partial \mathbf{C}_e^a}{\partial A_T'} \mathbf{R}_{0e} \end{bmatrix} \cdot \mathbf{P}_t - \begin{bmatrix} \mathbf{C}_e^a \frac{\partial \mathbf{R}_{0e}}{\partial \lambda_0'} & \mathbf{C}_e^a \frac{\partial \mathbf{R}_{0e}}{\partial B_0'} & \mathbf{C}_e^a \frac{\partial \mathbf{R}_{0e}}{\partial H_0'} \end{bmatrix} \cdot \mathbf{P}_s \tag{81}$$

3. Third term

Similarly, launch coordinate system coincides with launch inertial coordinate system at launch moment, so the radius of earth center in the launch inertial coordinate system can be represented by that in the launch coordinate system, thus,

$$\delta \mathbf{X}_{Pr3} = -\Delta\left(\boldsymbol{\omega}_e^a \times \mathbf{R}_{0a} \right) t - \Delta\left(\mathbf{C}_n^a(0) \ \ \mathbf{V}_s^n \right) \cdot t \tag{82}$$

Combing the analysis of apparent velocity gives

$$\delta \mathbf{X}_{Pr3} = \delta \mathbf{X}_{Pv3} \cdot t \tag{83}$$

4. Fourth term

The fourth term is the gravitational acceleration term, which can be obtained by integrating the error of apparent tracking velocity, written as

$$\delta X_{Pr4} = -\int_0^t \delta X_{Pv4} d\tau = -\int_0^t \int_0^u G_g(\tau) d\tau du \tag{84}$$

4.5.3 Relationship of the difference between telemetry data, tracking data and initial errors

According to the above analysis, the relationship of the difference between telemetry velocity and tracking velocity and initial errors can be concluded as follows

$$\begin{aligned} \delta \mathbf{X}_{Pv} &= \delta \mathbf{X}_{Pv1} + \delta \mathbf{X}_{Pv2} + \delta \mathbf{X}_{Pv3} + \delta \mathbf{X}_{Pv4} \\ &= \mathbf{G}_{vt} \cdot \mathbf{P}_t + \mathbf{G}_{vs} \cdot \mathbf{P}_s + \mathbf{G}_{vv} \cdot \mathbf{P}_v + \Delta \mathbf{v}_g \end{aligned} \tag{85}$$

where

$$\mathbf{G}_{vt1} = \frac{\partial \mathbf{C}_e^a}{\partial \lambda_T'} \cdot \mathbf{V}_e + \boldsymbol{\omega}_e^a \times \frac{\partial \mathbf{C}_e^a}{\partial \lambda_T'} \mathbf{r}_e - \left(\frac{\partial \boldsymbol{\omega}_e^a}{\partial \lambda_T'} \times \mathbf{R}_{0a} + \boldsymbol{\omega}_e^a \times \frac{\partial \mathbf{R}_{0a}}{\partial \lambda_T'} \right) - \frac{\partial \mathbf{C}_n^a(0)}{\partial \lambda_T'} \mathbf{V}_s^n \tag{86}$$

$$\mathbf{G}_{vt2} = \frac{\partial \mathbf{C}_e^a}{\partial B_T'} \cdot \mathbf{V}_e + \frac{\partial \boldsymbol{\omega}_e^a}{\partial B_T'} \times (\mathbf{C}_e^a \mathbf{r}_e) + \boldsymbol{\omega}_e^a \times \frac{\partial \mathbf{C}_e^a}{\partial B_T'} \mathbf{r}_e - \left(\frac{\partial \boldsymbol{\omega}_e^a}{\partial B_T'} \times \mathbf{R}_{0a} + \boldsymbol{\omega}_e^a \times \frac{\partial \mathbf{R}_{0a}}{\partial B_T'} \right) - \frac{\partial \mathbf{C}_n^a(0)}{\partial B_T'} \mathbf{V}_s^n \tag{87}$$

$$\mathbf{G}_{vt3} = \frac{\partial \mathbf{C}_e^a}{\partial A_T'} \cdot \mathbf{V}_e + \frac{\partial \boldsymbol{\omega}_e^a}{\partial A_T'} \times (\mathbf{C}_e^a \mathbf{r}_e) + \boldsymbol{\omega}_e^a \times \frac{\partial \mathbf{C}_e^a}{\partial A_T'} \mathbf{r}_e - \left(\frac{\partial \boldsymbol{\omega}_e^a}{\partial A_T'} \times \mathbf{R}_{0a} + \boldsymbol{\omega}_e^a \times \frac{\partial \mathbf{R}_{0a}}{\partial A_T'} \right) - \frac{\partial \mathbf{C}_n^a(0)}{\partial A_T'} \mathbf{V}_s^n \tag{88}$$

$$\mathbf{G}_{vs} = \begin{bmatrix} -\boldsymbol{\omega}_e^a \times \frac{\partial \mathbf{R}_{0a}}{\partial \lambda_0'} & -\boldsymbol{\omega}_e^a \times \frac{\partial \mathbf{R}_{0a}}{\partial B_0'} & -\boldsymbol{\omega}_e^a \times \frac{\partial \mathbf{R}_{0a}}{\partial H_0'} \end{bmatrix} \tag{89}$$

$$\mathbf{G}_{vv} = -\mathbf{C}_n^a(0) \tag{90}$$

$$\Delta \dot{\mathbf{v}}_g = -\Delta \mathbf{g}_a = -\begin{bmatrix} \frac{\partial \mathbf{C}_e^a}{\partial \lambda_T'} \mathbf{g}_e & \frac{\partial \mathbf{C}_e^a}{\partial B_T'} \mathbf{g}_e & \frac{\partial \mathbf{C}_e^a}{\partial A_T'} \mathbf{g}_e \end{bmatrix} \mathbf{P}_t \tag{91}$$

In the same manner the relationship of the difference between telemetry position and tracking position and initial errors can be concluded as follows

$$\begin{aligned} \delta \mathbf{X}_{Pr} &= \delta \mathbf{X}_{Pr1} + \delta \mathbf{X}_{Pr2} + \delta \mathbf{X}_{Pr3} + \delta \mathbf{X}_{Pr4} \\ &= \mathbf{G}_{st} \cdot \mathbf{P}_t + \mathbf{G}_{ss} \cdot \mathbf{P}_s + \mathbf{G}_{sv} \cdot \mathbf{P}_v + \Delta \mathbf{s}_g \end{aligned} \tag{92}$$

where

$$\mathbf{G}_{st1} = \frac{\partial \mathbf{C}_e^a}{\partial \lambda_T'} \cdot \mathbf{r}_e - \frac{\partial \mathbf{C}_e^a}{\partial \lambda_T'} \mathbf{R}_{e0} - \left(\frac{\partial \boldsymbol{\omega}_e^a}{\partial \lambda_T'} \times \mathbf{R}_{0a} + \boldsymbol{\omega}_e^a \times \frac{\partial \mathbf{R}_{0a}}{\partial \lambda_T'} \right) \cdot t - \frac{\partial \mathbf{C}_n^a(0)}{\partial \lambda_T'} \mathbf{V}_s^n \cdot t \tag{93}$$

$$\mathbf{G}_{st2} = \frac{\partial \mathbf{C}_e^a}{\partial B_T'} \cdot \mathbf{r}_e - \frac{\partial \mathbf{C}_e^a}{\partial B_T'} \mathbf{R}_{e0} - \left(\frac{\partial \boldsymbol{\omega}_e^a}{\partial B_T'} \times \mathbf{R}_{0a} + \boldsymbol{\omega}_e^a \times \frac{\partial \mathbf{R}_{0a}}{\partial B_T'} \right) \cdot t - \frac{\partial \mathbf{C}_n^a(0)}{\partial B_T'} \mathbf{V}_s^n \cdot t \tag{94}$$

$$\mathbf{G}_{st3} = \frac{\partial \mathbf{C}_e^a}{\partial A_T'} \cdot \mathbf{r}_e - \frac{\partial \mathbf{C}_e^a}{\partial A_T'} \mathbf{R}_{e0} - \left(\frac{\partial \boldsymbol{\omega}_e^a}{\partial A_T'} \times \mathbf{R}_{0a} + \boldsymbol{\omega}_e^a \times \frac{\partial \mathbf{R}_{0a}}{\partial A_T'} \right) \cdot t - \frac{\partial \mathbf{C}_n^a(0)}{\partial A_T'} \mathbf{V}_s^n \cdot t \tag{95}$$

$$\boldsymbol{G}_{ss} = \left[-\boldsymbol{C}_e^a \frac{\partial \boldsymbol{R}_{0e}}{\partial \lambda_0'} - \omega_e^a \times \frac{\partial \boldsymbol{R}_{0a}}{\partial \lambda_0'} t \quad -\boldsymbol{C}_e^a \frac{\partial \boldsymbol{R}_{0e}}{\partial B_0'} - \omega_e^a \times \frac{\partial \boldsymbol{R}_{0a}}{\partial B_0'} t \quad -\boldsymbol{C}_e^a \frac{\partial \boldsymbol{R}_{0e}}{\partial H_0'} - \omega_e^a \times \frac{\partial \boldsymbol{R}_{0a}}{\partial H_0'} t \right] \tag{96}$$

$$\mathbf{G}_{sv} = -\mathbf{C}_n^a(0) \cdot t \,, \;\; \Delta \dot{\mathbf{s}}_g = \Delta \mathbf{v}_g \tag{97}$$

Let $\delta \mathbf{X}_P = [\delta \mathbf{X}_{Pv} \;\; \delta \mathbf{X}_{Pr}]^T$, $\mathbf{P}_a = [\mathbf{P}_t \;\; \mathbf{P}_s \;\; \mathbf{P}_v]^T$, then the difference between the telemetry data and tracking data can be written in matrix form

$$\delta \mathbf{X}_P = \begin{bmatrix} \mathbf{G}_{vt} - \int_0^t \mathbf{G}_g dt & \mathbf{G}_{vs} & \mathbf{G}_{vv} \\ \mathbf{G}_{st} - \int_0^t \int_0^u \mathbf{G}_g d\tau du & \mathbf{G}_{ss} & \mathbf{G}_{sv} \end{bmatrix} \cdot \mathbf{P}_a = \begin{bmatrix} \mathbf{G}_v \\ \mathbf{G}_s \end{bmatrix} \cdot \mathbf{P}_a \tag{98}$$

By examining the above model, we can find that the correlation of the environmental function column corresponding to the geodetic latitude and height in the velocity domain, namely, $-\boldsymbol{\omega}_e^a \times \frac{\partial \mathbf{R}_{0a}}{\partial B_0'}$ and $-\boldsymbol{\omega}_e^a \times \frac{\partial \mathbf{R}_{0a}}{\partial H_0'}$ in the $\mathbf{G}_{vs}$ matrix, is large and the separation between them is not easy. But in the position domain, the property of initial error environmental function matrix is good therefore, the separation of initial errors is needed to perform in the position domain or velocity-position domain.

4.6 Separation model of instrumentation errors and initial errors

It is pointed out in the previous section that the guidance instrumentation systematic errors are contained in the telemetry data and the initial errors are primarily introduced during the data processing of tracking data. Consequently, in addition to the alignment errors and levelling errors of inertial platform and initial error parameters, the other error coefficients are separated. It follows from Eqs.(51) and (98) that the relationship involved in instrumentation error coefficients and initial errors as well as the difference between telemetry data and tracking data, which can be described as follows

$$\delta \mathbf{X} = \mathbf{S} \cdot \mathbf{D} - \mathbf{G} \cdot \mathbf{P}_a + \boldsymbol{\varepsilon} \tag{99}$$

where $\mathbf{S}$ is the environmental function matrix of instrumentation errors and $\mathbf{G}$ is the environmental function matrix of initial errors. This model is known as the separation model of instrumentation errors and initial errors and it is a linear model.

5. Simulated cases

In the previous section, the separation model of initial errors based on telemetry and tracking data and the separation model of instrumentation errors and initial errors are deduced in detail. In this section, numerical examples are given to verify the separation model of initial errors and instrumentation errors and initial errors.

5.1 Verification of separation model of initial errors

The telemetry and tracking data are obtained using the six-degree-of-freedom ballistic program. For the certain trajectory with 10000 kilometers of range, the initial errors are listed in Table 1.

Parameter	Error Value	Parameter	Error Value	Parameter	Error Value
Astronomical Longitude λ_T	30 arcsec	Geodetic Longitude λ_0	-20 arcsec	Initial Velocity V_x	-0.1m/s
Astronomical Latitude B_T	30 arcsec	Geodetic Latitude B_0	-20 arcsec	Initial Velocity V_y	-0.05m/s
Astronomical Azimuth A_T	120 arcsec	Geodetic Height H_0	-5 m	Initial Velocity V_z	0.1m/s

Table 1. The true values of initial errors.

During the simulation process, all the guidance instrumentation systematic errors are set to zero therefore, the difference between telemetry data and tracking data merely contain initial errors. Herein, define $\mathbf{Y} = \mathbf{G} \cdot \mathbf{P}_{a0}$, namely, $\mathbf{Y}$ is the difference between telemetry data and tracking data, which is calculated using the product of environmental function matrix of initial errors $\mathbf{G}$ and true values of initial errors $\mathbf{P}_{a0}$. Define $\boldsymbol{\delta}\mathbf{X}_P$ is the difference between telemetry data and tracking data obtained by the simulation data. Now, define $\boldsymbol{\delta}\mathbf{Y} = \boldsymbol{\delta}\mathbf{X}_P - \mathbf{Y}$ is the residual of the difference between telemetry data and tracking data. Simulation results are shown in the following figures, Fig.4 shows the difference between telemetry velocity and tracking velocity, δX_{P_v}; Fig.5 shows the difference between telemetry position and tracking position, $\boldsymbol{\delta}\mathbf{X}_{P_s}$; Fig.6 shows the residual of the difference between telemetry velocity and tracking velocity, $\boldsymbol{\delta}\mathbf{Y}_v$; and Fig.7 shows the residual of the difference between telemetry position and tracking position, $\boldsymbol{\delta}\mathbf{Y}_s$.

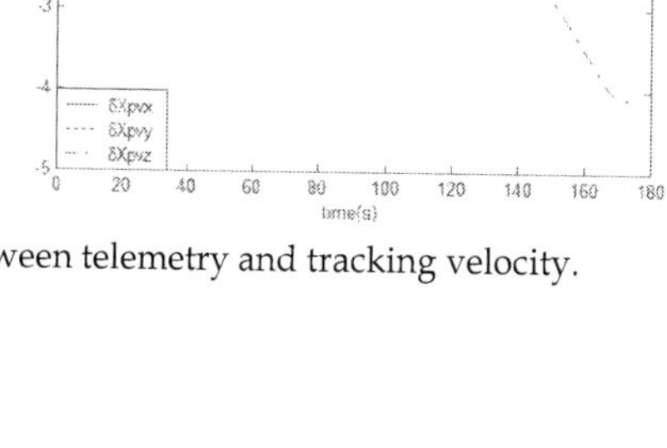

Fig. 4. The difference between telemetry and tracking velocity.

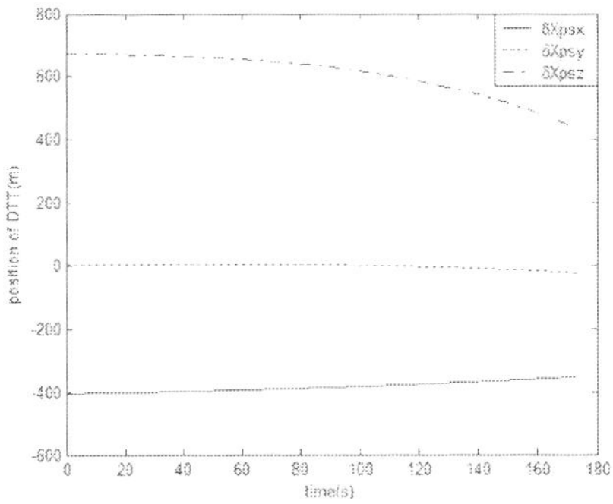

Fig. 5. The difference between telemetry and tracking position.

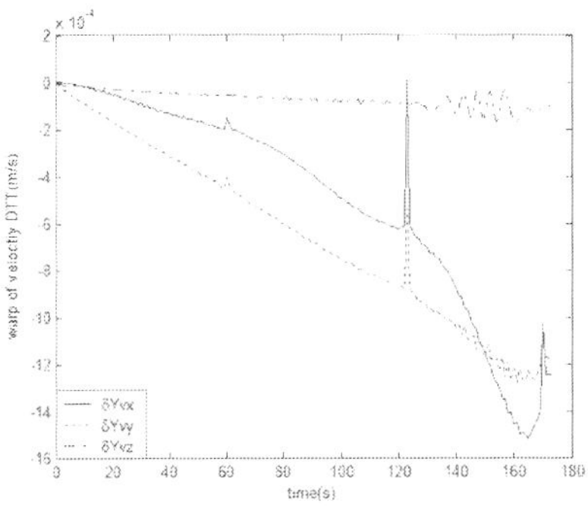

Fig. 6. The residual of the difference between telemetry and tracking velocity.

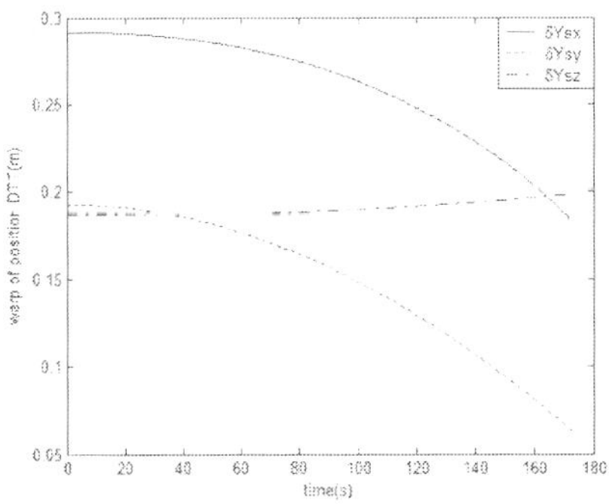

Fig. 7. The residual of the difference between telemetry and tracking position.

It is clearly seen from Figs. 4 and 6 that the differences between telemetry velocity and tracking velocity obtained by the two methods agree well. When the third stage engine shut down, the difference between telemetry velocity and tracking velocity is $(0.52, -0.53, -4.1)\text{m/s}$, while the largest residual computed by the two methods is $(-0.0015, -0.0013, -0.0002)\text{m/s}$, which is quite smaller than the difference between telemetry velocity and tracking velocity. Similarly, as seen in Figs. 5 and 7, when the third stage engine shut down, the difference between telemetry and tracking position is $(-400, -25, 672)\text{m}$, while the largest residual computed by the two methods is $(0.29, 0.19, 0.2)\text{m}$, which is quite smaller than the difference between telemetry position and tracking position. It follows that the separation model of initial errors are exact and the accuracy is fine.

Therefore, the initial errors can be estimated by using the computed difference between telemetry data and tracking data and the environmental function matrix of initial errors. In position domain, using the least-square estimation method we can have

$$\hat{\mathbf{P}}_a = (\mathbf{G}_s{}^T \cdot \mathbf{G}_s)^{-1} \mathbf{G}_s{}^T \boldsymbol{\delta}\mathbf{X}_p \tag{100}$$

The estimates of initial errors are given in Table 2.

	λ_T (arcsec)	B_T (arcsec)	A_T (arcsec)	λ_0 (arcsec)	B_0 (arcsec)	H_0 (m)	V_x (m/s)	V_y (m/s)	V_z (m/s)
True	30	30	120	-20	-20	-5	-0.1	-0.05	0.1
Est	30.013	29.987	120.01	-19.988	-20.007	-5.210	-0.0993	-0.049	0.1001

Table 2. The estimates of initial errors. Notes: True denotes the true value of parameter and Est denotes the estimates of parameter.

As it is seen from Table 2, the estimated accuracy of initial errors is high, such as astronomical longitude and latitude, azimuth, geodetic longitude and latitude, among others, of which the estimated relative error is smaller than 0.1%. Simultaneously, the estimated relative error of initial velocity is smaller than 1% and the estimated relative error of geodetic height is 4.2%.

It is necessary to point out that the variation of apparent acceleration due to the uncertainty of initial parameters in the error separation model mentioned above is not taken into consideration. In effect, the state of missile will change as the initial launch parameters change, subsequently the thrust and aerodynamic forces acting on the missile will vary. Simulation results indicate that the assumption that the factor is neglected is rational in the most cases. However, if there are errors in the position of vertical direction, then the large errors may be caused, for example, the variation of geodetic height will affect the shape of the trajectory severely. Although the error of geodetic height affect the apparent acceleration, this deviation of apparent acceleration can be measured onboard and reflected in both telemetry data and tracking data, which can be offset when computing the difference between telemetry data and tracking data. In the practical project, the ballistic missile is generally equipped with guidance system. Under the ideal situation, the error of apparent acceleration due to the initial errors can be completely offset therefore, the error of apparent acceleration will do no effect on the impact point.

5.2 Verification of separation model of instrumentation errors and initial errors

In the same manner the telemetry data and tracking data are generated by using the six-degree-of-freedom ballistic program with 10000 kilometers of range, and the initial errors are seen in Table 1. The model of guidance instrumentation systematic errors are given by Eqs.(22) and (23) and the levelling and alignment errors are not included.

Similarly, environmental function matrix of instrumentation error, $\mathbf{S}$, and environmental function matrix of initial errors, $\mathbf{G}$, are obtained to compute the difference between telemetry data and tracking data, $\mathbf{Y}$, which is defined as $\mathbf{Y} = \mathbf{S} \cdot \mathbf{D}_0 - \mathbf{G} \cdot \mathbf{P}_{a0}$. Simultaneously, $\boldsymbol{\delta}\mathbf{X}$ is the difference between telemetry and tracking data obtained by the simulation data. Likewise, define $\boldsymbol{\delta}\mathbf{Y} = \boldsymbol{\delta}\mathbf{X} - \mathbf{Y}$ is the residual. Simulation results are shown in the following figures, Fig.8 shows the difference between telemetry velocity and tracking velocity, $\boldsymbol{\delta}\mathbf{X}_v$; Fig.9 shows the difference between telemetry position and tracking position, $\boldsymbol{\delta}\mathbf{X}_s$; Fig.10 shows the residual of the difference between telemetry velocity and tracking velocity, $\boldsymbol{\delta}\mathbf{Y}_v$, and Fig.11 shows the residual of the difference between telemetry position and tracking position, $\boldsymbol{\delta}\mathbf{Y}_s$.

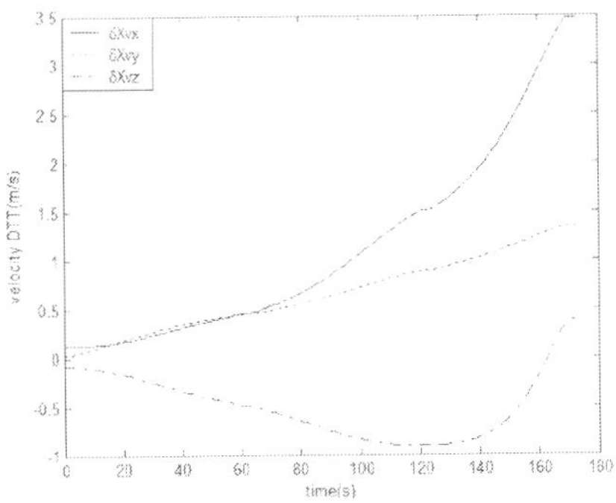

Fig. 8. The difference between telemetry and tracking velocity.

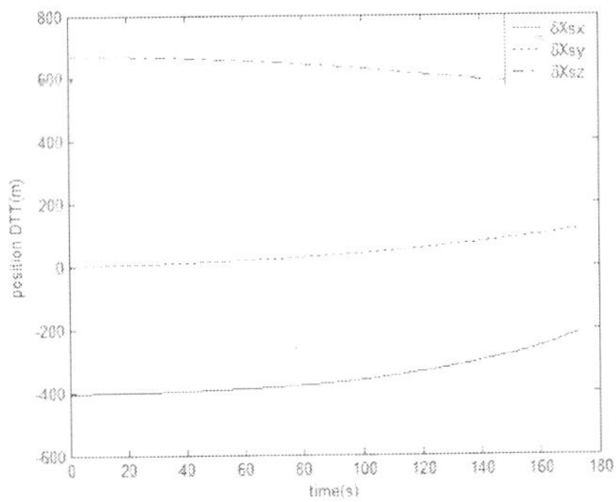

Fig. 9. The difference between telemetry and tracking position.

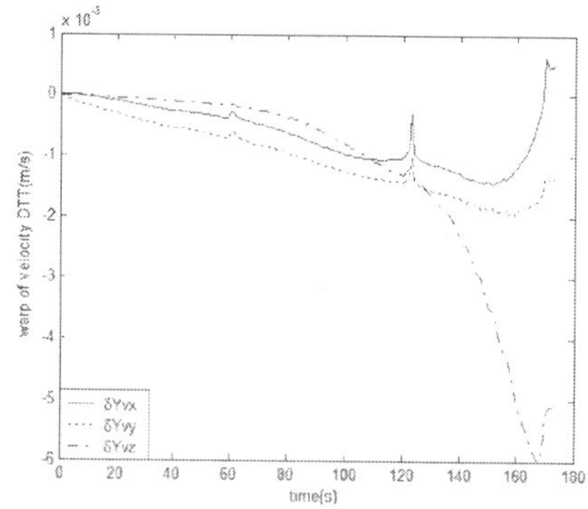

Fig. 10. The residual of the difference between telemetry and tracking velocity.

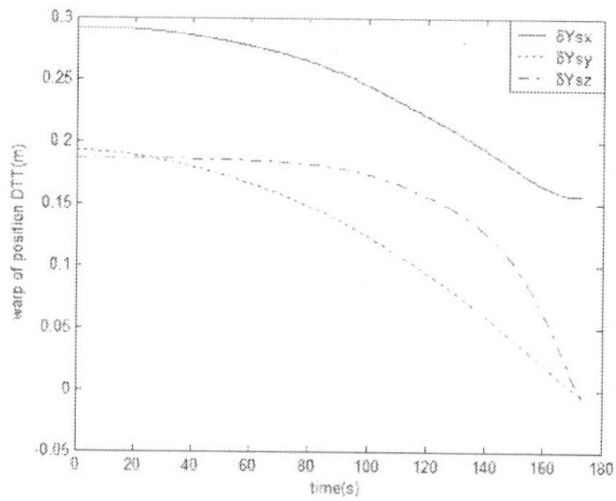

Fig. 11. The residual of the difference between telemetry and tracking position.

It is clearly seen from Figs. 8 and 10 that the differences between telemetry velocity and tracking velocity obtained by the two methods agree well. When the third stage engine shut down, the difference between telemetry velocity and tracking velocity is $(3.46, 1.34, -0.90)\text{m/s}$, while the largest residual computed by the two methods is $(-0.0015, -0.0019, -0.006)\text{m/s}$, which is quite smaller than the difference between telemetry velocity and tracking velocity. Similarly, as seen in Figs. 5 and 7, when the third stage engine shut down, the difference between telemetry position and tracking position is $(-400, -25, 672)\text{m}$, while the largest residual computed by the two methods is $(0.29, 0.19, 0.19)\text{m}$, which is quite smaller than the difference between telemetry position and tracking position. It follows that the separation model of instrumentation errors and initial errors are exact and precise.

The instrumentation errors and initial errors are estimated by using the above data. Selecting vector $\mathbf{K}=\begin{bmatrix}\mathbf{D}^T & \mathbf{P}_a^T\end{bmatrix}^T$ and letting $\mathbf{H}_s = \begin{bmatrix}\mathbf{S}_s^T & -\mathbf{G}_s^T\end{bmatrix}^T$, the in the position domain, the

$$\hat{\mathbf{K}} = (\mathbf{H}_s^T \mathbf{H}_s)^{-1} \mathbf{H}_s^T \delta\mathbf{X} \tag{101}$$

The estimates of error coefficients of gyroscope and accelerometer are given in Tables 3 and 4, respectively. The estimates of initial errors are given in Table 5.

	k_{g0x}	k_{g0y}	k_{g0z}	k_{g11x}	k_{g11y}	k_{g11z}	k_{g12x}	k_{g12y}	k_{g12z}
True	0.5	0.3	-0.5	-0.01	0.01	0.01	-0.01	0.02	0.02
Est	0.632	0.368	-0.503	-0.0139	0.0051	-0.0172	-0.0113	0.0200	0.0201

Table 3. The estimates of gyroscope error coefficients. (Units: deg/hour)

	$k_{a0x}\,(\mathrm{m/s^2})$	$k_{a0y}\,(\mathrm{m/s^2})$	$k_{a0z}\,(\mathrm{m/s^2})$
True	-2.0×10^{-3}	-2.0×10^{-3}	1.0×10^{-3}
Est	-2.0374×10^{-3}	-2.0086×10^{-3}	1.0826×10^{-3}
	k_{a1x}	k_{a1y}	k_{a1z}
True	5.0×10^{-4}	5.0×10^{-4}	5.0×10^{-4}
Est	5.0042×10^{-4}	5.0055×10^{-4}	3.8726×10^{-4}

Table 4. The estimates of accelerometer error coefficients.

	λ_T (arcsec)	B_T (arcsec)	A_T (arcsec)	λ_0 (arcsec)	B_0 (arcsec)	H_0 (m)	V_x (m/s)	V_y (m/s)	V_z (m/s)
True	30	30	120	-20	-20	-5	-0.1	-0.05	0.1
Est	30.586	30.198	116.25	-19.989	-20.007	-5.195	-0.0998	-0.049	0.1002

Table 5. The estimates of initial errors.

It is seen from Tables 3 through 5 that the instrumentation error coefficients and initial errors are well estimated in the position domain by using the separation model of instrumentation errors and initial errors mentioned above.

6. Conclusions

In this chapter, the separation model of initial launch parameter errors and guidance instrumentation systematic errors are formulated based on telemetry and tracking data. The calculation of difference between telemetry and tracking data is discussed in detail. It is generally considered that the telemetry data contain instrumentation errors while tracking data contain systematic errors and random measurement errors of exterior measurement equipment. Numerical examples are given for the verification of the separation by using six-degree-of-freedom trajectory program. Simulation results indicate that the separation model of initial errors and guidance instrumentation systematic errors can estimate the error coefficient well and is exact.

7. References

Barros A. S. & Rutledge D. N. (1998). Genetic Algorithm Applied to the Selection of Principal Components, Chemometrics and Intelligent Laboratory Systems, pp.65-81.

Cherkassky V. & Ma Y.Q. (2005). Multiple Model Regression Estimation, IEEE Trans on Neural Networks, Vol. 16, No. 4, 785-798.

Cortes C. & Vapnik V., (1995). Support-Vector Networks, Machine Learning, Vol(20), pp. 273～297.

Coulter J. E. & Meehan J. J. (1981). Test Methodology for Evaluation of the Input Axis of a Pendulous Integrating Gyro Accelerometer. AIAA81-1971.

Eduardo N. & Hugh D.W. (1999). Initial Calibration and Alignment of Low Cost Inertial Navigation Units for Land Vehicle Applications, Journal of Robotics Systems, Vol. 16, No. 2, pp. 81-92.

Forsberg R. & Sideris M. G. (1993). Geoid Computation by the Multi-band Spherical FFT Approach, manuscripta geodaetica, Vol. 18,No. 2, pp. 82—90.

Gore R. C. The Effect of Geophysical and Geodetic Uncertainties at Launch Area on Ballistic Missile Impact Accuracy, AD602214.

Jackson A. D. (1973). Continuous Calibration and Alignment Techniques for an All-attitude Inertial Platform, AIAA1973-865.

IEEE Standards Committee (1971). IEEE Standard Specification Format Guide and Test Procedure for Linear, Single-Axis, Pendulous, Analog Torque Balance Accelerometer, IEEE Std337-1972, , New York.

IEEE Standards Board (1973). IEEE Standard Specification Format Guide and Test Procedure for Single-Degree-of-Freedom Rate-Integrating Gyros, IEEE Std517-1974, Approved December 13.

John L. (1979). Characterization Testing of the MX AIRS. AIAA79-1888.

Liu Y. C., Fang H.R. and Zhang F. (2000). Telemetry and Telecommand System, National Defense Industry Press, Beijing, P.R.China.

Shattuck C.J.W. (1992). Technology and the PeaceKeeper, AIAA1992-1326.

Tony C. L. (2003). Development of U.S. Air Force Intercontinental Ballistic Missile Weapon Systems, Journal of Spacecraft and Rockets, Vol. 40, No. 4, pp. 491-509.

Titterton D. H. & Weston J. L. (1997). Strapdown Inertial Navigation Technology. London:United Kingdom, Peter Peregrinus.

Thompson A. A. (2000). Calibration of Inertial Sensors, AD20001121-025.

Wold S., Trygg J., Berglund A. et al. (2001). Some recent developments in PLS modeling. Chemometrics and Intelligent Laboratory Systems.

Yang H.B., Zhang S.F. and Cai H. (2007). Modeling and Parameters Estimation of Guidance Instrumentation Systematic Error and Initial Launched Parameters Error for Marine Missile, Journal of Astronautics, China, Vol. 28, No. 6, pp. 1638-1641.

Zheng W. (2006). Research on Effect of Geophysical Disturbance Factors on Hit Accuracy of Long-range Ballistic Missile and the Compensation Method for it, Graduate School of National University of Defense Technology Changsha，Hunan，P.R.China.